Lecture Notes in Artificial Intelligence   5221

Edited by R. Goebel, J. Siekmann, and W. Wahlster

Subseries of Lecture Notes in Computer Science

Bengt Nordström   Aarne Ranta (Eds.)

Advances in Natural Language Processing

6th International Conference, GoTAL 2008
Gothenburg, Sweden, August 25-27, 2008
Proceedings

 Springer

Series Editors

Randy Goebel, University of Alberta, Edmonton, Canada
Jörg Siekmann, University of Saarland, Saarbrücken, Germany
Wolfgang Wahlster, DFKI and University of Saarland, Saarbrücken, Germany

Volume Editors

Bengt Nordström
Aarne Ranta
Chalmers University of Technology
Department of Computer Science and Engineering
41296 Göteborg, Sweden
E-mail: {bengt, aarne}@chalmers.se

Library of Congress Control Number: Applied for

CR Subject Classification (1998): I.2.7, F.4.2-3, I.2, H.3, I.7

LNCS Sublibrary: SL 7 – Artificial Intelligence

ISSN 0302-9743
ISBN 978-3-540-85286-5 Springer Berlin Heidelberg New York

Springer is a part of Springer Science+Business Media

springer.com

© Springer-Verlag Berlin Heidelberg 2008

Typesetting: Camera-ready by author, data conversion by Scientific Publishing Services, Chennai, India
Printed on acid-free paper   SPIN: 12463534   06/3180   5 4 3 2 1 0

Preface

This volume contains the papers presented at GoTAL 2008, the 6th International Conference on Natural Language Processing, held on August 25–27, 2008, at Chalmers University of Technology in Gothenburg, Sweden. GoTAL was the sixth conference in the TAL series, preceded by FracTAL 1997 (Université de Franche-Comté, Besançon, France), VexTAL 1999 (Università Ca' Foscari di Venezia, Venice, Italy), PorTAL 2002 (Universidade do Algarve, Faro, Portugal), EsTAL 2004 (Universitat d'Alacant, Alicante, Spain), and FinTAL 2006 (University of Turku, Turku, Finland).

The conference received 107 submissions. Each submission was reviewed by three programme committee members or external reviewers. The committee finally accepted 44 papers to be presented at the conference and included in the proceedings. The conference programme also included three invited talks, which are the first three papers in this volume.

We are grateful to the programme committee members and the external reviewers for their careful and punctual work. The staff in the local organization team at Chalmers helped in a very professional way. The sponsors contributed, in particular, to the social programme planned for the conference. The invited speakers – Johan Bos, Lori Lamel, and Joakim Nivre – gave the scientific programme the broad, yet focused, profile that we wanted to achieve. And finally, it is essentially the authors of the submissions that created the substance of the conference and this volume, with all their good papers and their cooperative attitude.

The EasyChair software was used throughout the reviewing and editing process. It saved us a lot of work by doing exactly the things that could be automatized, in exactly the ways we expected.

June 2008

Bengt Nordström
Aarne Ranta

Organization

Local Organization

Björn Bringert
Håkan Burden
Rebecca Cyrén
Markus Forsberg
Harald Hammarström
Tiina Rankanen

Programme Committee

Olli Aaltonen	University of Helsinki, Finland
Walid El Abed	Nestle Corp., Switzerland
Jan Alexandersson	DFKI, Germany
Jorge Baptista	University of Algarve, Portugal
Tilman Becker	DFKI, Germany
Chris Biemann	Powerset, USA
Patrick Blackburn	INRIA Lorraine
Lars Borin	University of Gothenburg, Sweden
Johan Bos	University of Rome "La Sapienza," Italy
Johan Boye	SpeechAct, Sweden
Caroline Brun	Xerox Corp., France
Sylviane Cardey	University of Franche-Comté, France
Lauri Carlson	University of Helsinki, Finland
Rolf Carlson	KTH, Sweden
Alexander Clark	Royal Holloway University of London, UK
Robin Cooper	University of Gothenburg, Sweden
Walter Daelemans	University of Antwerp, Belgium
Rodolfo Delmonte	University of Venice, Italy
Elisabet Engdahl	University of Gothenburg, Sweden
Jan van Eijck	CWI Amsterdam, The Netherlands
Filip Ginter	University of Turku, Finland
Peter Greenfield	University of Franche-Comté, France
Philippe de Groote	INRIA Lorraine, France
Viggo Kann	KTH, Sweden
Kimmo Koskenniemi	University of Helsinki, Finland
Hans Leiß	LMU Munich, Germany
Oliver Lemon	University of Edinburgh, UK
Patricio Martinez Barco	University of Alicante, Spain
Adeline Nazarenko	University Paris-Nord, France

Joakim Nivre	Växjö University and Uppsala University, Sweden
Bengt Nordström	Chalmers University of Technology, Sweden
Pierre Nugues	University of Lund, Sweden
Guy Perrier	INRIA Lorraine, France
Elisabete Ranchhod	University of Lisbon, Portugal
Aarne Ranta	University of Gothenburg, Sweden (Chair)
Manny Rayner	University of Geneva, Switzerland
Tapio Salakoski	University of Turku, Finland
Karl-Michael Schneider	Textkernel, The Netherlands
Rolf Schwitter	Macquarie University, Australia
José Luis Vicedo	University of Alicante, Spain
Simo Vihjanen	Lingsoft Ltd., Finland
Annie Zaenen	Palo Alto Research Center, USA

External Reviewers

Krasimir Angelov
Björn Bringert
Håkan Burden
Maud Ehrmann
Samuel Eleutério
Oscar Ferrandez
Sergio Ferrández
Andrei Filip
Bruno Guillaume
Markus Forsberg
Caroline Hagege
Harald Hammarström
Rubén Izquierdo Beviá
Guillaume Jacquet
Kristofer Johannisson

Richard Johansson
Lauri Karttunen
Janna Khegai
Marco Kuhlmann
Joseph Le Roux
Peter Ljunglöf
Beáta Megyesi
Borja Navarro Colorado
Magnus Rosell
Fernando Ruiz-Rico
Markus Saers
Estela Saquete
Kamel Smaïli
David Tomás
Marcus Uneson

Sponsors

Centre for Language Technology, Gothenburg
City of Göteborg
Lingsoft Ltd., Helsinki

Table of Contents

Formal Semantics in the Real World

J. Bos

Linguistic Computing Laboratory
Department of Computer Science
University of Rome "La Sapienza", Italy
bos@di.uniroma1.it

Formal methods for the analysis of the meaning of natural language expressions have long been restricted to the ivory tower built by semanticists, logicians, and philosophers of language. It is only in exceptional cases that these methods make their way straight into open-domain natural language processing tools. Recently, however, this situation has changed. Thanks to (i) the development of treebanks, i.e., large collections of texts annotated with syntactic structures, (ii) robust statistical parsers trained on such treebanks, and (iii) the development of large-scale semantic lexica such as WordNet [1], VerbNet [2], PropBank [3], and FrameNet [4], we now have witnessed the development of wide-coverage systems that are able to produce formal semantic representations for open-domain texts.

One such system, developed by myself over the last four years, is Boxer, which follows the principles of Discourse Representation Theory (DRT) to construct and represent meaning of natural languages texts [5,6]. DRT is a formal theory of meaning, initially proposed by Hans Kamp [7] to solve various problems related to anaphoric pronouns. Throughout the years DRT faced various extensions and improvements and by now covers a wide range of semantic issues including plurals and tense [8], discourse segmentation and rhetorical structure [9], and presupposition [10]. Boxer constructs Discourse Representation Structures (DRSs, which are graphically displayed as boxes) with the help of Combinatory Categorial Grammar (CCG) for producing syntactic structure [11] and a typed lambda calculus to specify the syntax-semantics interface [12]. In conjunction with a robust CCG parser [13,14], Boxer achieves very high coverage ($> 98\%$ on the Wall Street Journal sections of the Penn Treebank [15]) on newswire text producing DRSs with neo-Davidsonian predicate-argument structure. These DRSs can be translated into standard first-order logic syntax and then fed into automated theorem provers and model builders to check for logical consistency or informativeness [12,16].

The existence of systems like Boxer is clear evidence that practicing formal semantics is not bound to pencil and paper exercises anymore, nor to implementations covering relatively small fragments of natural language. A case in point is the use of Boxer in real-world applications such as open-domain question answering [17]. These developments mark a milestone in the development of computational linguistics in general and computational semantics in particular. They also trigger new research questions, directions and challenges, including the identification of gaps between theory and practice, the inclusion of background

A. Ranta, B. Nordström (Eds.): GoTAL 2008, LNAI 5221, pp. 1–3, 2008.

knowledge, transferring theoretical ideas developed in isolation within different logical formalisms into one unifying framework [18], and the issue of evaluation.

In particular the evaluation issue is of major importance for further progress in the field. Modelling all nuances of meaning is an immense task — perhaps even impossible. The representations that Boxer produces for a text, as any rival system would, only characterise an *approximation* of its meaning. An interesting question to ask then is how good this approximation is. How do we measure the semantic adaquacy of systems like Boxer that claim are able to compute meaning? A timely question, but despite various proposals aiming to deal with this issue, as yet we cannot answer this question satisfactorily. Comparing a system's output with gold-standard semantic representations would be an obvious choice but annotated semantic corpora simply don't exist. Most promising are probably theory-neutral evaluation techniques such as recognising textual inference that we know from the FRACAS project [19], Monz and De Rijke [20], and the recent PASCAL challenges [21,22,23]. But such exercises are either considered artificial or fail to isolate semantic competence in systems [24].

References

1. Fellbaum, C. (ed.): WordNet. An Electronic Lexical Database. The MIT Press, Cambridge (1998)
2. Kipper, K., Korhonen, A., Ryant, N., Palmer, M.: A large-scale classification of english verbs. Language Resources and Evaluation 42(1), 21–40 (2008)
3. Kingsbury, P., Palmer, M.: From treebank to propbank. In: Proceedings of the 3rd LREC, Las Palmas, Canary Islands, Spain (2002)
4. Baker, C.F., Fillmore, C.J., Lowe, J.B.: The Berkeley FrameNet project. In: 36th Annual Meeting of the Association for Computational Linguistics and 17th International Conference on Computational Linguistics. Proceedings of the Conference, Université de Montréal, Montreal, Quebec, Canada (1998)
5. Bos, J.: Towards wide-coverage semantic interpretation. In: Proceedings of Sixth International Workshop on Computational Semantics IWCS-6, pp. 42–53 (2005)
6. Curran, J., Clark, S., Bos, J.: Linguistically motivated large-scale nlp with c&c and boxer. In: Proceedings of the 45th Annual Meeting of the Association for Computational Linguistics Companion Volume Proceedings of the Demo and Poster Sessions, Prague, Czech Republic, Association for Computational Linguistics, June 2007, pp. 33–36 (2007)
7. Kamp, H.: A Theory of Truth and Semantic Representation. In: Groenendijk, J., Janssen, T.M., Stokhof, M. (eds.) Formal Methods in the Study of Language, pp. 277–322. Mathematical Centre, Amsterdam (1981)
8. Kamp, H., Reyle, U.: From Discourse to Logic; An Introduction to Modeltheoretic Semantics of Natural Language, Formal Logic and DRT. Kluwer, Dordrecht (1993)
9. Asher, N.: Reference to Abstract Objects in Discourse. Kluwer Academic Publishers, Dordrecht (1993)
10. Van der Sandt, R.: Presupposition Projection as Anaphora Resolution. Journal of Semantics 9, 333–377 (1992)
11. Steedman, M.: The Syntactic Process. The MIT Press, Cambridge (2001)
12. Blackburn, P., Bos, J.: Representation and Inference for Natural Language. A First Course in Computational Semantics. CSLI (2005)

13. Hockenmaier, J.: Data and Models for Statistical Parsing with Combinatory Categorial Grammar. PhD thesis, University of Edinburgh (2003)
14. Clark, S., Curran, J.: Parsing the WSJ using CCG and Log-Linear Models. In: Proceedings of the 42nd Annual Meeting of the Association for Computational Linguistics (ACL 2004), Barcelona, Spain (2004)
15. Marcus, M.P., Santorini, B., Marcinkiewicz, M.A.: Building a large annotated corpus of english: The penn treebank. Computational Linguistics 19(2), 313–330 (1993)
16. Bos, J., Markert, K.: Recognising textual entailment with logical inference techniques. In: Proceedings of the Conference on Empirical Methods in Natural Language Processing (EMNLP 2005) (2005)
17. Bos, J.: The "La Sapienza" Question Answering System at TREC 2006. In et al., V., ed.: Proceeding of the Fifteenth Text RETrieval Conference, TREC-2006, Gaithersburg, MD (2006)
18. Pulman, S.: Formal and computational semantics: a case study. In: Proceedings of Seventh International Workshop on Computational Semantics IWCS-7 (2007)
19. Cooper, R., Crouch, D., Van Eijck, J., Fox, C., Van Genabith, J., Jaspars, J., Kamp, H., Pinkal, M., Milward, D., Poesio, M., Pulman, S.: Using the Framework. Technical report, FraCaS: A Framework for Computational Semantics, FraCaS deliverable D16 (1996)
20. Monz, C., de Rijke, M.: Light-weight inference for computational semantics. In: Blackburn, P., Kohlhase, M. (eds.) Workshop Proceedings ICoS-3, pp. 95–72 (2001)
21. Dagan, I., Glickman, O., Magnini, B.: The pascal recognising textual entailment challenge. In: Quiñonero-Candela, J., Dagan, I., Magnini, B., d'Alché-Buc, F. (eds.) MLCW 2005. LNCS (LNAI), vol. 3944, pp. 177–190. Springer, Heidelberg (2006)
22. Bar-Haim, R., Dagan, I., Dolan, B., Ferro, L., Giampiccolo, D.: The second pascal recognising textual entailment challenge. In: Proceedings of the Second PASCAL Challenges Workshop on Recognising Textual Entailment, Venice, Italy (2006)
23. Sekine, S., Inui, K., Dagan, I., Dolan, B., Giampiccolo, D., Magnini, B., eds.: Proceedings of the ACL-PASCAL Workshop on Textual Entailment and Paraphrasing. Association for Computational Linguistics, Prague (June 2007)
24. Bos, J.: Let's not argue about semantics. In: Proceedings of the 6th Language Resources and Evaluation Conference (LREC 2008), Marrakech, Morocco (2008)

Speech Processing for Audio Indexing*

Lori Lamel and Jean-Luc Gauvain

LIMSI-CNRS, BP 133, 91403 Orsay Cedex, France
{lamel,gauvain}@limsi.fr

Abstract. This paper addresses some of the recent trends in speech processing, with a focus on speech-to-text transcription as a means to facilitate access to multimedia information in a multilingual context. A brief overview of automatic speech recognition is given along with indicative performance measures for a range of tasks. Enriched transcriptions, that is enhancing the automatic word transcripts with meta-data derived from the audio data is discussed, followed by some hightlights of recent progress and remaining challenges in speech recognition.

1 Introduction

The last decade has witnessed major advances in spoken language technologies, with a growing interest in applications that rely on techniques for automatic structurization of multimedia, multilingual data. Although the different media types typically bring complementary information, for most documents much of the accessible content is provided by the audio and text streams. Thus speech and language processing technologies are key components for indexing. Some of the applications that can potentially make use of spoken language technologies are the creation and access to digital multimedia libraries, media monitoring services to provide selective dissemination of information based on automatic detection of topics of interest, and more generally speaking as News on Demand and Internet watch services which already are available for text documents. Developing speech technologies is by nature an interdisciplinary process, requiring knowledge and competence in a range of disciplines including signal processing, acoustics, phonetics, linguistics, artificial intelligence, etc. In addition to speech transcription, speech processing techniques can be used to provide other metadata, such as the language being spoken, the identity of the speaker, as well as to locate named entities or identify topics.

While the performance of speech recognition technology has dramatically improved for a number of 'dominant' languages (English, Mandarin, Arabic, French, Spanish, ...), generally speaking technologies for language and speech processing are available only for a small proportion of the world's languages. By several estimations there are over 6000 spoken languages in the world, but only about 15% of them also are written. Text corpora, which can be useful for training the language models used by speech recognizers, are becoming more and more readily available on the Internet. The site

* This work has been partially financed under the GALE program of the Defense Advanced Research Projects Agency, Contract No. HR0011-06-C-0022 and by OSEO under the Quaero program.

A. Ranta, B. Nordström (Eds.): GoTAL 2008, LNAI 5221, pp. 4–15, 2008.

`http://www.omniglot.com` lists about 800 languages that have a written form. According to `http://www.nvtc.gov/lotw` the top 10 languages on the Internet account over 80% of use, with the dominant language being English (almost 30%) and the second Chinese (14%). For speech recognition training purposes the best texts are speech transcripts, or texts that are close to spoken language. For prepared speech, such as broadcast news type data, newspaper texts are quite useful, and some efforts have been made to transform such material to better match spoken language [12]. For more conversational speech less formal texts are more appropriate and there have been recent effort to locate such data from the web, for example, from blogs [9].

It is difficult to estimate the amount of audio data on the Internet. A study by the University of Berkeley School of Information Management and Systems[1], attempts to estimate the proportions of different data types based on the file types and sizes. From these estimations of file size, about 30% of the files correspond to text data, about 20% image, 5% video and 3% audio. Considering worldwide sources of radio and television, about 100 million hours of original programming (about 20% from the US) are broadcast per year, representing about 10 terawords of data.

There have been numerous national and international projects addressing different aspects of processing multimedia, multilingual data for information access. Perhaps the longest running project is the National Science Foundation (NSF) Digital Libraries Informedia project (`http://www.informedia.cs.cmu.edu`), which started in the mid 1990s, aims to incorporate automatic text, speech, image and video processing to enable content-based search in multimedia digital archives. A list of ongoing national and European sponsored projects can be found on the web site of the Chorus coordinating action (`http://www.ist-chorus.org/projects.asp`), some of which include research on speech and audio processing.

During the last twenty years there has also been an accompanying growth in a support infrastructure for data collection, annotation and evaluation. Concerning data, the most notable actors are the Linguistic data consortium (LDC, `http://www.ldc.upenn.edu`), founded in 1992 with the goal of developing a mechanism for the creation of and the widespread sharing of linguistic resources for linguistic research, and the European Language Resources Association (ELRA, `http://www.elra.info`), founded in 1995 with the aim of promoting language resources and evaluation for the Human Language Technology sector. The Speech Group at the National Institute of Standards and Technology (NIST) has been organizing benchmark evaluations for a range of human language technologies (speech recognition, speaker and language recognition, spoken document retrieval, topic detection and tracking, automatic content extraction, spoken term detection) for over 20 years, recently extending to related multi-modal technologies[2]. Comparative evaluation of technologies in international campaigns is important in order to objectively assess the methods and models developed, and serves to increase the information exchange among participants. These evaluations require the development of methods and metrics to measure performance, as well as the annotation of

---

[1] `http://www2.sims.berkeley.edu/research/projects/how-much-info-2003`

[2] See `http://www.nist.gov/speech/tests` for a summary of previous and current evaluation campaigns.

development and test data. The post-evaluation workshops provide the opportunity for each participant to describe their research and development work in preparation for the evaluation, thus promoting the exchange of information. The most promising techniques are seen to be quickly adopted by other members of the research community, thus leading to rapid advances in the state-of-the-art.

Many of the recent advances can be attributed to the increased use of real world data, with its challenges and advantages. There has been a shift towards algorithms that can benefit from large corpora, and the development of methods to reduce the amount of supervision required for model training. While this paper focuses on speech recognition, there has been a trend to use corpus-based methods for other technologies, such as speech synthesis, speech understanding and machine translation of speech.

2   Speech Recognition Basics

Most state-of-the-art automatic speech recognition systems make use of statistical models, the principles of which have been known for many years [7,14]. From this point of view, speech is assumed to be generated by a language model which provides estimates of $\Pr(w)$ for all word strings w, and an acoustic model encoding the message w in the signal x, which is represented by a probability density function $f(x|w)$. Given the observed acoustic signal, the goal of speech recognition is to determine the most likely word sequence. The speech decoding problem thus consists of maximizing the probability of the word sequence w given the speech signal x, or equivalently, maximizing the product $\Pr(w)f(x|w)$. Considerable progress has been made in recent years in part due to the availability of large speech and text corpora, along with increased processing power which have allowed more complex models and algorithms to be implemented. The advances in acoustic, language and pronunciation modeling have enabled reasonable performance to be obtained for a range of data types and acoustic conditions.

The principle problems in speech recognition have been the focus of many years of research. The variability observed in the acoustic signal is due to multiple factors, including the linguistic message and the characteristics of the speaker, acoustic environment, recording conditions and transmission channel. Figure 1 shows the main components of a speech recognition system using statistical methods for training and decoding [19]. The main knowledge sources are the speech and text training data and the pronunciation lexicon. Acoustic and language model training relies on the preprocessing and normalization of the data. In general, speech data is manually transcribed, however recent research has been directed at reducing the need for supervision. Concerning the text corpus, after some initial processing to remove material unsuitable for sentence-based language modeling, such as tables and lists, the texts need to be normalized. This step, which helps reduce lexical variability and transforms the texts to better represent spoken language, is typically language specific. It includes rules to the process numbers, abbreviations and acronyms, and may also concern how hyphenated words, other compounds or words with apostrophes are treated.

The most popular language models for large vocabulary speech recognition [27] are n-gram models, which attempt to capture the syntactic and semantic constraints by estimating the frequencies of sequences of n words. The probability of a given

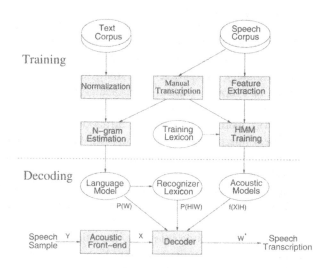

Fig. 1. System diagram of a speech recognizer based on statistical models, including training and decoding processes

word string $(w_1, w_2, ..., w_k)$ is approximated by $\prod_{i=1}^{k} \Pr(w_i | w_{i-n+1}, ..., w_{i-2}, w_{i-1})$, thereby reducing the word history to the preceeding $n-1$ words. A back-off mechanism is generally used to smooth the estimates of the probabilities of rare n-grams by relying on a lower order n-gram when there is insufficient training data, and to provide a means of modeling unobserved word sequences [15]. While 3- and 4-gram LMs are the most widely used, class-based n-grams, and adapted LMs are recent research areas aimed at improving LM accuracy.

Acoustic feature extraction is concerned with the choice and optimization of acoustic features in order to reduce model complexity while trying to maintain the linguistic information relevant for speech recognition. Acoustic modeling must take into account different sources of variability present in the speech signal: those arising from the linguistic context and those associated with the non-linguistic context such as the speaker and the acoustic environment and recording channel. Most state-of-the-art systems make use of hidden Markov models (HMMs) for acoustic modeling, which consists of modeling the probability density function of a sequence of acoustic feature vectors. The most widely used solutions model context-dependent phones and use a host of techniques such as parameter sharing, feature analysis, linear and non-linear transformation, noise compensation and discriminative training to improve model accuracy. Regarding the training data, the first 100-200 hours of representative data provide the most gain for acoustic modeling, with additional data giving only small improvements.

The pronunciation lexicon is the link between the representation at the acoustic-level (frames of features) and at the word level. At the lexical and pronunciation level, two main sources of variability are the dialect and individual preferences of the speaker. There are three main steps in designing a recognition lexicon: definition and selection of the vocabulary items, representation of each pronunciation entry using the basic acoustic units of the recognizer, and estimation of probabilities for pronunciation variants. Lexical coverage has a large impact on recognition performance, and the accuracy of the acoustic models is linked to the consistency of the pronunciations in the lexicon. The recognition vocabulary is usually selected to maximize lexical coverage for a given size lexicon. Since on average, each out-of-vocabulary (OOV) word causes more than a single error (usually between 1.5 and 2 errors), word list selection is an important design step. At LIMSI, word list selection is carried out by choosing the n most probable words after linear interpolation of unigram LMs trained on the different text sources so as to maximize the coverage on a set of development data. The vocabulary size, n is chosen so as to minimize the OOV rate while keeping a reasonable size and avoiding typos. The lexicon typically contains canonical pronunciations and frequent variants, which are generated either manually or by rule. Sometimes non-speech events and compound words or short phrases are also explicitly included as lexical entries.

Given the speech signal and the models (lexicon, acoustic and language), the job of the decoder is to determine the word sequence with the highest likelihood (MAP decoding) or maximizing the expected accuracy of the hypothesis (consensus decoding). The main decoding challenge for large vocabulary continuous speech recognition (LVCSR) is to design an efficient algorithm to explore the huge search space, for which it is generally impossible to carry out an exhaustive search. Many techniques have been proposed to reduce the needed computation by limiting the search space [6]. It has become common practice to use multi-pass decoding strategies which can limit the complexity of each individual decoding pass, allowing more complex models (additional knowledge) to be used progressively. Information is usually transmitted between passes via word graphs, containing the word hypotheses and their respective scores.

Table 1. Indicative speech recognition word error rates for different tasks and speaking styles

Task	Condition	Word Error
Dictation	read speech, close-talking mic.	3-4% (humans 1%)
	read speech, noisy (SNR 15dB)	10%
	read speech, telephone	20%
	spontaneous dictation	14%
	read speech, non-native	20%
Found audio	TV & radio news broadcasts	10-15% (humans 4%)
	documentaries	20-30%
	European Parliament	8%
	telephone conversations	20-30% (humans 4%)
	lectures (close mic)	20%
	lectures (distant mic)	50%

Table 2 gives some indicative word error rates for a range of speech recognition tasks and speaking styles. For a few of the tasks some measures of human performance are available. Studies comparing human and machine transcription performance [26,11,22] show that humans consistently do considerably (5 to 10 times) better than machines.

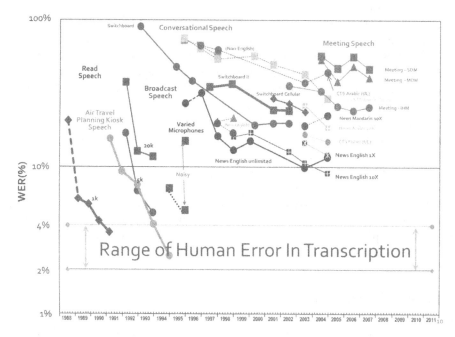

Fig. 2. NIST summary of automatic speech recognition evaluation history (May'07). The word error rate (WER) of the best system for each evaluation/task is shown. (Figure reprinted from [24].

The results in the top part of the table are for a dictation task, where under ideal conditions (i.e. the text is already prepared and the speaker uses a close-talking microphone in a quiet acoustic environment, and the goal is to speak to the machine), quite low error rates can be achieved. It can be noted however than even in this situation human performance is much better than the machine. Any perturbation, such as a noisy environment, a telephone acoustic channel, or accented speech from a non-native speaker results in a very significant increase in error rate. There is also a much higher error rate if the speaker does not read a text, but rather prepares the subject and formulates the ideas on the fly as shown by the entry labeled spontaneous dictation. The lower part of the table reports performance on some different types of 'found data,' that is data that was produced for independent purposes, but have been of interest to the research community since there are a range of potential applications that can be enabled via speech processing technologies. Broadcast data has been attracting growing interest since the task was introduced by DARPA over a decade ago. While initial error rates were quite high, today word error rates in the range of 10-15% have been reported on broadcast news data for a number of languages (English, French, Spanish, German, Dutch, Arabic, Mandarin, Portuguese, Japanese). A wide range in performance is observed for different data types, with quite low error rates for the speech of main announcers in recording studios, and much higher error rates for distant reporters, particularly when the acoustic channel or environment is poor. Similarly, the error rate can increase dramatically if the interactivity is high (interviews, debates). Documentaries are particularly challenging to transcribe, as the audio quality is often not very high, and there is a large proportion of voice over. The recent TC-STAR project (http://www.tc-star.org), which targeted speech-to-speech translation of unconstrained conversational speech from the European Parliament Plenary Sessions (EPPS), reported word error rates of about 8% for European English and Spanish. Word error rates on conversational telephone speech and lectures (http://chil.server.de) and meetings (http://www.amiproject.org) are substantially higher, reflecting some of the additional challenges of these domains.

Figure 2 summarizes the results of NIST sponsored benchmark speech recognition evaluations over the last 20 years. Each curve corresponds to a specific task, and plots the word error rate of the best system in each evaluation. The first evaluations were for read speech, with a move in the mid 1990's to conversation telephone speech and to broadcast data. Over time the amount of data used to train the speech recognizers increased along with model complexity (and vocabulary size). It can be seen that typically as the performance of the best systems approached 10%, more challenging tasks were introduced. The performance of humans is significantly better than that of machines for all types of real-world data.

3   Enriched Transcription

The speech signal encodes both the linguistic message and other types of information such as the characteristics of the speaker, the acoustic environment, the recording conditions and the transmission channel. Ideally we would like to identify as many of these characteristics as possible from the audio channel. For example, a first processing step can partition the audio signal, extracting acoustic-based meta-data and creating a description of the audio document in terms of the language(s) spoken, the speaker(s), accent(s), acoustic background, speaker's emotional state etc. Such information can be used to improve speech recognition performance, and to provide an enriched text output for downstream processing. The automatic transcription can also be used to provide information about the linguistic content of the data (topic, named entities, speech style, ...). By associating each word and sentence with a specific audio segment, an automatic transcription can allow access to any arbitrary portion of an audio document. If combined with other meta-data (language, speaker, entities, topics) access via other attributes can be facilitated. Enriched transcription also includes the inclusion of case and punctuation in the output.

Language and speaker recognition make use of similar modeling techniques as those use for speech recognition. There are two predominant approaches to language recognition, acoustic (Gaussian mixture) models) and phonotactic models [33]. Both types of systems require only untranscribed training data each target language of interest, but phonotactic-based systems are somewhat less sensitive to changes in recording conditions. Other techniques such as Support Vector Machines and system combination (fusion) have also been proposed. Speaker recognition [10] is the process of identifying a speaker from their voice. Two tasks are typically distinguished, speaker identification and speaker verification. For the former, the speaker is identified as one of a set of known speakers (closed task) or as none of them (open task). For the second task, given a speech sample, the system needs to decide if the sample was produced by a given speaker (the decision is yes or no). NIST (http://www.nist.gov/speech/tests) has been organizing language and speaker recognition benchmarks for conversational telephone speech since 1996.

Speech-to-text systems historically produce a case insensitive, unpunctuated output. In the context of the TC-STAR project tools to automatically add case and punctuation were developed [18]. Both linguistic and acoustic information (essentially pause and breath noise cues) are used to add punctuation marks in the speech recognizer output. This is done by rescoring a word lattice that has been expanded to permit punctuation marks after each word, sentences boundaries at each pause, with a specialized case sensitive, punctuated language model.

Speaker diarization, also referred to as speaker segmentation and clustering, has been of recent interest to the speech community. It is a useful preprocessing step for an automatic speech transcription system, in that it enables unsupervised speaker adaptation to be carried out at a cluster level, thus increasing the amount of available data which can improve transcription performance. The performance of diarization systems has been assessed in the Rich Transcription benchmarks(http://www.nist.gov/speech/tests/rt) under the DARPA EARS program, as well as in the CHIL, AMI and ESTER evaluation campaigns. One of the major issues is that the number of speakers is unknown a priori and needs to be automatically determined. In [8,31] speaker recognition techniques were shown to improve the performance of a diarization system. In these evaluations the goal was to correctly attribute speech segments to unidentified speakers in the audio document, that is there was no attempt to determine the true identity of the speaker.

Speaker diarization can also improve the readability of an automatic transcription by structuring the audio stream into speaker turns, in some cases by providing the true speaker identity. For example, in broadcast news programs, the speaker names are often explicitly stated, providing the true identities of those taking part in the show. A future aim is to combine speaker recognition techniques to identity speakers from a very large population. One of the goals in the QUAERO project (http://www.quaero.org)is to explore the novel use of the linguistic information produced by a speech recognizer to complement the information derived from the acoustics. The main idea of the 'Who's Who' procedure is to exploit the structure of broadcast data to automatically learn the names of speakers in a large unannotated corpus without the need for human intervention.

4   Some Recent Progress and Outstanding Challenges

One of the challenges for automatic language processing is the portability of technology across languages. Multilinguality is of particular interest for Internet-based applications, where information may first (or only) be available in another language than the user's mother tongue. A recent book [2] addresses issues in multilingual speech processing. Word error rates below 20% were reported for a number of languages [21]. With appropriately trained models, recognizer performance was observed to be more dependent upon the type and source of data, than on the language.

Speech recognizers for well-covered languages are typically trained on hundreds of hours of transcribed speech and hundreds of millions of words of texts. Thus data collection and preparation require significant investment, in terms of money, time and human effort. Reducing these costs is an important research direction (http://coretex.itc.it). For acoustic modeling, it has been proposed to use a speech recognizer [16,20,30] to reduce transcription costs. For some applications iterative training using automatic transcripts may be sufficient, whereas in other cases a human may need to correct the transcription. In the context of the DARPA EARS (http://w2.eff.org/Privacy/TIA/ears.php) program, extensive experiments were reported using 'quick' transcriptions to reduce the human annotator time for a conversational telephone speech task [17]. The approach has also adopted for use in the DARPA GALE (http://www.darpa.mil/ipto/programs/gale/gale.asp) program in order to reduce transcription costs and therefore provide more data. Acoustic model training requires an alignment between the audio signal and the phone models, which usually relies on a perfect orthographic transcription of the speech data and a good phonetic lexicon. Making use of these quick transcriptions has led to revisions in acoustic model training procedures to make them more flexible [25] and less dependent on a perfect transcription.

Obtaining resources is particularly difficult for 'lesser' represented languages that do not have a strong strategic (economic or security) push. Language preservation is important for cultural diversity, and transmission of cultural heritage (http://cmuspice.org, http://projects.ldc.upenn.edu/LCTL). A recent workshop addressed the topic of developing spoken languages technologies for under-resourced languages [1]. Given recent trends for computerization, such languages pose many new research challenges. In general it is relatively easy to obtain audio data, by recording radio or television programs. Finding text material in electronic form is often more difficult since many languages are poorly represented, if at all, on the Internet. For some languages there are no commonly adopted writing conventions or there may have been recent writing reforms which result in quite varied text materials. Another complication is that it is difficult to find people that have expertise in both the language of interest and in language processing. Written resources and a pronunciation dictionary are the most critical for todays technologies: reasonable acoustic models can be trained on several tens to hundreds of hours of data which can be obtained at a reasonable cost. Given that economic or political reasons are unlikely to support the development of technologies for many of these lesser languages, likely viable solutions will rely on new lightly supervised or unsupervised training techniques. Some work in this direction has been reported in [23,5] for pronunciation modeling, and a framework for the development of resources and models is being developed in the SPICE project (http://cmuspice.org). As mentioned earlier, only about 15% of the world's languages are written, so current word based modeling techniques cannot be directly applied to the remaining languages. For relatively small data collections, approaches based on phone-like units may provide a short-term solution for such languages [29].

Concerning language modeling, as the amount of available data has increased, most state-of-the-art systems use back-off n-gram language models which result from the interpolation of language models trained on non-overlapping subsets of the available language model training material. This allows different interpolated weights to be associated with different data subsets, thus increasing or reducing their importance. The interpolation weights are optimized on a set of development data. It is often the case that the

Table 2. Observed pronunciations for four inflected forms of the word 'interest' in American English broadcast news (BN) and conversational telephone speech (CTS) data

Word	Pronunciation	BN	CTS	Word	Pronunciation	BN	CTS
interest	IntrIst	238	488	interests	IntrIss	52	53
	IntXIst	3	33		IntrIsts	19	30
	InXIst	0	11		IntXIsts	3	2
					IntXIss	3	1
interested	IntrIstxd	126	386	interesting	IntrIst|G	193	1399
	IntXIstxd	3	80		IntXIst|G	8	314
	InXIstxd	18	146		InXIst|G	21	463

vast majority of training texts come from written sources (newspapers, newswires, ...), and audio transcripts represent only a small portion of the data. In the LIMSI Arabic speech-to-text system, the coefficients associated with the audio transcriptions, account for almost 0.5, even though these texts represent only about 1% of the available data. This highlights the importance of audio transcripts for language modeling of speech.

Although proposed a decade ago[13], Multi-Layer Perceptron (MLP) features have recently been attracting interest for large vocabulary speech recognition due to their complementarity with cepstral features [32]. Even though probabilistic features have never been shown to consistently outperform cepstral features in LVCSR, having different properties they can markedly improve the performance when used in conjunction with them. Connectionist models have also been shown to be effective for language modeling [28].

Concerning pronunciation modeling, most of todays state-of-the-art systems include pronunciation variants in the dictionary, associating pronunciation probabilities with the variants [3,4]. However, for large vocabulary systems most of the lexical items are never or only rarely observed. Table 4 shows the observed pronunciation counts for four inflected forms of the word 'interest' in about 100 hours American English broadcast news and conversational telephone speech data. It can be seen that the number of occurrences varies quite a bit for the different forms, and the data type. As can be expected there is a higher proportion of reduced forms are observed in CTS data than in BN data. Two main reductions are observed: the transformation of 'ter' into 'tr' (loss of the schwa) and the deletion of the 't' ('inter' is realized as 'iner'). In the recognition dictionary there are a number of similar, less frequent words: interestingly, disinterest, disinterested for which it would be nice to predict pronunciation variants, as well as for other words with a similar syllabic structure: interfere, interfering, interconnect, intercom, ... So an unresolved problem is how to accurately model pronunciation variants. It has been observed that a person will pretty much systematically choose a pronunciation variant, so one research direction is to develop style-specific or accent-specific pronunciations models, which could be adapted to a particular speaker.

Unsupervised model adaptation has been demonstrated to be quite successful for acoustic modeling, and is widely used in most state-of-the-art transcription systems. Several directions have been explored for adaptive language modeling with less convincing results [27]. Concerning pronunciation modeling, large amounts of data are needed to estimate accurate pronunciation probabilities. Where for acoustic modeling a few minutes of speech provides a fair amount of acoustic data for adaptation, this data only contains a few hundred words, many of which do not carry much information content. There are a few more phones for pronunciation modeling, however most are unlikely to be distinctive of the speaker/dialect.

5 Conclusion

Automatic speech recognition is a key technology for audio indexing. Recent progress has enabled the development of systems for a handful of languages that achieve word errors rates the order of 10 to 30% depending upon the type of data. Such performance levels are sufficient to support some near-term applications for structuring and mining spoken data collections, in particular those containing prepared speech. Higher error rates on the order of 20-50% have been reported for speech data from more interactive situations (interviews, debates, conversations, meetings). Transcriptions of speech data remain critical for language modeling, since 100 hours represents only about 1 million words of texts which is largely insufficient. Some recent efforts have been devoted to locating speech-like texts on the Internet.

References

1. International Workshop on Spoken Languages Technologies for Under-resourced languages, SLTU Hanoi, (May 2008), http://www.mica.edu.vn/sltu
2. Schultz, T., Kirchhoff, K. (eds.): Multilingual Speech Processing. Elsevier, Amsterdam (2006)
3. Bourlard, H., Furui, S., Morgan, N., Strik, H. (eds.): Modeling pronunciation variation for automatic speech recognition.In: Speech Communication, vol. 29(2-4) (November 1999) (Special issue)
4. Fosler-Lussier, E., Byrne, W., Jurafsky, D. (eds.): Pronunciation Modeling and Lexicon Adaptation.In: Speech communication, vol. 46(2) (June 2005) (Special issue)
5. Adda-Decker, M., Lamel, L.: Pronunciation variants across system configuration, language and speaking style. Speech Communication 29(2-4), 83–98 (1999)
6. Aubert, X.L.: An overview of decoding techniques for large vocabulary continuous speech recognition. Computer Speech & Language 16(1), 89–114 (2002)
7. Bahl, L.R., Baker, J.K., Cohen, P.S., Dixon, N.R., Jelinek, F., Mercer, R.L., Silverman, H.F.: Preliminary results on the performance of a system for the automatic recognition of continuous speech. In: IEEE ICASSP-1976, Philadelphia (April 1976)
8. Barras, C., Zhu, X., Meignier, S., Gauvain, J.L.: Multistage speaker diarization of broadcast news. IEEE Transactions on Audio, Speech and Language Processing 14(5), 1505–1512 (2006)
9. Bulyko, I., Ostendorf, M., Stolcke, A.: Gtting more mileage from web text sources for conversational speech language modeling using class-dependent mixtures. In: Hearst, M., Ostendorf, M. (eds.) HLT-NAACL 2003, Edmonton, March 2003, vol. 2, pp. 7–9 (2003)
10. Campbell, J.: Speaker Recognition: A Tutorial. Proc. of the IEEE 85(9) (September 1997)
11. Deshmukh, N., Duncan, R., Ganapathiraju, A., Picone, J.: Benchmarking Human Performance for Continuous Speech Recognition. In: Fourth International Conference on Spoken Language Processing, Philadelphia, October 1996, vol. 1(10) (1996)
12. Gauvain, J.L., Lamel, L., Adda, G.: The LIMSI Broadcast News Transcription System. Speech Communication 37(1-2), 89–108 (2002)

13. Hermansky, H., Sharma, S.: TRAPs - classifiers of TempoRAl Patterns. In: ICSLP 1998, Sydney (November 1998)
14. Jelinek, F.: Continuous Speech Recognition by Statistical Methods. Proc. of the IEEE 64(4), 532–556 (1976)
15. Katz, S.M.: Estimation of Probabilities from Sparse Data for the Language Model Component of a Speech Recognizer. IEEE Trans. Acoustics, Speech & Signal Processing ASSP-35(3), 400–401 (1987)
16. Kemp, T., Waibel, A.: Unsupervised Training of a Speech Recognizer: Recent Experiments. In: ESCA Eurospeech 1999, Budapest, Hungary, September 1999, vol. 6, pp. 2725–2728 (1999)
17. Kimball, O., Kao, C.L., Iyer, R., Arvizo, T., Makhoul, J.: Using Quick Transcriptions to Improve Conversational Speech Models. In: ICSLP 2004, Jeju, (October 2004)
18. Lamel, L., Gauvain, J.L., Adda, G., Barras, C., Bilinski, E., Galibert, O., Pujol, A., Schwenk, H., Zhu, X.: The LIMSI 2006 TC-STAR EPPS Transcription Systems. In: ICASSP, Honolulu, April 2007, pp. 997–1000 (2007)
19. Lamel, L., Gauvain, J.L.: Speech Recognition. In: Mitkov, R. (ed.) Chapter 16 in *OUP Handbook on Computational Linguistics*, pp. 305–322. Oxford University Press, Oxford (2003)
20. Lamel, L., Gauvain, J.L., Adda, G.: Lightly Supervised and Unsupervised Acoustic Model Training. Computer, Speech & Language 16(1), 115–229 (2002)
21. Lamel, L., Gauvain, J.L., Adda, G., Adda-Decker, M., Canseco, L., Chen, L., Galibert, O., Messaoudi, A., Schwenk, H.: Speech Transcription in Multiple Languages. In: IEEE ICASSP 2004, Montreal (April 2004)
22. Lippmann, R.P.: Speech recognition by machines and humans. Speech Communication 22(1), 1–16
23. Pellegrini, T., Lamel, L.: Experimental detection of vowel pronunciation variants in Amharic. In: LREC 2006, Genoa (2006)
24. Przybocki, M.: Technology Advancements have Required NIST Evaluations to Change Data and Tasks - and now Metrics. In: Presented at the ELRA Workshop on Evaluation, LREC 2008, Marrakesh (2008)
25. Stolcke, A., Chen, B., et al.: Recent innovations in speech-to-text transcription at SRI-ICSI-UW. IEEE Transactions on Audio, Speech, and Language Processing 14(5), 1729–1744 (2006)
26. van Leeuwen, D.A., van den Berg, L.G., Steeneken, H.J.M.: Human Benchmarks for Speaker Independent Large Vocabulary Recognition Performance. In: ESCA Eurospeech 1995, Madrid, pp. 1461–1464 (September 1995)
27. Rosenfeld, R.: Two decades of statistical language modeling: where do we go from here? Proc. IEEE 88(8), 1270–1278 (1999)
28. Schwenk, H.: Continuous space language models. Computer Speech and Language 21, 492–518 (2007)
29. Van Thong, J.M., Goddeau, D., Litvinova, A., Logan, B., Moreno, P., Swain, M.: SpeechBot: a speech recognition based audio indexing system for the web. In: RIAO 2000 Content-Based Multimedia Information Access, Paris, pp. 106–115 (April 2000)
30. Zavaliagkos, G., Colthurst, T.: Utilizing Untranscribed Training Data to Improve Performance. In: DARPA Broadcast News Transcription & Understanding Wshop (November 1998)
31. Zhu, X., Barras, C., Lamel, L., Gauvain, J.L.: Speaker Diarization: from Broadcast News to Lectures. In: Renals, S., Bengio, S., Fiscus, J. (eds.) MLMI 2006. LNCS, vol. 4299, pp. 396–406. Springer, Heidelberg (2006)
32. Zhu, Q., Stolcke, A., Chen, B.Y., Morgan, N.: Using MLP features in SRI's conversational speech recognition system. Interspeech 2005, 2141-2144, Lisbon (2005)
33. Zissman, M.A.: Comparison of Four Approaches to Automatic Language Identification of Telephone Speech. IEEE Trans. Speech and Audio Proc. 4(1), 31–44 (1996)

Sorting Out Dependency Parsing

Joakim Nivre

Uppsala University, Department of Linguistics and Philology
Växjö University, School of Mathematics and Systems Engineering
joakim.nivre@lingfil.uu.se
http://stp.lingfil.uu.se/~nivre/

Abstract. This paper explores the idea that non-projective dependency parsing can be conceived as the outcome of two interleaved processes, one that sorts the words of a sentence into a canonical order, and one that performs strictly projective dependency parsing on the sorted input. Based on this idea, a parsing algorithm is constructed by combining an online sorting algorithm with an arc-standard transition system for projective dependency parsing.

Keywords: parsing, sorting, non-projective dependency parsing.

1 Introduction

In syntactic parsing of natural language, we analyze sentences by constructing representations of their syntactic structure. Many different representations have been proposed for this purpose, but in this paper we will restrict our attention to *dependency graphs*. This form of representation, which comes out of a long tradition of theoretical work in dependency grammar [1,2,3,4], has recently enjoyed widespread interest in the computational linguistics community and have been used for applications as diverse as information extraction [5], machine translation [6], textual entailment [7], lexical ontology induction [8], and question answering [9]. We attribute this increase in interest to the fact that dependency graphs provide a transparent encoding of predicate-argument structure, which is useful for certain types of applications, together with the fact that they can be processed both efficiently and accurately, in particular using data-driven models that are induced from syntactically annotated corpora. Such models have recently been applied to a wide range of languages in connection with the CoNLL shared tasks on dependency parsing in 2006 and 2007 [10,11].

The dependency graph for a sentence is usually taken to be a directed tree, with nodes corresponding to the words of the sentence and with labeled arcs representing syntactic relations between words. For simplicity, it is often assumed that the single root of this tree is an artificial word ROOT prefixed to the sentence, as illustrated in Figure 1. One issue that is often debated is whether dependency graphs should also be assumed to be *projective*, that is, whether the yield of every subtree should be a continuous substring of the sentence. The dependency graph in Figure 1 fails to satisfy this condition, because the subtrees rooted at

A. Ranta, B. Nordström (Eds.): GoTAL 2008, LNAI 5221, pp. 16–27, 2008.

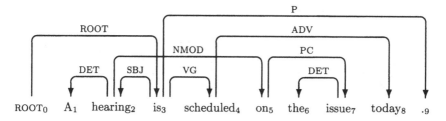

Fig. 1. Dependency graph for an English sentence (non-projective)

the words *hearing* and *scheduled* both have discontinuous yields (words 1, 2, 5, 6, 7 in the first case, words 4, 8 in the second). Most researchers today assume that, although projectivity is appealing from a computational point of view, it is too restrictive from a linguistic representational point of view, and most frameworks therefore allow non-projective dependency graphs for representing discontinuous linguistic constructions. This raises the question of how to parse such representations accurately and efficiently, given that most parsing algorithms proposed for natural language are limited to the derivation of continuous structures.

Current approaches to non-projective dependency parsing typically take one of two routes. Either they employ a non-standard parsing algorithm that is not limited to the derivation of continuous substructures, or they try to recover non-projective dependencies by post-processing the output of a strictly projective parser. The most well-known example of the former approach is the application of the Chu-Liu-Edmonds maximum spanning tree algorithm for directed graphs to dependency parsing [12], although other algorithms also exist [13,14]. The second approach is exemplified by pseudo-projective parsing [15], corrective modeling [16], and approximate second-order spanning tree parsing [17]. In this paper, we start exploring a third route, based on the idea that the parsing problem for dependency graphs can be decomposed into a *sorting problem*, where the input words need to be sorted into a canonical order, and a simpler *parsing problem*, where the ordered input is mapped to a strictly projective dependency graph.

The rest of the paper is structured as follows. Section 2 reviews the transition-based approach to projective dependency parsing, which is one of our building blocks. Section 3 introduces the idea of sorting the input words to facilitate parsing, defines the canonical sort order in terms of tree traversals, and presents a transition-based sorting algorithm. Section 4 puts the two building blocks together and presents an algorithm that simultaneously sorts the words in the input and constructs a projective dependency graph for the sorted input, a graph that may or may not be non-projective with respect to the original word order. Section 5 concludes and makes suggestions for future research.

2   Projective Dependency Parsing

The transition-based approach to dependency parsing has two key components. The first is a transition system for mapping sentences to dependency graphs;

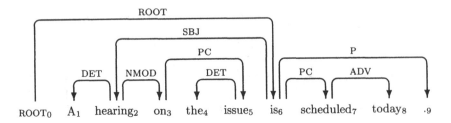

Fig. 2. Dependency graph for an English sentence (projective)

the second is a treebank-induced classifier for predicting the next transition for arbitrary configurations of the parser [18]. We will focus here on the first component and define a transition system that derives strictly projective dependency graphs, using a bottom-up, arc-standard parsing strategy, which is essentially a variant of the system described previously in [19,20,21]. But first of all, we need to define the notion of a dependency graph a little more precisely.

Given a set $L = \{l_1, \ldots, l_{|L|}\}$ of dependency labels, a *dependency graph* for a sentence $S = w_0 w_1 \cdots w_n$ (where $w_0 = $ ROOT) is a labeled directed graph $G = (V_S, A)$, where

1. $V_S = \{0, 1, \ldots, n\}$ is a set of nodes;
2. $A \subseteq V_S \times L \times V_S$ is a set of labeled directed arcs;

The set V_S of *nodes* (or *vertices*) is the set of non-negative integers up to and including n, each corresponding to the linear position of a word in the sentence (including ROOT). The set A of *arcs* (or *directed edges*) is a set of ordered triples (i, l, j), where i and j are nodes and l is a dependency label. Since arcs are used to represent dependency relations, we will say that i is the *head* and l is the *dependency type* of j. Conversely, we say that j is a *dependent* of i.

For a dependency graph $G = (V_S, A)$ to be well-formed we in addition require that it is a *tree* rooted at the node 0. This implies that there is a unique directed path from the root node to every other node of the graph, and that every node except the root has exactly one incoming arc. By contrast, we do *not* require that G is projective with respect to the sentence S, i.e., that the yield of every subtree of G forms a continuous substring of S (where the yield of a subtree is the set of words corresponding to nodes in the subtree).

As already noted, the dependency graph depicted in Figure 1 is not projective, since the subtrees rooted at nodes 2 and 4 do not have continuous yields. Note, however, that projectivity is not a property of the dependency graph in isolation, but only of the graph in combination with the word order of a sentence. Thus, the dependency graph in Figure 2, while isomorphic to the graph in Figure 1, is projective because the words of the sentence occur in a different order. We will return to this observation in the next section, but first we will concentrate on parsing sentences with strictly projective dependency graphs.

A transition system for dependency parsing consists of a set of *configurations* and *transitions* between configurations. Given a sentence $S = w_0 w_1, \cdots w_n$, we

Transition		Condition
LEFT-ARC$_l$	$([\sigma|w_i, w_j], \beta, A) \Rightarrow ([\sigma|w_j], \beta, A\cup\{(j,l,i)\})$	$i \neq 0$
RIGHT-ARC$_l$	$([\sigma|w_i, w_j], \beta, A) \Rightarrow ([\sigma|w_i], \beta, A\cup\{(i,l,j)\})$	
SHIFT	$(\sigma, [w_i|\beta], A) \Rightarrow ([\sigma|w_i], \beta, A)$	

Fig. 3. Transitions for projective dependency parsing

take a *configuration* to be a triple $c = (\sigma, \beta, A)$, where σ is a stack of words $w_i \in S$, β is a buffer of words $w_i \in S$, and A is a set of labeled directed arcs $(i, l, j) \in V_S \times L \times V_S$. When necessary, we use σ_c, β_c and A_c to refer to the different components of a configuration c, and we use G_c to refer to the dependency graph $G = (V_S, A_c)$ defined by c. Both the stack and the buffer will be represented as lists, although the stack will have its head (or top) to the right for reasons of perspicuity. Thus, $[\sigma|w_i]$ represents a stack with top w_i and tail σ, while $[w_j|\beta]$ represents a buffer with head w_j and tail β. We use square brackets for enumerated lists, e.g., $[1, 2, \ldots, n]$, with $[]$ for the empty list as a special case.

Given the notion of a parser configuration, we can now define a *transition* to be a (partial) function from configurations to configurations. The following set of transitions, defined more formally in Figure 3, are sufficient for projective dependency parsing:

1. The transition LEFT-ARC$_l$, parameterized for an arc label $l \in L$, updates a parser configuration with words w_i, w_j on top of the stack by adding the arc (j, l, i) to the arc set A and replacing w_i, w_j on the stack by w_j alone. This is a legal transition as long as $w_i \neq$ ROOT$_0$.

2. The transition RIGHT-ARC$_l$, parameterized for an arc label $l \in L$, updates a parser configuration with words w_i, w_j on top of the stack by adding the arc (i, l, j) to the arc set A and replacing w_i, w_j on the stack by w_i alone.

3. The transition SHIFT updates a parser configuration with the word w_i as the first word of the buffer by removing w_i from the buffer and pushing it onto the stack.

The transition system defined in Figure 3 is *complete* for the set of well-formed projective dependency graphs in the sense that, for any sentence $S = w_0w_1 \cdots w_n$ with projective dependency graph G, there is a transition sequence $(c_0, c_1, \ldots, c_m)$ such that:

1. $c_0 = ([w_0], [w_1, \ldots, w_n], \emptyset)$
2. $c_{i+1} = t_i(c_i)$ for some transition t_i $(0 \leq i < m)$
3. $G_{c_m} = G$

For example, the dependency graph for the sentence in Figure 2 is derived by the transition sequence given in Figure 4. Ideally, the system should also be *sound*

Transition	Stack (σ)	Buffer (β)	New Arc
	$[R_0]$	$[A_1, \ldots, {}_{.9}]$	
SHIFT	$[R_0, A_1]$	$[hearing_2, \ldots, {}_{.9}]$	
SHIFT	$[R_0, A_1, hearing_2]$	$[on_3, \ldots, {}_{.9}]$	
LA$_{DET}$	$[R_0, hearing_2]$	$[on_3, \ldots, {}_{.9}]$	$(2, DET, 1)$
SHIFT	$[R_0, hearing_2, on_3]$	$[the_4, \ldots, {}_{.9}]$	
SHIFT	$[R_0, \ldots, on_3, the_4]$	$[issues_5, \ldots, {}_{.9}]$	
SHIFT	$[R_0, \ldots, the_4, issues_5]$	$[is_6, \ldots, {}_{.9}]$	
LA$_{DET}$	$[R_0, \ldots, on_3, issues_5]$	$[is_6, \ldots, {}_{.9}]$	$(5, DET, 4)$
RA$_{PC}$	$[R_0, hearing_2, on_3]$	$[is_6, \ldots, {}_{.9}]$	$(3, PC, 5)$
RA$_{NMOD}$	$[R_0, hearing_2]$	$[is_6, \ldots, {}_{.9}]$	$(2, NMOD, 3)$
SHIFT	$[R_0, hearing_2, is_6]$	$[scheduled_7, \ldots, {}_{.9}]$	
LA$_{SBJ}$	$[R_0, is_6]$	$[scheduled_7, \ldots, {}_{.9}]$	$(6, SBJ, 2)$
SHIFT	$[R_0, is_6, scheduled_7]$	$[today_8, {}_{.9}]$	
SHIFT	$[R_0, \ldots, scheduled_7, today_8]$	$[{}_{.9}]$	
RA$_{ADV}$	$[R_0, is_6, scheduled_7]$	$[{}_{.9}]$	$(7, ADV, 8)$
RA$_{VG}$	$[R_0, is_6]$	$[{}_{.9}]$	$(6, VG, 7)$
SHIFT	$[R_0, is_6, {}_{.9}]$	$[]$	
RA$_P$	$[R_0, is_6]$	$[]$	$(6, P, 9)$
RA$_{ROOT}$	$[R_0]$	$[]$	$(0, ROOT, 6)$

Fig. 4. Transition sequence for parsing the English sentence in Figure 2

with respect to the set of well-formed projective dependency graphs, in the sense that every transition sequence derives a well-formed graph, which unfortunately is not the case. However, every dependency graph derived by a transition sequence is guaranteed to be a forest (set of trees), which means that it can trivially be converted to a well-formed dependency graph by adding arcs from the node 0 to all (other) root nodes.[1]

We define an *oracle o* to be a function from configurations to transitions such that, for any sentence S with (projective) dependency graph G, if $(c_0, c_1, \ldots, c_m)$ is the transition sequence that derives G for S, then $o(c_i) = t_i$ (for every i such that $0 \leq i < m$). That is, for every configuration c_i, the oracle returns the correct transition t_i out of c_i. Given an oracle, projective dependency parsing can be performed deterministically using the following algorithm:

PARSE($S = w_0 w_1 \cdots w_n$)
1 $c \leftarrow ([w_0], [w_1, \ldots, w_n], \emptyset)$
2 **while** $\beta_c \neq []$
3   SHIFT(c)
4     $t \leftarrow o(c)$
5   **while** $t \in \{\text{LEFT-ARC}_l, \text{RIGHT-ARC}_l\}$
6         $c \leftarrow t(c)$
7         $t \leftarrow o(c)$
8 **return** G_c

---

[1] For proofs of soundness and completeness for this transition system, see [20].

The parser is initialized to the configuration $c = ([w_0], [w_1, \ldots, w_n], \emptyset)$, where the stack σ_c contains the artificial root word ROOT, the buffer β_c contains all the real words of the sentence (in their linear order), and the arc set A_c is empty. The outer **while** loop is executed as long as there are words remaining in the buffer and starts by shifting the next word onto the stack after which it calls the oracle. The inner **while** loop is executed as long as the oracle predicts a LEFT-ARC$_l$ or RIGHT-ARC$_l$ transition and simply updates the configuration using the predicted transition and then calls the oracle again. After parsing is completed, the dependency graph G_c defined by the final configuration c is returned.

It is not hard to show that this algorithm terminates after at most $2n$ transitions, as it performs exactly n SHIFT transitions (one for each word initially in the buffer) and can perform at most n other transitions (since both LEFT-ARC$_l$ and RIGHT-ARC$_l$ reduce the size of the stack by 1). This means that, if oracle calls (lines 4 and 7) and transitions (lines 3 and 6) can be computed in constant time, then the time complexity of the parsing algorithm is $O(n)$ [20].

In order to build practical parsing systems, the oracle o has to be approximated by a classifier trained on data derived from a treebank. For every sentence S with dependency graph G, we construct a set of training instances of the form (c_i, t_i), where c_i is a parser configuration and t_i the correct transition out of c_i for the sentence. Training a classifier on such instances can be done using standard machine learning methods for discriminative classification, such as support vector machines or memory-based learning [22,23], and transition-based parsing using treebank-induced classifiers has been shown to give state-of-the-art parsing accuracy in several experimental evaluations [10,11,24]. For the rest of this paper, however, we will ignore the machine learning aspects and concentrate on the construction of a parsing algorithm that is not limited to projective graphs.

3   Sorting to Projective Order

As noted in the preceding section, the projectivity constraint on dependency graphs only holds in relation to a particular word order. And given a sentence $S = w_0 w_1 \cdots w_n$ with (non-projective) dependency graph G, it is always possible to find a permutation S' of S such that G is a projective dependency graph for S'. Moreover, since the graph structure remains the same, all the information about the syntactic structure encoded in G is preserved in this permutation. To take a concrete example, the sentence in Figure 1 can be permuted to the sentence in Figure 2 in order to make the dependency graph projective. In this section, we are going to explore the idea that this kind of permutation can be viewed as a sorting problem, which can be solved using standard sorting algorithms, and that this is a way of extending the transition-based dependency parsing method described in the preceding section to non-projective dependency graphs.

Let $S = w_0 w_1 \cdots w_n$ be a sentence with dependency graph $G = (V_S, A)$. We define the *projective order* of the words in S to be the order in which the corresponding nodes in V_S are visited in an inorder traversal of G starting at the root node 0, where the local order on a node and its children is given by the

Transition		Condition
SWAP	$(m, [\sigma|w_i, w_j|\sigma_m], \beta) \Rightarrow (m{+}1, [\sigma|w_j, w_i|\sigma_m], \beta)$	$i \neq 0$
SHIFT	$(m, \sigma, [w_i|\beta]) \Rightarrow (0, [\sigma|w_i], \beta)$	

Fig. 5. Transitions for sorting into projective order

arithmetic order $<$ on V_S induced by the original word order. The basic idea behind the notion of a projective order is to find a way to impose a linear order on the nodes of the dependency graph in such a way that we guarantee that every subtree has a continuous yield. This can be done in a variety of ways, but because we want to preserve as much as possible of the original word order, we choose an ordering that respects the original ordering of words corresponding to nodes that stand in a parent-child or sibling relation. We can exemplify this by returning to the sentence in Figure 1:

ROOT$_0$ A$_1$ hearing$_2$ is$_3$ scheduled$_4$ on$_5$ the$_6$ issue$_7$ today$_8$.$_9$

Given the dependency graph in Figure 1, the projective order of the words is the following (which corresponds to the word order of the sentence in Figure 2):

ROOT$_0$ A$_1$ hearing$_2$ on$_5$ the$_6$ issue$_7$ is$_3$ scheduled$_4$ today$_8$.$_9$

We now want to explore the idea that (non-projective) dependency parsing can be performed by sorting the words of a sentence into their projective order and deriving a strictly projective dependency graphs for the sorted input. In principle, we could use any one of the many algorithms that have been proposed for sorting, but our desire to combine sorting with a transition-based approach to parsing imposes certain constraints on the kind of algorithm that can be used. First of all, it should be an *online* algorithm, so that we can start sorting (and parsing) before having seen the end of the input, in an incremental left-to-right fashion. Secondly, it should be an *exchange sort*, which sorts by exchanging adjacent elements, so that sorting and parsing transitions can be defined on the same kinds of configurations. One algorithm that satisfies these constraints is *gnome sort*, which is similar to insertion sort, except that moving an element to its proper place is accomplished by a series of swaps, as in bubble sort. The worst-case time complexity of *gnome sort* is $O(n^2)$, but in practice the algorithm can run as fast as insertion sort and is very efficient on nearly sorted lists. This is an attractive property given that dependency graphs for natural language sentences tend to be very nearly projective, which means that the projective order will typically be close to the original word order [25,26].

In order to facilitate integration with the parser defined earlier, we first present a transition-based version of gnome sort, where a configuration is a triple $c = (m, \sigma, \beta)$, consisting of an index m and two lists σ and β, and where we use the two transitions defined in Figure 5. The idea is that the list β contains the list

Transition	m	List (σ)	Buffer (β)
	0	$[R_0]$	$[A_1, \ldots, .9]$
SHIFT	0	$[R_0, \mathbf{A_1}]$	$[\text{hearing}_2, \ldots, .9]$
SHIFT	0	$[R_0, A_1, \mathbf{hearing_2}]$	$[\text{is}_3, \ldots, .9]$
SHIFT	0	$[R_0, \text{hearing}_2, \mathbf{is_3}]$	$[\text{scheduled}_4, \ldots, .9]$
SHIFT	0	$[R_0, \ldots, \text{is}_3, \mathbf{scheduled_4}]$	$[\text{on}_5, \ldots, .9]$
SHIFT	0	$[R_0, \ldots, \text{scheduled}_4, \mathbf{on_5}]$	$[\text{the}_6, \ldots, .9]$
SWAP	1	$[R_0, \ldots, \text{is}_3, \mathbf{on_5}, \text{scheduled}_4]$	$[\text{the}_6, \ldots, .9]$
SWAP	2	$[R_0, \text{hearing}_2, \mathbf{on_5}, \text{is}_3, \text{scheduled}_4]$	$[\text{the}_6, \ldots, .9]$
SHIFT	0	$[R_0, \ldots, \text{scheduled}_4, \mathbf{the_6}]$	$[\text{issue}_7, \ldots, .9]$
SWAP	1	$[R_0, \ldots, \text{is}_3, \mathbf{the_6}, \text{scheduled}_4]$	$[\text{issue}_7, \ldots, .9]$
SWAP	2	$[R_0, \ldots, \text{on}_5, \mathbf{the_6}, \text{is}_3, \text{scheduled}_4]$	$[\text{issue}_7, \ldots, .9]$
SHIFT	0	$[R_0, \ldots, \text{scheduled}_4, \mathbf{issue_7}]$	$[\text{today}_8, .9]$
SWAP	1	$[R_0, \ldots, \text{is}_3, \mathbf{issue_7}, \text{scheduled}_4]$	$[\text{today}_8, .9]$
SWAP	2	$[R_0, \ldots, \text{the}_6, \mathbf{issue_7}, \text{is}_3, \text{scheduled}_4]$	$[\text{today}_8, .9]$
SHIFT	0	$[R_0, \ldots, \text{scheduled}_4, \mathbf{today_8}]$	$[.9]$
SHIFT	0	$[R_0, \ldots, .9]$	$[\,]$

Fig. 6. Transition sequence for sorting the English sentence in Figure 1 ($\sigma[m]$ in bold)

of remaining words to be sorted, while the list σ contains the words sorted so far, with the index m referring to the position in σ of the word that is being inserted into its proper place (with the first position having index 0). The two transitions work as follows:

1. The SWAP transition swaps the mth and $m+1$th words in σ and increments the index to $m+1$ (the position of the word in mth position before the swap).
2. The SHIFT transition takes the next word from β, inserts it at the head of σ and sets the index m to 0 (the position of the newly inserted word).

Note that we use the notation $[\sigma | w_i, w_j | \sigma_m]$ to refer to a list (with its head to the right) with a prefix of m words, followed by the words w_i and w_j and a tail σ of unspecified length.

Assume now that we have an *oracle* o, which maps each configuration to the correct transition (SWAP or SHIFT) in order to sort the words of a sentence into their projective order. Then sorting can be performed using an algorithm that is very similar to the parsing algorithm described in the previous section:

SORT($S = w_0 w_1 \cdots w_n$)
1 $c \leftarrow (0, [w_0], [w_1, \cdots, w_n])$
2 **while** $\beta_c \neq [\,]$
3   SHIFT(c)
4      $t \leftarrow o(c)$
5   **while** $t = $ SWAP
6          $c \leftarrow t(c)$
7          $t \leftarrow o(c)$
8 **return** σ_c

Transition		Condition
SWAP	$(m, [\sigma|w_i, w_j|\sigma_m], \beta, A) \Rightarrow (m{+}1, [\sigma|w_j, w_i|\sigma_m], \beta, A)$	$i \neq 0$
LEFT-ARC$_l$	$(m, [\sigma|w_i, w_j|\sigma_m], \beta, A) \Rightarrow (m, [\sigma|w_j|\sigma_m], \beta, A\cup\{(j,l,i)\})$	$i \neq 0$
RIGHT-ARC$_l$	$(m, [\sigma|w_i, w_j|\sigma_m], \beta, A) \Rightarrow (m, [\sigma|w_i|\sigma_m], \beta, A\cup\{(i,l,j)\})$	
SHIFT	$(m, \sigma, [w_i|\beta], A) \Rightarrow (0, [\sigma|w_i], \beta, A)$	

Fig. 7. Transitions for integrated sorting and parsing

The outer **while** loop is executed once for each word to be inserted into its place in the projective order, while the inner **while** loop is executed as many times as the word needs to be swapped with its neighbor in order to reach its place. To illustrate how this sort procedure works, Figure 6 shows the transition sequence for sorting the words of the sentence in Figure 1 into their projective order.

4   Integrated Sorting and Parsing

In the two previous sections, we have shown how to perform projective dependency parsing and how to sort the words of a sentence into their projective order, in both cases relying on oracles for predicting the next transition, which in practice can be approximated by classifiers trained on syntactically annotated sentences. In this section, we will put the two pieces together and define an algorithm that simultaneously sorts the words of a sentence into their projective order and derives a projective dependency graph for the sorted input, which may or may not be non-projective in relation to the original word order.

We let a *configuration* be a quadruple $c = (m, \sigma, \beta, A)$, where m, σ, and β are as in section 3, and where A is a set of dependency arcs as in section 2; we use the transitions in Figure 7, where SWAP and SHIFT are exactly as in section 3, and where LEFT-ARC$_l$ and RIGHT-ARC$_l$ have been modified to apply to the mth and $m{+}1$th word in σ instead of the first and second; and we use the following algorithm:

```
SORTPARSE(S = w₀w₁ ··· wₙ)
 1 c ← (0, [w₀], [w₁, . . . , wₙ], ∅)
 2 while βc ≠ []
 3     SHIFT(c)
 4     t ← o(c)
 5     while t = SWAP
 6         c ← t(c)
 7         t ← o(c)
 8     while t ∈ {LEFT-ARCₗ, RIGHT-ARCₗ}
 9         c ← t(c)
10         t ← o(c)
11 return Gc
```

Transition	m	List (σ)	Buffer (β)	New Arc
	0	[R_0]	[$A_1, \ldots, .9$]	
SHIFT	0	[R_0, A_1]	[$hearing_2, \ldots, .9$]	
SHIFT	0	[$R_0, A_1, \mathbf{hearing_2}$]	[$is_3, \ldots, .9$]	
LA$_{\text{DET}}$	0	[$R_0, \mathbf{hearing_2}$]	[$is_3, \ldots, .9$]	$(2, \text{DET}, 1)$
SHIFT	0	[$R_0, hearing_2, is_3$]	[$scheduled_4, \ldots, .9$]	
SHIFT	0	[$R_0, \ldots, is_3, \mathbf{scheduled_4}$]	[$on_5, \ldots, .9$]	
SHIFT	0	[$R_0, \ldots, scheduled_4, \mathbf{on_5}$]	[$the_6, \ldots, .9$]	
SWAP	1	[$R_0, \ldots, is_3, \mathbf{on_5}, scheduled_4$]	[$the_6, \ldots, .9$]	
SWAP	2	[$R_0, hearing_2, \mathbf{on_5}, is_3, scheduled_4$]	[$the_6, \ldots, .9$]	
SHIFT	0	[$R_0, \ldots, scheduled_4, \mathbf{the_6}$]	[$issue_7, \ldots, .9$]	
SWAP	1	[$R_0, \ldots, is_3, \mathbf{the_6}, scheduled_4$]	[$issue_7, \ldots, .9$]	
SWAP	2	[$R_0, \ldots, on_5, \mathbf{the_6}, is_3, scheduled_4$]	[$issue_7, \ldots, .9$]	
SHIFT	0	[$R_0, \ldots, scheduled_4, \mathbf{issue_7}$]	[$today_8, .9$]	
SWAP	1	[$R_0, \ldots, is_3, \mathbf{issue_7}, scheduled_4$]	[$today_8, .9$]	
SWAP	2	[$R_0, \ldots, the_6, \mathbf{issue_7}, is_3, scheduled_4$]	[$today_8, .9$]	
LA$_{\text{DET}}$	2	[$R_0, \ldots, on_5, \mathbf{issue_7}, is_3, scheduled_4$]	[$today_8, .9$]	$(7, \text{DET}, 6)$
RA$_{\text{PC}}$	2	[$R_0, hearing_2, \mathbf{on_5}, is_3, scheduled_4$]	[$today_8, .9$]	$(5, \text{PC}, 7)$
RA$_{\text{NMOD}}$	2	[$R_0, \mathbf{hearing_2}, is_3, scheduled_4$]	[$today_8, \ldots, .9$]	$(2, \text{NMOD}, 5)$
SHIFT	0	[$R_0, \ldots, scheduled_4, \mathbf{today_8}$]	[$.9$]	
RA$_{\text{ADV}}$	0	[$R_0, \ldots, is_3, \mathbf{scheduled_4}$]	[$.9$]	$(4, \text{ADV}, 8)$
RA$_{\text{VG}}$	0	[$R_0, hearing_2, \mathbf{is_3}$]	[$.9$]	$(3, \text{VG}, 4)$
LA$_{\text{SBJ}}$	0	[$R_0, \mathbf{is_3}$]	[$.9$]	$(3, \text{SBJ}, 2)$
SHIFT	0	[$R_0, is_3, .9$]	[]	
RA$_{\text{P}}$	0	[$R_0, \mathbf{is_3}$]	[]	$(3, \text{P}, 9)$
RA$_{\text{ROOT}}$	0	[R_0]	[]	$(0, \text{ROOT}, 3)$

Fig. 8. Transition sequence for parsing the English sentence in Figure 1 ($\sigma[m]$ in bold)

As before, the outer **while** loop is executed once for each word w_i ($1 \leq i \leq n$), which is inserted at the head of the list σ. The first inner **while** loop inserts w_i in its proper place, by performing the required number of SWAP transitions, and the second inner **while** loop adds the required number of arcs before the next word is shifted to σ. The parsing procedure is exemplified in Figure 8, which shows the transition sequence for parsing the sentence in Figure 1.

Provided that oracle predictions and transitions can both be performed in constant time,[2] the time complexity of the algorithm is $O(n^2)$ in the worst case but $O(n)$ in the best case where the input words are already sorted in the projective order. Since dependency graphs for natural language sentences tend to be very nearly projective, the algorithm can therefore be expected to be very efficient in practice.

---

[2] The time taken to compute the oracle prediction depends heavily on the time of classifier used but does not in general depend on the length of the input sentence. It can therefore be regarded as a constant in this context, corresponding to the grammar constant in grammar-based approaches to parsing.

5 Conclusion

In this paper, we have explored the idea that the general parsing problem for dependency graphs can be decomposed into a sorting problem and a simpler parsing problem restricted to projective dependency graphs. Based on this idea, we have constructed a parsing algorithm for non-projective dependency graphs by combining an online sorting algorithm with a projective parsing algorithm. The next important step in the exploration of this approach is to develop a practical parsing system by training classifiers to approximate the oracle used to predict the next transition. This methodology has previously proven successful for strictly projective dependency parsing, but it is an open question how well it will perform for the more complex problem of integrated sorting and parsing. Finally, it is worth emphasizing that the projective order and sorting algorithm proposed in this paper only define one of many conceivable realizations of the basic idea of integrated sorting and parsing. Exploring alternative orders and sorting strategies is another important area for future research.

References

1. Tesnière, L.: Éléments de syntaxe structurale. Editions Klincksieck (1959)
2. Sgall, P., Hajičová, E., Panevová, J.: The Meaning of the Sentence in Its Pragmatic Aspects. Reidel (1986)
3. Mel'čuk, I.: Dependency Syntax: Theory and Practice. State University of New York Press (1988)
4. Hudson, R.A.: English Word Grammar. Blackwell, Malden (1990)
5. Culotta, A., Sorensen, J.: Dependency tree kernels for relation extraction. In: Proceedings of the 42nd Annual Meeting of the Association for Computational Linguistics (ACL), pp. 423–429 (2004)
6. Ding, Y., Palmer, M.: Synchronous dependency insertion grammars: A grammar formalism for syntax based statistical MT. In: Proceedings of the Workshop on Recent Advances in Dependency Grammar, pp. 90–97 (2004)
7. Haghighi, A., Ng, A., Manning, C.D.: Robust textual inference via graph matching. In: Proceedings of the Human Language Technology Conference and the Conference on Empirical Methods in Natural Language Processing (HLT/EMNLP), pp. 387–394 (2005)
8. Snow, R., Jurafsky, D., Ng, A.Y.: Learning syntactic patterns for automatic hypernym discovery. In: Advances in Neural Information Processing Systems (NIPS) (2005)
9. Wang, M., Smith, N.A., Mitamura, T.: What is the Jeopardy Model? A quasi-synchronous grammar for QA. In: Proceedings of the 2007 Joint Conference on Empirical Methods in Natural Language Processing and Computational Natural Language Learning (EMNLP-CoNLL), pp. 22–32 (2007)
10. Buchholz, S., Marsi, E.: CoNLL-X shared task on multilingual dependency parsing. In: Proceedings of the 10th Conference on Computational Natural Language Learning (CoNLL), pp. 149–164 (2006)
11. Nivre, J., Hall, J., Kübler, S., McDonald, R., Nilsson, J., Riedel, S., Yuret, D.: The CoNLL 2007 shared task on dependency parsing. In: Proceedings of the CoNLL Shared Task of EMNLP-CoNLL 2007, pp. 915–932 (2007)

12. McDonald, R., Pereira, F., Ribarov, K., Hajič, J.: Non-projective dependency parsing using spanning tree algorithms. In: Proceedings of the Human Language Technology Conference and the Conference on Empirical Methods in Natural Language Processing (HLT/EMNLP), pp. 523–530 (2005)
13. Covington, M.A.: A fundamental algorithm for dependency parsing. In: Proceedings of the 39th Annual ACM Southeast Conference, pp. 95–102 (2001)
14. Nivre, J.: Incremental non-projective dependency parsing. In: Proceedings of Human Language Technologies: The Annual Conference of the North American Chapter of the Association for Computational Linguistics (NAACL HLT), pp. 396–403 (2007)
15. Nivre, J., Nilsson, J.: Pseudo-projective dependency parsing. In: Proceedings of the 43rd Annual Meeting of the Association for Computational Linguistics (ACL), pp. 99–106 (2005)
16. Hall, K., Novák, V.: Corrective modeling for non-projective dependency parsing. In: Proceedings of the 9th International Workshop on Parsing Technologies (IWPT), pp. 42–52 (2005)
17. McDonald, R., Pereira, F.: Online learning of approximate dependency parsing algorithms. In: Proceedings of the 11th Conference of the European Chapter of the Association for Computational Linguistics (EACL), pp. 81–88 (2006)
18. Nivre, J.: Inductive Dependency Parsing. Springer, Heidelberg (2006)
19. Nivre, J.: Incrementality in deterministic dependency parsing. In: Proceedings of the Workshop on Incremental Parsing: Bringing Engineering and Cognition Together (ACL), pp. 50–57 (2004)
20. Nivre, J.: Algorithms for deterministic incremental dependency parsing. Computational Linguistics (to appear)
21. Attardi, G.: Experiments with a multilanguage non-projective dependency parser. In: Proceedings of the 10th Conference on Computational Natural Language Learning (CoNLL), pp. 166–170 (2006)
22. Yamada, H., Matsumoto, Y.: Statistical dependency analysis with support vector machines. In: Proceedings of the 8th International Workshop on Parsing Technologies (IWPT), pp. 195–206 (2003)
23. Nivre, J., Hall, J., Nilsson, J.: Memory-based dependency parsing. In: Proceedings of the 8th Conference on Computational Natural Language Learning, pp. 49–56 (2004)
24. Nivre, J., Hall, J., Nilsson, J., Chanev, A., Eryiğit, G., Kübler, S., Marinov, S., Marsi, E.: Maltparser: A language-independent system for data-driven dependency parsing. Natural Language Engineering 13, 95–135 (2007)
25. Nivre, J.: Constraints on non-projective dependency graphs. In: Proceedings of the 11th Conference of the European Chapter of the Association for Computational Linguistics (EACL), pp. 73–80 (2006)
26. Kuhlmann, M., Nivre, J.: Mildly non-projective dependency structures. In: Proceedings of the COLING/ACL 2006 Main Conference Poster Sessions, pp. 507–514 (2006)

"I Know What You Feel": Analyzing the Role of Conjunctions in Automatic Sentiment Analysis

Ritesh Agarwal[1], T.V. Prabhakar[1], and Sugato Chakrabarty[2]

[1] Indian Institute of Technology Kanpur,
Kanpur, India 208016
[2] General Motors Technical Centre,
Bangalore, India 560066
onlyritesh@gmail.com, tvp@cse.iitk.ac.in, sugato.chakrabarty@gm.com

Abstract. We are interested in finding how people feel about certain topics. This could be considered as a task of classifying the *sentiment*: sentiment could be positive, negative or neutral. In this paper, we examine the problem of automatic sentiment analysis at *sentence level*. We observe that sentence structure has a fair contribution towards sentiment determination, and conjunctions play a major role in defining the sentence structure. Our assumption is that in presence of conjunctions, not all phrases have equal contribution towards overall sentiment. We compile a set of conjunction rules to determine relevant phrases for sentiment analysis. Our approach is a representation of the idea to use linguistic resources at phrase level for the analysis at sentence level. We incorporate our approach with support vector machines to conclude that linguistic analysis plays a significant role in sentiment determination. Finally, we verify our results on movie, car and book reviews.

Keywords: Sentiment Analysis, Linguistic Analysis, Natural Language Processing, Support Vector Machines, Machine Learning.

1 Introduction

Recent boom in the popularity and use of internet has resulted in easy and active exchange of information over weblogs and online discussion boards. This information usually conveys opinions of users on variety of products (e.g. automobiles, movies). A considerable effort has been made to analyze such information, called *Sentiment Analysis*. Sentiment analysis aims at classifying these reviews based on author's emotions. It finds useful application in fields like affective tutoring in e-learning systems [17], text summarization [5], quicker response times to market analysis etc. However, motivation to perform sentence level analysis arises from domains (like car) where users praise some features of the product, while being unhappy about some other features. In such cases, classifying entire review as positive or negative makes less sense, rather a deeper analysis is required.

Sentiment analysis is considered to be a difficult problem because: (1) It requires deeper understanding of sentence structure. (2) It requires proper evaluation of the attitude expressed by the opinion words. (3) Classification needs

A. Ranta, B. Nordström (Eds.): GoTAL 2008, LNAI 5221, pp. 28–39, 2008.
© Springer-Verlag Berlin Heidelberg 2008

to be done on the opinion expressed by the author which needs to be derived from the content of the text. While the presence of certain feeling words plays a major role in sentiment identification [13], the task becomes much more complex at sentence level due to the presence of mixed sentiment, sarcasm or irony, co-reference between subjects [11], and structure variations caused by the presence of conjuncts and negations.

In this work, we address a two level problem: (1) separating subjective and objective reviews (called *review identification* henceforth), and (2) classifying subjective reviews as positive or negative (called *sentiment analysis* henceforth). We observed that conjunctions occur with a high frequency in reviews, and they tend to affect the sentiment. Given a sentence with conjunction, our approach uses a set of conjunction rules to determine relevant phrases for overall sentiment determination. Consider this review:

"*The film compels, but overall the field of roughage dominates.*"

Both positive (*compels*) and negative (*roughage*) feeling words co-occur. A human can easily guess that the review is negative, but the task becomes complex for machines without any linguistic knowledge. In our approach, a parser would tell that *but* is used as a coordinating conjunct joining the two underlined verb and adverb phrases. Our conjunction rules will add that sentiment is dominated by the latter phrase, making it easier to classify this review as negative.

The rest of the paper is organized as follows. In the next section we briefly discuss the related work in the area of sentiment analysis. Section 3 studies the effect of conjunctions in sentiment analysis and explains our conjunction rules with examples. In Section 4 we compare various approaches and describe our proposed model alongwith the training and testing methodologies. In Section 5 we discuss the results and perform further analysis. Finally, in Section 6 we conclude our work and discuss possible future work.

2   Related Work

Much of the earlier research in sentiment analysis has been done at document level [1,11,13]. In previous approaches, major concern has been the co-occurrence of expressions, frequent patterns [3], document contents [1] and variations in feature selection for machine learning algorithms [8,11]. Their results show that supervised machine learning methods have been very promising at document level. Other approaches tried to gain advantage from linguistic knowledge sources [9,15] by adding polarity information of adjectives. Sentence level classification is considered significantly harder task [4,16]; these approaches are however, un-supervised in nature. They rely on the fact that sentiment terms of similar orientation tend to co-occur. A sentence level work (mostly unsupervised) has been done by [7], but they calculate phrase level polarities using General Inquirer[1] and Wordnet[2]. A phrase level work by [14] uses a large stable of clues

---

[1] http://www.wjh.harvard.edu/~inquirer
[2] http://wordnet.princeton.edu

marked with prior polarity to identify contextual polarities of phrases. Sentence level work by [6] finds productive synonyms and antonyms of an opinion bearing word through automatic expansion in Wordnet and uses them as feature sets of a classifier. Our work differs from previous works in these aspects: (1) Our focus is on classifying each sentence in a review as positive, negative or neutral. (2) We emphasize on sentence structure and conjunction analysis to locate dominating phrases in a sentence. (3) Our approach is supervised in nature and we verify our results using support vector machines on movie, car and book reviews. We also study the effect of combinations of various feature selection techniques like unigrams, n-grams and part-of-speech tags at sentence level.

3 Sentiment Analysis

In sentiment analysis, the essential issue is to identify the sentiments expressed in texts, and whether the expressions indicate positive (*favorable*) or negative (*unfavorable*) opinion. In topic classification problems, *what* is being communicated has been the major concern; whereas for sentiment analysis, we need to explore *how* is it being communicated.

3.1 Dependency Relations

Thematic relations[3] in a sentence explain the meaning of a noun phrase, as depicted by the verb present in the sentence. Example - "*Alice liked the movie*": *Alice* is an *agent*; *movie* is a *patient*. Major thematic relations include: *agent* – one who performs the action; *patient* – one who undergoes the action; and *experiencer* – one who receives an emotional input. English language often marks such thematic relations with prepositions (after, of, between, without, above etc.) and verbs. These are important in exploiting "*who liked what*" kind of relations and appear to be a good tool in deciding the subject-verb relationship. As an example, consider this review: "*We liked the movie as the locations were great*". Figure 1 shows the typed dependencies given by Stanford NLP Parser[4] for this review. Looking at the *nsubj* and *dobj* relationships, it becomes clear that "*we liked*", "*liked movie*" and "*great locations*" are the associated dependencies. Otherwise, high order n-grams based model is required to capture such relationships, increasing the dimensionality of feature space.

3.2 Effect of Conjunctions

Conjunctions are special words used to join different words, phrases or clauses together to form sentences, and define the relationship among their meanings. There are three main types of conjunctions:

---

[3] http://www.wikipedia.org

[4] We use the Stanford NLP parser available at http://nlp.stanford.edu/software/lex-parser.shtml

> *nsubj (liked-2, We-1)*
> *det (movie-4, the-3)*
> *dobj (liked-2, movie-4)*
> *mark (great-9, as-5)*
> *det (locations-7, the-6)*
> *nsubj (great-9, locations-7)*
> *cop (great-9, were-8)*
> *advcl (liked-2, great-9)*

Fig. 1. Typed dependencies for the example review

1. *Coordinating* conjuncts join one or more words of similar kind (like subject–subject, verb phrase–verb phrase). Examples: *and, nor, but, yet.*
2. *Correlative* conjuncts occur in pairs and they connect sentence elements of the same kind. Examples: *either-or, neither-nor, not only-but also.*
3. *Subordinating* conjuncts are adverbs used to connect secondary clauses to a main clause. Examples: *until, although, though, whereas, while, whether or not, even if.*

Conjunctions play a vital role in deciding the overall sentiment. Following examples will explain in detail:

Example 1. *"Dark and disturbing, yet compelling to watch."*

Here, yet is used as a coordinating conjunct, used to connect an adjective phrase and a noun phrase, having opposite sentiments. Clearly, the overall polarity is positive and dominated by the latter phrase. A system without conjunction analysis would fail to exploit this because of the presence of one positive and two negative feeling words.

Example 2. *"Not only unfunny, but also sad."*

This is an example of a correlative conjunct; they usually connect phrases with similar polarity. Using the usual negation word filtering techniques as in [2], first phrase will be marked as NOT_unfunny, changing its sentiment to positive. However, conjunction analysis will be able to preserve the actual relationship.

Example 3. *"Although bright, well-acted and thought-provoking, Heritage suffers from a laconic pace and a lack of traditional action."*

Example 3 illustrates the use of a subordinating conjunct, connecting an adjective phrase and noun phrase. This class of conjuncts when appear at the beginning of a sentence, usually connect phrases of opposite polarity. A system without conjunction analysis will be disguised by the presence of strong positive words in the adjective phrase.

Table 1. Examples of conjunction rules

1	if (conj='although' class='IN' begin=true)
2	if (Phrase1='VP' Phrase2='NP')
3	polarity = Phrase2; Phrase1 = !Phrase2;
4	if (Phrase1='FRAG' Phrase2='NP')
5	polarity = Phrase1 + Phrase2;
6	if (conj='but' class='CC' begin=false)
7	if (Phrase1='NP' Phrase2='NP')
8	polarity = Phrase2; Phrase1 = !Phrase2;
9	if (Phrase1='ADJP' Phrase2='SBAR')
10	polarity = Phrase1 + Phrase2;

3.3 Conjunction Rules

Based on Section 3.1 and Section 3.2, we compiled a set of about 50 conjunction rules, taking into account the way they affect the associated sentiment. The position of a conjunct in a sentence, alongwith the linguistic knowledge of phrases being joined, explains the behavior of that conjunct in sentiment determination. Our basic assumption is: "*Not all phrases joined by a conjunct have same level of significance in overall sentiment determination*". Table 1 cites some examples of our conjunction rules. In Line 1, *class='IN'*[5] checks if *although* occurs as a subordinating conjunct and *begin=true* ensures that this conjunct occurs at the beginning of the sentence. Line 2 checks if first phrase is a verb phrase and second phrase is a noun phrase. Line 3 states the rule and suggests that the sentiment of overall sentence is dominated by *Phrase2* (latter phrase). Line 3 gives additional information that the sentiments of *Phrase1* and *Phrase2* may be opposite. Similarly, Lines 6-10 state the rule for *but* as a coordinating conjunct. In Line 6, *begin=false* means that the conjunct may occur anywhere in the sentence, except the beginning. *As* an example, Figure 2 shows the parsed output for following review:

> "*Although shot with less style, skins is heartfelt.*"

Looking at the output of the parser in Figure 2, it becomes clear that *although* is used as a subordinating conjunct, connecting a verb phrase and a noun phrase. As, *although* occurs at the beginning of this sentence, from Line 2 of Table 1, we can say that the sentiment is dominated by the latter phrase, and the verb phrase becomes irrelevant for overall sentiment determination.

4 Evaluation Framework

4.1 Corpora

For our experiments, we have used three sentence level datasets. First dataset is in the movie domain where we use 5,331 positive, 5,331 negative and 5,000

---

[5] We follow the conventions from Penn Treebank tag set.

```
(ROOT
  (S
    (SBAR (IN although)
      (S
        (VP (VBD shot)
          (PP (IN with)
            (NP (JJR less) (NN style))))))
    (, ,)
    (NP (NNS skins))
    (VP (VBZ is)
      (ADJP (JJ heartfelt)))
    (. .)))
```

Fig. 2. Parsed output for the example review

neutral sentences, to train and test our classifiers. The positive and negative sentences are taken from Pang et al.'s [10] sentence polarity dataset (version 1.0) and neutral sentences are taken from Pang et al.'s subjectivity dataset (version 1.0)[6]. The polarity dataset contains about 21,000 different words (unigrams) and the average length of each sentence is 21 words. Second dataset is relatively smaller, comprising of car reviews collected from various car review websites[7]. After filtering out profane examples, three annotators hand annotated a corpus of about 8,000 sentences. These annotators had an agreement score of 68.90% on the original data, indicating ambiguities in sentence level analysis, even for humans. It is to be noted that we finally included only those sentences in our dataset that agreed to all the three annotators, leaving us with a set of 1,500 positive, 1,500 negative and 2,500 neutral sentences. Average length of these sentences is 20 words. This dataset contains about 6,900 different unigrams. Third dataset is a collection of book reviews collected from amazon website[8]. We mined the book reviews to extract one-line comments given by users before the start of each descriptive review. Reviews with 4 or 5 star rating were considered as positive, while 1 and 2 star reviews were taken as negative. This dataset contains 4000 positive and 4000 negative sentences[9] and consists of about 6,000 different unigrams with average length of each sentence being close to 14 words.

4.2   Experimental Settings

We perform 10-fold cross-validation (CV) experiments on all the three datasets using Joachims' (1999) SVM^{Light} package[10] with default parameter values[11].

---

[6] Both the datasets are available at http://www.cs.cornell.edu/people/pabo/movie-review-data

[7] www.carsurvey.org and www.motortrend.com

[8] www.amazon.com

[9] We do not experiment with neutral reviews in book domain

[10] Available at http://svmlight.joachims.org

[11] Default values gave the best results for all classifiers

For each fold, we take 90% of the total data for training our classifiers and remaining 10% as unseen test data. Let $f_1, f_2, .., f_k$ be a set of features that can appear in a sentence. In a sentence S_y, feature f_x is given a weight $w_{xy} = 1$ if f_x is present in S_y, otherwise $w_{xy} = 0$. Each sentence S_y is represented by the sentence vector $\vec{S_y} := (w_{1y}, w_{2y}, .., w_{ky})$ in the vector space model. Similar to [11], we experimented with frequency and presence of features, and found that even at sentence level, presence based approaches give better accuracies. To circumvent the problem of negations, we consider the manually constructed list of polarity-shifters from [5] and tag each word between a negation and next punctuation with NOT_ [2]. Similar to [9], we penalize longer reviews and neutralize their effect using length normalization. We perform cosine normalization [12], and observe that not performing normalization hurts the performance slightly. The cosine factor is computed as: $\sqrt{w_1^2 + w_2^2 + .. + w_n^2}$, where $w_1, w_2, .., w_n$ are the raw weights corresponding to the features present in the sentence.

4.3   Comparison of Methods

Majority Voting Approach: This method simply counts and compares the presence of positive and negative feeling words in a review. General Inquirer (GI) provides a list of 4,206 feeling words (1,915 positive and 2,291 negative). We perform stemming[12] on the dataset and also consider the effect of negation words preceding the feeling words, to achieve the results shown in Table 2. The columns show percentage accuracy for positive and negative sentences. As per Table 2, we get an accuracy of 68.8%, 71.6% and 50.1% for positive sentences in movie, car and book domains respectively. The accuracies on negative sentences are as low as 34.1%, 43.2% and 30.6% respectively. *GI + Conjunction* lists the accuracy when conjunction analysis approach is incorporated with GI. Incorporating conjunction analysis with GI improved the accuracies by almost 4-5% for both positive and negative categories. An observation of the results showed that 2,300 negative movie sentences were identified as positive indicating the presence of mixed sentiment or sarcasm, specially in negative reviews. These results also confirm the presence of positive sentiment words in negative reviews and vice-versa. This analysis motivates to incorporate conjunction analysis approach with supervised learning techniques like SVMs to achieve better accuracies.

Table 2. Accuracy in % of majority voting approach

Approach	Movie Dataset		Car Dataset		Book Dataset	
	Positive	Negative	Positive	Negative	Positive	Negative
GI	68.8	34.1	71.6	43.2	50.1	30.6
GI + Conjunction	73.4	38.5	76.2	46.7	51.9	31.5

---

[12] We used Porter stemming algorithm, available at http://tartarus.org/ ~martin/PorterStemmer/

Table 3. Average 10-fold CV precision/recall values in % for *review identification*

Approach	Movie Data		Car Data	
	Precision	Recall	Precision	Recall
Unigram	92.6	96.3	83.1	79.3
N-gram	**93.0**	96.4	83.9	81.0
Unigram + POS	92.7	96.3	82.0	79.3
Conjunction + N-gram	**93.0**	**96.6**	**84.1**	**81.4**

Table 4. Average 10-fold CV precision/recall values in % for *sentiment analysis*

Approach	Movie Data		Car Data		Book Data	
	Precision	Recall	Precision	Recall	Precision	Recall
Unigram	78.1	75.8	88.1	89.3	80.9	80.3
N-gram	78.6	76.8	89.0	91.1	81.1	80.6
Unigram + POS	76.4	75.1	87.5	89.7	80.1	80.4
Conjunction + Unigram	80.2	78.3	90.1	90.8	81.2	80.6
Conjunction + N-gram	**81.9**	**79.8**	**92.7**	**92.5**	**81.4**	**81.0**
Modified Conjunction	80.5	78.4	91.7	91.0	81.2	80.8

Unigrams: Rather than relying on a fixed set of sentiment words, we try to incorporate corpus-based learning with SVM. A set of all unique words present in the corpus, having frequency above a threshold (χ) are considered as features. While preparing the unigram list, negation words were handled as discussed in Section 4.2. In Tables 3 and 4, *Unigram* shows the results for *review identification* and *sentiment analysis* tasks respectively. On all the three datasets, $\chi = 2$ (frequency cut-off) appeared to give the best results. Clearly, learning methods with corpus statistics outperform the majority voting approach, achieving precisions of 78.1%, 88.1% and 80.9% for movie, car and book datasets respectively.

Bigrams/Trigrams: To capture the context in a better way and exploit the co-occurrence of sentiment expressions, we added frequent bigrams and trigrams to the unigrams list. Results are shown as *N-gram* in Tables 3 and 4 (frequency cut-off of $\chi = 3$ gave the best results). Negations were not handled explicitly as n-grams are supposed to capture their effect. *N-gram* gives better accuracy for both phases of the experiment. It is clear that bigrams and trigrams are able to capture the context in a better way as compared to unigrams. A drawback of including bigrams and trigrams is that they increase the complexity.

Parts-of-Speech Tags: To distinguish between different usages of same feature word, we added POS tags to unigrams. *Unigram + POS* lists the results for both the phases in Table 3 and Table 4. However, the precision drops to 76.4% for movie data, 87.5% for car data and 80.1% for book data. So, part-of-speech tags alone are not able to provide any additional benefit for the task of *sentiment analysis*. However, accuracies are almost similar to *N-gram* for *review identification* task.

Conjunction Analysis: Our approach *'Conjunction'* (Tables 3 and 4) is implemented as follows: Consider a sentence: "*abc phrase1 conj phrase2 pqr*", where *phrase1* and *phrase2* are phrases joined by the conjunct *conj*; *abc* and *pqr* may be any phrase, sentence or even null. If rule for *conj* (as in Table 1) says that *phrase2* dominates, then during training and testing our classifiers, we use this sentence as "*abc conj phrase2 pqr*". That means we simply ignore the irrelevant phrase as per the conjunction rule, and final sentence shortens in length.

Modified Conjunction: If rule for conjunction *conj* additionally states that sentiment of *phrase1* is opposite of *phrase2* (e.g. Line 3, Table 1), above sentence is used as "*abc NOT_phrase1 conj phrase2 pqr*", i.e. we reverse the polarity of *phrase1* to synchronize it with *phrase2* and try to improve classifier learning (*NOT_phrase1* is formed by prefixing *NOT_* before each word in *phrase1*). If no such rule exists, sentence remains same as in *Conjunction* approach. Features for *Modified Conjunction* are *n*-grams. Table 4 suggests that *Conjunction + N-gram* approach significantly improves the precision of *sentiment analysis* phase to 81.9% and 92.7% respectively for movie and car data. However, *review identification* accuracies are not much affected by this approach. We discuss this in detail in the following section.

5   Discussion and Further Analysis

Table 2 lists the percentage accuracy for the Majority Voting approach. For both positive and negative categories in our datasets, conjunction analysis incorporated with GI gives better accuracy. Conjunction analysis is comparatively less effective on book dataset because of improper grammatical structure of sentences. These results show that conjunction analysis is indeed able to remove few opposite sentiment feeling words from the sentences. Also, our belief that mixed sentiment reviews usually contain conjunctions appears to be true. This motivates for incorporating conjunction analysis with supervised learning techniques (like SVM) to achieve better results.

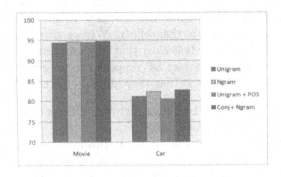

Fig. 3. Comparison of F_1 measures for *review identification*

Figure 3 plots the average F_1 measure of the 10-fold CV for *review identification*. It is clear that the *review identification* task is relatively simpler. If less complexity is desired, only unigrams can also be taken as features. We observed that movie dataset has 28,525 and 21,081 unigrams respectively for *review identification* and *sentiment analysis* tasks, indicating the existence of features peculiar to each task. However, *N-gram* is better than *Unigram*, which means that context is important for *review identification* task as well. As one might guess, for *review identification*, *Conjunction* approach is not much fruitful. This is because the discarded phrases in neutral sentences carry no sentiment anyways. Still the results are better than *Unigram* because some of the adjective and adverbial phrases, carrying feeling words, might get discarded by our conjunction rules. In Figure 3, lower F_1 measure on car dataset is mainly because of smaller corpus and objective sentences being wider in scope with lot of car domain knowledge. For example: *"Big projector, xenon lights are now standard on the coupe"* is actually a neutral sentence, despite the presence of adjectives.

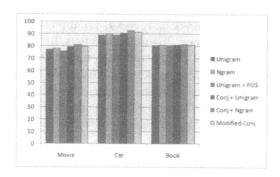

Fig. 4. Comparison of F_1 measures for *sentiment analysis*

Figure 4 plots the average F_1 measure of the 10-fold CV for *sentiment analysis*. It becomes clear that corpus based learning with unigrams is better than naive approach like Majority Voting. Since features of opposite class can also occur in a sentence (Section 4.3), machine learning based approaches are expected to perform better. POS tags slightly deteriorate the performance at sentence level: we guess, the benefit of being able to differentiate between feature usages is over-ruled by the inability to take into account the effect of negations and also the increased feature space dimensionality. Our approach based on conjunction analysis appears to give the best results with *n*-grams as features, as context is captured in a better way using *n*-grams. Our assumption that conjunctions affect sentence level sentiment is very much true. *Modified Conjunction* performs better than *N-gram* and even *Conjunction + Unigram*. So, our rules for conjunctions joining opposite sentiment phrases hold true. However, this approach is less accurate than *Conjunction + N-gram* because of the inability to efficiently negate a phrase; simply adding a *NOT_* before each word may not work accurately for all phrases. Finally, we hunch that higher accuracies on car reviews are because of: (1) Relatively smaller feature dimension (6,900 unigrams compared to 21,000 for movie reviews), and (2) We included only those reviews in the car dataset that agreed to all three annotators.

6 Conclusions and Future Work

Automatic sentiment analysis can never be perfect at sentence level: the sentiment of a statement depends on context, domain knowledge, sarcasm or irony - all of which are still far beyond the current classification techniques. However, we have shown that at sentence level, machine learning algorithms alone are effective for differentiating between subjective/objective reviews, but linguistic analysis becomes essential for sentiment analysis. While n-grams are able to capture context, they are unable to handle mixed sentiments that exist in reviews. We believe that not all phrases connected by a conjunct, have same level of significance in overall sentiment determination. We propose an approach based on conjunction analysis that determines phrases in a sentence which dominate the sentiment. On movie, car and book reviews, our approach when incorporated with SVM outperformed other non-linguistic classifiers. In future work, we would like to explore the applicability of our approach to perform sentiment analysis on documents. Our conjunction rules can be extended to cover all conjunctions in the language with deeper linguistic knowledge. Instead of relying on the frequency of feature words, a good feature selection criterion may be considered so as to limit the feature vector dimensionality and achieve better results.

References

1. Boiy, E., Hens, P., Deschacht, K., Moens: Automatic sentiment analysis in online text. In: Proceedings of International Conference on Electronic Publishing, pp. 349–360 (2007)
2. Das, S., Chen, M.: Yahoo! for amazon: Extracting market sentiment from stock message boards. In: Proceedings of the 8th Asia Pacific Finance Association Annual Conference (2001)
3. Dave, K., Lawrence, S., Pennock, D.M.: Mining the peanut gallery: opinion extraction and semantic classification of product reviews. In: WWW 2003: Proceedings of the 12th international conference on World Wide Web, pp. 519–528. ACM, New York (2003)
4. Gamon, M., Aue, A.: Automatic identification of sentiment vocabulary: Exploiting low association with known sentiment terms. In: Proceedings of the ACL Workshop on Feature Engineering for Machine Learning in Natural Language Processing, June 2005, pp. 57–64. Association for Computational Linguistics (2005)
5. Hu, M., Liu, B.: Mining opinion features in customer reviews. AAAI, Menlo Park (2004)
6. Kim, S.-M., Hovy, E.: Automatic detection of opinion bearing words and sentences. In: Companion Volume to the Proceedings of IJCNLP-2005, the Second International Joint Conference on Natural Language Processing, pp. 61–66 (2005)

7. Meena, A., Prabhakar, T.V.: Sentence level sentiment analysis in the presence of conjuncts using linguistic analysis. In: Amati, G., Carpineto, C., Romano, G. (eds.) ECIR 2007. LNCS, vol. 4425, pp. 573–580. Springer, Heidelberg (2007)
8. Mullen, T., Collier, N.: Sentiment analysis using support vector machines with diverse information sources. In: Proceedings of the Conference on Empirical Methods on Natural Language Processing, pp. 412–418 (2004)
9. Ng, V., Dasgupta, S., Arifin, S.M.N.: Examining the role of linguistic knowledge sources in the automatic identification and classification of reviews. In: Proceedings of the COLING/ACL on Main conference poster sessions, pp. 611–618. Association for Computational Linguistics (2006)
10. Pang, B., Lee, L.: Seeing stars: Exploiting class relationships for sentiment categorization with respect to rating scales. In: Proceedings of the ACL, pp. 115–124 (2005)
11. Pang, B., Lee, L., Vaithyanathan, S.: Thumbs up? sentiment classification using machine learning techniques. In: Proceedings of the 2002 Conference on Empirical Methods in Natural Language Processing (EMNLP) (2002)
12. Singhal, A., Buckley, C., Mitra, M.: Pivoted document length normalization. In: Research and Development in Information Retrieval, pp. 21–29 (1996)
13. Turney, P.D.: Thumbs up or thumbs down?: semantic orientation applied to unsupervised classification of reviews. In: ACL '02: Proceedings of the 40th Annual Meeting on Association for Computational Linguistics, pp. 417–424. Association for Computational Linguistics (2001)
14. Wilson, T., Wiebe, J., Hoffmann, P.: Recognizing contextual polarity in phrase-level sentiment analysis. In: HLT 2005: Proceedings of the conference on Human Language Technology and Empirical Methods in Natural Language Processing, pp. 347–354. Association for Computational Linguistics (2005)
15. Yi, J., Nasukawa, T., Bunescu, R., Niblack, W.: Sentiment analyzer: Extracting sentiments about a given topic using natural language processing techniques. icdm 00, 427–434 (2003)
16. Yu, H., Hatzivassiloglou, V.: Towards answering opinion questions: separating facts from opinions and identifying the polarity of opinion sentences. In: Proceedings of the 2003 conference on Empirical methods in natural language processing, Morristown, NJ, USA, pp. 129–136. Association for Computational Linguistics (2003)
17. Zhang, L., Barnden, J., Hendley, R., Wallington, A.: Exploitation in affect detection in open-ended improvisional text. In: Proceedings of the ACL Workshop on Sentiment and Subjectivity in Text, pp. 47–54. Association for Computational Linguistics (2006)

Automatic Annotation of Direct Reported Speech in Arabic and French, According to a Semantic Map of Enunciative Modalities

Motasem Alrahabi and Jean-Pierre Desclés

Maison de la Recherche – Université de Paris-Sorbonne
28, Rue Serpente, 75006 Paris, France
{motasem.alrahabi,jean-pierre.descles}@paris4.sorbonne.fr

Abstract. We present an analysis of the linguistic markers of the enunciative modalities in direct reported speech, in a multilingual framework concerning Arabic and French. Furthermore, we present a platform for automatic annotation of semantic relations, based on the Contextual Exploration method. This platform allows the automatic annotation and categorisation of quotational segments in both languages, exploiting a semantic map based on the notion of speaker commitment in enunciation.

Keywords: Automatic annotation, multilingual approach, commitment, semantic map, Contextual Exploration.

1 Introduction

Reported speech, both in the form of direct quotation and indirect paraphrases, is the most frequent expression found in newspapers, where it can occur in up to 90% of the sentences of the latter[1]. Nevertheless, the existing Natural Language Processing systems do not usually target on reported speech itself, since they mainly focus on an automated retrieval of quoted segments, without going further into neither the linguistic analysis of the introduction markers of the reported speech, nor the enunciative modality. The latter concerns, for instance, the position of the enunciator towards what he reports, or the manner in which he describes the reported enunciation or the attitude of the others speakers, etc.

Some research on the *Opinion Mining* uses automatic procedures, generally based on statistical methods, in order to assign a subjective or objective character to a word, a sentence or a text, and to determine the attitude of the speaker (orientation: positive, negative or neutral) or the degree (strength) of this attitude [3] ; [4] ; [5] ; [6]. This lexical approach seems to be limited because the terms in a certain context may have an emotional value which is exactly opposed to their values if considered individually, for example:

"This film should be brilliant. It sounds like a great plot, the actors are first grade, and the supporting cast is good as well, and Stallone is attempting to deliver a good performance. However, it can't hold up", cited in [7].

A. Ranta, B. Nordström (Eds.): GoTAL 2008, LNAI 5221, pp. 40–51, 2008.

Many researchers in this field have observed the same phenomenon and speak in favour of combining lexical information with more complex linguistic analysis: Polanyi and Zaenen [8] (cited in [9]), state the necessity of taking into consideration the negations, some connectors (*Although Boris is brilliant in math, he is a horrific teacher*) and the modal operators (*If Mary were a terrible person, she would be mean to her dogs*).

We can also mention other existing works [2] that develop a linguistic analysis of the modalities concerning events (in the aspectual sense). The term modality for the author refers to certain degrees of possibility, beliefs, opinions, evidentiality, etc., however the polysemy of modal auxiliaries (must, may...) is not taken into consideration.

In our work, we propose a linguistic analysis of enunicative modalities in direct reported speech (D-RS) in Arabic and French. This analysis takes into account the marks of the enunciator in the discourse (his attitude towards what is reported), and allows the organisation of modality values in a semantic map. This map is exploited by an automatic system of grammatical and discursive annotations, based on the Contextual Exploration. This method, unlike the above-stated approach [2], requires only the analysis of surface linguistic forms.

Our presentation is organized around two main lines: a linguistic one, which exposes the theoretical principles of the analysis and categorization of linguistic data; and an other, computational, which explains the architecture of the implemented system on the different processing levels.

2 Contextual Exploration Methodology

In the linguistic study of enunciation, the construction of an utterance (or a text) has to take into account some language operations such as predication, discourse operations and operations of commitment, the expression of which leaves a certain amount of surface linguistic traces. By analysing these linguistic indicators, the linguist is able to reconstruct, according to the process of abduction [10], the underlying operations of language production. Our methodology, the Contextual Exploration (CE) [11], is based on the analysis of these surface linguistic indicators, caracterising the textual representations used by the enunciator and which correspond to a given *point of view*[1] frame, such as citations, definitions or causal relations, etc. And because in natural languages the relationship between operations and linguistic indicators is rarely an one-to-one function, we need to explore the context in order to identify complementary *clues* that confirm or falsify the pertinence of the hypothesis first motivated by the indicators. The following example is analyzed by the CE' strategy:

أسَرَنا الكاتبة وهي تطرح علينا هذه العبارة الساخرة : « كل الشموس تشرق من طاقة الحاجّة أديبة، شمس الضفة العربية وشمس الـ 48 وشمس بوش » !

The writer fascinated us by giving to us this mocking sentence: "all suns rise from the dormer window of Hajja Adiba, the sun of the West Bank, the sun of 48th and the sun of Bush"!

---

[1] The notion of "point of view" in our approach corresponds to the analysis of a concrete task defined by the user.

In this example[2], the indicator of quotation is the quotation marks, and the complementary clues are combination of the verb « تَطرح » / « by giving » and the declarative noun « العِـــبارة » / « sentence ». As far as the modal clues are concerned, they are: « السّـــاخرة » / « mocking » which marks the attitude of the speaker ; « أَسَرَتنا » / « fascinated us » and « ! », that denote the attitude of the enunciator.

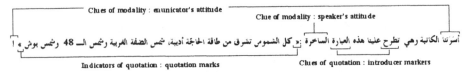

The linguistic analysis performed by the CE method does not rely on any preliminary morpho-syntactic analysis or statistical method, and is composed mainly of two parts of procedure made by the linguist: one that consists in studying various types of texts in different languages and distinguishes between two types of linguistic markers: indicators and clues ; and another that concerns CE's rules and exploits these markers (by using a CE engine), in order to find the surface level markers of the textual representations corresponding to the given *point of view*.

This method has been used in different computer applications, such as automatic summarization [12] [13] [14], extraction of causal relationships [15] and relationships between concepts [16].

3   The Linguistic Markers of Enunciative Modalities in D-RS

The notion of modality has been studied from many different perspectives: Logic, Philosophy and Linguistics [28] ; [29] ; [30]. In the field of Linguistics, modality can be considered from a syntactic, semantic or enunciative perspective.

We shall consider modality in an enunciative approach, according to Ch. Bally [31], E. Benveniste [32] and A. Culioli [33], so we distinguish between the enunciator and the speaker [34]: in reported speech, the enunciator makes a commitment to the utterance in its totality (*the author*), and the speaker is the third person quoted by the author, the "*last enunciator who directly makes commitment to the predicative relation*" [35].

In the theory of Enunciation, the commitment of an enunciator of an utterance introduces aspect and tense variations or enunciative modalities, marked in the utterance by traces that the enunciator leaves in his speech. In our case, these traces can manifest themselves in the introductory portion of the direct speech in different forms: they may indicate the enunciator's position towards what is reported, describe the speaker's attitude towards what is being said (in general) or towards what the speaker himself is saying; or refer to the relationship between the speaker and the enunciator, etc. In each of the processed languages, the enunciative modality markers in D-RS are either those that introduce the citation, or other markers that are otherwise appointed.

---

[2] *http://www.arabicstory.net*

3.1 Citational Linguistic Markers

The term *reported speech* covers a number of forms [17]: direct and indirect speech, free indirect speech, direct speech introduced by *"that"* [18], etc. We are particularly interested in direct reported speech (quotations). This linguistic act permits the enunciator to make a commitment for what is said or written by the speaker, without modifying it.

As we have already mentioned above, we can distinguish two types of linguistic markers: indicators and clues. For us, the indicators of D-RS are typographical signs (in French, Arabic and also in a number of many other languages) that define the scope of the D-RS. These signs are the quotation marks surrounding the clause[3], sometimes preceded by a colon (therefore the clause constitutes a syntactically independent sentence) or by the conjunction '*that*'.

As to the contextual clues for D-RS, they are the declarative linguistic markers that introduce or succeed the citation:

- verbs (*X underline{denied} the facts:* *"…"*): Arabic examples: ...زعم, أعلن, عبّر عن, أشار إلى; French examples: *écrire, souligner, avouer, affirmer, critiquer, …*
- nouns (*This is underline{the declaration of} X:* *"…"*): Arabic examples: اعلان, تصريح, بيان; French examples: *déclaration, annonce, slogan, appel...*
- gerunds (*X affirmed this underline{by adding}:* *"…"*): Arabic ex.: ...قائلا, مضيفا, مؤكداً; French examples: *en soulignant, en affirmant, en ajoutant...*
- adverbials (*underline{According to X}:* *"…"*): Arabic ex.: ...بحسب, نقلا عن, على ذمة, وفقا لـ; French examples: *d'après, selon...*

We note that in French, unlike Arabic, verbs can be positioned in the middle of the citation ("…, *affirme-t-il, …*").

3.2 Linguistic Modality Markers

In a D-RS, the enunciator can take into account the oral or written speech of the speaker, or describe the speaker's attitude towards his own speech or that of his interlocutor. On the other hand, the enunciator can show his position towards what he reports. We shall see in more detail some of these enunciative relationships:

- The enunciator reports the speaker's declaration (*he says, he declares, he adds, he repeats,* etc.). The latter makes a commitment to the predicative relation without getting involved.
- The enunciator reports the speaker's commitment (*he confirms, he asserts, he certifies,* etc.). The latter takes the responsibility for the matter of the clause. This language act is a commitment concerning the validity of a predicative relation.
- The enunciator describes the relationship between the speaker and the interlocutor: this relationship can be related to the volutive modalities (*to encourage, to forbid, to command*) or to evaluative modalities (*to make fun, to denounce, to apologize*). In a question, for example, the speaker demands the

---

[3] We do not take into consideration the '*textual islands*' (*She criticised the president's "machiavelism"*).

commitment of the interlocutor in regard to the content suggested by the speaker (*he asked his son: "..."*).
- The enunciator relates the act of locution (*I say that X said: « ... »*)
- The enunciator makes a commitment to the truth of the locution act: *I affirme / it's sur that X said: « ... » ;*
- The enunciator indicates a judgement on the spatio-temporal realisation of the predicative relation: *X said in Goteborg yesterday that: « ... »*.
- The enunciator makes commitment on the evaluative modalities that pertain to the veracity of the speaker's utterance (an *untrue* declaration, *a credible* explanation...) or on positive or negative values (*good / bad* explanation...).
- The enunciator makes commitment on the evaluative modalities pertaining on his own attitude (*happily he confessed...*) or to the attitude of other speakers who are implied in the reported enunciation (sincerity: *to pretend* ; agreement/disagreement: *wrongly* ; pronunciation: *to babble*).

These modalities can be marked by the choice of the declarative expression introducing the citation seen above (*to say, to whisper...*). But they can also be tagged by polysemic declarative markers (*to make fun of, to humiliate...*) or by non declarative markers that denote the speaker's attitude for example (*to interrupt, to blush...*). Other grammatical categories are also to be observed, such as adverbs (*alas, finally*) and adjectives (*untrue, credible*).

Among the markers of modality, some expressions introducing citations, especially the verbs, have been subject to diverse syntactic, semantic and pragmatic analysis [19] ; [20] ; [21] ; [22] ; [23] ; [24] ; [25]; [26] ; [27]. The analysis that we have adopted here differs on several points: the linguistic markers of the reported speech and modality concern all lexical categories (verbs, nouns, adverbs...) ; these markers have been studied cross-linguistically (Arabic and French); the framework is that of the Enunciative Linguistics where the mark of the enunciator is analysed in the discourse ; finally, this work is carried out in the perspective of automatic language processing and our final goal is to provide automatic applications that respond to concrete needs.

4 Categorisation of the Enunciative Modalities: Semantic Map

We have analysed, in a contrastive manner, the markers of enuncicative modalities in Arabic and French and we then organized them according to a semantic map, based on the principle of commitment [35], [36].

This semantic map (SM) is a "linguistic ontology" of grammatical or discursive categories, interlinked by the elements of specification, opposition, application, value attribution, etc. It corresponds to one or more *points of view*. The values of the SM (the nodes of the graph) are represented in texts by different indicators and clues (node instances) in one language or another[4], and by the CE rules that are associated to these instances. Thus, we have organised the enunciative relations [37] in the following figure:

---

[4] Some values of the SM can be attested in one language and not in another.

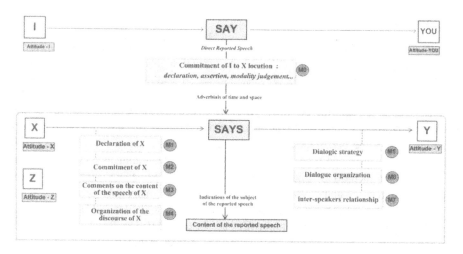

Fig. 1. Semantic Map of enunciative modalities in D-RS

The fundamental dialogical dipole is between the enunciator (I) and the co-enunciator (YOU). The (I) reports to (YOU) the utterance of a speaker (X), absent from the dialogue. In the same way, the D-RS is centered on the dialogical relation speaker-interlocutor. All the enunciative relations in this SM are under the commitment of the enunciator. Some of them concern the simple I-YOU speech relation (M0), and others concern the D-RS (M1 to M7).

The categories M1 to M4 denote the relation between the speaker and his utterance ; the categories M5 to M7 indicate the relation between the speaker and the interlocutor. We have also added other categories to the SM, in order to describe the attitudes of the different speakers implicated in the D-RS: Attitude-I, Attitude-YOU, Attitude-X (speaker), Attitude-Y (interlocutor) and Attitude-Z (speaker absent).

The categories of the SM can be related by application, incompatibility, specification, etc. In this way, the spatio-temporal category that depends on the enunciator can be applied to all the sub-categories from M0 to M7. Similarly, all the categories contain other sub-classes, such as assertion of the speaker, that can take several values (individual assertion, universal or collective assertion, etc. [35]).

5   Program Implementation of the Automatic Annotation

The applicative part of our work [38] consists in the implementation of an automatic annotation tool for grammatical or discursive categories. This tool, EXCOM[5], is composed by a CE engine and the supplementary modules[6] connected to it.

The automatic annotation requires pre-processing of the linguistic resources, which means: corpora segmentation, markers organization and CE rules construction.

---

[5] For "EXploration COntextuelle Multilingue". Our system in its second edition is freely available online for the use of researchers on the following address: https://www.excom.fr
[6] For the implementation we have used Java, XML, JDOM, XLINK, JNLP, etc.

5.1 Automatic Segmentation

In our work, the segmentation of a text into smaller parts helps in determining the search fields for linguistic markers, and the textual segments which are to be annotated. This consists in defining the boundaries of sections, titles, paragraphs and sentences.

The sections are determined by the presence of titles in the text, the titles are defined by several heuristics[7], and the paragraphs are delimited by the sign of carriage return. In order to split the paragraphs into sentences, we used a set of rules, which can be modified by the user, and based on disambiguation of typographical signs[8] and linguistic terms[9]. This method [39] takes into account the difficulties encountered in Arabic (lack of capitalization and of vocalization) and in French (many abbreviations).

The input files for the segmentation module are raw text files in UTF-8 encoding, in different languages, and the output files are in the XML DocBook format for articles. The results of segmentation are satisfactory, however they must be evaluated in a large scale, and improved, for example, by the identification of item lists and the hierarchy between titles and sub-titles.

5.2 Automatic Annotation

The core of the EXCOM architecture (Fig. 2) consists of a CE engine that manipulates the CE rules and linguistic markers associated with the annotations. The annotation process consists in the research of the indicators in the search fields defined by the segmentation process. The presence of indicators calls the application of CE rules and then the conditions of these rules are examined (research of contextual clues). If all the conditions are satisfied, the CE engine either attributes the corresponding annotation to the segment, or calls (recursively) another CE rule.

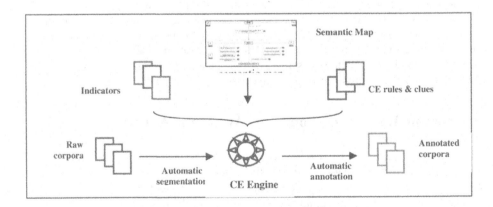

Fig. 2. Simplified architecture of the platform EXCOM

---

[7] For example, if the line is not longer than n words and if it is terminated by colon.

[8] For example: period, semicolon, question mark, etc.

[9] Connectors like *but, however, nevertheless, so that*, etc.

As to the CE rules, they are automatically generated (with XML format) by using a graphical user interface that offers the possibility of defining and modifing all of the functional parameters of the CE engine, in order to separate maximally the data from the implementation. The efficiency of the CE rules corresponds to the functionalities of localization and disambiguation of markers, offered by the CE engine, such as for example:

- The hierarchy between the indicators that carry the semantic meaning of the category in question and the contextual clues. From a theoretical perspective, this principle is fundamental for us and concerns one of the differences between the CE method and other context analysis methods.
- The contextual clues can be of two types: positive (their presence is obligatory) and negative (their presence cancels the action of annotation).
- The markers (indicators or clues) can be either linguistic units (words or regular expressions), or already annotated segments (in an already annonated text).
- The targeting of a part of a text can be specified and used as search field by using the XML structure of the file and the identified titles in the segmented document (for ex.: find indicators in all the titles, or find indicators in the last sentence of the second paragraph of the first section).
- The research of the contextual clues is carried out in the context of the indicators: before, after or inside the indicator (for ex.: a morphem in a word).
- Different types of clues can be combined by logical operators: between the positive clues, before and after the indicator, between the negative clues, before and after the indicator. These operators can be: AND, OR, XOR. (for ex. looking at clues before OR exclusively (XOR) after indicators).
- An order can be defined between the positive and the negative clues in the context before or after each indicator (for ex.: in the context before the indicator, a negative clue cannot occur before a positive clue).
- Meta-rules can be set by the user in order to define priority between rules or the navigation mode in the semantic map (this second section is under construction).

The annotation of the segments contains the following meta-data: the semantic category of the annotation, the class of the indicator that has triggered the annotation, the identifier of the CE rule that has carried out the annotation, etc. This information allows the linguist to improve the rules, as well as the relevance of the linguistic markers.

This is an example of a simple EC rule for the citation, in a declarative form:

```
CE rule # 5:
Given P the following research space: all sentences of the first paragraph of the last section
If (indicator from the class "2-quotes" exists in P)
If (in the before-indicator-context does not exists a negative clue from the class "references")
If (in the middle-indicator context exists a positive clue from "declaration-verb-reversed")
Then: Give the semantic annotation "quotation-middle-conclusive" to P
```

This rule can annotate some sentences found in the first paragraph of the last section of an article which carry a conclusive value in addition to their enunciative modality. For example:

"Nevertheless, <u>he concludes</u>, this rapprochement between the European business companies is one of the challenges of tomorrow".

Once the texts are annotated, the user can then proceed to the post-processing treatment by using a module which compiles all annotated segments of the corpus in a database, with an interface allowing the navigation between these segments and their original contexts.

6 Evaluation

We set up a first evaluation test consisting in the judgment of the capacity of the system to categorize[10] the marked segments of quotations, according to the SM. The corpus on which we worked was composed of 250 texts of journalistic articles per language handling various subjects[11]. We made preliminary tests on 80 % of the corpus aiming the EC rules adjustment. Then we performed the evaluation test on the other part of the texts (20 %).

Based on the results on each corpus, we extracted randomly 39 segments annotated according to the following three semantic categories[12]:

1) the declaration of the speaker without commitment to the content (category M1), for instance, *X says: "..."* ;
2) the commitment of the speaker in regard to the content (category M2): for instance, *X affirms: "..."* ;
3) the enunciator's comments about the speech of the speaker, concerning the degree of the sincerity of the speaker or the truth of his speech (category M3): for instance, *X claims: "..."*.

The test consisted then in asking the subjects (15 French-speaking persons[13], and 9 Arabic-speaking persons[14]) to annotate manually the 39 extracted segments, according to the same semantic categories. For each segment the subjects had to choose one of the proposed categories and assign it to the sentence. For the calculation of the evaluation measures, we have used the evaluation interface EVA-2[15].

In order to calculate the precision and recall measures, the "correct" annotations were determined on the basis of the set of human annotations. These correct annotations are defined as the most frequent annotations attributed by the subjects. The results for the Arabic and French corpus are the following:

---

[10] As for quotations localization by means of typographical indicators, no evaluation has been made due to the relative simplicity of the task.

[11] The French corpus was taken from the following newspapers: *Le Monde Diplomatique, le Figaro, l'Humanité* and *Libération* ; and the Arabic one from: *Al-Nahar, AL-Ahram, Tishreen, Al-Jazeera, Al-Sabah, Al-Alam* and *Al-Quds*.

[12] The only restriction was that the segment numbers by category had to be the same for both languages.

[13] PhD and Master students of Human Sciences Department of Paris-Sorbonne University and Paris 7 - Denis Diderot University.

[14] Arabic-speaker students of Sorbonne Univ., Paris-Jussieu Univ., Lyon and Damascus Univ.

[15] *Evaluation d'Annotation Automatique*, developed by I. Atanassova and M. Bertin (LaLIC).

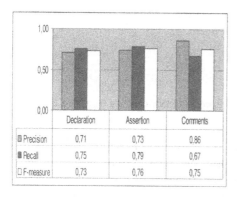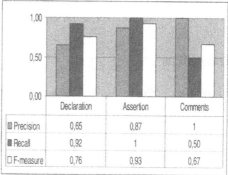

Fig. 3. The results of evaluation on the Arabic (left) and French (right) corpora

7 Perspectives

Our first evaluation results are quite encouraging. We are currently drawing up a deeper protocol for the evaluation of all categories in the SM, in order to validate this part of the work.

These tests have allowed us to draw comparisons between French and Arabic on several levels. First, we have noticed that in Arabic the surface forms are generally more polysemous than in French, especially the forms that have a three-letter root. This difficulty, already well known [40] ; [41] ; [42] ; [43], is due to the morphological ambiguity in Arabic caused, above all, by the absence of vocalisation, the agglutination and the relatively free word order in a sentence. To resolve this problem, we have used clues for the disambiguation of certain markers, in order to validate or not their correspondence to the researched forms. Secondly, we remark that the occurrences of direct speech in French texts and the use of enunciative modalities are much more frequent than in texts in Arabic. Finally, we should elaborate more our reflexion on our categorization of the assertion class and its sub-categories. Some of these categories were manually annotated as a declaration.

As the annotation procedure is independent of a given *point of view* (the D-RS in our case) and of the processed languages (Arabic and French), it is absolutely possible to annotate other types of texts with different linguistic resources, in different languages and according to other *points of view*. The annotation platform has also been then tested in the following works: identification of the hypotheses in biological articles in English[16], annotation of D-RS in Korean[17] and of events in articles in French and Polish[18]. These works are in progress and will be published shortly. It becomes also conceivable, in futur work, to intersect the annotations according to different semantic maps, such as, for example, that of D-RS and the SM of bibliosemantics or contact between people (meetings).

---

[16] Desclés J., Ecole Normal Supérieure de Paris.
[17] Suh J., Seoul Women's Univ.
[18] Gwiazdecka E., Univ. of Warsaw.

Acknowledgments. The authors would like to thank all readers of this paper, and everyone who participated in the evaluation tests.

References

1. Bergler, S.: Conveying Attitude with Reported Speech. In: Shanahan, J.C., Qu, Y., Wiebe, J. (eds.) Computing Attitude and Affect in Text: Theory and Applications. Springer, Heidelberg (2005)
2. Sauri, R., Verhagen, M., Pustejovsky, J.: Annotating and recognizing event modality in text. In: Proceedings of the 19th international Flairs conference, Florida (2006)
3. Riloff, E., Wiebe, J., Wilson, T.: Learning subjective nouns using extraction pattern bootstrapping. In: Proceedings of the 7th Conference on Natural Language Learning, pp. 25–32 (2003)
4. Wiebe, J., Wilson, T., Bruce, R., Bell, M., Martin, M.: Learning Subjective Language. Computational Linguistics 30, 277–308 (2004)
5. Yu, H., Hatzivassiloglou, V.: Towards answering opinion questions: Separating facts from opinions and identifying the polarity of opinion sentences. In: Proceedings of the Conference on Empirical Methods in Natural Language Processing, pp. 129–136 (2003)
6. Turney, P.: Thumbs up or thumbs down? Semantic orientation applied to unsupervised classification of reviews. In: Proceedings of the 40th Annual Meeting of the Association for Computational Linguistics, Philadelphia, pp. 417–424 (2002)
7. Pang, B., Lee, L., Vaithyanathan, V.: Thumbs up? Sentiment classification using machine learning techniques. In: Proceedings of the 2002 Conference on Empirical Methods in natural language processing, pp. 79–86 (2002)
8. Polanyi, L., Zaenen, A.: Shifting attitudes. In: Lagerwerf, L., Spooren, W. (eds.) Determination of information and tenor in texts: Multidisciplinary approaches to discourse, Nodus Publikationen, pp. 61–69 (2003)
9. Bestgen, Y., Fairon, C., Kevers, L.: Un baromètre affectif effectif. In: Purnelle, G., Fairon, C., Dister, A. (eds.) Actes des septième Journées internationales d'Analyse statistique des Données Textuelles, Louvain-la-Neuve, pp. 182–191 (2004)
10. Peirce, Ch. The Collected Papers vol. V: Pragmatism and Pragmaticism. Harvard University Press, Cambridge, MA (1934)
11. Desclés, J.-P., Jouis, C., Oh, H.-G., Reppert, D.: Exploration Contextuelle et sémantique: un système expert qui trouve les valeurs sémantiques des temps de l'indicatif dans un texte. In: Herin-Aime, R., Dieng, J.-P., Regourd, J.P. (eds.) Knowledge modeling andexpertise transfer, pp. 371–400. Amsterdam (1991)
12. Berri, J.: Contribution à la méthode d'Exploration Contextuelle: Applications au résumé automatique et aux représentations temporelles. Réalisation informatique du système SERAPHIN, Thèse de doctorat, Université de ParisIV-Sorbonne, Paris (1996)
13. Minel, J.-L.: Filtrage sémantique, du résumé automatique à la fouille de textes. Hermès, Paris (2002)
14. Blais, A., Desclés, J.-P., Djioua, B.: Le résumé automatique dans la plate-forme EXCOM, Digital Humanities, Paris (2006)
15. Jackiewicz, A.: La notion de cause pour le filtrage de phrases importantes d'un texte. In: International Conference on Natural Language Processing and Industrial Applications, Moncton, Canada (1996)
16. Le Priol, F.: A data processing sequence to extract terms and semantics relations between terms. In: 10th Human Centered Processes Conference, pp. 241–248 (1999)

17. Rosier, L.: Le discours rapporté. Histoire, théories, pratiques, Duculot, Paris et Bruxelles (1999)
18. Bruna-Cuevas, M.: le discours indirect introduit par que. Le français moderne 54(1), 28–50 (1996)
19. Gross, M.: Méthodes en syntaxe, Hermann, Paris (1975)
20. Charolles, M.: Exercices sur les verbes de communication. Pratiques 9, 83–107 (1976)
21. Lamiroy, B., Charolles, M.: Les verbes de parole et la question de l'(in)transitivité. In: colloque lexique et grammaire, Thessaloniki (2003)
22. Mourad, G.: Analyse informatique des signes typographiques pour la segmentation de textes et l'extraction automatique de citations: Réalisation des Applications informatiques, SegATex et CitaRE, thèse de doctorat, Université de Paris-Sorbonne (2001)
23. Austin, J.: How To Do Things With Words. Oxford University Press, Oxford (1962)
24. Searle, J.-R.: les actes du langage: essai philosophique du langage, Hermann, Paris (1972)
25. Vanderveken, D.: Les actes de discours, Mardaga, Liège (1988)
26. Ross, J.-R.: On declarative sentences. In: Jacobs, R.-A., Rosen-baum, P.-S. (eds.) Readings in english transformational grammar, Massachussets (1970)
27. Banfield, A.: Le style narratif et la grammaire des discours direct et indirect. Change 16(17), 190–226 (1973)
28. Bybee, J., Perkins, R., Pagliuca, W.: The Evolution of Grammar: tense, aspect and modality in the languages of the world. The University of Chicago Press, Chicago (1994)
29. Palmer, F.R. (ed.): Mood and Modality. Cambridge University Press, Cambridge (1986)
30. Nuyts, J.: Modality: overview and linguistic issues, in The expression of modality, pp. 1–26. Mouton de Gruyter, Berlin (2006)
31. Bally, Ch.: Linguistique générale et linguistique française, Francke, Berne (1932)
32. Benveniste, E.: Problèmes de linguistique générale 1, Gallimard, Paris (1966)
33. Culioli, A.: sur quelques contradictions en linguistiques. Communications 20, 83–91 (1973)
34. Desclés, J.-P.: Quelques opérations énonciatives. In: David, J. (ed.) Logique et niveaux d'analyse linguistique, Klinckseieck, Paris, pp. 213–242 (1976)
35. Desclés, J.-P., Guentcheva, Z.: Enonciateur, locuteur, médiateur. Les Rituels du dialogue, Nanterre: Société d'ethnologie, Recherches thématiques 6, 79–112 (2000)
36. Desclés, J.-P.: Prise en charge, engagement et désengagement, Anvers (2007)
37. Alrahabi, M., Desclés, J.-P.: Vers une carte sémantique du discours rapporté. In: 75th congrès de l'ACFAS, Trois-Rivières (2007)
38. Alrahabi, M., Ibrahim, A.H., Desclés, J.-P.: Semantic Annotation of Reported Information in Arabic. In: Flairs 2006, Floride (2006)
39. Alrahabi, M., Djioua, B., Desclés, J.-P.: Annotation Sémantique des Énonciations en Arabe. In: Inforsid 2006, Hammamet (2006)
40. Alrahabi, M., Mourad, G., Djioua, B.: Filtrage sémantique de textes en arabe. In: JEP-TALN 2004, Fès (2004)
41. Alrahabi, M.: Désambiguiser par le contexte, le cas de la graphie alef-noun en arabe. In: vers de nouveaux accès aux savoirs, Paris (2006)
42. Diab, M., Kadri, H., Daniel, J.: Automatic Tagging of Arabic Text: From raw text to Base Phrase Chunks. In: Proceedings of HLT-NAACL (2004)
43. Dichy, J.: On lemmatization in Arabic. In: Proceedings of the Workshop on Arabic Language Processing, Toulouse (2001)

Type-Theoretical Bulgarian Grammar

Krasimir Angelov

Chalmers University of Technology, Computer Science and Engineering,
SE-412 96 Göteborg, Sweden

Abstract. We describe a type-theoretical resource grammar for Bulgarian in the Grammatical Framework (GF). The grammar allows parsing and generation of natural language text to and from abstract syntax representation. The representation is common for all languages in the resource library in GF which makes it possible to translate between any of the two supported languages and to have multilingual text authoring. We developed formalized grammar rules for Bulgarian and we show how the language specifics fit into this multilingual setting.

1 Introduction

Grammatical Framework (GF) [1] is a grammar formalism based on the type theory and there is a high-level language with compiler and interpreter for it. Within the framework a resource grammar library was developed that contains grammars for ten languages: one Slavic language: Russian [2], three Scandinavian languages: Swedish, Danish and Norwegian, three Romance languages: Italian, Spanish and French, two Germanic languages: English and German and finally one Finno-Ugric language: Finnish. There is also a still unfinished grammar for Arabic [3]. We added the eleventh language - Bulgarian.

Although this is not the first Slavic language in the library, this is the first South-Slavic language. Russian itself is East-Slavic and it differs significantly both in morphology and syntax. Furthermore, Bulgarian belongs to the Balkan linguistic area and has some characteristic properties such as a complete loss of case declension, lack of verb infinitive forms and the development of a definite article.

The GF grammars can share common code via inheritance and parametricity [4]. This is already used to capture the similarities between the Scandinavian and the Romance languages. There are common Scandinavian and Romance modules from which the concrete grammars are inherited. Although this can not be easily done for Bulgarian and Russian, the Bulgarian grammar is a good common ground candidate for Serbian and Macedonian since they are of the same family and of the same language area.

The grammar has two levels in GF: abstract and concrete. The abstract level is language independent and represents the original textual sentence as a typed lambda term (abstract syntax). The concrete level gives the mapping from a given lambda term to its concrete textual representation. It is possible to have multiple concrete syntaxes for each abstract syntax. This allows one language

A. Ranta, B. Nordström (Eds.): GoTAL 2008, LNAI 5221, pp. 52–64, 2008.

to be translated into another or to simultaneously generate equivalent texts in different languages.

Furthermore, the grammars in GF are divided into resource grammars and application grammars. The resource grammars have a wider coverage and are linguistically oriented but they can be highly ambiguous. The application grammars reuse the already existing resource grammars but specialize them in a specific context. In this way they are less ambiguous and usually they are extended with an application specific dictionary.

The grammar that we developed is a resource grammar. On top of it, the developer could create an application specific grammar with a very limited linguistic knowledge. It could be started with an English grammar which then could be translated to Bulgarian just by introduction of new lexicon since the abstract syntax representation is common for all languages.

The current abstraction proved to be enough for many dialog and text generation projects (KeY, TALK, WebALT). For that reason constructions that are not covered in the current abstract syntax are out of the scope of the current project. We found that the current design provides sufficient abstraction and we did not have to change it in order to fit the new language.

In the next sections we first explain the morphology and then the most important parts of the grammar: noun, verb and adjective phrases, numerals, declarative sentences, questions and imperative utterances. Comparative examples are given mainly in English but where it is more appropriate there are also examples from other languages.

2   Morphology

The grammar has a complete morphology for adjectives, nouns, verbs, numerals and pronouns. The full word classification is given in [5] where the words are divided in 187 paradigms. Each paradigm in GF is defined as a function that takes the base form and produces a table with all possible word forms.

GF has a small parallel dictionary of 350 words that is translated to all languages and is used mainly for development and testing purposes. Another small dictionary of about one hundred words contains structural words like pronouns, prepositions and quantifiers. These dictionaries are translated to Bulgarian as well. In addition there is a bigger dictionary of 57805 words that is only for Bulgarian and defines the base form, the part of speech category and its inflection paradigm. The dictionary is an import of all adjectives, nouns and verbs from the BGOffice project.[1]

In the abstract syntax the words are defined as constants of some of the lexical categories. For example in the Lexicon the words red, go and apple are declared as:

fun *red_A*   : *A* ;
   go_V   : *V* ;
   apple_N : *N* ;

---

[1] http://bgoffice.sourceforge.net

The corresponding linearization rules in the concrete syntax for Bulgarian are[2]:

lin red_A   = *mkA076* "červen" ;
  apple_N = *mkN041* "jabâlka" ;
  go_V   = *actionV* (*mkV186* "otivam") (*mkV146* "otida") ;

Here the numbers 076, 041, 186 and 146 are the paradigm numbers given in Krustev [5]. The verbs have two base forms which correspond to perfective and imperfective aspect. The usage of verb aspect is explained in section 4.

For comparison we also give the linearization rules for English:

lin red_A   = *duplADeg* "red" ;
  apple_N = *regN* "apple" ;
  go_V   = *mk5V* "go" "goes" "went" "gone" "going" ;

In English *apple* is a regular noun and it is defined with the *regN* function. In contrast *red* is defined with *duplADeg* because it doubles the ending consonant in the comparative form. The verb *go* itself is irregular and it is defined by enumerating all its forms.

The application grammars are supposed to use their own context specific dictionaries but when it is appropriate they can reuse the already existing one. The advantage of having a context specific dictionary is that it is much less ambiguous. For example the Bulgarian word *vreme* in general has the meaning of either time, weather or tense. Despite this an application in the weather forecast area will use the second translation while an application for airport service is more likely to use the first one and neither of them will use the tense meaning.

3   Noun Phrases

The nouns in Bulgarian are divided into four genders: masculine animate, masculine inanimate, feminine and neuter. There are two numbers singular and plural. The main noun forms are illustrated on fig. 1.

In the sentence the noun modifiers (adjectives, numerals) are in gender and number agreement with the noun. The inflection for all modifiers except the cardinal numerals does not distinguish between masculine animate and masculine inanimate so they have effectively merged into a single gender. For the cardinals there is a distinct masculine animate form (mǎžkolična forma).

dvama mǎže two men

dva učebnika two textbooks

The animate gender includes all human masculine words like man, teacher and king while others like *kon* (horse) are inanimate despite that they are alive. Most informal grammars do not mention the existence of four genders and describe the masculine animate form as an exception. In the formalized rules it behaves exactly as a separate gender and this is not something uncommon in the other Slavic languages. For example in Czech there is a much clearer distinction between masculine animate and masculine inanimate in the declension system. In Bulgarian the animate gender is not fully developed.

---

[2] In the paper we use the scientific transliteration of cyrilic but the actual grammar is in cyrilic.

In the rest of the section we will state masculine gender when there is no distinction between animate and inanimate and we will specify it explicitly otherwise.

Bulgarian and Macedonian are the only Slavic languages that developed definite article. The article is a clitic and attaches to the end of the first nominal in the noun phrase that is noun, adjective, pronoun or numeral. Its form depends on the ending of the nominal and on the case when the nominal is a masculine singular noun. The masculine nouns use full definite article (*pălen opredelitelen člen*) when they are in singular and they have the role of subject in the sentence. The definite noun forms are recorded in the inflection tables together with the singular and the plural forms.

There is also a vocative form used for a noun identifying the object being addressed: *mǎžo, ženo*. The vocative form is a remnant from the old vocative case in the Old Church Slavonic.

The masculine inanimate nouns have also a special plural form used for counting and after the determiner *njakolko* (few):

mnogo učebnici   many textbooks
njakolko učebnika few textbooks
dva učebnika   two textbooks

Although some masculine animate nouns also have countable forms, their usage in the literary language is discouraged [6]. One exception is the case of homonyms with animate and inanimate meanings. In this case they are two different abstract syntax constants in GF and are treated properly. The usage of the countable forms for masculine animate in our grammar is not supported.

Sg+Indef	Sg+Def	SgDefNom	Pl+Indef	Pl+Def	English	Gender
mǎž	*mǎža*	*mǎžǎt*	*mǎže*	*mǎžete*	man	masc animate
učebnik	*učebnika*	*učebnikǎt*	*učebnici*	*učebnicite*	textbook	masc inanimate
momče	*momčeto*	*momčeto*	*momčeta*	*momčetata*	boy	neut
žena	*ženata*	*ženata*	*ženi*	*ženite*	woman	feminine

Fig. 1. Noun Forms

In the concrete syntax the category N is represented by the record:
lincat $N = \{s : NForm \Rightarrow Str; \; g : DGender\}$;
where NForm is:
param *NForm* = *NF Number Species*
      | *NFSgDefNom*
      | *NFPlCount*
      | *NFVocative*
      ;

The *Number, Species* and *DGender* parameters are defined on figure 2. Here the *NF* constructor represents the common case while *NFSgDefNom, NFPlCount* and *NFVocative* represent the forms with full definite article, the countable form and the vocative. When the noun does not have some of the special forms then the corresponding normal singular or plural form is filled in.

The noun is the head of the common noun (*CN*) phrase. The phrase is formed by these three functions:

fun *UseN*   : *N* → *CN* ;
    UseN2   : *N2* → *CN* ;
    ComplN2 : *N2* → *NP* → *CN* ;
    AdjCN   : *AP* → *CN* → *CN* ;

Here *N2* is a category of the relational nouns and *AP* is the adjective phrase. The common noun itself is the head of the noun phrase (*NP*) formed by:

fun *DetCN* : *Det* → *CN* → *NP* ;
    DetSg : *Quant* → *Ord* → *Det* ;
    DetPl : *Quant* → *Num* → *Ord* → *Det* ;
    every_Det, someSg_Det, somePl_Det : *Det* ;
    much_Det, many_Det : *Det* ;
    few_Det : *Det* ;

The first two determiners are synthetic and they combine quantifiers with ordinal and/or cardinal numerals. The *Quant* category specifies the definiteness. It has two members *DefArt* and *IndefArt* which in English generate the "a" and "the" articles. In Bulgarian there is no indefinite article and the noun phrase is just unchanged. When the *DefArt* is chosen then it adds the definite article to the first nominal in the noun phrase. The selection of the first nominal is ensured by a system of parameters in *DetSg*, *DetPl* and *AdjCN*.

The determiners also specify whether the noun has to be in singular, plural or countable plural form. Singular is used with *DetSg*, *DetPl* with cardinal one and with the lexical determiners *someSg_Det* (*njakoj, njakoja, njakoe*) and *much_Det* (*mnogo*). The determiners *somePl_Det* (niakoi), *many_Det* (mnogo) and *DetPl* without numeral (*NoNum*) require the noun to be in plural. Finally *few_Det* (nijakolko) and *DetPl* with any cardinal greater than one select a countable form for the noun.

In the *N* category the *g* field is of type *DGender* (fig. 2) and this allows the right numeral inflection in *DetPl*. At the same time the agreement in NP:

lincat *NP* = {*s* : *Role* ⇒ *Str*; *a* : *Agr*} ;

param *Number* = *Sg* | *Pl* ;
    Person = *P1* | *P2* | *P3* ;
    Gender = *Masc* | *Fem* | *Neut* ;
    DGender = *MascA* | *Masc* | *Fem* | *Neut* ;
    Species = *Indef* | *Def* ;
    Case   = *Acc* | *Dat* ;

    AForm   = *ASg Gender Species*
          | *ASgMascDefNom*
          | *APl Species*
          ;

oper   Agr   = {*gn* : *GenNum* ; *p* : *Person*} ;

Fig. 2. Inflection Parameters

contains only the simplified *Gender* which does not make a distinction between masculine animate and masculine inanimate. This reflects the fact that the adjectives and the verb participles have only one form for masculine.

The *Role* parameter plays the role of the case in the other languages. The role can be either subject (*RSubj*) or object (*RObj c*, where *c* is of type *Case*). In the other languages there is a nominative case which is used to mark the subject and is equivalent to our *RSubj* role. In Bulgarian it is more useful to distinguish between case and role because the case is also used as a synthesized parameter in the medial and phrasal verbs and also in the prepositions. In these situations the case is always accusative or dative and never nominative. In fact the Bulgarian language is mostly analytic and the case makes a distinction only for the pronouns and the definite forms in masculine.

4   Verb Phrases

The verb category is the most complex. There are three simple verb tenses (present, aorist, imperfect) and three synthetic participles (perfect, plusquam-perfect, present participle). These synthetic forms are used in six other compound tenses: future, past future, present perfect, past perfect, future perfect and past future perfect. There are also passive voice and imperative, conditional and inferential moods.

In addition almost all verbs come in pairs with equivalent lexical meanings but with different aspects. For example *otivam* and *otida* are two different verbs which are both translated as "go" in English but they express different aspects in Bulgarian. The former is with imperfective aspect and represents the event in action while the letter is with perfective aspect and represents the event as a whole together with its start and end. The grammar has only one abstract syntax constant for each lexical meaning and for that reason the verbs are coupled together in pairs. Which verb will be used in the linearization depends on the grammatical tense and aspect.

The verb category *V* in the concrete syntax is defined as:

param *VForm = VPres*   *Number Person*
            | *VAorist*   *Number Person*
            | *VImperfect*   *Number Person*
            | *VPerfect*   *AForm*
            | *VPluPerfect*   *AForm*
            | *VPresPart*   *AForm*
            | *VPassive*   *AForm*
            | *VImperative*   *Number*
            | *VGerund*

            ;

    VType = VNormal
            | *VMedial*   *Case*
            | *VPhrasal*   *Case*

            ;

        Aspect = Imperf | *Perf* ;
lincat *V* = {*s* : *Aspect* ⇒ *VForm* ⇒ *Str*; *vtype* : *VType*} ;

The inherent *VForm* parameter is a mixture of tenses, voices and moods because it enumerates all possible morphological forms. The compound tenses and moods are not listed because they are formed on the level of the *VP* category.

The *VType* parameter marks two special kinds of verbs medial and phrasal:

Bulgarian	English	VType
Az rabotja	I work	VNormal
Az se smeja	I smile	VMedial Acc
Az si spomnjam	I remember	VMedial Dat
Men me trese	I shiver	VPhrasal Acc
Na men mi lipsvaš	I miss you	VPhrasal Dat

The medial verbs express middle voice but syntactically are marked with the passive voice particle *se/si*. The difference is that they either cannot be used without it (a) or they have different meanings if they are used without it (b-c):

a * *Az boja*
b *Az se kazvam ...* | My name is ...
c *Az kazvam ...* | I say ...

The passive/middle voice is marked with the clitic *se* for accusative or *si* for dative. Similarly, the phrasal verbs are always coupled with the clitic form of the personal pronoun in accusative or dative. The number and person agreement is marked on the clitic instead of on the verb. The subject in the sentence is inflected as an object in the specified case. The choice of accusative or dative case for both the medial and phrasal verbs depends only on the verb so it is specified in its lexical definition. In the lexicon the medial and phrasal verbs are created with these functions:

$$medialV : V \rightarrow Case \rightarrow V$$
$$phrasalV : V \rightarrow Case \rightarrow V$$

First a normal verb form is created with some of the *mkV* function and after that it is modified with *medialV* or *phrasalV*.

A verb forms a verb phrase *VP* with the following constructors:

fun *UseV*   : $V \rightarrow VP$;
  ComplV2 : $V2 \rightarrow NP \rightarrow VP$;
  ComplV3 : $V3 \rightarrow NP \rightarrow NP \rightarrow VP$;

Here the *V2* and *V3* categories have a structure similar to *V* and contain the transitive and ditransitive verbs. The *VP* category itself is defined as:

lincat *VP* = { *s* :   Tense
           $\Rightarrow$ *Anteriority*
           $\Rightarrow$ *Polarity*
           $\Rightarrow$ *Agr*
           $\Rightarrow$ *Bool*
           $\Rightarrow$ *Aspect*
           $\Rightarrow$ *Str* ;
        } ;

There are also other fields but only the *s* field is shown because the others are not relevant for the explanation. The first two parameters *Tense* and *Anteriority* define the tense system in the resource library. The supported tenses are present, past, future and conditional[3]. In English the anteriority distinguishes between the simple and the perfect tenses. This system of tense and anteriority is over-simplified. There are 8 different combinations of *Tense* and *Anteriority* but this is not enough to cover all Bulgarian and even some English tenses. For example there are two past tenses - past imperfect and aorist, but only the second one is currently supported in the grammar. It is usually translated as past simple in English. In addition there is a past future tense which is translated as "was going to" tense but the "going to" tense is also not supported. This is overcome in the Romance grammar where the concrete syntax has more tenses than the abstract syntax. They are not accessible from the common API but still can be used from language specific modules. Currently only the minimal number of tenses is implemented for Bulgarian. The tense system in the resource library is just an intersection between the tenses of all supported languages.

The verb phrase in Bulgarian has a complex structure where clitics and aux-iliary verbs are combined with the main verb to form a phrase [7]. The basic components are the pronoun and the reflexive clitics, the *li* clitic, the *da, ne* and *šte* articles and the auxilary verb *săm* (be). The particle *ne* marks phrases with negative polarity (the *Polarity* parameter is *Neg*) and it is always in the beginning of the phrase. The *li* clitic marks questions and is added after the first stressed word in the verb phrase. The future tense is formed with the *šte* particle and the auxiliary verb *săm* is used in the perfect tenses.

Most languages distinguish between progressive and finite actions. In English this is expressed with the so called -ing verb forms or gerund. In the grammar the verb phrases use nonprogressive tenses by default. This could be changed with the function:

ProgrVP : *VP* → *VP*

It converts the phrase "work" for example to the continuous phrase "am working". For Bulgarian the same function deals with the lexical aspect of the verb. In the lexicon all verbs come in pairs: one with perfective aspect and one with imperfective. The perfective aspect is the default but when the *ProgrVP* function is applied it is replaced with the imperfective.

An important exception is the present tense when the perfective aspect can-not be used. In this case the imperfective aspect is used regardless of whether the *ProgrVP* function is applied or not. The imperfective aspect in present tense is ambiguous and can have the meaning of both progressive and finite action. The parser from Bulgarian will produce two different abstract trees from the verb *otivam*: *(UseV go_V)* and *(ProgrVP (UseV go_V))*. In the opposite direc-tion from abstract tree to English phrase the linearizer will produce both "go" and "going".

---

[3] This is actually a mood but it is defined as a tense because it is parallel to the other tenses.

Another kind of ambiguity exists between the reflexive verb phrases and the phrases with passive voice. In the grammar they are created with these functions:

$ReflV2 : V2 \rightarrow VP$

$PassV2 : V2 \rightarrow VP$

It was already mentioned that the reflexive verbs are marked with the clitic *se* or *si*, but the same construction might mean passive voice as well [6]. The following sentences:

Pesenta se pee

Pesenta e pjata (passive participle)

both have the meaning of "the song is sung" (passive voice) but the first has also the meaning of "the song sings itself" (reflexive verb). Of course the second meaning is rejected from the common knowledge that the song cannot sing. On the other side, the second sentence is ambiguous between present and present perfect while the first one is not - *pesenta se e pjala*.

The grammar does not try to disambiguate between the tenses or between passive voice and reflexive verb because this would require external common sense knowledge which is beyond the scope of the current project. Instead, the phrases marked with *se/si* are parsed as reflexive and the phrases formed with the passive participle are parsed as passive but the anteriority parameter remains ambiguous in the abstract tree.

The Balkan languages are known to lack verb infinitives and Bulgarian is not an exception. Instead, the Bulgarian language has developed the *da* complex [7]. The particle *da* is placed in the beginning of the verb phrases in the cases when we expect an infinitive in the other languages. The main verb itself can be in any tense and it is aggreement with the subject.

One place where infinitives are used in the other languages is the *VV* category. It contains verbs which take another verb in infinitive form as a complement. For example in Russian it is *Ja dolžen hodit'* (I must go) but *Ja hožu* (I go). In English usually the infinitive coincides with the present, singular, first person. In Bulgarian these phrases are translated with *da* complex:

Az trjabva da hodja

Az hodja

here the main verb (*hodja*) is in present simple while the *VV* verb (*trjabva*) can be in any tense, anteriority and polarity. Although *da* complexes with other conjugations of the main verbs are also possible the abstract syntax does not have constructions that require that.

5   Adjective Phrases

The adjectives have forms for masculine, feminine and neuter in singular and a separate form for plural which is common for all genders. There are also definite and indefinite forms. The *A* category definition is:

lincat $A = \{s : AForm \Rightarrow Str\}$;

There are also comparative and superlative forms which are formed analyticaly on the *AP* level.

krasiv	beautiful
po-krasiv ot nego	more beautiful than he
naj-krasiv	most beautiful

The examples are generated from the following abstract syntaxes:

PositA beautiful_A

ComparA beautiful_A (UsePron he_Pron)

OrdSuperl beautiful_A

For comparison, in German the comparative and superlative forms are synthethic (schön - schöner als er - schönst) but they still use the same abstract syntax.

The AP clauses are attached to the common nouns with the function:

fun *AdjCN : AP → CN → CN* ;

and are in gender and number agreement with the noun.

6 Numerals

The basic building blocks of the numerals are the digits from one to nine. They are divided in three groups. The first group includes only the digit one. It has forms for masculine (*edin*), feminine (*edna*) and neuter (*edno*). There is also a form for plural (*edni*) which is used to refer to a group as a whole. The second group includes the digit two. It has forms for masculine animate (*dvama*), masculine inanimate (*dva*) and a common form for feminine and neuter (*dve*). All other digits are in the third group. They have separated form for masculine animate and a common form for all other genders. There are also definite and indefinite forms.

The cardinal and ordinal numbers in Bulgarian are also marked morphologicaly (*edin-părvi, dve-vtori*).

The *Digit* category is defined as:

param *CardOrd = NCard DGenderSpecies*
              | NOrd AForm ;
       DForm   = unit | teen | ten | hundred ;
lincat *Digit = {s : DForm ⇒ CardOrd ⇒ Str}* ;

The *DForm* parameter enumerates all numeral forms which are defined syntheticaly.

edno	edinadeset	deset	sto
one	eleven	ten	hundred

A similar parameter exists in the other grammars but it usually has different values. For example in Arabic there are forms only for unit and ten. All other numerals are formed analytically. Since the parameters are only in the concrete syntax on an abstract level, the numerals have uniform representation in all languages.

7 Clauses and Declarative Sentences

The simplest clause is formed by *PredVP*:

lincat *Cl = {s : Tense ⇒ Anteriority ⇒ Polarity ⇒ Order ⇒ Str}* ;
fun   *PredVP : NP → VP → Cl* ;

It just combines one noun phrase and one verb phrase. The *NP* category has an agreement as a synthesized parameter which is passed by *PredVP* to the verb as an inherent parameter. This guarantees the subject-verb agreement in the clause. The clause does not have fixed tense, anteriority and polarity. Instead they are given as an inherent parameters which are fixed on the sentence (S) level:

fun *UseCl* : *Tense* → *Ant* → *Pol* → *Cl* → *S* ;

Here *Tense*, *Ant* and *Pol* are syntactic categories whose constructors does not have linearizations but just fix the corresponding *Tense*, *Anteriority* and *Polarity* parameters in *Cl*. The constructed sentences can be used to construct utterances or they could be embedded in other sentences.

8   Imperative Sentences

The GF resource grammars have a limited support for imperative sentences. Basically, you can turn any verb phrase to *Imp* and from it an imperative utterance can be formed with positive or negative polarity:

fun *ImpVP*   : *VP* → *Imp* ;
        UttImpSg, UttImpPl, UttImpPol : *Pol* → *Imp* → *Utt* ;

In the formation of the *Imp* category, the verb phrase is turned into imperative mood and after that it is negated if negative polarity is specified.

9   Questions

There are various ways to form a question in GF. The two basic constructors are *QuestCl* and *QuestVP*. The first one creates yes/no questions and the second one creates wh-questions:

fun *QuestCl* : *Cl* → *QCl* ;
        QuestVP : *IP* → *VP* → *QCl* ;
        UseQCl   : *Tense* → *Ant* → *Pol* → *QCl* → *QS* ;

Just like with the definitive sentences, the above constructors create clauses which do not have fixed tense and polarity. The *UseQCl* create interrogative sentences (QS) and fixes the tense and polarity.

In Bulgarian the questions are formed with the *li* clitic. It can appear either in the verb phrase or in the noun phrase and it indicates whether we are asking about the action or about the subject. In the GF grammar only the first option is used. The reason is that questions like "Do you work?" usually ask about the action. The opposite question is "Is it you who work?". This is an idiomatic construction and has different translations in the different languages; anyway it still can be translated literally in Bulgarian and is still grammatical.

10   Future Work

There are many constructions that are not covered in the abstract syntax. Some are very language specific while others are more or less common. The right abstraction is not always obvious but it is also not necessary to have a single abstraction for all languages. Having a single language independent abstraction is definitely an advantage because then the application level grammar is just a parameterized module built on top of the abstract syntax. If there is not a single abstraction, then a language dependent abstract syntax can be used and the application level grammar will use different resource modules.

One immediate candidate for further extension is the tense system. A language specific module could be provided that implements all possible tenses, aspects and moods. However, the common abstract syntax could still work with the already existing language independent abstraction.

Other candidates are the pronouns. In Bulgarian the personal pronoun is quite often avoided because it is clear from the verb conjugation. For example:

(Ti) Govoriš li bălgarski? — Do you speak Bulgarian?

The pronoun *ti* is often skipped because it is clear from the verb conjugation that the subject is in third person singular. The generated sentence is still grammatically correct but the construction is used only for clarity or to stress the pronoun itself. In this respect it makes sense to have stressed and unstressed forms of the pronouns where the unstressed form will be just empty when the pronoun is in subject position. The same construction can be used also for the other pro-drop languages.

The possessive pronouns in Bulgarian have definite and indefinite forms: *moja-mojata* (my), *tvoja-tvojata* (your). The definite form is used to specify one particular object that belongs to the subject. In both cases in English my/your is used. This could be illustrated in Italian where both "la mia penna" and "una mia penna" (my pen) are possible. The difference is that in Bulgarian the definite article is a clitic and it attaches to the first word in the NP phrase which is the pronoun, so we have two different forms for the possessive pronouns.

11   Conclusion

The grammar does not cover all aspects of the language and it cannot be used to parse arbitrary text. This limits its usage in applications like information extraction and question answering where the input is often assumed to be free text. Despite this GF has been proven useful for dialog systems, text generation applications and for software localization where a well defined controlled language is used. The Bulgarian grammar can be successfully applied in the same areas. It is even more important for multilingual systems because with GF the translation can be done automatically or at least semi-automatically.

References

1. Ranta, A.: Grammatical Framework: A Type-Theoretical Grammar Formalism. Journal of Functional Programming 14(2), 145–189 (2004)
2. Khegai, J.: GF parallel resource grammars and Russian. In: Proceedings of the COLING/ACL on Main conference poster sessions, Association for Computational Linguistics (2006), pp. 475–482 (2006)

3. Dada, A.E., Ranta, A.: Implementing an Open Source Arabic Resource Grammar in GF. In: Perspectives on Arabic Linguistics XX. John Benjamins Publishing Company (June 2007)
4. Ranta, A.: Modular Grammar Engineering in GF. Research on Language & Computation 5(2), 133–158 (2007)
5. Krustev, B.: The Bulgarian Morphology in 187 type tables. NI, Bulgaria (1984)
6. Pashov, P.: A Bulgarian Grammar, Hermes, Plovdiv, Bulgaria (1999)
7. Avgustinova, T.: Word Order and Clitics in Bulgarian. PhD in Philosophy, der Universitat des Saarlandes, Saarbrucken (1997)

A Compact Arabic Lexical Semantics Language Resource Based on the Theory of Semantic Fields

Mohamed Attia, Mohsen Rashwan, Ahmed Ragheb, Mohamed Al-Badrashiny, Husein Al-Basoumy, and Sherif Abdou

The Engineering Company for the Development of Computer Systems; RDI, 171st Al-Haram Av., 12111, Giza, Egypt
{m_Atteya,Mohsen_Rashwan,Ragheb,Mohammed.Badrashiny, Basoumy,sAbdou}@RDI-eg.com

Abstract. Applications of statistical Arabic NLP in general, and text mining in specific, along with the tools underneath perform much better as the statistical processing operates on deeper language factorizations than on raw text. Lexical semantic factorization is very important in this regard due to its feasibility, high level of abstraction, and the language independence of its output.

In the core of such a factorization lies an Arabic lexical semantic DB. While building this LR, we had to go beyond the conventional exclusive collection of words from dictionaries and thesauri that cannot alone produce a satisfactory coverage of this highly inflective and derivative language.

This paper is hence devoted to the design and implementation of an Arabic lexical semantics LR that enables the retrieval of the possible senses of any given Arabic word at a high coverage.

Instead of tying full Arabic words to their possible senses, our LR flexibly relates morphologically and PoS-tags constrained Arabic lexical compounds to a predefined limited set of semantic fields across which the standard semantic relations are defined. With the aid of the same large-scale Arabic morphological analyzer and PoS tagger in the runtime, the possible senses of virtually any given Arabic word are retrievable.

Keywords: Arabic, AWN, coverage, language factorization, language resource, lexical compounds, lexical semantics, LR, morphology, morpho-PoS constraining, PoS tagging, semantic fields, semantic mapping, semantic relations, text mining, word net, word senses.

1 Introduction

This paper presents an Arabic lexical semantics LR that is composed of the following four logical components:

1- A compact basis set of predefined semantic fields; i.e. word senses.
2- Lexical semantics relational data base (RDB) where the Arabic lexical compounds from a given lexicon are one-to-many mapped to semantic fields both in the forward and backward directions.

A. Ranta, B. Nordström (Eds.): GoTAL 2008, LNAI 5221, pp. 65–76, 2008.
© Springer-Verlag Berlin Heidelberg 2008

3- A set of predefined standard semantic relations; e.g. antonymy, hyponymy, entailment ... etc.

4- An RDB connecting the semantic fields to one another via none, one, or multiple standard semantic relations.

In what follows; the need for this LR is first manifested in sec. 2. Next, the criteria that governed the design of the LR is manifested in sec. 3, hence the design itself is dissected in sec. 4 and the process of building the LR is explained in sec. 5.

Finally, sec. 6 compares this LR to the Arabic Word Net (AWN) which seems to be the most relevant one to ours.

2 Need for This LR

While the wide spectrum of text mining applications might perform patterns detection/comparison for many tasks by directly processing raw text, performance gets better and better as the mining is done on deeper and deeper linguistic analysis of this text given the same algorithms, training corpora, and computational power.

Mathematically, as we delve deeper in linguistic analysis (e.g. from morphological, to semantic ...) resolving more and more complex relations, the raw text is factorized into more fundamental - and typically less numerous - atomic entities to be dealt with. This in turn reveals more concentrated statistical correlations and reduces the dimensionality of the problem, which both sharpen the effectiveness of the mining process. [8], [9], [11], [12]

The importance of language factorization gets more and more magnified as the vocabulary and structure of the subject language gets richer. In fact, while Arabic is on the extreme of richness as per its vocabulary when regarded as full-form words, this language is also on the extreme of compactness of atomic building entities due to its systematic and rich derivative and inflective nature. [1], [2], [6], [24] This positions language factorization not only as a performance boosting enhancement to Arabic text mining tasks, but also as a necessity for producing workable applications with useful output.

Among the fundamental and feasible factorizations in this regard comes Arabic morphological analysis, Part-of-Speech (PoS) tagging, and lexical semantic analysis.

3 Design Criteria of the LR

In order to meet the abovementioned need, our Arabic lexical semantic analyzer had to rely on an Arabic lexical semantics LR built according to the following criteria:

1- Originality of the source Arabic lexical semantic knowledge base. This means the LR, esp. its lexical side, should be designed in accordance with the intricate specifics of the Arabic language from the very beginning. This is a missing feature in other similar LR's like the Arabic Word Net (AWN). [5]

2- Widest coverage of possible Arabic lexical compounds, and semantic relations. Unless the highly derivative and inflective nature of Arabic is effectively handled, the runtime retrieval miss ratio of input words vs. the (inevitably limited) terms explicitly covered by the source of raw Arabic lexical semantics would be unacceptably high. So, this LR must go beyond the simplistic vocabulary-based model for maximally covering input Arabic terms and tying them to their possible senses/semantic fields.

3- Compactness of the resulting LR. Such an LR should never be huge in size not only in order to avoid prohibitive development, reviewing, and updating cost & time, but also to keep the LR development process from being excessively error-prone. So, this LR should be cleverly designed with a pacified growth of lexical/semantic relations versus the size of lexicon entries and semantic fields.

4- Independence and simplicity of the LR. Just like any professionally built LR; independence from the applications and from any LR development tools, as well as the simplicity of the LR format, are vital implicit aspects of this LR design.

5- Minimum implementation and updating cost. Less than 100 man-months within 2 calendar years had been allocated for building, refining, and verifying this LR. So, design decisions were always made in favor of the smaller, the clearer, the cleaner, and the faster choices. It was not always straightforward to satisfy this aspect together with the other ones of the criteria.

4 Design Description of the LR

To produce a sound Arabic lexical semantics LR complying with the abovementioned criteria, the implemented design relied on the following key concepts and choices:

4.1 Source of Raw Arabic Lexical Semantics

The published literature had been surveyed for sound semantic knowledge bases crafted originally for the Arabic language by specialized Arabic linguistics teams led by credible experts. [6], [16], [17], [19], [20], [22], [23], [24], [25]

Neatly based on the theory of semantic fields [10], [21], the Grand Thesaurus [22] containing over 35,000 explicit Arabic lexical entries and relying on around 1,800 semantic fields has been elected to be our initial source of raw Arabic lexical semantics. Other sources are also used for the refinement and enrichment of the LR.

4.2 Arabic Lexical Compounds and Morpho-PoS Constraining

In order to avoid a prohibitively high runtime retrieval miss-ratio of input Arabic words versus the terms covered by the source(s) of raw Arabic lexical semantics[1], Arabic *lexical compounds* and *morpho-PoS constraining* are introduced as two powerfully flexible concepts for taming the highly inflective and derivative nature of Arabic.

Instead of full-form words, the units of the lexical side in the lexical semantics DB of the LR are encoded as lexical compounds composed of the underlying morphemes that are flexible to be fully or partially matched against the morphemes composing the input words.

A morpheme code is explicitly mentioned *only if* its exact existence in the lexical compound is necessary to imply the semantic field(s) tied to this lexical compound. If

---

[1] The size of lexical entries in any such source has an order of magnitude of $O(10^{4.5})$ while that of the generable Arabic lexical compounds via inflection and derivation is $O(10^7)$.

the existence of *any* morpheme containing a certain PoS tag is only necessary to imply those semantic field(s), the code of this PoS tag with a negative sign is mentioned in place of that morpheme. A *don't-care* code (assigned -1000) in some place signifies that the morpheme at that place is semantically neutral.

Illustrative examples on morpho-PoS constrained lexical compounds are provided in tables 4 and 5 in section 5 below.

To realize such design concepts, RDI's Arabic morphological and PoS tagging factorization models are adopted in this LR. [1], [2], [3]

4.2.1 Arabic Morphological and PoS-Tagging Factorization Models from RDI

This Arabic morphological model assumes the canonical structure uniquely representing any given Arabic word w to be a quadruple of morphemes so that $w \rightarrow q = (t: p, r, f, s)$ where p is prefix code, r is root code, f is pattern (or form) code, and s is suffix code. The type code t can signify words belonging to one of the following 4 classes: *Regular Derivative* (w_{rd}), *Irregular Derivative* (w_{id}), *Fixed* (w_f), or *Arabized* (w_a).

Prefixes & suffixes; P and S, the 4 classes applied on patterns; F_{rd}, F_{id}, F_f, and F_a, and only 3 classes applied on roots[2]; R_d, R_f, and R_a constitute together the 9 categories of morphemes in this model. The total number of morphemes of all these categories in this model is around 7,800. With such a limited set of morphemes, the dynamic coverage exceeds 99.8% measured on large Arabic text corpora excluding transliterated words.

While table 1 on the next page shows this model in application on few representative sample Arabic words, the reader is kindly referred to [2] for the detailed documentation of this Arabic morphological factorization model and its underlying lexicon along with the dynamics of the involved morphological analysis/synthesis algorithms.

Table 1. Exemplar Arabic morphological analyses

Sample word	Word type	Prefix & prefix code	Root & root code	Pattern & pattern code	Suffix & suffix code
فَمَا	Fixed	فَ 2	اَلَّذِي 87	مَا 48	- 0
تَتَنَاوَلُه	Regular Derivative	تَ 86	ن و ل 4077	تَفَاعَلَ 176	ـه 8
الْكِتَابَات	Regular Derivative	الـ 9	ك ت ب 3354	فِعَال 684	ـات 27
الْعِلْمِيَّة	Regular Derivative	الـ 9	ع ل م 2754	فِعْل 842	ـيَّة 28
مِنْ	Fixed	- 0	مِنْ 63	مِنْ 118	- 0
مَوَاضِيع	Regular Derivative	- 0	و ض ع 4339	مَفَاعِيل 93	- 0
مُتَّخَذة	Irregular Derivative	- 0	أ خ ذ 39	مُتَّخَذ 13	ـة 26

---

[2] The roots are common among both the regular and irregular derivative Arabic words.

On the other hand, our Arabic PoS-tagging model relies on a compact set of Arabic PoS tags containing only 62 tags covering all the possible atomic context-free syntactic features of Arabic words. While many of these Arabic PoS tags may have corresponding ones in other languages, few do not have such counterparts and may be specific to the Arabic language.

This PoS tags-set has been extracted after thoroughly scanning and decimating the morpho-syntactic features of the 7,800 morphemes in our morphologically factorized Arabic lexicon. Completeness, atomicity, and insurability of the scanned morpho-syntactic features were the criteria adhered to during that process.

Due to the atomicity of our Arabic PoS-tags as well as the compound nature of Arabic morphemes in general, the PoS labels of Arabic morphemes are represented by PoS tags-vectors. Each morpheme in our Arabic factorized lexicon is hence labeled by a PoS tags-vector as exemplified by table 2 on the next page.

Table 2. PoS labels of sample Arabic morphemes

Morpheme	Type & Code	Arabic PoS tags vector label
الـ	P 9	[Definitive] [ال التعريف]
سيـ	P 125	[Future, Present, Active] [استقبال، مضارع، مبني للمعلوم]
مُفَاعِل	F_{rd} 482	[Noun, Subjective Noun] [اسم، اسم فاعل]
اسْتِفْعَال	F_{rd} 67	[Noun, Noun Infinitive] [اسم، مصدر]
مَلَائِك	F_{id} 29	[Noun, No SARF, Plural] [اسم، ممنوع من الصرف، جمع]
هُوَ	F_f 8	[Noun, Masculine, Single, Subjective Pronoun] [اسم، مذكر، مفرد، ضمير رفع]
ذُو	F_f 39	[Noun, Masculine, Single, Adjunct, MARFOU'] [اسم، مذكر، مفرد، مضاف، مرفوع]
ـات	S 27	[Feminine, Plural] [مؤنث، جمع]
ـوَنَهُمْ	S 427	[Present, MARFOU', Subjective Pronoun, Objective Pronoun] [مضارع، مرفوع، ضمير رفع، ضمير نصب]
يَتَان	S 195	[Relative Adjective, Feminine, Binary, Non Adjunct, MARFOU'] [نسب، مؤنث، مثنى، غير مضاف، مرفوع]

While the Arabic PoS-tagging of stems is retrieved from the PoS label of the pattern only, not the root's, the PoS-tagging of the affixes is obtained from the PoS labels of the prefix and suffix. So, the Arabic PoS-tagging of a quadruple corresponding to a morphologically factorized input Arabic word is given by the concatenation of its PoS labels of the prefix, the pattern, and suffix respectively after eliminating any redundancy.

While table 3 on the next page shows the Arabic PoS-tagging of few sample words, the reader is kindly referred to [3] and chapter 3 of [1] for the detailed documentation of this Arabic PoS-tagging model along with its underlying PoS tags-set.

Table 3. PoS tags-vectors of sample Arabic words

Sample word	Arabic PoS tags vector
فَمَا	[Conjunction, Noun, Relative Pronoun, Null Suffix] [عطف، اسم، اسم موصول، لا لاحقة]
تَتَنَاوَلُه	[Present, Active, Verb ,Objective Pronoun] [مضارع، مبني للمعلوم، فعل، ضمير نصب]
الكِتَابَات	[Definitive, Noun, Plural, Feminine] [ال التعريف، اسم، جمع، مؤنّث]
العِلمِيَّة	[Definitive, Noun, Relative Adjective, Feminine, Single] [ال التعريف، اسم، نسب، مؤنّث، مفرد]
مِنْ	[Null Prefix, Preposition, Null Suffix] [لا سابقة، حرف، لا لاحقة]
مَوَاضِيع	[Null Prefix, Noun, No SARF, Plural, Null Suffix] [لا سابقة، اسم، ممنوع من الصرف، جمع، لا لاحقة]
مُتَّخَذَة	[Null Prefix, Noun, Objective Noun, Feminine, Single] [لا سابقة، اسم، اسم مفعول، مؤنّث، مفرَد]

4.3 Arabic Lexical Compounds and Morpho-PoS Constraining

All the components of this LR are formally structured as relational databases (RDB) which guarantees both its independence and simplicity.

4.4 Multi-level Indirect Semantic Mapping

Instead of the infeasible direct semantic mapping of the whole Arabic vocabulary across itself with a size complexity of $O(V^2)$; V is the huge vocabulary size of Arabic, our LR is designed for the multi-level semantic mapping; $w_i \leftrightarrow LC_m \leftrightarrow SF_u \leftrightarrow SFv \leftrightarrow LC_n \leftrightarrow w_j$.

Input Arabic words w_i are analyzed into morpho-PoS constrained lexical compounds LC_m which are in turn mapped in the inverse direction of the lexical semantics RDB to semantic fields SF_u.

The semantic fields are semantically interrelated through an $S \times S$ matrix per each defined semantic relation; where S is the size of the predefined basis set of semantic fields.[3] The third step of the mapping is hence possible.

Navigating our lexical semantics RDB in the forward direction can infer the possible LC_n that correspond to the semantic fields SF_v obtained in the previous step.

Morphological and PoS-tagging models help again at the last link in the chain of indirect semantic mapping across all the generable Arabic words.

Given that $S \ll V^{\backprime} \ll V$; where $V^{\backprime}$ is the number of core lexical compounds mentioned explicitly in our LR, the size complexity of the indirect semantic mapping approach is then $O(S^2 + S \cdot V^{\backprime}) = O(S \cdot V^{\backprime})$ which is much more tractable than $O(V^2)$ of the direct semantic mapping.

---

[3] This size has typically an order of magnitude of $O(10^{3.5})$.

5 The Building Process of the LR

The sources of raw Arabic lexical semantics knowledge base are usually organized so that the semantic fields/word senses are the primary keys that recall the terms belonging to them. Assuming such sources, the process of building our Arabic lexical semantics LR proceeds as follows:

1- After adding each distinct semantic field in the raw source to the basis set of semantic fields, the terms belonging to each field are linguistically reviewed to explicitly add/remove any missing/irrelevant terms under this semantic field.
2- Each of these Arabic terms is analyzed to obtain its morphological as well as PoS-tagging factorization, and is hence encoded as a morpho-PoS constrained lexical compound as previously explained in section 4.2.
3- This lexical semantic knowledge base obtained so far is then formally structured as an RDB with the semantic fields acting as the primary keys. This is called the *forward* Arabic lexical semantics RDB of which table 4 on the next page shows a sample fragment:

Table 4. A fragment of the forward lexical semantic RDB

Semantic Field	Lexical Compound	Morphological–PoS Tagging Constraints of Lexical Compound							Meta Semantic Fields	
		Q_1					Q_2	...		
		t	p	r	f	s				
⋮	⋮	⋮	⋮	⋮	⋮	⋮	⋮	⋮	⋮	⋮
	...	.	...	...	...	...	...	...	...	...
(النَّفَائِسُ), Authoring, 466	أَطْرُوحَة	1	-1000	2484	785	-48	×	×		
	بَحْثٌ	1	-1000	211	817	-1000	×	×		
	تَأْلِيفٌ	1	-1000	128	526	-1000	×	×		
	رِسَالَة	1	-1000	1565	684	-48	×	×		
	مُؤَلَّفٌ	1	-1000	128	519	-1000	×	×		
	سِجِلٌّ	2	-1000	1893	208	-1000	×	×		
	سِفْرٌ	1	-1000	1964	842	-1000	×	×		
	كِتَابٌ	1	-1000	3354	684	-1000	×	×		
	كِتَابَة	1	-1000	3354	684	-48	×	×		
	مَبْحَثٌ	1	-1000	211	792	-1000	×	×		
	زَبُورٌ	1	-1000	1728	671	-1000	×	×		
	مَخْطُوط	1	-1000	1155	779	-1000	×	×		
	مُصَنَّف	1	-1000	2364	519	-1000	×	×		
	...		...	...	...	...	...	...		
⋮	⋮	⋮	⋮	⋮	⋮	⋮	⋮	⋮	⋮	⋮

The detailed documentation of the building process of this forward Arabic lexical semantics RDB, written by Attia et al., is freely downloadable at http://www.rdieg.com/rdi/downloads/process_of_building_the_forward_Arabic_lexical_semantic_db.pdf

4- Using SQL operations, this forward RDB is automatically inverted so that the lexical compounds act as the primary keys. A sample fragment of this *inverse* lexical semantic RDB is shown by table 5 on the next page.

5- While building the inverse RDB, a special *back-off* row is inserted per each distinct root in the inverse RDB in order to further attenuate the runtime retrieval miss ratio of input words. The lexical compound of a back-off row mentions only the root morpheme explicitly, and all the other morphemes (prefix, pattern, and suffix) as *don't care*.

If an input word matches none of the explicitly registered derivatives of some root in the inverse RDB, the corresponding back-off row is resorted to. The recalled semantic fields of such a row are the union of the recalled semantic fields of all the registered derivatives of its root in the inverse RDB.

6- The basis set of semantic fields are interrelated via a matrix per each predefined standard semantic relation. So far, in addition to *relatedness*, the following 20 semantic relations [22] are defined in our Arabic lexical semantic LR:

1- *Antonymy.*
2- *Approximate Synonymy.*
3- *"Whole→Part"* relation.
4- *"Part→Whole"* relation.
5- *Hyponymy; "is-a-special-type-of"* relation.
6- Inverse of no. 5: *"is-a-general-type-of"* relation.
7- *Hyponymy; "is-a-member-of"* relation.
8- Inverse of no. 7: *"includes-several"* relation.
9- *Hyponymy; "is-originated-from"* relation.
10- Inverse of no. 9: *"is-the-origin-of"* relation.
11- *Hyponymy; "is-integrally-included-in"* relation.
12- Inverse of no. 11: *"includes-integrally"* relation.
13- *Causality: "is-a-cause-of"* relation.
14- Inverse of no. 13: *"due-to"* relation.
15- *Conditionality; "is-conditional-on"* relation.
16- Inverse of no. 15: *"is-a-condition-for"* relation.
17- *Temporal locality: "is-a-time-for"* relation.
18- Inverse of no. 17: *"occurs-during"* relation.
19- *Spatial locality: "is-a-place-of"* relation.
20- Inverse of no. 19: *"takes-place-in"* relation.

7- The totality of these matrices is then unified in one formal RDB compatible with the format of our LR.

It should be noted that the development team followed a *cross-checking* policy for ensuring the quality of this LR whose first edition had been completed in Oct. 2007 followed by a more refined one in mid. 2008.

Table 5. A sample fragment of the inverse Arabic lexical semantic RDB

String	Lexical compound											Possible semantic fields						
	Q_1					Q_2												
	t	r	f	p	s	t	r	f	p	s	…	SF_1	SF_2	SF_3	SF_4	SF_5	SF_6	…
ك ت ب	1	3354	-1000	-1000	-1000	…	-1000	-1000	-1000	-1000	…	الاستثمار 1800	العقود 450	الرياضة 179	المالية 466	الكتابة 1678	الإدارة 590	…
كتابـ	1	3354	176	-1000	-1000	…	-1000	-1000	-1000	-1000	…	العقود	-	-	-	-	-	…
اكتتب	1	3354	249	-1000	-1000	…	-1000	-1000	-1000	-1000	…	الاستثمار	-	-	-	-	-	…
اكتتب في	1	3354	249	-1000	-1000	3	42	132	-1000	-1000	…	الاستثمار	-	-	-	-	-	…
اكتتب	1	3354	280	-1000	-1000	…	-1000	-1000	-1000	-1000	…	الاستثمار	-	-	-	-	-	…
كاتب	1	3354	457	-1000	-1000	…	-1000	-1000	-1000	-1000	…	الرياضة	-	-	-	-	-	…
مكتبة	1	3354	487	-1000	-1000	…	-1000	-1000	-1000	-1000	…	العقود	الرياضة	المالية	الكتابة	الإدارة	-	…
كتب	1	3354	859	-1000	-1000	…	-1000	-1000	-1000	-1000	…	العقود	الرياضة	المالية	الكتابة	الإدارة	-	…
كتاب	1	3354	648	-1000	-1000	…	-1000	-1000	-1000	-1000	…	الرياضة	الرياضة	المالية	الكتابة	الإدارة	-	…
كتابة	1	3354	648	-1000	-48	…	-1000	-1000	-1000	-1000	…	الرياضة	المالية	الكتابة	-	-	-	…
…	…	…	…	…	…	…	…	…	…	…	…	…	…	…	…	…	…	…

6 Comparison with AWN

Disseminated LR's relevant to ours, esp. Word Nets and Thesauri are surveyed; [4], [5], [7], [13], Visual Thesaurus; http://www.VisualThesaurus.com.

Among those LR's; the beta release of the Arabic Word Net (AWN) www. GlobalWordNet.org/AWN/, www.LDC.UNPENN.edu, announced in Mar. 2007, has apparently been found closest and hence been thoroughly investigated and compared to our Arabic lexical semantics LR.

Interestingly, each of the two has shown superior/inferior complementary aspects to the other. While the AWN has a richer taxonomized set of semantic fields, and can also map to sister Word Nets in other languages (esp. English), our LR on the other hand has much richer semantic relations, much more explicit lexical entries, and much lower miss-ratio versus input words due to lexical compounds, morph-PoS constraining as well as the back-off.

A concise comparison between the two LR's is given in table 6 below.

Table 6. AWN vs. our Arabic Lexical Semantics LR

Feature	AWN	Our LR
Underlying theories	*Semantic Fields*, and *Componential Analysis of Semantic Fields*	*Semantic Fields*, and *Componential Analysis of Semantic Fields*
Data format of LR	Hierarchical	RDB
Current no. of lexical entries	≈ 12,038	≈ 40,000
Current no. of semantic fields	5,861	1,824
Semantic relations defined	*Hyponymy* only	20 semantic relations (see section 5 above)
Auxiliary technologies	None	*Morphological* and *PoS-Tagging* factorization
Back-off upon mismatches	None	To the semantic fields of the root
Mapping to other languages	Many; esp. *English*	None

7 Conclusion

This paper has presented a large-scale Arabic lexical semantics LR with a wide coverage of the huge generable Arabic vocabulary. Based on the theory of semantic fields, the raw source content of this LR is primarily drawn from the best experts' works crafted originally for the Arabic language.

Packaged as an RDB, the primary key of this LR in its inverse format is a morphologically and PoS-tags constrained lexical compound that provokes in real time, using an Arabic morphological analyzer and PoS tagger, the semantic fields it may belong to. The relatively compact predefined set of semantic fields addresses the most common, if not all, the context-free word senses.

The standard semantic relations are labeled in matrices across that set of semantic fields which, indirectly along with the morphological & PoS-tags constraining, enables semantically relating virtually any possible couple of Arabic lexical compounds.

The mostly language independent issue of disambiguating the retrieved word senses has deliberately been located outside the scope of the presented LR and left to the applications layer that can benefit from numerous works reported in the rich published literature on that concern.

Acknowledgments. Building this Arabic semantic LR has taken off in late 2005 out of the need for a reliable Arabic lexical semantic analyzer to power the diverse applications of the 3-year "Arabic Text Mining" project funded by the "Data Mining & Computer Modeling" (DMCM) "Centre of Excellence" (CoE) which is the first centre within the national R&D CoE's initiative launched by the Egyptian Ministry of Communications and Information Technology: www.MCIT.gov.eg/Centers_Excellence.aspx.

References

I- References in English

1. Attia, M.: Theory and Implementation of a Large-Scale Arabic Phonetic Transcriptor, and Applications. PhD thesis, Dept. of Electronics and Electrical Communications, Cairo University (2005), http://www.RDI-eg.com/RDI/Technologies/paper.htm
2. Attia, M.: A Large-Scale Computational Processor of the Arabic Morphology, and Applications, M.Sc. thesis, Dept. of Computer Engineering, Faculty of Engineering, Cairo University (2000), http://www.RDI-eg.com/RDI/Technologies/paper.htm
3. Attia, M., Rashwan, M.: A Large-Scale Arabic POS Tagger Based on a Compact Arabic POS Tags Set, and Application on the Statistical Inference of Syntactic Diacritics of Arabic Text Words, Proceedings of the Arabic Language Technologies and Resources Int'l Conference; NEMLAR, Cairo (2004),
   http://www.RDI-eg.com/RDI/Technologies/paper.htm
4. Black, W., Elkateb, S., Rodriguez, H., Alkhalifa, M., Vossen, P., Fellbaum, C.: Introducing the Arabic Word Net Project (2006), http://NLPweb.kaist.ac.kr/gwc/pdf2006/74.pdf
5. Diab, M.: The Feasibility of Bootstrapping an Arabic Word Net Leveraging Parallel Corpora and an English Word Net. In: Proceedings of the Arabic Language Technologies and Resources Int'l Conference; NEMLAR, Cairo (2004)
6. Dichy, J., Hassoun, M.: The DINAR.1 (DIctionnaire INformatisé de l'ARabe, version 1) Arabic Lexical Resource, an outline of contents and methodology. The ELRA news letter 10(2) (April-June 2005)
7. Ghonaimy, M.A.: A Tutorial Review on Word Nets. In: Proceedings of the 4th Conference on Language Engineering; CLE 2003, the Egyptian Society of Language Engineering (ESLE) (2003)
8. Hearst, M.: Untangling Text Data Mining. In: Proceedings of the 37th Annual Meeting of the Association for Computational Linguistics (ACL), (1999), http://www.sims.Berkeley.edu/~hearst/papers/acl99/acl99-tdm.html
9. Jurafsky, D., Martin, J.H.: Speech and Language Processing: An Introduction to Natural Language Processing, Computational Linguistics, and Speech Processing. Prentice-Hall, Englewood Cliffs (2000)
10. Lehrer, A.: Semantic Fields and Lexical Structures, Amsterdam-London (1974)

11. Riloff, E., Jones, R.: Learning Dictionaries for Information Extraction Using Multi-level Boot-strapping. In: Proceedings of AAAI (1999)
12. Schütze, H., Manning, C.D.: Foundations of Statistical Natural Language Processing. The MIT Press, Cambridge (2000)
13. Vossen, P.: Euro Word Net; General Document, Version 3, Final, University of Amsterdam (2002), http://www.hum.uva.nl/~ewn
14. Yaseen, et al.: Building Annotated Written and Spoken Arabic LR's in NEMLAR Project. In: LREC 2006 conference Genoa-Italy (May 2006), http://www.lrec-conf.org/lrec2006

II- References in Arabic

15- [Abdul Kareem H. Gabal, 1997] "في علم الدلالة"، د.عبد الكريم حسن جبل، دار المعرفة الجامعية، الإسكندرية، 1997.

16- [Hanna Ghaleb, 2003] "كنز اللغة العربية"، د. حنا غالب، لبنان ناشرون، 2003م.

17- [Ibraheem Al-Yazijy] "نجعة الرائد في المترادف والمتوارد"، إبراهيم اليازجي، مكتبة لبنان، بيروت.

18- [Ibraheem Anees, 1952] "دلالة الألفاظ"، د. إبراهيم أنيس، مكتبة الأنجلو المصرية، 1952.

19- [La Rousse, 1988] "المعجم العربي الأساسي "، المنظمة العربية للتربية والثقافة والعلوم، لاروس، 1988م.

20- [Mahmoud I. Siny et al., 1993] "المكنز العربي المعاصر"، د. محمود إسماعيل صيني – وآخرون، مكتبة لبنان، بيروت، الطبعة الأولى، 1993م.

21- [Mukhtaar Umar, 1998] "عِلْمُ الدَّلالةِ"، د. أحمد مختار عمر، عالَمُ الكُتُب، الطَّبْعَةُ الخَامِسةُ، 1998م.

22- [Mukhtaar Umar et al., 2002] "المَكْنَزُ الكَبِيرُ"، د. أحمد مختار عمر – وآخَرُونَ، دارُ نَشْرِ "سُطُور" المملكة العربية السعودية، الطَّبْعَة الأُولَى، 2002م.

23- [Rafael Nakhla] "المنجد في المترادفات والمتجانسات"، الأب رفائيل نخلة اليسوعي، دار المشرق.

24- [Sulayman Fayyaadh, 1990] "الحُـــقولُ الدَّلاليَّةُ الصَّرْفيَّةُ لِلأفْعالِ العَرَبيَّةِ"، سُلَيْمان فَيَّاض، دارُ المَرِّيخ بالرِّياضِ، 1990م.

25- [Wagdy R. Ghaly, 1996] "معجم المترادفات العربية الأصغر "، وجدي رزق غالي، مكتبة لبنان، بيروت، الطبعة الأولى، 1996م .

Automatically Extracting Personal Name Aliases from the Web

Danushka Bollegala*, Taiki Honma, Yutaka Matsuo, and Mitsuru Ishizuka

The University of Tokyo, Hongo 7-3-1, Tokyo, 113-8656, Japan
{danushka,honma}@mi.ci.i.u-tokyo.ac.jp,
matsuo@biz-model.t.u-tokyo.ac.jp,
ishizuka@i.u-tokyo.ac.jp

Abstract. Extracting aliases of an entity is important for various tasks such as identification of relations among entities, web search and entity disambiguation. To extract relations among entities properly, one must first identify those entities. We propose a novel approach to find aliases of a given name using automatically extracted lexical patterns. We exploit a set of known names and their aliases as training data and extract lexical patterns that convey information related to aliases of names from text snippets returned by a web search engine. The patterns are then used to find candidate aliases of a given name. We use anchor texts to design a word co-occurrence model and use it to define various ranking scores to measure the association between a name and a candidate alias. The ranking scores are integrated with page-count-based association measures using support vector machines to leverage a robust alias detection method. The proposed method outperforms numerous baselines and previous work on alias extraction on a dataset of personal names, achieving a statistically significant mean reciprocal rank of 0.6718. Experiments carried out using a dataset of location names and Japanese personal names suggest the possibility of extending the proposed method to extract aliases for different types of named entities and for other languages. Moreover, the aliases extracted using the proposed method improve recall by 20% in a relation-detection task.

1 Introduction

Precisely identifying entities in web documents is necessary for various tasks such as relation extraction [16], search and integration of data [9] and entity disambiguation [14]. Nevertheless, identification of entities on the web is difficult for two fundamental reasons: first, different entities can share the same name (lexical ambiguity); secondly, a single entity can be designated by multiple names (referential ambiguity). As an example of lexical ambiguity the name *Jim Clark* is illustrative. Aside from the two most popular namesakes, the formula-one racing champion and the founder of Netscape, at least 10 different people are listed among the top 100 results returned by Google for the name. On the other

---

* Research Fellow of the Japan Society for the Promotion of Science (JSPS).

A. Ranta, B. Nordström (Eds.): GoTAL 2008, LNAI 5221, pp. 77–88, 2008.

hand, referential ambiguity occurs because people use different names to refer to the same entity on the web. For example, the American movie star *Will Smith* is often called the *the Fresh Prince* in web contents. Although lexical ambiguity, particularly ambiguity related to personal names, has been explored extensively in the previous studies of name disambiguation [14,4], the problem of referential ambiguity of entities on the web has received much less attention. In this paper, we specifically examine on the problem of automatically extracting the various references on the web to a particular entity.

For an entity e, we define the set A of its aliases to be the set of all words or multi-word expressions that are used to refer to e on the web. For example, *Godzilla* is a one-word alias for *Hideki Matsui*, whereas the alias *the Fresh Prince* contains three words and refers to *Will Smith*. Various types of terms are used as aliases on the web. For instance, in the case of an actor, the name of a role or the title of a drama (or a movie) can later become an alias for the person (e.g., *Fresh Prince, Knight Rider*). Titles or professions such as *president, doctor, professor*, etc. are also frequently used as aliases. Variants or abbreviations of names such as *Bill* for *William* and acronyms such as *J.F.K.* for *John Fitzgerald Kennedy* are also types of name aliases that are observed frequently on the web.

Identifying aliases of a name is important for extracting relations among entities. For example, Matsuo et al. [16] propose a social network extraction algorithm, in which they compute the strength of the relation between two individuals A and B by the web hits for the conjunctive query, *"A" AND "B"*. However, both persons A and B might also appear in their alias names in web contents. Consequently, by expanding the conjunctive query using aliases for the names, a social network extraction algorithm can accurately compute the strength of a relationship between two persons.

Searching for information about people on the web is an extremely common activity of Internet users. Around 30% of search engine queries include personal names [1]. However, retrieving information about a person merely using his or her real names is insufficient when that person has nicknames. Particularly with keyword-based search engines, we will only retrieve pages which use the real name to refer to the person about whom we are interested in finding information. In such cases, automatically extracted aliases of the name are useful to expand a query in a web search, thereby improving recall.

Our contributions in this paper are two fold:

- We propose a lexical pattern-based approach to extract aliases of a given name using snippets returned by a web search engine. We propose an algorithm to automatically generate lexical patterns using a set of real-world name-alias data.
- To select the best aliases among the extracted candidates, we propose numerous ranking scores based upon two approaches: a word co-occurrence model using anchor texts, and page-counts returned by a search engine. Moreover, using real world name alias data, we train a ranking support vector machine to learn the optimal combination of individual ranking scores to leverage a robust alias extraction method.

2   Related Work

The problem of extracting aliases of a given name can be considered as a special case of the more general problem of extracting the words Y that have a given relation R with a word X. For example, extracting hyponyms [10], synonyms [13], meronyms [5] are specific instances of this general problem of relation extraction. Manually created or automatically extracted lexico-syntactic patterns have been successfully used to identify various relations between words [17,18]. For example, patterns such as X *is a* Y and X *such as* Y are typically used to introduce hypernyms, whereas, X *of a* Y and X's Y are frequently used with meronyms. However, alias extraction poses several unique challenges that separates it from the more general relation extraction problem. Firstly, personal names and their aliases are not typically listed in manually created dictionaries. Therefore, an alias extraction algorithm must first extract a possible set of candidate aliases for a given name and then verify each extracted candidate. Secondly, names and aliases can be multi-word expressions. For example, in the case of *Will Smith*, who has a two-word alias *fresh prince*, it is inaccurate to extract *fresh* as an alias. Thirdly, unlike hypernyms or meronyms, it is not obvious as to which lexical patterns convey useful clues related to aliases of a given name. This makes it difficult to manually create a sufficiently large list of lexical patterns to cover various types of name aliases. In addition to above mentioned challenges, the lack of evaluation benchmark dataset for aliases makes it difficult to compare and evaluate different approaches. Although it is relatively easy to manually verify whether an extracted candidate is a correct alias of a given name, it is not always possible to obtain a list of all the aliases of a name, which makes it difficult to compute the recall or coverage of an alias extraction algorithm.

Alias identification is closely related to the problem of cross-document coreference resolution, in which the objective is to determine whether two mentions of a name in different documents refer to the same entity. Bagga and Baldwin [3] proposed a cross-document coreference resolution algorithm by first performing within-document coreference resolution for each individual document to extract coreference chains, and then clustering the coreference chains under a vector space model to identify all mentions of a name in the document set. However, the vastly numerous documents on the web render it impractical to perform within-document coreference resolution to each document separately and then cluster the documents to find aliases.

In personal name disambiguation the goal is to disambiguate various people that share the same name (*namesakes*) [14,4]. Given an ambiguous name, most name disambiguation algorithms have modeled the problem as one of document clustering, in which all documents that discuss a particular individual of the given ambiguous name are grouped into a single cluster. However, the name disambiguation problem differs fundamentally from that of alias extraction because, in name disambiguation the objective is to identify the different entities that are referred by the same ambiguous name; in alias extraction, we are interested in extracting all references to a single entity from the web.

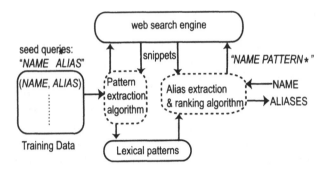

Fig. 1. Outline of the proposed method

Approximate string matching algorithms have been used for extracting variants or abbreviations of personal names (e.g. matching *Will Smith* with the first name initialized variant *W. Smith*) [8]. Rules in the form of regular expressions and edit-distance-based methods have been used to compare names. However, an inherent limitation of such string matching approaches is that they cannot identify aliases which share no words or letters with the real name. For example, approximate string matching methods would not identify *Fresh Prince* as an alias for *Will Smith*.

Hokama and Kitagawa [11] propose an alias extraction method that is specific to the Japanese language. For a given name p, they search for the query "** koto p*" and extract the context that matches the asterisk. The Japanese word *koto*, roughly corresponds to *also known as* in English. However, *koto* is a highly am-biguous word in Japanese that can also mean *incident, thing, matter, experience* and *task*. As reported in their paper, many noisy and incorrect aliases are ex-tracted using this pattern, which requires various post-processing heuristics that are specific to Japanese language to filter-out the incorrect aliases. Moreover, manually crafted patterns do not cover various ways that convey information about name aliases. In contrast, we propose a method to leverage such lexical patterns automatically using a training dataset of names and aliases.

3   Method

The proposed method is outlined in Fig.1 and comprises two main components: pattern extraction, and alias extraction and ranking. Using a seed list of name-alias pairs, we first extract lexical patterns that are frequently used to convey information related to aliases on the web. The extracted patterns are then used to find candidate aliases for a given name. We define various ranking scores using the hyperlink structure on the web and page counts retrieved from a search engine to identify the correct aliases among the extracted candidates.

3.1   Extracting Lexical Patterns from Snippets

Many modern search engines provide a brief text snippet for each search result by selecting the text that appears in the web page in the proximity of the query.

Such snippets provide valuable information related to the local context of the query. For names and aliases, snippets convey useful semantic clues that can be used to extract lexical patterns that are frequently used to express aliases of a name. For example, consider the snippet returned by Google[1] for the query *"Will Smith * The Fresh Prince"*.

> ...Rock the House, the duo's debut album of 1987, demonstrated that **Will Smith**, aka **the Fresh Prince**, was an entertaining and amusing storyteller...

Fig. 2. A snippet returned for the query *"Will Smith * The Fresh Prince"* by Google

Here, we use the wildcard operator * to perform a *NEAR* query and it matches with one or more words in a snippet. In Fig.2 the snippet contains *aka* (i.e. *also known as*), which indicates the fact that *fresh prince* is an alias for *Will Smith*. In addition to *a.k.a.*, numerous clues exist such as *nicknamed, alias, real name is, nee*, which are used on the web to represent aliases of a name. Consequently, we propose the shallow pattern extraction method illustrated in Fig.3 to capture the various ways in which information about aliases of names is expressed on the web. Lexico-syntactic patterns have been used in numerous related tasks such as extracting hypernyms [10] and meronyms.

Given a set S of (NAME, ALIAS) pairs, the function *ExtractPatterns* returns a list of lexical patterns that frequently connect names and their aliases in web-snippets. For each (NAME, ALIAS) pair in S, the *GetSnippets* function downloads snippets from a web search engine for the query *"NAME * ALIAS"*. Then, from each snippet, the *CreatePattern* function extracts the sequence of words that appear between the name and the alias. Results of our preliminary experiments demonstrated that consideration of words that fall outside the name and the alias in snippets did not improve performance. Finally, the real name and the alias in the snippet are respectively replaced by two variables [**NAME**] and [**ALIAS**] to create patterns. For example, from the snippet shown in Fig.2, we extract the pattern [**NAME**] *aka* [**ALIAS**]. We repeat the process described above for the reversed query, *"ALIAS * NAME"* to extract patterns in which the alias precedes the name.

Once a set of lexical patterns is extracted, we use the patterns to extract candidate aliases for a given name as portrayed in Fig.4. Given a name, $NAME$ and a set, P of lexical patterns, the function *ExtractCandidates* returns a list of candidate aliases for the name. We associate the given name with each pattern, p in the set of patterns, P and produce queries of the form: *"NAME p *"*. Then the *GetSnippets* function downloads a set of snippets for the query. Finally, the *GetNgrams* function extracts continuous sequences of words (*n*-grams) from the beginning of the part that matches the wildcard operator *. Experimentally, we selected up to 5-grams as candidate aliases. Moreover, we removed candidates

---
[1] www.google.com

Algorithm 1: EXTRACTPATTERNS(S)

comment: S is a set of (NAME, ALIAS) pairs

$P \leftarrow null$
for each $(NAME, ALIAS) \in S$
$\quad$ **do** $\begin{cases} D \leftarrow \text{GetSnippets}("NAME * ALIAS") \\ \textbf{for each} \text{ snippet } d \in D \\ \quad \textbf{do } P \leftarrow P + \text{CreatePattern}(d) \end{cases}$
return (P)

Fig. 3. Given a set of (NAME, ALIAS) instances, extract lexical patterns

---

Algorithm 2: EXTRACTCANDIDATES($NAME, P$)

comment: P is the set of patterns

$C \leftarrow null$
for each pattern $p \in P$
$\quad$ **do** $\begin{cases} D \leftarrow \text{GetSnippets}("NAME \ p \ *") \\ \textbf{for each} \text{ snippet } d \in D \\ \quad \textbf{do } C \leftarrow C + \text{GetNgrams}(d, NAME, p) \end{cases}$
return (C)

Fig. 4. Given a name and a set of lexical patterns, extract candidate aliases

that contain only stop words such as *a*, *an*, and *the*. For example, assuming that we retrieved the snippet in Fig.3 for the query *"Will Smith aka *"*, the procedure described above extracts *the fresh* and *the fresh prince* as candidate aliases.

3.2 Ranking of Candidates

Considering the noise in web-snippets, candidates extracted by the shallow lexical patterns might include some invalid aliases. From among these candidates, we must identify those which are most likely to be correct aliases of a given name. We model this problem of alias recognition as one of ranking candidates with respect to a given name such that the candidates which are most likely to be correct aliases are assigned a higher rank. First, we define various ranking scores to measure the association between a name and a candidate alias using two approaches: co-occurrences in inbound anchor texts of a url and page-counts retrieved from a search engine. Next, we integrate those ranking scores using ranking support vector machines (SVMs) [12] to leverage a robust ranking function.

3.3 Co-occurrences in Anchor Texts

Anchor texts have been studied extensively in information retrieval and have been used in various tasks such as synonym extraction, query translation in cross-language information retrieval, and ranking and classification of web pages [7], However, anchor texts have not been exploited fully in Semantic Web applications. We revisit anchor texts to measure the association between a name and its aliases on the web. Anchor texts pointing to a url provide useful semantic clues related to the resource represented by the url. For example, if the majority of inbound anchor texts of a url contain a personal name, it is likely that the remainder of the inbound anchor texts contain information about aliases of the name.

We define a name p and a candidate alias x as *co-occurring*, if p and x appear in two different inbound anchor texts of a url u. Moreover, we define *co-occurrence frequency* (**CF**) as the number of different urls in which they co-occur. We can use this definition to create a contingency table like that shown in Table 1. Therein, C is the set of candidates extracted by the algorithm described in Fig.4, V is the set of all words that appear in anchor texts, $C - \{x\}$ and $V - \{p\}$ respectively denote all candidates except x and all words except the given name p, k is the co-occurrence frequency between x and p. Moreover, K is the sum of co-occurrence frequencies between x and all words in V, whereas n is the same between p and all candidates in C. N is the total co-occurrences between all word pairs taken from C and V. To measure the strength of association between a name and a candidate alias, using Table 1 we define nine popular co-occurrence statistics: chi-squared measure (**CS**), Log-likelihood ratio (**LLR**), hyper-geometric distributions (**HG**) and the six measures shown in Table 2. Because of the limited availability of space, we omit the definitions of these measures (see Manning and Schutze [15] for a detailed discussion).

Table 1. Contingency table for a candidate alias x

	x	$C - \{x\}$	C
p	k	$n - k$	n
$V - \{p\}$	$K - k$	$N - n - K + k$	$N - n$
V	K	$N - K$	N

Table 2. Anchor text-based co-occurrence measures

Measure	Definition	Measure	Definition
CF	k	**tfidf**	$k \log \frac{N}{K+1}$
PMI	$\log_2 \frac{kN}{Kn}$	**cosine**	$\frac{k}{\sqrt{n}+\sqrt{K}}$
Dice	$\frac{2k}{n+K}$	**Overlap**	$\frac{k}{\min(n,K)}$

A frequently observed phenomenon related to the web is that many pages with diverse topics link to so-called *hubs* such as Google, Yahoo, or MSN. Two anchor texts might link to a hub for entirely different reasons. Therefore, co-occurrences coming from hubs are prone to noise. To overcome the adverse effects of a hub h when computing co-occurrence measures, we multiply the number of co-occurrences of words linked to h by a factor $\alpha(h, p)$, where

$$\alpha(h, p) = \frac{t}{d}. \tag{1}$$

Here, t is the number of inbound anchor texts of h that contain the real name p, and d is the total number of inbound anchor texts of h. If many anchor texts that link to h contain p (i.e. larger t value), then the reliability of h as a source of information about p increases. On the other hand, if h has many inbound links (i.e. larger d value), then it is likely to be a noisy hub and gets discounted when multiplied by $\alpha(<< 1)$. Intuitively, Eq.1 boosts hubs that are likely to contain information related to p, while penalizing those that contain various other topics.

3.4   Page-Count-Based Association Measures

In previous section we defined various ranking scores using anchor texts. However, not all names and aliases are equally well represented in anchor texts. Consequently, in this section, we define word association measures that consider co-occurrences not only in anchor texts but in the web overall. Page counts retrieved from a web search engine for the conjunctive query, $p \cap x$, for a name p and a candidate alias x can be regarded as an approximation of their co-occurrences in the web. We define the four measures shown in Table 3 using page-counts retrieved from a search engine. Therein, the function $H(q)$ denotes the page-counts for a query q. **WebDice** and **WebPMI** [6] respectively are based on the Dice coefficient and pointwise mutual information. In WebPMI, L is the number of pages indexed by the web search engine, which we approximated as $L = 10^{10}$ according to the number of pages indexed by Google. **Prob**$(x|p)$ and **Prob**$(p|x)$ respectively denote the conditional probabilities of a candidate (x) given a name (p) and a name given a candidate.

Table 3. Page-count-based association measures

Measure	Definition	Measure	Definition
WebPMI	$\log_2 \frac{L \times H(p \cap x)}{H(p) \times H(x)}$	Prob(p|x)	$\frac{H(p \cap x)}{H(x)}$
WebDice	$\frac{2 \times H(p \cap x)}{H(p) + H(x)}$	Prob(x|p)	$\frac{H(p \cap x)}{H(p)}$

3.5   Training

Using a dataset of name-alias pairs, we train a ranking support vector machine [12] to rank candidate aliases according to their strength of association with a name. For a name-alias pair we define three feature types: anchor text-based co-occurrence measures, web page-count-based association measures, and frequencies of observed lexical patterns. The nine co-occurrence measures: **CF, tfidf, CS, LLR, PMI, HG, cosine, overlap, Dice** (Table 2) are computed with and without weighting for hubs to produce $18(2 \times 9)$ features. Moreover, the four page-count-based association measures defined in Table 3 and the frequency of lexical patterns extracted by algorithm 1 are used as features in training the ranking SVM. If numerous patterns connects a name and a candidate alias in snippets, then the confidence of the candidate alias as a correct alias of the name increases. During training, ranking SVMs attempt to minimize the number of discordant pairs in the training data, thereby improving the average precision. The trained SVM model is used to rank the set of candidates that were extracted for a name. Finally, the highest-ranking candidate is selected as the alias of the name.

Table 4. Lexical patterns with the highest F-scores

patterns for personal names	F-score
* aka [NAME]	0.335
[NAME] aka *	0.322
[NAME] better known as *	0.310
[NAME] alias *	0.286
[NAME] also known as *	0.281
* nee [NAME]	0.225
patterns for location names	**F-score**
[NAME] nickname the *	0.739
[NAME] is nicknamed the *	0.723
[NAME] employment nickname *	0.627
[NAME] state flag or *	0.589
[NAME] nicknamed the *	0.5567
[NAME] is called the *	0.3199

Table 5. Comparison with baselines and previous work

Method	MRR	Method	MRR
SVM (Linear)	0.6718	Prob($p\|x$)	0.1414
SVM (Quad)	0.6495	CS(h)	0.1186
SVM (RBF)	0.6089	CF	0.0839
Hokama & Kitagawa	0.6314	cosine	0.0761
tfidf(h)	0.3957	tfidf	0.0757
WebDice	0.3896	Dice	0.0751
LLR(h)	0.3879	overlap(h)	0.0750
cosine(h)	0.3701	PMI(h)	0.0624
CF(h)	0.3677	LLR	0.0604
HG(h)	0.3297	HG	0.0399
Dice(h)	0.2905	CS	0.0079
Prob($x\|p$)	0.2142	PMI	0.0072
WebPMI	0.1416	overlap	0.0056

4   Experiments

To train and evaluate the proposed method, we create three name-alias datasets[2]: the English personal names dataset (50 names), the English place names dataset (50 names), and the Japanese personal names (100 names) dataset. Both our English and Japanese personal name datasets include people from various fields of cinema, sports, politics, science, and mass media. The place name dataset contains aliases for the 50 U.S. states. Aliases were manually collected after referring various information sources such as Wikipedia and official home pages. The anchor texts collection we used to compute the measures in Table 2 contains $24,456,871$ anchor texts pointing to $8,023,364$ unique urls.

Algorithm 1 extracts over 8000 patterns for the 50 English personal names in our dataset. We rank the patterns according to their F scores to identify the patterns that accurately convey information about aliases. F score of a pattern s is computed as the harmonic mean between the precision and recall of the pattern:

$$\text{Precision}(s) = \frac{\text{No. of correct aliases retrieved by } s}{\text{No. of total aliases retrieved by } s},$$

$$\text{Recall}(s) = \frac{\text{No. of correct aliases retrieved by } s}{\text{No. of total aliases in the dataset}}.$$

Table 4 shows the patterns with the highest F scores extracted using English personal names. As shown in the table, unambiguous and highly descriptive patterns are extracted by the proposed method. Experimentally, we selected the top ranked 200 patterns as features for training. Interestingly, among the extracted pattens we found patterns written in languages other than English, such as *de son vrai nom* (French for *his real name*) and *vero nome* (Italian for *real name*).

---

[2] www.miv.t.u-tokyo.ac.jp/danushka/aliasdata.zip

In Table 5, we compare the proposed SVM-based method against various individual ranking scores (baselines) and previous studies of alias extraction Hokama and Kitagawa [11]) on Japanese personal names dataset. We used linear, polynomial (quadratic), and radial basis functions (RBF) kernels for ranking SVM. Mean reciprocal rank (MRR) [2] is used to evaluate the various approaches. If a method ranks the correct aliases of a name on top, then it receives a higher MRR value. As shown in Table 5, the best results are obtained by the proposed method with linear kernels (SVM(Linear)). Both ANOVA and Tukey HSD tests confirm that the improvement of SVM(Linear) is statistically significant ($p<0.05$). A drop of MRR occurs with more complex kernels, which is attributable to overfitting. Hokama and Kitagawa's method which uses manually created patterns, can only extract Japanese name aliases. Their method reports an MRR value of 0.6314 on our Japanese personal names dataset. In Table 5 we denote the hubweighted versions of anchor text-based co-occurrence measures by (h). Among the numerous individual ranking scores, the best results are reported by the hubweighted tfidf score (tfidf(h)). It is noteworthy that, for anchor text-based ranking scores, the hub-weighted version always outperforms the non-hub-weighted counterpart, which justifies the proposed hub-weighting method. Among the four page-count-based ranking scores, WebDice reports the highest MRR. It is comparable to the best anchor text-based ranking score, tfidf(h). The fact that $Prob(x|p)$ gives slightly better performance over $Prob(p|x)$ implies that we have a better chance in identifying an entity given its real name than an alias.

Table 6. Overall performance

Table 7. Aliases extracted by the proposed method

Dataset	MRR	AP
English Personal Names	0.6150	0.6865
English Place Names	0.8159	0.7819
Japanese Personal Names	0.6718	0.6646

Real Name	Extracted Aliases
David Hasselhoff	**hoff, michael knight, michael**
Courteney Cox	**dirt lucy, lucy, monica**
Al Pacino	**michael corleone**
Teri Hatcher	**susan mayer, susan,** mayer
Texas	**lone star state,** lone star, lone
Vermont	**green mountain state,** green,
Wyoming	**equality state, cowboy state**
Hideki Matsui	**Godzilla, nishikori, matsui**

In Table 6 we evaluate the overall performance of the proposed method on each dataset using MRR and average precision (AP) [2]. Different from the mean reciprocal rank, which focuses only on rank, average precision incorporates consideration of both precision at each rank and the total number of correct aliases in the dataset. Both MRR and average precision have been used in rank evaluation tasks such as evaluating the results returned by a search engine. With each dataset we performed a 5-fold cross validation. As shown in Table 6, the proposed method reports high scores for both MRR and average precision on all three datasets. Best results are achieved for the place name alias extraction task. Table 7 presents the aliases extracted for some entities included in our datasets. Overall, the proposed method extracts most aliases in the manually created gold standard (shown in bold).

Table 8. Effect of aliases on relation detection

Real name only			Real name and top alias		
Precision	Recall	F	Precision	Recall	F
.4812	.7185	.4792	.4833	.9083	.5918

We evaluate the effect of the extracted aliases on a real-world relation detection task. First, we manually classify 50 people in the English personal names dataset, depending on their field of expertise, into four categories: *music, politics, movies,* and *sports*. Then, we measure the association between two people using the pointwise mutual information (WebPMI) as defined in Table 3. We then use group average agglomerative clustering (GAAC) to group the people into four clusters. Initially, each person is assigned to a separate cluster. In subsequent iterations, GAAC merges the two clusters with the highest correlation. We terminate the GAAC process when exactly four clusters are formed. Ideally, people who work in the same field should be clustered into the same group. We use the *B-CUBED* method [3] and compute the precision, recall and *F*-score for each name in the dataset and average the results over the number of people in the dataset. Table 8 shows performance of clustering when only the real name is used and the real name disjunctively coupled with the top alias extracted by the proposed method for the name. The use of aliases significantly improves recall (ca. 20%) and consequently the *F* score. This significant improvement in recall can be attributed to the discovery of relations between entities that use not only their real names but also numerous aliases. In such cases, using only the real name would extract only a fraction of the relations between the entities under consideration. By considering not only real names but also aliases, it is possible to discover relations that are unidentifiable solely using real names.

5   Conclusion

We proposed a lexical-pattern-based approach to extract aliases of a given name. The extracted candidates were ranked using various ranking scores computed using the hyperlink structure on the web and page-counts retrieved from a search engine. The proposed method reported high MRR scores on three different datasets and outperformed numerous baselines and a previously proposed method. Moreover, the extracted aliases significantly improved recall in a relation detection task.

References

1. Artiles, J., Gonzalo, J., Verdejo, F.: A testbed for people searching strategies in the www. In: Proc. of SIGIR 2005, pp. 569–570 (2005)
2. Baeza-Yates, R.A., Ribeiro-Neto, B.A.: Modern Information Retrieval. ACM Press, New York (1999)

3. Bagga, A., Baldwin, B.: Entity-based cross-document coreferencing using the vector space model. In: Proc. of COLING 1998, pp. 79–85 (1998)
4. Bekkerman, R., McCallum, A.: Disambiguating web appearances of people in a social network. In: Proc. of WWW 2005, pp. 463–470 (2005)
5. Berland, M., Charniak, E.: Finding parts in very large corpora. In: Proc. of ACL 1999, pp. 57–64 (1999)
6. Bollegala, D., Matsuo, Y., Ishizuka, M.: Measuring semantic similarity between words using web search engines. In: Proc. of WWW 2007, pp. 757–766 (2007)
7. Chakrabarti, S.: Mining the Web: Discovering Knowledge from Hypertext Data. Morgan Kaufmann, San Francisco (2003)
8. Galvez, C., Moya-Anegon, F.: Approximate personal name-matching through finite-state graphs. Journal of the American Society for Information Science and Technology 58, 1–17 (2007)
9. Guha, R.V., McCool, R., Miller, E.: Semantic search. In: Proc. of WWW 2003, pp. 700–709 (2003)
10. Hearst, M.A.: Automatic acquisition of hyponyms from large text corpora. In: Proc. of COLING 1992, pp. 539–545 (1992)
11. Hokama, T., Kitagawa, H.: Extracting mnemonic names of people from the web. In: Sugimoto, S., Hunter, J., Rauber, A., Morishima, A. (eds.) ICADL 2006. LNCS, vol. 4312, pp. 121–130. Springer, Heidelberg (2006)
12. Joachims, T.: Optimizing search engines using clickthrough data. In: Proc. of KDD 2002 (2002)
13. Lin, D.: Automatic retrieval and clustering of similar words. In: Proc. of COLING 1998, pp. 768–774. Association for Computational Linguistics, Morristown (1998)
14. Mann, G.S., Yarowsky, D.: Unsupervised personal name disambiguation. In: Proc. of CoNLL 2003, pp. 33–40 (2003)
15. Manning, C., Schutze, H.: Foundations of Statistical Natural Language Processing. MIT Press, Cambridge (1999)
16. Matsuo, Y., Mori, J., Hamasaki, M., Ishida, K., Nishimura, T., Takeda, H., Hasida, K., Ishizuka, M.: Polyphonet: An advanced social network extraction system. In: Proc. of WWW 2006 (2006)
17. Ravichandran, D., Hovy, E.: Learning surface text patterns for a question answering system. In: Proc. of ACL 2002, pp. 41–47 (2001)
18. Snow, R., Jurafsky, D., Ng, Y.: Learning syntactic patterns for automatic hypernym discovery. In: Proc. of NIPS 2005 (2005)

An Efficient Statistical Approach for Automatic Organic Chemistry Summarization

Florian Boudin[1], Juan-Manuel Torres-Moreno[1,2],
and Patricia Velázquez-Morales[1]

[1] Laboratoire Informatique d'Avignon
339 chemin des Meinajariès, BP1228
84911 Avignon Cedex 9, France
{florian.boudin,juan-manuel.torres}@univ-avignon.fr
[2] École Polytechnique de Montréal
Département de génie informatique
CP 6079 Succ. Centre Ville H3C 3A7
Montréal (Québec), Canada

Abstract. In this paper, we propose an efficient strategy for summarizing scientific documents in Organic Chemistry that concentrates on numerical treatments. We present its implementation named YACHS (Yet Another Chemistry Summarizer) that combines a specific document preprocessing with a sentence scoring method relying on the statistical properties of documents. We show that YACHS achieves the best results among several other summarizers on a corpus made of Organic Chemistry articles.

1 Introduction

Over 1.7 million new Chemistry articles were published in 2007[1], thereby most of scientists today are on *information overload*. Information extraction technology arose in response to the need for efficient processing of documents in specialized domains. Scientists, especially chemists, want to be able to promptly access information concealed in a document in addition to the author's abstract that is often too concise or not satisfying. Automatically producing summaries from Organic Chemistry documents is a challenging but critical task for chemical information retrieval. *Text Summarization* is the process of distilling the most important information from a source (or sources) to produce an abridged version for a particular user and task [1]. There are many uses of text summarization in everyday activities, we are familiar with summaries such as headlines, reviews or digests. Introduced by [2] in the late 1950's, text summarization was characterized by the use of a surface level approach (i.e. exploiting term frequencies). The first entity-level approaches based on syntactic analysis appeared in the early 1960's [3] while the use of location features and cue phrases was not developed until later [4]. The investigations reported by [5] at the Chemical Abstracts Service

---

[1] See Chemical Abstracts Publication Record, *http://www.cas.org/*

A. Ranta, B. Nordström (Eds.): GoTAL 2008, LNAI 5221, pp. 89–99, 2008.
© Springer-Verlag Berlin Heidelberg 2008

(CAS) provide further insight into the effectiveness of automatic summarization in particular domain areas. Corpus-based approaches were introduced by [6] with a trainable summarization system using a collection of text/summaries pairs as training set. A Bayes classifier algorithm takes each sentence and, based on features such as cue phrases, sentence length or location, computes a probability that it should be included in the summary. Thereafter, [7] have extended this model using decision tree rules instead of bayesian classifiers. Rhetorical status was proposed by [8] to summarize scientific articles (Computational Linguistic conference articles) that can highlight the new contribution of the source article. The main drawback of this approach is that it depends on manually constructed resources (metadiscourse features are manually annotated). [9] proposes to combine semantic-based and frequency-distribution approaches for extractive text summarization in biomedical documents. However, this approach requires a difficult concept identification process. Benefits of automatic abstracting are now clearly identified: it is inexpensive compared to human effort and, unlike humans, it is consistent and avoid subjectivity and variability observed in human abstracts. Typically, summarization systems are two-phased, consisting of a content selection step followed by a generation step. Firstly, text fragments (most often sentences) are assigned a score that reflects how important they are. The highest-ranking material can then be arranged and displayed as an "extract". This paper presents YACHS (Yet Another Chemistry Summarizer), a summarization system that generates extracts from scientific articles in a specialized domain, Organic Chemistry. The motivation behind this work is to allow non-experts users to access information contained in high-end scientific documents by dynamically generating extracts. Specifically, through statistical entity level approaches, we seek to produce highly informative extracts that can stand in place of the original author's abstracts as surrogates.

2   Method

2.1   Pre-processing

The first question we are concerned with is whether classical Natural Language Processing (NLP) tools are reasonably consistent across the Organic Chemistry domain (no significant performance loss). The answer is clearly no. Tools such as parsers, taggers or chunkers achieve very poor on these documents without requiring a strenuous, costly and often manual adaptation phase. Issues encountered by classical tools are due to domain specificity: very wide vocabulary, long sentences containing *noise* (citations, chemical formulas, tables, pictures references, etc.), high quantity of *hapax legomena*[2], etc.

The basic idea is to represent the document within the vector space model introduced by [10] and apply specific numeric treatments to select the most salient sentences. An n-dimensional term-space Γ, where n is the number of different terms found in the document, is constructed. One convenient way to represent

---

[2] Terms which only appears once in a document.

the document in Γ is a matrix $M = [a_{x,y}]_{x=1...m; \ y=1...n}$ where m is the number of sentences and n the number of different terms. In this interpretation, every row of M is a vector $\vec{s}_x$ representing the sentence x in which each component is the term frequency within the sentence.

In order to reduce the size of the matrix M and accordingly cut down the computational complexity, sentences are filtered and normalized (see Table 1). In written language, some words carry more *meaning* than others. Thereby, a stop-words elimination phase is performed **(1)** to delete non representative words (words such as '*the*', '*of*', '*in*'... are removed). One standard pre-processing would normalize character case, remove punctuation and special characters **(2)**. However, important information about chemical compounds may be lost during the filtering process (e.g. '1,2-*dienes*' is transformed into '*dienes*'). Besides if word normalization (in our case stemming[3]) is applied afterwards **(3)**, erroneous information is brought in the sentence (e.g. '1,2-*dienes*' is transformed into '*dien*'). We propose to perform a chemical compounds detection to protect these terms during the normalization process **(2′)**. Finally stemming is performed only on non-chemical terms **(3′)**. Chemical compounds are detected within sentences

Table 1. Example of sentence pre-processing

Original	Cycloalkynes are known to isomerize to the 1,2-dienes under basic conditions.
(1)	Cycloalkynes known isomerize 1,2-dienes under basic conditions.
(2)	cycloalkynes known isomerize dienes under basic conditions
(3)	cycloalkyn know isomer dien under basic condit
(2′)	**cycloalkynes** know isomerize **1,2-dienes** under basic conditions
(3′)	**cycloalkynes** *know isomer* **1,2-dienes** *under basic condit*

using a combination of two classifiers. The first one is a Bayes classifier trained on 3-grams of letters whereas the second one uses pattern matching with a small number of manually written rules (7 rules). Each sentence is tokenized in words and each word is classified by the two classifiers, precision is prioritized by using the AND combination (a word has to be classified as chemical compound by the two classifiers). This hybrid approach (statistical and symbolic) for chemical term recognition achieves very good results on a test corpus composed by Organic Chemistry articles [12].

2.2   Sentence Ranking

Once sentences are pre-processed, a combination of features (also called metrics) is used to assign a score to each sentence. That score reflects how important the sentences are in relation to the whole document. The main advantage of this approach is that *zero knowledge* is required and that makes the system fully

---

[3] The Porter Stemmer algorithm [11] is used to normalize words by removing commoner morphological and inflexional endings from words.

adjustable to any language and/or domain. This section formally describes the metrics calculated by YACHS.

Authors normally conceive titles as circumscribing the topic of the document. Sentences sharing words, containing words related to or similar with the title are likely to be relevant. Following this assumption, two metrics computing similarity measures between a sentence and the title have been implemented. The first measure is the well known cosine angle [10] between a sentence and the title vectorial representations in Γ. The main weakness of *cosine* and more generally of all similarity measures using words for tokens is that they are relying too much on term normalization. Their performance dramatically decrease with wrongly or non normalized words. We propose a second similarity measure based on the Jaro-Winkler distance [13] that can bridge morphologically similar words in order to smooth normalization and misspelling errors. The original Jaro-Winkler measure, denoted Jw, uses the number of matching characters and transpositions to compute a similarity score between two terms, giving more favourable ratings to terms that match from the beginning (see examples in Table 2). We have extended this measure to calculate the similarity between a sentence s_x and the title t (see Table 3):

$$\mathrm{Jw}_e(s_x, t) = \frac{1}{|t|} \cdot \sum_{w_i \in t} \max_{w_j \in S'} \mathrm{Jw}(w_i, w_j) \tag{1}$$

where S' is the term set of s_x in which the terms w_j that already have maximized $\mathrm{Jw}(w_i, w_j)$ are removed.

Table 2. Examples of Jaro-Winkler distance (Jw) between words

Word 1	Word 2	Jw
nucleophile	nucleophilic	0.94515
nucleophile	electrophile	0.47643
diphenyl	1,1-Diphenylmethanone	0.35516
1,1-Diphenylmethanone	nucleophile	0.11038

Experiments have shown that sentence position within the document is a very important feature [1]. Indeed, the information is not homogeneously spread across the document but scattered tidily by the author respecting universally accepted writing rules. Document beginnings and endings usually contain sentences that are highly relevant because their original goals are to present and sum up the topic. Sentence position is therefore used as metric, denoted P (Equation 2), by computing a normalized parabolic function depending on the total number of sentence m in the document.

$$P_x = \frac{(x - \lceil \frac{m}{2} \rceil)^2}{\lfloor \frac{m}{2} \rfloor^2} \tag{2}$$

Table 3. Example of similarity measures between the title and a sentence ($\mathbf{T}_{preproc.}$ and $\mathbf{S}_{preproc.}$ are the pre-processed title and the pre-processed sentence)

Title	Generation of Cycloalkynes by Hydro-Iodonio-Elimination of Vinyl Iodonium Salts
Sentence	Cycloalkylidenecarbene can provide a ring-expanded cycloalkyne via 1,2-rearrangement.
$\mathbf{T}_{preproc.}$	*generat* **cycloalkynes** *hydro-iodonio-elimination* **vinyl iodonium salt**
$\mathbf{S}_{preproc.}$	**cycloalkylidenecarbene** *provid ring expand* **cycloalkyne** *via rearrang*
cosine	0 (no co-occurrencies)
JW_e	0.43348

where $\lceil x \rceil$ is the ceiling function that returns the smallest integer not less than x and $\lfloor x \rfloor$ is the floor function that returns the highest integer less than or equal to x.

We have implemented four other metrics relying on numerical treatments, they are computed on the matrix M (previously introduced in section 2.1). The first one is the sum of word frequencies, denoted F (Equation 3), that uses the frequencies of words in sentences. Sentences that are containing a high number of *informative* words (words remaining after pre-processing) are considered relevant.

$$F_x = \sum_{y=1}^{n} a_{x,y} \tag{3}$$

The second metric, denoted C (Equation 4), relies on the number of chemical compounds detected in the sentence giving a penalty to sentences that do not contain any chemical compounds.

$$C_x = \begin{cases} 1 & \text{if } x \text{ contains at least one chemical compound} \\ 0 & \text{Otherwise} \end{cases} \tag{4}$$

The third metric, denoted I (Equation 5), represents the interaction relationship between sentences. The underlying idea is that sentences containing words that are used in other sentences are statistically more representative for the document [14].

$$I_x = \sum_{\substack{y=1 \\ a_{x,y} \neq 0}}^{n} \sum_{\substack{z=1 \\ z \neq x}}^{m} a_{z,y} \tag{5}$$

The last metric, denoted H (Equation 6), is the sum of the Hamming distances computed on the sentence pair words [14]. The idea is to give more weight to pairs of words that appears independently in sentences. Synonyms and topic-related words generally are, according to the Hamming distance, high weighted. In order to compute this metric, a second matrix denoted M_h is constructed from M. M_h is a $n \times n$ triangular matrix constructed from word co-occurrences between sentence pairs:

$$M_h = [h_{i,j}]_{i=1...n;\ j=1...n}$$

$$h_{i,j} = \sum_{x=0}^{m} \begin{cases} 1 & \text{if } a_{x,i} \neq a_{x,j} \\ 0 & \text{Otherwise} \end{cases}$$

$$H_x = \sum_{i=1}^{n-1} \sum_{j=i+1}^{n} \begin{cases} h_{i,j} & \text{if } a_{x,i} \neq 0 \text{ and } a_{x,j} \neq 0 \\ 0 & \text{Otherwise} \end{cases} \tag{6}$$

Sentences are scored by using a equiprobable linear combination[4] of the normalized metrics (i.e. ranged in $[0,1]$) described above. A ranked sentences list is produced by the system allowing to construct the extract by arranging the high scored sentences until the desired size is reached.

3   Experimental Settings

Considerable interest has been expressed and effort expended in attempting to evaluate automatically the quality of the summaries. There exists two different types of evaluation: extrinsic and intrinsic [15]. Extrinsic evaluations measure the quality of a summary based on how it affects certain tasks. In intrinsic evaluations, summary's quality is evaluated by an analysis of its content. Most existing automated evaluation methods work by comparing the produced summaries to one or more reference summaries (ideally, produced by humans). In order to evaluate our system, we have collected a testing set from *http://pubs.acs.org*. The testing set is composed by 100 pairs of articles/abstracts coming from different journals (Organic Letters, Accounts of Chemical Research and Journal of Organic Chemistry) of different years (respectively 2000-2002, 2005-2007 and 2007-2008), different authors and topics. Each document has been cleaned up manually from the PDF (or HTML) version (figures, bibliographic references, special characters, etc. have been removed). By ways of comparison the corpus used in the Document Understanding Conference (DUC)[5] 2005 competition was also composed of 100 sets. Table 4 shows some statistics about the testing set.

3.1   Performance Measures

To evaluate the quality of our generated summaries, we choose to use the ROUGE[6] [16] evaluation toolkit, that has been found to be highly correlated with human judgments [17]. ROUGE-N is a N-gram recall measure calculated between a candidate summary and one or more reference summaries. In our experiments ROUGE-1, ROUGE-2 and ROUGE-SU4 will be computed. Each generated extract will be

---

[4] Other combinations might be considered, but a large training corpus is required to tune the parameters.

[5] Document Understanding Conferences are competitions on text summarization conducted since 2000 by the National Institute of Standards and Technology (NIST), *http://www-nlpir.nist.gov*

[6] ROUGE is available at *http://haydn.isi.edu/ROUGE/*

Table 4. Testing corpus description

Journal	Year	Number	Sentences	Words
Organic Letters	2000-2008	63	5.313	104.588
Accounts of Chemical Research	2005-2006	10	979	18.337
The Journal of Organic Chemistry	2007-2008	27	2.631	66.242
Total	-	100	8.923	189.167

evaluated by comparison with the author's abstract. The size of the produced extracts is set at 5% of the original document (in sentence number) with a minimum of three sentences. This value corresponds to the average compression rate observed on the evaluation corpus (average compression rate is $5, 39\%$).

4   Results

The first experiment is focused on the study of metrics. Figure 1 shows the ROUGE results of each metric alone and their combination. As we can see from these results, the combination, denoted by Combi., always outperforms the best metric alone. The most discriminant metrics are the similarity measures with the title (Jw_e and *cosine*) and the interaction relationship between sentences (I). The title similarity measures allow to focus the summary on the document main topic, delineated by the author. The similarity measure Jw_e that we propose is globally the most discriminant metric, its ability to bridge morphologically similar words is well adapted for Organic Chemistry documents. The interaction metric uses the networks built by words within the document to compute a relevance score, sentences that are constructed with terms appearing in many other sentences are selected. These sentences are judged as being the most representative to the document because they are containing most of the information.

A second evaluation compares YACHS to a generic statistical summarizer and a baseline on the corpus of manually segmented documents (see Figure 2). We use

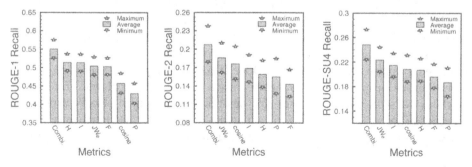

Fig. 1. ROUGE-1, ROUGE-2 and ROUGE-SU4 recall scores for each metric independently and for their combination (denoted Combi.)

the Cortex summarizer [14] which is based on the same approach that YACHS, namely a combination of relevance metrics, but without the chemical compounds detection process and the powerful Jw_e metric. The baseline is generated by arranging n sentences selected randomly from the document, n being 5% of the document sentence number with a minimum of three sentences. In order to smooth the baseline results, the average of 100 baseline evaluations is used in our experiments. YACHS achieves the best results among the ROUGE evaluations. It confirms that the specialized pre-processing and sentence scoring are well adapted to process domain specialized (Organic Chemistry) documents.

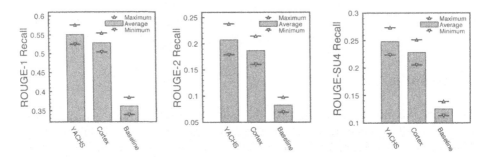

Fig. 2. ROUGE-1, ROUGE-2 and ROUGE-SU4 recall scores of YACHS, Cortex and the random baseline

The last evaluation models a real world summarization task: a plain text is given as input (without manual sentence segmentation), each summarizer has to produce an extract of size equals to 5% of the original document (in sentence number). We compare YACHS to six extractive summarizers and one baseline, results are shown in Figure 3. YACHS, Cortex and the baseline use the same automatic sentence segmentation process which consists in a standard sentence boundaries detection system enriched with lists of abbreviations. The other systems using their own sentence splitters. The baseline is generated by arranging n sentences selected randomly from the document, n being 5% of the document sentence number with a minimum of three sentences. Again, the average of 100 baseline evaluations is used in our experiments. MEAD[7] is a centroid based summarizer [18] that extract sentences according to three features: sentence centrality within the cluster, sentence position within the document and weighted similarity with the title. Open Text Summarizer[8] (OTS) [19] is an Open Source project that, similarly to MEAD, use statistical word-frequency methods to score sentences that are beforehand parsed. It also incorporates an English language lexicon with synonyms and cue terms. Pertinence Summarizer[9] performs linguistic processing of a document to generates an extract,

---

[7] Available at *http://www.summarization.com/mead/*
[8] Available at *http://libots.sourceforge.net*
[9] Available at *http://www.pertinence.net/ps/*

the sentence scoring method considering general and specialized (Chemistry) linguistic markers. Besides, two frequency-based summarizers are evaluated: Copernic[10] summarizer and the AutoSummarize feature of Microsoft Word. Exact details of their algorithms are unfortunately not documented.

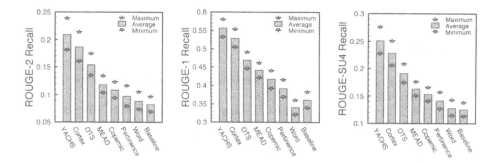

Fig. 3. Comparison of the ROUGE-1, ROUGE-2 and ROUGE-SU4 recall scores for the seven summarizers and the random baseline

YACHS and Cortex clearly stand out from the crowd. These two methods perform significantly better than the other systems (and the baseline) confirming that these statistical techniques work well for Organic Chemistry documents. YACHS achieves the best results among all summarizers proving that specialized pre-processing and adapted sentence scoring are features allowing to generate better specialized extracts.

5   Conclusion

In this paper we have described an efficient approach for automatically generating extracts from documents in Organic Chemistry. Through experiments performed on a corpus composed of scientific articles, we have showed that our approach (implemented in the YACHS[11] system) achieves promising results. This work represent a good starting point but do show a critical point: a lot of information is lost during document pre-processing. Indeed, pictures, tables or captions, that are removed during PDF (or HTML) to text conversion, are containing salient information that can be used to enhance extracts. Among the others, there are several points that would be worthy of further investigation:

– Use multi-media information (pictures, texts, tables, etc.) to generate extracts.
– Fuse text summarization and Question Answering (QA) to model real-world complex QA, in which a question cannot be answered by simply stating a name, date, quantity, etc.

---

[10] Available at *http://www.copernic.com/en/products/summarizer/index.html*
[11] An demonstration version of YACHS is available at `http://daniel.iut.univ-metz.fr/yachs`

Acknowledgement

We are grateful to Pr. Alain Krief and Julie Henry for our useful talks. This work was partially supported by the *Laboratoire de chimie organique de synthèse*, FUNDP (*Facultés Universitaires Notre-Dame de la Paix*), Namur, Belgium and by the *Agence Nationale de la Recherche*, France, project RPM2.

References

1. Mani, I., Maybury, M.T.: Advances in Automatic Text Summarization. MIT Press, Cambridge (1999)
2. Luhn, H.P.: The Automatic Creation of Literature Abstracts. IBM Journal of Research and Development 2(2), 159 (1958)
3. Climenson, W.D., Hardwick, N.H., Jacobson, S.N.: Automatic Syntax Analysis in Machine Indexing and Abstracting. American Documentation 12(3), 178–183 (1961)
4. Edmundson, H.P.: New Methods in Automatic Extracting. Journal of the ACM (JACM) 16(2), 264–285 (1969)
5. Pollock, J.J., Zamora, A.: Automatic Abstracting Research at Chemical Abstracts Service. Journal of Chemical Information and Computer Sciences 15(4), 226–232 (1975)
6. Kupiec, J., Pedersen, J., Chen, F.: A Trainable Document Summarizer. In: 18th annual international ACM SIGIR conference on Research and development in information retrieval, pp. 68–73. ACM Press, New York (1995)
7. Mani, I., Bloedorn, E.: Machine Learning of Generic and User-focused Summarization. In: 15th National Conference on Artificial intelligence (AAAI), pp. 820–826. AAAI Press, Menlo Park (1998)
8. Teufel, S., Moens, M.: Summarizing Scientific Articles: Experiments with Relevance and Rhetorical Status. Computational Linguistics 28(4), 409–445 (2002)
9. Reeve, L.H., Han, H., Brooks, A.D.: The use of Domain-Specific Concepts in Biomedical Text Summarization. Information Processing and Management 43(6), 1765–1776 (2007)
10. Salton, G., Wong, A., Yang, C.S.: A Vector Space Model for Automatic Indexing. Communications of the ACM 18(11), 613–620 (1975)
11. Porter, M.F.: An Algorithm for Suffix Stripping. Program 14, 130–137 (1980)
12. Boudin, F., Torres-Moreno, J.M.: Mixing Statistical and Symbolic Approaches for Chemical Names Recognition. In: Gelbukh, A. (ed.) CICLing 2008. LNCS, vol. 4919, pp. 334–349. Springer, Heidelberg (2008)
13. Winkler, W.E.: The State of Record Linkage and Current Research Problems. Statistics of Income Division 4, 73–79 (1999)
14. Torres-Moreno, J.M., Velazquez-Morales, P., Meunier, J.G.: Condensés de textes par des méthodes numériques. In: Journées internationales d'Analyse statistique des Données Textuelles (JADT), vol. 2, pp. 723–734 (2002)
15. Spärck Jones, K., Galliers, J.R.: Evaluating Natural Language Processing Systems: An Analysis and Review. Springer, Heidelberg (1996)
16. Lin, C.Y.: Rouge: A Package for Automatic Evaluation of Summaries. In: Workshop on Text Summarization Branches Out, pp. 25–26 (2004)

17. Dang, H.T.: Overview of DUC 2005. In: Document Understanding Conference (DUC) (2005)
18. Radev, D.R., Blair-Goldensohn, S., Zhang, Z.: Experiments in Single and Multi-Document Summarization Using MEAD. In: Document Understanding Conference (DUC) (2001)
19. Yatsko, V.A., Vishnyakov, T.N.: A Method for Evaluating Modern Systems of Automatic Text Summarization. Automatic Documentation and Mathematical Linguistics 41(3), 93–103 (2007)

Augmenting Word Space Models for Word Sense Discrimination Using an Automatic Thesaurus[*]

Hiram Calvo

Center for Research in Computing, National Polytechnic Institute
Mexico City, 07738, Mexico
hcalvo@cic.ipn.mx, hiramcalvo@gmail.com

Abstract. This paper presents an algorithm for Word Sense Discrimination that divides the global representation of a word into a number of classes by determining for any two occurrences whether they belong to the same sense or not. We rely on the notion that words that are used in similar contexts will have the same or a closely related meaning, thus, given a target word, we group its dependency co-occurrences in a Word Space Model. Each cluster represents a distinct meaning or sense of that word. We experiment with augmenting the bag of words of each cluster of co-occurrences, the dictionary of sense definition, and augmenting both. Then we count the number of intersections of each word of the bag of clustered senses and the bag of the dictionary of senses following the Lesk method. We find an increase in recall and a decrease in precision when augmenting. However, the best resulting F-measure is for the option of augmenting the both dictionary of senses and the bag of words from the clusters.

1 Introduction

In several natural language applications such as text mining, information retrieval or question answering, it is convenient to have disambiguated sentences. Word Sense Discrimination divides the occurrences of a word into a number of classes by determining for any two occurrences whether they belong to the same sense or not [15]. Approaches to this problem rely on the notion that words that are used in similar contexts will have the same or a closely related meaning [10], thus Word Sense Discrimination (WSDisc) can be seen as grouping multiple occurrences of a given target word into clusters, where each cluster represents a distinct meaning or sense of that word [11].

Following Salton and McGill [14] and Schütze [15], we model context as a vector space model for sense discrimination. This model is related to the Latent Semantic Analysis [4, 6] and has been adapted to Word Sense Disambiguation (WSDisc), for example, by Schütze [15] and Purandare and Pedersen [11]. Following them, each

---

[*] This work was done under partial support of Mexican Government (SNI, SIP-IPN, COFAA-IPN, and PIFI-IPN). We thank to Ted Pedersen and our anonymous reviewers for their useful comments and discussion.

A. Ranta, B. Nordström (Eds.): GoTAL 2008, LNAI 5221, pp. 100–107, 2008.

dimension corresponds to a word, and each vector represents the co-occurrence with other words.

Several techniques have been used for improving WSDisc, such as using syntactic relationships instead of bigram co-occurrences (See [8] and [16]), other techniques include augmenting the Vector Space with content-words that occur in the glosses of each word in Machine Readable Dictionaries (manually created MRD) [11]. In this work, we explore with both improvements, using syntactic dependency relationships, and augmenting the vector space with related words; however we use automatically obtained related words from an automatically created thesaurus instead of a manually created MRD.

In the following sections we give details of our implementation, as well as details of experiments and results.

2 Vector Space Model and Clustering

2.1 Construction of the Context Vector Space Model

Each context in which a target word occurs in a set of test data is represented by a vector. The set of vectors conforms what is called a vector space model. A vector space model (or *term vector model*) is an algebraic model for representing text documents as vectors of identifiers, such as, for example, words. They have been used in information retrieval systems long ago since 1960s with the SMART system [2] developed at Cornell University in the 1960s by the group leaded by Gerard Stalton[1].

The vector space model we use is a symmetric table, constructed by adding up the dependency relations co-occurrences, normalized by dividing by the number of times

Table 1. Fragment of Vector Space Model for the word 'band'

	atenta-do	sonar	asal-tante	ase-sino	al-bum	fre-cuencia	delic-tivo	seques-trador	infor-mación	partici-pación	co-meter
atentado 'attack'		0.00	0.00	0.00	0.00	0.00	0.00	0.00	1.19	4.40	**194.03**
sonar 'to sound'	0.00		0.00	0.00	**14.3**	**18.44**	0.00	0.00	0.31	0.34	0.00
asaltante 'robber'	0.00	0.00		0.00	0.00	0.00	0.00	0.00	0.00	0.00	5.53
asesino 'killer'	0.00	0.00	0.00		0.00	0.00	0.00	0.00	0.75	0.00	7.72
álbum 'album'	0.00	**14.30**	0.00	0.00		0.00	0.00	0.00	0.00	2.04	0.00
frecuencia 'frequency '	0.00	**18.44**	0.00	0.00	0.00		4.20	0.00	6.06	0.21	5.47
delictivo 'delictive '	0.00	0.00	0.00	0.00	0.00	4.20		0.00	0.35	0.39	0.00
secuestrador 'kidnapper '	0.00	0.00	0.00	0.00	0.00	0.00	0.00		1.06	0.00	5.43
información 'information '	1.19	0.31	0.00	0.75	0.00	6.06	0.35	1.06		0.69	0.33
participación 'participation'	4.40	0.34	0.00	0.00	2.04	0.21	0.39	0.00	0.69		0.00
cometer 'commit '	**194.03**	0.00	5.53	7.72	0.00	5.47	0.00	5.43	0.33	0.00	

---

[1] Michael Lesk was among the contributors of this group.

each word occurs. This matrix is obtained exclusively from the dependency relations extracted from the corpus *Prensaw* in Spanish. This corpus consists of 4 years of 4 mexican newspapers. The size of *Prensaw* is more than 1GB of text. We use the Spanish parser DILUCT [3] for extracting the dependency relationships from this text[2]. See Table 1 for an example of this matrix.

Table 1 shows only 12 x 12 cells of the total 345 x 345 features for the word *banda* 'band'. We adjust the threshold automatically to obtain matrices between 250 and 350 rows (and equal number of columns, as matrices are symmetric). The threshold is adjusted by increasing the number of pairs occurrences (as *banda, delincuente* 'band, robber') needed to be considered in the wordspace matrix. Each cell is divided by the number of occurrences of both words. Values are multiplied by 10^8 because resulting values are too small due to a big number of occurrences of words individually.

$$cell(w_1, w_2) = \frac{freq(w_1, w_2)}{freq(w_1) \cdot freq(w_2)} \cdot 10^8$$

As an example, consider the first column of Table 1; it is possible to see that *cometer* 'commit' and *atentado* 'attack' are highly related (it is almost a collocation in Spanish, since other combinations sound strange, as for 'make' an 'attack'). The second column shows that *sonar* 'to sound' is highly related to *album* and *frequencia* 'frequency'.

Table 2. CLUTO clustering for the Dependency Context Vector Space of *banda* 'band'

Cluster	Size	ISim	ESim	Descriptive	Discriminating
0	46	0.399	0.027	presunto 0.9%, captura 0.7%, organización 0.7%, robar 0.6%	país 2.8%, grupo 1.9%, momento 1.8%, año 1.7%
1	20	0.210	0.004	internet 27.1%, radio 25.4%, red 9.6%, espectro 7.8%, frecuencia 6.0%	internet 16.5%, banda 15.1%, radio 15.1%, espectro 5.4%, red 3.7%
2	25	0.199	0.005	canción 24.9%, grabar 13.4%, disco 8.7%, álbum 6.8%, interpretar 6.0%	canción 12.9%, grabar 10.0%, interpretar 5.0%, álbum 4.7%
3	27	0.193	0.040	grupo 25.6%, organización 6.5%, movimiento 6.2%, músico 4.9%	grupo 14.4%, movimiento 5.8%, gira 4.3%, músico 4.0%
4	69	0.158	0.018	momento 7.1%, vez 4.2%, año 3.4%, nombre 3.3%, país 3.0%	momento 4.7%, vez 2.7%, lugar 2.4%, cuenta 2.2%
5	32	0.124	0.006	oscilar 9.7%, llegar 9.4%, derecha 5.4%, hacer 4.8%, ubicar 3.4%	oscilar 6.5%, llegar 5.3%, derecha 2.9%, hacer 2.5%
6	32	0.133	0.012	méxico 29.2%, estados 8.0%, país 6.4%, droga 6.2%, parte 2.9%	méxico 17.9%, estados 5.7%, droga 4.1%, romper 2.5%
7	29	0.127	0.006	flotación 9.0%, cotización 8.6%, precio 7.2%, fluctuación 4.8%, control 4.6%	flotación 7.2%, cotización 6.2%, precio 4.9%, fluctuación 4.0%
8	34	0.120	0.001	narcotráfico 24.3%, arizmendi 6.8%, delito 5.6%, arellano 5.5%, asesinar 4.6%	narcotráfico 12.4%, arizmendi 5.4%, arellano 4.2%, delito 3.4%
9	31	0.134	0.015	policía 20.5%, delincuente 9.7%, militar 6.5%, elemento 4.7%, terrorista 4.0%	policía 12.3%, delincuente 6.1%, militar 3.7%, pandilleros 3.6%

[2] We have made available the Spanish dependency relationships and their count at http://hiramcalvo.com/diluct/resources/ in Ted Pedersen's ngram format.

Table 3. Examples of w ordbags to be intersected for *banda* 'band'

bagclu (fragment)	bagdir
0:asaltante, asesino, armada, delictivo, rival, neza, vocalista, colaboración, alternar, flotación, ladrón, legendario, arizmendi, operar, mafioso, especializado, pertenencia, dedicada, desmembrar, deslizamiento, robo, criminal, desintegrar.	**banda.1:** Cinta que se coloca cruzada sobre el pecho y que es señal de un cargo o una distinción *Ex:* ha conseguido unas cuantas bandas, incluyendo la novedosa de Miss Internet
1:sonar, frecuencia, servicio, información, acceso, través, comunicación, ampliar, concesión, conexión, transmitir, escuchar, transmisión, radio, espectro,	**banda.2:** Tira de tela u otro material *Ex:* unas bandas de lona, unas bandas de velcro *Syn:* tira, cinta
2:álbum, video, dedicar, tocar, interpretar, canción, éxito, sonido, cantar, musical, conformar, componer, grabar, estilo, músico, ritmo, presentación, tema, película, concierto, disco, incluir, género, música, producción	**banda.3:** Conjunto de músicos que tocan juntos *Ex:* banda de jazz, banda de cornetas y tambores *Syn:* grupo *Collo:* banda militar, banda de música, banda de rock, banda musical
3:ofrecer, miembro, iniciar, participación, organizar, británico, civil, acompañar, jazz, colaborar, trabajo, existencia, integrante, gira, pertenecer, participar, apoyo, dirigir, paramilitar, jóvenes, líder, unir, integrar, encabezar, compañero, apoyar,	**banda.4:** Grupo de personas que se une con fines comunes, especialmente delictivos *Ex:* banda de atracadores, banda de traficantes *Syn:* grupo *Collo:* banda armada, banda callejera, banda de delincuentes, banda juvenil, banda militar, banda organizada, banda paramilitar, banda terrorista, banda ultra
4:imponer, vivir, ir, regresar, seguir, surgir, llevar, decir, encontrar, ver, traer, primero, hacer, nacer, crear, pasar, grande, propio, to mar, considerar, oscilar, rebasar, mexicano, acercar, abandonar, poder, jugar, existir, ubicar, nueva,	
5:cabeza, límite, 22, 20, nombre, cuenta, salida, paso, escenario, jugada, 25, tierra, punto, 10, viento, propuesta, 15, año, momento, vez, extremo, izquierda, fin, calle, centro, mano, derecha, grado, lugar, 30, carrera	**banda.5:** Zona lateral de un objeto o lugar *Ex:* recorrió toda la banda derecha con el balón cosido a sus botas *Syn:* margen, lateral, lado, costado *Collo:* banda derecha, banda izquierda, línea de banda, saque de banda
6:estado, ciudad, tráfico, mundo, comercio, intereses, negociación, guerra, llegada, formar, traficante, presidente, pueblo, resto, comunidad, gobierno, política, país, tradición, diferencia, movimiento, historia, alianza, territorio, estados, sur,	**banda.6:** Conjunto de animales que pertenecen a una misma especie y se desplazan en grupo *Ex:* banda de gaviotas *Syn:* bandada, manada
7:cambio, respecto, mecanismo, peso, instrumento, internacional, calidad, precio, control, acuerdo, mantener, tipo, dólar, cambiaria, objetivo, mercado, área, permitir, base, fluctuación, régimen, acción, capacidad, baja, operación,	**banda.7:** Intervalo de frecuencias entre dos puntos que permite transmitir una señal por medio de ondas electromagnéticas *Ex:* los radiofaros trabajan en la banda 280 *Syn:* frecuencia *Collo:* banda de frecuencia
8:secuestrador, cometer, crimen, asesinato, secuestro, delincuencia, sicario, lucha, tiro, droga, actividad, aprehensión, investigación, persona, captura, organizado, pistoleros, involucrar, delito, combate, asalto, organización, combatir, violencia, caso, narcotráfico, vínculo, sujeto, víctima, impunidad, nexo,	
9:detener, utilizar, grupo, argentino, seguridad, enfrentar, elemento, colonia, presunto, decena, proteger, acabar, actuación, ataque, protección, intervenir, jefe, barrio, presencia,.	

2.2 Clustering of the Context Vectors

CLUTO is a family of data clustering software tools [12]. We use *vcluster* version 2.1.1 to cluster the rows of the Vector Space Model (like the fragment shown in Table 1), using the co-ocurrences of each word as features. We used direct k-way clustering. CLUTO computes a direct k-way clustering as follows [13]: Initially, a set of k objects is selected from the data sets to act as the seeds of the k clusters. Then, for each object, its similarity to these k seeds is computed, and it is assigned to the cluster corresponding to its most similar seed. This forms the initial k-way clustering. This clustering is then repeatedly refined so that it optimizes a desired clustering criterion function. This optimization is performed using a randomized incremental optimization algorithm that is greedy in nature, has low computational requirements, and produces high-quality solutions [17].

In Table 2 we show an example of clustering of meanings for the word *banda* 'band'. **Isim** shows the internal similarity of each cluster, **Esim** shows the external similarity with other clusters, and the descriptive and discriminating features for each cluster. Features are words which co-occurr with the word to desambiguate.

Different senses of "banda" can be spotted from the descriptive words for each cluster. Cluster #0 would correspond to *banda de delincuentes* 'robbers band', Cluster #1 to *banda de frecuencia* 'frequency band' (AM, FM,...), Cluster #3 to *organized band*, etc. Cluster #7 is interesting, since it shows a meaning that is not present in Spanish Wordnet or Minidir (the inventory of senses used for Spanish Senseval-3 [9]). It is related to *banda de flotación*, which means an interval where Mexican peso fluctuates in comparison to U.S. dollar.

We experimented with several parameter combinations. We obtained better results with the co-relational coefficient and no less than 10 clusters. For less than 10 clusters, meanings tend to clutter. Using more clusters leads to several clusters corresponding to one meaning in WordNet or Minidir, which is not indeed a problem, since we can map several clusters to a single sense in Minidir. In all experiments we set the number of classes to 10.

2.3 Mapping of Clusters to Sense's Inventory

For evaluation, clusters must be mapped to an inventory of senses. For our experiments, we used Minidir from Senseval-3 Spanish Lexical Test[3]. We used intersection of word-bags following the Simplified Lesk approach [5] with all words weighted as 1 (i.e., no IDF as in [5]). See Table 3 for an example of the words belonging to each cluster (**bag-clu**) and the words from Minidir (**bagdir**). The Senseval-3 task for Spanish is slightly different from English, since they supply a Minidir which includes *ex*amples, *syn*onyms and frequent *collo*cations, whereas in the English test the sense directory is taken from WordNet. The resulting mappings are shown in Table 3 with connecting lines.

2.4 Evaluation

Once the clusters are mapped to senses, their words (**bagclu**) can be intersected using Simple Term Matching (STM) as in the Simplified Lesk algorithm with the words from the Senseval-3 Lexical Sample Test of Spanish (**bagtest**) to find the correct sense; so that we are using the algorithm of intersection of words (STM) twice: Once for mapping **bagclu** to **bagdir**, and then to intersect **bagclu** with **bagtest**.

The **results** are: precision: 48.87%, recall: 28.68%, uncovered cases: 42.10%, F-Measure: 33.35. We have not applied any *augmentation* of the bags of words yet.

3 Augmenting the Word Space Model with a Thesaurus

We created a thesaurus following the Lin method described in [7]. The corpus used to create the thesaurus was the whole Encarta encyclopaedia 2004 in Spanish [1]. It has 18.59 M tokens, 117,928 types in 73MB of text, 747,239 sentences, and 39,685 definitions. See Table 4 for an example of similar words obtained from this corpus[4].

---

[3] See http://www.lsi.upc.es/~nlp/senseval-3/Spanish.html and [9] for a description of this test and information about the 46 words which make up test. Each word has in average 91 instances with a standard deviation of $\sigma=30.29$. In total there are 4195 instances.

[4] The Lin Distributional Thesaurus from Encarta is available at http://hiramcalvo.com/resources

Table 4. Example of similar words using Lin similarity method

word w	similar word w'	English	$sim_{lin}(w,w')$
guitarrista	*pianista*	pianist	0.141
'guitarist'	*fisiólogo*	physiologist	0.139
	educador	teacher	0.129
devoción	*afecto*	affection	0.095
'devotion'	*respeto*	respect	0.091
	admiración	admiration	0.078
leer	*editar*	to edit	0.078
'to read'	*traducir*	to translate	0.076
	publicar	to publish	0.072

We used a thesaurus from this corpus because this corpus is smaller than *prensaw*[5], and we considered that an encyclopaedia is wide enough to consider many different words; however we should be aware that the different word distribution of Encarta vs. *prensaw* may influence the outcome. All augmentations considered only the top 10 similar words for each word in the bag, thus, multiplying the size of the bag by 10.

There are four ways to use the thesaurus from Encarta on the first mapping (**bagclu** to **bagdir**):

0. No augmentation (See results of Section 2.4).
1. Augmenting the matrix, **before** clustering, with similar words, i.e., for each word, add its top n similar words. That results in a (345 x n) x (345 x n) matrix. This option adds a considerable quantity of noise, so it was not further explored.
2. Augmenting **bagclu**: Adding the top n similar words for each content word in **bagclu**.
3. Augmenting **bagdir**: Adding the top n similar words for each content word in **bagdir**.
4. Augmenting both **baclu** and **bagdir**

Table 5. Results of WSDisc Augmenting the Word Space Model

encarta	Precision	Recall	uncovered	F-measure	Description
0	**48.87**	28.68	42.10	33.35	raw
2	45.34	33.71	23.67	36.92	aug. bagclu
3	41.91	32.35	23.64	35.38	aug. bagdir
4	42.26	**34.89**	**18.63**	**37.55**	aug. both
prensaw	Precision	Recall	uncovered	F-measure	desc.
0	**46.33**	38.53	18.51	41.52	raw
2	40.00	38.50	4.15	39.21	aug. bagclu
3	42.73	40.73	5.06	41.65	aug. bagdir
4	42.58	**41.80**	**2.23**	**42.18**	aug. both

---

[5] The algorithm to obtain a Lin-Thesaurus from *prensaw* might take up to one month due to the increased combination of words.

Table 6. Results of Senseval-3 systems

System	Supervised	Precision	Recall	Coverage	F-measure
IRST	Yes	84.20%	84.20%	100.0%	84.20
UA-SRT	Semi	84.00%	84.00%	100.0%	84.00
UMD	Yes	82.48%	82.48%	100.0%	82.48
UNED	Yes	81.76%	81.76%	100.0%	81.76
SWAT	Yes	79.45%	79.45%	100.0%	79.45
D-SLSS	Yes	74.29%	75.02%	100.0%	74.65
CSUSMCS	Yes	67.84%	67.82%	99.9%	67.83
UA-NSM	No	61.93%	61.93%	100.0%	61.93
UA-NP	No	84.31%	47.27%	56.1%	60.58
Baseline (MFS)	--	67.72%	67.72%	100.0%	67.72

The results are shown in Table 5, for Context Vector Space Models obtained from the *prensaw* corpus and the *encarta* corpus separatedly. Note that we did not explore option 1 since it resulted in very big tables with a high amount of noise.

4 Conclusions and Future Work

Compared with the similar system of Purandare and Pedersen [11], their system achieves similar results (42.35% F-measure with no gloss augmentation vs. 46.9% F-measure with gloss augmentation). It is important to notice that results are not directly comparable, because they test against the Senseval-2 Lexical Sample test in English. In addition, they report an increase of F-measure, while they do not report the particular values of precision and recall.

It is important to note the following differences between our system and Purandare and Pedersen's: Our system is based on dependency relationships for building the Word Space Model, whereas their system is based on co-occurrences in a window of size 3. Secondly, we do not perform matrix packing (SVDPack). Third, we augment the WSM using an automatically created thesaurus instead of a manually obtained MRD.

We show in Table 6 the results of other systems at the Spanish Lexical Sample Test of Senseval-3 [9]. The baseline was calculated as the most frequent sense from MiniDir. Compared with these results, the overall results of our system fall below the baseline, and below the unsupervised systems (which achieve 61.92 and 60.58 respectively). Such systems work only for nouns; our system works for every part of speech. The evaluation of our system considering only nouns (18 of 46 words) yields very similar results than for all words.

In general, the best F-measure is obtained by augmenting both the bag of directory of senses (**bagdir**) and the bag of words of the clustered senses (**bagclu**). Both augmentations sum to each other. Coverage rises notably when using a bigger corpus such as *prensaw* for the wordspace model (WSM). We think that using an even larger WSM might attain better results. In addition, when using the same corpus for WSM and for the Lin-Thesaurus, the increase on performance is more noticeable.

We think that using resources such as thesaurus and WSM clearly benefit WSD. In a future work, we should experiment with applying these resources to more complex algorithms for WSD, aside from WSDisc. As for WSDisc, as future work, we plan to experiment with other clustering algorithms that find the number of classes automatically, as we set always 10 clusters. We should explore the impact of varying the number of neighbors for augmentation; and experiment with distributional thesaurus obtained from different sources, particularly from *prensaw*.

References

1. Biblioteca de Consulta Microsoft Encarta 2004, Microsoft Corporation (1994–2004)
2. Buckley, C., Salton, G.: Optimization of Relevance Feedback Weights. In: Annual International ACM-SIGIRr Conference on Research and Development in Information Retrieval (SIGIR 1995), pp. 351–357. ACM Press, New York (2004)
3. Calvo, H., Gelbukh, A.: DILUCT: An Open-Source Spanish Dependency Parser Based on Rules, Heuristics, and Selectional Preferences. In: Kop, C., Fliedl, G., Mayr, H.C., Métais, E. (eds.) NLDB 2006. LNCS, vol. 3999, pp. 164–175. Springer, Heidelberg (2004)
4. Deerwester, S., Dumais, S.T., Furnas, G.W., Landauer, T.K., Harshman, R.: Indexing by latent semantic analysis. Journal of the American Society for Information Science 41, 391–407 (1990)
5. Kilgarriff, A., Rosenzweig, J.: Framework and results for English SENSEVAL. Computers and the Humanities 34(1-2) (2000)
6. Landauer, T.K., Foltz, P.W., Laham, D.: An introduction to latent semantic analysis. Discourse Processes 25, 259–284 (1998)
7. Lin, D.: An information-theoretic measure of similarity. In: Proceedings of ICML 1998, pp. 296–304 (1998)
8. Lin, D.: Automatic retrieval and clustering of similar words. In: Proceedings of COLING/ACL 1998, Montreal, Canada (1998)
9. Márquez, L., Taulé, M., Martí, M.A., Artigas, N., García, M., Real, F., Ferres, D.: Senseval-3: The Spanish lexical sample task. In: Senseval-3 Third international Workshop on the Evaluation of Systems for the Semantic Analysis of Text, ACL, USA, pp. 47–52 (2004)
10. Miller, G.A., Charles, W.G.: Contextual correlates of semantic similarity. Language and Cognitive Processes 6(1), 1–28 (1991)
11. Purandare, A., Pedersen, T.: Word sense discrimination by clustering contexts in vector and similarity spaces. In: Proceedings of the Conference on Computational Natural Language Learning, Boston, MA, pp. 41–48 (2004)
12. Rasmussen, M., Karypis, G.: gCLUTO: An Interactive Clustering, Visualization, and Analysis System - Dep. Comput. Sci. Eng., Univ. Minnesota, Tech. Rep. TR (2004)
13. Rasmussen, M.D., Deshpande, M.S., Karypis, G., Johnson, J., Crow, J.A., Retzel, E.F.: wCLUTO: A Web-Enabled Clustering Toolkit. Plant Physiology 133(2), 510–516 (2003)
14. Salton, G., McGill, M.: Introduction to modern IR. McGraw-Hill, New York (1983)
15. Schütze, H.: Automatic word sense discrimination. Comp. Linguistics 24(1), 97–123 (1998)
16. van der Plas, L., Bouma, G.: Syntactic contexts for finding semantically similar words. In: van der Wouden, T., et al. (eds.) Computational Linguistics in the Netherlands, Selected Papers from the Fifteenth CLIN Meeting, Utrecht, LOT. pp. 173–184 (2004)
17. Zhao, Y., Karypis, G.: Empirical and Theoretical Comparisons of Selected Criterion Functions for Document Clustering. Machine Learning 55(3), 311–331 (2004)

Plagiarism Detection Based on Singular Value Decomposition

Zdenek Ceska

Department of Computer Science and Engineering, Faculty of Applied Sciences,
University of West Bohemia, Univerzitni 22, 306 14 Pilsen, Czech Republic
zceska@kiv.zcu.cz

Abstract. Plagiarism is a widely spread problem that is the main focus of interest these days. In this paper, we propose a new method solving associations of
phrases contained in text documents. This method, called SVDPlag, employs
Singular Value Decomposition (SVD) for this purpose. Further, we discuss
other approaches to plagiarism detection and compare them with our method.
To examine the efficiency of plagiarism detection methods, we used
an experimental corpus of 950 text documents about politics, which were created from the standard CTK corpus. The experiments indicate that our approach
significantly improves the accuracy of plagiarism detection and overcomes
other methods.

Keywords: Plagiarism, Copy Detection, Natural Language Processing, Phrases,
N-grams, Singular Value Decomposition, Latent Semantic Analysis.

1 Introduction

In recent years, the growing popularity of plagiarism has raised general awareness and
searching for new protections has started. Although various protections have been
developed for CDs, DVDs, and other media, it always contains a vulnerability that is
later exploited to bypass the protection. The Internet can be considered as a particular
case of public media where whatever can be found. Thanks to its wide popularity, it is
an inexhaustible source of information. If we take a brief look at the content of the
Internet, we discover that most of the information distributed on CDs, DVDs, and
some other media is available in an unprotected form.

The aim is not to protect the information, but looking for the plagiarists and punish
them. The main advantage of this approach rests in psychology since every plagiarism
may be identified by comparing it with a database of existing works. Plagiarism in
written text is in the center of public interest for its wide use in education, research,
politics, etc. A tool for identification plagiarism among various text documents is
required by every institution you can think of. For instance, it is crucial for education
system, because many students try to submit someone else's works.

Clough [4, 5] and Maurer [13] carried out an observation of the current state of
plagiarism in written text. In this paper, we are going deeper to propose an advanced
plagiarism detection method specialized in written text. It is the center of our attention

A. Ranta, B. Nordström (Eds.): GoTAL 2008, LNAI 5221, pp. 108–119, 2008.
© Springer-Verlag Berlin Heidelberg 2008

due to its wide use and general public demands for new approaches. Paraphrasing is still a key issue for plagiarism detection and therefore further development is required. We employed the Latent Semantic Analysis (LSA) framework to infer the latent semantic associations and subsequently determine the document similarity. During this process, LSA applies Singular Value Decomposition (SVD). An essential goal of our method is to process all selected documents together.

The following text is organized as follows. Section 2 describes the current state of the art in the field of plagiarism detection. Section 3 proposes our method based on SVD. The comparison of our method with other existing approaches is presented in Section 4. Finally, Section 5 summarizes our results and proposes some improvements for future work.

2 Related Work

In the field of Information Retrieval (IR), Vector Space Model (VSM) has been often employed. This method computes the cosine measure between two documents according to the occurrence frequencies of single words. In the field of plagiarism detection we can regard it as a baseline. An implementation of this method can be found, for instance, in Detection of Duplicate Defect Reports [14].

Shivakumar and Garcia-Molina introduced the most famous Relative Frequency Model (RFM), which is partly derived from the VSM. In 1995, they developed SCAM system [16] based on RFM. Later in 1996, they proposed an improvement [17] to reach better accuracy and scalability. This system uses single words as features for plagiarism detection. A similar approach was used in COPS system [3] as well. The only one difference is that it uses whole sentences as features instead of single words.

The previous two methods employed mainly single words as features. The main disadvantage is that it detects rather the topic similarity than the real text overlap. On the other hand, COPS uses whole sentences, where the only one word mismatch causes the failure of the sentence matching. The proper solution seems to be the use of phrases since they contain only simple ideas. Therefore, the modern plagiarism detection turned to identification of overlapping phrases.

In 2006, Lane presented system Ferret [10, 11] based on comparison of common trigrams. The resulting similarity is computed according to the Jaccard-Tanimoto coefficient [12]. Analogously, Bao used this approach in a study dealing with plagiarism in academic conference papers [1].

Some other approaches for plagiarism detection have been developed, such as PPChecker [7] or Hoad&Zobel [6]. Although, they improve the accuracy of plagiarism detection, single words are still being utilized. For instance, PPChecker identifies a certain plagiarism pattern based on three decision conditions, i.e. word overlap, word difference, and size overlap. Hoad&Zobel proposed several modifications to the traditional VSM. Some of the similarity measures, they proposed, improve the score of separation of the correctly plagiarized documents from the incorrectly ones. In some cases, they slightly improve the accuracy.

3 The Proposed Plagiarism Detection Method

To achieve better results, we decided to employ SVD in the field of plagiarism detection. Generally, SVD is a tool for LSA to infer the latent semantic associations between two different entities [2, 9]. In our case we deal with phrases contained in text documents.

We can imagine phrases as word N-grams of a concrete length n, i.e. a sequence of n words. With the help of N-grams, we are able to identify the overlapping parts of text documents. Although the document overlap can be sufficient to identify plagiarism, we propose to employ SVD to infer the latent semantics based on statistical computations of large data. The following text describes our method SVDPlag in detail. Fig. 1 is just the presentation of our system which is based on the proposed method.

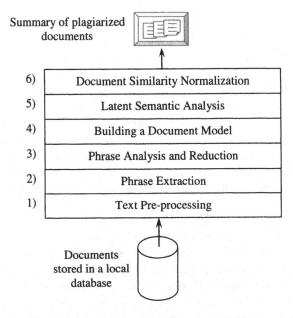

Fig. 1. Scheme of the system based on SVDPlag

3.1 Text Pre-processing

Text pre-processing is an important step for every Natural Language Processing (NLP) task to achieve outstanding results. In SVDPlag we use stop-word removal and lemmatization. Stop-word removal is the most fundamental NLP technique, which removes all common and inconvenient words from the text. In our case, we use it as a necessary data reduction technique. Lemmatization is the process of determining the lemma for a given word [18]. In contrast to Stemming, it involves techniques such as understanding the context and determining the part of speech of a word.

3.2 Phrase Extraction

The second step retrieves simple ideas from the text. For this purpose, we extract word N-grams of a specified length from the pre-processed text. Recent experiments have shown that the most suitable length of N-grams lies between 2 and 7. For our experiments, introduced in the following section, we used N-grams of the length 1 to 5. Indeed, 1-grams are just single words that do not identify any text overlap and therefore the accuracy of the used method significantly decreases. We employed single words just to make a comparison with the VSM and RFM method. On the other hand, N-grams having length 6 or more are not able to identify fine-grained text modifications. Thus, the accuracy of the used method decreases as quickly as the length of N-grams increases.

3.3 Phrase Analysis and Reduction

Analysis and reduction is an essential step that should follow every data extraction. The longer phrases, in terms of N-grams, are extracted, the higher amount of distinct phrases has to be compared to identify plagiarized documents. This can seem to be a disadvantage of longer phrases; however, we have to take into account that not all phrases have the same importance. If we employ a feature selection technique, the amount of phrases can be significantly reduced.

The most simple and from our point of view the best method for plagiarism detection is a Document Frequency (DF) feature selection. According to the document frequency we can simply determine if the given phrase is important or not. The phrases existing just in one document are removed right away since they cannot be plagiarized in any other document. Moreover, we propose to remove such phrases that are contained in more than $\mu + \sigma$ documents, where μ is the mean document frequency and σ is the standard deviation from the mean document frequency. In other words, it removes all common phrases from the documents.

Table 1. Number of phrases before and after reduction of a sample of 1000 pieces of news obtained from the standard CTKcorpus. We use the DF feature selection for N-gram reduction.

N-gram length	Number of original phrases	Number of reduced phrases	Average phrase occurrence freq.
1	30550	15343	7.45
2	128449	28206	1.76
3	169093	23337	1.34
5	189621	18281	1.18
7	195999	15549	1.13
9	199421	13536	1.10

Table 1 presents the number of phrases after the DF feature selection. As you can see, the number of phrases after reduction decreases with the increasing length of N-grams. The main reason is that longer phrases more often occur just in one document and are subsequently removed. For phrases of the length 5, the reduction ratio achieves about 10. Thus, we are able to reduce the number of phrases in a significant way and accelerate the further processing in terms of time consumption.

3.4 Building a Document Model

This part deals with a simplified description of text documents. We propose a phrase-by-document model considering occurrence frequencies of phrases contained in the examined documents. These relationships are depicted in a matrix form, where columns represent phrases and rows represent documents. Let matrix A be an n-by-m rectangular matrix to be composed of n vectors $[A_1, A_2, ..., A_m]$, where the vector A_i represents phrases contained in document i. Then, each vector A_i is composed of m elements $a_{i,j}$ representing the weighted occurrence frequency of phrase j in document i, as depicted in Equation 1. This equation is a modification of the standard TF-IDF weighting [15] we propose for initialization of matrix A.

$$a_{i,j} = \begin{cases} \dfrac{1}{2} + \dfrac{PF_{i,j} \cdot \log\left(\dfrac{|N|}{DF_j}\right)}{2 \cdot \max\limits_{i}\left(PF_{i,j}\right) \cdot \log(|N|)} & \text{if phrase } j \text{ occurs in document } i \\ \\ 0 & \text{otherwise} \end{cases} \tag{1}$$

$PF_{i,j}$ represents the occurrence frequency of phrase j in document i, DF_j represents the number of documents where phrase j occurs, and finally $|N|$ is the number of all documents. The difference in comparison to TF-IDF rests in IDF normalization. We divide it by $\log(|N|)$ in order to $a_{i,j} \in <0.5, 1>$. On the other hand, if phrase j does not occur in document i, then $a_{i,j} = 0$. This weighting mechanism yields the best result for SVD that is employed in the following subsection.

3.5 Latent Semantic Analysis

In this step, we infer the latent semantic associations among phrases contained in the examined documents. We apply SVD to decompose matrix A into three independent matrices U, Σ, and V. All these matrices can be decomposed in a reduced latent space k to perform the best k-rank approximation of A so that singular values $\sigma_{k+1}, \sigma_{k+2}, ..., \sigma_m$ are replaced by 0, where $1 \leq k \leq m$. Then, matrix U is an n-by-k column orthonormal, whose columns are phrase singular vectors. Σ is a k-by-k diagonal matrix without negative and zero numbers that represents singular values.

$$\sigma_1 \geq \sigma_2 \geq ... \geq \sigma_k > \sigma_{k+1} = ... = \sigma_m = 0 \tag{2}$$

A characteristic feature of SVD is that the singular values on the diagonal are placed in descending order and satisfy Equation 2. Matrix V^T is a k-by-m row orthonormal, whose rows are document singular vectors.

Fig. 2 presents the decomposition in a more detailed fashion. After the decomposition, matrix V^T is an essential building element for further processing since it contains independent profile vectors of the examined documents.

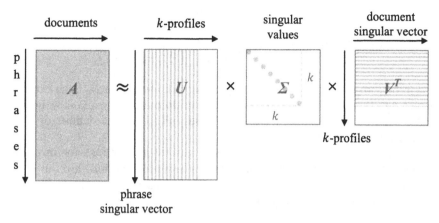

Fig. 2. Singular value decomposition of a phrase-by-document matrix

3.6 Document Similarity Normalization

The last step computes the mutual pairwise document similarity. Before we use matrix V^T, single elements of all document profiles must be rescaled with the corresponding singular values, as shown in Equation 3.

$$B = \Sigma \times V^T \qquad (3)$$

Finally, we compute the mutual pairwise correlation according to Equation 4, where the columns of matrix B are length-normalized. The resulting sim_{SVD} is a symmetric matrix where each pair of documents is evaluated by a score representing the percentage similarity.

$$sim_{SVD} = \left\| B \right\|^T \times \left\| B \right\| \qquad (4)$$

Although everything might seem to have been solved now, the opposite is true. Let us have a look at Fig. 3; we remember the reduction process employed in the third step. Actually, this has to affect the measure of similarity because of the smaller set of phrases considered during the decomposition. Thus, sim_{SVD} obtains much higher score for such documents where vast majority of phrases are removed as meaningless.

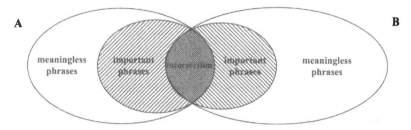

Fig. 3. An intersection of two sets of phrases

$$sim(R,S) = sim_{SVD}(R,S) \cdot \sqrt{\frac{|ph_{orig}(R)|}{|ph_{red}(R)|} \cdot \frac{|ph_{orig}(S)|}{|ph_{red}(S)|}} \qquad (5)$$

Therefore, we propose to modify the evaluation in matrix sim_{SVD}. Such expression is depicted in Equation 5, where the evaluation of documents R and S is weighted by the ratio between the number of original phrases $|ph_{orig}|$ and the number of phrases after reduction $|ph_{red}|$.

The resulting evaluation corresponds with general assumptions for measure of similarity. Now, let us define threshold τ that determines a minimal level of similarity. If similarity between two document R and S is greater than τ, we consider such documents as plagiarized, see Equation 6.

$$plagiarized(R,S) = \begin{cases} true & if \ sim(R,S) > \tau \\ false & if \ sim(R,S) \leq \tau \end{cases} \qquad (6)$$

4   Evaluation Measures

To compare our proposed method SVDPlag with other approaches, we decided to use a standard mechanism well-known from IR. We define precision p and recall r according to Equations 7 and 8, where *relevant* represents a set of documents to be selected as plagiarized by users and *retrieved* is a set of documents to be selected as plagiarized by the examined algorithm.

$$p = \frac{|relevant \cap retrieved|}{|retrieved|} \qquad (7)$$

$$r = \frac{|relevant \cap retrieved|}{|relevant|} \qquad (8)$$

In the following figures, we use a more representative measure F_1 depending on threshold τ, where τ determines a minimal level of similarity. Measure F_1 combines precision and recall, as depicted in Equation 9.

$$F_1 = \frac{2 \cdot p \cdot r}{p + r} \qquad (9)$$

Although precision and recall suite well for most of tasks, we recommend include in a complementary measure [6] especially developed for plagiarism detection. This measure combines *highest false match* (HFM) and *separation* (SEP), where HFM is the highest percentage given to an incorrect result and SEP is the difference between the lowest correct result and the HFM. Because a high HFM is acceptable in case the SEP is high too and vice versa for the low score, both the SEP and HFM need to be considered together. The ratio between the SEP and HFM provides a useful measure how plagiarism is separated from original documents. Equation 10 expresses the ratio we call SH.

$$SH = \frac{SEP}{HFM} \tag{10}$$

5 Experiments

For our initial experiments, we gathered a collection of 150 plagiarized text documents in Czech language. This collection was created manually by students from the standard CTK corpus. We selected 300 articles from the politics and used them as a baseline to create the plagiarized documents. Subsequently, students were assigned to combine two or more randomly selected articles by the following rules:

- Take paragraphs from the selected articles and create a new article
- Remove about 20% of sentences from the new article
- Remove about 10% of single words
- Exchange about 20% of sentences from different paragraphs
- Exchange about 10% of words from different sentences
- Exchange the order of several paragraphs, sentences, and words
- Insert several new words to get the sentence meaning

As result we obtained 150 plagiarized documents where the underlying articles are known. Then we mixed up the plagiarized documents with the original 300 articles and appended it by 500 other articles of the same topic. Thus, we obtained an experimental corpus, which contained 950 text documents about politics.

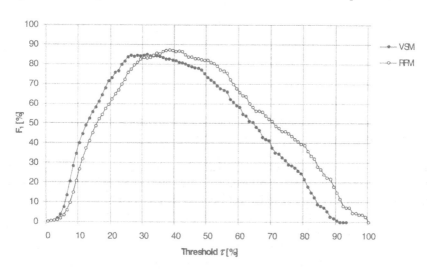

Fig. 4. The dependency of measure F_1 on threshold τ for plagiarism detection based on VSM and RFM

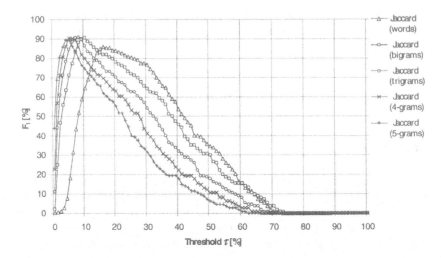

Fig. 5. The dependency of measure F_1 on threshold τ for plagiarism detection based on Jaccard-Tanimoto coefficient using single words, bigrams, trigrams, 4-grams, and 5-grams

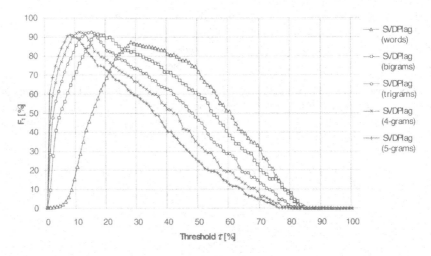

Fig. 6. The dependency of measure F_1 on threshold τ for plagiarism detection based on SVD using single words, bigrams, trigrams, 4-grams, and 5-grams

We focused our attention on the comparison of our method SVDPlag to other available approaches for plagiarism detection. We selected VSM approach used, for instance, in Detection of Duplicate Defect Reports [14], and RFM approach employed in SCAM system [16]. Further, we selected Jaccard-Tanimoto coefficient using N-grams of different length, which was employed in Ferret system [10] or in a study of academic conference papers [1]. All these methods employ the same pre-processing and feature selection as introduced in Section 3.1, 3.2, and 3.3.

Fig. 4 presents the dependency of measure F_1 on threshold τ for VSM and RFM plagiarism detection methods. As you can see, both curves are quite wide, because only word matches are searched. There is no problem to determine the right threshold τ due to the flatness around the maximum of F_1. On the other hand, it reaches lower score because more unrelated documents are recognized as plagiarized. RFM slightly overcomes VSM because it computes an asymmetric measure taking into account a document is a subset of another one. Thus, it better evaluates such pairs of documents that have different number of features.

The following method is the one based on Jaccard-Tanimoto coefficient. Fig. 5 presents various dependency curves for single words, bigrams, trigrams, 4-grams, and 5-grams. All curves, as obvious, are narrower in comparison with VSM and RFM. Moreover, the longer N-gram is used the narrower the curve is. Jaccard-Tanimoto coefficient evaluates the pairs of related documents with a lower score. Therefore, the peak F_1 is reached for very low threshold τ. By virtue of narrow curves, peak values are obtained just for a short interval of τ.

Finally, Fig. 6 presents the dependency of measure F_1 on threshold τ for SVDPlag. In comparison to Jaccard-Tanimoto, the curves are slightly wider. Thus, it is easier to determine the right threshold. Although the curves are wider, SVDPlag achieves better F_1 score and overcomes the other methods for each N-gram length we used.

Table 2 summarizes peak F_1 achieved for a concrete threshold τ during the experiments. Moreover, we present measure HFM, SEP, and SH for all the methods using various N-gram lengths. As obvious from the table, SVDPlag overcomes the other methods. The best results yield SVDPlag for phrase match of four consecutive words, i.e. 4-gram. Jaccard-Tanimoto yields the best results for trigrams; however, it achieves only 90.82% for F_1 compared to 92.57% in case of SVDPlag. As you can see, SVDPlag has very similar results for trigrams and 4-grams as well. The same situation occurs in Jaccard-Tanimoto, where bigrams, trigrams, and 4-grams get similar results. From this observation, we can state that 4-grams are convenient not only for our SVDPlag method.

Now, let us have a look at HFM, SEP, and SH. The longer N-gram match is used the lower HFM and SEP is. It is obvious because less number of N-gram matches is found. As result, SH slightly increases because SEP does not decrease as quickly as HFM. This is the reason why we recommend using longer N-grams for plagiarism detection since they better separate documents and make fewer mistakes between two

Table 2. The best results achieved for F_1, HFM, SEP, and SH

Method	Threshold τ	F_1	HFM	SEP	SH
VSM	30%	84.97%	76.67%	66.01%	0.8610
RFM	37%	87.03%	85.12%	65.84%	0.7734
Jaccard (words)	16%	85.84%	56.07%	51.73%	0.9227
Jaccard (bigrams)	10%	90.56%	55.35%	53.33%	0.9635
Jaccard (trigrams)	8%	90.82%	50.00%	48.76%	0.9753
Jaccard (4-grams)	6%	90.53%	45.12%	44.34%	0.9827
Jaccard (5-grams)	4%	89.36%	40.25%	39.76%	0.9878
SVDPlag (words)	28%	87.31%	72.09%	60.12%	0.8339
SVDPlag (bigrams)	17%	91.36%	70.72%	56.28%	0.9231
SVDPlag (trigrams)	15%	92.48%	65.32%	61.93%	0.9480
SVDPlag (4-grams)	12%	92.57%	61.21%	59.16%	0.9665
SVDPlag (5-grams)	8%	91.03%	56.45%	55.08%	0.9756

unrelated documents. Thus, 4-grams are also a good choice for Jaccard-Tanimoto despite of the fact that the measure F_1 is slightly worse.

In our comparison, we regard VSM and RFM just as the baseline because they can compete neither with Jaccard-Tanimoto nor SVDPlag. Moreover, SVDPlag that employs only single words as features overcomes both VSM and RFM.

5 Conclusion

In this paper, we proposed a new plagiarism detection method based on SVD. It solves associations among phrases contained in the examined documents to infer the mutual similarity of all pairs of the documents. According to Lancaster [8], SVDPlag can be classified both as a Structural and Corpal method.

From our observation of existing techniques for plagiarism detection and the experiments we performed, it is evident that SVDPlag overcomes the other methods. SVDPlag achieves the best results for 4-grams at the threshold level τ of 12%. Under these circumstances measure F_1 achieves 92.57% on the experimental corpus. This corpus is composed of 950 documents about politics, which were obtained from the standard CTK corpus.

In view of the future we intend to enlarge our experimental corpus and add topics focused not only on politics. Further, we are going to examine our method in detail. The aim is to find the influence of text pre-processing on the quality of results. There are some possibilities to improve our method with an advanced word normalization technique using, for instance, the WordNet thesaurus. The further possibility rests in weighting mechanism used for phrase occurrence frequencies. In our method, we used a modification of the TF-IDF weighting. Another solution might be, for instance, entropy weighting.

Acknowledgments. This research was supported in part by National Research Programme II, project 2C06009 (COT-SEWing).

References

1. Bao, J., Malcolm, J.: Text Similarity in Academic Conference Papers. In: Proceedings of the 2nd International Plagiarism Conference. The Sage, Gateshead (2006)
2. Berry, M., Dumais, S., O'Brein, G.: Using Linear Algebra for Intelligent Information Retrieval. SIAM Review 37(4), 573–595 (1995)
3. Brin, S., Davis, J., Garcia-Molina, H.: Copy Detection Mechanisms for Digital Documents. In: Proceedings of the ACM SIGMOD Annual Conference, San Jose, Canada (1995)
4. Clough, P.: Plagiarism in natural and programming languages: An overview of current tools and technologies. In: Internal Report CS-00-05, Department of Computer Science, University of Sheffield (2000)
5. Clough, P.: Old and new challenges in automatic plagiarism detection. In: Plagiarism Advisory Service, vol. 10, Department of Computer Science, University of Sheffield (2003)
6. Hoad, T., Zobel, J.: Methods for Identifying Versioned and Plagiarised Documents. In: Proceedings of the 30th Annual International ACM SIGIR Conference on Research and Development in Information Retrieval, Amsterdam, The Netherlands, pp. 825–826 (2007) ISBN 978-1-59593-597-7

7. Kang, N., Gelbukh, A., Han, S.: PPChecker: Plagiarism Pattern Checker in Document Copy Detection. In: Sojka, P., Kopeček, I., Pala, K. (eds.) TSD 2006. LNCS (LNAI), vol. 4188, pp. 661–667. Springer, Heidelberg (2006)
8. Lancaster, T., Culwin, F.: Classification of Plagiarism Detection Engines. E-journal ITALICS 4(2) (2005) ISSN 1473-7507
9. Landauer, T., Foltz, P., Laham, D.: An Introduction to Latent Semantic Analysis. Discourse Processes 25, 259–284 (1998)
10. Lane, P., Lyon, C., Malcolm, J.: Demonstration of the Ferret Plagiarism Detector. In: Proceedings of the 2nd International Plagiarism Conference, Newcastle (2006)
11. Lyon, P., Malcolm, J., Dickerson, B.: Detecting short passages of similar text in large document. In: Proceedings of Conference on Empirical Methods and Natural Language Processing, Pittsburgh, USA, pp. 118–125 (2001)
12. Manning, C., Schutze, H.: Foundation of Statistical Natural Language Processing. MIT Press, Massachusetts Institute of Technology, Cambridge (1999)
13. Maurer, H., Kappe, F., Zaka, B.: Plagiarism – A Survey. Journal of Universal Computer Science 12(8), 1050–1084 (2006)
14. Runeson, P., Alexanderson, M., Nyholm, O.: Detection of Duplicate Defect Reports Using Natural Language Processing. In: Proceedings of the IEEE 29th International Conference on Software Engineering, pp. 499–510 (2007)
15. Salton, G., Buckley, C.: Term-Weighting Approaches in Automatic Retrieval. Journal of Information Processing and Management 24(5), 513–523 (1988)
16. Shivakumar, N., Garcia-Molina, H.: SCAM: A copy detection mechanism for digital documents. In: Proceedings of the 2nd International Conference in Theory and Practice of Digital Libraries, Austin, USA (1995)
17. Shivakumar, N., Garcia-Molina, H.: Building a Scalable and Accurate Copy Detection Mechanism. In: Proceedings of the 1st ACM DL International Conference, Besheda (1996)
18. Toman, M., Tesar, R., Jezek, K.: Influence of Word Normalization on Text Classification. In: Proceedings of the 1st International Conference on Multidisciplinary Information Sciences & Technologies, Merida, Spain, vol. 2, pp. 354–358 (2006) ISBN 84-611-3105-3

Networking Multiword Units

Matthieu Constant[1] and Patrick Watrin[2]

[1] Université Paris-Est, IGM & CNRS
[2] Université catholique de Louvain, Cental

Abstract. This paper details a network infrastructure for representing and sharing multiword units. It enables connecting local networks describing linguistic semi-fixed components in the form of local grammars.

1   Introduction

Multiword units (MWUs) have deep impact on Natural Language Processing (NLP) because their lexical, syntactic or semantic behaviour is often unpredictable from their individual words [14]. In the past twenty years, researches pointed out the lack of data resources of these expressions and attempted to build broad-coverage lexicons, such as [7, 5, 6].

Local grammars (LGs) [8] have been shown of great interest to represent multiword units and especially those involving some degree of lexical and syntactic variability [16, 13, 4]. Their easy integration in NLP applications is also very convenient like in [9, 15, 3]. They are in the form of Recursive Transition Networks (RTNs) that describe word sequences in a factorized and structured manner. They form linguistic components that can be reused by other local grammars. Nevertheless, in pratice, local grammars are often stored on isolated machines and their components cannot be directly used by others. Our objective is to connect these local networks in order to facilitate collaborative work, to share them freely with the community and use them in NLP applications.

This paper describes an infrastructure for networking LGs and details different implemented services facilitating importation, access and publishing. This network is formed of three layers: (1) a formal network (RTN) representing word sequences; (2) a linguistic network combining linguistic components in the form of local networks; (3) a collaborative network connecting linguistic components of different authors. First, we describe local grammars as linguistic recursive networks and illustrate it with MWUs[1]. Next, we detail a colaborative infrastructure connecting local grammars together and the different services implemented. We finally present the current state of the system, which contains local grammars compatible with platforms Unitex [10] and Outilex [2].

2   Local Grammars as Linguistic Recursive Networks

The MWUs we are dealing with are contiguous semi-fixed collocations[2] of two or more words, that can be considered as lexical units. There exist many varieties such as

---

[1] LGs can formalize other types of linguistic units (e.g. chunks or phrases). We decided to focus on MWUs because they are considered key elementary units in many modern applications.

[2] The continuity of the collocation is not strict because it might contain adjectival or adverbial inserts like in *ministre [français] de l'Agriculture* ([French] minister of Agriculture).

A. Ranta, B. Nordström (Eds.): GoTAL 2008, LNAI 5221, pp. 120–125, 2008.

nominal collocations (e.g. *red wine*), light verb constructions (*to have the impression*), compounds (e.g. *of course, close to*), auxiliary predicates (e.g. *continue to <verb>*), named entities such as time adverbials (*January 12, 2007*) or person names (*George W. Bush*), and so on. Some of them accept lexical variations. For instance, in the expression *(gold+silver+bronze) medal*, the modifier paradigm is limited to a small semantic class. When lexical variation is limited to classes of few elements, this type of expressions might be listed in dictionaries. Nevertheless, some expressions accept larger variations that are not suitable to be listed in the form of dictionaries. For instance, the expression *world champion* may vary in *(E+defending+reigning) (European+African+...) champion*. In that case, it is more convenient to describe the variation with a more compact formalism like local grammars.

A local grammar [8] is a recursive transition network [17]. It is composed of recursive automata which transition labels can be either lexical items or calls to other automata. There exist a main automaton which is the entry point of the network. These grammars theoretically recognize algebraic languages. Numerical expressions are a typical kind of expressions the description of which local grammars is best suited for. A significant interest is that linguistic components described by local grammars can be used by other local grammars by means of a simple reference. For instance, the compound locative preposition *around ten meters east of* is recognized by the simple local grammar given in figure 1. This grammar combines linguistic components defined

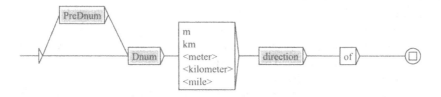

Fig. 1. Locative preposition

in other automata. `PredDnum` is an automaton that describes all possible numerical predeterminers such as *around, approximatively*. `Dnum` points out the automaton representing numbers. `Direction` is an automaton that recognizes different directions such as *west, north, southwest*. This grammar can be integrated to a larger grammar of compound prepositions by a simple reference to its axiom automaton.

3   A Collaborative Network Insfrastructure

3.1   A Decentralized Architecture

In theory, a LG can use components of other LGs. Nevertheless, in pratice, authors do not have an overview of available components and they cannot directly use them in their own grammars because they are stored on isolated machines. We propose a decentralized network infrastructure to handle this issue. It consists of a set of HTTP servers (see figure 2). These servers are only used as repositories of LGs, that are managed independently of each others by their respective owners. Reporitories are in the most part

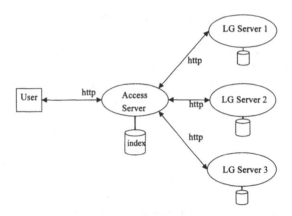

Fig. 2. Architecture

located on the own web site of the grammar authors. A user that needs to get access to the LGs, uses an access server including an index. The queries are processed with the use of this index that gathers all data information of the network. The decentralized architecture is then invisible for the user.

Each repository includes a collection of packages of local grammars. A package is an archive including a set of (recursive) automata, a license and documentations in XML and HTML. This documentation contains information such as authors, language, linguistic description, entry points (main automata), required preprocessing and linguistic resources (e.g. dictionaries). An automaton of a given package can call any automaton contained in a package referenced by the system. A system of automata referencing has been developped for that purpose.

The index contains precise information on repository packages, especially on the linguistic content. In its current state, it contains the following information: addresses of all repositories; packages (language, repository, path); terms used in the documentations and in the automata; dependency between the automata (which automata call which automata); entry points of the network (main automata).

3.2   Web Services

As any network containing data, this infrastucture requires some services to make it useful. In addition of a manager that helps publishing packages and importing grammars on local machines, we implemented a network browser and a search engine gathered in GraalWeb, a Java Applet[3].

The search engine has been implemented to help users to find grammars. The query is a set of terms occurring either in the automata or in the documentation. The computation of the query produces a list of automata sorted according to their relevancy to the query. This tool is based on standard Information Retrieval techniques [1] by using space vector models for representing queries, automata and documentations. We developped three techniques to search grammars according to their lexical content. The first

---

[3] http://igm.univ-mlv.fr/~mconstan/library

one consists in considering that the terms of an automaton are its lexical items. The similarity rate between an automaton and a query is the cosine between their respective vectors. The second technique (independent from the query) consists in computing a popularity rate for each automaton by using the PageRank technique used for Google search engine [11]: the more an automaton is called by popular automata, the more it is popular. We called this procedure *GrammarRank* as a tribute to its well-known inspiration. The third technique consists in combining lexicon and dependency. It is based on the fact that a term used in an automaton is also indirectly used by an automaton calling it. Our algorithm propagates terms in the inverted dependency graph of the library. Recent similar experiments have been conducted successfully for information retrieval on the web like in [12]. The final score of a retrieved automaton combines the three techniques the scores of which are assigned coefficients. When searching in the documentation content of the packages, we use a variant of the first technique. If a package is relevant, solely the main automata are listed.

The implemented browser provides global and detailed views of the network. Firstly, all available packages are listed and their documentation can be seen to get an overview of the linguistic content. The structure of the dependency between the automata of a package can be visualized in the form of a tree like in file system browsers. Each automaton can be explored in detail with a graph viewer implemented from Unitex source code. A call to another automaton is considered as an hypertext link that can be followed to be vizualized (by a simple mouse click). The browser is also used to follow the inverted dependency of the library, i.e. to get the list of automata that calls the current automaton, select one and vizualize it.

The manager tool especially provides a functionality that projects a local grammar of a package (including external components) on the filesytem of a local machine by keeping the structure of the network.

4   Current State

The networked library currently contains local grammars compatible with formats and resources of the Unitex and Outilex platforms. It includes 6 repositories and 9 packages. In total, 1,496 automata including 11 main automata, are referenced by the system. The network has 33,577 states and 77,978 transitions. For instance, we consider that the automaton in figure 1 has 7 states and 7 transitions. The dependency graph is composed of 5,258 edges. Two languages are represented: English and French. Several types of MWU grammars are referenced: sequences of determiners in French, e.g. *la plupart des dix* (most of the ten), named entities (location, organizations, persons, time) in French and English, sequences of verbs in French and English (*has continued to be afraid of eating*), locative prepositions in French (*ten meters west of*).

5   Conclusion and Future Work

The network infrastructure and services described in this paper aims at sharing local grammars of linguistic phenomena (especially, MWUs) in the NLP community. It has the specificity of being decentralized: authors have their grammars on their own web site. An indexer is in charge of centralizing all the information on an access server. Users can freely publish, access and import grammars from it in a transparent manner. This library is presently limited to Unitex grammars, but we intend to extend it to other formats. We also plan to provide a corpus that have been annotated by the application of all grammars in order to show their coverage. The size of the library is rather small but it is slowly growing. We hope that it will encourage NLP researcher to share their grammars trough the system and then help new significant advances in the domain.

References

[1] Baeza-Yates, R., Ribeiro-Neto, B.: Modern Information Retrieval. Addison-Wesley, Reading (1999)

[2] Blanc, O., Constant, M.: Outilex, a platform for Text Processing. In: Proc. of Coling-ACL on Interactive Presentation Sessions, Sydney, Australia, pp. 73–76 (2006)

[3] Blanc, O., Constant, M., Watrin, P.: Segmentation in super-chunks with a finite-state approach. In: Proc. of the Workshop on Finite State Methods for Natural Language Processing, Potsdam, Germany (2007)

[4] Català, D., Baptista, J.: Spanish Adverbial Frozen Expressions. In: Proc. of the Workshop on A Broader Perspective on Multiword Expressions, Prague, pp. 33–40 (2007)

[5] Copestake, A., Lambeau, F., Villavicencio, A., Bond, F., Baldwin, T., Sag, I.A., Flickinger, D.: Multiword expressions: linguistic precision and reusability. In: Proc. of the Third conference on Language Resources and Evaluation, Las Palmas, Canary Islands, pp. 1941–1947 (2002)

[6] Grégoire, N.: Design and Implementation of a Lexicon of Dutch Multiword Expressions. In: Proc. of the Workshop on A Broader Perspective on Multiword Expressions, Prague, Czech Republic, pp. 17–24 (2007)

[7] Gross, M.: Lexicon-Grammar and the Syntactic Analysis of French. In: Proc. of the 10th International Conference on Computational Linguistics, Stanford, California (1984)

[8] Gross, M.: The construction of local grammars. In: Roche, E., Schabes, Y. (eds.) Finite-State Language Processing, pp. 329–352. The MIT Press, Cambridge (1997)

[9] Nam, J., Choi, K.: A Local-Grammar-based Approach to Recognizing of Proper Names in Korean Texts. In: Zhou & Church (eds.). Proc. of the Workshop on Very Large Corpora. ACL/Tsing-hua University/Hong-Kong University of Science and Technology, pp. 273–288 (1997)

[10] Paumier, S.: The Unitex Manual (2006), http://igm.univ-mlv.fr/~unitex/

[11] Page, L., Brin, S., Motwani, R., Winograd, T.: The PageRank Citation Ranking: Bringing Order to the Web. Stanford Digital Technologies (1998)

[12] Qin, T., Liu, T.-Y., Zhang, X.-D., Chen, Z., MA, W.-Y.: A study of relevance propagation for web search. In: Proc. of The 28th Annual International ACM SIGIR Conference. ACM Press, New York (2005)

[13] Ranchhod, E., Carvalho, P., Mota, C., Barreiro, A.: Portuguese Large-scale Language Resources for NLP Applications. In: Proc. of Language Resources and Evaluation Conference, Lisbon, pp. 1755–1758 (2004)

[14] Sag, I.A., Baldwin, T., Bond, F., Copestake, A.A., Flickinger, D.: Multiword Expressions: A Pain in the Neck for NLP. In: Ivan, A. (ed.) Proc. of the Third International Conference on Computational Linguistics and Intelligent Text Processing, pp. 1–15. Springer, London (2002)

[15] Senellart, J., Plitt, M., Bailly, Ch., Cardoso, F.: Resource alignment and implicit transfer. Machine translation in the information age, MT Summit, pp. 317–323 (2001)

[16] Silberztein, M.: Finite-state description of the french determiner system. Journal of French Language Studies 13(2) (2003)

[17] Woods, W.A.: Transition network grammars for natural language analysis. Communications of the ACM 13(10) (1970)

Searching for Part of Speech Tags That Improve Parsing Models

Martín Ariel Domníguez[1] and Gabriel Infante-Lopez[1,2]

[1] Grupo de Procesamiento de Lenguaje Natural
Universidad Nacional de Córdoba - Argentina
{gabriel,mdoming}@famaf.unc.edu.ar
[2] Consejo Nacional de Investigaciones Científicas y Técnicas

Abstract. We introduce a technique for inducing a refinement of the set of part of speech tags related to verbs. We cluster verbs according to their syntactic behavior in a dependency structure setting. The set of clusters is automatically determined by means of a quality measure over the probabilistic automata that describe words in a bilexical grammar. Each of the resulting clusters defines a new part of speech tag. We try out the resulting tag set in a state-of-the art phrase structure parser and we show that the induced part of speech tags significantly improve the accuracy of the parser.

1 Introduction

A part-of-speech (POS) tag is a linguistic category of words that are characterized by their particular syntactic behaviors. These POS tags are usually defined within a syntactic theory and supervised algorithms for parsing use them as they are defined.

A given definition of POS tags may not be the best for supervised algorithms for parsing; words might be grouped differently in order to improve parsing performance. Our main research question is: Can we redefine the set of POS tags so that when a state-of-the-art parser is trained using the new set its performance improves? We answer this question by presenting an algorithm that induces sets of POS tags capable of improving state-of-the-art-parsing performance. We show that our POS tag sets improve parsing by means of encoding some additional linguistic information into the new set of tags, which is clearly useful for the parsing model.

We extract information from dependency trees based on Bilexical Grammars [1]. In Bilexical Grammars there are two automata for each word in the lexicon. These automata model, respectively, right and left dependents. We cluster words whose automata are "similar", and we treat each cluster as a new POS tag.

We design a procedure that implements this simple idea; a procedure that aims at finding the best possible POS tag set clustering words whose automata show similar behaviors. The procedure is defined as an optimization problem. As every in optimization problem, we define the quality measure it has to optimize, its search space, and strategy it should follow to find the optimal POS tag set among all possible tag sets.

A. Ranta, B. Nordström (Eds.): GoTAL 2008, LNAI 5221, pp. 126–137, 2008.

The *search space* also defines the type of information that will be codified into the POS tags. Different syntactic features are used to generate different search spaces and, consequently, different resulting POS tag sets. The *quality measure* for a tag set is computed by tagging a dependency tree-bank using the POS tag to be evaluated, inducing a bilexical grammar and evaluating the grammar's quality, so that the quality measure for POS tags is evaluated using quality measures for bilexical grammars. Finally, the *strategy* for traversing the search space is implemented using Genetic Algorithms.

The set of new POS tags can be used to retag a phrase structure corpus. In our case, we retag the Penn Treebank (PTB) [2] to test our new sets of POS tags in a phrase structure setting. POS tag sets are evaluated using Collins parser [3] by means of Bikel's implementation [4]. We add our new POS tags to the training material, we re-train the parser and we evaluate the parser performance, showing a significant improvement on parsing results.

The rest of the paper is organized as follows. Section 2 provides details on how to compute the quality measure, Section 3 explains how to build and traverse the search space, Section 4 explain how the new tag sets are used for training a phrase structure parser and it also reports the performance for the different tag sets we built. Section 5 gives an overview of different approaches to the same problem from the literature and it hints some possible future directions. Finally, Section 6 concludes the paper.

2   Quality Measure for Tag Sets

This section introduces the quality measure q that we used for evaluating and optimizing POS tag sets. This measure is defined using a further quality measure q' for a particular flavor of bilexical grammars. Briefly speaking, the quality q of a tag set C is computed by means of retagging a dependency tree-bank with C, inducing a bilexical grammar B from it, and computing a quality function q' on B.

This section introduces our flavor of bilexical grammars, it shows how bilexical grammars are induced from dependency tree-banks and how the measure q is defined in terms of q'. It also discusses why we think q is a good measure of the quality of a tag set C.

2.1   Bilexical Grammars

Bilexical grammars are a formalism in which lexical items, such as verbs and their arguments, can have idiosyncratic selective influences on each other. Formally, our flavor of a *bilexical grammar* B is a 3-tuple $(C, \{r_c\}_{w \in C}, \{l_c\}_{c \in C},)$ where:

- C is a set of POS tags, which contains a distinguished symbol ROOT.
- For each tag $c \in C$, l_c and r_c are a pair of probabilistic automata with start symbols S_{l_c} and S_{r_c} respectively. Each automaton accepts some regular subset of C^*.

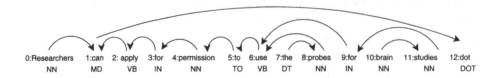

Fig. 1. Tree extracted from the PTB, file `wsj_0297.mrg` and transformed to a dependency tree

In our definition there are two automata per POS tag instead of two automata per word, as in the original definition. In the rest of the paper we refer to our flavor of bilexical grammars directly as bilexical grammars.

A *dependency tree* is a tree whose nodes (internal and external) are labeled with tags from C; the root is labeled with the symbol ROOT. The children ('dependents') of a node are ordered in a sequence with respect to each other and the node itself, so that each node may have both *left children* that precede it and *right children* that follow it. A dependency tree T is *grammatical* if, for every tag token c that appears in the tree, l_c accepts the (possibly empty) sequence of c's left children (from right to left), and r_c accepts the sequence of c's right children (from left to right).

2.2 Induction of Bilexical Grammars

Bilexical grammars can be induced from a dependency tree-bank by inducing two automata for each tag in C. Once the tag set C is defined, the induction of a bilexical grammar is straightforward. The induction of Bilexical Grammars is carried out in a supervised fashion. Our training material comes from Sections 02–21 of the PTB. Trees are first transformed to dependency trees using Collins rules as implemented by Bikel's parser. All words in the PTB are removed and original POS tags are replaced by tags in a given tag set C. This means that for each candidate POS tag set C the training material has to be rewritten.

Once the training material reflects the tag set C, two bags T_L^c and T_R^c of *strings* for each tag c in C are extracted. An example illustrates the extraction procedure better: Figure 1 shows a dependency tree and Table 1 shows some of the bags of left and right dependents

Table 1. Bags of left and right dependents extracted from dependency tree in Figure 1. Left dependents are to be read from right to left. All displayed sets are singletons.

Word #	i	T_L^i	T_R^i
0	NN	{NN}	{NN}
1	MD	{MD NN}	{MD VB DOTSYB}
2	VB	{VB}	{VB IN}
3	IN	{IN}	{IN NN}
4	NN	{NN}	{NN TO}

that are extracted. Note that in the example, the tag set C is the PTB tag set, and all sets of strings displayed in the table are strings extracted from the example tree only. In the actual setting, T_L^c and T_R^c are built joining strings coming from all trees in the tree-bank.

Once T_L^c and T_R^c are extracted, two probabilistic automata A_L^c and A_R^c are built. For this purpose, we use the *minimum discrimination information* (MDI) [5] algorithm. The MDI algorithm receives as arguments a bag of strings and it outputs a probabilistic deterministic automata that accepts and generalizes over the input bag of strings. The algorithm has a unique parameter `alpha`, which we optimize during the grammar optimization phase as explained in Section 3. Since a bilexical grammar is defined through its automata, once all automata A_L^c and A_R^c, c in C are induced, the bilexical grammar associated to the tag set C is completely defined.

2.3 Quality Measure for Grammars

The measure q' for bilexical grammars is based on two quality measures for probabilistic automata [6]. The first, called *test sample perplexity* (PP), is the *per symbol log-likelihood* of strings belonging to a test sample according to the distribution defined by the automaton. The minimal perplexity $PP = 1$ is reached when the next symbol is always predicted with probability 1, while $PP = |\Sigma|$ corresponds to uniformly guessing from an alphabet Σ of size $|\Sigma|$. The second measure is given by the number of *missed samples* (MS). A missed sample is a string in the test sample that the automaton fails to accept. One of such instance suffices to have PP undefined. Since an undefined value of PP only witnesses the presence of at least one MS we count the number of MS separately, and compute PP without considering MS. The test sample that is used to compute PP and MS comes from all trees in sections 00-01 of the PTB. These trees are transformed to dependency trees and they reflect tag sets C as the training material.

We can now define the measure q' for bilexical grammars. q' has two parts, one considering all automata related to right-hand side dependents, and one considering left-hand side. To simplify our exposition, we give the component referring to the right-hand side; the other component is obtained by replacing R in the superscripts with L.

Let $C = \{c_1, \ldots, c_n\}$ be a candidate tag set. Let $A_R^{c_i}$, $i = 1, \ldots, n$ be the automata induced as described previously. Let $PP_R^{c_i}$ and $MS_R^{c_i}$ be the values of PP and MS respectively for the automaton $A_R^{c_i}$. We combine all values of PP_i and MS_i to obtain a quality value for the whole grammar.

PP and MS values can not simply be summed up as the importance of an automaton is proportional to the number of times it is used in parsing, as a consequence we combine the different values of PP and MS using weights. Define $p_R^{c_i} = |T_R^{c_i}|/|T_R|$, where $i = 1, \ldots, n$; where T_R is union of all $T_R^{c_i}$; we view $p_R^{c_i}$ as the probability of using the automata $A_R^{c_i}$. Let $E[MS_C^R]$ and $E[PP_C^R]$ be the *expected value of* MS *and* PP *for a right automata*, defined as $E[MS_C^R] = \sum_{i=1}^n p_R^{c_i} MS_R^{c_i}$, and $E[PP_C^R] = \sum_{i=1}^n p_R^{c_i} PP_R^{c_i}$, respectively. Let $E[MS_C^L]$ and $E[PP_C^L]$ be the corresponding values for the left sides. The expected values depend on a tag set, hence the subscript C.

The quality measure q' for a bilexical grammar B is defined using $E[\mathrm{PP}_C^R]$, $E[\mathrm{MS}_C^R]$, $E[\mathrm{PP}_C^L]$ and $E[\mathrm{MS}_C^L]$. Formally, the function q'_{C_0} that we minimize for grammars is

$$q'_{C_0}(B) = \begin{cases} \|X\| + k \text{ if } E[\mathrm{PP}_C^R] > E[\mathrm{PP}_{C_0}^R] \\ \|X\| + k \text{ if } E[\mathrm{MS}_C^R] > E[\mathrm{MS}_{C_0}^R] \\ \|X\| + k \text{ if } E[\mathrm{PP}_C^L] > E[\mathrm{PP}_{C_0}^L] \\ \|X\| + k \text{ if } E[\mathrm{MS}_C^L] > E[\mathrm{MS}_{C_0}^L] \\ \|X\| \qquad \text{otherwise,} \end{cases}$$

where

$$X = (E[\mathrm{PP}_C^R], E[\mathrm{MS}_C^R], E[\mathrm{PP}_C^L], E[\mathrm{MS}_C^L]),$$

$$\|(x_1, x_2, \ldots, x_n)\| = \sqrt{x_1^2 + x_2^2 + \ldots + x_n^2},$$

k is a constant used to penalize configurations that we know are not part of the set of possible solutions, and C_0 is the set of POS tags defined by the PTB. Finally, the function $q(C)$ for a given candidate POS tag C is defined as $q'(B)$ where B is the bilexical grammar that can be induced using C as the tag set. Note that, q' and q are essentially the same function, they only differ on the type of the argument they take. Given that q uses C_0 as a referent, we can see q as a function that penalizes POS tag sets whose expected values of PP and MS are worse than those values obtained by the PTB tag set. Better values of MS and PP for a grammar mean that its automata capture better the regular language of dependents by producing most strings in the automata target languages with fewer levels of perplexity.

Another point of view on q comes from formal language theory: for a given tag c, the automata A_R^c and A_L^c model the probabilistic regular language of right and left dependents respectively. The idea behind q' is that these probabilistic languages might be better described as the disjoint union of several smaller probabilistic regular languages. The two measures (PP and MS) in which q is based, indirectly measure the diversity of languages that are associated to each POS tag. Such analysis was first introduce in [6]. As we show in the next section, the optimization tries to detect which are these several languages and to define a new POS tag for each of them.

3 Building and Traversing the Search Space

The search space is built by means of 2 elements: a subset V of PTB POS tags and a function f called *feature*. V is the portion of the PTB tag set that we want to refine. f is a function that takes two arguments, a dependency tree t and a number i. The number i refers to the i-th node, from left to right, in the dependency tree t. Since words in the yield of t are in direct correspondence to its nodes, the index i also corresponds to the i-th word in the yield of t. A feature returns some information around the i-th node in the tree; they are meant to characterize the dependents a verb might take. Figure 2 lists a few features and it shows examples of features applied to the tree in Figure 2.

> **VerbAllDepth:** the number of nodes labeled with $\{\texttt{VB},\texttt{VBD},\texttt{VBN},\texttt{VBZ},\texttt{MD},\texttt{TO}\}$ in the path that goes from node i to the ROOT node. $f(t,6) = 3$.
> **VerbDepth:** the number of nodes labeled with $\{\texttt{VB},\texttt{VBD},\texttt{VBN},\texttt{VBZ},\texttt{MD}\}$ in the path that goes from node i to the ROOT node. $f(t,6) = 2$.
> **VerbVBDepth:** the number of nodes labeled with $\{\texttt{VB},\texttt{VBD},\texttt{VBN},\texttt{VBZ}\}$ in the path that goes from node i to the ROOT node. $f(t,6) = 1$.
> **NumSib:** the number of sibling. $f(t,2) = 1$.
> **NumDep:** the number of dependents. $f(t,6) = 2$.
> **NumChanges:** the number of times the label changes in consecutive nodes in the path that goes from node i to the ROOT node. $f(t,10) = 7$.
> **Depth:** The length of the path that goes from node i to the ROOT node. $f(t,6) = 5$.
> **GFather:** The POS tag of the grand-father of node i. $f(t,6) = NN$.
> **FstRightDep:** The POS tag of first dependent to the right of node i. $f(t,6) = NONE$.

Fig. 2. Description and examples of some of the features we used. Examples are obtained using t as the tree in Figure 1.

Given f and V, the search space is built using a 2-step procedure. The first step defines an *initial tag* set Ci while the second uses Ci to define the family of all possible candidate tag sets in the search space. The initial tag set is built by applying $f(t,i)$ to all trees t in the tree-bank, and for their words i that have their original tags in the PTB tag set. The result of applying f to one tree t and to one word w of t whose tag belongs to V is added to Ci. Suppose that the tree in Figure 1 is processed for building Ci with feature *father*, and $V = \{VB\}$; then tags VB-MD and VB-TO are added to Ci. Formally, Ci is defined as $(O - V) \cup Img(f)$ where O is the set of PTB POS and $Img(f)$ is the image of f.

If original tags are replaced by the results of f, the training material can be completely retagged. In the previous example, VB-MD and VB-TO replace VB in position 2 and 6 respectively.

The second step builds the family of possible candidate tag set. The search space for feature f and tag set V is defined as all possible tags sets that are the product of merging arbitrary tags $c_1, \ldots, c_k, c_i$ in Ci. Building a tag set C by merging tags $c_1, \ldots, c_k$ means that a new tag symbol t is introduced and that C is defined as $Ci - \{c_1, \ldots, c_k\} \cup t$. Merging tags also means that the training material has to be rewritten; this is done by replacing tags $c_1, \ldots c_k$ by tag t.

Since the family of possible tag sets is constructed by merging subsets of the initial tag set, the size of the search space is exponential. The traversing strategy for inspecting the search space is based on Genetic Algorithms. Genetic Algorithms need for their implementation (1) A definition of individuals: our individuals codify both a value of `alpha` to be used for building the automata and candidate tag set of the training material. (2) A fitness function defined over individuals: the quality measure q' we defined in Section 2.3. (3) A strategy for evolution: we apply two different operations to genes, namely crossover and mutation; crossover gets 0.95 probability of being applied,

Table 2. A subset of a new POS tag set which shows entries corresponding to the new tags related to VB calculated with feature Depth

new POS	Feature Value	new POS	Feature Value	new POS	Feature Value
NEWTAG_1	6	NEWTAG_4	4	NEWTAG_7	11
NEWTAG_2	2	NEWTAG_5	5	NEWTAG_8	7,12
NEWTAG_3	8	NEWTAG_6	10	NEWTAG_9	17,18,20,15,24
NEWTAG_10	1,16,13,9	NEWTAG_11	0,3,14		

while mutation gets 0.05. We select individuals using the *roulette wheel strategy* [7]. Finally, at each generation the population consists of 50 individuals; we let the population evolve for 100 generations. The outcome of our optimization method is a set of new tags. The algorithm also outputs a table that assigns a new tag to each possible outcome of the feature used during the optimization procedure . This table, together with the feature f, can be used for retagging the training material with the new set of POS tags. For example, using Table 2 together with feature Depth it is possible to calculate the new tag for word number 4 of Figure 3 (a). Note that feature Depth(4) returns 1 and that Table 2 states that for words with value 1 for this feature should receive NEWTAG_10. Words that are originally not tagged with VB keep their old tags.

As such, the algorithm for inducing our POS tag sets is a mixture between algorithms for inducing automata and genetic algorithms. Genetic algorithms were chosen because they provide a direct map from our problem to their representation. Genetic algorithms are used to search for the best way to merge POS tags from the initial tagging. Measure PP was chosen because it is the standard measure to evaluate automata (c.f., [5]). Before trying genetic algorithms we tried out standard clustering algorithms, but the failure to capture the idea behind the q measure.

4   Parsing with New Sets of Tags

All tags computed in the previous section encode information regarding some syntactic feature. Even though these features are computed using dependency trees, the information codified in the new tags help phrase structure parsers to improve their performance. Our tag sets are introduced in the training material of a supervised parsing model.

4.1   Rewriting the Training Material

The parser is trained in a modified version of Sections 02–21 of the PTB. All trees in those sections are modified to reflect the new set of POS tags: Our tags are introduced as new nodes above the original POS tags, as depicted in Figure 3 (b), by adding a new node with the new tag (in the example, NEWTAG_10) above the original node (VB). The new tag comes from the retagging schema for dependency trees returned by our optimization algorithm as explained in the previous section.

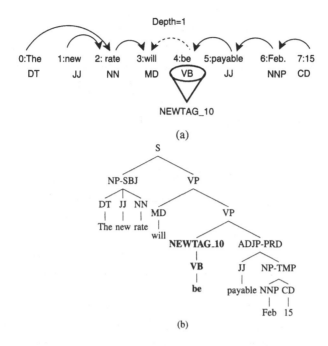

Fig. 3. (a) Tag `NEWTAG_10` is assigned to word number 4. (b) The new tag is introduced in the phrase structure above the original tag.

Note that instead of replacing the original POS tags with the new POS tags, we choose to add an extra-node above the original POS tag. The reason for the extra-node is given by the way the parser deals with POS tagging: The parser might guess the POS tags or they can be given with the sentence. Formally, the parser can be fed either with a sequence of pairs $\langle (w_1, c_1), \ldots, (w_k, c_k) \rangle$, w_i and c_i being words and tags respectively or with a sequence of words $\langle w_1, \ldots, w_k \rangle$.

If extra-nodes are not used in the training material, we can not resort to the first type of sequences because syntactic trees are needed to obtain the correct sequence of POS tags. In other words, in order to tag the sentence with our new POS tag set, we need to know the syntactic tree that yields the sentence, which is not available during testing. The extra-nodes are used to reflect a new set of POS tags. Adding one extra-node above each original POS tag allows reflecting one of our POS tag sets, while using two extra-nodes we can reflect two of our sets of new POS tags.

Still, without using extra-nodes, the second type of sequences can be used. We tried out replacing old tags with our new tags and we let the parser guess the correct new POS tags. Unfortunately, the performance of such approach drops dramatically. We believe that this is due to the fact that the tagger that is being used inside the parser is incapable of recovering our tags. We speculate that, since new POS tags encode syntactic information, they can not be recovered with a POS tagger; however, this point requires further research.

It is important to note that the generative model that results from training in our own version of the training material does not suffer from the extra nodes. In order to empirically try this out, we carried out a dummy experiment consisting of adding an extra node CLUSTER above the tag VB in the training material. That is, we just add an extra node that does not codify extra information. The resulting model reports the same result as the original model. This experiment shows that the generative model that is built from the material containing the extra node behaves exactly as the model without extra nodes.

4.2 Modifying the Parser's Training Algorithm

The parser's training algorithm was modified to make it aware of the new set of POS tags. During the training phase, Bikel's parser transforms phrase structure trees into dependency trees. During this process, the parser uses a function to determine the head symbol of each constituent. The aforementioned function uses a *head-definition table* that provides all the necessary information for finding heads in context-free grammar rules. Since entries in this table are non-terminal symbols, the table should be aware of the new set of extra-nodes that were introduced in the training material.

There are two different ways to make the head finding function aware of the new set of non-terminals: The first approach adds the new set of labels to the head-definition table. This approach is straightforward but it presents some problems when features are applied to redefine more than one syntactic category. The second approach changes the algorithm that computes heads using the head-definition table so that the new POS are completely ignored. The second approach is the one we use in our experiments.

4.3 Experimental Results

The results reported in this sections were performed on sentences in Section 23 of the PTB. Since the parser returns trees with extra-nodes, they are deleted *before* evaluation. Standard measures of labeled precision and labeled recall are reported.

We tested 17 different features applied to different sets of tags related to verbs. None of our experiments showed significant decrease in parsing performance, but many showed significant increases. Table 3 reports 11 experimental results, 10 of them show improvements. Features were selected without any optimization method. We selected features by hand using intuitions provided in [8] and by selecting new features that take into consideration the syntactic structure above a tree node. Such information was shown to be useful in [9] and it is not being modeled by Collins' model.

Each row displays the feature that was used (see Table 2 for explanation), the tag set that was redefined, the results on labeled precision, labeled recall and the significance level *pval* of the result; the latter was computed against baseline results. The baseline row reports the performance of Bikel implementation for Collins model.

The table is divided in three. The upper part shows statically significant results. The middle part provides an example of a feature that does decrease parser performance but whose decrease is not statistically significant. The bottom part reports results where features are combined with statistically significant improvements. In all cases, we consider a result statistically significant if its significance level *pval* is below 0.05. Performance is measured using `evalb` script while significance is measured using Bikel's *Randomized Parsing Evaluation Comparator* script.

Table 3. Experiments result. The middle part shows a feature whose performance results decreases. The bottom part shows features combinations.

Num.	Feature	Tags	L. R.	L. P.	pval R.	pval P.	F_1
	Baseline		88,53	88,63			0,8858
(1)	Depth	VB,MD	88,64	88,78	0,067	0,020	0,8871
(2)	Depth	VBN,VB,MD	88,65	88,86	0,120	0,004	0,8875
(3)	gFather	VB,MD	88,69	88,80	0,047	0,044	0,8874
(4)	gFather	VBN,VB,MD	88,64	88,80	0,160	0,047	0,8872
(5)	NumChanges	VB,MD	88,69	88,80	0,030	0,020	0,8874
(6)	NumChanges	VBN,VB,MD	88,62	88,81	0,200	0,030	0,8871
(7)	VerbAllDepth	VBN,VB,MD	88,67	88,79	0,047	0,024	0,8873
(8)	VerbDepth	VBN,VB,MD	88,67	88,78	0,069	0,051	0,8872
(9)	**VerbVBDepth**	**VBN,VB,MD**	**88,70**	**88,83**	**0,017**	**0,008**	**0,8876**
(10)	NumSib	VBN, VB,MD	88,66	88,77	0,079	0,048	0,8871
(11)	FstRightDep	VB	88,52	88,57	0,439	0,260	0,8854
(2)-(9)	Depth-VerbVBDepth	VBN,VB,MD-VBN,VB,MD	88,68	88,86	0,081	0,010	0,8876
(2)-(4)	Depth-gFather	VBN,VB,MD-VBN,VB,MD	88,62	88,82	0,210	0,020	0,8872

From Table 3, it can be seen that the combination of features (2) and (4) does not necessarily improve the results obtained by each of the features separately. For this particular example, the parser loses both performance and significance. We think that the reason for the decrease lies in the fact that the parser suffers the extra number of rules that it is has to handle. Recall from the previous section that two extra-nodes are added for every possible combination of new POS tags. Combination of features are not intended to obtain the best performance, but to investigate the impact of the combination. We tried also to combine two features by using their Cartesian product in the GA search space. In this way, we could rewrite the training material by using only one extra-node which combines both features. However, the resulting number of new tags obtained was too large and the parsing performance decreased significantly.

Our experimental results show that even though our approach hardly increases the performance figures for Bikel's parser, improvements are significant. We think that this is due to the syntactic information codified in the new set of extra-nodes. In some cases, e.g., when gFather feature is used, non-local information is stored in these extra-nodes. The experimental results show that not only the parser is able to recover the extra-nodes but it is also capable of taking advantage of the information stored in these nodes. Our approach minimally modifies the learning algorithm; we can state that the underlying parsing model has been left intact. Our approach mainly modifies the training material trying to incorporate information that is present there but which is not currently used by the parser.

5   Related and Future Work

Two relatively recent approaches studied the use of automatic split of non-terminals to improve parsing performance. In [10] the authors induce a parsing model by using a generative process which starts with a standard PCFG and splits each non-terminal in a fixed number of categories. The resulting model is a generative unlexicalized grammar named PCFG-LA. Using this parser they obtained a F_1 measure comparable to state of the art unlexicalized parsers. Similarly, in [11] the authors induce a PCFG grammar using an automatic split and merge of non-terminal symbols to maximize the likelihood of training treebank. The hierarchical split and merge used also captures linguistic phenomena that used to be added manually in previous works. Furthermore, they obtain a lexicalized parser model with a performance comparable to the parser in [12], though the grammar induced is significantly smaller. In contrast, our approach uses an automatic unlexicalized split only for pre-terminal symbols, and we use the new POS set to rewrite the training material for a given parser to improve its performance.

Rewriting the training material is an important aspect of our paper that has been studied in the literature. For example, [13] present a technique that induces better performing PCFGs. They split and factorize *non-terminals* that have been detected as structural zeros in a given training material. Our approach differs from theirs in that we split only *pre-terminal* and that our splitting is based on syntactic behavior.

Klein and Manning [14] split POS tags related to verbs in order to detect constituents. They did this in the context of induction of rules for grammars. All categories used, such as transitive, intransitive, etc., were set in advance. In [15] the authors use a fixed number of categories that are based on universal language rules to build an unsupervised POS tagger. In contrast to the latter two approaches, our approach induces all categories automatically and, moreover, the resulting categories are tested in phrase structure-grammars, providing a better way to asses the quality of the resulting tags.

Our tags were tested by means of one particular parsing model. Clearly, the set of experiments we present here can be run using other parsing models. We think that such experiments can help understanding how different models take advantage of the information that is coded in our non-terminals. Since our tags are built using dependency trees, we believe that they can better help parsers that do not rely so heavily on dependencies (e.g., [12,16]) as Collins model. During our experiments we could not directly replace old POS tags with our new tags because the parser's built in tagger did not handle our tags correctly. This puts forward questions that require further research, such as: can we build POS taggers that are able to recover complex tags that encode deep syntactic information?, or, more generally, which information can be coded in tags so that it can be recovered using taggers? Some answers to this question have been given in the literature [17].

6   Conclusions

We introduced an algorithm that induces sets of POS tags. These tag sets are the result of clustering words with similar syntactic behavior. Word behaviors were characterized by means of probabilistic regular automata in a dependency syntax setting. We showed that the resulting tags encode syntactic information that was used by an state-of-the-art parser to significantly improve its performance.

References

1. Eisner, J.: Bilexical grammars and a cubictime probabilistic parser. In: Proceedings of IWPT 2004 (1994)
2. Marcus, M., Santorini, B.: Building a large annotated corpus of English: The Penn treebank. Computational Linguistics 19, 313–330 (1993)
3. Collins, M.: Three generative, lexicalized models for statistical parsing. In: ACL 1997 (1997)
4. Bikel, D.: On the Parameter Space of Generative Lexicalized Statistical Parsing Models. PhD thesis, University of Pennsylvania (2004)
5. Thollard, F., Dupont, P., de la Higuera, C.: Probabilistic DFA inference using Kullback-Leibler divergence and minimality. In: Proc. ICML, Stanford (2000)
6. Infante-Lopez, G., de Rijke, M.: Alternative approaches for generating bodies of grammar rules. In: Proc. 42nd ACL (2004)
7. Gen, M., Cheng, R.: Genetic Algorithms and Engineering Design. John Wiley, Chichester (1997)
8. Infante-Lopez, G.: Two-Level Probabilistic Grammars for Natural Language Parsing. PhD thesis, Universiteit van Amsterdam (2005)
9. Klein, D., Manning, C.: Accurate unlexicalized parsing. In: Proc. 41st ACL (2003)
10. Matsuzaki, T., M.Y.: Probabilistic cfg with latent annotations. In: ACL (2005)
11. Petrov, S., Barrett, L., Klein, D.: Learning accurate, compact, and interpretable tree annotation. In: ACL (2006)
12. Charniak, E.: A maximum-entropy-inspired parser. In: NAACL 2000 (2000)
13. Mohri, M., Roark, B.: Probabilistic context-free grammar induction based on structural zeros. In: HLT-NAACL 2006 (2006)
14. Klein, D., Manning, C.: Distributional phrase structure induction. In: CoNLL 2001 (2001)
15. Schone, P., Jurafsky, D.: Language-independent induction of part of speech class labels using only language universals. In: IJCAI 2001 (2001)
16. Henderson, J., Titor, I.: Data-defined kernels for parse reranking derived from probabilistic models. In: ACL (2005)
17. Osborne, M.: Shallow parsing as part-of-speech tagging. In: Conll. (2000)

A POS-Based Word Prediction System for the Persian Language

Masood Ghayoomi[1] and Ehsan Daroodi[2]

[1] Nancy 2 University, Nancy, France
masood29@gmail.com
[2] Iran National Science Foundation, Tehran, Iran
darrudi@insf.org

Abstract. Word prediction is the problem of guessing the words which are likely to follow in a given text segment by displaying a list of the most probable words that could appear in that position. In this research, we designed and implemented three word predictors for Persian. Our baseline is a statistical-based system which uses language models. The first system uses word statistics; in the second one we use the main syntactic categories of a Persian POS tagged corpus; and the last one uses the main syntactic categories along with their morphological, syntactic and semantic subcategories. Using KeyStroke Saving (KSS) as the most important metrics to evaluate systems' performance, the primary word-based statistical system achieved 37% KSS, and the second system that used only the main syntactic categories with word-statistics achieved 38.95% KSS. Our last system which used all of the available information to the words get the best result by 42.45% KSS.

Keywords: word prediction, statistical language modeling, POS tagging.

1 Introduction

A word prediction system facilitates the typing of text for users with physical or cognitive disabilities. As the user enters each letter of the word, the system displays a list of most likely completions of the partially typed word. As the user continues typing more letters, the system updates the suggestion list accordingly. If the required word is in the list, the user can select it with a single keystroke. Then, the system tries to predict the next word. It displays a list of suggestions to the user, who can select the next intended word if it appears in the list. Otherwise, the user can enter the first letter of the next word to restrict the suggestions. The process continues until the completion of the text.

For someone with physical disabilities, each keystroke is an effort; as a result, the prediction system saves the user's energy by reducing his or her physical effort. Additionally, the system assists the user in the composition of the well-formed text qualitatively and quantitatively (Fazly, 2002). Moreover, the system helps to increase the user's concentration (Klund and Novak, 2001).

Traditionally, word predictors have been built based on statistical language modeling (SLM; Gustavii and Pederssen, 2003). SLM could be merely based on the

A. Ranta, B. Nordström (Eds.): GoTAL 2008, LNAI 5221, pp. 138–147, 2008.

probability of a sequence of n given words (n-gram), or a combination of the sequence of words themselves taking advantage of the Part-of-Speech (POS) tags of the words. Using such knowledge of the language makes predictions more appropriate. A number of word prediction systems are available today for languages such as English and Swedish that use the linguistic knowledge of these languages.

This paper discusses the design and implementation of a word prediction SLM based system which uses the POS tags for Persian text.

2 Related Work

Early prediction systems that were developed in the 1980s were used as writing assistance systems for people with learning difficulties. Those early systems mainly suggested the high frequency words that matched the partially typed word and ignored the entire previous context (Swiffin et al, 1985) such as SoothSayer, and PAL (Booth et al, 1990) for English. PAL has been shown to save over 50% of keystrokes. Systems like Profet (Carlberger et al, 1997a; Carlberger et al, 1997b) for Swedish, and WordQ (Nantais et al, 2001; Shein et al, 2001) for English are among the examples that use word unigram and bigram sequences. Profet has saved keystrokes by 26.1% (Carlberger, 1997). Ghayoomi (2004) reports the first attempt to develop a word prediction system for Persian. His system simply used the statistical knowledge of uni-, bi- and trigram word models in algorithms. It is further reported that this system saves keystrokes by 57.57% (Ghayoomi and Assi, 2005). The best result that their system has achieved experimentally is 65.46% KSS after adaptation of the system to the user's writing style (Ghayoomi, 2006).

Using solely statistical word knowledge for prediction often results in the suggestion of inappropriate words syntactically. In contrast, by using the POS tags of a language in prediction algorithms, we can filter the inappropriate words in the predictions. Systems such as Syntax PAL (Morris et al, 1992) for English, Prophet (Carlberger, 1997) for Swedish are among the examples which have used syntactic knowledge of the language in predictions. Syntax PAL has decreased the problems of using PAL and has made it possible for the users to write longer and more complicated sentences (Wood, 1996). Prophet saved 33% keystrokes (Carlberger, 1997) compared to the earlier version, Profet.

This paper discusses the design and implementation of a word predictor for Persian using the bi, tri-, and quadrogram word statistics, and the bi-, tri-, and quadrogram POS tag statistics of the language. The paper also compares a system that solely uses word statistics with the designed systems that use word statistics as well as POS tags.

3 Language Models

3.1 *N*-Gram Word Modeling

The task of predicting the next word can be stated as attempting to estimate the probability function P:

$$P(W_n|W_1,\ldots, W_{n-1})$$

In such a stochastic problem, we use the previous word(s), the history, to predict the next word. To give reasonable prediction to the words which appear together, we try to use the Markov assumption that only the last few words affect the next word (Fazly, 2002). So if we construct a model where all histories restrict the word that would appear in the next position, we will then have an $(n-1)^{th}$ order Markov model or an n-gram word model (Manning and Schütze, 1999; Jurafsky and Martin, 2000).

3.2 Knowledge Modeling

The systems that merely use statistical modeling for prediction often present words that are syntactically, semantically or pragmatically inappropriate (Rosenfeld, 1994; McCoy and Demasco, 1995). Syntactic prediction is a method that tries to present words that are appropriate syntactically in a particular position within the sentence. This means that knowledge from the syntactic structure of the language is used. In syntactic prediction, POS tags of all the words in a corpus are identified and the system uses this knowledge for making predictions (Fazly, 2002; Woods, 1996). Statistical syntax and rule-based grammars are two general syntactic prediction methods.

3.2.1 Statistical Syntax

This approach uses the sequence of syntactic categories and POS tags for predictions. The appearance of a word in this method is based upon the correct usage of syntactic categories. In other words, the Markov assumption about n-gram word tags is used. Fazly (2002) has discussed three methods that can be used to obtain statistical knowledge about the syntax: (a) POS tags only, (b) previous word and two previous POS tags, and (c) linear combination.

In the system presented here, we have used the three previous words as well as their syntactic knowledge in order to predict the following word.

4 Some Properties of Persian

Persian is a member of the Indo-European language family and has many features in common with them in terms of morphology, syntax, phonology, and lexicon.

Although Persian uses a modified version of the Arabic alphabet, it is worth noting that Arabic is from the Semitic family of languages and the two languages differ from one another in many respects. One important point which is related to the topic of the present research is that there are a number of graphemes which represent the same spoken sound. The alphabet used in Persian is more appropriate for the Arabic sound system. For instance, the letters 'ز', 'ذ', 'ض' and 'ظ' are four letters of the alphabet in both Persian and Arabic. However, all of these letters are pronounced the same way in Persian, namely /z/, while, they are each pronounced differently in Arabic. Persian writing system is right to left, the same as Arabic, but quite distinct from the European languages that have a left to right writing system.

Persian letters have joined or non-joined forms; i.e., based on the position that the letters appear within a word, they have different forms. The vocabulary of Persian has been greatly influenced by Arabic and to some extent by French in which a great number of words are borrowed from these two languages.

Space is a word boundary for Persian words. There is also pseudo-space behaving as a morpheme boundary within a word.

Persian is a null-subject language with SOV word order in unmarked structures. Word order is relatively free in Persian. The subject mood is widely used. Verbs are inflected in the language and they indicate tense and aspect, and agree with subject in person and number. The language does not make use of gender.

5 Word Prediction Algorithms

Suppose the user is typing a sentence and the following sequence has been entered so far from right to left according to the Persian writing system:

$$W_i \qquad PW_i \qquad PPW_i \qquad PPPW_i \qquad \ldots$$

Where $PPPW_i$, PPW_i and PW_i are the most recently completed words, and W_i is the current word that is going to be predicted or completed. Let W be the set of all words in the lexicon that would likely appear in that position. Our statistical prediction algorithm first attempts to estimate the probability of each candidate word's POS, (t_{Wi}), according to the previous tags (t_{PWi}), (t_{PPWi}), and (t_{PPPWi}). Then, it tries to estimate the probability of the candidate word in the current position, (W_i), according to the previous words (PW_i), (PPW_i), and ($PPPW_i$); i.e., $P(w_i, t_{Wi} \mid PW, t_{PWi}, PPW_i, t_{PPWi}, PPPW_i, t_{PPPWi})$

Then the algorithm selects the N most appropriate words from W that are likely to be the user's intended words, where N is usually between 1, 5, 9 or 10 based on the experiment done by Soede and Foulds (1986). The general approach is to estimate the probability of each candidate word, $W_i \in W$, being the user's required word in that context based on the POS tags of the preceding words.

6 Methodology

6.1 Corpus

The corpus that we have used in our research consists of about ten million tokens; it also contains about 143 thousand types. It seems to be a balanced corpus in the sense that to be a good representative of the language in terms of source, genre, style, registers, and theme[1]. 80 percent of the available texts are written, and 20 percent are dialog transcriptions. The source of the data is the Internet, publications, magazines, journals, newspapers, and various circular letters.

For our purposes, we have divided the corpus into three parts: nine million tokens as training corpus; one million as developing corpus; and half a million as test corpus.

6.2 Annotation

To annotate the corpus in our research, some inflectional morphemes are automatically added to the stems. Instead of a space, a pseudo-space is used between the components of a word to make the separated morphemes to become joined to each other

---

[1] This corpus is provided by the Research Center for Intelligent Signal Processing.

in order to form a complete word. The spelling of certain words was replaced by a list of accepted spellings.

The corpus is tagged both automatically and manually. First, a POS tagger was trained manually. The most important reason to tag them manually was in order to be able to distinguish homographs in terms of both syntactic distribution and semantic features. Then, based on the context, the corpus was tagged automatically. The accuracy of the tagger was experimentally over 90%. Finally, the corpus was checked again manually to remove bugs and problems. Homographs and scientific texts were problematic for the tagger. Other problems were with genitive (Ezafe[2]), words not existent in the lexicon, and some multicategorical functional words such as 'این' /in/ (this), 'آن' /ān/ (that). The examples below show problems in tagging 'ساعت' /sā?at/ (watch).

There are 19 POS tags as main syntactic categories in the corpus along with morphological, syntactic, and semantic subcategories. Example (1) below illustrates how tags are ordered in terms of their hierarchy:

(1)   این ساعت دو هزار تومان ارزش دارد.

in *sā?at* *do hezār* *tumān* *arzeš dārad.*
this watch two thousand Thamen   worth has
'This watch is worth two thousand Thamens'.

The tag order of 'sā?at' in this example is N, SING, COM. Its main syntactic category is 'noun'; and its semantic subcategories are 'single' and 'common'.

Compare these categories and subcategories with example (2) below:

(2)   ساعت دو آنجا می‌آیم.

sā?at-e   *do*   *ānjā*   *mi'āyam*
hour-genitive   two   there progressive-come-I
'I am coming there by two o'clock.'

The tag order of 'sā?at-e' in this example is N, SING, TIME, GEN. Its main syntactic category is 'noun'; its semantic subcategories are 'single' and 'time'; and genitive (Ezafe) is its syntactic subcategory (Bijankhan, p.c).

6.3 Tokenization

For the tokenization process, we used a software written in Visual Basic to compute, the needed statistics. The software ran on the training corpus to compute word bi- , tri-, and quadrograms. The software was then used to extract POS bi-, tri- and quadrograms of the main categories only. The software was finally used to extract POS bi-, tri- and quadrograms of the main categories with their morphological, syntactic, and semantic subcategories. Space was considered as a word boundary, and alphanumeric characters were treated as words. Finally, all words along with their POS tags (unigram) were extracted from the corpus as the main lexicon of the system. These sources of information for the system were organized in hash tables.

---

[2] Ezafe in Persian is a vowel /e/. It is a genitive case marker; and it has only phonetic representation but is not written. It functions something like 'of' in English.

6.4 Solving Sparseness

Since a big corpus includes only a fraction of n-grams, increasing n makes the distribution of the events rarer. We have used the Simple Linear Interpolation (SLI) method (Manning and Schütze, 1999) to smooth the probability distribution. The developed corpus was used to compute the lambda values of both word and POS n-gram models to solve the sparse data problem. We have used the Boosting Algorithm to compute the lambda values (Freund and Shapire, 1996).

7 Implementation

7.1 The Algorithm

The architecture of our algorithm is shown in Figure 1. The system we developed has four major components: (a) the statistical information extracted from the training corpus for the prediction algorithm, (b) the component computing lambda values for solving the sparseness of both word and POS n-gram models, (c) the predictive program that tries to suggest words to the simulated user, and (d) a simulated user that types the test text.

Component (c) has two parts: word completion and word prediction. The prediction algorithm first completes the partially spelled word and then it predicts the next probable words and presents them in the suggestion list. The simulated typist is a perfect user who always chooses the desired word when it is available in the prediction list and does not miss it.

7.2 Performance Measures

Following Woods (1996) and Fazly (2002), we used three standard performance metrics to evaluate our system.

Keystroke Saving (KSS) is referred to the percentage of keystrokes that the user saves by using the word prediction system. A higher value for keystroke saving implies a better performance. Hit Rate (HR) is the percentage of correct words that appear in the suggestion list without entering any letters of the following word. A higher hit rate also implies a better performance. Keystroke until Prediction (KuP) refers to the average number of keystrokes that the user enters for each word before it appears in the prediction list. A lower value for this measure implies a better performance.

8 Results

Since the corpus we used to develop our systems was different from the Persian corpus used by Ghayoomi (2004) and Ghayoomi and Assi (2005), our obtained results were not comparable with the output of their systems.

One of the differences of their corpus with the one we used in our research is in terms of the number of tokens in their training, development, and test corpus. Their training corpus contained of about 6 million tokens; the development corpus about 850 thousand tokens; and the test corpus about 13 thousands tokens.

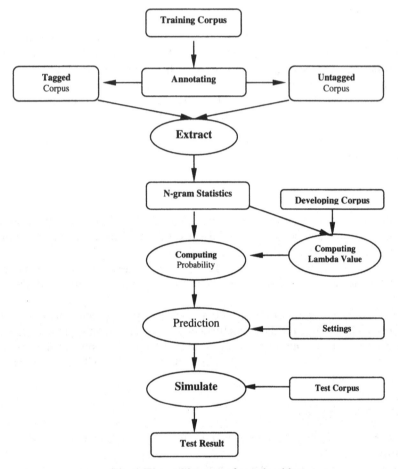

Fig. 1. The architecture of our algorithm

The other difference is the genre of their corpus in which only newspaper texts have been gathered for the training, development, and test corpus. Quite contrary in our corpus it has contained a wider coverage of genres.

The *n*-gram word models that have been used in their algorithms are merely word statistics of uni-, bi-, and trigram. They have not benefited from the POS tags of the words; while we developed and tested our system in three different scenarios.

The first test used only bi-, tri- and quadrogram word models; we called it System A. A second system was tested using the described *n*-gram word models along with the words' POS bi-, tri- and quadrograms of the main syntactic categories only; we called it System B. Finally the system was tested using the described *n*-gram word models along with the words' POS *n*-grams of both the main syntactic categories and their morphological, syntactic, and semantic subcategories; we called this System C.

The test corpus was given to the simulated typist. It contained half a million tokens, and 1,950,000 characters; white space was not treated as a character. The reason for not considering space is that after selecting any word, a space will automatically be entered which results in a saved keystroke. On the other hand, to select a word from the list, one of the Function Keys, F1 through F9, are required to be pressed in order to drag and drop the intended word into the text being typed. The result is that the keystroke which was saved by entering the automatic space would now be lost.

The virtual typist is a Visual C^{++} program that reads in each text letter by letter. After reading each letter, it determines what the correct prediction for the current position is. The prediction program is then called and a list of suggestions is returned to the user. The user searches the prediction list for the correct one. If the correct prediction is found in the list, the user increases the amount of correct predictions by the predictor. The correctly predicted word is then completed and the user continues to read the rest of the text.

The results obtained from using the various n-gram models are presented in table 1 for only 9 suggestions in the prediction list:

Table 1. Summary of the results obtained by using word and POS n-gram models from the test corpus

	KSS%	HR%	KuP
System A	37	43.56	2.13
System B	38.95	46.08	1.98
System C	42.45	56.20	1.53

As shown in table 1, higher KSS and HR and the lowest KuP were obtained when the system used the word statistics and syntactic knowledge of the language (systems B and C); compared to the model which only used word statistics (system A). But this differentiation is not very remarkable between systems A and B when only words and the first main syntactic categories are used for prediction. Probably the reason is that the main syntactic categories are too noisy for the system, and the 2% better performance is achieved by simply doing minor filtering the sequence of words by considering the main syntactic categories that belong to the words. System C had the best performance among the developed systems, since it has used all of the word and syntactic knowledge available to the system; so having more syntactic information available to the words would highly improve predictions.

The 42.45% KSS means that for each 100 characters that the user is required to type to enter a text segment, at least 42 characters are entered by the system, and the rest, the remaining 58 characters, were entered by the user. 56% of words, more than half of the user's required words, appeared in the prediction list before entering any of the letters of the following word. At least one keystroke is needed by the user to type a word on the system while the average length of words for the corpus we used was 3.86.

9 Conclusion

By using POS tags of Persian in the word prediction algorithm, we achieved a higher keystroke saving rate. Since every keystroke is an effort for disabled users, the result obtained is very important for users with disabilities.

Moreover, there is a significant difference between the performances of the system that uses all of the available syntactic knowledge which achieved a sudden increase in KSS, comparing to the one that uses mere word statistic knowledge.

Using the POS tags of the language allows the system to filter words in the predictions list that are syntactically inappropriate in a particular position within the sentence. Thus, it would increase the user's confidence to enable him or her to select words from the prediction list that can result in better written sentences, along with imposing a lower cognition load on him or her. This feature is useful for users with cognitive disabilities, specially the ones suffering from aphasia.

10 Further Work

To achieve higher percentage of KSS, we are planning to add the feature of adaptability of the system to the user's writing style. By adapting itself to the user, the system would gradually improve its performance. Also, it is necessary to add a POS tager to the system in order to identify the POS tags of new words and tag them automatically.

Bibliography

Booth, L., Beattie, W., Newell, A.: I know what you mean. Special Children, pp. 26-27 (1990)

Carlberger, J.: Word Prediction: Design and Implementation of a probabilistic Word Prediction Program. Master dissertation. Royal Institute of Technology. Stockholm (1997)

Carlberger, A., Magnuson, T., Carlberger, J., Wachtmeister, H., Hunnicutt, S.: Probability-based word prediction for writing support in dyslexia. In: Barner, R., Heldner, M., Sullivan, K., Wretling, P. (eds.) Proceedings of Fonetik 1997 Conference, vol. 4, pp. 17–20 (1997a)

Carlberger, A., Carlberger, J., Magnuson, T., Hunnicutt, M.S., Palazuelos-Cagigas, S.E., Navarro, S.A.: Profet, a new generation of word prediction: An evaluation study. In: Copestake, A., Langer, S., Palazuelos-Cagigas, S. (eds.) Natural Language Processing for Communication aids, In Proceedings of a workshop sponsored by ACL, Madrid, Spain, pp. 23–28 (1997b)

Fazly, A.: The Use of Syntax in Word Completion Utilities. Master dissertation. University of Toronto, Canada (2002)

Freund, Y., Shapire, R.E.: Experiments with new boosting algorithm. In: Proceedings of ICML (1996)

Ghayoomi, M.: Word Prediction in Computational Processing of the Persian Language. Master dissertation. Iran: Islamic Azad University, Tehran Central Branch (2004)

Ghayoomi, M.: Using word prediction systems for users with disabilities: A case study. In: Proceedings of the 2nd Workshop on the Persian Language and Computer, Tehran University, Iran, June 27-28, 2006, pp. 216–225 (2006)

Ghayoomi, M., Assi, S.M.: Word prediction in a running text: A statistical language modeling for the Persian language. In: Proceedings of the Australasian Language Technology Workshop, University of Sydney, Australia, Dec. 10-11, 2005, pp. 57–63 (2005)

Gustavii, E., Pettersson, E.: A Swedish Grammar for Word Prediction. Uppsala University, Stockholm (2003)

Jurafsky, D., Martin, J.H.: Speech and Language Processing: An Introduction to Natural Language Processing, Computational Linguistics, and Speech Recognition. Prentice-Hall, New Jersey (2000)

Klund, J., Novak, M.: If word prediction can help, which program do you choose? (2001), http://trace.wisc.edu/docs/wordprediction2001/index.htm

Manning, C.D., Schütze, H.: Foundations of Statistical Natural Language Processing. MIT Press, Cambridge (1999)

McCoy, K., Demasco, P.: Some application of natural language processing to the field of augmentative and alternative communication. In: Proceeding of the IJCAI – 1995 Workshop on Developing AI Applications for People with Disabilities (1995)

Morris, C., Newell, A., Booth, L., Arnott, J.: Syntax pal: A system to improve the written syntax of language-impaired users. Assistive Technology 4(2), 51–59 (1992)

Nantais, T., Shein, F., Johansson, M.: Efficacy of the word prediction algorithm in WordQ. In: Proceedings of the 24th Annual Conference on Technology and Disability, RESNA (2001)

Rosenfeld, R.: Adaptive Statistical Language Modeling: A Maximum Entropy Approach. PhD. dissertation. Pittsburgh, Canegie Mellon University (1994)

Shein, F., Nantais, T., Nishiyama, R., Tam, C., Marshall, P.: Word cuing for persons with writing difficulties: WordQ. In: The16th Annual International Conference on Technology and Persons with Disabilities, California State University at Northridge, Los Angeles, CA (March 2001)

Soede, M., Foulds, R.A.: Dilemma of prediction in communication aids and mental load. In: Proceedings of the 9th Annual Conference on Rehabilitation Technology, pp. 357–359 (1986)

Swiffin, A.L., Pickering, J.A., Arnott, J.L., Newell, A.F.: PAL: An effort efficient portable communication aid and keyboard emulator. In: Proceedings of the 8th Annual Conference on Rehabilitation Technology, pp. 197–199 (1985)

Wood, M.E.J.: Syntactic Pre-Processing in Single-Word Prediction for Disabled People. Ph.D. dissertation. University of Bristol, Bristol (1996)

A Graph Based Method for Building Multilingual Weakly Supervised Dependency Parsers

Jagadeesh Gorla, Anil Kumar Singh, Rajeev Sangal, Karthik Gali, Samar Husain, and Sriram Venkatapathy

Language Technologies Research Centre, IIIT, Hyderabad, India
{jagadeesh,anil,samar,sriram}@research.iiit.ac.in,
{sangal,karthikg}@students.iiit.ac.in

Abstract. The structure of a sentence can be seen as a spanning tree in a linguistically augmented graph of syntactic nodes. This paper presents an approach for unlabeled dependency parsing based on this view. The first step involves marking the chunks and the chunk heads of a given sentence and then identifying the intra-chunk dependency relations. The second step involves learning to identify the inter-chunk dependency relations. For this, we use an initialization technique based on a measure we call Normalized Conditional Mutual Information (NCMI), in addition to a few linguistic constraints. We present the results for Hindi. We have achieved a precision of 80.83% for sentences of size less than 10 words and 66.71% overall. This is significantly better than the baseline in which random initialization is used.

Keywords: Weakly Supervised Learning, Dependency Parsing, Multilingual Processing, South Asian Languages, Association Measures.

1 Introduction

Parsing a sentence can be described as finding the correct syntactic structure of that sentence according to a particular formalism. Most of the work on parsing so far can be categorized as either based on rules or based on supervised learning [8,24,6,4,1]. Fairly good parsers are available for English [3] and for some other languages [7]. Some of the latest work was presented at the CoNLL Shared Task Session of EMNLP-CoNLL 2007 [17]. There has also been work on learning models of dependency trees [16,22,21,23,25,15]. However, many other languages of the world still lack good parsers. This is mainly because these languages do not have the resources required for building either rule based parsers (extensive computational grammars) or supervised parsers (treebanks). Since the researchers working on most of these languages usually happen to be short of funding and other support, we need to find reasonably good methods for unsupervised or weakly supervised parsing, either for direct use or for making the task of creating treebank like resources easier.

A sentence can be seen as a graph consisting of syntactic units as the nodes and dependency relations as the edges. The weight of an edge represents the degree of association between the two nodes. We can view the syntactic structure of the sentence as the best spanning tree for that graph. There has been some previous work where

A. Ranta, B. Nordström (Eds.): GoTAL 2008, LNAI 5221, pp. 148–159, 2008.

the problem of parsing was modeled as finding the maximum spanning tree (MST) in a graph representing the sentence [14,13]. Our work is in a similar direction. We also represent the sentence as a graph, but we have 'chunks' rather than words as the nodes. This is because we are focusing on languages which have fixed word order inside chunks, but which can have relatively free order as far as chunks are concerned. One example of such languages are the languages of the South Asian linguistic area [10]. Having chunks as the nodes reduces the complexity of the problem significantly and is likely to increase the accuracy. Another justification for doing this is that the intra-chunk dependencies in these languages are very easy to find by using some simple rules, as we will explain later. It is also relatively quite easy to identify the chunks using a few rules defined in terms of the part of speech (POS) tags. It should be noted that the notion of a chunk as used by us is somewhat specific to our purposes, i.e., identifying dependency relations. So, for our purposes, a chunk is a sequence of words inside which the order of words is fixed and the dependencies are very easily identifiable. This is why we do not make the assumption that a chunker is available for the languages concerned, as we can identify the 'chunks' using some simple rules.

One assumption that we do make is that a POS tagger is available for the concerned language. The parsing algorithm runs over the sequence of POS tags for the given sentence. This assumption is valid for several South Asian languages [19,20], even though there is still a lot of scope for improving the accuracy of the POS taggers. For learning dependency relations, we can either use manually POS tagged data (if available), or we can use the output of the POS tagger on a raw corpus. In our experiments, we do the latter. Due to this and the other reasons mentioned above, our method can be easily extended for other similar languages, even though we have experimented only on Hindi so far.

During the last few years there has been a steady progress in the area of unsupervised parsing [2,12], but most of the work is based on phrase structure grammars, rather than dependency grammars. Very few efforts have been made towards building unsupervised or weakly supervised dependency parsers. Klein and Manning had [12] proposed a hybrid approach, which combines constituency and dependency models. This approach yielded 77.6% f-score on WSJ-10 corpus.

The model learnt using the method described in this paper can also be used as Dependency Language Model [11]. This could be an important application of the work even if the parser, as it is, may not be directly usable for some practical applications.

2 Overview of the Parsing Method

In the training phase, our method requires a raw text corpus and a POS tagger. The corpus is first POS tagged. After that, we identify the chunks, chunk heads and the intra-chunk dependencies using simple rules (see Section-3). From then on, we basically work with sequences of POS tags of chunk heads.

To create the parsing (training) model, we have designed a non-projective weakly supervised dependency parsing algorithm to learn the dependency relations between the head words of chunks using an Expectation-Maximization (EM)-like iterative algorithm. The approach that we describe in this paper to create the initial dependency

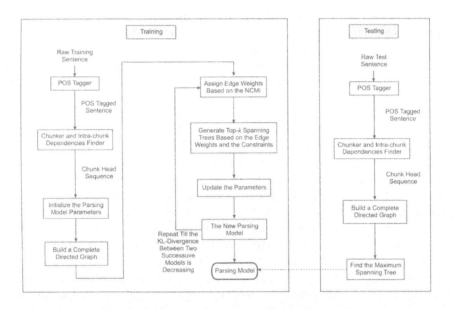

Fig. 1. Overview of the parsing method based on syntactic structure as the best spanning tree in a linguistically augmented graph of syntactic nodes

model uses a measure called Normalized Conditional Mutual Information (NCMI) along with a few linguistic constraint which are applicable across all the major South Asian languages.

In this proposed approach to build a parser, no treebank is required and it can also be applied to other free order languages by changing the linguistic constraints, which are very few in number. All the rules and the model parameters of parsing model in this approach are based on only POS tags.

One of the reasons for using a sequence of POS tags for learning is that the dependency relations between two words mostly depend on their POS tags, since words of the same POS tags are usually mutually substitutable. This is an established practice and was used by Klein [12]. Also, as we are using some rules to identify the chunks and chunk heads, it is easy to define such rules on tags instead of lexical items.

Figure-1 illustrates the basic ideas used in the method described in this paper.

3   Syntactic Properties of the Languages Covered

As indicated earlier, our method is suitable for languages with certain properties. These properties include a relatively free word order nature. 'Relatively' because the order within a chunk may be fixed and languages like Hindi are verb final languages. A sentence in such languages is typically divided into non-overlapping phrases (chunks), and these chunks can occur in any order without affecting the core meaning of the sentence. Each chunk consists of one content word, referred to as the *head word H*, and several other words, which are function words F. The head of the chunk is the main element of the chunk and it carries the meaning of the chunk and can occur independently. For example, consider the following Hindi sentences:

S1:   *[merI nayI <u>kiwAba</u>] [<u>rAma</u>] [paDZa rahA hE]*.
      [my new book] [Ram] [is reading]
S2:   *[<u>rAma</u>] [merI nayI <u>kiwAba</u>] [paDZa rahA hE]*.
      [Ram] [my new book] [is reading]

Both the sentences S1 and S2 convey the same meaning, even though *[merI nayI kiwAba]* and *[rAma]* are swapped in S2. Here *[merI nayI <u>kiwAba</u>]* and *[<u>rAma</u>]* are noun chunks and *[paDZa rahA hE]* is a verb chunk. The chunks are (internally) fixed word order units, but they can be combined in almost any order. The underlined word in each chunk is the head word and the other words are function words.

One important condition while building a dependency parser for South Asian languages is that we can not apply the projectivity constraint because these languages are relatively free word order languages. Our study of the dependency relations inside the chunks clearly shows that, almost always, the words inside the chunk modify the head of that chunk.

In our experiments, we have used some rules which generalize to many South Asian languages. Some of these rules used by the Chunker and Intra-chunk Dependency Finder (CIDF) are given below[1]:

1. r1: (QFNUM | QF | INTF | QFN | JJ)* (NN | (NNPC)* NNP | (NNC)* NN | PRP) (PREP | NLOC | RP | SYM)*
2. r2: (NEG)* (VRB | NVB | VJJ | VFM | VAUX) + (PREP | NLOC | RP | SYM)*
3. r3: (RB)+
4. r4: (CC)+
5. r5: (JJ)+

The rule $r1$ is used for identifying noun chunks in a sentence, $r2$ is for verb chunks, $r3$ is for adverbs, $r4$ is for conjunctions, and $r5$ is for adjectives. These rules are applied one after the other (i.e., in the order given above) to identify the different chunks in the given sentence.

We have conducted some experiments to evaluate the performance of the CIDF. The precision for chunking is 77%, for intra-chunk dependencies it is 96%, and for finding the head of the chunk it is 98%. There are some issues still to be resolved, e.g. if PRP NN is a tag sequence then it is difficult to decide whether to combine them as a chunk or not. If the PRP is a demonstrative PRP then it will be a chunk, otherwise there will be two different chunks. This situation is not currently handled by the CIDF.

4   Weakly Supervised Dependency Parsing Model

In this section, we present an approach to create an weakly supervised dependency parsing model using chunks head sequences. It captures the strength of a dependency relation between any two chunk head tags at a particular distance.

---

[1] We are using a POS tagset which has been designed for many Indian languages. The details are available at http://shiva.iiit.net/SPSAL2007/downloads.php

4.1   Notation

We view the sentences of a language L as sequences of word tokens drawn from some set of word types or vocabulary of L. Let $V = \{t_0, t_1, \cdots t_v\}$ be the vocabulary of the language L and $S =< x_0, x_1, \cdots, x_n >$ be a sentence of n words such that $x_0 = ROOT$, $\forall n$ such that $x_n \in V$. Let $C = \{S_0, S_1, \cdots S_N\}$ be the set of N sentences in the language L. Let $G_S = (V_S, E_S)$ be a complete directed graph of a sentence S such that,

1. the set of vertices $V_S = \{x_0, x_1, \cdots, x_n\}$
2. the set of edges $E_S = \{< x, y >_S | \forall x, y \in V_S\}$

where G_S is a graph such that each word in the sentence is a node and there is a directed edge between every pair of nodes, corresponding to the dependencies. By definition, G_S is a digraph. G_S encodes all possible dependencies among the words (actually, chunk heads) of the sentence S. Thus, every possible dependency graph of S must be a subgraph of G_S. Let $< x, y >_S$ represent the edge from x to y in the sentence S.

Let $x \rightarrow^+ y$ be a dependency relation that is true if and only if there is a non-empty directed path from node x to node y in some graph under consideration. A directed spanning tree of a graph G_S that originates out of a particular node $x_r \in V_S$, is any subgraph $T = (V_T, E_T)$ such that,

1. $V_T = V_S$ and $E_T \subseteq E_S$
2. $\forall x_j \in V_T$, $x_r \rightarrow^+ x_j$ if and only if $x_r \neq x_j$
3. If $< x_i, x_j >_S \in E_T$, then:
   $< x_m, x_j >_S \notin E_T \forall x_m \neq x_i$

Let $T(G_S)$ be the set of all directed spanning trees of the graph G_S. As McDonald et al. [14] noted, there is a one-to-one correspondence between spanning trees of G_S and dependency graphs of S. This implies that $T(G_S)$ is the set of all possible projective and non-projective dependency graphs for the sentence S.

For a given sentence S, using the parsing model, we can estimate the conditional probability $P(T|S)$ and the parser finds the most likely parse of the sentence using:

$$T_{best} = \arg\max_T P(T|S) \tag{1}$$

We assume that each dependency decision is independent. The class of dependency models which follow this assumption are called **edge-factored models** [18,14]. Under this assumption, every edge in G_S of a sentence S is associated with a score $Score(x, y) \geq 0$ that maps edge between x and y to a real valued score ranging from 0 to 1. These scores represent the likelihood of the dependency relation occurring from word x to y. We refer to this score as the dependency score of x being the head of y and we denote it by $Score(x, y)$. The way $Score(x, y)$ is calculated depends on the framework in which it is being used. For example, in a generative probabilistic model such as Paskin's [18] it could represent the conditional probability of x being generated by y.

Based on the above assumption, we define $P(T|S)$ as follows:

$$P(T|S) = \prod_{(x, y) \in E_T} Score(x, y) \tag{2}$$

We can also write T_{best} of a sentence S as follows:

$$T_{best} = \arg \max_{T \in T(G_S)} P(T|S) = \arg \max_{T \in T(G_S)} \prod_{(x,y) \in E_T} Score(x, y)$$

Here, $Score(x, y)$ represents the probability of x being the head of y. It can also be represented as $P(x|y)$. McDonald et al.[14] showed that this can be solved in $O(n^2)$ time using the Chu-Liu-Edmonds algorithm for standard digraphs [5,9]. We will use the parsing algorithm proposed by McDonald et al.[14] to parse a given test sentence, once the training has been completed.

We need to estimate the parsing model parameters, i.e., $P(x|y)$ to find T_{best} for a sentence. Before describing the way $Score(x, y)$ (or $P(x|y)$) is estimated, we define the following:

1. We denote the sum of the scores of all the possible output parses of a given input sentence S as Z_S:

$$Z_S = \sum_{T \in T(G_S)} P(T|S) = \sum_{T \in T(G_S)} \prod_{(x, y) \in E_T} P(x|y)$$

   where $x, y \in V_S$
2. The expected value (or the dependency score) of each edge in G_S for a sentence S is represented as $< P(x|y) >_S$ and is computed as:

$$< P(x|y) >_S = \sum_{T \in T(G_S)} P(T|S) \times I(< x, y >, T)$$

   where $I(< x, y >, T)$ is an indicator function that is equal to 1 when the edge $< x, y >$ is in the tree T and is zero otherwise.

An estimate based on the identities of the two tokens alone is problematic and the lexical distance between the words will strongly influence the likelihood of one word modifying other [6]. So, we include the distance while deciding whether two words are related or not. We estimate, $< P(x|y, d) >_S$, i.e., the probability of x being the head of y at a lexical distance d, instead of just $P < (x|y) >_S$.

4.2 Language Model for Parameter Estimation

In principle, a language model recovers the probability of a sentence $P(S)$ over all possible T given S by estimating the joint probability $P(S, T)$:

$$P(S) = \sum_T P(S, T) \tag{3}$$

In practice, we approximate $P(S)$ to the sum of tree scores (probabilities) of k best probable trees generated for the sentence S. Let $T_k(S)$ be the set of k best probable trees generated for the sentence. Each tree $T \in T_k(S)$ is the most probable tree for sentence S when each word of the sentence is taken as the root node.

$$P(S) = \sum_T P(S,T) \approx \sum_{T \in T(T_k(S))} P(S,T) = \sum_{T \in T(T_k(S))} \prod_{(x,y,d) \in E_T} < P(x|y,d) >_S$$

To generate the trees in $T_k(S)$, we first generate a single child, $x_r \in V_S$, of $ROOT$ and then we select the single best incoming edge of each node x_g such that $x_g \in V_S$, $x_g \neq x_r$ and T_{x_r} should satisfy the spanning tree properties (no cycles). In other words, T_{x_r} is the directed maximum spanning tree of G_S generated from the node x_r. In this way, in each tree, we have to choose the head of each word (incoming edge) in the sentence S based on the probability of each edge, i.e., $P(x|y,d)$, where x, $y \in V_S$.

It is very unlikely that the same sentence will appear in the training data and the test data. We thus approximate $< P(x|y, d) >_S$ by $P(x|y, d)$ and estimate the dependency probability from the training sentences, where x, $y \in V$. From now onwards, we denote $P(x|y, d)$ as $P^d_{x, y}$.

Let t_a, $t_b \in V$. We can estimate the maximum likelihood $P^d_{t_a, t_b}$ by maximizing the log-likelihood $\sum_{c=1}^N log(P(S_c))$ subjected to the normalization constraints:

$$\sum_{t_a} P^d_{t_a, t_b} = 1 \tag{4}$$

and

$$P^d_{t_a, t_b} \geq 0 \tag{5}$$

Let x_{ci} be the ith word of S_c. By solving the above constraint optimization problem with the usual Lagrange multipliers method, we get the probability $P^d_{t_a t_b}$ as:

$$P^d_{t_a t_b} = \frac{\sum_{c=1}^N \frac{1}{Z_{S_c}} \sum_{\substack{x_{ci}=t_a \\ x_{cj}=t_b}} < P^d_{x_{ci},x_{cj}} >_{S_c}}{\sum_{c=1}^N \frac{1}{Z_{S_c}} \sum_{t_a,d} \sum_{\substack{x_{ci}=t_a \\ x_{cj}=t_b}} < P^d_{x_{ci},x_{cj}} >_{S_c}} \tag{6}$$

$P^d_{t_a, t_b}$ are the maximum likelihood parameters for the dependency parsing model. We estimate these parameters from the head tagged corpora using an EM-like iterative algorithm described below.

Learning the Dependency Parsing Model. To create a dependency model, we first create the chunk head corpus by running a tagger on a corpus (21857 sentences) followed by running the CIDF on the tagged corpora, which gives the head corpus. We then apply the following three steps to create the parsing model:

1. Initialize the parsing model parameters
2. For each sentence in the chunk head corpus:
    (a) Construct a complete weighted directed graph with the nodes as chunk heads and the edge weights as the parsing model weights between the chunk heads
    (b) Find out what is the possible root of the sentence, i.e., is it CC or VFM

(c) Find out the possible parse trees of the sentences by finding the MST of the graph by taking the each possible root as the head of the sentence, i.e., take the possible root as the child of the dummy root and generate the MST.

3. Estimate $P^d_{t_a, t_b}$ from the set of generated trees and update the weight of each parameter and create a new model

4. Repeat from the step-2(b) with newly estimated edge weights in step-3 until the KL-divergence between the two successive models is decreasing

5   Creating Initial Parsing Model

The effectiveness of the dependency model is highly dependent on the initial dependency model weights. We initialize the dependency model using a measure called Normalized Conditional Mutual Information (NCMI) and a few linguistic constraints. NCMI is a measure of association between distant word (or POS tag) pairs, i.e., two words occurring at a particular distance d. We use NCMI between two tags as an initial undirected dependency score between them.

First we define a measure called Conditional Mutual Information (CMI), which is a modified version of the mutual information measure that takes into account the extra variable of the lexical distance between the words. The condition in the 'conditional' is the value of the distance. CMI is calculated as:

$$CMI(x, y, d) = p(x, y, d)log\frac{p(x, y, d)}{p(x)p(y)}$$ (7)

where x, y are the POS tags and d is the distance between x and y.

All CMI scores are then normalized to get the $NCMI$ ($NCMI \in [0, 1]$), which is calculated as:

$$NCMI = \frac{CMI - min(CMI)}{max(CMI) - min(CMI)}$$ (8)

As mentioned earlier, $NCMI$ gives the measure of association or interdependency score between the two tags at a particular distance. It does not represent the exact measure of dependency between two tags, but is an approximation to the measure of dependency which can be effectively used for initialization.

5.1   Dependency Constraints

Based on the linguistic reality and the frequencies of occurrence of dependency relations, we have defined a small set of constraints that any valid dependency tree must satisfy.

A tree is considered a valid dependency tree of sentence iff:

1. It has either a main verb (VFM) or a conjunction (CC) as the root of the dependency tree

2. It does not have any adjective (JJ) as the head of any verb (VFM, VJJ, VRB)

3. It does not have any noun (NN) as a child of a pronoun (PRP)
4. It does not have a dependency relation between two conjunctions (CCs) or two main verbs (VFMs).
5. If there is an adverb (RB) or a non-finite adverbial (VRB) then it modifies (i.e., is the child of) its closest main verb (VFM)
6. Two nouns (NN) are not related at a lexical distance greater than 2.

The first three constraints are based on the linguistic reality while the rest are based on frequencies.

5.2 Generating Initial Dependency Trees

This section describes the method to generate the initial set of dependency trees for each sentence using the NCMI scores and the dependency constraints and then creating the initial model from the trees. We know that the NCMI score is a rough measure of the strength of a dependency relation between two tags. From the constraints given above, we also know that two conjunctions (CC) or two main verbs (VFM) or two nouns (NN) at a lexical distance of more than 2 are not related. This means that we can modify the NCMI scores between two conjunctions, main verbs or nouns at lexical distance more than 2 to 0 (weak dependency score). And so on for other constraints. The modified NCMI scores are used to generate the most likely dependency trees for a given sentence.

Let S be the sentence and g_s be the weighted undirected complete graph of S constructed using the words/tags of the sentence as nodes. Following are the steps to generate the initial dependency trees for a sentence S:

1. Construct g_s by taking words/tags of S as nodes and the $NCMI$ score as edge weight.
2. Modify the weights of the edges connecting the node tag VNN or VRB or RB in g_s to its closest [2] VFM node in the graph to 1 (strong dependency score).
3. Generate the set of M maximum spanning trees of g_s.
   Each spanning tree of g_s represents the possible undirected dependency tree of the sentence S and the tree score (product of edge scores) represents the likelihood of tree being the undirected dependency tree of S.
4. Generate the set of directed trees from each undirected tree by taking each possible head (CC and VFM) as a root and converting the undirected tree to a directed tree by assigning directions to each edge as going out from the parent towards the child.

After applying the above steps on the sentences, we get the set of most likely parse trees of the sentences and their scores ($P(S, T)$). The basic intuition here is that once we modify the edge weights using the constraints, when generating the top M-spanning trees, edges with strong dependency score are likely to be included in the top MSTs. Once the initial possible trees are generated for each sentence, we can estimate the initial parsing model parameters by calculating P_{t_a, t_b}^d as described in the previous section. One important observation here is that we are estimating the parsing model parameters

---

[2] Here closeness is in terms of the lexical distance between the nodes in the sentence.

using the trees generated based on the NCMI scores modified by the linguistic constraints and these linguistic constraints are used only in estimating the initial parameter values.

5.3 Parsing

The output of the training model (or learning model) described in the above sections are the dependency relations between tags at a particular distance with their corresponding probabilities. To parse a new (test) sentence, we apply the following steps:

1. Run the POS tagged and the CIDF and find chunks, chunk heads and intra-chunk dependency relations
2. Construct a complete weighted graph of the sentence by taking the chunk heads as nodes and assigning the parsing model weights for the tag-tag-distance triples to the edges
3. Compute the Maximum Spanning Tree of the sentence graph using the Chu-Liu-Edmonds algorithm [5,9]

The output MST gives us the most likely parse of the sentence.

6 Experimental Setup and Results

As not much parsed data is available for Indian Languages, we used raw (unannotated) text to build a parser and tested the parser accuracy on 1997 human tagged sentences (these sentences were not the part of the training corpus). For training, we tagged 22187 sentences using a POS tagger for which the reported performance is 88.8%. We calculated the NCMI scores between the tags at a maximum lexical distance d of 20. We used the standard evaluation metric used in supervised parsing techniques to evaluate the parser performance, i.e.:

$$Accuracy = \frac{correct\ dependency\ relations}{total\ relations}$$

We conducted two main experiments. The first was on sentences of length less than ten words and the second was on sentences of all lengths. We calculated the performance for both the sets of sentences. The results are shown in **Table-1** and **Table-2**. Note that these results are only for the accuracy of inter-chunk head dependency relations. The precision of the CIDF for intra-chunk dependency identification was found to be 88.69%, 83.21% and 90.50% for Hindi, Telugu and Bengali, respectively. Since the CIDF is able to find intra-chunk relations much more accurately, the overall performance of the parser will be greater than shown in **Table-1**, even more so because the average length of sentence in the training data was 20.34, whereas it was only 10.14 after the chunking step.

We also conducted an experiment where the initialization was performed with random values. The performance is this case (for sentences of all lengths) was 48.44%. The performance when initialization was performed with the NCMI scores modified by the linguistic constraints was 66.71%. This clearly shows that our method of initialization is making a significant difference to the performance.

Table 1. Parser Evaluation: Sentence Length and Initialization Method

Sentence Length	Accuracy
≤ 10	80.83%
Overall	66.71%

Initialization	Accuracy
Random (Baseline)	48.44%
Only NCMI	64.13%
NCMI + Constraints	66.71%

7   Future Work

There are several possible areas of further research as an extension of this work. One of them is improving the learning and parsing algorithms. Right now, the parser is using only the tags to learn the dependency relations. Since we know that lexical information can be crucial in parsing, we can use such information, especially the post-positions or case markers, to make the parser more accurate. Such improvements can perhaps make the parser practically usable. One other very important area for future work is domain adaptation of the parser for restricted domains as has been successfully attempted for many other languages [17].

8   Conclusion

In this paper we presented a method for weakly supervised dependency parsing. This method is based on the idea that the problem of parsing can be defined as the computation of the best spanning tree in the complete graph generated from the syntactic units of the sentence, where these units are the nodes in the graph. In our case, we select chunks as the units because our focus was on South Asian languages which have fixed word order but free chunk order. Also, it is very easy to identify the chunks relevant for our purposes as well as to identify the intra-chunk dependencies. We described an algorithm for learning the parsing model from POS tagged sequences prepared from the unannotated training data. A novel way was used to initialize the parameters of the model (i.e., weights of the edges between two tags at particular distances). This method of initialization used a measure of association called Normalized Conditional Mutual Information (NCMI) and application of a few simple linguistic constraints. Our parser achieved an accuracy of 80.80% for sentence of length less than ten and 66.71% for sentences of all lengths. We were also able to show that our method of initialization significantly increased the performance of the parser over the baseline of random initialization.

References

1. Bharati, A., Sangal, R.: Parsing free word order languages using the paninian framework. In: Proceedings of Annual Meeting of Association for Computational Linguistics, pp. 105–111 (1993)
2. Bod, R.: An all-subtrees approach to unsupervised parsing. In: Proceedings of COLING-ACL (2006)

3. Charniak, E.: A maximum-entropy-inspired parser. In: Proceedings of the Annual Meeting of the North American Chapter of the Association for Computational Linguistics (ACL) (2000)
4. Charniak, E., Johnson, M.: Coarse-to-fine n-best parsing and maxent discriminative reranking. In: Proceedings of the Annual Meeting of the Association for Computational Linguistics (ACL) (2005)
5. Chu, Y., Liu, T.: On the shortest arborescence of a directed graph. Science Sinica 14, 1396–1400 (1965)
6. Collins, M.: Head-driven statistical models for natural language parsing. PhD thesis, University of Pennsylvania (1999)
7. Collins, M., Hajic, J., Brill, E., Ramshaw, L., Tillmann, C.: A statistical parser for czech. In: Proceedings of the 37th Meeting of the Association for Computational Linguistics (ACL), pp. 505–512 (1999)
8. Doran, C., Egedi, D., Hockey, B.A., Srinivas, B., Zaidel, M.: Xtag system: a wide coverage grammar for english. In: Proceedings of the 15th conference on Computational linguistics, Morristown, NJ, USA, pp. 922–928. Association for Computational Linguistics (1994)
9. Edmonds, J.: Optimum branchings. Journal of Research of the National Bureau of Standards (1967)
10. Emeneau, M.B.: India as a linguistic area. Linguistics 32, 3–16 (1956)
11. Gao, J., Suzuki, H.: Unsupervised learning of dependency structure for language modeling. In: ACL 2003, pp. 521–528. Association for Computational Linguistics (2003)
12. Klein, D.: The Unsupervised Learning of Natural Language Structure. PhD thesis, Stanford University (2004)
13. McDonald, R.: Discriminative learning and spanning tree algorithms for dependency parsing. PhD thesis, University of Pennsylvania (2006)
14. McDonald, R., Crammer, K., Pereira, F.: Online large-margin training of dependency parsers. In: Proceedings of the Annual Meeting of the Association for Computational Linguistics (ACL) (2005)
15. McDonald, R., Satta, G.: On the complexity of non-projective data-driven dependency parsing. In: Proceedings of the International Conference on Parsing Technologies (IWPT) (2007)
16. Nivre, J.: An efficient algorithm for projective dependency parsing. In: Proceedings of International Workshop on Parsing Technologies, pp. 149–160 (2003)
17. Nivre, J., Hall, J., Kübler, S., McDonald, R., Nilsson, J., Riedel, S., Yuret, D.: The CoNLL 2007 shared task on dependency parsing. In: Proceedings of the CoNLL Shared Task Session of EMNLP-CoNLL 2007, pp. 915–932 (2007)
18. Paskin, M.A.: Grammatical bigrams. In: Proceedings of NIPS, pp. 91–97 (2001)
19. Avinesh, P.V.S., Karthik, G.: Part-of-speech tagging and chunking using conditional random fields and transformation based learning. In: Proceedings of the IJCAI 2007 Workshop on Shallow Parsing in South Asian Languages, Hyderabad, India (2007)
20. Rao, D., Yarowsky, D.: Part of speech tagging and shallow parsing for indian languages. In: Proceedings of the IJCAI-07 Workshop on Shallow Parsing in South Asian Languages, Hyderabad, India (2007)
21. Smith, D.A., Eisner, J.: Bootstrapping feature-rich dependency parsers with entropic priors. In: Proceedings of the 2007 Joint Conference on Empirical Methods in Natural Language Processing and Computational Natural Language Learning (EMNLP-CoNLL), pp. 667–677
22. Smith, D.A., Smith, N.A.: Probabilistic models of nonprojective dependency trees. In: Proceedings of the 2007 Joint Conference on Empirical Methods in Natural Language Processing and Computational Natural Language Learning (EMNLP-CoNLL), pp. 132–140
23. Smith,N.A.: Discovery of linguistic relations using lexical attraction. PhD thesis (1998)
24. Yoshinaga, N., Miyao, Y., Torisawa, K., Tsujii, J.: Efficient LTAG parsing using HPSG parsers. In: Proc. of PACLING, pp. 342–351 (2001)
25. Yuret,D.: Discovery of linguistic relations using lexical attraction. PhD thesis (1998)

A Web-Based Self-training Approach for Authorship Attribution[*]

Rafael Guzmán-Cabrera[1,2], Manuel Montes-y-Gómez[3],
Paolo Rosso[2], and Luis Villaseñor-Pineda[3]

[1] FIMEE, Universidad de Guanajuato, México
guzmanc@salamanca.ugto.mx
[2] NLE Lab, DSIC, Universidad Politécnica de Valencia, Spain
prosso@dsic.upv.es
[3] LabTL, Instituto Nacional de Astrofísica, Óptica y Electrónica, México
{mmontesg,villasen}@inaoep.mx

Abstract. As any other text categorization task, authorship attribution requires a large number of training examples. These examples, which are easily obtained for most of the tasks, are particularly difficult to obtain for this case. Based on this fact, in this paper we investigate the possibility of using Web-based text mining methods for the identification of the author of a given poem. In particular, we propose a semi-supervised method that is specially suited to work with just few training examples in order to tackle the problem of the lack of data with the same writing style. The method considers the automatic extraction of the unlabeled examples from the Web and its iterative integration into the training data set. To the knowledge of the authors, a semi-supervised method which makes use of the Web as support lexical resource has not been previously employed in this task. The results obtained on poem categorization show that this method may improve the classification accuracy and it is appropriate to handle the attribution of short documents.

1 Introduction

Nowadays, there is a lot of information available in digital format. This situation has produced a growing need for tools that help people to find, organize and analyze all these resources. In particular, text categorization [14], the automatic assignment of free text documents to one or more predefined categories, has emerged as a very important component in many information management tasks. Most of these tasks are of thematic nature, such as newswire and spam filtering, whereas some others are non-thematically restricted, for instance, authorship attribution and sentiment classification.

The state-of-the-art approach for automatic text categorization considers the application of a number of statistical and machine learning techniques, including Bayesian classifiers, support vector machines, nearest neighbour classifiers and artificial neural networks [14]. A major difficulty with this kind of supervised techniques is that they

---

[*] This work was done under partial support of CONACYT-Mexico (43990, C01-39957), MCyT-Spain (TIN2006-15265-C06-04) and PROMEP (UGTO-121).

A. Ranta, B. Nordström (Eds.): GoTAL 2008, LNAI 5221, pp. 160–168, 2008.

commonly require a great number of labelled examples (training instances) to construct an accurate classifier. Unfortunately, because a human expert must manually label these examples, the training sets are extremely small for many application domains. In order to overcome this problem, recently many researchers have been working on semi-supervised learning algorithms (for an overview see [15]). It has been showed that by augmenting the training set with additional unlabelled information it is possible to improve the classification accuracy using different learning algorithms such as naïve Bayes [12], support vector machines [8], and nearest-neighbour algorithms [19].

In line with these current works, we have proposed a new semi-supervised method for text categorization [5, 6]. This method differs from previous approaches in two main issues. On the one hand, it does not require a predefined set of unlabelled training examples, instead it considers their automatic extraction from the Web. On the other hand, it applies a self-training approach that selects instances not only considering their labelling confidence by a base classifier, but also their correspondence with a web-based labelling[1]. This method has been applied with success in thematic text classification tasks, indicating that it is possible to automatically extract discriminative thematic information from the Web. The method was evaluated on training sets of different sizes demonstrating its usefulness for dealing with very small data sets. As an example of this fact, our method improved the categorization of natural disaster news by 26% using a naïve Bayes classifier and a small training set with 10 examples per class [5].

In this paper, we investigate the application of the proposed web-based self-training method in a non-thematic classification task, namely, authorship attribution. This task confronts the method with new challenges since an author may write about several topics as well as a topic may be treated by different authors. Therefore, in this task, words by themselves do not allow distinguishing among classes; it is necessary to take into account how words are used together (i.e., the author's writing style). In order to make harder the evaluation, we focus our experiments on poem classification where documents are usually very short and their vocabulary and structure are very different from everyday –web– language.

The rest of the paper is organized as follows. Section 2 introduces the task of authorship attribution and discusses some representative works. Section 3 describes our web-based self-training approach for text classification. Then, Section 4 presents some evaluation results on poem classification by author. Finally, Section 5 depicts our conclusions.

2 Authorship Attribution

Authorship attribution is the task of identifying the author of a given text. It can be considered as a classification problem, where a set of documents with known authorship are used for training, and the aim is to automatically determine the corresponding author of an anonymous text.

---

[1] Given that each unlabelled example is downloaded from the Web using a set of automatically defined class queries, each of them has a default category or web-based label.

There are several methods for authorship attribution. These methods may be clustered in the following three main approaches:

Stylometric measures as document features. This approach considers features such as the length of words and sentences as well as the richness of the vocabulary [7, 10]. Its results are not conclusive, but they have shown that these features are not sufficient for the task. It seems that they vary depending on the genre of the text, and that they lost most of their meaning when dealing with short texts.

Syntactic cues as document features. This approach uses a set of style markers. These markers go beyond the stylometric measures by integrating information related to the structure of the language, which is obtained by an in depth syntactic analysis of documents [2, 4, 17]. Mainly, texts are characterized by the presence and frequency of certain syntactic structures. This characterization is very detailed and relevant; unfortunately, it is computationally expensive and even impossible to build for languages lacking of robust text-processing resources (e.g. POS tagger, syntactic parser, etc.). Besides, it is also clearly influenced by the length of documents.

Word-based document features. This approach includes at least three different kinds of methods. The first one characterizes documents using a set of functional words, ignoring content words since they tend to be highly correlated with the document topics [1, 21]. This kind of methods works properly, but it is also affected by the size of documents. In this case, the document length not only influences the frequency of occurrence of the functional words but also their sole presence. The second kind of methods applies the traditional bag-of-words representation and uses single content-words as document features [9]. It is very robust and produces excellent results when there is a noticeable relation between authors and topics. Finally, a third kind of method considers word n-gram features, i.e., features consisting of sequences of n consecutive words. It attempts to capture the language structure of texts by simple word sequences instead of by complex syntactic structures [13]. Somehow, its purpose is to obtain a rich characterization of texts without performing an expensive syntactic analysis. Nevertheless, due to the feature explosion, it tends to use only n-grams up to three words.

In contrast to all these works, this paper does not propose another document representation for authorship attribution, it describes instead a new semi-supervised learning method that allows working with small training sets. As expected, our web-based self-training classification method may be applied along with all these kinds of features. However, given that our interest is to have a general approach for authorship attribution that allows analyzing documents of different sizes and domains, we have decided to mainly explore the use of word-based features, in particular, n-grams.

3   Our Text Categorization Method

Figure 1 shows the general scheme of our semi-supervised text classification method. It consists of two main processes. The first one deals with the corpora acquisition from the Web, whereas the second one focuses on the self-training learning approach [11]. The following sections describe in detail these two processes.

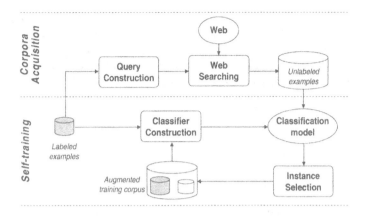

Fig. 1. General overview of our classification method

3.1 Corpora Acquisition

This process considers the automatic extraction of unlabeled examples from the Web. In order to do this, it first constructs a number of queries by combining the most significant words for each class; then, using these queries, it looks at the Web for some additional training examples related to the given classes.

Query Construction. In order to form queries for searching the Web, it is necessary to previously determine the set of relevant words for each class in the training corpus. The criterion used for this purpose is based on a combination of frequency of occurrence and information gain of words. We consider that a word w_i is relevant for a class C if it satisfies the following two conditions:

1. The frequency of occurrence of w_i in C is greater than the average occurrence of all words (happening more than once) in that class. That is:

$$f_{w_i}^C > \frac{1}{|C'|} \sum_{\forall w \in C'} f_w^C \text{ , where } C' = \left\{ w \in C \middle| f_w^C > 1 \right\}$$

2. The information gain of w_i is positive, that is $IG_{w_i} > 0$.

Once obtained the set of relevant words per class, it is possible to construct the corresponding set of queries. Founded on the method by Zelikovitz and Kogan [20], we decide to construct queries of three words. This way, we create as many queries per class as all three-word combinations of its relevant words. We measure the significance of a query $q = \{w_1, w_2, w_3\}$ to the class C as indicated below:

$$\Gamma_C(q) = \sum_{i=1}^{3} f_{w_i}^C \times IG_{w_i}$$

Web Searching. The next action is using the defined queries to extract from the Web a set of additional unlabeled text examples. Based on the observation that most significant queries tend to retrieve the most relevant web pages, our method for searching the Web determines the number of downloaded examples per query in a direct proportion to its Γ-value. Therefore, given a set of M queries $\{q_1, ..., q_M\}$ for class C, and considering that we want to download a total of N additional examples per class, the number of examples to be extracted by a query q_i is determined as follows:

$$\Psi_C(q_i) = \frac{N}{\sum_{k=1}^{M} \Gamma_C(q_k)} \times \Gamma_C(q_i)$$

3.2 Self-training Learning

As we previously mentioned, the purpose of this process is to increase the classification accuracy by gradually augmenting the originally small training set with the examples downloaded from the Web. Our algorithm for self-training learning is an adaptation of a method proposed elsewhere [16]. It mainly considers the following steps:

1. Build a weak classifier (C_l) using a specified learning method (l) and the training set available (T).
2. Classify the unlabeled web examples (E) using the constructed classifier (C_l). In order words, estimate the class for all downloaded examples.
3. Select the best m examples ($E_m \subseteq E$) based on the following two conditions:
   a. The estimate class of the example corresponds to the class of the query used to download it. In some way, this filter works as an ensemble of two classifiers: C_l and the Web (expressed by the set of queries).
   b. The example has one of the m-highest confidence predictions.
4. Combine the selected examples with the original training set ($T \leftarrow T \cup E_m$) in order to form a new training set. At the same time, eliminate these examples from the set of downloaded instances ($E \leftarrow E - E_m$).
5. Iterate σ times over steps 1 to 4 or repeat until $E_m = \varnothing$. In this case σ is a user specified threshold.
6. Construct the final classifier using the enriched training set.

4 Evaluation on Authorship Attribution

4.1 Experimental Setup

Corpus. Given that there is not a standard data set for evaluating authorship attribution methods, we had to assemble our own corpus. This corpus was gathered from the Web and consists of 353 poems written by five different authors [3]. Table 1 resumes some statistics about this corpus. It is important to notice that, on the one hand, the collected poems are very short texts (172 words in average), and on the other hand, that all of them correspond to contemporary Mexican poets. In particular, we were very careful in selecting modern writers in order to avoid the identification of authors by the use of anachronisms.

Table 1. Corpus Statistics

Poets	Number of documents	Word forms	Word tokens	Number of Phrases	Average Word Tokens by Document	Average Phrases by Document
Efraín Huerta	48	3831	11352	510	236.5	22.3
Jaime Sabines	80	3955	12464	717	155.8	17.4
Octavio Paz	75	3335	12195	448	162.6	27.2
Rosario Castellanos	80	4355	11944	727	149.3	16.4
Rubén Bonifaz	70	4769	12481	720	178.3	17.3

Baseline Configurations. Because of the difficulty of comparing our approach with other previous works (mainly because of the absence of a standard evaluation corpus), we performed several experiments in order to establish a baseline. These experiments consider the use of four different kinds of word-based features: (i) functional words, (ii) content words, (iii) the combination of functional and content words, and (iv) word n-grams. Table 2 shows the results corresponding to each one of these kinds of word-based features.

Table 2. Baseline Configurations

Features	Accuracy	Macro Average Precision	Average Recall
Functional words	0.41	0.42	0.39
Content words	0.73	0.78	0.73
All kind of words	0.73	0.78	0.74
n-grams (unigrams plus bigrams)	0.78	0.84	0.79
n-grams (from unigrams to trigrams)	0.76	0.84	0.77

Our main interest in this first experiment was to determine a baseline configuration for our subsequent experiments. Because of that, we used in all cases the same classification algorithm (namely, the naïve Bayes classifier), the same technique for dimensionality reduction (information gain) as well as the same evaluation schema (a 10-cross-fold validation). In all experiments, we used the implementations facilitated by the WEKA machine-learning environment [18].

The results shown in Table 2 are very interesting since they confirm some of our major assumptions. First, functional words by themselves do not help to capture the writing style of short texts. Second, content words contain some relevant information to distinguish among authors, even when all documents correspond to the same genre and discuss similar topics. Third, the lexical collocations, captured by word n-gram sequences, are useful for the task of authorship attribution. Fourth, due to the feature explosion and the small size of the corpus, the use of higher n-gram sequences not necessarily improves the classification performance.

4.2 Experimental Results

This section describes the application of the proposed semi-supervised method to the task of authorship attribution. The method, as depicted in Section 3, includes two main processes: the corpora acquisition from the Web and the self-training learning approach. Following, we detail some results from both of them.

The central task for corpora acquisition is the automatic construction of a set of queries that expresses the relevant content of each class. Using these queries, we collected from the Web a set of 2,400 snippets per class, obtaining 12,000 additional unlabeled examples. Then, we applied the self-training method for constructing the final poem classifier.

It is important to point out that there is not a clear criterion to determine the parameters m and σ of a self-training method [11]. In our case, we determined the number of unlabeled examples that must be incorporated into the training set at each iteration based on the following condition: the added information –expressed in number of words– must be proportionally small with respect to the original training data. This last condition is very important because of the small size of poems (176 words on average). In particular, we decided to incorporate 60 unlabeled examples per iteration ($m = 60$), approximately 10 examples per class. However, it is necessary to perform further experiments in order to determine the best value of m for this task.

Table 3. Training/test data sets

Poets	Training Set	Test Set	Word forms (in Training Set)
Efraín Huerta	38	10	2827
Jaime Sabines	64	16	2749
Octavio Paz	60	15	2431
Rosario Castellanos	64	16	3280
Rubén Bonifaz	56	14	3552
Total	*282*	*71*	*8377*

For this new experiment, we organized the corpus in a different way with respect to the baseline experiment described in Section 4.1 The corpus was divided in two data sets: training (with 80% of the labelled examples) and test (with 20% of the examples). The idea was to carry out the experiment in an almost-real situation, where it is not possible to know in advance all the vocabulary. This is a very important aspect to take into account in poem classification since poets tend to employ a very rich vocabulary. Table 3 shows some numbers about this collection.

Taking into account the results described in the previous section, we decided to use n-grams as document features. We mainly performed two different experiments. In the first one we used bigrams as features, whereas in the second one we used trigrams. Table 4 shows the results corresponding to the first five iterations of the method. As can be observed, the integration of new information improved the baseline results. In particular, the best result was obtained at the second iteration when using bigrams. We suppose this behaviour was due because bigrams are better suited to look for the most used collocations of an author from a small corpus; for trigrams –we presume– it is necessary to have more information.

Table 4 also shows the vocabulary's growing: aproximately 300 new words per iteration. Due to this increment it was possible to correctly classify more poems from the very first iteration. However, this increment was also the reason for the accuracy decrement in subsequent iterations where several non-relevant words were inserted into the training set.

Table 4. Accuracy percentages after the training corpus enrichment

n-grams	Initial Accuracy	Iteration				
		1	2	3	4	5
Bigrams	78.9	80.3	**82.9**	80.3	78.9	78.9
Trigrams	74.6	74.7	78.8	**80.3**	80.3	78.7
Vocabulary Size	8377	8732	9019	9319	9676	9915

Although being preliminary results, it is surprising to verify that it is feasible to extract useful examples from the Web for the task of authorship attribution. In fact, our intuition suggested the opposite: given that poems tend to use rare and improper word combinations, the Web seemed not to be an adequate source of relevant information for this task.

5   Conclusions

This paper proposed a novel approach for authorship attribution based on a web-based self-training learning method. This method differs from others in that: (i) it is specially suited to work with few training examples, and (ii) it considers the automatic extraction of additional training knowledge from the Web.

In general, the achieved results allow us to formulate the following preliminary conclusions:

- Our web-based self-training classification method seems to be portable to non-thematic tasks. In particular, the achieved results in authorship attribution support this observation.
- The proposed method for authorship attribution, which uses n-gram features and a semi-supervised learning approach, could outperform most common approaches for authorship attribution. Furthermore, our method, contrary to other current approaches, is not affected by the small size of the texts, and avoids using any sophisticated linguistic analysis of documents.
- The proper identification of an author, even from a poem, must consider both stylometric and topic features of documents. Therefore, our conclusion points to use word-based features such as word n-grams.

Finally, it is important to comment that it is necessary to achieve a detailed analysis of current results as well as to perform further experiments in order to define better empirical criteria for selecting the values of the parameters m and σ.

References

1. Argamon, S., Levitan, S.: Measuring the Usefulness of Function Words for Author-ship Attribution. Association for Literary and Linguistic Computing/ Association Com-puter Humanities, University of Victoria, Canada (2005)
2. Chaski, C.: Who's at the Keyword? Authorship Attribution in Digital Evidence Investiga-tions. International Journal of Digital Evidence 4(1) (2005)

3. Coyotl-Morales, R.M., Villaseñor-Pineda, L., Montes-y-Gómez, M., Rosso, P.: Authorship Attribution using Word Sequences. In: Martínez-Trinidad, J.F., Carrasco Ochoa, J.A., Kittler, J. (eds.) CIARP 2006. LNCS, vol. 4225, Springer, Heidelberg (2006)
4. Diederich, J., Kindermann, J., Leopold, E., Paas, G.: Authorship Attribution with Sup-port Vector Machines. Applied Intelligence 19(1), 109–123 (2003)
5. Guzmán-Cabrera, R., Montes-y-Gómez, M., Rosso, P., Villaseñor-Pineda, L.: Improving Text Classification using Web Corpora. In: 5th Atlantic Web Intelligence Conference, AWIC 2007. Advances in Soft Computing, vol. 43. Springer, Heidelberg (2007)
6. Guzmán-Cabrera, R., Montes-y-Gómez, M., Rosso, P., Villaseñor-Pineda, L.: Taking Advantage of the Web for Text Classification with Imbalanced Classes. In: Gelbukh, A., Kuri Morales, Á.F. (eds.) MICAI 2007. LNCS (LNAI), vol. 4827. Springer, Heidelberg (2007)
7. Holmes, D.: Authorship Attribution. Computers and the Humanities, vol. 28, pp. 87–106. Kluwer Academic Publishers, Dordrecht (1995)
8. Joachims, T.: Transductive inference for text classification using support vector machines. In: Proceedings of the Sixteenth International Conference on Machine Learning (1999)
9. Kaster, A., Siersdorfer, S., Weikum, G.: Combining Text and Linguistic Document Representations for Authorship Attribution. In: 28th Int. Workshop Stylistic Analysis of Text for Information Access, SIGIR 1, MPI, Saarbrücken (2005)
10. Malyutov, M.B.: Authorship Attribution of Texts: a Review. Proceedings of the program Information transfer held in ZIF. University of Bielefeld, Germany (2004)
11. Mihalcea, R.: Co-training and Self-training for Word Sense Disambiguation. In: Proc. of the Conference on Natural Lenguage Learning (CoNLL 2004), Boston, USA (2004)
12. Nigam, K., Mccallum, A.K., Thrun, S., Mitchell, T.: Text classification from labeled and unlabeled documents using EM. Machine Learning 39(2/3), 103–134 (2000)
13. Peng, F., Schuurmans, D., Keselj, V., Wang, S.: Augmenting Naïve Bayes Classifiers with Statistical Languages Models. Information Retrieval 7, 317–345 (2004)
14. Sebastiani, F.: Machine learning in automated text categorization. ACM Computing Surveys 34(1), 1–47 (2002)
15. Seeger, M.: Learning with labeled and unlabeled data. Technical report, Institute for Adaptive and Neural Computation, University of Edinburgh, Edinburgh, United Kingdom (2001)
16. Solorio, T.: Using unlabeled data to improve classifier accuracy, Master Degree Thesis, Computer Science Department, INAOE, Mexico (2002)
17. Stamatatos, E., Fakotakis, N.: Computer-Based Authorship Attribution Without Lexical Measures. Computers and the Humanities 35, 193–214 (2001)
18. Witten, I.H., Frank, E.: Data Mining-practical Machine Learning Tools and Techniques whit Java Implementation. Morgan Kaufmann, San Francisco (2000)
19. Zelikovitz, S., Hirsh, H.: Integrating background knowledge into nearest-Neighbor text classification. In: Advances in Case-Based Reasoning, ECCBR Proceedings (2002)
20. Zelikovitz, S., Kogan, M.: Using Web Searches on Important Words to Create Background Sets for LSI Classification. In: 19th International FLAIRS conference, Melbourne Beach, Florida (May 2006)
21. Zhao, Y., Zobel, J.: Effective and Scalable Authorship Attribution Using Function Words. In: Lee, G.G., Yamada, A., Meng, H., Myaeng, S.-H. (eds.) AIRS 2005. LNCS, vol. 3689, pp. 174–189. Springer, Heidelberg (2005)

Parsing Discontinuous Phrase Structure with Grammatical Functions

Johan Hall[1] and Joakim Nivre[2]

[1] Växjö University, Sweden
johan.hall@vxu.se
[2] Växjö University, Sweden and Uppsala University, Sweden
joakim.nivre@vxu.se

Abstract. This paper presents a novel technique for parsing discontinuous phrase structure representations, labeled with both phrase labels and grammatical functions. Phrase structure representations are transformed into dependency representations with complex edge labels, which makes it possible to induce a dependency parser model that recovers the phrase structure with both phrase labels and grammatical functions. We perform an evaluation on the German TIGER treebank and the Swedish Talbanken05 treebank and report competitive results for both data sets.

1 Introduction

Data-driven parsing is a popular method for deriving the syntactic representation of a sentence by inducing a parser model from a treebank of syntactically annotated sentences of a given language. However, there is often a discrepancy between the original treebank annotation and the representations used by the parser. Take for instance parsers trained on the Penn Treebank, where it is often the case that function labels and empty categories are not recovered by the parser. Notable exceptions, among others, are Musillo and Merlo [1], who enrich the parser output with function labels, and Gabbard et al. [2], who recover both function labels and empty categories.

For German, the Negra annotation scheme is the basis for the annotation of both the Negra Corpus [3] and the TIGER treebank [4]. The Negra annotation scheme uses a combination of dependency and phrase structure representations, and encodes both local and non-local dependencies, which sometimes results in discontinuous phrases. Data-driven parsing of these two German treebanks often involve a simplification of the syntactic representation, and it is common to restrict the task to deriving only the continuous phrase structure and only the phrase labels. Kübler et al. [5] recover grammatical functions, but not discontinuities. By contrast, Plaehn [6] parses discontinuous phrase structure using a probabilistic extension of discontinuous phrase structure grammar (DPSG), but evaluation is restricted to only phrase labels.

This paper describes how a data-driven dependency parser can be turned into a phrase structure parser that recovers both continuous and discontinuous

A. Ranta, B. Nordström (Eds.): GoTAL 2008, LNAI 5221, pp. 169–180, 2008.

phrases with both phrase labels and grammatical functions.[1] Evaluation is carried out on two treebanks: the German TIGER treebank [4] and the Swedish Talbanken05 treebank [7]. Both treebanks are encoded in the TIGER-XML format, but use different annotation schemes. The parser system induces a parser model from the original treebanks by automatically transforming the phrase structure representations into dependency representations. Our method for parsing phrase structure with grammatical functions consists of four steps:

1. Transform phrase structures into dependency graphs that encode the inverse transformation in complex edge labels.
2. Train a transition-based dependency parser on dependency graphs derived in step 1.
3. Parse new sentences using the parser model induced in step 2.
4. Apply the inverse transformation to dependency graphs produced in step 3, using the information encoded in the complex edge labels.

This paper is structured as follows: Section 2 describes the target syntactic representation, and shows how this representation is transformed to a dependency representation and back. In section 3 we explain how the transformed dependency graphs are parsed with a transition-based dependency parser. Section 4 presents the experimental evaluation and discusses the results, while section 5 compares our results to previous work. Finally, section 6 concludes.

2   Syntactic Representations

We have selected two treebanks for evaluating our approach that are both encoded in the TIGER-XML treebank encoding format [8], which is generic format for representing various corpora and treebanks. This format allows a treebank creator, in a straightforward way, to encode continuous and discontinuous phrase structures with phrase labels but also with grammatical functions.[2] The format is well-suited for deriving a dependency representation of a phrase structure, because of all the information at hand (especially the grammatical functions are very useful).

Our approach is not restricted to treebanks encoded in TIGER-XML, but we have used treebanks encoded in TIGER-XML as the target encoding format because it allows discontinuous phrase structure with grammatical functions. To define our algorithms for transforming a phrase structure representation to a dependency representation and back, we need a formal framework. In this framework, the syntactic representation of a sentence can be encoded either as a *phrase structure graph* G_P or as a *dependency graph* G_D. The two representations are equivalent in the sense that we can convert between them without loss of information, but whereas G_P corresponds to the representation found in the

---

[1] We have used MaltParser 1.1, which can be downloaded free of charge from following page: http://www.vxu.se/msi/users/jha/maltparser/
[2] We have ignored the secondary edges in TIGER-XML.

treebank, G_D is the representation used internally by the parser. Our notion of phrase structure graph is inspired by the notion of *syntax graph* defined by König and Lezius [9].

Definition 1. Let L_{NT} be the set of *non-terminal labels* (phrase labels) and let L_E be the set of *edge labels* (grammatical functions). A *phrase structure graph* G_P for a sentence $x = (w_1, \ldots, w_n)$ is a quintuple $G_P = (V_{NT}, V_T, E_P, <, R_P)$, where

1. V_{NT} is a finite set of non-terminal nodes, labeled by elements of L_{NT},
2. V_T is a non-empty finite set of terminal nodes, one for each $w_i \in x$,[3]
3. E_P is a set of directed edges (v_i, v_j) $(v_i \in V_{NT}, v_j \in V_{NT} \cup V_T)$, labeled by elements of L_E,
4. $<$ is a linear order on V_T (defined by the order of words in x),
5. $R_P \in (V_{NT} \cup V_T)$ is the root node.

A phrase structure graph G_P is well-formed if it is a directed tree rooted at R_P.

Definition 2. Let L_{NT} and L_E be as in definition 1. A *dependency graph* G_D for a sentence $x = (w_1, \ldots, w_n)$ is a quadruple $G_D = (V_T, E_D, <, R_D)$, where

1. V_T is a non-empty finite set of terminal nodes, one for each $w_i \in x$, plus an extra root node v_0,
2. E_D is a set of directed edges (v_i, v_j) $(v_i, v_j \in V_T)$, labeled by complex labels (l_E, p_E, p_{NT}, a), where
   (a) l_E is an edge label in L_E,
   (b) p_E is a sequence (or path) of edge labels in L_E,
   (c) p_{NT} is a sequence (or path) of phrase labels in L_{NT},
   (d) a is a positive integer,
3. $<$ is a linear order on V_T (defined by the order of words in x),
4. R_D is the root node v_0.

A dependency graph G_D is well-formed if it is a directed tree rooted at R_D.

Figure 1 shows a German sentence from the TIGER treebank with its phrase structure graph (top) and dependency graph (bottom).[4] The elements of a complex edge label (l_E, p_E, p_{NT}, a) for an edge $(v_i, v_j) \in E_D$ in the dependency graph have the following interpretation:

- The label l_E is the grammatical function of the highest non-terminal node $v_k \in V_{NT}$ such that v_j is the lexical head of v_k in G_P.
- The sequence p_E is the path of grammatical functions from v_j to v_k in G_P.
- The sequence p_{NT} is the path of phrase labels from v_j to v_k in G_P.
- The integer a is the attachment level of v_k with respect to the non-terminal nodes that have v_i as their lexical head in G_P.

---

[3] We assume that terminal nodes are labeled with part-of-speech tags as well as word forms.

[4] Note that sequence elements in the complex edge labels in the dependency graph are separated by a vertical bar |.

The transformation $G_P \rightarrow G_D \rightarrow G_P$ involves several steps and the rest of this section is structured according to these steps. The first step is to find the head child for each non-terminal node in the phrase structure graph G_P. The second step builds a dependency graph G_D according to the heads identified in the first step, where the inverse transformation is encoded in the complex edge labels of G_D. To make this more understandable, we go through an example of the transformation $G_P \rightarrow G_D$. Finally, we define the inverse transformation $G_D \rightarrow G_P$.

2.1 Head Identification

The first steps are basically the steps that are used to convert a phrase structure to a dependency graph. One way of doing this is to traverse the phrase structure graph from the root node and identify the head-child v_{hc} and the lexical head v_{hcl} for all nodes $v \in V_{NT}$ in a recursive depth-first search. The algorithm is defined in the following way:

IDENTIFY-HEAD(v, HR)
1 **if** $v \in V_T$
2   **return** v
3 **else**
4    $v_{hc} \leftarrow$ IDENTIFY-HEADCHILD(v, HR)
5    $v_{hcl} \leftarrow$ IDENTIFY-HEAD(v_{hc}, HR)
6   **for** $i = 1$ **up to** NUMBEROFCHILDREN(v)
7   **if** GET-CHILD$(v, i) \neq v_{hc}$
8        $v_{lc} \leftarrow$ IDENTIFY-HEAD$($GET-CHILD$(v, i), HR)$
9   SET-TERMINALHEAD(v_{lc}, v_{hcl})
10   **return** v_{hlc}

The algorithm starts from the root R_P and visits all nodes in the phrase structure graph, but it is only the non-terminals that will be assigned a head-child v_{hc} and a lexical head v_{hcl}; if the node v is a terminal then it is its own lexical head. The function IDENTIFY-HEADCHILD takes the current node v and the head rules HR and returns the head-child v_{hc} of v according to the head rules. The head rules can be very simple, such as: Take the leftmost terminal child as the head-child if it exists; otherwise take the leftmost non-terminal child. But the head rules can also be more complex with a priority list for each phrase type. The next step is to find the lexical head of the head-child v_{hcl} by invoking the function IDENTIFY-HEAD recursively. Finally, the algorithm iterates over all children of node v, and if the child returned by GET-CHILD(v, i) is different from the head-child v_{hc}, SET-TERMINALHEAD assigns the lexical head v_{hcl} as the head of the lexical terminal child v_{lc} returned by recursively invoking IDENTIFY-HEAD. In other words, after we have visited all nodes in the phrase structure graph, all non-terminal nodes V_{NT} have been assigned a head-child and a lexical head, and all terminal nodes V_T (except the terminal node that is the lexical head-child of the root R_P) have been assigned another terminal node as head. The latter assignment contains all the information need to derive an unlabeled dependency graph.

2.2   Phrase Structure Graph → Dependency Graph

The next step builds a labeled dependency representation that encodes the inverse transformation in the edge labels of the dependency graph. The function CREATE-DEPENDENCYGRAPH defines this algorithm as follows:

CREATE-DEPENDENCYGRAPH(V_T, E_D)
1   **for** $i = 1$ **up to** $|V_T|$
2       $v_{pt} \leftarrow v_i$
3   **while** $v_i = $ GET-LEXICALHEAD(v_{pt})
4   **if** $\exists$GET-PARENT(v_{pt})
5               $v_{pt} \leftarrow$ GET-PARENT(v_{pt})
6       $l_E \leftarrow$ GET-EDGELABEL(v_{pt})
7       $p_E \leftarrow$ GET-EDGELABEL-PATH($v_i, v_{pt}, "|"$)
8       $p_{NT} \leftarrow$ GET-PHRASELABEL-PATH($v_i, v_{pt}, "|"$)
9       $a \leftarrow 0$
10   **if** $v_{pt} \in V_{NT}$
11          $v_{hc} \leftarrow$ GET-HEADCHILD(v_{pt})
12   **while** $v_{hc} \in V_{NT}$
13              $a \leftarrow a + 1$
14              $v_{hc} \leftarrow$ GET-HEADCHILD(v_{pt})
15   **if** $\exists$GET-TERMINALHEAD(v_i)
16   ADD-EDGE(E_D, GET-TERMINALHEADINDEX(v_i), $v_i, (l_E, p_E, p_{NT}, a)$)
17   **else**
16   ADD-EDGE($E_D, v_0, v_i, (l_E, p_E, p_{NT}, a)$)

For each terminal node $v_i \in V_T$, we first identify the parent v_{pt} of the highest non-terminal node of which v_i is the lexical head. This is done by traversing the phrase structure upwards, invoking the function GET-PARENT until we encounter a non-terminal node for which v_i is *not* the lexical head. The next steps find the first three elements of the complex label for the edge going into v_i: the grammatical function l_E (line 6), the path of grammatical functions p_E (line 7), and the path of phrase labels p_{NT} (line 8). If $v_i = v_{pt}$, there are no paths to encode, which is indicated by $p_E = p_{NT} = *$. Moreover, the lines 9–14 calculate the attachment level a of the path of nodes from v_i to v_{pt} by following the head-child as long as it is a non-terminal. Finally, an edge (v_j, v_i) is added to the set of directed edges E_D with the complex edge label (l_E, p_E, p_{NT}, a), where j is either the index of the terminal head of the terminal v_i or the special root node $R_D = v_0$.

2.3   Example

Figure 1 illustrates the procedure of encoding the phrase structure graph as a dependency graph with complex edge labels for a German sentence. For this example, we have used very simple head rules to identify the head-child for each non-terminal: Select the leftmost lexical child if present; otherwise use the leftmost non-terminal child. The phrase VP has one lexical child *verlangen* and therefore this child will be both the head-child and the lexical head of VP. By contrast, the phrase NP has no lexical child and therefore the head-child is the leftmost non-terminal AVP. The lexical head of NP is the token *nicht* because

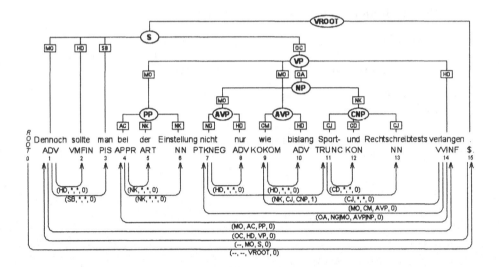

Fig. 1. The sentence s4962 is taken from the TIGER treebank and a possible translation is: "Nevertheless, when hiring, you should not only, as before, require a sport and spelling test.". The phrase structure graph is illustrated above the sentence and the derived dependency graph below the sentence.

it is the lexical head of AVP. Because VP dominates NP the lexical head of VP *verlangen* will be the head of the terminal *nicht*, and this is illustrated with an edge in the dependency graph from *verlangen* to *nicht*.

The edge between these two terminals is labeled with a complex label (OA, NG|MO, AVP|NP, 0), which consists of four sublabels (l_E = OA, p_E = NG|MO, p_{NT} = AVP|NP, $a = 0$). The first sublabel OA is the grammatical function above NP. The sublabel NG|MO encodes the path of grammatical functions from the lexical head *nicht* to NP. The phrase labels are encoded in the same way in the third sublabel AVP|NP. Finally, the fourth sublabel indicates the attachment level of the non-terminal NP. In this case, NP should be attached directly under the non-terminal VP and the sublabel is therefore 0. By contrast, the edge from *nicht* to *Sport-* with the label (NK, CJ, CNP, 1) has the attachment level 1, which means that the non-terminal CNP should be attached to NP, which is one level up in the structure with respect to the head *nicht*.[5] We can also see that the discontinuous NP gives rise to a non-projective edge from *nicht* to *Sport-*.

2.4 Dependency Graph → Phrase Structure Graph

The last step of our presented strategy is to make the inverse transformation from a dependency graph to a phrase structure graph. This is done by a bottom-up and top-down process on the dependency graph. The algorithm is defined in the function CREATE-PHRASESTRUCTUREGRAPH:

---

[5] If the attachment level had been 0, then the non-terminal CNP would have been attached to the non-terminal AVP instead of the non-terminal NP.

CREATE-PHRASESTRUCTUREGRAPH(V_T)
1 **for** $i = 1$ up to n
2 $(l_E, p_E, p_{NT}, a) \leftarrow$ GET-EDGELABEL(v_i)
2 $v_{pt} \leftarrow$ BUILD-PATH(p_E, p_{NT})
3 **for** $i =$ GET-NUMBEROFDEPENDENTS(v_0) down to 1
4 ATTACH-PATH(GET-DEPENDENT(v_0, i))

For each node v_i in the dependency graph, we invoke the function BUILD-PATH, which restores the path of non-terminal nodes with phrase labels and grammatical functions for each terminal using the information in the sublabels p_E and p_{NT} of the incoming edge. After this bottom-up process we have a lineage from v_i to the highest non-terminal node of which v_i is the lexical head. The top-down process then traverses the dependency graph recursively from the root(s) by invoking the function ATTACH-PATH, which is defined as follows:

ATTACH-PATH(v_i)
1 $v_{pt} \leftarrow$ GET-PATHTOP(v_i)
2 $v_{ph} \leftarrow$ GET-PARENT(GET-HEAD(v_i))
3 $(l_E, p_E, p_{NT}, a) \leftarrow$ GET-EDGELABEL(v_i)
4 $k \leftarrow 0$
5 **while** $k < a$ **and** $\exists$GET-PARENT(v_{ph})
6 $k \leftarrow k + 1$
7 $v_{ph} \leftarrow$ GET-PARENT(v_{ph})
8 **if** GET-HEAD(v_i) = v_0 **or** $v_{ph} \in V_T$
9 ATTACH-ROOT(v_{pt}, l_E)
10 **else**
11 ADD-EDGE(v_{ph}, v_{pt}, l_E)
12 **for** $j = 1$ up to GET-NUMBEROFDEPENDENTS(v_i)
13 ATTACH-PATH(GET-DEPENDENT(v_i, j))

The function ATTACH-PATH uses a pre-order depth-first search to attach the lineage of a node to its head lineage or to the root of the phrase structure graph. First, the algorithm starts by assigning v_{pt} the highest non-terminal (or terminal) of the lineage by invoking GET-PATHTOP. In lines 2–7, the algorithm traverses the head lineage a steps up in the structure to find v_{ph}, where a is the attachment level defined in the sublabel a of the complex edge label (l_E, p_E, p_{NT}, a).[6]

If the current node v_i has the root of the dependency graph as its head, then the highest non-terminal node v_{pt} of the lineage will be the root R_P of the phrase structure graph, and the function ATTACH-ROOT is invoked.[7] If the node v_i does not attach to the root, then an edge from v_{ph} to v_{pt} is added with the sublabel

---

[6] The function GET-HEAD returns the head of v_i in the dependency graph. During parsing it is possible that the attachment level is higher than the number of nodes in the lineage and therefore the loop condition checks whether the parent node exists or not.

[7] The if statement also contains the condition $v_{ph} \in V_T$, which is possible during parsing. The function ATTACH-ROOT also hides two special cases, which can occur during parsing: if $v_{pt} \in V_T$, then a non-terminal node is inserted with a default root label, and if the root R_P already has been assigned a node, then v_{pt} will be a child of the root R_P.

l_E of the complex edge label (l_E, p_E, p_{NT}, a). Finally, all dependents of the node v_i are visited recursively by invoking ATTACH-PATH.

3 Parsing

Section 2 describes how we can transform phrase structure representations to dependency representations, which makes it possible to recover the phrase structure with both phrase labels and grammatical functions. The next natural step is to find a way of parsing these dependency representations. McDonald and Nivre [10] define global, exhaustive, graph-based parsing and local, greedy, transition-based parsing, which are two different approaches to data-driven dependency parsing with almost the same performance. For our parsing experiments, we have chosen to implement the transition-based approach, because we believe that it makes it easier to handle the large number of distinct edge labels that occur in our dependency representations.

The basic idea of transition-based parsing is to derive dependency graphs using a greedy parsing algorithm that approximates a globally optimal solution by making a sequence of locally optimal choices. Since discontinuous phrases are transformed into non-projective dependency graphs we need a way to manage such graphs. Covington [11] presents an incremental parsing strategy for dependency representations that can recover non-projective graphs in quadratic time. Nivre [12] formulates this parsing strategy as follows:

PARSE($x = (w_1, \ldots, w_n)$)
1 **for** $j = 1$ **up to** n
2   **for** $i = j - 1$ **down to** 0
3   LINK(i, j)

The operation LINK(i, j) is nondeterministic and either adds an edge (v_i, v_j) (with some label), adds an edge (v_j, v_i) (with some label), or does nothing at all. Our parser system uses history-based feature models for predicting the outcome of the operation LINK(i, j). The complex edge labels defined in section 2 will result in a large set of distinct edge labels, and to make it more feasible we divide prediction into nine feature models. First, we have a model for predicting one of the three possible operations. If the prediction is to do nothing then the nondeterminism is resolved, but if the prediction is either a right edge (v_i, v_j) or a left edge (v_j, v_i), the system continues by predicting the complex edge label. There are four models, one for each sublabel, for predicting a label for a right edge operation and four models for a left edge.

All symbolic features are then converted to numerical features and we use the quadratic kernel of the LIBSVM package [13] for mapping histories to parser actions and edge labels.

4 Experiments

The evaluation of the presented method is divided into two experiments. First, we want to validate the transformation of phrase structure representations to dependency representations by transforming them back to phrase structure without losing any information about the structure and the labels. Secondly, we want to train a parser model based on the transformed dependency representations, parse new sentences using the parser model, and then apply the inverse transformation to the parsed dependency graphs.

A secondary goal of designing our parser system is to take a TIGER-XML document as input for training a parser model and output a TIGER-XML document after completing the parse and the inverse transformation.[8] We have chosen to use two treebanks that are both encoded in TIGER-XML, but with different annotation schemes. The first data set is the TIGER treebank version 2.1 [4], which contains 50 472 sentences (888 238 tokens) of German newspaper text, with an average sentence length of 17.6 tokens, and 54 distinct part-of-speech tags. The German data set contains 22.5% discontinuous phrases, but many of the discontinuities are due to punctuation being attached to the root. The second data set is taken from the professional prose section of the Swedish treebank Talbanken05 [7], containing 6100 sentences (97 335 tokens). More precisely we use the Deep Phrase Structure version. The average sentence length is 16.0 tokens, there are 252 distinct part-of-speech tags, and 1.2% of the phrases are discontinuous.

Our first experiment verified for both treebanks that all well-formed phrase structures can be transformed to dependency graphs and back to phrase structures with all phrases and edges correctly labeled.[9]

For the second experiment we used a pseudo-randomized method to divide the data into 10 sections, where sentence i is allocated to section i mod 10. During optimization of the two parsing models we used sections 1–9 and for the final evaluation we trained two parser models on sections 1–9 and tested on section 0.[10]

The results on the final test set (section 0) are shown in table 1. For both treebanks we present four rows of results. The first two rows contain results with gold standard part-of-speech tags (tagging accuracy = TA = 100%). The last two rows contain results where the input has been tagged automatically (tagging accuracy = TA). Both sets of results are divided into two groups: evaluation on all sentences (∞) and evaluation on all sentences up to 40 words long (40). Every row presents an evaluation according to the F_1-score, which is the harmonic mean of recall (R) and precision (P), that is, $F_1 = (2PR)/(P + R)$. The column UF_1 shows the unlabeled F_1-Score, which means that unlabeled recall UR is defined as the percentage of phrases in the final test set which are correctly found by our parser system. Notice that correctly means that the two phrases dominate

---

[8] It is impossible to recover exactly the same TIGER-XML document with its metadata and the numbers of the identifiers in the same way as the treebank creator.

[9] Talbanken05 contains six malformed structures: s1549, s2908, s2326, s3355, s4035 and s5903. TIGER contains two malformed structures: s46234 and s50224; TIGER also contains one well-formed structure with one token (s39172), where the lonely token is not the root of the structure which is the case for all other one token sentences in TIGER.

[10] In the evaluation on TIGER we used 45424 sentences for training and 5048 sentences for testing, and on Talbanken05 5490 for training and 610 for testing.

Table 1. Parsing accuracy; TA = tagging accuracy; SL = sentence length; F_1 = F_1-score; M = exact match; U = unlabeled; P = phrase labels; E = edge labels; L = labeled (both phrase and edge labels); T = includes incoming edge labels to terminals

Treebank	TA	SL	UF_1	PF_1	EF_1	LF_1	UM	PM	EM	LM	TEM	TLM
TIGER	100	∞	81.35	78.69	70.95	69.32	39.10	36.53	32.21	30.69	29.69	29.44
		40	82.55	79.93	72.44	70.79	40.44	37.78	33.35	31.77	30.74	30.48
	97.0	∞	77.50	74.04	66.69	64.82	34.31	31.56	28.39	26.92	25.87	25.61
		40	78.76	75.33	68.16	66.27	35.48	32.63	29.39	27.87	26.78	26.52
Talbanken05	100	∞	76.82	73.97	66.96	65.33	32.30	30.16	22.95	22.13	18.36	17.87
		40	79.80	76.90	70.09	68.34	33.16	30.98	23.57	22.73	18.86	18.35
	84.2	∞	70.85	66.72	59.77	58.03	25.25	22.46	17.87	16.72	13.93	13.44
		40	73.47	69.21	62.23	60.46	25.93	23.06	18.35	17.17	14.31	13.80

the same terminals. The unlabeled precision UP is defined as the percentage of phrases proposed by our parser system which are actually correct according to the structures in the treebank. The column PF_1 presents results where also phrase labels are required to be correct; for EF_1, edge labels must be correct; and for LF_1 both phrase labels and edge labels must match. The metric UM is the unlabeled exact match, that is, the proportion of sentences that are assigned the completely correct unlabeled phrase structure, while PM, EM and LM are the corresponding metrics for phrase labels, edge labels, and all labels, respectively. The metrics TEM and TLM are the same as EM and LM except that they also consider edge labels going into terminals, which are ignored in all other metrics.

The results with gold-standard part-of-speech tags show that the parser can reconstruct the phrase structure with an F_1-score of 81.35 for TIGER and 76.82 for Talbanken05, and that it is able to recover the phrase structure with all phrase labels and all edge labels going into non-terminals with an F_1-score of 69.32 for TIGER and 65.33 for Talbanken05. The parser recovers the complete structure of a sentence with all its labels (phrase labels and both incoming edge labels to non-terminals and terminals) with an accuracy of 29.44 for TIGER and 17.87 for Talbanken05.

If we replace the gold-standard part-of-speech tags with part-of-speech tags that have been assigned by a part-of-speech tagger with a tagging accuracy of 97.0 for TIGER and 84.2 for Talbanken05,[11] we can recover discontinuous and continuous phrase structure with all its labels and edge labels with an F_1-Score of 64.82 for TIGER and 58.03 for Talbanken05.

In addition to the results in table 1, we have investigated the precision and recall with respect to discontinuous phrases only. For TIGER, discontinuous phrases have an unlabeled recall of 53.6% and an unlabeled precision of 62.9%, when evaluated on all sentences and tagged data. This is an encouraging result, given that discontinuous phrases are generally harder to parse correctly than continuous phrases, which shows that the parser can learn to process a

---

[11] Unfortunately, the Talbanken05 tagger suffers from sparse data due to the large part-of-speech tagset (over 250 distinct tags) and the small data set.

very significant proportion of these structures. Unfortunately, the results for Talbanken05 are much more disappointing in this respect, with an unlabeled precision and recall of approximately 1% for discontinuous phrases under the same conditions. The most likely explanation for this result is that discontinous phrases are simply too rare in the Swedish treebank for the parser to be able to learn how to process them. Comparing the two data sets, we find not only that the German training set is ten times larger than the Swedish one, but also that discontinuous phrases are twenty times more frequent.

5   Related Work

It is difficult to compare our results with other published results on German and Swedish, because of different data sets and experimental setup. The most obvious comparison for German is the work of Plaehn [6], which is the only previous work that we can find that recovers both discontinuous and continuous structures. Plaehn reports an F_1-score of 73.16 (evaluation metric PF_1 and sentence length $SL <= 15$) for the Negra treebank using an agenda-based chart parser. The closest comparable result for our parser is 75.33, but this result includes sentences up to a length of 40 tokens and is based on three times as much training data. Dubey [14] uses an unlexicalized parser which employs smoothing and suffix analysis and is capable of parsing continuous phrase structure with an F_1-Score of 76.3 for Negra (PF_1 and $SL <= 40$). This score is higher than our result (75.33), but Dubey has removed all discontinuous phrases, which arguably makes the parsing task easier. The score 66.27 for LF_1 and $SL <= 40$ is also competitive, if we compare with Kübler et al. [5], who report 51.41 F_1-score (LF_1 and $SL <= 35$) on the Negra treebank using the unlexicalized, markovized PCFG version of the Stanford parser.

For Swedish and Talbanken05 we could only find one paper on parsing phrase structure. Hall et al. [15] report an F_1-Score of 74.88 (PF_1 and $SL <= 100$) with gold standard part-of-speech tags using a dependency parser on a hybrid representation of phrase structure and dependency. This can be compared with our score of 73.97 (PF_1 and $SL < \infty$), but the results of Hall et al. [15] are again based on a simplified representation, where all phrases that do not have at least one terminal child have been removed.

6   Conclusion

We have presented a technique for syntactic parsing that makes it possible for a transition-based dependency-driven parser to recover both discontinuous and continuous phrase structure, labeled with both phrase labels and grammatical functions. The evaluation on two treebanks shows state-of-art results for parsing the TIGER treebank and the Talbanken05 treebank. The second contribution of this paper is a lossless method for automatically transforming phrase structure representations to dependency representations and back to phrase structure representations.

References

1. Musillo, G., Merlo, P.: Lexical and Structural Biases for Function Parsing. In: Proceedings of the Ninth International Workshop on Parsing Technologies (IWPT), pp. 83–92 (2005)
2. Gabbard, R., Marcus, M., Kulick, S.: Fully Parsing the Penn Treebank. In: Proceedings of the Human Language Technology Conference of the North American Chapter of the ACL, pp. 184–191 (2007)
3. Skut, W., Krenn, B., Brants, T., Uszkoreit, H.: An Annotation Scheme for Free Word Order Languages. In: Proceedings of the Fifth Conference on Applied Natural Language Processing (ANLP), pp. 314–321 (1997)
4. Brants, S., Dipper, S., Hansen, S., Lezius, W., Smith, G.: The TIGER Treebank. In: Proceedings of the Workshop on Treebanks and Linguistic Theories Sozopol, pp. 1–18 (2002)
5. Kübler, S., Hinrichs, E.W., Maier, W.: Is it Really that Difficult to Parse German. In: Proceedings of the 2006 Conference on Empirical Methods in Natural Language Processing (EMNLP 2006), pp. 111–119 (2006)
6. Plaehn, O.: Computing the Most Probable Parse for a Discontinuous Phrase Structure Grammar. In: Bunt, H. (ed.) New Technologies in Parsing Technology, pp. 283–298. Kluwer Academic Publishers, Dordrecht (2005)
7. Nivre, J., Nilsson, J., Hall, J.: Talbanken 2005: A Swedish Treebank with Phrase Structure and Dependency Annotation. In: Proceedings of the fifth international conference on Language Resources and Evaluation, pp. 1392–1395 (2006)
8. Mengel, A., Lezius, W.: An XML-based Representation Format for Syntactically Annotated Corpora. In: Proceedings of the 2nd International Conference on Language Resources and Evaluation, vol. 1, pp. 121–126 (2000)
9. König, E., Lezius, W.: The TIGER Language - A Description Language for Syntax Graphs, Formal Definition. Technical report, Institut fr Maschinelle Sprachverarbeitung, University of Stuttgart (2003)
10. McDonald, R., Nivre, J.: Characterizing the Errors of Data-Driven Dependency Parsing Models. In: Proceedings of the 2007 Joint Conference on Empirical Methods in Natural Language Processing and Computational Natural Language Learning (EMNLP-CoNLL 2007), pp. 122–131 (2007)
11. Covington, M.A.: A Fundamental Algorithm for Dependency Parsing. In: Proceedings of the 39th Annual ACM Southeast Conference, pp. 95–102 (2001)
12. Nivre, J.: Incremental Non-Projective Dependency Parsing. In: Proceedings of Human Language Technologies: The Annual Conference of the North American Chapter of the Association for Computational Linguistics, pp. 396–403 (2007)
13. Chang, C.C., Lin, C.J.: LIBSVM: A Library for Support Vector Machines (2001)
14. Dubey, A.: What to do when Lexicalization fails: Parsing German with Suffix Analysis and Smoothing. In: Proceedings of the 43rd Annual Meeting of the Association for Computational Linguistics (ACL), pp. 314–321 (2005)
15. Hall, J., Nivre, J., Nilsson, J.: A Hybrid Constituency-Dependency Parser for Swedish. In: Proceedings of the 16th Nordic Conference of Computational Linguistics (NODALIDA), pp. 284–287 (2007)

How Can the Term Compositionality Be Useful for Acquiring Elementary Semantic Relations?

Thierry Hamon[1] and Natalia Grabar[2]

[1] LIPN – UMR 7030, Université Paris 13 – CNRS, 99 av. J-B Clément,
F-93430 Villetaneuse, France
thierry.hamon@lipn.univ-paris13.fr
[2] Université Paris Descartes, UMR_S 872, Paris, F-75006 France
INSERM, U872, Paris, F-75006, France
natalia.grabar@spim.jussieu.fr

Abstract. Acquiring and enriching lexical resources is crucial for various areas of the computational linguistics applications, especially in specialized domains. In this paper, we propose a high-quality method exploiting the compositionality of complex terms issued from a structured terminology in order to infer three kinds of semantic relations (synonymy, hierarchical and meronymy) between words or terms. The approach has been applied and evaluated on the Gene Ontology biomedical terminology: 1,273 is-a, 178 part-of and 921 synonymy relations have been inferred and show a precision over 90%. We analyze these results and the possibility of their cross-validation through a graph representation.

1 Introduction

Detection of semantic similarity between terms is an important but heavy step within various natural language processing (NLP) applications. For instance, tasks like query expansions, information retrieval, knowledge extraction or terminology matching highly rely on such information and would generate different results according to whether the semantic proximity between two terms (*i.e.*, *aromatic amino acid family anabolism* and *aromatic amino acid family biosynthesis*) is established or not. In order to help the NLP applications, specific lexica, offering various semantic relations (hyperonymy, meronymy and synonymy) as well as morphological and orthographic variants, can be used. But, depending on languages and on specialized areas, such resources are not equally well described.

We can mention the availability of morphological resources for common language [1,2] and for medical area [3,4,5]. We can also mention the common language resource of synonyms WordNet [6] for English, although the corresponding resources for other languages are not freely available. Notice that the initiative for fitting this resource for the medical area [7] is still ongoing, and that there is no initiative for the creation of a similar resource for the NLP processing of biological documents. Besides, lexica with hierarchical or meronymy relations, especially in specialized areas, are not available. The purpose of our work is to

A. Ranta, B. Nordström (Eds.): GoTAL 2008, LNAI 5221, pp. 181–192, 2008.

fill in this gap in the biological domain. Within this area, several terminologies are created and continuously updated. We propose to reuse them in order to infer lexica of semantically related words or terms specific to biology. The relationships aimed include synonymy, hyperonymy and meronymy. All these relationships can be used for computing the semantic similarity between words and terms [8,9,10]. Moreover, they are basic resources for structuring terminologies as well as a way to improving the sensitivity of information retrieval and extraction applications.

The proposed novel method provides high-quality results. This method is language-independent. It exploits the compositionality of complex terms extracted from structured terminologies and is based on the identification of their syntactic invariants. The main originality of our work is that the same method is applied for inferring various semantic relationships as far as input material is correctly constrained.

2   Material

Our main material is Gene Ontology [11] (*GO*), which goal is to produce a structured, common, controlled vocabulary for describing the roles of genes and their products in any organism. *GO* terms convey three types of biological meanings: biological processes, molecular functions and cellular components. Within *GO*, terms are structured through three types of relations: (1) hierarchical subsumption or hyperonymy, also called **is-a** relation; (2) meronymy or **part-of** relation; (3) and synonymy. Synonyms are grouped within the same concept, which are related between them through hierarchical and **part-of** relations.

For instance, within the concept GO:0009073, the preferred term *aromatic amino acid family biosynthetic process* has several synonyms (*i.e.*, *aromatic amino acid family anabolism, aromatic amino acid family biosynthesis*). This concept is related to the concept GO:0008652 *amino acid biosynthetic process* through a hierarchical relation.

The used version of *GO* provides 24,537 **is-a** and 2,726 **part-of** relations, while synonymy relations are established among 18,315 terms and their 13,850 synonyms.

3   Method

Often within biomedical terminologies, terms are coined on the same syntactic and compositional scheme which can be exploited in order to induce the elementary relations between simple terms. For instance, the *GO* concept GO:0009073 contains the following synonyms, which show the compositionality through the substitution of one of their components (underlined):

aromatic amino acid family biosynthesis
aromatic amino acid family anabolism
aromatic amino acid family formation
aromatic amino acid family synthesis

Fig. 1. Parsing syntactic trees of the terms *aromatic amino acid family anabolism* and *aromatic amino acid family biosynthesis* for the acquisition of synonymous relations

It is possible to exploit this scheme and to induce the following paradigm of elementary synonyms: *biosynthesis, anabolism, formation, synthesis*. We propose a method for generalizing this observation for the acquisition of various elementary semantic relationships. Like in the given examples, the method exploits compositional structure of terms and relies on existence of structured terminologies. The notion of compositionality assumes that the meaning of a complex expression is fully determined by its syntactic structure, the meaning of its parts and the composition function [12]. In our work, the syntactic analysis of terms is crucial: it normalizes the representation of terms through their head and expansion components and it prepares thus the syntactic dependencies computing.

In the following of this section, we first present the approach for achieving the syntactic analysis of terms (section 3.1) and then the compositionality-based method for acquisition of lexical resources (section 3.2).

3.1   Preprocessing and Syntactic Analysis: Ogmios

Figure 2 presents general workflow scheme implemented for computing elementary relations existing within *GO*. For this, *GO* terms are preprocessed through the Ogmios linguistic annotation platform [13] in order to automatically analyze these terms and generate their syntactic analysis. As result, all terms are parsed into their head and expansion components. The used tools are developed in Perl5 language.

The Ogmios platform is adapted to the processing of large amount of data and, moreover, can be easily tuned to a specialized domain. Through this platform, several types of linguistic processing are performed. First, the TagEN [14] tool is applied for the recognition on named entities (*i.e.*, gene names, chemical products). Its application at the beginning of linguistic pipeline helps the forthcoming segmentation into words and sentences. Indeed, the recognition of named entities allows disambiguating special characters, such as punctuation marks, dashes, slashes, etc, widely used within named entities in biology and often altering the segmentation into words and sentences.

After the segmentation, the GeniaTagger [15] tool is applied in order to perform POS-tagging and lemmatization.

The final step within the Ogmios platform is the shallow syntactic analysis of terms in order to syntactically parse them. This task is carried out thanks to the rule-based term extractor YATEA [16]. Syntactic dependencies between term components are computed according to assigned POS tags and shallow parsing rules. Thus, each term is considered as a syntactic binary tree (figure 1) composed of two elements: head component and expansion component. For

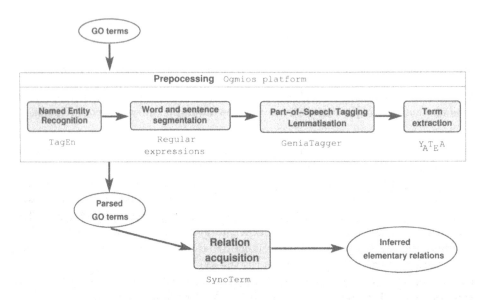

Fig. 2. General flowchart of the method

instance, in terms of syntactic dependencies, *anabolism* is the head component of *aromatic amino acid family anabolism* term, while *aromatic amino acid family* is its expansion component. It goes without saying that each complex component (*i.e.*, *aromatic amino acid family*) is also syntactically parsed, which can give place to inferring even more elementary relations. Moreover, because we used the syntactic structure of the terms, their surface form is not an obstacle for their alignment. For instance, once two synonym terms like *replication of mitochondrial DNA* and *mtDNA replication* are lemmatized and syntactically analyzed, *replication* is recognized to be their head component and *mitochondrial DNA* and *mtDNA* their expansion components (figure 3).

Such analyzed *GO* terms are then aligned through specific compositional rules and ready for detection of elementary semantic relations within *GO* terms.

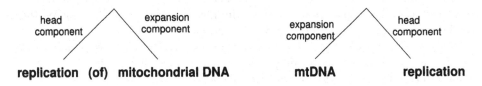

Fig. 3. Parsing syntactic trees of synonym terms *replication of mitochondrial DNA* and *mtDNA replication* with surface syntactic variation for the acquisition of synonymous relations

3.2   Acquisition of Elementary Relations

In this work, the compositionality-based method designed for the terminology structuring through corpora [17], is adapted to inferring elementary relations between simple terms. The method is applied for the acquisition of synonymy, hierarchical and **part-of** relations, as described below. It should be noticed that the method is recursive and each inferred elementary relation can then be propagated in order to infer new elementary relations, and thus to generate a more exhaustive lexicon with a given relationship.

Acquisition of Synonymy Relations. For the acquisition of synonymy relations, we consider that if the meaning $\mathcal{M}$ of two complex terms A rel B and A' rel B is given as following:

$$\mathcal{M}(A\ rel\ B) = f(\mathcal{M}(A), \mathcal{M}(B), \mathcal{M}(rel))$$

$$\mathcal{M}(A'\ rel\ B) = f(\mathcal{M}(A'), \mathcal{M}(B), \mathcal{M}(rel))$$

for a given composition function f, if A rel B and A' rel B are complex synonymous terms and if B is identical, then the synonymy relation between simpler terms A and A' can be inferred. The method takes into account the syntactic structure of complex terms. The fully parsed terms are represented as a terminological network, within which the deduction of the elementary synonymy relations is based on the three rules:

R1. If two terms are synonymous and their expansion components are identical, then an elementary synonymy relation is inferred: the pair {*anabolism, biosynthesis*} is inferred from the original synonymy relation between *acetone anabolism* and *acetone biosynthesis* where the expansion component *acetone* is identical in both terms (figure 1).

R2. If both terms are synonymous and their head components are identical, then an elementary synonymy relation is inferred: the pair {*endocytic, endocytotic*} is inferred from the synonymy relation between *endocytic vesicle* and *endocytotic vesicle* where the head component *vesicle* is identical.

R3. If both terms are synonymous and either their head or expansion components are synonymous, then an elementary synonymy relation is inferred: the pair {*nicotinamide adenine dinucleotide, NAD*} is inferred from the synonymy relation between *nicotinamide adenine dinucleotide catabolism* and *NAD breakdown* where the head components {*catabolism, breakdown*} are already known synonymous.

Acquisition of Hierarchical and Part-of Relations. The same method is applied for the acquisition of hierarchical (or **part-of**) relations. For this, original pairs are composed of the GO hierarchical (or **part-of**) pairs. Thus, if the meaning $\mathcal{M}$ of two complex terms A rel B and C rel B are given as following:

$$\mathcal{M}(A\ rel\ B) = f(\mathcal{M}(A), \mathcal{M}(B), \mathcal{M}(rel))$$

$$\mathcal{M}(C\ rel\ B) = f(\mathcal{M}(C), \mathcal{M}(B), \mathcal{M}(rel))$$

for a given composition function f, if A rel B and C rel B are complex terms related through hierarchy (or **part-of** relation) and if B is identical, then the hierarchical (or **part-of**) relation between simpler terms A and C can be inferred.

(a) Parsing tree of the terms *cell activation* and *astrocyte activation* related through a hierarchical relation

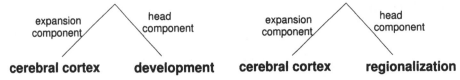

(b) Parsing tree of the terms *cerebral cortex development* and *cerebral cortex regionalization* related through a **part-of** relation

Fig. 4. Parsing syntactic trees for the acquisition of hierarchical and **part-of** relations

For the acquisition of these relations we exploit the same three rules. For instance, figure 4 exemplifies rules R2 and R1, where one of components of the original terms is identical. On figure 4(a), original terms are two biological processes: *cell activation* GO:0001775 and *astrocyte activation* GO:0048143. They have between them hierarchical relation: *cell activation* is the hierarchical parent to *astrocyte activation*. Further to their syntactic analysis and application of the compositional rule R2, the hierarchical relation between their expansion components *cell* ⇒ *astrocyte* can be inferred.

Similarly, on figure 4(b), original terms are two biological processes: *cerebral cortex development* GO:0021987 and *cerebral cortex regionalization* GO:0021796. They have between them **part-of** relation: *cerebral cortex regionalization* is a part of a more large biological process *cerebral cortex development*. Further to their syntactic analysis and application of the compositional rule R1, the **part-of** relation between their head components *development* ⇒ *regionalization* can be inferred.

Notice that another work [18] aimed at the acquisition of elementary hierarchical relations from structured terminologies. Their approach relies on string substitution within identical lexical contexts, while in the work we propose we perform a more rich NLP approach by syntactically analysing terms and applying compositionality-based transformation syntactic rules.

4   Results and Discussion

23,899 *GO* terms have been fully parsed through the Ogmios platform. The three compositional rules have been then applied and allowed to infer elementary synonyms (n=921), is-a (n=1,273) and **part-of** pairs (n=178). We present and discuss these results. For the inferred synonymy relations, we present also their productivity (number of original *GO* pairs which allowed to infer them).

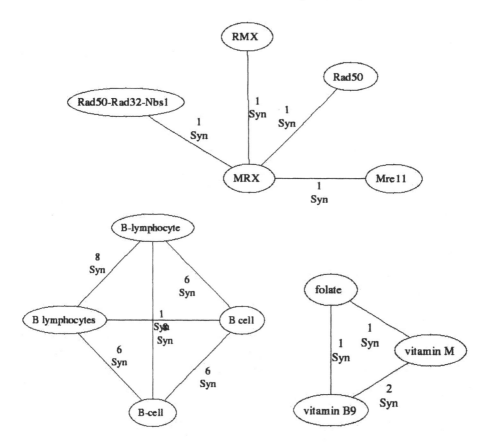

Fig. 5. Connected components (CCs) presenting elementary synonymy relations. Components can have various shapes: star-shaped connection between nodes for *MRX* CC, or cliques (strongly connected components) for the two other CCs.

4.1   Elementary Synonyms

The 921 inferred elementary synonyms have been grouped into 627 connected components (CCs) – groups of synonyms which are linked between them. For instance, the CC *MRX* of figure 5 contains five elementary synonyms (*MRX, Rad50-Rad32-Nbs1, RMX, Rad50* and *Mre11*) inferred from the *GO* concept GO:0030870 which preferred term is *MRX complex*. Elementary synonymy relations are labelled *Syn* on figures, and numbers indicate their productivity (number of original *GO* pairs from which an elementary relation has been inferred). In this CC, the preferred elementary term *MRX* is linked to all its synonyms – this is a star-shaped CC. The two other CCs are strongly connected, or cliques: all their nodes are related between them. Observing synonyms through their CCs, rather than pairs of synonyms (*i.e.*, {*MRX, Rad50*}, {*B-cell, B-lymphocyte*}, {*B-cell, B cell*}, {*vitamin B9, vitamin M*}) gives a more global view of their semantics. In this way, the contextual nature of synonyms, which can influence their acceptance, is more easily detected within CCs though terms or their relations.

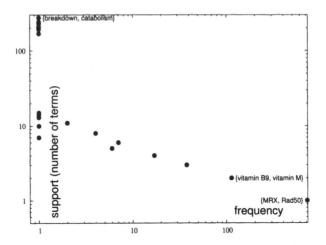

Fig. 6. Productivity of the inferred elementary synonyms within *GO* (logarithmic scale)

Productivity of the elementary synonyms within *GO* is presented on figure 4.1 (scaled logarithmically). Its axes represent the support (number of original *GO* synonyms that allow to infer a given pair of elementary synonyms) and the frequency of each support value. Pairs, which productivity values are concentrated near the top left corner, are the more reliable: their meaning and use are the most common. For instance, {*breakdown, catabolism*} is the most productive (and reliable) synonym pair: it is inferred within 274 *GO* synonyms and appears to be a fundamental notion in biology. At the other end, we have pairs like {*MRX, Rad50*} or {*vitamin B9, vitamin M*} inferred from one or two original synonyms. As their meaning seems to be more specific, they may convey more specific semantics. Besides, such rare pairs represent nearly 80% (n=722) of the whole set of the inferred synonyms.

4.2   Elementary Hierarchical and Part-of Relations

We inferred 1,273 hierarchical and 178 `part-of` elementary relations. Figure 7 presents two of the generated connected components.

Most of the acquired hierarchical pairs (85%, n=1089) are inferred from only one pair of original *GO* terms. This is the case for *differentiation* ⇒ *fate cell commitment* and *differentiation* ⇒ *germination* pairs on figure 7(a) and with the relations on figure 7(b). The most frequent elementary hierarchical pair is *membrane* ⇒ *part*. It is found within nine *GO* term pairs, for instance, within the following cellular components terms:

> *vacuolar part* (GO:0044437) ⇒ *vacuolar membrane* (GO:0005774)
> *peroxisomal part* (GO:0044439) ⇒ *peroxisome membrane* (GO:0005778)
> *endoplasmic reticulum part* (GO:0044432) ⇒ *endoplasmic reticulum membrane* (GO:0005789)

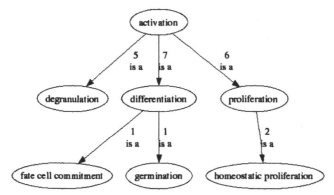

(a) CC of elementary hierarchical relations of *activation*.

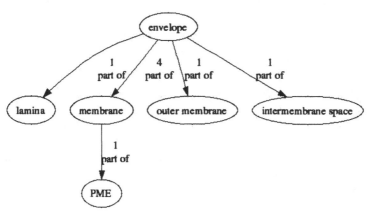

(b) CC of elementary **part-of** relations of *envelope*.

Fig. 7. Connected components of elementary hierarchical and **part-of** relations. Numbers indicate the productivity of the inferred pairs within original *GO* terms.

As for elementary **part-of** relations, the most frequent one is *development* ⇒ *morphogenesis*. It is acquired within 46 *GO* term pairs, denoting mostly biological processes, for instance:

> *compound eye development* (GO:0048749) ⇒ *compound eye morphogenesis* (GO:0001745)
> *Bolwig's organ development* (GO:0055034) ⇒ *Bolwig's organ morphogenesis* (GO:0001746)
> *neural plate development* (GO:0001840) ⇒ *neural plate morphogenesis* (GO:0001839)
> *endothelial cell development* (GO:0001885) ⇒ *endothelial cell morphogenesis* (GO:0001886)

First evaluation of the acquired resources showed that the quality of synonyms is very good (over 90% precision). Evaluation of hierarchical and **part-of**

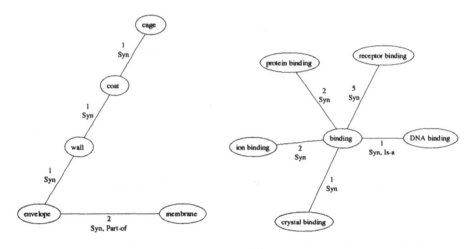

Fig. 8. Connected components with lexical inclusions, hierarchical and part-of relations (possible weak points of connected components)

relations is still ongoing. Recall of these resources could not be evaluated because there is no reference data for this kind of lexica. Nevertheless we assume that a better POS-tagging and then shallow parsing would improve detection of the semantic relations within terms. Our results showed also that the redundancy of use of elementary synonyms is very high: productivity of several pairs is greater than 100 original *GO* term pairs. Redundancy within hierarchical and part-of relationships is rather small.

5   Conclusion and Perspectives

In this paper, we propose a compositionality-based method for inferring different types of elementary semantic relations from structured terminologies in order to help the natural language processing applications. The method relies on syntactic analysis of terms and exploits three compositional rules. The main originality of this work is that the same approach is applied for inferring different types of semantic relations: synonymy, hierarchical and part-of relations. The semantic nature of the source term pairs has to be constrained, while the NLP part of the method remains the same.

The inferred resources are useful for different NLP applications, particularly for those initiated by Philip Resnik [8] for computing the semantic distance between terms.

The presented work has several perspectives. For instance, the inferred elementary relations can be used for enriching the existing terminologies through the detection of additional synonymous or hierarchically related terms. For this, the reverse method should be applied on corpora [17].

This method is language-independent, and it is possible to apply it to other languages as far as (1) the required linguistic processing can be realized and (2) semantic relations between complex terms are available. In the biomedical area, we plan to apply our method on the UMLS resource [3], or more specifically the MeSH [19] or Snomed [20] terminologies which are available in several languages.

Additionally, the inferred resources can be used for their cross-validation. For instance, if the same elementary relation is inferred as being synonymy and hierarchical, it can help detecting possibly weak points within network of the generated relations and ambiguities or inconsistencies within original terminologies. As shows figure 8, some of the inferred relations are indeed ambiguous:

- *envelope* and *membrane* are found to be both synonymously and part-of related;
- *binding* and *DNA binding* are found to be both synonymously and hierarchically related.

In this perspective, the three relationships between elementary terms (synonymy, hierarchical and part-of) can be cross-validated between them. This would prepare the human validation of the inferred resources which must be thoroughly evaluated still.

References

1. Burnage, G.: CELEX - A Guide for Users. Centre for Lexical Information, University of Nijmegen (1990)
2. Hathout, N., Namer, F., Dal, G.: An experimental constructional database: the MorTAL project. In: Boucher, P. (ed.) Morphology book. Cascadilla Press, Cambridge (2001)
3. N.L.M.: UMLS Knowledge Sources Manual. National Library of Medicine, Bethesda, Maryland (2007), http://www.nlm.nih.gov/research/umls/
4. Schulz, S., Romacker, M., Franz, P., Zaiss, A., Klar, R., Hahn, U.: Towards a multilingual morpheme thesaurus for medical free-text retrieval. In: Medical Informatics in Europe (MIE) (1999)
5. Zweigenbaum, P., Baud, R., Burgun, A., Namer, F., Jarrousse, E., Grabar, N., Ruch, P., Duff, F.L., Thirion, B., Darmoni, S.: Towards a Unified Medical Lexicon for French. In: Medical Informatics in Europe (MIE) (2003)
6. Fellbaum, C.: A semantic network of english: the mother of all WordNets. Computers and Humanities. EuroWordNet: a multilingual database with lexical semantic network 32(2-3), 209–220 (1998)
7. Smith, B., Fellbaum, C.: Medical wordnet: a new methodology for the construction and validation of information. In: Proc of 20th CoLing, Geneva, Switzerland, pp. 371–382 (2004)
8. Resnik, P.: Semantic similarity in a taxonomy: An information-based measure and its application to problems of ambiguity in natural language. Journal of Artificial Intelligence Research (JAIR) 11, 95–130 (1999)
9. Bousquet, C., Jaulent, M.C., Chatellier, G., Degoulet, P.: Using semantic distance for the efficient coding of medical concepts. In: Annual Symposium of the American Medical Informatics Association (AMIA), Los Angeles, CA, pp. 96–100 (2000)
10. Lord, P., Stevens, R., Brass, A., Goble, C.: Investigating semantic similarity measures across the Gene Ontology: the relationship between sequence and annotation. Bioinformatics 19(10), 1275–1283 (2003)

11. Gene Ontology Consortium: Creating the Gene Ontology resource: design and implementation. Genome Research 11, 1425–1433 (2001)
12. Partee, B.H.: In: Landman, F., Veltman, F. (eds.) Compositionality (1984)
13. Hamon, T., Nazarenko, A., Poibeau, T., Aubin, S., Derivière, J.: A robust linguistic platform for efficient and domain specific web content analysis. In: RIAO 2007, Pittsburgh, USA (2007)
14. Berroyer, J.F.: Tagen, un analyseur d"entits nommes: conception, development et valuation. In: Mmoire de D.E.A. d'intelligence artificielle, UniversitParis-Nord (2004)
15. Tsuruoka, Y., Tateishi, Y., Kim, J.D., Ohta, T., McNaught, J., Ananiadou, S., Tsujii, J.: Developing a robust part-of-speech tagger for biomedical text. In: Bozanis, P., Houstis, E.N. (eds.) PCI 2005. LNCS, vol. 3746, pp. 382–392. Springer, Heidelberg (2005)
16. Aubin, S., Hamon, T.: Improving term extraction with terminological resources. In: Salakoski, T., Ginter, F., Pyysalo, S., Pahikkala, T. (eds.) FinTAL 2006. LNCS (LNAI), vol. 4139, pp. 380–387. Springer, Heidelberg (2006)
17. Hamon, T., Nazarenko, A., Gros, C.: A step towards the detection of semantic variants of terms in technical documents. In: International Conference on Computational Linguistics (COLING-ACL 1998), Université de Montréal, Montréal, Quebec, Canada, pp. 498–504 (1998)
18. Verspoor, C.M., Joslyn, C., Papcun, G.J.: The gene ontology as a source of lexical semantic knowledge for a biological natural language processing application. In: SIGIR workshop on Text Analysis and Search for Bioinformatics, pp. 51–56 (2003)
19. National Library of Medicine Bethesda, Maryland: Medical Subject Headings (2001), http://www.nlm.nih.gov/mesh/meshhome.html
20. Côté, R.A.: Répertoire d'anatomopathologie de la SNOMED internationale, v.3.4. Université de Sherbrooke, Sherbrooke, Québec (1996)

Training Statistical Language Models from Grammar-Generated Data: A Comparative Case-Study

Beth Ann Hockey[1], Manny Rayner[2], and Gwen Christian[3]

[1] UCSC UARC, Mail Stop 19-26
NASA Ames Research Center
Moffet Field, CA 94035
bahockey@ucsc.edu
[2] University of Geneva, TIM/ISSCO
40 bvd du Pont-d'Arve
CH-1211 Geneva 4, Switzerland
Emmanuel.Rayner@issco.unige.ch
[3] Dept of Linguistics
UC Santa Cruz
gwenlle@gmail.com

Abstract. Statistical language models (SLMs) for speech recognition have the advantage of robustness, and grammar-based models (GLMs) the advantage that they can be built even when little corpus data is available. A known way to attempt to combine these two methodologies is first to create a GLM, and then use that GLM to generate training data for an SLM. It has however been difficult to evaluate the true utility of the idea, since the corpus data used to create the GLM has not in general been explicitly available. We exploit the Open Source Regulus platform, which supports corpus-based construction of linguistically motivated GLMs, to perform a methodologically sound comparison: the same data is used both to create an SLM directly, and also to create a GLM, which is then used to generate data to train an SLM. An evaluation on a medium-vocabulary task showed that the indirect method of constructing the SLM is in fact only marginally better than the direct one. The method used to create the training data is critical, with PCFG generation heavily outscoring CFG generation.

1 Introduction

Non-trivial speech recognition always requires some kind of language model [1]. At least in the world of research, it has generally been assumed that language models are best constructed using some kind of data-driven process; the most common alternative in practice is the N-gram grammar. We will generically refer to models built in this way as "Statistical Language Models" or SLMs.

SLMs perform extremely well when there is adequate training data available, but in practice this is not always the case. When training data is limited or,

A. Ranta, B. Nordström (Eds.): GoTAL 2008, LNAI 5221, pp. 193–204, 2008.

in the worst case, completely unavailable, an alternative method is to construct the language model as a hand-coded grammar [2,3,4,5]. We will refer to models of this kind as "Grammar-based Language Models" or GLMs. GLMs appear to be particularly suitable for applications which require high levels of accuracy, and which will also be used by expert users, who can reasonably be expected to produce a high percentage of in-coverage material [6,7,8,9]. The distinction between SLMs and GLMs is by no means black-and-white. SLMs can contain embedded GLM-style subgrammars that define simple types of phrase like dates or times [10]. In the other direction, once a GLM has been created, it is possible to use available data to perform statistical tuning, which technically transforms the GLM into a type of SLM. We will have more to say about this later.

Statistical tuning of a GLM is certainly one way to add some of the advantages associated with SLMs. It fails, however, to address the key problem, which is brittleness. In general, grammar-based speech recognition tends to be unforgiving for naive users, since it gives results only for utterances within grammar coverage. This suggests another compromise position between the two methodologies. As noted, SLMs clearly perform well when they are trained on enough data. The grammar in a GLM can also be used to *generate* data; this data can be used to train an SLM. The hope is that the result will combine the advantages of both methodologies. The final language model is an SLM, so it will not be subject to brittleness; but since this language model is created from a GLM, it will be possible to achieve reasonable performance without large amounts of training data.

Although the idea of creating SLMs from GLM-generated data has been used successfully in more than one study [11,12], one cannot help feeling that there is something, methodologically speaking, that is slightly suspicious about it. It is always clear what data has been used to construct an SLM; it is, however, much harder to be quantative about the process of building a GLM. When a grammar writer hand-codes a grammar, there are always utterances that they have in mind to cover. If those items were recorded as the grammar was built, they would constitute a corpus that represented what data the hand-coded grammar was "trained" on. The same corpus could be used for other purposes, in particular for explicit training of an SLM. It is certainly possible *a priori* that this would produce a recognizer that yielded just as good performance as one built through the roundabout route of first creating a grammar, and then using it to generate training data. However, grammar-writers are rarely, if ever, methodical enough to write down all their example sentences, and comparisons of the kind suggested are hard to carry out in practice.

This kind of problem is inherent in any comparison between data-driven machine learning and hand-coded rules. However, the Regulus project offers an approach to address this problem. Regulus [13] is an Open Source toolkit for spoken language system development, which builds grammar based language models for the commercial Nuance[1] platform using example-based methods driven by small corpora of examples. In [14], it was shown how Regulus made possible

---

[1] Nuance 8.5 was used for the work discussed in this paper.

a methodologically fair comparison between a GLM and a normal SLM on a medium-vocabulary speech-understanding task; the same data could be used explicitly to build both language models, rendering irrelevant any speculation about intangible grammar-writer's intuitions.

The paper also showed up another potential methodological pitfall. When recognizers derived from the two language models were compared in terms of Word Error Rate (WER) on a corpus which contained data both in-coverage and out-of-coverage with respect to the GLM, the SLM-based recognizer produced slightly better performance. Further analysis, however, revealed that the raw WER scores were in fact very misleading; they represented the average of better performance of the SLM on out-of-coverage data, and worse performance on in-coverage data. Performance of both recognizers on the out-of-coverage data (WER = 48% for SLM and 58% for GLM) was however so bad as to be essentially uninteresting in the context of the speech translation task, which required precise, fine-grained analysis[2]. Conversely, performance on in-coverage data showed a WER for the GLM (6%) that was less than half that of the SLM (13%), an extremely useful improvement. This is by no means the first study which has shown up the weakness of WER as a metric for evaluating speech *understanding*, as opposed to raw speech *recognition* [15].

In the present paper, we use the Regulus platform and a methodology which borrows several elements from [14] to evaluate the idea of creating SLMs from GLM-generated training data. This approach makes it possible to address the key methodological problems in a sound way, which has not been the case in previous studies. The paper is organized as follows. Section 2 describes the framework that we have adopted for performing the language modeling experiments. Section 3 describes the experiments performed. Section 4 summarizes the results and draws conclusions for language modeling in sparse data situations.

2 Experimental Framework

As discussed in the previous section, a key problem with earlier work has been the impossibility of knowing what "seed corpus" was used to construct the hand-coded grammars used to generate the SLM training data. The Regulus platform allows us to address these issues head-on, since it makes the role of the seed corpus completely explicit. The basic idea is to start with a general resource grammar, and then use the seed corpus to drive an example-based process that creates the final domain-specific language model. We now present a brief overview of how this is done; the details of the various compilation steps are described in [13, Chapters 9 and 10].

The Regulus release contains a fairly substantial domain-independent feature grammar for English [13, Chapter 8], which also contains a function-word lexicon of about 500 words. The grammar developer adds to them a domain-specific lexicon containing the necessary content words, a domain-specific seed corpus,

---

[2] In tasks involving coarse-grained speech understanding, for example call-routing, this difference might have been more important.

and a set of "operationality criteria", whose role will be explained shortly. These resources constitute the input to the grammar creation process. The Regulus parser is first used to convert the seed corpus into a set of parse trees. The operationality criteria then define how each tree is to be cut up into a number of subtrees. The rules in each subtree are collapsed into a derived rule. The set of all such derived rules constitutes a specialised version of the original feature grammar.

By construction, the specialised feature grammar produces analyses compatible with those of the original grammar, and covers all the examples in the seed corpus, but will in general have coverage strictly less than that of the original grammar. The specialised feature grammar is next subjected to another compilation phase, which converts it into a CFG grammar in Nuance's GSL notation. Finally, the seed corpus can optionally be used a second time, as training data to convert the CFG grammar into a PCFG grammar. This final conversion stage is performed by the Nuance `compute-grammar-probs` utility.

Nuance contains another utility, `generate`, which can be used to generate an arbitrary number of sentences from a GSL-formatted CFG grammar. We also wrote a utility of our own, which performs generation on GSL-formatted PCFG grammars produced by the Regulus compilation process. Both Nuance's `generate` and our own generation utility work by sampling the space of generated utterances, starting with the root symbol and expanding non-terminals until the result contains only terminals. The critical difference is that `generate`, when randomly choosing a rule to expand a non-terminal N, assigns equal weights to all the productions where N occurs on the LHS. Our PCFG generation utility, in contrast, weights the productions with the probabilities attached to them.

To recapitulate, the process we have just outlined allows us to use a grammar to generate training data for building an SLM, but does it in a way which makes completely explicit which corpus data was used to construct the generation grammar itself. In effect, the "seed corpus" reifies the linguistic intuitions used to build the generation grammar. This has several very useful consequences. In particular, since the seed corpus is just a normal domain corpus, it is also possible to use it directly to train an SLM.

The concrete experiments we describe were performed using English corpora and an English Regulus grammar taken from MedSLT [16], a medium-vocabulary Open Source speech translation system for medical domains. Vocabulary size was 458 words. Most of the detailed aspects of the MedSLT system are not relevant here, but one turned out to be potentially useful. Translation in the system is interlingua-based: source-language representations are translated into interlingua representations, and then into target-language representations. The space of well-defined interlingua representations is defined by means of another Regulus grammar [17]. Not all representations licensed by the source-language grammar produce well-formed interlingua; it can be the case that constraints are hard to formulate at the source-language level, but easy to capture in interlingua. This means that the interlingua can be used as another source of information. Since some of the randomly generated utterances do not produce well-formed interlingua after being passed through the source-language-to-interlingua transfer phase, it is possible to treat the combination of the transfer rules and the interlingua definition as a filter.

The actual construction of the SLMs was performed using the Nuance Say-Anything© utilities. Each SLM was a class trigram model, created using Good-Turing discounting. The classes were defined using a Regulus utility which extracted sets of words with similar syntactic and semantic properties from the relevant specialized grammars. The properties for each class were defined by specifying a small number, usually two or three, paradigm words, and computing the least common generalization of the corresponding lexicon entries.

In the next section, we describe the concrete experiments we carried out using this basic framework.

3   Experiments

We used all of the following different kinds of corpus as input to train SLMs:

Seed. The original "seed corpora". This consisted of 948 examples.
CFG-generated. Corpora generated from a CFG grammar derived by Regulus from the seed corpus. We created datasets of several different sizes.
PCFG-generated. Corpora generated from a PCFG grammar derived by Regulus from the seed corpus. We created datasets of several different sizes.
CFG-generated-filtered. Corpora generated by a CFG grammar derived by Regulus from the seed corpus, and then filtered by removing utterances which do not give rise to well-formed interlingua. We created datasets of several different sizes.
PCFG-generated-filtered. Corpora generated by a PCFG grammar derived by Regulus from the seed corpus, and then filtered by removing utterances which do not give rise to well-formed interlingua. We created datasets of several different sizes.

We evaluated the quality of the resulting SLMs by using them to perform recognition on the 810-utterance dataset described in [14], which consisted of spontaneously generated utterances collected during studies carried out on naive subjects who had not been involved in system development. 514 of these utterances (63%) were within the coverage of the GLM grammar, and 296 out of coverage.

The main results from the experiments are presented in Tables 1 to 6. As in [14], we calculate WER and Sentence Error Rate (SER) both for the full datasets, and also for the subset consisting only of in-coverage utterances. Our primary reason for using SER as a metric is that it enables us to apply the McNemar sign test, in order to evaluate the significance of differences between recognition performance of different versions. We present significance as one of the following: "not significant", "significant at $P < 0.05$", "significant at $P < 0.01$" and "significant at $P < 0.001$". In the rest of this section, we discuss the implications of the results.

3.1   Different Types of Corpora

Tables 1 and 2 presents results contrasting different methods for building the SLM training corpora; the first line, for the GLM built using the "seed" corpus, is intended to provide a reference point. Line 2 shows the SLM built from the "seed" corpus. The other recognizers were all built from GLM-generated training corpora of the same size. The small size of these corpora reflects the fact that CFG generation (lines 3 and 4) produces very low-grade data. The interlingua-based filtering operation discards over 99% of it; 4281 was the number of utterances left by filtering from an initial CFG-generated set of 500K utterances, and the other corpora were then truncated to that length[3] Line 3 shows results for unfiltered, and line 4 for filtered data. Lines 5 and 6 are PCFG-generated sets, with and without interlingua filtering.

Several immediate conclusions can be drawn. First, as shown by line 1 in Table 2, PCFG generation is vastly superior to CFG. Given that CFG-generated data clearly did not deliver interesting performance, we only used PCFG-generated data for the other experiments.

A more interesting result (line 2 in Table 2) is that even the best SLM trained on PCFG-generated data (line 6 in Table 1) is not clearly better than the one trained directly from the original "seed" corpus (line 2, same table). The PCFG-generated data produces a better WER; however, its SER is significantly worse.

Table 1. Recognition performance for SLMs trained on different types of generated data. "Size" = number of utterances in training set; "WER" = Word Error Rate on test set of in-coverage and out of coverage material; "SER" = sentence error rate on test set of in-coverage and out of coverage material. GLM results included for comparison.

	Version	size	WER	SER
1	seed corpus GLM	948	21.96%	50.62%
2	seed corpus SLM	948	27.74%	58.40%
3	CFG/unfiltered	4281	49.0%	88.4%
4	CFG/filtered	4281	44.68%	85.68%
5	PCFG/unfiltered	4281	25.98%	65.31%
6	PCFG/filtered	4281	25.81%	63.70%

Alhough interlingua filtering does result in some improvement (lines 4 and 5 in Table 2), it does not have a very large effect on PCFG-generated data, and in fact the difference in SER is not significant.

Finally, lines 6 and 7 in Table 2 show that the plain GLM recognizer produces significantly better performance than any of the other versions. It should

---

[3] To test for the possibility of bias in the truncated unfiltered corpora, we created both "head" (taken from the beginning of the larger file) and "tail" (taken from the end) versions of the needed size. Performance on the head and tail versions was nearly the same, leading us to conclude that it is unlikely that the truncation procedure is creating a skewed corpus. The head versions are used in the paper.

Table 2. Significance of differences between some of the versions of the recogniser listed in Table 1, according to the McNemar sign test performed on SER. Significantly better results are marked in **bold**.

	First	Second	Score	Significance
1	CFG/unfiltered	**PCFG/unfiltered**	12–199	$P < 0.001$
2	**seed corpus SLM**	PCFG/filtered	87–44	$P < 0.001$
3	**seed corpus SLM**	CFG/unfiltered	244–15	$P < 0.001$
4	CFG/unfiltered	**CFG/filtered**	27–49	$P < 0.05$
5	PCFG/unfiltered	PCFG/filtered	16–29	not significant
6	**seed corpus GLM**	seed corpus SLM	124–47	$P < 0.001$
7	**seed corpus GLM**	PCFG/filtered	142–36	$P < 0.001$

be noted, however, that the generated training sets produced in these first experiments are quite small. The next set of experiments investigates what happens as they are made larger.

3.2 Increasing the Size of the Training Set

When SLMs are trained on human-generated data, performance usually improves for some time as more data is added. A common rule of thumb when building commercial SLM-based systems is that one should aim to collect about 20 000 utterances. Tables 3 and 4 presents results for SLMs trained off PCFG-generated corpora of increasing size. As in the first set of experiments, unfiltered data sets were truncated to make them equal in size to the corresponding filtered ones; the labels "50K", "1000K" and "1500K" indicate the number of utterances in the original unfiltered PCFG-generated set, prior to truncation. The amount of training data was incremented until addition of data no longer resulted in an improvement in the error rates.

The recognizers trained on filtered data continued to improve as we increased the size of the training set (lines 1 and 2, Table 4), though the improvement

Table 3. Recognition performance as training set size increases. "Size" = number of utterances in training set; test set includes both in-coverage and out of coverage; "WER" = Word Error Rate; "SER" = sentence error rate.

	Version	size	WER	SER
1	seed corpus GLM	948	21.96%	50.62%
2	seed corpus SLM	948	27.74%	58.40%
3	50K PCFG/unfiltered	16 619	24.84%	62.47%
4	50K PCFG/filtered	16 619	23.80%	59.51%
5	1000K PCFG/unfiltered	331 328	24.12%	58.77%
6	1000K PCFG/filtered	331 328	23.62%	57.28%
7	1500K PCFG/unfiltered	497 798	24.38%	59.88%
8	1500K PCFG/filtered	497 798	23.76%	57.16%

Table 4. Significance of differences between some of the versions of the recogniser listed in Table 3, according to the McNemar sign test performed on SER. Significantly better results are marked in **bold**.

	First	Second	Score	Significance
1	50K PCFG/filtered	**1000K PCFG/filtered**	22–40	$P < 0.05$
2	1000K PCFG/filtered	1500K PCFG/filtered	4–5	not significant
3	50K PCFG/unfiltered	**1000K PCFG/unfiltered**	22–52	$P < 0.001$
4	**1000K PCFG/unfiltered**	1500K PCFG/unfiltered	11–2	$P < 0.05$
5	1000K PCFG/unfiltered	seed corpus SLM	68–71	not significant
6	1500K PCFG/unfiltered	seed corpus SLM	68–80	not significant
7	1500K PCFG/filtered	seed corpus SLM	75–65	not significant
8	1500K PCFG/filtered	**1000K PCFG/unfiltered**	27–14	$P < 0.05$
9	1000K PCFG/unfiltered	**seed corpus GLM**	33–99	$P < 0.001$
10	1500K PCFG/unfiltered	**seed corpus GLM**	32–107	$P < 0.001$
11	1500K PCFG/filtered	**seed corpus GLM**	36–89	$P < 0.001$

between the largest set (497 798 utterances) and the second-largest (331 328 utterances) was not significant. With unfiltered data, we were surprised to discover that moving from 331 328 utterances to 497 798 utterances actually *degraded* performance (line 4, Table 4). It is not clear why this should be, but we can at least note that the filtering operation appears to make the data less noisy.

The best recognizer trained on unfiltered data (line 5, Table 3) had lower WER than the "seed corpus" SLM recogniser (line 2, same table). SER, however, was almost the same between these two versions, and the difference was not significant (line 5, Table 4). The best recognizers trained on filtered data (lines 6 and 8, Table 3) did better, and outscored the "seed corpus" SLM on both WER and SER. The difference on SER, however, was again not significant (line 7, Table 4). The difference between the best filtered and the best unfiltered versions was significant (line 8, Table 4), again supporting the claim that filtering helps.

In terms of both WER and SER, however, all versions were still clearly inferior to the GLM recognizer (lines 9–11, Table 4). Since the superiority of the GLM is most marked on in-coverage data, our third set of experiments focussed on this.

3.3   In-Coverage Performance

The third and final set of experiments measured performance only on the 514-utterance subset of the data that was within the coverage of the GLM. As pointed out earlier, comparisons between GLM and SLM models depend heavily on the mix of in-coverage and out of coverage data encountered in the test data. Performance of both models is generally dismal on out-of-coverage data, and consequently not very interesting; performance on in-coverage data is a more useful metric. The results of these tests are shown in Tables 5 and 6.

The relationships between most of the scores are similar to those in Table 3 above. Two points are worth noting. First, as expected, restriction to in-coverage data increases the difference between the GLM recognizer and the others in terms

Table 5. Recognition performance as training set size increases, on in-coverage material only. "Size" = number of utterances in training set; "WER" = Word Error Rate; "SER" = sentence error rate.

	Version	size	WER	SER
1	seed corpus GLM	948	7.00%	22.37%
2	seed corpus SLM	948	14.40%	42.02%
3	50K PCFG/unfiltered	16 619	14.13%	46.11%
4	50K PCFG/filt	16 619	12.76%	40.86%
5	1000K PCFG/unfiltered	331 328	11.83%	38.91%
6	1000K PCFG/filtered	331 328	11.21%	36.58%
7	1500K PCFG/unfiltered	497 798	12.35%	40.66%
8	1500K PCFG/filtered	497 798	11.25%	36.19%

of both WER and SER; for both metrics, we see a relative decrease of over 35% between results for the GLM and the best of the other versions. The second point, rather more interestingly, is that the best SLM version is now the one created from filtered PCFG-generated data (line 8, Table 5). This version is significantly better than the "seed corpus" SLM (Table 6, line 7).

Table 6. Significance of differences between some of the versions of the recogniser listed in Table 5, evaluated on in-coverage data only, according to the McNemar sign test performed on SER. Significantly better results are marked in **bold**.

	First	Second	Score	Significance
1	50K PCFG/filtered	**1000K PCFG/filtered**	16–38	$P < 0.01$
2	1000K PCFG/filtered	1500K PCFG/filtered	2–4	not significant
3	50K PCFG/unfiltered	**1000K PCFG/unfiltered**	15–52	$P < 0.001$
4	**1000K PCFG/unfiltered**	1500K PCFG/unfiltered	11–2	$P < 0.05$
5	1000K PCFG/unfiltered	seed corpus SLM	69–53	not significant
6	1500K PCFG/unfiltered	seed corpus SLM	68–61	not significant
7	**1500K PCFG/filtered**	seed corpus SLM	74–44	$P < 0.01$
8	1000K PCFG/unfiltered	**seed corpus GLM**	13–98	$P < 0.001$
9	1500K PCFG/unfiltered	**seed corpus GLM**	12–106	$P < 0.001$
10	1500K PCFG/filtered	**seed corpus GLM**	17–88	$P < 0.001$
11	**1500K PCFG/filtered**	1000K PCFG/unfiltered	25–11	$P < 0.05$

4   Summary and Conclusions

The idea of creating a statistical language model by using a grammar to generate training data has been known for some time, but previous attempts to evaluate it objectively have run into methodological difficulties. The study we have presented here has solved what we view as the key problem. By using the trainable Regulus grammar-development framework, we have been able to quantify the data that was used to create the grammar. This has made it possible for us to compare, on the one hand, the indirect method of using the data first to create a grammar, which then creates training data for an SLM, and on the other the direct method of simply creating an SLM from the original seed corpus. We have also compared the utility of generating SLM training data using CFG and PCFG versions of the grammar, investigated the effect of filtering the generated data using the Med-SLT interlingua, and looked at the relationship between the size of the generated training set and the quality of the SLM it produces. Our experiments have used English grammars and data from the Open Source MedSLT project.

The key result, as we see it, is that the indirect method of constructing the SLM actually turns out to be only marginally better than the direct one. When measured on the whole dataset (Tables 3 and 4), several of the versions produced better WER. However, only the best one yielded any reduction in SER, this reduction was not statistically significant, and producing it required the extra interlingua-based filtering step. This is consistent with the intuition that the GLM grammar essentially contains only a little more information than the corpus used to create it. The SLM trained from the PCFG-generated corpus does in fact produce a slight improvement over the one trained from the "seed" corpus. We hypothesize that this improvement is due to a combination of two factors. First, the PCFG generation process probably helps, in effect, to smooth the training data; second, it seems reasonable to believe that the general resource grammar used to build the GLM contributes at least some information.

Restricting evaluation only to in-coverage data did finally produce a result where an SLM recognizer trained on generated data significantly outperformed the one trained on the seed corpus. This is again, unfortunately, still not very interesting, since the main point of the SLM is to achieve greater robustness on out-of-coverage material; as we had expected, the GLM recognizer strongly outperformed all the SLM versions on the in-coverage material.

An incidental result that we found interesting was the large difference between the models trained on PCFG-generated data and those trained on CFG-generated data. In retrospect, this should not have been entirely surprising. However, looking at previous work, it is worth noting that although [11] used PCFG generation, [12] appeared not to. The experiments where we increased the size of the generated corpus suggest that one needs to produce quite a large amount of data, on the order of hundreds of thousands of sentences, before performance tops out.

In conclusion, we think we can reasonably claim to have put the idea of using grammars to create SLM training data on a sounder theoretical footing. Although the results reported here are more negative than positive, we hope that the methodology we present will open new possibilities for research in this area.

Acknowledgments

We would like to thank Nuance for giving us access to the proprietary software used in this research. Work by Manny Rayner was funded by the Fonds National de la Recherche Scientifique (FNRS) under the project "A Swiss Platform for Controlled Language Spoken Dialog Applications".

References

1. Rabiner, L.: A tutorial on hidden Markov models and selected applications in speech recognition. Proceedings of the IEEE 77(2), 257–286 (1989)
2. Moore, R.: Using natural language knowledge sources in speech recognition. In: Proceedings of the NATO Advanced Studies Institute, pp. 115–129 (1998)
3. Dowding, J., Hockey, B., Gawron, J., Culy, C.: Practical issues in compiling typed unification grammars for speech recognition. In: Proceedings of the 39th Annual Meeting of the Association for Computational Linguistics, Toulouse, France, pp. 164–171 (2001)
4. Rayner, M., Dowding, J., Hockey, B.: A baseline method for compiling typed unification grammars into context free language models. In: Proceedings of Eurospeech 2001, Aalborg, Denmark, pp. 729–732 (2001)
5. Bos, J.: Compilation of unification grammars with compositional semantics to speech recognition packages. In: Proceedings of the 19th International Conference on Computational Linguistics, Taipei, Taiwan (2002)
6. Stent, A., Dowding, J., Gawron, J., Bratt, E., Moore, R.: The CommandTalk spoken dialogue system. In: Proceedings of the Thirty-Seventh Annual Meeting of the Association for Computational Linguistics, pp. 183–190 (1999)
7. Knight, S., Gorrell, G., Rayner, M., Milward, D., Koeling, R., Lewin, I.: Comparing grammar-based and robust approaches to speech understanding: a case study. In: Proceedings of Eurospeech 2001, Aalborg, Denmark, pp. 1779–1782 (2001)
8. Rayner, M., Hockey, B., Renders, J., Chatzichrisafis, N., Farrell, K.: A voice enabled procedure browser for the International Space Station. In: Proceedings of the 43rd Annual Meeting of the Association for Computational Linguistics (interactive poster and demo track), Ann Arbor, MI (2005)
9. Chatzichrisafis, N., Bouillon, P., Rayner, M., Santaholma, M., Starlander, M., Hockey, B.: Evaluating task performance for a unidirectional controlled language medical speech translation system. In: Proceedings of the HLT-NAACL International Workshop on Medical Speech Translation, New York, pp. 9–16 (2006)
10. Wang, Y.-Y., Acero, A., Chelba, C., Frey, B., Wong, L.: Combination of statistical and rule-based approaches for spoken language understanding. In: Proceedings of the 7th International Conference on Spoken Language Processing (ICSLP), Denver, CO, pp. 609–612 (2002)
11. Jurafsky, A., Wooters, C., Segal, J., Stolcke, A., Fosler, E., Tajchman, G., Morgan, N.: Using a stochastic context-free grammar as a language model for speech recognition. In: Proceedings of the IEEE International Conference on Acoustics, Speech and Signal Processing, pp. 189–192 (1995)
12. Jonson, R.: Generating statistical language models from interpretation grammars in dialogue systems. In: Proceedings of the 11th EACL, Trento, Italy (2006)
13. Rayner, M., Hockey, B., Bouillon, P.: Putting Linguistics into Speech Recognition: The Regulus Grammar Compiler. CSLI Press, Chicago (2006)
14. Rayner, M., Bouillon, P., Chatzichrisafis, N., Hockey, B., Santaholma, M., Starlander, M., Isahara, H., Kanzaki, K., Nakao, Y.: A methodology for comparing grammar-based and robust approaches to speech understanding. In: Proceedings of the 9th International Conference on Spoken Language Processing (ICSLP), Lisboa, Portugal, pp. 1103–1107 (2005)

15. Wang, Y.Y., Acero, A., Chelba, C.: Is Word Error Rate a good indicator for spoken language understanding accuracy. In: Proceedings of Eurospeech 2003, Geneva, Switzerland, pp. 609–612 (2003)
16. Bouillon, P., Rayner, M., Chatzichrisafis, N., Hockey, B., Santaholma, M., Starlander, M., Nakao, Y., Kanzaki, K., Isahara, H.: A generic multi-lingual open source platform for limited-domain medical speech translation. In: Proceedings of the 10th Conference of the European Association for Machine Translation (EAMT), Budapest, Hungary, pp. 50–58 (2005)
17. Bouillon, P., Halimi, S., Nakao, Y., Kanzaki, K., Isahara, H., Tsourakis, N., Starlander, M., Hockey, B., Rayner, M.: Developing non-European translation pairs in a medium-vocabulary medical speech translation system. In: Proceedings of LREC 2008, Marrakesh, Morocco (2008)

A Mixed Method Lemmatization Algorithm Using a Hierarchy of Linguistic Identities (HOLI)

Anton Karl Ingason[1], Sigrún Helgadóttir[2], Hrafn Loftsson[3],
and Eiríkur Rögnvaldsson[1]

[1] Department of Icelandic, University of Iceland
Árnagarður v/Suðurgötu, 101 Reykjavik, Iceland
[2] The Árni Magnusson Institute for Icelandic Studies
Neshagi 16, 107 Reykjavik, Iceland
[3] School of Computer Science, Reykjavik University
Kringlan 1, 103 Reykjavik, Iceland
anton@akademia.is, sigruhel@hi.is, hrafn@ru.is, eirikur@hi.is

Abstract. We present a new mixed method lemmatizer for Icelandic, *Lemmald*, which achieves good performance by relying on IceTagger [1] for tagging and The Icelandic Frequency Dictionary [2] corpus for training. We combine the advantages of data-driven machine learning with linguistic insights to maximize performance. To achieve this, we make use of a novel approach: Hierarchy of Linguistic Identities (HOLI), which involves organizing features and feature structures for the machine learning based on linguistic knowledge. Accuracy of the lemmatization is further improved using an add-on which connects to the Database of Modern Icelandic Inflections [3]. Given correct tagging, our system lemmatizes Icelandic text with an accuracy of 99.55%. We believe our method can be fruitfully adapted to other morphologically rich languages.

Keywords: lemma, lemmatization, normalization, machine learning, BLARK, Icelandic, Lemmald, IceTagger.

1   Introduction

Lemmatization is the task of finding the base form – the *lemma* – of a given word form. The process is similar, while not identical, to the task of stemming which removes affixes from a word and returns the stem, the largest common part shared by morphologically related forms. Lemmatization and stemming are normalization techniques which serve the purpose of creating a connection between related words or word forms. Such a normalization is important in various natural language processing (NLP) applications, such as text classification and information extraction, because it brings out actual grammatical or semantic relations which are otherwise not accessible by the software (e.g. [4,5,6]).

In this paper, we describe *Lemmald*, a new lemmatizer for Icelandic, written in Java. Since Icelandic is a highly inflected language, one of the most important units in an Icelandic BLARK (Basic Language Resource Kit) [7] is an effective

A. Ranta, B. Nordström (Eds.): GoTAL 2008, LNAI 5221, pp. 205–216, 2008.

lemmatizer. Until now, the only available lemmatizer for Icelandic has been the language-independent CST Lemmatizer which has been trained for Icelandic [8]. A practical motivation for developing another lemmatizer for Icelandic is, for example, to be able to integrate it easily with other tools in the *IceNLP* toolkit which is currently being developed [9]. Furthermore, the existence of *Lemmald* gives the Icelandic NLP community the possibility of further improving the accuracy in lemmatization without having to rely on a language-independent lemmatizer. Unique aspects of the Icelandic language can thus by directly mirrored in the program code.

The tagset we use for Icelandic is the one developed for the Icelandic Frequency Dictionary corpus (IFD) [2]. It consists of about 700 different POS tags, where each character in the tag string corresponds to a single morphosyntactic category. The first character always marks the part of speech. Thus, the sentence *Hún mætti manninum* 'She met the man' will be tagged like this:

(1) Hún   fpven
    mætti   sfg3eþ
    manninum   nkeþg

The meaning of the tags is as follows: **fpven**: pronoun (f) - personal (p) - feminine (v) - singular (e) - nominative (n); **sfg3eþ**: verb (s) - indicative (f) - active (g) - 3rd person (3) - singular (e) - past (þ); **nkeþg**: noun (n) - masculine (k) - singular (e) - dative (þ) - suffixed article (g).

In addition to dealing with a large tagset, an Icelandic NLP tool must address the fact that several word formation processes are very active in the language. Any given text is likely to contain a number of new compounds or derived forms which a data-driven solution has not encountered when trained using a corpus. To handle this, some kind of a compound analyzer is an important tool.

Lemmald uses a new algorithm for lemmatizing morphologically rich languages, combining data-driven machine learning methods and linguistic knowledge. The lemmatizer relies on three external NLP resources developed in previous projects. It uses the rule-based POS tagger *IceTagger* [1] for tagging its input and it is trained using the IFD corpus. Furthermore, *Lemmald* can optionally be run with the Database of Modern Icelandic Inflections (DMII) [3] as an add-on for improved results.

Our evaluation shows that, given correct tagging, *Lemmald* lemmatizes with an accuracy of 98.54%. Using the DMII as an add-on further improves the result to an accuracy of 99.55%. We consider this success an indication of the tool being ready to be used in practical situations for purposes of linguistic research or commercial software development.

The paper is organized as follows. In Sect. 2, we discuss related work concerned with normalizing text. Section 3 presents the external NLP resources used by *Lemmald*, and Sect. 4 describes some language specific issues when lemmatizing Icelandic. Section 5 describes our algorithm and in Sect. 6 we present an evalution of our system and the CST Lemmatizer. We conclude, in Sect. 7, with a summary.

2   Related Work

A frequently cited example of text normalization is the Porter Stemming Algorithm [10]. Development of the algorithm is motivated by the idea that "the performance of an IR system will be improved if [related] term groups [...] are conflated into a single term". The Porter Stemmer removes suffixes from a word form until the "stem" is found. The stem may or may not be a linguistically "correct stem" but in most cases serves well the purpose of reducing the size and complexity of the data in the text it processes. For this purpose, the use of a stemmer instead of a lemmatizer is often desirable, because it can make a connection between a noun and a verb with the same stem which frequently reflects an actual semantic relation. However, the method of suffix stripping does not bring out such connections in irreglar inflection (e.g. *good*, *better*) – a job better suited for a lemmatizer (given that the lemmatizer can handle such irregularities). Actually, the advantages of both approaches can be combined to a considerable extent by running a lemmatizer first and subsequently stemming the lemmatized form.

The CST Lemmatizer [11] and the Euroling Stemmer [12] have been used for normalizing text in the Nordic languages, cf. [13]. Those two normalization systems represent the difference between stemming and lemmatization and also the other main distinction in software of this kind – that is the difference between hand-crafted and machine learned rules. The Euroling Stemmer uses only hand-crafted rules while the CST Lemmatizer uses only machine learned rules.

The method used by the CST Lemmatizer involves discovering suffix substitution rules by examining a tagged and lemmatized training corpus. When applying the rules to input data the rule with the longest suffix that matches the input word (and tag if present) is selected. The training phase is responsible for organizing the suffix substitution rules to maximize the probability of the longest matching suffix in the rule set, resulting in a correct lemma.

There are two main differences between our *Lemmald* and these techniques. Instead of focusing entirely on either hand-crafted rules or machine learning, we attempt to combine linguistic knowledge with machine learning. Then we attempt to use this combination to select from rules that apply minimally. By rules that apply minimally, we mean that we use the shortest suffixes that will map an input word to its lemma because *Lemmald* does not base its decisions on suffix length. In the evaluation of *Lemmald*, we compare our results with running the CST Lemmatizer on the same data as presented in Section 6.

3   External NLP Resources

3.1   Tagged Icelandic Corpus

Lemmald is designed to be trained on a tagged and lemmatized corpus. The only such corpus available for Icelandic is the IFD corpus. The IFD corpus contains about 590k tokens, where each token consists of a word form, a manually corrected POS (morphosyntactic) tag, and a lemma. This kind of data is well suited for training NLP tools, but the main weakness is that most of the texts in the corpus are literary works and thus the corpus may not represent other text categories as well. In terms of our lemmatizer it may perform slightly better if the input resembles literary texts.

3.2 IceTagger

Our lemmatizer can lemmatize text that has already been tagged, but in the common case of untagged texts, *Lemmald* uses IceTagger to tag the input before lemmatization is performed. Evaluations have indicated that IceTagger gives the correct tag about 91.5% of the time [1].

This relatively low tagging accuracy, compared to related languages, seems to limit the possibility of lemmatization which is based on the tag as well as the word form. However, the impact of incorrect tagging is quite low, since most tagging errors do not involve selecting the wrong word class (noun, verb, etc.), but rather incorrect subfeatures such as case, number, and gender in ambiguous word forms. Such an error does not affect lemmatization, because, for example, the lemma for a noun is the same irrespective of case. Indeed the accuracy in lemmatization is remarkably higher than the tagging accuracy. Accuracy when tagging Icelandic only with respect to word class has been measured as high as 98.14% [14] which is substantially higher than when including all subfeatures.

3.3   Database of Modern Icelandic Inflections

Although it is possible to achieve relatively good results using only data from the IFD corpus, a larger database of words can improve the results by filling in the gaps. Therefore, we have included the option of running *Lemmald* with an add-on which communicates with the DMII. Note that the DMII does not contain any frequency data and thus complements, rather than replaces, the IFD corpus.

The DMII is a huge database and its size causes some practical issues in terms of implementation and performance. For our purposes, we use a format where the data is contained within a table and each row consists of a set of a word form, a tag and a lemma. All combinations of grammatical categories for nouns, verbs and adjectives are included and in total there are over 5 million rows in the table. Note that other word classes are closed and are thus well covered by the IFD corpus. Our add-on is designed to communicate with any database management system which contains such a table and supports JDBC connections. In our development tests, we used MS SQL Server which worked quite efficently but frequent database queries will nevertheless affect the performance of any software. Thus, the improved lemmatization is traded for slower execution speeed when running the DMII add-on.

4   Language Specific Issues

When lemmatizing an unknown word in a language which uses suffixes for encoding grammatical distinction, it seems intuitive to search for the longest known ending of the unknown word. This method is indeed frequently used in lemmatization (e.g. [11]). However, applying longest match substitution blindly to Icelandic words can lead to mistakes.

Consider, for example, the word *götusópari* 'street sweeper' which is a compound made of the genitive of the noun *gata* 'street' and a noun derived from the verb *sópa*, using the affix *-ari* 'one who does what the verb expresses' (similar to the English *-er*). The masculine noun *götusópari* does not appear in the 590K word IFD corpus nor does the noun *sópari* 'sweeper'. On the other hand, the neuter noun *pari* (dative form of *par* 'pair') does exist in the corpus. Using longest match analysis for unknown words results in the incorrect lemma *götusópar*, while the correct result would be an unmodified *götusópari*. In *Lemmald*, we still use longest match analysis for cases where other methods fail, but first we attempt to analyze compounds using other more precise modules.

Examples like *götusópari* are particularly difficult to handle, because both the word itself and its second half, *sópari*, (the grammatical head) are unknown. Usually, compound analysis for unknown word forms is easier when both parts are known. However, it is not always enough to know both parts because of the problem of compound ambiguity. Consider, for example, the feminine plural noun *álfelgur* 'alumininum rims'. Even if our lemmatizer recognizes the parts *ál* 'aluminium' and *felgur* 'rims' it might mistake the *ál-felgur* compound for *álf-elgur* 'elf moose', because of compound ambiguity.

Compound analysis may also fail because of what we might call *partially unknown word parts*. This occurs when both parts of the compound are known as word forms, but the grammatical head (the rightmost part) does not exist in the corpus in a context where it fully agrees with the provided morphosyntactic tag. Maintaining an agreement between the input tag and decisions of the lemmatizer is important, because on most occasions, the occurrence of a partially unknown compound can be attributed to a minor distinction within the inner structure of the tag. Perhaps a particular noun has the same written form in the nominative case and the accusative case, but the corpus only contains the accusative form.

An example of an Icelandic compound which could possibly be partially unknown is *drengja-móður* 'mother of boys'. The compound is in no way unusual Icelandic but it is unlikely to appear in a corpus. The word form *drengja-móður* is identical in the accusative, dative and genetive case. Even if the first part of the compound *drengja* 'boys' was known and the second *móður* 'mother' also – a problem would rise if the input *móður* is in genitive case but is only known in accusative case in the corpus. This can of course happen irrespective of whether the genitive form is a part of a compound or not. Thus, a mechanism is needed to fall back to an agreement on, say, word class and gender, even if it is impossible to also confirm agreement on case using the limited corpus.

To resolve this, we present the idea of a *Hierarcy of Linguistic Identities* (HOLI) for Icelandic. It uses a simple linguistic insight to maintain a mostly data-driven machine learning approach when lemmatizing compounds, while falling back to nonperfect data in a linguistically sensible way when there are gaps in the training data.

5   Algorithm

5.1   Overview

We define the task of lemmatizing an Icelandic word as the one of implementing the function *getLemma(wordForm, tag)*. This definition implies that for a given word form and tag there exists one and only one correct lemma and it also leaves all issues of context sensitivity to the task of determining the tag. In this sense, our method is identical to the one of the CST Lemmatizer. The observation that an input of word form and tag corresponds to a unique lemma holds for almost all cases in Icelandic and the rare exceptions represent an insignificant part of lemmatization errors. Thus, the input to *Lemmald* consists of a wordform and a morposyntactic tag, whose format is described in Sect. 1. The tag can be obtained by using any POS tagger for Icelandic, but, as discussed in Sect. 3, we use IceTagger for this purpose.

Lemmald uses a mixed method approach to perform its task. The main method is the HOLI method mentioned in the previous section. However, further techniques are required to handle special cases, such as compound analysis, umlaut substitution and various systematic exceptions to Icelandic morphology. Finally, the add-on that connects to the DMII can be used for improved results. Units of functionality are organized into modules that can be turned on or off by adjusting configuration parameters of the program. The modules are as follows: (1) Hierarchy of Linguistic Identities Analysis, (2) Compound Analysis, (3), Umlaut substitution, (4) Post processing, (5) Database of Modern Icelandic Inflections Lookup.

5.2   Hierarchy of Linguistic Identities

It is a challenge for a data-driven NLP method to handle input that it does not recognize from its training data. When working with fully known data patterns is not an option, some kind of fallback to a more general method is inevitable and the goal of machine learning is of course to be able to apply learned patterns to new data. However, it may not be the best strategy to think of the problem exclusively from the point of view of machine learning, because the success of such an approach also depends on the features fed to the machine and the structure of those features. This is where linguistic insights can be important, as Manning has recently emphasized [15].

When dealing with the Icelandic tagset of about 700 different tags, data sparseness problems are bound to occur and handling them well is essential. Our approach to this task makes use of a HOLI. An example of a data sparseness gap which can be resolved by HOLI analysis is if a corpus does not contain a particular case of a noun. Consider, for example, the previously mentioned word form *móður*, which may be the accusative, dative or genitive case of the feminine noun *móðir* 'mother' (singular). This word can also be a masculine singular form of an adjective which means 'winded, out of breath'. The format of the morphosyntactic tag for an Icelandic noun has four characters; the first character 'n' stands for noun, the second character is for gender, the third is for number and the fourth is for case. The noun *móður* can thus have the following tags: *nveo, nveþ, nvee*, where the second letter stands for feminine and the final letter stands for accusative, dative and genitive case, respectively. The adjective *móður* has the tag *lkensf* which stands for adjective, masculine, singular, nominative, strong declension, and positive degree, respectively.

Let us imagine that the lemmatizer is asked to lemmatize the word *móður* with the tag *nvee* (noun, genitive), and while the genitive form of 'mother' is not present in the training data there are a few occurrences of the identical accusative and dative forms. If the tag was treated as one unit having no structure and the fallback mechanism would just pick the most frequent lemma for the word form according to the corpus, we might get the adjective form *móður* if the adjective happened to occur frequently in the training data. Therefore, we generate four levels of identities for $<móður,nvee>$ from specific to general:

```
(2) word        tag
    -------------
    móður       nvee
    móður       nv
    [any]       nvee
    móður       [any]
```

Note that this particular hierarchy may not be the optimal representation of a noun, it is simply something we have found to work well for our purpose. We create an intermediate level of specificness for *feminine noun (nv)*, but we do not use number and case for creating such identities – those are just reflected in the full tag string. The study of how it is best to construct hierarchies of linguistic features is a complex issue. An example of such work in linguistics is the feature tree in phonology (e.g. [16]).

When matching input words to machine learned rules, the lemmatizer goes for the most specific matching identity. Note that when making a decision based on specificness like here, we use strict domination of the most specific level relevant to the given input. A lower ranking identity has no significance if it is possible to base a decision on a higher ranking identity. In this sense, our model is similar to Optimality Theory [17]. In the case of the genitive *móður*, it would be the identity *feminine noun* resulting in correct lemmatization even if there were no useful clues for lemmatizing the word according to its genitive case.

During the training phase, a HOLI is generated for every pair of word form and tag encountered in the training data (the IFD corpus) along with a rule which correctly lemmatizes the given word. An example HOLI along with the corresponding lemmatization rules for $<móður,nveo>$ is as follows:

```
(3) word        tag       rule
    ----------------------------
    móður       nveo      ur>ir
    móður       nv        ur>ir
    [any]       nveo      ur>ir
    móður       [any]     ur>ir
```

The rule is the minimal suffix substitution needed to map the full word form to its lemma. In a second run through the corpus, the full hierarchy is again generated for each word and tested against all matching rules created in the previous run, in order to obtain a score for each combination of identity+rule depending on how often that combination results in a correct lemma. The score is recorded in a rule database along with the identity and the rule. This score is used to select a rule if more than one possible rule is available within a specificness level.

If the lemmatizer knows the above rules for $<móður,nveo>$ but has not seen $<móður,nvee>$ it can not use the most specific identity in that case. Then it must try a lower ranking one. The HOLI for $<móður,nvee>$ is shown in (2). The most specific known identity is $<móður,nv>$ and therefore the rule $ur>ir$ is applied resulting in the correct lemma $móðir$. Without the intermediate level of specificness, there would have been a conflict between the noun form $móður$ and the identical masculine adjective which might have given the rule $r>r$, resulting in a lemmatization error.

Using a HOLI, we can still rely on machine learning to perform most of the work and save time that would otherwise be spent on manually writing linguistic rules. The HOLI takes care of "coming up with" linguistic insights such as picking a pattern from a feminine noun instead of a masculine noun, or a pattern from a noun rather than an adjective where appropriate. This way we can combine some of the advantages of data-driven and linguistic rule-based NLP.

It is important to note that the key observation here is the general idea of combining linguistic structure with how the machine learns, not this particular implementation. A strictly machine learning motivated study would probably treat the word form and the tag as two features with no internal structure. Even if such an approach attempted to "machine learn" the internal structure of the tag it could not make use of the linguistic understanding of "specificness" we employ with little effort here. This sort of thinking provides opportunities for linguistics to contribute to NLP without switching from machine-learning to hand-crafted rules. Instead of choosing between the approaches, they are combined.

5.3 Compound Analysis

By checking for the existance of an identity of the most specific level (which is identical to a dictionary lookup), the compound analyzer determines if the input word is known. This happens before the HOLI analysis and if the word is known, there is no reason to attempt compound analysis. In contrast, an unknown word can go through up to three levels of compound analysis: strict analysis, loose analysis and longest match analysis which is attempted only if the previous methods fail.

Strict analysis requires that both parts of the compound are known and that the tag of the the latter part (the grammatical head) is known to exist for that word form. Loose analysis has the same requirements for the grammatical head, but tries to construct a well formed first part using a few known Icelandic derivation methods. If the word is still unknown and is longer than 6 letters an attempt is made to find the longest matching known ending while requiring that the first part has at least one vowel. Should the compound analysis result in a successfully split compound, the grammatical head is sent to HOLI analysis along with its tag.

Let us, for example, say that the input is the noun *<hestaskip,nheo>* 'horse ship'. Strict analysis then determines that while this is an unknown word it is probably a compound made of the parts *hesta-skip* since *hesta* is a known word and *skip* is known to have the tag *<nheo>*. Then the input to the HOLI module becomes *<skip,nheo>* and the compound analyzer makes sure that the first part *hesta* is added to the result before it is returned.

All of the above methods can of course fail to find a probable compound analysis of the input word as is supposed to happen if the word is not really a compound, but a (simple) unknown word. Then a HOLI analysis takes over.

Although the compound analyzer works in most cases, it is a module which can without a doubt be improved. The authors hope to develop an independent and powerful unit for this task in future research as a contribution to the Icelandic BLARK.

5.4   Umlaut Substitution, Post-Processing and DMII Lookup

Umlaut substitution is a known issue in the lemmatization of other Germanic languages (e.g. [18]). For common words, the automatically generated rules in the HOLI analysis take care of changing 'ö' in an inflected form to 'a' in the lemma, but to make sure that this happens in less common words as well, every rule which removes the umlaut trigger 'u' causes the umlaut substitution module to reverse its effect in an affected root if appropriate.

For example, if the rule $u>a$ is applied to the noun *tösku* 'bag' (accusative, dative or genitive) the resulting lemma without umlaut substitution would be **töska*. The umlaut module of *Lemmald* corrects this by substituting the 'ö' in the root for 'a' giving the correct lemma *taska*.

A few systematic errors appear in the output of the lemmatizer due to irregularities in Icelandic morphology. Some of those, particularly the ones that result in consonant clusters which violate constraints of Icelandic phonology, are corrected using a list of substitutions which is applied after all other modules have finished their work. The program must be taught to perform u-epenthesis when its machine-learned rules result in word final consonant clusters like *-kr* replacing them with *-kur*.

As previously mentioned, the program can be configured to communicate with the DMII using an add-on. The format of the database we use consists of just over 5 million rows, each containing a word form and a tag along with the corresponding lemma. If turned on, this module is run before the HOLI analysis. This improves precision of the lemmatization while slowing it down.

6   Evaluation

To evaluate the performance of *Lemmald*, and the effect of the modules it uses, we ran a 10-fold cross validation test on the IFD corpus where the size of each training set was about 530k tokens and each test set contained about 60k tokens. We used the word forms and the manually corrected morphosyntactic tags from the corpus and measured the success of *Lemmald* in finding the correct lemma for each token. We also trained the CST Lemmatizer using the IFD corpus and performed an identical evaluation – with and without tags in the input. The results are presented in Table 1, where mean accuracy is shown. In the first row the success for the HOLI method without any additional modules is shown and in each of the following rows one module is added to improve accuracy. The last row contains the results of our evaluation of the CST Lemmatizer. Note that, while assuming correct tagging is useful for evaluating different lemmatization methods, real world results will in most cases rely on machine tagged text which negatively affects accuracy. A preliminary test with one test set containing approximately 10,000 words was performed using *Lemmald*. This test showed a drop in accuracy of about 1.5% between lemmatizing correctly tagged text and a text tagged with IceTagger. The accuracy of the lemmatization is still much higher than the accuracy of the machine tagging, because, as pointed out earlier, most tagging errors do not affect lemmatization.

Table 1. Results

Lemmald	Tagged Input	Untagged Input
Basic (HOLI only)	97.85%	
+ Compound Analysis	98.38%	
+ Umlaut Substitution	98.42%	
+ Post processing	98.54%	
+ DMII	99.55%	
CST Lemmatizer		
	98.99%	93.15%

The CST Lemmatizer trained on the IFD Corpus reaches 98.99% accuracy when applied to correctly tagged text. A comparable number for *Lemmald* is 98.54%, which is obtained by omitting the use of the DMII. The difference is statistically significant ($\alpha < 0.001$). However, the difference between the best result for *Lemmald*, 99.55% obtained when the DMII is used, is significantly higher than the result with the CST lemmatizer (98.99%). Adding the DMII should have the same effect on the CST Lemmatizer resulting in an even higher accuracy. However, the above comparision has already confirmed that the CST Lemmatizer performs better than *Lemmald* when trained on the same data so we have not implemented such an evalution setting. Instead, we focus on measuring the effect of each specialized module.

Taking a closer look at the *Lemmald* column in Table 1, we can see that every language specific module contributes to the accuracy of the lemmatizer. This clearly shows that addressing language specific issues does matter for the performance. The language independent aspects of *Lemmald* are still a little behind the CST Lemmatizer. The reason for this is that within a level of specificness in the HOLI, *Lemmald* uses a very primitive way of choosing between rules. In such a situation there is no linguistic evidence to base the decision on and a very simple score mechanism is employed. By improving the decision making on this level, we believe the combination of our linguistically inspired method and the powerful tools of data-driven methods can result in an Icelandic lemmatizer which outperforms both systems evaluated here. Currently, there are examples of each lemmatizer failing in a situation where the other succeeds. The strenghts of the HOLI method in dealing with data sparseness in a large tagset is in many cases successful, but in other cases when there is ambiguity within a specificness level the method fails. We intend to improve our system in a future version so that it covers most or all cases that can be learned in a language independent way and goes beyond that when used with the language specific modules. Thus, we believe that future versions of *Lemmald* (without using DMII) will outperform the CST Lemmatizer and the former could therefore be used in favour of the latter. Additionally, as mentioned in Sect. 1, *Lemmald* allows for an easy integration into the IceNLP toolkit, because both units are implemented in Java.

7 Conclusion

We have shown that the combination of linguistic knowledge with data-driven machine learning can resolve issues that are difficult to handle when using one of the approaches exclusively. Machine learning is essential to save the time otherwise needed for hand-crafting linguistic rules. However, using linguistics to determine features and feature structures can combine the advantges of both approaches. Our way to achieve such combination in lemmatization is based on a Hierarchy of Linguistic Identities. More important than this particular implementation of such a HOLI, is the idea that a similar approach can be used in a number of NLP tasks. We believe it is important to move away from viewing the field as "just a branch of applied machine learning" [15] and towards the strenghts of a truly cross disciplinary field. NLP may have "caught up with what statisticians and machine learning people have discovered in 400 years" [15] but now it is time to catch up with the knowledge of linguistics.

Lemmald is ready to be used in combination with other Icelandic BLARK units in various practical situations in linguistic reasearch and commercial software development. However, we will continue to improve the system and aim to increase the lemmatization accuracy in future versions. This will involve more intelligent machine learning to deal with cases where our method fails and development of a more advanced compound analyser.

References

1. Loftsson, H.: Tagging Icelandic text: A linguistic rule-based approach. Nordic Journal of Linguistics 31(1), 47–72 (2008)
2. Pind, J., Magnússon, F., Briem, S.: [The Icelandic Frequency Dictionary]. The Institute of Lexicography, University of Iceland, Reykjavik (1991)

3. Bjarnadóttir, K.: Modern Icelandic Inflections. In: Holmboe, H. (ed.) Nordisk Sprogteknologi 2005. Museum Tusculanums Forlag, Copenhagen (2005)
4. Korenius, T., Laurikkala, J., Järvelin, K., Juhola, M.: Stemming and lemmatization in the clustering of finnish text documents. In: CIKM 2004: Proceedings of the thirteenth ACM international conference on Information and knowledge management, pp. 625–633. ACM, New York (2004)
5. Braschler, B., Ripplinger, B.: How Effective is Stemming and Decompounding for German Text Retrieval? Information Retrieval 7(3-4), 291–316 (2004)
6. Airio, E.: Word normalization and decompounding in mono- and bilingual IR. Information Retrieval 9(3), 249–271 (2006)
7. Krauwer, S.: The Basic Language Resource Kit (BLARK) as the First Milestone for the Language Resources Roadmap. SPECOM-2003, Moscow, Russia, Accessed 01.04.2008 (2003), http://www.elsnet.org/dox/krauwer-specom2003.pdf
8. Cassata, F.: Automatic thesaurus extraction for Icelandic. BSc Final Project, Department of Computer Science, Reykjavik University (2007)
9. Loftsson, H., Rögnvaldsson, E.: IceNLP: A Natural Language Processing Toolkit for Icelandic. In: Proceedings of Interspeech 2007, Special Session: Speech and language technology for less-resourced languages, Antwerp, Belgium (2007)
10. Porter, M.: An algorithm for suffix stripping. Program 14(3), 130–137 (1980)
11. Jongejan, B., Haltrup, D.: The CST Lemmatiser. Center for Sprogteknologi, University of Copenhagen version 2.9 (2005)
12. Carlberger, J., Dalianis, H., Hassel, M., Knutsson, O.: Improving precision in information retrieval for Swedish using stemming. In: Proceedings of NODALIDA 2001 – 13th Nordic conference on computational linguistics (2001)
13. Dalianis, H., Jongejan, B.: Hand-crafted versus Machine-learned Inflectional Rules: The Euroling-SiteSeeker Stemmer and CST's Lemmatiser. In: LREC 2006: Proceeding of the International Conference on Language Resources and Evaluation (2006)
14. Helgadóttir, S.: Testing Data-Driven Learning Algorithms for PoS Tagging of Icelandic. In: Holmboe, H. (ed.) Nordisk Sprogteknologi 2004. Museum Tusculanums Forlag, Copenhagen (2005)
15. Manning, C.: Focusing on Linguistic Representations [abstract]. In: The Natural Language and Speech Processing Colloquium, Stanford, January 19 (2005)
16. Kenstowicz, M.: Phonology in Generative Grammar (Blackwell Textbooks in Linguistics). Blackwell Publishers, Malden (1993)
17. Prince, A., Smolensky, P.: Optimality Theory: Constraint Interaction in Generative Grammar. Manuscript, Rutgers University and University of Colorado at Boulder. ROA [ROA #537] (1993/2002), http://roa.rutgers.edu/
18. Lezius, W., Rapp, R., Wettler, M.: A freely available Morphological Analyzer, Disambiguator, and Context Sensitive Lemmatizer for German. In: Proceedings of the COLING-ACL, pp. 743–747 (1998)

Semantic Roles in Valency Lexicon of Czech Verbs: Verbs of Communication and Exchange*

Václava Kettnerová, Markéta Lopatková, and Klára Hrstková

Charles University in Prague, Institute of Formal and Applied Linguistics
{kettnerova,lopatkova,hrstkova}@ufal.mff.cuni.cz

Abstract. We introduce a project to enhance a valency lexicon of Czech verbs with semantic roles. For this purpose, we make use of FrameNet. At the present stage, frame elements from FrameNet have been mapped to valency complementations of verbs of communication and verbs of exchange. The feasibility of this task has been proven by the achieved inter-annotator agreement – 95.6% for the verbs of communication and 91.2% for the verbs of exchange. As a result, we have obtained 37 semantic roles for the verbs of communication and 34 for the verbs of exchange, based on frame elements of upper level semantic frames from FrameNet.

1 Introduction

Semantic roles play a key role in NLP tasks in which semantic interpretation is necessary, as information extraction, question answering, or summarization [1]. In this paper, we report on labeling VALLEX valency complementations with more verb-specific semantic roles. For this purpose, we exploit frame elements from FrameNet.

As a first step, we experimented with two groups of verbs with divergent semantic and morphosyntactic properties, verbs of communication and verbs of exchange. First semantic frames from FrameNet were manually assigned to these verbs.[1] Then their valency complementations were linked with frame elements. Manual annotation is highly time consuming, however, it allows us to reach the desired quality.

2 Two Lexical Resources: VALLEX and FrameNet

In this section, we briefly characterize two lexical resources: VALLEX which takes into account mainly syntactic criteria and semantically oriented FrameNet.

Valency Lexicon of Czech verbs VALLEX. The Valency Lexicon of Czech Verbs, Version 2.5 (VALLEX 2.5)[2] provides information on the valency

---

* The research reported in this paper is carried under the project of the Ministry of Education, Youth and Sports No. MSM0021620838 (Objects of Research), under the grants LC536 (Center for Computational Linguistics II) and GA UK 7982/2007.

[1] This part of the experiment is described in [2].

[2] http://ufal.mff.cuni.cz/vallex/2.5/

A. Ranta, B. Nordström (Eds.): GoTAL 2008, LNAI 5221, pp. 217–221, 2008.
© Springer-Verlag Berlin Heidelberg 2008

structure of Czech verbs in their particular senses: primarily, the number of valency complementations, their type (labeled with functors), and their possible morphological forms. VALLEX 2.5 describes 2,730 lexeme entries containing around 6,460 lexical units, 'senses' (LUs), see [3].

VALLEX 2.5 has a rather syntactic approach to valency, see [4]. Five functors are determined for verb arguments: 'Actor', 'Patient', 'Addressee', 'Effect', and 'Origin'. However, not having verb-specific meaning, this tight set does not reflect similarities and differences in verb meaning. E.g., the following verbs remain indistinct, despite being semantically different:

(1) *Petr.*ACT *prodal Pavlovi.*ADDR *motorku.*PAT
Eng. *Peter.*ACT *has sold Paul.*ADDR *the motorbike.*PAT
(2) *Učitel.*ACT *vysvětlil dětem.*ADDR *pravidla.*PAT *hry*
Eng. *The teacher.*ACT *has explained the rules.*PAT *of the game to the children.*ADDR

Thus introducing verb-specific semantic roles to VALLEX allows us to capture relations between semantically similar verbs. Moreover, it enables us to make inferences on lexical entailments of verbs.

FrameNet. FrameNet[3] is an on-line lexical resource for English. It documents semantic and syntactic properties of each word in each of its senses, see [5]. FrameNet covers more than 10,000 LUs, i.e., pairs consisting of a word and its meaning.

The descriptive framework of FrameNet is based on *frame semantics*. The *semantic frame* (SF) represents a schematic representation of a particular situation involving various participants, *frame elements* (FEs). These are defined for each SF separately.

FrameNet records frame-to-frame relation (including FEs-to-FEs relation) in the form of a hierarchical network. The relation of 'Inheritance', i.e., the hyperonymy / hyponymy relation, represents the most important one – the semantics of the parent frame corresponds equally or more specifically to the semantics of its child frames.

3   Mapping Frame Elements from FrameNet to Valency Complementations in VALLEX

As a first step, we translated each LU belonging to the verbs of communication and to the verbs of exchange from Czech to English.[4] The total number of translated Czech LUs was 341 for the verbs of communication and 129 for the verbs of exchange.

Two human annotators were asked to indicate an appropriate SF for each given Czech LU. Then they assigned FE(s) of this SF to argument(s) of the

---

[3] http://framenet.icsi.berkeley.edu/
[4] The on-line dictionary at http://www.lingea.cz/ was used.

given Czech LU. More than one FE could be assigned to a single argument ('Ambiguous annotation of FEs'). When no FE corresponded to a particular argument, the annotators concluded that the given FE was missing. For the overall statistics, see Table 1.

Table 1. Overall statistics on the annotations of FEs

	annotator 1		annotator 2	
	Com	Exch	Com	Exch
Annotations of arguments from VALLEX	1088	479	1088	479
Unambiguous annotations of FEs	869	435	879	416
Ambiguous annotations of FEs	453	88	435	142
Marked as missing FEs	47	47	34	50

Inter-Annotator Agreement. Table 2 summarizes the inter-annotator agreement (IAA) and Cohen's κ statistics [6] on the total number of assigned FEs. IAA was measured only in the cases of match of SFs. Both the exact and intersection match of FEs (when both the annotators chose the same FEs regardless of other variants of ambiguous annotations) gave satisfactory results for both the verbs of communication (84.6% and 95.6%) and the verbs of exchange (85.4% and 91.2%). The κ statistics represents an evaluation metric that reflects average pairwise agreement corrected for chance agreement. The achieved levels represent significant results even in case of the exact match of FEs.

Table 2. Inter-annotator agreement and κ statistics

	IAA [%]		κ	
	Com	Exch	Com	Exch
Exact match of FEs	84.6	85.4	0.83	0.84
Intersection match of FEs	95.6	91.2	0.95	0.91

4   Exploiting Frame Elements as Semantic Roles

1185 FEs (in which the annotators concurred) were mapped to 1088 arguments of the verbs of communication and 433 FEs were assigned to 479 arguments of the verbs of exchange.

As for **ambiguous assignment of FEs**, the annotators mapped more than one FE to a single argument especially due to a variety of lexical entailments imposed by a verb on such an argument. E.g., two valency slots of the verb *zmínit se^{pf}* 'to mention' were assigned ambiguously – (i) the FEs 'Speaker' and 'Medium' were mapped to 'Actor' and (ii) 'Message' and 'Topic' to 'Patient':

(1) *Peter^{Speaker} did not mention (that he had moved away from her wife.)^{Message}*

(2) *This resolution^{Medium} mentions the problem^{Topic} of the refugee camp.*

Frame Elements as Semantic Roles. We enhanced VALLEX with semantic roles based on the FEs from the SFs from upper levels of the relation of 'Inheritance' – we made use of the ancestor FEs belonging to the SFs from the appropriate level of the relation of 'Inheritance', see [2].

Figure 1 illustrates the relation of 'Inheritance' between core FEs from the SFs 'Giving', 'Commerce_sell', and 'Renting_out'. We mapped the FEs 'Donor', 'Recipient', and 'Theme' from the ancestor SF 'Giving' to the appropriate arguments of the Czech LUs to which the descendant SFs 'Renting_out' and 'Commerce_sell' were assigned.

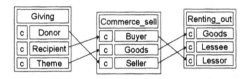

Fig. 1. The FEs-to-FEs relation of 'Inheritance' of the SFs 'Giving', 'Commerce_sell', and 'Renting_out'

As a result, 37 core FEs from nine SFs – belonging to the upper levels of the relation of 'Inheritance', [2] – were applied as semantic roles to the arguments of the **verbs of communication**. (We introduce only core FEs as the most important ones.):

1. 'Communication': 'Communicator', 'Medium', 'Message', 'Topic'
2. 'Statement': 'Medium', 'Message', 'Speaker', 'Topic'
3. 'Communication_response': 'Addressee', 'Message', 'Speaker', 'Topic', 'Trigger'
4. 'Judgment_communication': 'Communicator', 'Evaluee', 'Expressor', 'Medium', 'Reason', 'Topic'
5. 'Chatting': 'Interlocutor_1', 'Interlocutor_2'
6. 'Prohibiting': 'Principle', 'State_of_affairs'
7. 'Request': 'Addressee', 'Medium', 'Message', 'Speaker', 'Topic'
8. 'Reporting': 'Authorities', 'Behavior', 'Informer', 'Wrongdoer'
9. 'Commitment': 'Addressee', 'Medium', 'Message', 'Speaker', 'Topic'

(Note that the FEs with the same name cannot be confused across different SFs.) The arguments of the **verbs of exchange** were labeled with 34 core FEs as semantic roles, arisen from ten SFs from the upper levels of the relation of 'Inheritance':

1. 'Giving': 'Donor', 'Recipient', 'Theme'
2. 'Getting': 'Recipient', 'Theme'
3. 'Replacing': 'Agent', 'New', 'Old'
4. 'Exchange': 'Exchanger_1', 'Exchanger_2', 'Theme_1', 'Theme_2'
5. 'Robbery': 'Perpetrator', 'Source', 'Victim'
6. 'Hiring': 'Employee', 'Employer', 'Field', 'Position', 'Task'
7. 'Transfer': 'Donor', 'Recipient', 'Theme', 'Transferors'
8. 'Frugality': 'Behavior', 'Resource', 'Resource_controller'

9. 'Taking': 'Agent', 'Source', 'Theme'
10. 'Supply': 'Purpose_of_recipient', 'Recipient', 'Supplier', 'Theme'

As a result, the FEs from the upper level SFs cover 95.4% of arguments of the verbs of exchange and almost 53% of arguments of the verbs of communication. The considerable difference is due to the low coverage of the relation of 'Inheritance' for the verbs of communication (only 68% of assigned SFs are connected by this relation for the time being). In the future, we plan to continuously increase the coverage following the progress made in FrameNet.

5 Conclusion

We have presented an experiment with enhancing the valency lexicon of Czech verbs, VALLEX 2.5, with semantic roles derived from FrameNet. As a first step, we mapped frame elements to arguments of the verbs of communication and the verbs of exchange. The attained inter-annotator agreement has proved the feasibility of this task. Then we labeled their arguments with semantic roles based on the frame elements from the upper level semantic frames of the relation of 'Inheritance' – 37 and 34 semantic roles are determined for the verbs of communication and the verbs of exchange, respectively. In the future, we plan to expand this experiment to other groups of verbs and we intend to exploit the obtained data for summarization of Czech texts.

References

1. Gildea, D., Jurafsky, D.: Automatic Labeling of Semantic Roles. Computational Linguistics 28, 245–288 (2002)
2. Kettnerová, V., Lopatková, M., Hrstková, K.: Semantic Classes in Czech Valency Lexicon: Verbs of Communication and Verbs of Exchange. In: Proceedings of the 11th International Conference on Text, Speech and Dialogue (in print)
3. Žabokrtský, Z., Lopatková, M.: Valency Information in VALLEX 2.0: Logical Structure of the Lexicon. The Prague Bulletin of Mathematical Linguistics 87, 41–60 (2007)
4. Panevová, J.: Valency Frames and the Meaning of the Sentence. In: Luelsdorff, P.L. (ed.) The Prague School of Structural and Functional Linguistics, pp. 223–243. John Benjamins, Amsterdam (1994)
5. Ruppenhofer, J., Ellsworth, M., Petruck, M.R.L., Johnson, C.R., Scheffczyk, J.: FrameNet II: Extended Theory and Practice (2006),
   http://framenet.icsi.berkeley.edu/book/book.html
6. Carletta, J.: Assessing agreement on classification tasks: The Kappa statistic. Computational Linguistics 22, 249–254 (1996)

Automatic Generation of Frequent Case Forms of Query Keywords in Text Retrieval

Kimmo Kettunen

University of Tampere, Department of Information Studies,
Kanslerinrinne 1, FIN-33014 Tampere, Finland
Kimmo.kettunen@uta.fi

Abstract. This paper presents implementations of generative management method for morphological variation of query keywords. The method is called FCG, Frequent Case Generation. It is based on the skewed distributions of word forms in natural languages and is suitable for languages that either have fair amount of morphological variation or are morphologically very rich. The paper reports implementation and evaluation of automatic procedures of variant query keyword form generation with short and long queries of CLEF collections for English, Finnish, German and Swedish. The evaluated languages show varying degrees of morphological complexity.

1 Introduction

Morphological variation of textual words and keywords is a well known issue in information retrieval (IR) and needs some sort of management. Roughly put, the need for managing the variation of keywords increases as the morphological complexity of the language increases. For languages like English, it is not crucial, but for languages like Finnish, Turkish, Russian etc. it is much more important for better retrieval results. The first answers to management of morphological variation of keywords in IR have been manual term truncation and stemming. Later, lemmatization has been added to the repertoire. Generation of inflectional stems and generation of full word forms have been used less, although they also offer a suitable solution to the problem [1].

Kettunen [2] has divided the methods of keyword variation management into two groups: reductive and generative. The main idea behind reductive methods is that varying word forms are somehow reduced so that relationships between query keywords and index words can be detected. These methods demand both reductive analysis of textual data bases for index formation and reduction of query keywords. What is here called reductive methods have generally been named conflation in the IR literature [3], and the methods include stemming and lemmatization. Methods that generate inflectional stems or full word forms from a given input form may be called generative. With generative methods of keyword variation management textual indexes are left in their original form without any linguistic processing. Reductive methods have been used far more than generative so far, although also generative methods should be of interest e.g. in present web retrieval systems, where very large multilingual indexes may be impractical for reductive methods.

A. Ranta, B. Nordström (Eds.): GoTAL 2008, LNAI 5221, pp. 222–236, 2008.

In this paper we shall report IR results of restricted automatic generation of varying query keyword forms for four languages. With English, Finnish, German, and Swedish we have used CLEF 2003 materials. Our purpose is to show the feasibility of the Frequent Case Generation method that has been simulated earlier with languages that are morphologically different: one of the languages, English, is morphologically simple; German and Swedish are somehow complex and Finnish morphologically quite complex in the sense, that it has lots of word form variation that needs to be taken account for. We shall show that by generating the most frequent forms of nominal query keywords quite good IR performance is achieved.

2 The FCG Method

The FCG method has been earlier presented for management of morphological variation of query words with Finnish, Swedish, German and Russian in Kettunen and Airio [4] and Kettunen and colleagues [5]. The FCG method and its language specific evaluation procedure are characterized as follows:

1) For a morphologically sufficiently complex language the distribution of nominal case/other word forms is first studied through corpus analysis. The used corpus can be quite small, because variation at this level of language can be detected even from smaller corpuses. Variation in textual styles may affect slightly the results, so a style neutral corpus is the best.
2) After the most frequent (case) forms for the language have been identified with corpus statistics, the IR results of using only these forms for noun and adjective keyword forms are tested in a well-known test collection. As a comparison the best available reductive keyword and index management method (lemmatization or stemming) is used, if such is available. The number of tested FCG retrieval procedures depends on the morphological complexity of the language: more procedures can be tested for a complex language, only a few for a simpler one.
3) After evaluation, the best FCG procedure with respect to morphological normalization is usually distinguished. The testing process will probably also show that more than one FCG procedure is giving quite good results, and thus a varying number of keyword forms can be used for different retrieval purposes, if necessary.

It should be noted, that the FCG method does not usually outperform golden standard, usage of a lemmatizer, for morphologically complex languages. It provides, however, a simple and usually easily implementable alternative for lemmatization for languages that might lack language technology tools for information retrieval.

Based on this method, Kettunen and Airio [4] first evaluated four different FCG procedures in two different full-text collections of Finnish, TUTK (with graded relevance assessments, Sormunen [6]) and CLEF 2003 (with binary relevance). The results of [4] showed that frequent case form generation works in full-text retrieval of inflected indexes in a best-match query system (Inquery) and competes at best well with the gold standard, lemmatization, for Finnish. The best FCG procedures in

Kettunen and Airio. [4], FCG_9 and FCG_12[1], achieved about 86 % of the best average precisions of FINTWOL lemmatizer in TUTK and about 90 % in CLEF 2003. Kettunen and colleagues [5] tested the method with three new languages, German, Russian and Swedish. With German and Swedish the results were positive, but Russian results were reported to be inconclusive most obviously due to the limits of the Russian collection used.[2]

So far the process of FCG query keyword generation has been simulated in tests, but we have now implemented fully automatic query generation using word form generators of four languages: English, Finnish, German and Swedish. Three of the languages are morphologically at least moderately rich and English has been included to see, how a morphologically simple language behaves with the same approach.

3   Materials and Methods

CLEF collections for English, Finnish, German and Swedish were utilized in this study. The used retrieval system was Lemur [8]. Lemur combines an inference network retrieval model with language models, which are thought to give more sound estimates for word probabilities in documents [9, 10]. In Table 1, the number of documents and topics with relevant documents in each collection is shown.

Table 1. Collections used in the study

Language	Collection	Collection size (docs)	Topics	IR system
EN	CLEF 2003	169 477	54	Lemur
FI	CLEF 2003	55 344	45	Lemur
DE	CLEF 2003	294 809	56	Lemur
SV	CLEF 2003	142 819	54	Lemur

3.1   Query Formation and Linguistic Tools Used

Our query formation for all of the languages was based on application of a same type of routine: topics of the collection were first preprocessed and then lemmatized with the lemmatizers FINTWOL, SWETWOL, GERTWOL and ENGTWOL from Lingsoft Ltd. for Finnish, Swedish, German and English. Stop words were omitted. From the base forms of topical words we generated the actual queries with word form generators for each language followingly:

---

[1] Here 9 and 12 denote number of variant keyword forms used in the procedure. These figures are a fraction of all the possible grammatical noun forms (1872 - ≈ 2000) and 35-46 % of the productive noun forms (26).

[2] The limits of the Russian CLEF collection are most clearly expressed in Savoy [7].

- generation was used only for nouns and adjectives in the topics (except for English, where only nouns are inflected in cases), all words of other parts of speech were left in the form they were in the topic
- only one base form interpretation for each word in the output of lemmatizer was used for generation (first nominal interpretation given by the lemmatizer)
- if the lemmatizer was not able to give a base form analysis for the topic word, it was anyhow given to the generator for generation: this would produce sometimes right generations and sometimes false generations depending on which form the word happened to be in the topic; Assumedly wrong generations will not harm queries because they usually match nothing but right generations might boost performance of the query. This tactic also makes the generation more independent of the lexicons of lemmatizers, which anyhow lack words.

Generators for the four languages were obtained from different sources, free and commercial. Generator for English was obtained from the University of Sussex [11]. For Swedish we used Grim generator [12] from Nada KTH with Java interface of Martin Hassel; the functionality of the generator can be seen also from the Grim web page[3]. For Finnish we obtained Teemapoint's generator FGEN[4] and for German Canoo's WMTRANS[5]. Three of the generators, English, Finnish and Swedish, are rule based and lexiconless, German generator uses large lexicons for generation. The generators were embedded in the query generation process of each language with Unix scripts. The way they were used emulates use in an interactive search system: a user would give the keywords in their base forms and inflected forms of these would be generated using the generator. In our case, the base forms of topical words are produced by lemmatizers of each language. The process of query generation is shown schematically in Figure 1.

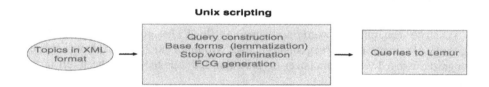

Fig. 1. Generation of queries using FCG generation[6]

3.2 Queries

CLEF topics have the following structure: each topic has three parts, title, description and narrative as in the topic #200 in German:

---

[3] http://skrutten.nada.kth.se/grim/

[4] www.teemapoint.com

[5] http://www.canoo.com/wmtrans/home/index.html

[6] Due to lack of space no example scripts are included here. Model scripts can be shown upon request.

```
<top>

<num> C200 </num>

<DE-title> Hochwasser in Holland und Deutschland </DE-
title>

<DE-desc> Finde statistische Angaben über die Ho-
chwasserkatastrophe in Holland und Deutschland im Jahre
1995. </DE-desc>

<DE-narr> Relevante Dokumente sollen das Ausmaß des
Schadens beziffern, der durch die Überschwemmungen ent-
stand, die 1995 in Deutschland und den Niederlanden
stattfanden. Die Dokumente sollen die Wirkung des durch
Überschwemmung verursachten Schadens hinsichtlich der
Anzahl von Menschen oder Tieren, die evakuiert wurden,
und/oder hinsichtlich der ökonomischen Verluste bezif-
fern.</DE-narr>

</top>
```

Out of these three parts a query can be formulated using either all the three parts or some combination of parts, usually title and description. We chose to use title and description parts to make long queries and titles only to make short queries that resemble Web queries in the number of words.

The FCG queries were structured with Lemur's #SYN operator so, that all the generated morphological variants of the base form were combined by the same #SYN operator. This way they are handled and weighted as instances of the same form by the query program. As an example a generated title query #200 for Swedish is shown:

```
<query> #combine(#syn(översvämning översvämningar
översvämningarna översvämningen) #syn(holland )
#syn(tyskland ))</query>
```

As can be seen, only the word *översvämning* ('flood') has got generated forms during query construction, whereas country names (*Holland* and *Tyskland*) have not been recognized either by the lemmatizer or generator and thus they have been left in the original form.

3.3 Distributions

The prerequisite for applying the FCG method is that distributions of nominal case forms for the language need to be known so that only the most frequent nominal forms are generated for keywords in the FCG query construction process. For Finnish, German and Swedish, Kettunen and Airio [4] and Kettunen and colleagues. [5] had analyzed and published the distributions of nouns and adjectives, and we used the same forms in the FCG generation now. For English we needed distributional data.

We analyzed English word form distributions for nouns from three different samples: 228 084 nouns from the Brown corpus, which is morphologically tagged and disambiguated material [13], a sample of 42 064 words from NY Times [14] and 38 723 word forms from the CLEF collection's English material (from Glasgow Herald).

The last two samples were run through ENGTWOL lemmatizer and all noun interpretations given by the lemmatizer were counted.

As expected, almost all of the nouns in different corpora of English are in singular or plural nominative. The majority of forms (72–76.5 %) were in singular nominative and 21.8–26.4 % in plural nominative depending on the corpus. The occurrences of genitive were very rare (0.9–1.7 % in plural and singular). Only proper nouns have a bigger share of genitive, as analyzed from the Brown corpus, which distinguishes proper nouns from common nouns. Out of 43 154 proper noun tokens in the Brown corpus 39 045 (90.5 %) were in singular nominative, and 1351 (3.1 %) were in plural nominative. 2716 forms (6.3 %) were in singular genitive and 42 forms (0.1 %) in plural genitive.

From this kind of distribution and scarcity of variation in word forms follows that only generation of English plural nominative besides singular nominative form should yield fairly good IR results. The situation is basically the same as with the so called s-stemmer, but in reverse: while s-stemmer removes plural and genitive *s*, we generate plural forms with the *s* [3]. This procedure is named En-FCG_2 in the tests. To see the effect of full paradigm generation we also made an En-FCG procedure which includes genitive forms. This procedure is named En-FCG_2G in the tests.

4 Results

4.1 Results of English Queries

It was to be expected that English would not benefit much from any of the variation management methods used. So far usually a stemmer that combines both inflectional and derivational stemming has achieved best results for English IR, but the difference between doing nothing and the best method is usually small [15, 16]. For English we compared lemmatization, Snowball stemmer [17], plain query words and the two En-FCG procedures. Table 2 shows results of our short English queries in mean average precisions (MAP, given by trec.eval program) for all the runs and Table 3 shows the results of long queries. Compared methods are coded in the tables as follows: Lemmas (ENGTWOL lemmatizer), Plain (plain query keywords), Stems (Snowball stemmer), EN-FCG_2 (only nominative forms in singular and plural) and En-FCG_2G (En-FCG_2 + genitive).

Table 2. English results, title queries, MAP

Lemmas	Plain	Stems	En-FCG_2	En-FCG_2G
0.4102	0.4065	0.4287	0.4201	0.4256

Table 3. English results, title-description queries, MAP

Lemmas	Plain	Stems	En-FCG_2	En-FCG_2G
0.4671	0.4467	0.4809	0.4591	0.4472

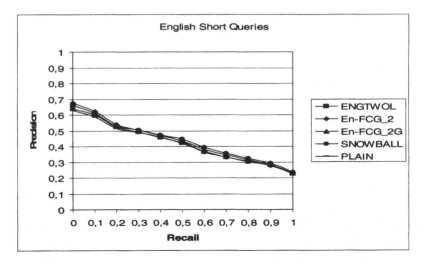

Fig. 2. P/R graphs of short English queries

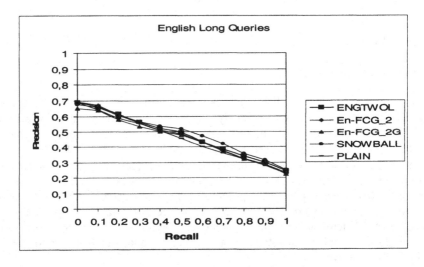

Fig. 3. P/R graphs of long English queries

Figures 2 and 3 show the P/R graphs of short and long English queries.

All the methods perform almost at the same level, and the best mean average precision is achieved by Snowball stemmer both in short and long queries. Lemmatization does not perform very well with English short queries, and it is the second worst method there. With long queries it performs better, being the second best method. Overall the difference of doing nothing to query words and the best achieved results is small, only 2.22 % with short queries and 3.42 % with the long ones. Generation of plural nominative forms for English nouns in En-FCG_2 with short queries increases MAP about 1.5 % compared to plain query words, and slightly less with long queries. En-FGC_2G with added genitive forms performs only slightly better than En-FCG_2 with short queries, but worse with long queries.

Statistical significance of the results was tested using the Friedman test, using the version in Conover [18]. None of the differences between different methods were statistically significant for English.

4.2 Results of Finnish Queries

Finnish was morphologically the most complex language in our tests. Kettunen and Airio [5] had used four different FCG procedures in their tests, but two of the procedures with least word forms did not yield too good IR results. Thus for Finnish we compared two FCG procedures with 9 and 12 variant query word forms with lemmatization, Snowball stemmer and plain query words. Table 4 shows our Finnish results for short queries in mean average precisions for all the runs, and Table 5 shows the results of long queries. The methods compared are coded in the tables as follows: Lemmas (FINTWOL lemmatizer, compounds split in the index), Plain (plain query keywords), Stems (Snowball stemmer), FCG_12 (twelve forms of six cases in singular and plural) and FCG_9 (three cases in singular and plural and three cases in singular only).

Table 4. Finnish results, title queries, MAP

Lemmas	Plain	Stems	FCG_12	FCG_9
0.4525	0.3041	0.3841	0.4028	0.4021

Table 5. Finnish results, title-description queries, MAP

Lemmas	Plain	Stems	FCG_12	FCG_9
0.5071	0.3753	0.4624	0.4804	0.4734

Figures 4 and 5 show the P/R graphs of short and long queries of Finnish.

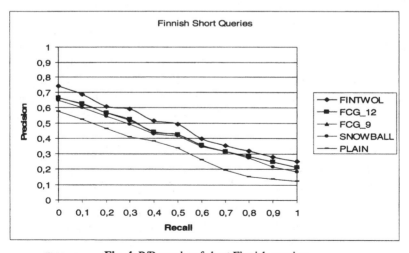

Fig. 4. P/R graphs of short Finnish queries

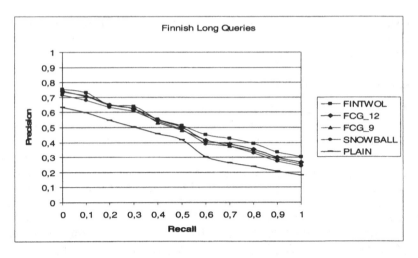

Fig. 5. P/R graphs of long Finnish queries

As can be seen from the results, FINTWOL lemmatizer performs best with short queries and both of the FCG procedures perform about 5 % below it, but slightly better than Snowball stemmer. With long queries situation is similar: FINTWOL yields also best results, and both of the Finnish FCG procedures perform very well being slightly better than Snowball stemmer. The difference of FGCs to lemmatizer is 2.7 – 3.4 per cent.

Comparing the statistical significance of the performance of the methods using the Friedman test gave significant differences (p < 0.01) for the entire set of methods. Statistically significant pairwise differences (p ≤ 0.01) within short and long queries were found between all the variation management methods and plain queries using the Friedman test. There were no statistically significant pairwise differences between lemmatization, stemming and the FCG procedures.

4.3 Results of Swedish Queries

For Swedish we compared lemmatization, the Snowball stemmer, plain query words and two FCG procedures. Table 6 shows results of short queries for Swedish in mean average precisions for all the runs, and Table 7 shows results for long queries. The methods compared are coded in the tables as follows: Lemmas (SWETWOL lemmatizer, compounds split in the index), Plain (plain query keywords), Stems (Snowball stemmer), Sv-FCG_4 (four forms) and Sv-FCG_2 (two forms). The μ value below the

Table 6. Swedish results, title queries, MAP

Lemmas	Plain	Stems	Sv-FCG_4	Sv-FCG_2
0.3896 (μ= 800)	0.2950 (μ= 2500)	0.3618 (μ= 900)	0.3620 (μ= 900)	0.3472 (μ= 900)

Table 7. Swedish results, title-description queries, MAP

Lemmas	Plain	Stems	Sv-FCG_4	Sv-FCG_2
0.4505 (μ= 800)	0.3738 (μ= 2500)	0.4145 (μ= 1500)	0.3913 (μ= 500)	0.3635 (μ= 1100)

MAP shows the used μ parameter value, which gave the best result for runs (default being 2500 with the Dirichlet smoothing [9]).

Figures 6 and 7 show the P/R graphs of short and long queries of Swedish.

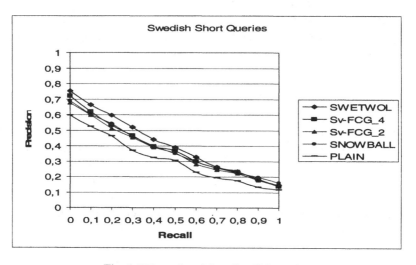

Fig. 6. P/R graphs of short Swedish queries

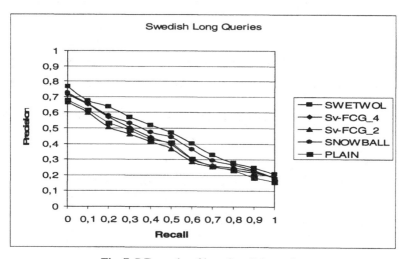

Fig. 7. P/R graphs of long Swedish queries

Our Swedish results for short queries are along the lines of earlier results of [5]. The baseline given by the plain query words with Lemur is 5 % higher than with Inquery used in Kettunen and colleagues [5], and so are also other results. Lemmatization performs best with short queries, and the difference to the best Swedish FCG is about 2.7 %. Snowball stemmer performs at the same level as the best Sv-FCG procedure.

With long queries SWETWOL lemmatizer is the best method and Snowball stemmer performs second best. Sv-FCGs do not perform very well, and FCG_2 performs worse than unprocessed query words with long queries.

Comparing the statistical significance of the performance of the methods using the Friedman test gave significant differences ($p < 0.01$) for the entire set of methods. Statistically significant pairwise differences ($p \leq 0.01$) for short queries were found between SWETWOL, Sv-FCG_4, Sv-FCG_2, Snowball and plain queries using the Friedman test. With long queries SWETWOL stemmer was significantly better than plain queries and both Sv_FCGs. Snowball stemmer was also statistically significantly better than Sv_FCG_2.

4.4 Results of German Queries

For German we compared also lemmatization, Snowball stemmer, plain query words and two German FCG procedures. Table 8 shows the results of German short queries in mean average precisions for all the runs, and Table 9 the results of long queries. The methods compared are coded in the tables as follows: Lemmas (GERTWOL lemmatizer, compounds split in the index), Plain (plain query keywords), Stems (Snowball stemmer), De-FCG_4 (four forms) and De-FCG_2 (two forms).

Figures 8 and 9 show the P/R graphs of short and long queries of German.

Table 8. German results, title queries, MAP

Lemmas	Plain	Stems	De-FCG_4	De-FCG_2
0.3524 ($\mu= 2500$)	0.2854 ($\mu= 2300$)	0.3354 ($\mu= 2000$)	0.2962 ($\mu= 1800$)	0.3029 ($\mu= 2800$)

Table 9. German results, title-description queries, MAP

Lemmas	Plain	Stems	De-FCG_4	De-FCG_2
0.4456 ($\mu= 1500$)	0.3842 ($\mu= 2400$)	0.4332 ($\mu= 2000$)	0.4158 ($\mu= 700$)	0.3937 ($\mu= 700$)

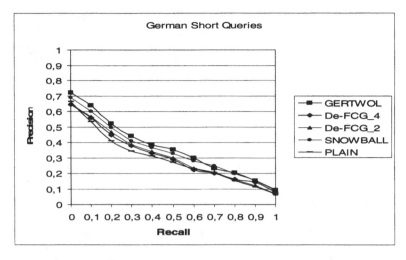

Fig. 8. P/R graphs of short German queries

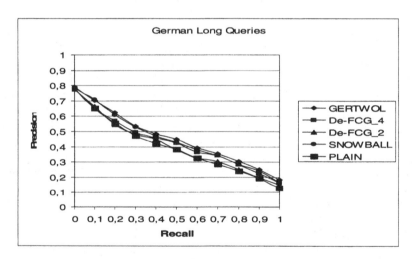

Fig. 9. P/R graphs of long German queries

The results of German short queries seem to be the worst of all the results. The difference between doing nothing and the best De-FCG procedure is only 1.83 % in short queries, opposed to over 4 % earlier with Inquery in Kettunen and colleagues [5]. Lemmatization did not perform very well with Inquery, but with Lemur it performs clearly best. Plain query words perform also quite well with Lemur.

Lemmatization was the best method also with long queries. Snowball stemmer is the second best method with long German queries, but De-FCG_4 performs also quite well here, being only 2.98 % behind GERTWOL lemmatizer. The gap between De-FCG_4 and plain query words is at best 3.13 % with long queries.

Comparing the statistical significance of the performance of the methods using the Friedman test gave significant differences ($p < 0.01$) for the entire set of methods for short queries. Statistically significant pairwise differences ($p \leq 0.01$) for short queries were found between lemmatization and plain queries and between lemmatization and both of the De-FCG procedures. Also Snowball stemmer was statistically significantly better than plain queries and both of the De-FCG procedures. With long queries statistical significance test of the methods using the Friedman test gave significant differences ($p < 0.01$) for the entire set of methods. In pairwise comparisons GERTWOL and Snowball stemmer were significantly better than plain queries and De-FCG_2 procedure.

5 Discussion and Conclusion

We have now set up and evaluated *automatized* FCG query generation with four languages that are morphologically different. English is morphologically simple, Swedish and German moderately complex, and Finnish the most complex of all. English FCGs performed quite well: they gained better mean average precisions than lemmatization (with short queries) or plain query words and were only slightly beyond performance of Snowball stemmer in a setting, where the overall difference between the best and worst method will anyhow be small regardless of the morphological tools used. This shows that the usage of FCG style generation for languages with little morphological variation in words is a feasible alternative to lemmatization and stemming, if morphological tools need to be used with text retrieval.

Our "mid-level" languages with respect to morphological complexity, Swedish and German, got partly expected and partly worse than expected FCG results. Swedish results for short queries were reasonably good, and results for long queries slightly worse. German results were worse than expected, as the German FCGs were only slightly better than plain query words with short queries. In long queries the gap was slightly bigger. Lower than expected German results are most obviously due to the fact, that the German generator version from Canoo uses a 100 000 word lexicon[7] for generation and all the other generators are lexiconless and thus able to cope better with unknown words. Canoo's generator was unable to generate any inflected forms for about 100 (19 %) of the nominal query words, because they were left either unanalyzed by GERTWOL or otherwise unknown to the generator. Most of these words are either proper names or compound nouns, which many times lack from dictionaries, but are important for the queries. This emphasizes the limits of the lexical lemmatizers and generators and also limits of simulated query procedures used in Kettunen and colleagues [5]: upper limits of performance achieved with simulation may not be achieved with real word generation programs, which have their restrictions. Also impact of the retrieval system needs consideration. As the results of [4, 5] were achieved with InQuery, change of retrieval system to Lemur changes some of the results. Overall plain query words fare better with Lemur than with InQuery, but also other methods yield better results, and thus the relative differences between doing nothing and morphological processing are almost the same with all the languages. This emphasizes the pragmatic or empirical nature of IR as Robertson states [19].

---

[7] A lexicon with 210 000 base forms is also available. Usage of the larger generation lexicon might yield better results, but as also GERTWOL's capability to analyze topical words to base forms affects the end result, the larger generation lexicon may not help much.

Our Finnish results were good as the results of FCG procedures were only about 2.5-5 % worse than results of lemmatization and slightly better than results of the Snowball stemmer. Finnish FCGs behaved consistently in both short and long queries, being always statistically significantly better than plain query words, and never worse than lemmatization or stemming. FCG procedures fared actually slightly better with Lemur than with Inquery, gaining about 2 % in MAP with both short and long queries.

Our aim in this paper has been setting up an automatized query generation system for several languages with purpose to show feasibility of the FCG method that has been simulated earlier. The results of four languages, although not totally compatible with earlier results, show that the method works well with word forms generators taken off-the-shelf from different sources in a new retrieval system. On the basis of these and earlier findings and common knowledge about word form distributions in texts of natural languages, it is to be expected, that the method will work for other languages of equal morphological complexity as well. Applications of the proposed restricted generation method include in particular Web IR for languages poor in morphological resources and with at least moderate amount of morphological variation that needs management in full-text retrieval. Also the multi-linguality of a web index [20] can be dealt with the approach. As the indexes consist of mixture of word forms in different languages with no linguistic processing (lemmatization or stemming), language specific FCG procedures will yield better retrieval results than usage of plain query words in random textual forms or especially base forms. A natural continuation for work done in this paper would thus be evaluation of web retrieval using the FCG method for a group of different languages showing different degrees of morphological complexity.

Acknowledgements

This work was supported by the Academy of Finland grant number 124131. We wish to thank Ms. Eija Airio, Dept. of Information Studies, University of Tampere, for implementing all the Unix scripts for the query processes.

References

1. Sparck-Jones, K., Tait, J.I.: Automatic Search Term Variant Generation. Journal of Documentation 40, 50–66 (1984)
2. Kettunen, K.: Reductive and Generative Approaches to Morphological Variation of Keywords in Monolingual Information Retrieval. Acta Universitatis Tamperensis 1261. University of Tampere, Tampere (2007)
3. Frakes, W.B.: Stemming algorithms. In: Frakes, W.B., Baeza-Yates, R. (eds.) Information Retrieval. Data Structures and Algorithms, pp. 131–160. Prentice Hall, Upper Saddle River (1992)
4. Kettunen, K., Airio, E.: Is a Morphologically Complex Language Really that Complex in Full-Text Retrieval? In: Salakoski, T., Ginter, F., Pyysalo, S., Pahikkala, T. (eds.) FinTAL 2006. LNCS (LNAI), vol. 4139, pp. 411–422. Springer, Heidelberg (2006)
5. Kettunen, K., Airio, E., Järvelin, K.: Restricted Inflectional Form Generation in Management of Morphological Keyword Variation. Information Retrieval 10, 415–444 (2007)

6. Sormunen, E.: A Method for Measuring Wide Range Performance of Boolean Queries in Full-text Databases. Acta Universitatis Tamperensis 748. University of Tampere, Tampere (2000)
7. Savoy, J.: Searching Strategies for the Bulgarian Language. Information Retrieval 10, 509–529 (2007)
8. The Lemur Toolkit for Language Modeling and Information Retrieval, http://www.lemurproject.org/
9. Metzler, D., Croft, W.B.: Combining the Language Model and Inference Network Approaches to Retrieval. Information Processing and Management Special Issue on Bayesian Networks and Information Retrieval 40, 735–750 (2004)
10. Grossman, D.A., Frieder, O.: Information Retrieval. Algorithms and Heuristics, 2nd edn. Springer, Netherlands (2004)
11. Minnen, G., Carrol, J., Pearce, D.: Applied Morphological Processing of English. Natural Language Engineering 7, 207–223 (2001)
12. Knutsson, O., Pargman, T.C., Eklundh, K.S., Westlund, S.: Designing and Developing a Language Environment for Second Language Writers. Computers and Education, An International Journal 49 (2001)
13. Brown Corpus Manual, http://khnt.hit.uib.no/icame/manuals/brown/INDEX.HTM
14. TDT2 Multilanguage Text Version 4.0, http://www.ldc.upenn.edu/Catalog/CatalogEntry.jsp?catalogId=LDC2001T57
15. Airio, E.: Word normalization and decompounding in mono- and bilingual IR. Information Retrieval 9, 249–271 (2006)
16. Hollink, V., Kamps, J., Monz, C., de Rijke, M.: Monolingual Document Retrieval for European Languages. Information Retrieval 7, 33–52 (2004)
17. Snowball, http://snowball.tartarus.org/
18. Conover, W.J.: Practical Nonparametric Statistics, 3rd edn. Wiley, New York (1999)
19. Robertson, S.: Salton Award Lecture. On Theoretical Argument in Information Retrieval. ACM Sigir Forum 34, 1–10 (2000)
20. Rasmussen, E.M.: Indexing and Retrieval for the Web. In: Cronin, B. (ed.) Annual Review of Information Science and Technology, vol. 37, pp. 91–124 (2003)

Definition Extraction
with Balanced Random Forests

Łukasz Kobyliński[1] and Adam Przepiórkowski[2,3]

[1] Institute of Computer Science, Warsaw University of Technology,
ul. Nowowiejska 15/19, 00-665 Warszawa, Poland
L.Kobylinski@elka.pw.edu.pl
[2] Institute of Computer Science, Polish Academy of Sciences,
ul. Ordona 21, 01-237 Warszawa, Poland
adamp@ipipan.waw.pl
[3] Institute of Informatics, University of Warsaw,
ul. Banacha 2, 02-097 Warszawa, Poland

Abstract. We propose a novel machine learning approach to the task of identifying definitions in Polish documents. Specifics of the problem domain and characteristics of the available dataset have been taken into consideration, by carefully choosing and adapting a classification method to highly imbalanced and noisy data. We evaluate the performance of a Random Forest-based classifier in extracting definitional sentences from natural language text and give a comparison with previous work.

1 Introduction

Natural Language Processing (NLP) tasks often involve heavily imbalanced data, with a dominating "uninteresting" class and a minority "interesting" class. One such task is that of definition extraction, where a set of sentences is to be classified into definitional and non-definitional sentences. There may be as many as 20 non-definition sentences for any single definition sentence in an instructive text, but it is the latter class that a definition extraction system is interested in.

The usual Machine Learning (ML) classifiers, ranging from naïve bayesian methods, through decision trees, perceptrons and various lazy learners, to the currently very popular classifiers based on Support Vector Machines (SVMs) and on Adaboost, do not work well in such cases, even when trained with subsampling (of uninteresting examples) or oversampling (of the interesting examples). The problem is that such classifiers attempt to minimise the overall error rate, rather than concentrating on the interesting class. In case of a dataset with a 1:20 ratio of interesting to uninteresting cases, it is difficult to beat a classifier uniformly assigning each new item to the uninteresting class: such a classifier reaches the overall accuracy higher than 95%, but at the cost of misclassifying all the interesting cases!

The problem of heavily imbalanced data has already been addressed in the ML community, where most solutions consist either in the assignment of a high

A. Ranta, B. Nordström (Eds.): GoTAL 2008, LNAI 5221, pp. 237–247, 2008.

cost to the misclassification of the minority class or in subsampling and/or over-sampling. A novel approach to the problem has been proposed in Chen *et al.* 2004 and it consists in a modification of the Random Forest (Breiman, 2001) classifier.

Random Forest (RF) is a homogeneous ensemble of unpruned decision trees (e.g., CART, C4.5), where — at each node of the tree — a subset of all attributes is randomly selected and the best attribute on which to further grow the tree is taken from that random set. Additionally, Random Forest is an example of the bagging (bootstrap aggregating) method, i.e., each tree is trained on a set bootstrapped[1] from the original training set. Decisions are reached by simple voting.

Balanced Random Forest (BRF; Chen *et al.* 2004) is a modification of RF, where for each tree two bootstrapped sets of the same size, equal to the size of the minority class, are constructed: one for the minority class, the other for the majority class. Jointly, these two sets constitute the training set.

The aim of this paper is to demonstrate that BRF is a technique well-suited to the difficult problem of definition extraction and, by extension, other NLP tasks. When trained on the dataset of Polish instructive texts introduced in Przepiórkowski *et al.* (2007b,a), BRF-based classifiers give better results than manual definition extraction grammars (Przepiórkowski *et al.*, 2007a), the usual ML classifiers, even when sequentially combined with some *a priori* linguistic knowledge (Degórski *et al.*, 2008), or a linear combination of such ML classifiers and complete manual grammars (Przepiórkowski *et al.*, 2008).

In what follows we first introduce the attribute space assumed here (§2), then describe the used classification approach (§3) and present the results of our experiments (§4). Finally, we outline work conducted previously in the field (§5) and conclude with possibilities of further research (§6).

2   Feature Selection

Employing any machine learning approach to unstructured data requires that data is represented in the form of feature values, either binary, numeric or nominal. We use a relatively straightforward approach of n-gram representation of the sentences in the available document set. Each sentence is represented by a vector of binary values, where each value indicates whether a particular n-gram is present in the corresponding sentence. The n-grams consist of base forms of words, their parts of speech and grammatical cases that appear in the greatest number of sentences in all documents. We individually count the occurrences of each of the n-grams in sentences marked as definitions and non-definitions. Both lists are then combined and a number of most common entries is selected to form a dictionary of features used for sentence description.

---

[1] That is, examples in such a bootstrapped training set are uniformly and randomly drawn *with replacement* from the original training set. As a result, some examples will be repeated while other will not make it to the bootstrapped set.

Even by limiting the length of generated n-grams to $n \leq 3$ and having a choice of three distinct n-gram types: base word form (further denoted as *base*), part of speech of the word (*ctag*) and its grammatical case (*case*), we face a problem of many possible dictionary configurations, selecting from the set of $3^1 + 3^2 + 3^3 = 39$ possibilities. Including too many n-gram types would result in a an extremely large attribute space, while including too few in reducing the potential classification accuracy. We approached the problem by measuring the average value of the χ^2 statistic of each of the possible n-gram types with respect to the class attribute. This was performed on a training set consisting of all the available documents, on the basis of 100 n-grams for each of the 39 types. Table 1 presents a list of the 20 n-gram types with the highest average χ^2 value.

Table 1. Top 20 values of the χ^2 statistic of possible n-gram permutations

rank	n-gram	average χ^2	rank	n-gram	average χ^2
1	*base*	21.04	11	*base base ctag*	16.70
2	*ctag ctag case*	18.91	12	*ctag base ctag*	16.29
3	*ctag base*	18.53	13	*ctag ctag base*	14.77
4	*base case*	18.45	14	*ctag case*	14.69
5	*base ctag*	17.92	15	*ctag ctag ctag*	14.63
6	*base base*	17.81	16	*base ctag case*	14.52
7	*base base case*	17.73	17	*base base base*	14.33
8	*ctag base case*	17.43	18	*ctag*	13.88
9	*ctag ctag*	17.11	19	*ctag case ctag*	13.65
10	*ctag base base*	16.73	20	*base ctag ctag*	13.59

Unfortunately, just taking a number of attributes from the top of this list does not guarantee the best possible selection of n-gram types. This is because certain attribute pairs may be statistically dependent and introducing both of them into the dictionary would result in noise, instead of meaningful data for the classifier. Having experimented with different attribute configurations, we have chosen the following heuristic procedure of attribute selection: we take one attribute at a time from the sorted list, starting from the top, and reject these n-grams of length $n = 3$, for which another trigram with one of the same feature types has already been selected. The resulting set of 10 selected n-gram types is presented in Table 2.

Table 2. The selected set of n-gram types

no.	n-gram	no.	n-gram
1	*base*	6	*base base*
2	*ctag ctag case*	7	*ctag ctag*
3	*ctag base*	8	*ctag case*
4	*base case*	9	*base base base*
5	*base ctag*	10	*ctag*

For comparison purposes, we also present here the results of experiments on a dataset from the work of Degórski *et al.* 2008, where the set of n-grams has been selected in a different manner and using a different set of attributes. Specifically, this dataset, referenced later as the "baseline dataset", has been created by using the 100 most common uniform unigrams, bigrams and trigrams of base forms, parts of speech and cases (i.e., *base*, *base-base*, ..., *ctag-ctag-ctag*).

3   Classifying Imbalanced Data

As noted earlier, the available dataset of definitional and non-definitional sentences is highly imbalanced and consists of 10830 sentences, 546 of which contain — or are a part of — definitions. Consequently, any successful classification-based approach to extraction of definitions from this data must take into consideration — either explicitly or implicitly — the difference in training samples from both categories.

The most common way of dealing with imbalanced data is introducing appropriately weighted costs for specific classes or sampling the available training set. Balanced Random Forest is an approach where equalizing the influences of classes is not performed externally to classification algorithm by evaluating weights, but is integrated in the very process. Here, for the task of extracting definitions from a set of documents by sentence classification, we use the following algorithm, based on Chen *et al.* 2004:

- split the training corpus into definitions and non-definitions; let us assume that there are n_d definitions and n_{nd} non-definitions, where $n_d < n_{nd}$;
- construct k trees, each in the following way:
  - draw a bootstrap sample of size n_d of definitions, and a bootstrap sample of the same size n_d of non-definitions;
  - learn the tree (without pruning) using the CART algorithm, on the basis of the sum of the two bootstrap samples as the training corpus, but:
  - at each node, first select at random m features (variables) from the set of all M features ($m < M$; selection without replacement), and only then select the best feature (out of these m features) for this node; this random selection of m features is repeated for each node;
- the final classifier is the ensemble of the k trees and decisions are reached by simple voting.

We have chosen the value of m to be equal to $\sqrt{M}$ in all the experiments.

As Random Forest is a well known classifier and widely covered in the literature, it also allows having a greater insight into the results produced by the BRF approach. RFs have been verified to be suitable both for large and highly dimensional data, as is the case in natural language processing. They also provide means of estimating the classification error rate without performing a full cross-validation procedure and for estimating variable importance and variable interactions. In our current experiments we have not performed such estimations, as we are more interested in selecting the optimal set of n-gram types, than comparing the importance of particular features.

4   Experimental Results

We use several statistical parameters to describe and compare the results of the proposed classification approach: recall and precision are the most commonly calculated information retrieval performance measures. We assume the sentences marked as definitions to be the set of relevant documents in the retrieval task:

$$precision = \frac{|\{\text{definitions}\} \cap \{\text{retrieved sentences}\}|}{|\{\text{retrieved sentences}\}|} \tag{1}$$

$$recall = \frac{|\{\text{definitions}\} \cap \{\text{retrieved sentences}\}|}{|\{\text{definitions}\}|} \tag{2}$$

For a single-valued performance indicator, we use the F-measure, both in the form used in the previous papers on Polish definition extraction (marked as F_α) and in the more common sense (marked as F_β). For F_1 we just use F_1 (as $F_{\alpha=1} = F_{\beta=1}$):

$$F_\alpha = \frac{(1+\alpha) \cdot precision \cdot recall}{\alpha \cdot precision + recall} \tag{3}$$

$$F_\beta = \frac{(1+\beta^2) \cdot precision \cdot recall}{\beta^2 \cdot precision + recall} \tag{4}$$

Finally, we also calculate the area under the ROC curve (AUC), which is another single-valued measure of retrieval accuracy, but not tied to a single probability threshold value, like the F-measure. Still, because in the task of definition extraction we are more interested in maximizing the recall value (in other words: minimizing the false negative rate), we compare all further experiment results on the basis of $F_{\alpha=2}$ and $F_{\beta=2}$ values.

Our initial experiments aimed at verifying whether any additional preprocessing of the available data, commonly applied to text classification problems, would result in improving the accuracy of definition extraction. Firstly, we have included the information about the relative position of an n-gram in a sentence into the feature vector. By dividing the sentences into three equal parts and counting the n-gram occurrences in each of the parts separately, we have increased the attribute space three times, but achieved no increase in performance (Table 3). We may speculate that the positional information introduced too much noise, as the available dataset was too small to benefit from the significantly larger feature space.

Similarly, there was no gain in definition extraction accuracy after including the information about the actual number of occurrence counts of particular n-grams in the analyzed sentences. This may also be explained by a relatively small size of the available dataset and sparseness of the feature vector. The calculated numbers of occurrences were negligibly small and provided no additional information to the classifier.

Finally, applying a stop-list of most common words and filtering non-alphanumeric characters from the documents also proved to reduce both the value of $F_{\alpha=2}$ and $F_{\beta=2}$ measures. Thus, neither of the attribute modifications and data

Table 3. The influence of additional preprocessing steps on classification accuracy. Ten-fold cross-validation results, with 100 iterations of random trees generation.

dataset	precision	recall	F_1	$F_{\alpha=2}$	$F_{\alpha=5}$	$F_{\beta=2}$	$F_{\beta=5}$	AUC
base	18.1%	66.1%	28.4%	**35.1%**	45.9%	**43.2%**	60.0%	82.4%
n-gram position	16.2%	63.9%	25.9%	32.3%	42.9%	40.2%	57.4%	81.2%
n-gram occurrence	17.2%	65.0%	27.2%	33.7%	44.4%	41.8%	58.7%	81.4%
base form stoplist	17.3%	63.0%	27.2%	33.5%	43.7%	41.2%	57.2%	81.4%

preprocessing steps mentioned above have been used in further experiments. A detailed comparison of each of the approaches has been presented in Figure 2a.

In an effort to determine the optimal size of feature space for classification, we have conducted a series of experiments with an increasing number of n-grams used for sentence representation (Table 4 and Figure 1a). On the basis of the results, we have decided to use 100 n-grams of each type in further experiments, as increasing their number above that threshold does not seem to have any positive influence on the classification accuracy. By choosing that number, we obtained a training set consisting of 10830 instances and 929 attributes (as there are less than 100 different n-grams of the type *ctag*).

Table 4. The influence of the number of used n-grams of each type on classification accuracy. Ten-fold cross-validation results, with 100 iterations of random trees generation.

n-grams	precision	recall	F_1	$F_{\alpha=2}$	$F_{\alpha=5}$	$F_{\beta=2}$	$F_{\beta=5}$	AUC
10	14.4%	57.7%	23.1%	28.8%	38.5%	36.0%	51.7%	76.6%
20	17.2%	63.7%	27.1%	33.5%	43.9%	41.4%	57.7%	81.7%
30	18.7%	65.4%	29.0%	35.6%	46.1%	43.6%	59.6%	82.7%
40	19.1%	66.8%	29.7%	36.4%	47.1%	44.5%	61.0%	82.6%
50	19.3%	67.9%	30.1%	37.0%	47.9%	45.2%	62.0%	83.1%
60	19.3%	67.2%	29.9%	36.7%	47.5%	44.9%	61.3%	82.9%
70	19.1%	66.8%	29.8%	36.5%	47.2%	44.6%	61.0%	83.2%
80	19.7%	67.2%	30.4%	37.2%	47.9%	45.3%	61.5%	83.7%
90	19.8%	69.4%	30.8%	37.8%	49.0%	46.2%	63.3%	84.5%
100	20.1%	70.1%	31.2%	**38.3%**	49.6%	**46.8%**	64.0%	83.8%
110	19.6%	68.1%	30.4%	37.3%	48.2%	45.6%	62.2%	84.1%
120	19.6%	67.8%	30.4%	37.3%	48.1%	45.5%	61.9%	84.1%

As the accuracy of Random Forest classification depends heavily on the number of generated random trees used in voting, we have conducted the experiments both on the current dataset and on the baseline dataset provided by Degórski *et al.* 2008 for several different numbers of iterations (Tables 5 and 6, Figure 1b). We have performed ten-fold cross-validation experiments instead of counting the out-of-bag error of the bagging classifier, so as to make the results

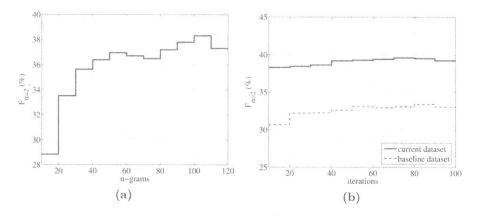

Fig. 1. 1a Performance of classification with respect to the number of used n-grams, 1ba comparison between classification performance using the baseline dataset and the current dataset for different number of iterations

as closely comparable with those of Degórski *et al.* 2008 as possible. The detailed comparison of both sets, with respect to BRF classification accuracy for the number of iterations which proved to give the best results for each of the sets, is presented in Figure 2b.

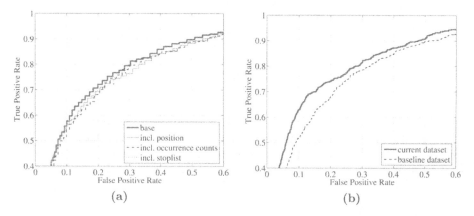

Fig. 2. ROC curve of classification: 2a using additional data preprocessing steps, 2b using the baseline dataset and the current dataset

As may be seen from the results of the consecutive experiments, increasing the number of generated random trees improves the accuracy of definitional sentences classification only up to a certain point. Above that threshold the performance reaches a plateau and no further iterations are necessary.

While the use of Balanced Random Forest classification method alone significantly improves the definition extraction performance over other pure machine

Table 5. Ten-fold cross-validation results of the baseline dataset classification

iterations	precision	recall	F_1	$F_{\alpha=2}$	$F_{\alpha=5}$	$F_{\beta=2}$	$F_{\beta=5}$	AUC
100	15.1%	63.0%	24.4%	30.6%	41.2%	38.6%	56.2%	80.6%
200	16.1%	64.3%	25.8%	32.2%	42.9%	40.3%	57.7%	81.3%
300	16.2%	63.8%	25.9%	32.3%	42.8%	40.2%	57.3%	81.6%
400	16.5%	63.6%	26.2%	32.6%	43.1%	40.5%	57.3%	81.6%
500	16.8%	64.1%	26.6%	33.1%	43.7%	41.0%	57.9%	81.7%
600	16.7%	63.9%	26.5%	32.9%	43.5%	40.9%	57.7%	81.7%
700	16.9%	63.6%	26.7%	33.1%	43.5%	40.9%	57.5%	81.8%
800	17.0%	64.1%	26.9%	**33.4%**	43.9%	**41.3%**	58.0%	81.9%
900	16.9%	63.6%	26.7%	33.1%	43.5%	40.9%	57.5%	81.9%
1000	16.9%	64.0%	26.8%	33.2%	43.7%	41.1%	57.8%	81.9%

Table 6. Ten-fold cross-validation results of the current dataset classification

iterations	precision	recall	F_1	$F_{\alpha=2}$	$F_{\alpha=5}$	$F_{\beta=2}$	$F_{\beta=5}$	AUC
100	20.1%	70.1%	31.2%	38.3%	49.6%	46.8%	64.0%	83.8%
200	20.5%	68.7%	31.5%	38.5%	49.3%	46.7%	63.0%	84.4%
300	20.6%	68.7%	31.7%	38.7%	49.5%	46.8%	63.0%	84.5%
400	21.0%	69.2%	32.2%	39.2%	50.0%	47.4%	63.6%	84.6%
500	21.1%	68.9%	32.3%	39.3%	50.0%	47.4%	63.4%	84.7%
600	21.2%	68.9%	32.5%	39.4%	50.1%	47.5%	63.4%	84.7%
700	21.4%	69.0%	32.6%	**39.6%**	50.3%	**47.7%**	63.6%	84.7%
800	21.3%	69.0%	32.5%	39.5%	50.3%	47.7%	63.6%	84.8%
900	21.1%	68.7%	32.3%	39.2%	49.9%	47.3%	63.2%	84.8%
1000	21.2%	68.7%	32.4%	39.3%	50.0%	47.4%	63.2%	84.8%

learning based approaches (e.g., as reported by Degórski *et al.* 2008), it is worth pointing out that a careful feature selection is an equally important step. We achieve an over 18% increase in accuracy, as indicated by the $F_{\alpha=2}$ measure, by describing the sentences with a more representative set of attribute types.

5 Previous Work

To the best of our (and Google's) knowledge, there is no previous NLP work taking advantage of the Balanced variety of RFs. Apparently, the first NLP applications of the plain Random Forests are those reported in Nielsen and Pradhan 2004, for PropBank-style (Kingsbury and Palmer, 2002) role classification, and in Xu and Jelinek 2004 (followed by a series of papers by the same authors, culminating in Xu and Jelinek 2007), where they are used in the classical language modelling task (predicting a sequence of words) for speech recognition and give better results than the usual *n*-gram based approaches.

On the other hand, there is some substantial previous work on definition extraction, as this is a subtask of many applications, including terminology extraction (Pearson, 1996), the automatic creation of glossaries (Klavans and Muresan, 2000, 2001), question answering (Miliaraki and Androutsopoulos, 2004; Fahmi and Bouma, 2006), learning lexical semantic relations (Malaisé *et al.*, 2004; Storrer and Wellinghoff, 2006) and the automatic construction of ontologies (Walter and Pinkal, 2006). Despite the current dominance of the ML paradigm in NLP, tools for definition extraction are invariably language-specific and involve shallow or deep processing, with most work done for English (Pearson, 1996; Klavans and Muresan, 2000, 2001) and other Germanic languages (Fahmi and Bouma, 2006; Storrer and Wellinghoff, 2006; Walter and Pinkal, 2006), as well as French (Malaisé *et al.*, 2004).

When ML methods are used, it is in combination with linguistic processing. For example, Fahmi and Bouma 2006 applied a robust wide-coverage parser of Dutch to select candidate definition sentences, which were then subject to an ML classifier. They experimented with three classifiers (Naïve Bayes, SVM and Maximum Entropy) and a number of possible feature configurations and obtained the best results for the Maximum Entropy classifier and feature configurations, which included some syntactic features.

For Polish, first attempts at constructing definition extraction systems are described — in the context of other Slavic languages — in Przepiórkowski *et al.* 2007b, and improved results are presented in Przepiórkowski *et al.* 2007a. In that work definitions were identified on the basis of a manually constructed partial grammar (a cascade of regular grammars over morphosyntactically annotated XML-encoded texts), with the best grammar giving the precision of 18.7% and recall of 59.3%, which amounts to $F_{\alpha=2} = 34.4\%$. Przepiórkowski *et al.* 2007a note that these relatively low results are at least partially due to the inherent difficulty of the task: the inter-annotator agreement measured as Cohen's κ is only 0.31 (the value of 1 would indicate perfect agreement, the value of 0 — complete randomness). The same dataset was used in the experiments reported here.

An approach more directly comparable to ours is presented in Degórski *et al.* 2008. The general idea is analogous to that of Fahmi and Bouma 2006: first candidate definition sentences are selected via linguistic methods and then they are classified using ML methods. What is novel in Degórski *et al.* 2008 is the very basic character of the linguistic knowledge (a small low-precision collection of n-grams typical for definitions, including the copula, sequences corresponding to *that is* and *i.e.*, etc.), and the use of ensembles of classifiers in the second stage. The best results reported there, the precision of 19.9%, recall of 69.2%, and $F_{\alpha=2} = 38.0\%$, are significantly better than those of Przepiórkowski *et al.* 2007a, but still, despite some use of *a priori* language-specific knowledge, worse than the pure ML results reported here.

6   Conclusions and Future Work

Our currently reported results seem to restore hope in the machine learning approach to the vaguely specified task of definition extraction from a small set of text documents. It is usually the case that the smaller, less structured and more noisy the available training data, the lesser is the advantage of such methods over hand-crafted rules and grammars, utilizing linguistic knowledge. Thus, achieving better results in such circumstances by a pure machine learning approach seems to justify the necessary work on feature and classification method selection.

It would still be interesting to combine the current classification method with manually constructed grammars, similarly as in Degórski et al. 2008, to see if such a sequential processing scheme would further improve the definition extraction performance. On the basis of the experiments described there, we might expect a considerable increase in retrieval precision, at the cost of a slight decrease in recall.

Acknowledgements

We are very grateful to Prof. Jacek Koronacki for suggesting the use of Balanced Random Forests in the task of definition extraction and his further helpful comments. We also thank the anonymous reviewers for providing valuable remarks.

References

Breiman, L.: Random forests. Machine Learning 45, 5–32 (2001)

Chen, C., Liaw, A., Breiman, L.: Using random forest to learn imbalanced data. Technical Report 666, University of California, Berkeley (2004), http://www.stat.berkeley.edu/tech-reports/666.pdf

Degórski, Ł, Marcińczuk, M., Przepiórkowski, A.: Definition extraction using a sequential combination of baseline grammars and machine learning classifiers. In: Proceedings of the Sixth International Conference on Language Resources and Evaluation (LREC 2008). ELRA, Forthcoming (2008)

Fahmi, I., Bouma, G.: Learning to identify definitions using syntactic features. In: Proceedings of the EACL 2006 workshop on Learning Structured Information in Natural Language Applications (2006)

Kingsbury, P., Palmer, M.: From TreeBank to PropBank. In: Proceedings of the Third International Conference on Language Resources and Evaluation, LREC 2002, pp. 1989–1993. ELRA, Las Palmas (2002)

Klavans, J.L., Muresan, S.: DEFINDER: Rule-based methods for the extraction of medical terminology and their associated definitions from on-line text. In: Proceedings of the Annual Fall Symposium of the American Medical Informatics Association (2000)

Klavans, J.L., Muresan, S.: Evaluation of the DEFINDER system for fully automatic glossary construction. In: Proceedings of AMIA Symposium (2001)

Lin, D., Wu, D. (eds.): Proceedings of the 2004 Conference on Empirical Methods in Natural Language Processing (EMNLP 2004). ACL, Barcelona (2004)

Malaisé, V., Zweigenbaum, P., Bachimont, B.: Detecting semantic relations between terms in definitions. In: Ananadiou, S., Zweigenbaum, P. (eds.) COLING 2004 CompuTerm 2004: 3rd International Workshop on Computational Terminology, Geneva, Switzerland, pp. 55–62 (2004)

Miliaraki, S., Androutsopoulos, I.: Learning to identify single-snippet answers to definition questions. In: Proceedings of COLING 2004, Geneva, Switzerland, pp. 1360–1366 (2004)

Nielsen, R.D., Pradhan, S.: In: Lin,, Wu (eds.) Mixing weak learners in semantic parsing, pp. 80–87 (2004)

Pearson, J.: The expression of definitions in specialised texts: a corpus-based analysis. In: Gellerstam, M., Järborg, J., Malmgren, S.G., Norén, K., Rogström, L., Papmehl, C. (eds.) Proceedings of the Seventh Euralex International Congress, Göteborg, pp. 817–824 (1996)

Przepiórkowski, A., Degórski, Ł, Wójtowicz, B.: On the evaluation of Polish definition extraction grammars. In: Vetulani, Z. (ed.) Proceedings of the 3rd Language & Technology Conference, Poznań, Poland, pp. 473–477 (2007a)

Przepiórkowski, A., Degórski, Ł, Spousta, M., Simov, K., Osenova, P., Lemnitzer, L., Kuboň, V., Wójtowicz, B.: Towards the automatic extraction of definitions in Slavic. In: Piskorski, J., Pouliquen, B., Steinberger, R., Tanev, H. (eds.) Proceedings of the Workshop on Balto-Slavonic Natural Language Processing at ACL 2007, Prague, pp. 43–50 (2007b)

Przepiórkowski, A., Marcińczuk, M., Degórski, Ł.: Dealing with small, noisy and imbalanced data: Machine learning or manual grammars? In: Sojka, P., Kopeček, I., Pala, K. (eds.) Text, Speech and Dialogue: 9th International Conference (TSD 2008), Brno, Czech Republic, September 2008. LNCS (LNAI). Springer, Berlin (2008)

Storrer, A., Wellinghoff, S.: Automated detection and annotation of term definitions in German text corpora. In: Proceedings of the Fifth International Conference on Language Resources and Evaluation, LREC 2006, ELRA, Genoa (2006)

Walter, S., Pinkal, M.: Automatic extraction of definitions from German court decisions. In: Proceedings of the 21st International Conference on Computational Linguistics and 44th Annual Meeting of the Association for Computational Linguistics, Sydney, Australia, pp. 20–28 (2006)

Xu, P., Jelinek, F.: In: Lin,, Wu (eds.) Random forests in language modeling, pp. 325–332 (2004)

Xu, P., Jelinek, F.: Random forests and the data sparseness problem in language modeling. Computer Speech and Language 21(1), 105–152 (2007)

Reviewing and Evaluating
Automatic Term Recognition Techniques

Ioannis Korkontzelos, Ioannis P. Klapaftis, and Suresh Manandhar

Department of Computer Science, The University of York
Heslington, York, YO10 5NG, UK
{johnkork,giannis,suresh}@cs.york.ac.uk

Abstract. Automatic Term Recognition (ATR) is defined as the task
of identifying domain specific terms from technical corpora. *Termhood-based* approaches measure the degree that a candidate term refers to a
domain specific concept. *Unithood-based* approaches measure the attach-
ment strength of a candidate term constituents. These methods have
been evaluated using different, often incompatible evaluation schemes
and datasets. This paper provides an overview and a thorough evaluation of state-of-the-art ATR methods, under a common evaluation
framework, i.e. corpora and evaluation method. Our contributions are
two-fold: (1) We compare a number of different ATR methods, showing
that *termhood-based* methods achieve in general superior performance.
(2) We show that the number of independent occurrences of a candidate term is the most effective source for estimating term nestedness,
improving ATR performance.

Keywords: automatic term recognition, ATR, term extraction.

Introduction

A terminology bank (vocabulary) contains the terms, which refer to the concepts
of a domain. Constructing such a vocabulary is crucial, because it is the starting
point for many applications such as machine translation, indexing, and ontology learning [8]. Manual construction is time-consuming, error-prone, labour-
intensive and unable to deal with the rapid growth of technical terms. ATR
targets at solving these obstacles.

ATR techniques can be divided into two broad categories: *unithood-based* and
termhood-based ones [8]. *Unithood* refers to the attachment strength of the constituents of a candidate term. *Termhood* refers to the degree that a candidate
term is related to a domain-specific concept. For example, in an eye-pathology
corpus, *"soft contact lens"* is a valid term, which has both high *termhood* and
unithood. However, its frequently occurring substring *"soft contact"*, has high
unithood and low *termhood*, since it does not refer to a key domain concept.

Unithood-based methods, such as *t-test, χ^2-test, Log-likelihood (LL)* [3] and
pointwise mutual information (PMI) [1], have been thoroughly evaluated for
the task of collocation extraction [3,4,2,14]. In [3,4] the authors show that LL

A. Ranta, B. Nordström (Eds.): GoTAL 2008, LNAI 5221, pp. 248–259, 2008.

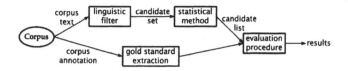

Fig. 1. Experimental procedure

performs better than the other statistical measures due to its milder tendency
to overestimate rare events.

Given that *unithood*- and *termhood-based* methods capture different types of
information, it is still unclear whether the former are able to perform better
than the latter methods, such as *C Value* [5] and *Statistical Barrier (SB)* [13].
Furthermore, most *ATR* methods [5,3,1,13] have been evaluated using different
technical corpora, under different evaluation frameworks, with different sets of
parameters depending on the domain and test corpus. This lack of a common
evaluation scheme complicates the interpretation of results. It is unclear which
are the strengths and weaknesses of each method, making unmanageable the
choice of an appropriate *ATR* method as a starting point for other applications.

This paper provides an overview of the field of *ATR* and evaluates a number of linguistic and statistical approaches using two English corpora i.e. the
GENIA[6] and the *PennBioIE* [9] corpus. Figure 1 presents a block diagram of
our experimental procedure. A linguistic filter is applied on the corpus text to
identify candidate terms. Then, a statistical method ranks these candidates, to
create a list in decreasing order of scores. The evaluation scheme compares this
list to the gold standard terms, generated by the corpus annotation. The scheme
consists of a manually annotated corpus, and an evaluation method which as-
sesses the performance of *ATR* methods at a fine-grained scale; i.e. increments
of 0.5% of their candidate term ranked list, based on the one proposed in [16].

Our contributions are two-fold: firstly, we extensively compare state-of-the-art
approaches to *ATR* under a common evaluation scheme. We show that *termhood-
based* approaches, which take into consideration the nestedness of a candidate
term into others, such as *C Value* and *SB*, have in general superior performance
over methods which measure the strength of association among the tokens of
a multi-word candidate term, such as *LL* and *PMI*. Secondly, after further ex-
perimentation with different statistical approaches to nestedness we show that
the independent occurrences[1] of a term is the most effective source of nestedness information, clearly improving the performance of ATR methods, in this
evaluation setting.

The rest of the paper is structured as follows: Sections 1 and 2 review linguistic
filtering and statistical approaches, respectively. Section 3 presents the evaluation
scheme, the experimental results and comments on them. Section 4 concludes
this paper.

---

[1] Number of occurrences on its own; without being nested within others candidate
terms.

1   Linguistic Filters

Initial *ATR* research focused on exploiting the parts-of-speech (*PoS*) of multi-word expression constituents. As a result, different pattern-based models (linguistic filters) were proposed, to identify terms. For example, the linguistic filter in formula 2 would recognise terms consisting of nouns (*N*) or adjectives (*A*). The choice of linguistic filter depends on the language and the domain of the corpus and the application [5]. If the target is to identify terms with high recall an open filter should be used, such as the one in formula 3, which applies on numbers (*#*) and prepositions (*P*).

In this paper, four lenient *PoS* filters were employed to capture as many terms as possible. Their performance was experimentally compared. The most basic, *Nouns*, accepts sequences of *Ns*, only, since terms mainly consist of *Ns*. The second, *A&N*, applies on sequences consisting of *As* and *Ns* ending with a *N* (formula 1). The third linguistic filter, *J&K* (formula 2) was introduced by Justeson and Katz [7] and has been widely used. Its first part is identical to *A&N*, whereas the second applies on sequences which start with one or more *Ns* or *As*, continue with a *N* followed by a *P* and end with zero or more *Ns* or *As* followed by a *N*. Justeson and Katz [7] used this filter to extract multi-word terms from large text collections in a variety of domains -metallurgy, space engineering and nuclear energy-, reporting coverage of 97% (99% if *Ps* are allowed).

$$(A|N)^+ \, N \tag{1}$$
$$(\, (A|N)^+ \mid (A|N)^* \, (NP)? \, (A|N)^* \,) \, N \tag{2}$$
$$(\, (A|N|\#)^+ \mid (A|N|\#)^* \, (NP)? \, (A|N|\#)^* \,) \, N \tag{3}$$

Nouns and *A&N* extract sequences of *As*, *Ps* and *Ns*. However, our initial experimental projections show that approximately 6% of *GENIA* gold standard terms contain numbers. To capture those, we extended *J&K* to *J&K#* (formula 3), so as to accept numbers (*#*) whenever it accepts *Ns* or *As*.

2   *ATR* Statistical Approaches

Approaches to *ATR* have been largely based on statistical information. However, most of them include some linguistic part; usually a linguistic filter, to produce a list of candidate terms (section 1). The statistical part assigns to each candidate term, *ct*, a score, indicating how likely *ct* is a valid term. The most simple statistical measure is the *frequency of occurrence* (*FR*), which captures terms occurring frequently in the corpus. *FR* is used as a baseline in our evaluation.

2.1   Termhood-Based Methods

C Value [5] focuses on nested terms. The basic intuition is that a candidate term, *ct*, should occur frequently on its own, not nested in other candidate terms. For example, in an eye-pathology corpus, *"soft contact lens"* is a valid term, possibly occurring frequently. However, its substring *"soft contact"* is not an actual term and should not be extracted, since it occurs frequently as nested [5].

However, the nested frequency of ct is not a reliable measure of its nestedness, since it does not take into account the number of different candidate terms, in which ct appears as nested. For example, consider the following terms in the domain of real time systems: *"real time clock"*, *"real time systems"*, *"real time group"* and *"real time expert system"*. The fact that they all contain *"real time"* as substring, increases its possibility to be a term.

Consequently, the nestedness, NST, of ct is defined as the fraction of its nested frequency over the number of distinct candidate terms, in which it appears as nested. The length of a ct in tokens, $|ct|$, is also taken into account. The longer ct is, the more likely ct is an actual term.

$$NST(ct) = \frac{1}{P(T_{ct})} * \sum_{b \in T_{ct}} f(b)) \tag{4}$$

In order to compute a *termhood* value, Frantzi et al. [5] subtract the nestedness, NST, of ct from its *frequency of occurrence*, $f(ct)$. In case that ct appears as nested, C *Value* is defined by the upper branch of equation 5, where T_{ct} is the set of candidate terms, in which ct appears as nested, $P(T_{ct})$ is its cardinality and $L(ct) = log_2(|ct|)$. In the opposite case, ct is assigned a value based on its length and *frequency of occurrence* (lower branch of equation 5).

$$CV(ct) = \begin{cases} (f(ct) - NST(ct))L(ct), \text{ nested } ct \\ f(ct)L(ct), \text{ otherwise} \end{cases} \tag{5}$$

NC Value incorporates contextual information into the *C Value ATR* process. It consists of three parts. Firstly, *C Value* is applied on a corpus cp, to extract a ranked list of candidate terms, l. Secondly, the top n candidate terms are selected from l. For each of these, its context words cw are collected, using a window of $\pm w$ words around it. Context words can be nouns, adjectives or verbs. For each cw, the following weight is computed as: $w(cw) = \frac{t(cw)}{n}$, where $t(w)$ is the number of candidate terms cw appears with.

Thirdly, the *C Value* ranked list is refined by applying the weights $w(cw)$ to compute a context factor, CF, for each ct. The context factor of a $ct \in l$ is formally defined by equation 6, where C_{ct} is the set of context words of ct, b is an element of C_{ct}, $f_{ct}(b)$ is its *frequency of occurrence* as a context word and $w(b)$ is its weight as a context word. In the case that b was not encountered during the stage of creating the list of context words it is assigned a 0 weight. *NC Value* is computed as the linear interpolation of *C Value (CV)* and CF (equation 7).

$$CF(ct) = \sum_{b \in C_{ct}} f_{ct}(b) * w(b) \tag{6}$$

$$NCV(ct) = 0.8 * CV(ct) + 0.2 * CF(ct) \tag{7}$$

Statistical Barrier (SB) [13] is another *ATR termhood-based* approach, which assumes that terms having complex structure are made of existing simple terms.

Thus, they first measure the *termhood* of single words, and then use it to measure the *termhood* of complex terms. The basic intuition is that if a single word N, expresses a key concept of a domain, then N occurs not only frequently, but also in various ways. Thus, there will be a number of valid terms containing N. This potential relationship between single words and multi-word candidate terms is exploited to perform *ATR*.

In particular, after *PoS* tagging a given corpus, Nakagawa [13] extracts a list of single words. Let $R(N)$ and $S(N)$ be two functions that calculate the number of distinct words that adjoin N or N adjoins, respectively. Then, for each candidate term, $ct = N_1, N_2, \ldots, N_k$ a score is calculated (equation 8).

$$IMP(ct) = (\prod_{i=1}^{k}((R(N_i) + 1) * (S(N_i) + 1))))^{1/2k} \tag{8}$$

Nakagawa [13] notes that the frequency of independent occurrences of candidate terms have a significant impact on the term recognition process. Independent occurrences are the ones, where the candidate term ct, is not nested to any other candidate term. To incorporate this, *IMP* is multiplied by the *marginal frequency*, $MF(ct)$, the number of independent occurrences of ct (equation 9).

$$SB(ct) = IMP(ct)MF(ct) \tag{9}$$

2.2 Unithood-Based Methods

Termhood-based methods focus on measuring how likely a candidate term, ct, is a domain-specific concept, by considering nestedness information. On the contrary, *unithood-based* methods attempt to identify if the constituents of a multi-word candidate term form a collocation rather than co-occurring by chance.

Log-likelihood (LL) [3] is a *unithood-based* measure. For bigram terms, $ct = N_1 N_2$, LL compares the observed frequency counts with the counts that would be expected, if N_1 and N_2 were co-occurring assuming independence: $P(N_1, N_2) = P(N_1)P(N_2)$. A high LL means that observed and expected values diverge significantly, indicating that N_1 and N_2 do not co-occur by chance. Contrarily, a LL close to 0 indicates that N_1 and N_2 co-occur by chance.

For the computation, two tables are created. The first one, OT, holds the observed counts taken from the corpus. The second, ET, contains the expected values assuming independence (table 1). LL can then be calculated using equation 10, where n_{ij} is the i, j cell of OT, m_{ij} is the i, j cell of ET and $T = \sum_i^j n_{ij}$.

$$LL = 2 * \sum_{i,j} n_{ij} \cdot \log\left(\frac{n_{ij}}{m_{ij}}\right), \quad \text{where} \quad m_{ij} = \frac{\sum_k n_{ik} * \sum_k n_{kj}}{T} \tag{10}$$

For N-grams, where $N > 2$, there are more than one hypothesized models to compare against the observed counts. For example, table 2 shows the different hypothesized models for trigrams. We use the extended LL [11], in order to

Table 1. Observed (OT) and expected (ET) value tables. Bigram: "gene expression".

OT	N_1	$\neg N_1$
N_2	$n_{11} = 563$	$n_{12} = 702$
$\neg N_2$	$n_{21} = 1,085$	$n_{22} = 57,553$

ET	N_1	$\neg N_1$
N_2	$m_{11} = 35.44$	$m_{12} = 1,229.56$
$\neg N_2$	$m_{21} = 1,612.56$	$m_{22} = 55,940.44$

Table 2. Hypothesized models for trigrams

$\text{Model}_1 = \dfrac{P(N_1 N_2 N_3)}{(P(N_1)P(N_2)P(N_3))}$	$\text{Model}_2 = \dfrac{P(N_1 N_2 N_3)}{(P(N_1 N_2)P(N_3))}$
$\text{Model}_3 = \dfrac{P(N_1 N_2 N_3)}{(P(N_1)P(N_2 N_3))}$	$\text{Model}_4 = \dfrac{P(N_1 N_2 N_3)}{(P(N_1 N_3)P(N_2))}$

calculate LL values for each hypothesized model. For each model a different table of expected values is computed, while the observed values table remains the same for all. Then, for each model LL is calculated (equation 10). The model with the lowest LL value best represents the N-gram, since when a model is a good fit the observed values are close to the expected ones.

Pointwise mutual information (PMI) [1] is an information theoretic measure applied for N-gram terms. For bigrams, PMI quantifies the distance between the joint distribution of N_1 and N_2 and the joint distribution if N_1 and N_2 were independent. Equation 11 shows the PMI formula for bigram terms. If N_1, N_2 are independent: $P(N_1, N_2) = P(N_1) * P(N_2)$, then PMI is 0. For N-grams of $N > 2$, there are more than one hypothesized models to compare against the joint distribution of N-gram constituents. The process is similar to the process followed in LL. For each model we calculate different PMI values, and we choose the one with the lowest PMI value, i.e. the model which best represents the observed counts. For example, the PMI formula for the ith 3-gram model of table 2 is $log(\text{Model}_i)$.

$$PMI(N_1, N_2) = \log \frac{P(N_1, N_2)}{P(N_1)p(N_2)} \tag{11}$$

3   Evaluation

3.1   Experimental Setting

For evaluation, the *GENIA* [6] and the *PennBioIE* [9] were used (table 3). Both corpora consist of *MEDLINE* abstracts, $2,000$ and $2,257$ respectively, and their terms are manually annotated.

For *PennBioIE* [9] evaluation we excluded annotations of quantitative values and units. In *GENIA*, annotation terms are not part of the text, but of separate *xml* attributes. Thus, *GENIA* gold standard (GS) is created by collecting these *xml* values and cleaning most non-alphanumerical characters. We observed that

Table 3. *GENIA* and *PennBioIE* corpus statistics

	sentences	tokens	terms	distinct terms	terms types
GENIA	18,546	454,848	97,876	35,947	36
PennBioIE	32,692	712,551	76,535	13,759	22

Table 4. *GS* term counts and candidate term counts per ling. filter and term length.

Length	GENIA					PennBioIE				
	GS	N	A&N	J&K	J&K#	GS	N	A&N	J&K	J&K#
Any	28,142	29,751	69,457	85,978	138,251	7,447	46,519	80,205	99,194	178,939
2-grams	12,654	17,103	33,021	33,021	36,866	4,034	28,489	44,072	44,072	58,086
3-grams	9,051	8,813	21,401	28,071	37,146	1,820	11,421	22,530	31,930	49,570
4-grams	3,839	3,199	9,356	15,204	29,803	821	4,157	8,629	14,945	35,746
5-grams	1,559	1,020	3,699	6,339	18,099	388	1,486	3,070	5,447	20,019
6-grams	606	297	1,317	2,239	9,005	207	694	1,172	1,822	9,105

in a few cases annotation tokens are not lemmatized (e.g. "activators of transcription", "activating function") or erroneous (e.g. "latent proviru"). However, we hypothesize that a corpus with low level of noise is acceptable for our purposes. Both *GENIA* and *PennBioIE* text was similarly cleaned. Then, both corpora were tokenized and part-of-speech (*PoS*) tagged using the GENIA tagger[2].

The first and sixth column of table 4 shows *GS* term counts of *GENIA* and *PennBioIE*, respectively. The following columns present candidate term counts, identified by each linguistic filter, for each corpus. The filters are shown in order of descending strictness. For example, the *A&N* filter identified far fewer candidates than the *J&K*. However, even the most strict filter, *Nouns*, creates more candidate terms than the valid ones. Note that, for each column, the count of candidates of any length (row 1, table 4) is not equal to the sum of all *N*-grams, because candidates of any length include sequences up to 12 tokens long.

The standard evaluation metrics Precision (*P*) and Recall (*R*) [12,15] (equation 12) were used for evaluating *ATR* statistical methods. *F-Score* is defined as the weighted harmonic mean of *P* and *R*: $2 \left(R^{-1} + P^{-1} \right)^{-1}$.

$$P = \frac{\# \text{ correctly identified terms}}{\# \text{ identified terms}} \qquad R = \frac{\# \text{ correctly identified terms}}{\# \ GS \text{ terms}} \qquad (12)$$

Table 5 shows *R* and *P* for every linguistic filter for candidates of any length and *N*-grams for both corpora. We observe that the less strict a filter is, the higher the *R* and the lower the *P*. *A&N* seems to achieve the best compromise between *R* and *P*. *ATR* statistical methods re-rank the list of candidates, with a target to output the actual terms higher. Thus, considering the whole list, the performance of all statistical methods is the same (table 5).

---

[2] www-tsujii.is.s.u-tokyo.ac.jp/GENIA/tagger

Table 5. R (%) and P (%) per linguistic filter and length of candidate term

Length	GENIA								PennBioIE							
	Nouns		A&N		J&K		J&K#		Nouns		A&N		J&K		J&K#	
	R	P	R	P	R	P	R	P	R	P	R	P	R	P	R	P
Any	35.4	33.5	80.2	32.5	80.2	26.3	85.4	17.4	37.2	6.0	63.1	5.9	63.7	4.8	76.1	3.2
2-grams	48.1	35.6	88.0	33.7	88.0	33.7	90.6	31.1	52.6	7.5	78.1	7.1	78.0	7.1	90.6	6.3
3-grams	31.9	32.8	80.4	34.0	80.5	25.9	84.5	20.6	26.8	4.3	60.7	4.9	61.6	3.5	73.1	2.7
4-grams	21.3	25.5	67.0	28.7	70.4	17.8	78.9	10.2	15.8	3.1	42.8	4.1	45.2	2.5	56.5	1.3
5-grams	14.9	22.7	63.8	26.9	64.2	15.8	77.0	6.6	4.7	1.2	17.1	2.2	18.7	1.3	38.3	0.7
6-grams	9.2	18.9	54.5	25.1	54.5	14.7	71.0	4.8	3.9	1.3	13.0	2.3	13.5	1.5	24.6	0.6

Table 6. Executed experiments on each corpus

Candidate term length	Any, 2-grams, 3-grams, 4-grams, 5-grams, 6-grams
Linguistic filter	Nouns, A&N, J&K, J&K#
ATR stat. approach	NC Value, PMI (N-grams only)
	LL (N-grams only), SB (Nouns and A&J only)

As discussed in section 2, the *Log-likelihood* (*LL*) method can only be applied separately for sequences of a specific length. We implemented the extended *LL* algorithm for N-grams, $N \in [2, 6]$. There are only 433 *GENIA GS* terms and 177 *PennBioIE GS* terms longer than 6 tokens, very few to experiment with (table 4). The results of the *LL* algorithm for different values of N are not comparable to each other. Thus, we set separate experiments up for each value of $N \in [2, 6]$.

For example, for 2-grams we first apply a linguistic filter to identify candidates of which we keep 2-grams only. Next, 2-grams are re-ranked according to one of the implemented statistical methods. Evaluation is performed towards the 2-gram *GS* terms. Experiments for the other values of N were set up identically.

Except for N-grams, we ran experiments taking into account sequences of any length, higher than 2. For each one, candidate terms are identified using one of our four linguistic filters. Then, one of *C-Value*, *NC-Value* or *SB* re-ranking method is applied. Evaluation uses the whole *GS* term set. Note that the *SB* method makes sense only when following the *Nouns* or the *A&N* linguistic filter.

The *NC Value* algorithm takes as input a list of candidates, ranked by the *C Value* algorithm and is subject to two parameters: the percentage of the list, starting from the top, that it will take into account to identify context terms and the size of the context window. We experimented using values 5%, 7.5% and 10% for the former one and 2, 4, 6, 8, 10 for the latter.

Table 6 shows all executed experiments, referring to the combination of length of candidate terms, filtering and statistical approach used. To visualise the results, we used an approach similar to the one indicated in [16]. R and P values were calculated at 0.5% increments on the list of candidates and plotted on graphs, such as figure 2. For each increment on the list, P refers to the ratio of true positives over the overall number of candidates and R refers to the ratio of

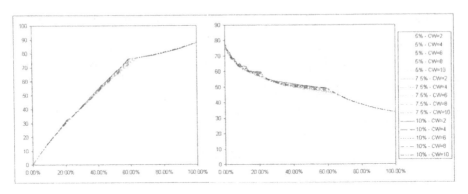

Fig. 2. *GENIA* 2-grams, J&K filter, *NC Value* results, *R* and *P*

true positives over the number of *GS* terms. The x-axis shows the percentage of the list taken into account. *Frequency of occurrence* (*FR*) is used as baseline.

Intuitively, the *P* curve of a bad performing method would be relatively horizontal indicating that the true positives were dispersed uniformly throughout the list rather than pushed towards the top. Contrarily, the *P* curve of a well-performing method would be 100% until the percentage point at which all *GS* terms would have been retrieved, where a sharp decrease would occur [11].

3.2   Results

Figure 2 shows the 2-gram *P* and *R* curves of *NC Value* for 15 parameter combinations (see subsection 3.1), using the *J&K* linguistic filter on *GENIA* corpus. We observe that different combinations do not affect the results. This behaviour remains the same for all linguistic filters and for all term lengths. Interestingly, for all the above experiments the performance of *C* and *NC Value* is almost identical, both for *GENIA* and *PennBioIE*.

Figure 3 shows the *F-Score* performance for 3-gram candidate terms of *GENIA* and *PennBioIE* as identified by the *Nouns* linguistic filter. We observe that *termhood-based* methods outperform *unithood-based* ones. *SB*, *C* and *NC Value* perform similarly with *SB* having a slightly better *F-Score* on *GENIA*. *PMI* curves are below the baseline on both corpora. On the contrary, *LL* outperforms the baseline of *FR* on *PennBioIE* but not on *GENIA*. Possible reasons for the behaviour of *LL* and *PMI* are discussed in subsection 3.3. The ranking of *ATR* methods remains the same as in figure 3 for any *N*-gram using both the *Nouns* and the *A&N* linguistic filter, on both corpora.

The performance for *N*-gram candidate terms as identified by *J&K* and *J&K#* demonstrate the following trends: On *GENIA* the highest performance is achieved by *C* and *NC Value* methods throughout the plots. The remaining methods in order of decreasing *F-Score* are: *FR*, *LL* and *PMI*. The bigger *N* is, the closer *FR*, *LL* and *PMI* curves are to each other.

On *PennBioIE*, the performance differences between *FR*, *LL*, *C* and *NC Value* are insignificant, while *PMI* clearly performs worse. In this corpus we observe

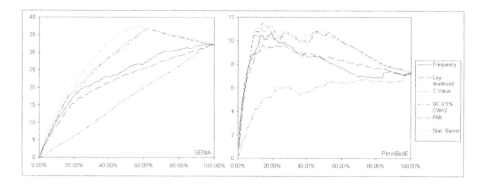

Fig. 3. *GENIA* and *PennBioIE* 3-grams, Noun filter, *F-Score*

that *termhood-based* methods have a comparable performance with the baseline. 6-gram results follow the same trends in general, but they are not very reliable due to the small number of candidates.

On both corpora for candidates of any length identified by *Nouns* and *A&N*, *SB*, *C* and *NC Value* methods exceed the baseline of *FR*, achieving similar levels of performance. Using the *J&K* and *J&K#* on *GENIA* (*PennBioIE*), the performances of *C*, *NC Value* and *FR* are similar for increments up to 10% (on both corpora) of the candidate list. For increments between 10% and 30% (50% for *PennBioIE*), *FR* performs better than *C* and *NC Value*. After 30% (50%), *C* and *NC Value* perform better than *FR*.

3.3 Discussion

Our results (section 3.2) show that *termhood-based* methods re-rank the candidate list better than *unithood-based* methods or equally well, irrespective of the candidate terms length and linguistic filter used. A possible reason is that *unithood-based methods* measure the strength of attachment of the candidate term constituents, in effect assigning high scores to candidate terms, which might not refer to domain concepts. For example, in *GENIA*, *"allergic inflammatory"*, substring of the term *"allergic inflammatory disease"*, occurs at least equally often as the term, although the former is not a term itself.

The only setting in which a *unithood-based* method (*LL*) performed equally well to the *termhood-based* methods was when using *J&K* or *J&K#* to extract *N*-gram candidates from *PennBioIE*. A possible explanation for this peculiarity is the limited amount of nestedness information in *PennBioIE*, which degrades the performance of *termhood-based* approaches. Particularly for 3-grams, the average nested frequency in *PennBioIE* is 1.03, while in *GENIA* is 1.16. Note that *PennBioIE* is almost double the size of *GENIA* (table 3).

PMI overestimates rare events, which dominate the candidate term lists. For example, *A&N* identifies 69, 457 *GENIA* candidate terms, out of which 52, 998 (76.3%) occur only once, and 16, 459 twice. *LL* outperforms *PMI*, due to its milder tendency in overestimating rare events.

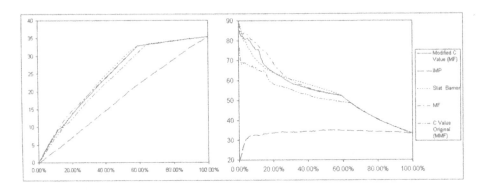

Fig. 4. *GENIA* sequences of any length, *Nouns* filter, various methods, *R* and *P*

C and *NC Value* exploit nestedness information, in the sense that the more often a candidate appears as nested, the less likely it is a valid term. *SB* considers this information through *MF* counts. *NC Value* attempts to improve *C Value* by exploiting contextual information. However, unsuccessfully, under our evaluation scheme. To investigate this, we adjusted the interpolation constant of equation 7 to assess the contribution of the *CF* only $(NCV(ct) = 0 * CV(ct) + 1 * CF(ct))$. *P* curves are almost uniform across most of the plot.

SB exploits two sources of information: Firstly, *IMP* (equation 8), assumes that complex terms consist of existing simple terms. Secondly, *MF* (equation 9), refers to the marginal frequency counts. To evaluate the contribution of each, we executed two experiments, which re-rank the candidate term list taking into account *IMP* and *MF* separately. Interestingly, *P* of *IMP* is roughly uniform on *GENIA* (figure 4), which means that it contributes negatively to *SB*. On the contrary, *MF* successfully redistributes candidates towards the top of the list. Thus, the corresponding *P* curve is higher than the curve of *SB* in the x-axis interval [0%, 30%]. *PennBioIE* experiments verified these results.

C Value suggests that the higher the nested frequency of a candidate term, *ct*, the less likely it is a valid term, conditional to the number of distinct candidate terms, in which *ct* appears as nested. Hence, *C Value* calculates a weighted version of marginal frequency (*MMF*), $f(ct) - NST(ct)$ (formula 5). $NST(ct)$ is the ratio of the frequency of the candidate as nested over the number of distinct terms, in which it appears nested. To examine the effect of *MMF* in *C Value*, we replaced the *MMF* in the *C Value* formula with *MF*. Results show that the modified version of *C Value* performs better i.e. *MF* captures nestedness better than *MMF*. However, *MF* outperforms even this modified version of *C Value*, for increments up to 25% of the candidate list for *GENIA* and 55% for *PennBioIE*.

4   Conclusion

We reviewed and evaluated state-of-the-art linguistic filtering and statistical *ATR* methods under a common evaluation scheme. Our results indicate that:

(1) *termhood-based* methods have in general superior performance over *unithood-based* ones, and (2) that the number of independent occurrences of a candidate term is the most effective source of nestedness information for *ATR*.

References

1. Church, K.W., Hanks, P.: Word association norms, mutual information, and lexicography. Computational Linguistics 16(1), 22–29 (1990)
2. Dias, G., Kaalep, H., Muischnek, K.: Automatic Extraction of Verb Phrases from Annotated Corpora: A Linguistic Evaluation for Estonian. In: EACL/ACL Workshop on Collocations, Toulouse, France (2001)
3. Dunning, T.E.: Accurate Methods for the Statistics of Surprise and Coincidence. Computational Linguistics 19(1), 61–74 (1993)
4. Evert, S., Krenn, B.: Methods for the qualitative evaluation of lexical association measures. In: ACL, Morristown, NJ, USA (2001)
5. Frantzi, K.T., Ananiadou, S., Mima, H.: Automatic recognition of multi-word terms: the C-value/NC-value method. International Journal on Digital Libraries 3(2), 115–130 (2000)
6. Gu, B.: Recognizing Nested Named Entities in GENIA corpus. In: HLT-NAACL BioNLP Workshop, New York, pp. 112–113 (2006)
7. Justeson, J.S., Katz, S.M.: Technical terminology: some linguistic properties and an algorithm for identification in text. Natural Language Engineering 1(1), 9–27 (1995)
8. Kageura, K., Umino, B.: Methods of automatic term recognition: a review. Terminology 3(2), 259–289 (1996)
9. Kulick, S., Bies, A., Liberman, M., Mandel, M., Mcdonald, R., Palmer, M., Schein, A., Ungar, L., Winters, S., White, P.: Integrated Annotation for Biomedical Information Extraction. In: Hirschman, L., Pustejovsky, J. (eds.) HLT-NAACL BioLINK Workshop, Boston, Massachusetts, USA, pp. 61–68 (2004)
10. Manning, C., Schutze, H.: Foundations of Statistical Natural Language Processing. Chapter: Collocations. MIT Press, Cambridge (1999)
11. Mcinnes, B.T.: Extending the Log Likelihood Measure to Improve Collocation Identification. Master's thesis. University of Minnesota (2004)
12. Mikheev, A., Moens, M., Grover, C.: Named Entity recognition without gazetteers. In: EACL, Bergen, Norway, pp. 1–8 (1999)
13. Nakagawa, H.: Automatic Term Recognition based on Statistics of Compound Nouns. Terminology 6(2), 195–210 (2000)
14. Pecina, P., Schlesinger, P.: Combining Association Measures for Collocation Extraction. In: ACL, Sydney, Australia (2006)
15. Radev, D., Teufel, S., Saggion, H., Lam, W., Blitzer, J., Qi, H., Elebi, A., Liu, D., Drabek, E.: Evaluation challenges in large-scale document summarization. In: ACL, Sapporo, Japan (2003)
16. Wermter, J., Hahn, U.: Collocation extraction based on modifiability statistics. In: COLING, Morristown, NJ, USA (2004)

Finding Text Boundaries and Finding Topic Boundaries: Two Different Tasks?

Alexandre Labadié and Violaine Prince

LIRMM
161 rue Ada
34392 Montpellier Cedex 5, France
{labadie,prince}@lirmm.fr
http://www.lirmm.fr

Abstract. The goal of this paper is to demonstrate that usual evaluation methods for text segmentation are not adapted for every task linked to text segmentation. To do so we differentiated the task of finding text boundaries in a corpus of concatenated texts from the task of finding transitions between topics inside the same text. We worked on a corpus of twenty two French political discourses trying to find boundaries between them when they are concatenated, and to find topic boundaries inside them when they are not. We compared the results of our distance based method to the well known c99 algorithm.

Keywords: Topic detection, topic change, evaluation methods, text segmentation.

Introduction

The huge amount of text available on the Internet and other media, allows users to access more and more information. The drawback of this abundance is that information is less and less relevant and workable. Many research fields, such as information retrieval (IR), try to solve this problem by formating data and/or selecting information the more accurately possible. Text segmentation significantly helps improving methods used in these domains since it is considered as one of the fundamental actions in IR [14],[18] .

There are many distinct tasks labeled as 'text segmentation'. For instance, identifying and extracting text from multimedia support where it is mixed with pictures or videos is called as such [13]. The task of grouping words into morphemes or bigger linguistic units is sometimes also referred as text segmentation (e.g. in written Asiatic languages where words boundaries are not easy to assess[26], [27]). In this paper, we concentrate on '**topic based text segmentation**'. This type of process tries to find the topical structure [9] of a text and thus provide a possible thematic decomposition of a given document [21]. Most texts do not talk about only one topic. The bigger the documents, the more

A. Ranta, B. Nordström (Eds.): GoTAL 2008, LNAI 5221, pp. 260–271, 2008.

topics they include. The goal of topic based text segmentation is to find where
a topic begins and where it ends, within a text. For practical purposes, we will
use the name 'text segmentation' to refer to topic based text segmentation.

Basically, the goal of text segmentation is to divide a text into multiple segments which are thematically coherent and distinct. Each of these text segments
should ideally bear one topic, but topics could be complex units from a rhetorical point of view, needing explanations, examples or argumentations. This brings
out the question of defining the concept of a topic. Browsing literature shows
that there are several definitions of a topic and a large body of works in (topical) text segmentation. Generally speaking, a topic is: *the subject matter of a
conversation or discussion*. In linguistics, it is defined as: *the part of the proposition that is being talked about (predicated)*. Thus one may admit that the topic
of a text segment is *what talking is about*. So, the goal of an automatized text
segmentation could be simplified into dividing a text in segments, each sentence
of which "talks about" the same subject.

To evaluate automatic methods of text segmentation, most papers (among
which [6] and [7] are representative examples) use a common protocol: They
concatenate multiple texts, and consider each of them as an instance of a thematically coherent text segment. They assume that retrieving text boundaries in
a concatenation and segmenting topically a text are equivalent tasks. Although
they might appear as syntactically similar, semantically, actions are very different. A concatenation of texts is not designed by an author as a discourse
instance, in the way that collecting and grouping several papers on a subject
does not make a dissertation about that subject. In this paper, we will question the commonly admitted hypothesis that finding boundaries of concatenated
texts and finding boundaries of topic segments are the same task, by presenting two complementary approaches: First, common text segmentation methods
which similarly process text boundaries and in text topic boundaries, and second, our approach, which separates both tasks (all described in section 2). Then
we will compare one segmentation method of the first type(Choi's c99 algorithm) and our method on the same set of data a French political discourse
corpus in section 3. Results will definitely separate the methods capabilities:
Common segmentation methods get good results in finding text boundaries, but
their performances drop when handling in text topic boundaries, whereas our
method shows rather fair results in text boundaries whereas it scores satisfyingly
in topic boundaries detection. This section discusses the benefits of considering
text boundaries detection and topic change as two different task that should be
evaluated differently. We will conclude on possible other approaches of evaluating
text segmentation methods.

1   Existing Methods and the Task (Tasks?)

As said in introduction, literature is abundant on the subject, and mostly methods
divide into two main categories: Supervised ones, more or less data dependent, and
unsupervised methods, trying to avoid the liabilities of learning. In this paper we

concentrate on unsupervised methods, since they can be evaluated on corpora as broadly distinct as possible, which is a better case for evaluation.

1.1 Main Approaches for Unsupervised Text Segmentation

Within this subfield, there are also several methods of text segmentation, but they can be classified into three main approaches.

Similarity Text Segmentation Methods. These methods consider each text sentence as an atomic element in their analysis and represent it as a vector which, most of the time, is built with the frequency of each term (TF) of the text after the text has been stemmed and purged of useless words with the help of a stop list. To give more weight to 'important' words, the inverse document frequency (IDF) is also quite often present.

The goal of such methods is to measure the gap between sentences, relying on the angle between vectors . A mathematical measure such as the cosine (which is the most used) as a similarity (more exactly, a dissimilarity) measure leads to build similarity matrices, which are employed to search for boundaries in the text.

One of the most efficient similarity based method is probably Choi's C99 algorithm [6]. C99 uses the similarity matrix to build local ranking of proximity between sentences. The more similar to their neighbors the sentences are, the higher their ranks. The lowest rank in the new built ranking matrix shows the boundary between the two main parts of the text. These two parts are then considered as two independent texts, and the algorithm is applied on each part. The algorithm stop when the lowest rank detected is the last sentence of the analyzed part of the text.

Graphical Text Segmentation Methods. By using a graphical representation of TF, it is easier to see how terms are dispatched all over the text. [10] uses this kind of representation in IR. The principle is quite simple, each word is represented by one or more dots on a a bi-dimensional graphic. The number and positions of dots depend on where and how many times the word appears in the text. For example, a word appearing in sentence i and sentence j will be represented by four dots : (i, i), (i, j), (j, i) and (j, j). Parts of the text where a strong term is repeated appear on the graphic as dot clouds.

This visual approach of TF representation has been used by [23] to develop his DotPlotting algorithm, which identifies text segments by finding the boundaries of the most dense dot clouds. Reynard computes the density of an area of the graphic by dividing the number of dots by the surface of the area. Then the algorithm finds the text segment boundaries by maximizing the density of the dot clouds and/or minimizing the size of "empty" areas in the graphic.

Graphical methods inspired also the one developed by [11], which considers the text segmentation issue as a picture segmentation issue. The authors used an anisotropic diffusion algorithm on a graphic representation of the text distance matrix. By doing so, their algorithm strengthens the divergence between dense areas and boundaries.

Lexical Chains Text Segmentation Methods. Lexical chains text segmentation links multiple occurrences of the same term in a text to form a chain. When the distance between two occurrences of a term is too important, the chain is considered broken. This distance is generally the number of sentences between two consecutive occurrences of one word.

Segmenter [12], is software based on this approach with a little specificity: The number of sentences breaking the word chain depends on the syntactic class of the word, thus enhancing discrimination.

Another lexical chain based algorithm, is the $TextTiling$ algorithm developed by [8]. A **consistency score** is given to each text block depending the following block. This score is computed on the basis of a first "lexical" score given to each pair of consecutive sentences. The 'lexical' score is obtained by computing some parameters between two consecutive pairs. These parameters are typically the number of common words between the two pairs, the number of new words and the number of still active lexical chains in the considered sentences. So, the score of each text segment is a normalized scalar product of each pairs score. If a text segment has a very different score from the next and previous text segments, there is a change of topic in this text segment.

1.2   Limits in Current Text Segmentation

All these approaches have in common the almost exclusive use of lexical cohesion [20], which means that they only look for similar and/or different words to find text segments or boundaries. If a few use syntactic information, it is limited to the word part-of-speech tag (noun, verb, adjective, etc.). In natural language, the word/constituent function also bears information. If a noun is the subject of a verb, it could mean something totally different from what it means if it were its object. This lack of syntactic information is one of the limits of such word-based methods.

Another limitation of lexical cohesion based methods which as been pointed by [25], is the intensive use of synonyms as a stylistic effect. In many languages, and particularly in French, the language on which we experiment, repeating several times the same word in a paragraph or even a short text is considered unsightly. This massive use of synonyms makes these approaches quite inefficient as they are based on the exact repetition of words. It is possible to use some semantic resources like WordNet to counterbalance this, but languages requiring such a use of synonyms have also great polysemy issues. So, doing so only changes the problem into another.

More specifically, Bestgen and Piérard [2] have observed that, if these methods are quite efficient at finding text boundaries in a corpus of concatenated texts, they get poor results at finding in text topic segments [2] . These results can be explained by the differences between a whole text and just a segment of it. A text, is a complete entity. With a beginning (generally described as the introduction), a main body (development) and an end (conclusion). So, a text is self-sufficient in terms of information and structure. It does not need any contextual information to be understood. On the other side, a text segment is just a part of a bigger entity. If the text is the 'main topic' then segments are 'sub-topics' and the relation between main and sub is a semantic relation for sure. As an incomplete entity, the segment needs other segments to bear any meaning. Lexical cohesion based methods need a lot of information to be efficient, and most of the time a single topic segment does not bear enough of it. Moreover, as an incomplete entity, it has to refer to other parts of the text to be linked with it, in the way a subtopic is also related to its parent, child or brother subtopic in a topical tree [19].

1.3   Transeg: A Distance Based Method

We have developed a distance based text segmentation specifically designated to find topic variations inside the text called Transeg.

Textual Representation. The first step of our approach is to convert each text sentence into a semantic vector obtained using the French language parser SYGFRAN [3]. These vectors are Roget like semantic vectors [24], but using the Larousse thesaurus [16] as a reference. Sentence vectors are recursively computed by linearly combining sentence constituents, which are themself computed by linearly combining word vectors. The weights of each word vectors is the result of a constituents and dependencies syntactic analysis[1]. So, these vectors bear both the semantic and the syntactic information of the sentence.

Text Segmentation. Using this sentence representation, we try to find transition zones inside the text. The notion of transition zone come from the idea that topic change boundaries inside a text are not isolated sentences, but small groups of sentences. To find them, we slide a window along the text, considering each half of the window as a potential segment (fig. 1). Each potential text segment is then represented by one vector, which is a weighted barycenter of its sentence vectors. We added a stylistic information by giving a better weight to first sentences, relying on the fact that introductions bear the important information [15],[17]. Then we compute a distance (we call it thematic distance) between the two barycenter, and consider it as the window central sentence transition score.

Transition zones are successive sentences with a transition score greater than a threshold. This threshold is the result of a detailed observation of DEFT'06 political corpus. We computed distances on many discourses and their topic segments (the sum of their sentences were around 100000) and obtained an average distance of 0.45 and a σ of 0.08. Boundary sentences are selected in the transition zones. A more detailed description of this approach can be found in [22].

In our first implementations of this method we used the angular distance to compute transition score. In this paper we used an extended version of the concordance distance first proposed by [5].

---

[1] The formula is given in [4] and has no relation with Kendall's (1948) measure of concordance.

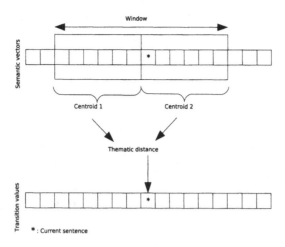

Fig. 1. Giving a transition score to each sentences

Concordance Distance. Semantic vectors resulting from the analysis have 873 components and most of them are not even activated. With so much null values in the vector the angular distance is not enough discriminant. The goal of the concordance distance is to be more discriminant by not only considering the vectors components values, but their ranks to.

Considering two vectors A and B, we sorted their values from the most activated to the less activated and chose to keep only the first values of the new vectors ($\frac{1}{3}$ of the original vector). A_{sr} and B_{sr} are respectively the sorted and reduced versions of A and B. Obviously A_{sr} and B_{sr} could have no common strong component (so the distance will be 1), but if they have some we can compute two differences :

The rank difference: if i is the rank of C_t a component of A_{sr} and $\rho(i)$ the rank of the same component in B_{sr}, we have :

$$E_{i,\rho(i)} = \frac{(i - \rho(i))^2}{Nb^2 + (1 + \frac{i}{2})} \tag{1}$$

Where Nb is the number of values kept.

The intensity difference: We also have to compare the intensity of common strong components. If a_i is the intensity of i rank component from A_{sr} and $b_{\rho(i)}$ the intensity of the same component in B_{sr} (its rank is $\rho(i)$), we have:

$$I_{i,\rho(i)} = \frac{\|a_i - b_{\rho(i)}\|}{Nb^2 + (\frac{1+i}{2})} \tag{2}$$

These two differences allow us to compute an intermediate value P:

$$P(A_{sr}, B_{sr}) = (\frac{\sum_{i=0}^{Nb-1} \frac{1}{1 + E_{i,\rho(i)} * I_{i,\rho(i)}}}{Nb})^2 \tag{3}$$

As P concentrate on components intensities and ranks, we introduce the overall components direction by mixing P with the angular distance. If $\delta(\boldsymbol{A}, \boldsymbol{B})$ is the angular distance between $\boldsymbol{A}$ and $\boldsymbol{B}$, then we have:

$$\Delta(\boldsymbol{A_{sr}}, \boldsymbol{B_{sr}}) = \frac{P(\boldsymbol{A_{sr}}, \boldsymbol{B_{sr}}) * \delta(\boldsymbol{A}, \boldsymbol{B})}{\beta * P(\boldsymbol{A_{sr}}, \boldsymbol{B_{sr}}) + (1 - \beta) * \delta(\boldsymbol{A}, \boldsymbol{B})} \tag{4}$$

Where β is a coefficient used to give more weight (or less) to P. It is easy to prove that neither P nor $\Delta(\boldsymbol{A_{sr}}, \boldsymbol{B_{sr}})$ are symmetric.

But $\Delta(\boldsymbol{A_{sr}}, \boldsymbol{B_{sr}})$ was designed in a context of text classification, to compare text vectors to class vectors. As only the likelihood of a text to the class center had to be measured, $\Delta(\boldsymbol{A_{sr}}, \boldsymbol{B_{sr}})$ did not need to be symmetric. But in our context of text segmentation we needed a symmetric value. even if $\boldsymbol{A}$ come before $\boldsymbol{B}$ in a text, $\boldsymbol{A}$ is not more important than $\boldsymbol{B}$. So the final concordance distance $D(\boldsymbol{A}, \boldsymbol{B})$ we use, is:

$$D(\boldsymbol{A}, \boldsymbol{B}) = \frac{\Delta(\boldsymbol{A_{sr}}, \boldsymbol{B_{sr}}) + \Delta(\boldsymbol{B_{sr}}, \boldsymbol{A_{sr}})}{2} \tag{5}$$

2   Experiment and Result on French Political Discourses

To test the assumption that text and topic boundaries detection are different tasks, we have set up an experiment comparing C99 and our method. Both are unsupervised, therefore not data sensitive (they do not learn, don't adapt to data specificities, therefore a given corpus could be used several times with no effect on results). The first has been tested on concatenated texts by its author, the second has been tested on both concatenated texts and un-concatenated texts in the DEFT'06 [1] competition (an equivalent of TREC Novelty task for French). So in order to compare methods, we tried them on a set of concatenated texts and we measured their scores according to our two criteria : text boundaries detection, in text topic boundaries detection. The following subsections describe data, experiments and results.

2.1   Data: A Corpus of French Political Discourse

We chose a corpus of concatenated French political discourses, extracted from the training corpus proposed in the workshop DEFT'06 [1], which proposed several other corpora, but we chose to work on political discourses, for two main reasons:

- As they were identified by experts, internal boundaries looked less artificial than just beginnings of concatenated texts.
- As an argumentative text, the topical structure of a political discourse should be more visible than other more mundane texts. The mentioned workshop was about finding topic boundaries in three different corpora in politics (the one we chose) law and science but we discarded the other domains because of several biases that could be introduced by artificial devices (words such as 'article' in European law texts or paragraph line break that was questionably considered as a topic frontier in the science corpora by the organizers).

There was a lot of noise inside the political corpus. Some discourses were exclusively in capital letters, which is quite annoying when processing a language like French, that discriminates words according to accents on vowels. And some of the "discourses" were, in fact, interviews. So, we manually selected, separated and cleaned discourses from this corpus and created two different corpora:

- Each discourse separately with its internal topic boundaries.
- All discourses concatenated. We only kept the first sentence of each discourse as a boundary (internal topic boundaries were ignored).

From an original corpus of more than $30,0000$ sentences of a questionable quality we extracted 22 discourses totalizing $1,895$ sentences and $54,551$ (Table 1). No information on the discourses were at our disposal, except the beginning of topic segments (which could have been beginnings of texts or real topic boundaries), so this manual cleaning of the corpus took lot of time and significantly reduced the amount data. But it was a necessity to have a workable data set.

The original corpus, full of noise (entire sentences in capital letter, empty sentences, punctuation repetition, etc.), brings some discredit on the DEFT'06 workshop results. But, noise is a common problem in natural language processing and as it should be done with, it should not invalidate the DEFT'06 experiment. In our case, as we tried to differentiate two tasks commonly considered as one, we needed the cleanest data set possible.

2.2   Experiments

We set up a first run of both Transeg and the LSA augmented c99 Choi algorithm on the concatenated discourses, and a second one on each discourse separately. We chose to use the latest version of c99 because it is commonly recognized as one of the best text segmentation methods (if not the best at all). To be sure that there is not any implementation error, we used the 1.3 binary release that can be downloaded on Choi's personal Linguaware Internet page (`http://www.lingware.co.uk/homepage/freddy.choi/software/software.htm`).

To evaluate the results of both methods, we used the DEFT'06 workshop tolerant recall and precision ([1]). These recall and precision count as relevant potential boundary sentences which are in a window around the boundary sentence identified by experts. This evaluation give a better idea of algorithms efficiency on the task of finding inner texts topic boundaries and does not have a significant influence on the task of finding texts boundaries. The team of DEFT'06 saw in [1] that the use of either strict or tolerant measure had no effect on the ranking of the submissions they had to evaluate.

We computed the $FScore$ with these tolerant recall and precision, using the well known formula:

$$FScore = \frac{(\beta^2 + 1) * recall * precision}{\beta^2 * precision + recall} \tag{6}$$

With $\beta = 1$.

We have to note that both method consider first sentences of texts as a boundaries and that every first sentence of each text is considered as a boundary when computing recall, precision and *FScore* (so both methods have always at least one good answer).

2.3   Results

All results were multiplied by 100 for legibility purpose. First of all, we see that results are not spectacular (be it in table 1 or table 2). *FScore* is a very strict measure, even when softened by using tolerant recall and precision. The best *FScore*, obtained by Transeg in run 2 text 9, is of 85.72% for a precision of 75% and a recall of 100% and the worst is of 5.72%. This give us a good view of the quality of current text segmentation methods and of the progresses we can make in this domain.

Considering run 1, c99 has a better *FScore* and precision than Transeg. This confirm our initial postulate that c99 is better than us at finding texts boundaries. But, we also see that both methods have overall bad results. When watching in detail the results of both methods we see that:

– C99 bring back only 15 potential boundaries also it should have bring back at least 22 (one for each text). And only 2 of them are in the tolerance window.
– Transeg bring back 190 potential boundaries (which is far to much), for only 7 in the tolerance window.

These results are significant of the differences between the two approaches. Transeg has been conceived to be very sensitive to variations. So on the many sentences composing the corpus, it detected many variations. Transeg is clearly too sensitive for such tasks. C99 detected far less variations and seem far less sensitive, why? C99 is designed to detect brutal changes in the lexical field. As our corpus is exclusively composed of political discourses, texts are quite uniform. This could explain its overall bad results (even if better than us) on run 1.

Considering run 2, Transeg has a better *FScore* on 16 on the 22 composing the corpus. On these 16 texts our recall is always better or equal to c99 and our *FScore* are from 20% (text 1) to 329% (text 9) better than c99 ones. Transeg has also the best *FScore* of both runs with 85.72% on text 9. C99 has a better *FScore* on 6 texts, but it is at best twice Transeg *FScore* on the same text. Anyway, we should notice that c99 has comparatively good precision on most of the texts. Thus, when examining texts where c99 is better we see that they are in two categories: - Texts with few boundaries. C99 seems to be very effective on short texts with just one inner topic boundary. With few boundaries identified, and first sentences always identified as boundaries, mathematically c99 has a

Table 1. Results of run 1

	Words	Sentences	Transeg			c99		
			Precision	Recall	FScore	Precision	Recall	FScore
All texts concatenated	54,551	1,895	3.68%	31.82%	3.3%	13.33%	9.09%	**5.41**

Table 2. Results of run 2

	Words	Sentences	Transeg			c99		
			Precision	Recall	FScore	Precision	Recall	FScore
Text 1	617	22	50%	33.33%	**40%**	33.33%	33.33%	33.33%
Text 2	3,042	100	33.33%	37.5%	**35.3%**	50%	12.5%	20%
Text 3	2,767	92	42.86%	85.71%	**57.14%**	20%	14.29%	16.67%
Text 4	1,028	40	33.33%	33.33%	**33.33%**	20%	33.33%	25%
Text 5	4,532	157	12.5%	18.18%	**14.82%**	16.67%	9.09%	11.76%
Text 6	5,348	212	8.7%	18.18%	11.76%	20%	18.18%	**19.04%**
Text 7	1,841	47	100%	42.86%	**60%**	100%	14.29%	25%
Text 8	1,927	74	60%	33.33%	**42.86%**	100%	11.11%	20%
Text 9	1,789	53	75%	100%	**85.72%**	25%	16.67%	20%
Text 10	1,389	31	33.33%	20%	12.5%	100%	20%	**16.67%**
Text 11	2,309	81	30%	50%	**37.5%**	33.33%	16.67%	22.22%
Text 12	7,193	211	15.38%	16.25%	**8.88%**	33.33%	3.13%	5.72%
Text 13	6,097	305	20.59%	33.33%	**25.46%**	17.65%	14.29%	15.78%
Text 14	1,417	57	40%	33.33%	**36.36%**	100%	16.67%	28.58%
Text 15	3,195	79	40%	8%	13.34%	66.67%	8%	**14.28%**
Text 16	1,995	60	66.67%	28.57%	40%	57.14%	57.14%	**57.14%**
Text 17	558	16	33.33%	33.33%	33.33%	50%	66.67%	**57.14%**
Text 18	696	25	100%	37.5%	**54.54%**	40%	25%	30.76%
Text 19	678	26	33.33%	33.33%	33.33%	50%	66.67%	**57.14%**
Text 20	1,388	57	50%	66.67%	**57.14%**	100%	16.67%	28.58%
Text 21	3,127	110	62.5%	25%	**35.72%**	40%	10%	16%
Text 22	1,618	40	60%	75%	**66.66%**	100%	25%	40%

very good precision on such short texts (text 10 for example). - Enumerations. Text 6 for example, which is quite big, is a record of the government spokesman where he enumerates dealt subject during the weekly minister reunion. So it is basically an enumeration of different subjects with different vocabularies and no real transition between the different segments.

3   Conclusion

In this paper we presented strong evidences that finding text boundaries in a corpus of concatenated texts and finding topic segments inside a specific text are two different task that need (at least) two different approaches. As we already said in the introduction and in the first section, lexical cohesion based methods are more efficient at identifying entire texts in a corpus of concatenated texts than at finding topic boundaries inside texts. . On the opposite methods integrating syntactic, semantic and/or stylistic information seem to be more sensitive to small variation inside a text and are more appropriated when it come to find topic segments inside a text. So, developing methods specifically for one or another of these tasks could be a better approach than the current one consisting in considering the two tasks as one.

Judging these results we should also consider evaluation methods specifically designated for each task. If it is easy to create data set to evaluate methods that find texts boundaries inside a huge amount of concatenated texts. It is far more difficult to find data sets where inner topic segments are identified. Such corpus need at least one linguistic or domain expert to identify each potential topic boundaries, which is very time consuming even for a small amount of text. And one expert is probably not enough. Due to the subjectivity of such task, it is better to ask two groups of expert to generate the corpus. The first to propose boundaries and the second to validate. This would be far more time consuming and cost consuming than only one expert of course.

We were lucky to have the DEFT'06 corpus to test our method. But, topic boundaries, in this corpus, were identified by people managing the government Internet site. They are supposed to be political experts and to have the skills to find change of topics inside a political discourse. But are their boundaries all exact ? And a better question, are their choices the only right ones ? As we already said, topic based text segmentation is a subjective task as well as other natural language processing tasks like automatic summary for example. Maybe are we doing wrong by trying to evaluate these tasks on generated (automatically or by experts) data sets. We are envisaging other ways of evaluating these methods, by, for example, asking experts to evaluate the result of the automatic method and not to generate corpus.

Finally, we should notice the complementarity of both tasks and both approaches. If it is hard consider a fusion of both approaches, the development of an automatic process choosing between methods that concentrate on finding texts and methods that concentrate on finding inner topic segments could be of great help in a domain such as IR.

References

1. Azé, J., Heitz, T., Mela, A., Mezaour, A., Peinl, P., Roche, M.: Présentation de deft 2006 (defi fouille de textes). In: Proceedings of DEFT 2006, vol. 1, pp. 3–12 (2006)
2. Bestgen, Y., Piérard, S.: Comment évaluer les algorithmes de segmentation automatiques? essai de construction d'un matriel de référence. In: Proceedings of TALN 2006 (2006)
3. Chauché, J.: Un outil multidimensionnel de l'analyse du discours. In: Proceedings of Coling 1984, vol. 1, pp. 11–15 (1984)
4. Chauché, J., Prince, V.: Classifying texts through natural language parsing and semantic filtering. In: Proceedings of LTC 2003 (2007)
5. Chauché, J., Prince, V., Jaillet, S., Teisseire, M.: Classification automatique de textes partir de leur analyse syntaxico-sémantique. In: Proceedings of TALN 2003, 55–65 (2003)
6. Choi, F.Y.Y.: Advances in domain independent linear text segmentation. In: Proceedings of NAACL-2000, 26–33 (2000)
7. Choi, F.Y.Y., Wiemer-Hastings, P., Moore, J.: Latent semantic analysis for text segmentation. In: Proceedings of EMNLP, pp. 109–117 (2001)

8. Hearst, M.A.: Text-tilling: segmenting text into multi-paragraph subtopic passages. Computational Linguistics, 59–66 (1997)
9. Hearst, M.A., Plaunt, C.: Subtopic structuring for full-length document access. In: Proceedings of the ACM SIGIR-1993 International Conference On Research and Development in Information Retrieval, 59–68 (1993)
10. Helfman, J.: Similarity patterns in language. Visual Languages, 173–175 (1994)
11. Ji, X., Zha, H.: Domain-independant segmentation using anisotropic diffusion and dynamic programming. In: Proceedings of ACM/SIGIR Conference of Research and Developpement in Information Retrieval (2003)
12. Kan, M., Klavans, J.L., McKeown, K.R.: Linear segmentation and segment significance. In: Proceedings of WVLC-6, pp. 197–205 (1998)
13. Karatzas, D.: Text Segmentation in Web Images Using Color Perception and Topological Features. ECS Publications, UK (2003)
14. Kaszkiel, M., Zobel, J.: Passage retrieval revisited. In: Proceedings of theTwentieth International Conference on Research and Development in Information Access (ACMSIGIR), pp. 178–185 (1997)
15. Labadié, A.: Chauché: Segmentation thématique par calcul de distance sémantique. In: Proceedings of DEFT 2006, vol. 1, pp. 45–59 (2006)
16. Larousse: Thésaurus Larousse - des idées aux mots, des mots aux idées. Larousse, Paris (1992)
17. Lelu, A., C.M., Aubain, S.: Coopération multiniveau d'approches non-supervises et supervises pour la detection des ruptures thématiques dans les discours présidentiels franais. In: Proceedings of DEFT 2006(2006)
18. Llopis, F., Ferrandez, A., Vicedo, J.L.: G. In: Gelbukh, A. (ed.) CICLing 2002. LNCS, vol. 2276, pp. 373–380. Springer, Heidelberg (2002)
19. McCoy, K., Cheng, J.: Focus of attention: Constraining what can be said next. In: Paris, C., Swartout, W., Mann, W. (eds.) Natural Language Generation in Artificial Intelligence and Computational Linguistics (1991)
20. Morris, J., Hirst, G.: Lexical cohesion computed by thesaural relations as an indicator of the structure of text. Computational Linguistics 17, 20–48 (1991)
21. Ponte, J.M., Croft, W.B.: Text segmentation by topic. In: European Conference on Digital Libraries, pp. 113–125 (1997)
22. Prince, V., Labadié, A.: Text segmentation based on document understanding for information retrieval. In: Kedad, Z., Lammari, N., Métais, E., Meziane, F., Rezgui, Y. (eds.) NLDB 2007. LNCS, vol. 4592, pp. 295–304. Springer, Heidelberg (2007)
23. Reynar, J.C.: Topic Segmentation: Algorithms and Applications. Phd thesis, University of Pennsylvania (1998)
24. Roget, P.: Thesaurus of English Words and Phrases. Longman, London (1852)
25. Sitbon, L., Bellot, P.: Evaluation de méthodes de segmentation thématique linéaire non supervisés après adaptation au franais. In: Proceedings of TALN 2004 (2004)
26. Wu, Z., Tseng, G.: Chinese text segmentation for text retrieval: Achievements and problems. Journal of the American Society for Information Science 44, 532–542 (1993)
27. Yang, C.C., Li, K.W.: A heuristic method based on a statistical approach for chinese text segmentation. Journal of the American Society for Information Science and Technology 56, 1438–1447 (2005)

Tamil Question Classification Using Morpheme Features

S. Lakshmana Pandian and T.V. Geetha

Department of Computer Science & Engineering
Anna University, Chennai, India
lpandian72@yahoo.com, rctamil@annauniv.edu

Abstract. Question classification plays an important role in question answering systems. This paper presents the Conditional Random field (CRF) model based on Morpheme features for Tamil question classification. It is a process that analyzes a question and labels it based on its question type and expected answer type (EAT). The selected features are the morpheme parts of the question terms and its dependent terms. The main contribution in this work is in the way of selection of features for constructing CRF Model. They discriminates the position of expected answer type information with respect to question term's position. The CRF model to find out the phrase which contains the information about EAT is trained with tagged question corpus. The EAT is semantically derived by analyzing the phrase obtained from CRF engine using WordNet. The performance of this morpheme based CRF model is compared with the generic CRF engine.

Keywords: Classification, Machine Learning.

1 Introduction

Question Classification (QC) is an important component of Question Answering System (QAS). QC strives to match a question into one or more categories which are defined in terms of type of answer expected. The purpose of QC is to reduce a large number of answer candidates by filtering out the possible answer candidate for the type of question and the type of expected answer. Every question class places some semantic restriction on the type of answer required within intern helps in the location of the correct answer. QA systems depend on information retrieval technique for answer extraction. In this context, QC provides important clues for answer selection and extraction and hence a good QC system improves performance of the overall QA system. QC helps in minimizing search space by generating the appropriate queries to the information retrieval system.

One of the important issues to be decided for QC is the question/answer type taxonomy. There are a number of taxonomies that exists including flat and hierarchical taxonomies but they are different in size.

In this work, we use two level hierarchical answer type taxonomy having total of 50 answer type. We used Tamil questions corpus which has been derived by translating the TREC question corpus of 5500 questions. Tamil is a morphologically rich language and we exploit these morpheme feature variances and WordNet [4]

A. Ranta, B. Nordström (Eds.): GoTAL 2008, LNAI 5221, pp. 272–283, 2008.

semantics for the purpose of QC. A morpheme is defined as the smallest part of a language that can be regularly assigned a meaning.

This remaining part of this paper is organized as Section 2 describes the different approaches being implemented for QC. Section 3 describes taxonomies for question types. Section 4 explains our original work for Tamil QC. Section 5 describes the experiment conducted on our work for Question classification. Section 6 outlines the results. In Section 7, we conclude this work and its future work.

2   Related Work

There are basically two approaches to QC, one of which uses regular expression and hand written grammar rules to analyse the question to determine the answer type. Though hand written grammar rules have been used successfully for question classification, this approach is time consuming, that rules are often brittle, the number of answer handle is limited and it is difficult to extend the answer types to more specific types.

The other approach is the probabilistic techniques which includes machine learning and language modeling. This approach to QC tries to find out the probability of a question given a question class [8]. In this approach language model is created for each question class from a large corpus of question tagged with the question class. Various models like unigram and bigram are used to predict the class of given question. Pinto, in his work, he used Named Entity tag in addition to the words in the question for building the language model [8]. Wei Li combined unigram, bigram and language models with an absolute discount smoothing technique and a back off bigram model for QC [11].

The other important probabilistic approach of QC is machine learning technique. SVM has been used extensively for QC. Li & Roth have used SNoW learning architecture for classifying a question into one of 50 possible classes. They used two simple classifiers one for coarse and the other for fine classification. The features used by Snow for QC include words part-of-speech (POS) tags, chunks, Named Entities, head chunks and semantically related words [12]. Dell Zhang and Lee have used SVM for QC where bag of words and bag of n-grams are used as features. Here, the n-grams are word sequences represented as binary feature vector. Since QC is multiclass problem, one against one strategy has been used by them [3]. Vijay Krishnan et.al induced a Conditional Random Field (CRF) to identify informer spans and built a meta-classifier using a linear SVM on the CRF output [10].

In our work, CRF model has been used for classifying Tamil questions. The morpheme feature variance property of the morphologically rich Tamil language is the main role of this work.

3   Question Classification

Classifying questions into categories is a key task during question analysis, since it allows filtering out unrelated documents and applying more tuned extraction rules in the candidate sentences. To address this, we used a set of 50 fine categories. These categories are obtained from TREC corpus. Table 1 illustrates some of the categories currently used in our QA system for factoid type questions. Table 2 illustrates some of the categories currently used in our QA system for definitional type questions. Table 3 illustrates some of the categories currently used in our QA system for List type questions.

Table 1. Expected Answer Type category for factoid type

Coarse category	Fine Category
Abbreviation	Abb, exp
Entity	Animal ,body, color ,creative , currency, dis.med., event, food, Instrument, lang., letter, other, plant, Continued, Evaluation, Class, Product ,religion, sport, substance, Symbol, technique, term, vehicle, word
Human	Group, ind, title,
Location	city, country, mountain other, state,
Numeric	Date, count, money, period, volsize, other, speed, perc, code, dist, temp, ordinal, weight, Class, order, other, period, size

Table 2. Expected Answer Type category for Definitional type

Coarse category	Fine Category
Description	Definition, description, Manner, reason
Human	Description

Table 3. Expected Answer Type category for List type

Coarse category	Fine Category
Entity	Animal ,body,color ,creative , currency, dis.med., event, food Instrument, lang., letter, other, plant Continued, Evaluation, Class Product ,religion, sport, substance Symbol, technique, term, vehicle word
Human	Group, title,
Location	city, country, mountain other, state,

We have included yes or no questions and List type questions along with given translated question. The problem of classification is to predict a single class variable y given a vector of features $x = (x_1, x_2, \ldots, x_k)$. We classify the question into four main categories namely factoid type, yes or no type, definitional type or List type question. These questions are further classified into coarse categories and fine categories as shown in the corresponding tables.

4 The Proposed Question Classifier System

This work is organized as shown in the block diagram. The Morphological analyser is used for separating morpheme components of words. These morpheme components are used to compute the POS type of the word. The second phase is to chunk the phrases like verb phrase, noun phrase by exploiting CRF chunker. The third phase is to extract features which are used in the next phase called morpheme based CRF classifier to identify the phrase which contains the information about the required answer type. Then the phrase analyzer analyses the phrase for identification of answer type. This section is organized to explain the various phases in the form of sub–sections.

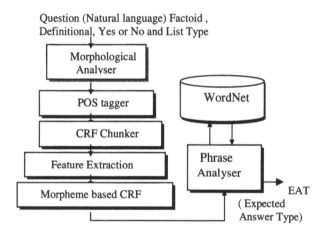

Fig. 1. Question type classification

4.1 Morphological Analyser (Atcharam)

The available Linguistic tools like 'Atcharam – Morphological Analyzer for Tamil' [1], is used as processing tools in the question analysis module. Morphological Analyzer is a tool used to identify every morpheme parts of a word. It breaks a word into its root word and associated morphemes. [1].

4.2 POS Tagger

Tamil is a morphologically rich language resulting in its relatively free word order characteristics. Normally most Tamil words take on more than one morphological suffix; often the number of suffixes is 3 with the maximum going up to 13. The role of the sequence of the morphological suffixes attached to a word in determining the part-of-speech tag is an interesting property of Tamil language. In this work we have identified 79 morpheme components, which can combine to form about 2000 possible combination of integrated suffixes. Two basic parts of speech namely noun and verb are mutually distinguished by their grammatical inflections. In Tamil, noun grammatically marks number and cases. Tamil nouns basically take on eight cases. The normal morphological derivatives of Tamil nouns are as follows

Root Noun + [Plural Marker]+[Oblique]+[Case Marker]

The normal morphological derivative of Tamil Verb is as follows

Root Verb + [Tense Marker] + [Verbal Participle Suffix] + [Auxiliary verb] $^{(1 \text{ to } 4)}$ + [Tense Marker] + [Person, Number, Gender]

In addition, adjective, adverb, pronoun, postposition are also some root words that take suffixes. In this work, we have used a tagged corpus of 4,70,910 words which have been tagged with 35 POS categories in a semi automatic manner using an available morphological analyzer [5] which separates root word and all morpheme components. It also provides the type of root word using lexicon. The value 1 to 4 indicated as power denotes maximum 4 auxiliary can occur for a single verb.

4.3 CRF Chunker

In partially free word order language, the order of words in a single phrase is a sequential one. In this characteristic point of view, the features to be considered in designing a CRF model are its POS type, Last end morpheme component and Previous to last end morpheme component of a word. The size of the window is 3 words.

The centre word of the window is considered as zeroth position. The sequence from left to right of 3 words snippet is -1 0 1. The zeroth position word are considered to be chunk tagged as B, I or O .The features of designed language specific CRF model for chunking are shown in table 4.

Table 4. The List of features for Chunking

The state features are $POS(-1), POS(0), POS(1), E_{l-1}(-1), E_{l-1}(0), E_{l-1}(1), E_l(-1), E_l(0), E_l(1)$ **The transition features** $POS(-1)/POS(0), POS(0)/POS(1), \, , E_{l-1}(-1)/E_{l-1}(0), E_{l-1}(0)/E_{l-1}(1), E_l(-1)/E_l(0), E_l(0)/E_l(1), POS(-1)/POS(0)/POS(1), E_{l-1}(-1)/E_{l-1}(0)/E_{l-1}(1)$ and $E_l(-1)/E_l(0))/P(E_l(1)$

This CRF model has trained by a large tagged corpus with the required features mentioned in this Model. The trained CRF model is used for separating the phrases in the question.

4.4 Feature Extraction

The combinations of morphemes of a word include more information for discriminating the required information for computing question type. This property leads us to exploit the morpheme components for the construction of this morpheme based CRF model. The following features are extracted and arranged in sequence as follows

Table 5. The List of features for Morpheme based CRF model

Word (Qw-1)	Root_type(Qw-1)	M_end (QW-1)
Word (Qw)	Root_type (Qw)	M_ end (QW)
Word (Qw+1)	Root_type(Qw+1)	M_end (QW+1)

In this table QW denotes the word position of the question terms in the given question. QW-1 denotes previous word to the question term . Similarly, QW+1 denotes next word of question term. The function called Word provides the term of the question in the corresponding position specified by its parameter. The Root_type function provides the type of the root component of the word at the specified position. M_end provides the lost morpheme part of the word in the corresponding position. Here is the case we consider the question term, previous and next word of the question term for features of morpheme based CRF model.

4.5 Model Representation

Conditional Random Fields (CRF). Conditional random fields (CRFs) are undirected graphical models developed for labeling sequence data [6]. CRFs directly model $p(x \mid z)$, the *conditional* distribution over the hidden variables x given observations z. This model is different from generative models such as Hidden Markov Models or Markov Random Fields, which apply Bayes rule to infer hidden states [9]. CRFs can handle arbitrary dependencies between the observations z, which gives them substantial flexibility in using high-dimensional feature vectors.

The nodes in a CRF represent hidden states, denoted $x = < x_1, x_2 \ldots x_n >$, and data, denoted z. The nodes x_i, along with the connectivity structure represented by the undirected edges between them, define the conditional distribution $p(x \mid z)$ over the hidden states x. Let C be the set of cliques (fully connected subsets) in the graph of a CRF. Then, a CRF factorizes the conditional distribution into a product of *clique potentials* $\phi_c(z, x_c)$, where every c ε C is a clique in the graph and z and x_c are the observed data and the hidden nodes in the clique c, respectively. Clique potentials are functions that map variable configurations to non-negative numbers. Intuitively, a potential captures the "compatibility" among the variables in the clique: the larger the potential value, the more likely the configuration.

Using clique potentials, the conditional distribution over hidden states is written as

$$p(x \mid z) \;=\; \frac{1}{Z(z)} \prod_{c \in C} \phi_c(z, x_c) \tag{1}$$

where $Z(z) = \sum_{x} \prod_{c \in C} \phi_c(z, x_c)$ is the normalizing partition function. The computation of this partition function can be exponential in the size of x. Hence, exact inference is possible for a limited class of CRF models only. Potentials $\phi_c(z, x_c)$ are described by log-linear combinations of *feature functions* f_c i.e.,

$$\phi_c(z, x_c) = \exp(w_c^T \cdot f_c(z, x_c)) \tag{2}$$

Where w_c^T is a weight vector, and $f_c(z, x_c)$ is a function that extracts a vector of features from the variable values. Using feature functions, we rewrite the conditional distribution (1) as

$$p(x \mid z) = \frac{1}{Z(z)} \exp\left\{ \sum_{c \in C} w_c^T \cdot f_c(z, x_c) \right\} \tag{3}$$

Generic CRF. The generic CRF model is designed by the words state features and transition features by considering the sequence of 3 words by arranging the question term in center position.

Table 6. List of Features for Generic CRF Model

State features	Transition features
Word (Qw-1), Pos(Qw-1)	Word (Qw)/ Word (Qw-1),
Word (Qw), Pos(Qw)	Word(Qw+1)/ Word (Qw),
Word (Qw+1), Pos(Qw-1)	POS(Qw)/POS(Qw-1),
	POS(Qw+1)/ POS (Qw)

The straight lines represent the state features and the curved lines represent the transition features. The center Word is the position of question term of question. The Position at which the term contains the EAT information is labeled as -1, 0, 1. The label 0 refers the position of question term as reference. Label -1 denotes the previous term of the question term and 1 refers the next term of question term.

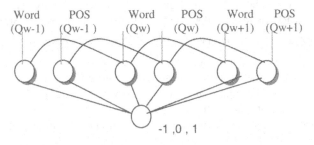

Fig. 2. Graphical Representation of Generic CRF model

Morpheme Based CRF. The question statement is preprocessed so as to arrange the features which discriminate the position of expected answer type information with respect to question terms position. The main contribution of this work is the way of selection of features for constructing CRF Model. The list of features in the Cliques considered as unigram.

Table 7. List of Features for Morpheme Based CRF Model

State Features	Transition features
Word (Qw-1), Root_type (Qw-1), end(QW-1),Word (Qw), Root_type (Qw), end (QW) Word (Qw+1), Root_type(Qw+1), end(QW+1),End(Qw-1)/Root(Qw-1) End(Qw)/Root(Qw) End(Qw+1)/Root(Qw+1)	End(Qw)/ End(Qw-1) End(Qw+1)/ End(Qw)

The following graph explains the totals features along with its position in the question. The centre three nodes correspond to Word, root and Morpheme end of the question word. The left side three nodes correspond to Word, root and Morpheme end of the previous word of question word and the right side three nodes correspond to Word, root and Morpheme end of the next word of question word. The horizontal edges represent the conditional features and the slanting edges represent individual features.

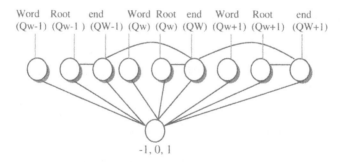

Fig.3. Graphical Representation of Morpheme based CRF model

4.6 Phrase Analyser

The phrase chunk which incurred the EAT information is further analysed to compute the fine category of EAT with the help of Tamil WordNet. Tamil WordNet is the network of lexical relations between lexical items in Tamil. Lexical items are related to one another in the hierarchical dimension as taxonomies (which show hyponymy-hypernymy and meronymy-holonymy relationship) and non-hierarchical dimension as opposites (which include complementaries, antonyms, antipodals, counterparts, reversives and converses) and synonyms. Also words are related to one another due to their derivational as well as collocational meaning. Componential analysis which studies meanings of lexical items in terms of meaning components or features can help to capture the above mentioned net work of relations in a more systematic way [10].

If the phrase chunk is a noun phrase, the hypernym of head term of the phrase chunk is the most probable expected answer type. On the other hand, the phase chunk is as Verbal phrase the event which imply the verb is the expected answer type. When the Question phrase implied as the EAT information term, the rule is formed by the lexical term which denote question word itself categories the expected answer type.

5 Experiment

The question corpus for evaluating this work is prepared by translating the TREC question corpus with 5452 questions into Tamil. In addition that we formulate 300 questions for yes or No type questions and 500 list type questions manually. The total question corpus is then tagged with POS tagger. The POS tagged corpus is then tagged by Phrase Chunker as next level tagging. The tagged corpus is manually analyzed and further tagged the position of phrase in which the expected answer type information inhered. From the tagged corpus, 5252 questions are selected in such a way that they uniformly distributed the types of questions for the CRF model training. The remaining 1000 questions which are not included in the training are used for testing. Table 8 shows an example for various processes of question classification.

Table 8. Example for a Tamil question

SL. No	Question	Translation	Word	Root type		end
1	இந்தியாவின் தேசிய பறவை எது?	What is the national bird of India?	இந்தியா	adjective	இன்	-3
			தேசிய	adjective	null	-2
			பறவை	noun	null	-1
			எது	quesword	null	0
			?	ques symbol	null	1

Position of Expected answer type -1   ie பறவை (bird)

The word பறவை is in the phrase chunk of Noun Phrase
இந்தியாவின் தேசிய பறவை (National animal of India)

The expected answer type is 'bird'

The question focus is இந்திய தேசிய பறவை (National animal of India)

This question category is <Factiod, entity, bird>

6   Results and Evaluation

The results are tabulated in table 9 and table 10 for each question types by conducting test on QC with generic CRF model and QC with Morpheme based CRF model respectively.

Table 9. QC with generic CRF model

Question↓ Answer →	No of Question	Correct	Wrong	Inexact	Accuracy
Fact	678	442	122	114	65.19
List	134	98	15	21	73.13
Definitional	126	93	19	14	73.81
Yes or No	62	43	11	8	69.35
Total	1000	676	167	157	67.60

Table 10. QC with morpheme based CRF model

Question ↓ Answer →	No of Question	Correct	Wrong	Inexact	Accuracy
Fact	678	491	92	95	72.41
List	134	120	5	9	89.55
Definitional	126	108	8	10	85.71
Yes or No	62	54	6	2	87.09
Total	1000	773	111	116	77.30

Table 11. Computation for Row means and Grand means

	Fact	List	Defni	Y or N	Row totals	Row means
Generic CRF	65.19	73.13	73.81	69.35	281.48	70.37
Morpheme Based CRF	72.41	89.55	85.71	87.09	334.76	83.69
Column Total	137.60	162.68	159.52	156.44	Grand total =616.24	
Column Means	68.8	81.34	79.76	78.22	Grand mean =77.03	

$V_r = 4 [(70.37\text{-}77.03)^2 + (83.69\text{-}77.03)^2] = 354.84$

$V_c = 2 [(68.80\text{-}77.03)^2 + (81.34\text{-}77.03)^2 + (79.76\text{-}77.03)^2 + (78.22\text{-}77.03)^2] = 190.35$

$V = [(65.19\text{-}77.03)^2 + (73.13\text{-}77.03)^2 + (73.81\text{-}77.03)^2 + (69.35\text{-}77.03)^2 + (72.41\text{-}77.03)^2 +$
$\quad (89.55\text{-}77.03)^2 + (85.71\text{-}77.03)^2 + (87.09\text{-}77.03)^2] = 579.386$

$V_e = V - V_r - V_c$
$\quad = 34.196$

Table 12. Analysis of Variance

Variation	Degree of Freedom	Mean Square	F
V_r =354.84	1	354.84	31.154 df :1,3
V_c = 190.35	3	63.45	5.57 df:3,3
V_e= 34.196	3	11.39	
V = 579.386	7		

The results are analysed by two factor experiments. Using the long method, test at the 0.05 level of significance whether there is a significant difference in identifying expected answer type due to Generic and Morpheme based CRF.

Hypothesis: both models accuracy are same

At the 0.05 level of significance with 1, 3 degrees of freedom, $F_{0.95}$=10.1. Then, since 31.154 > 10.1, we can reject the hypothesis that the row means are equal and conclude that at the 0.05 level there is significant deference in performance of Morpheme based CRF model.

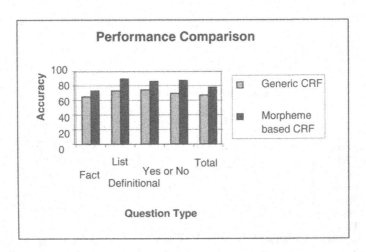

Fig. 4. Pictorial representation of performance comparison

7 Conclusion

This paper presents a CRF model for Tamil QC. The morpheme variants of morphologically rich type of language embed much information to predict the dependency of terms. This concept is a crux idea for morphologically rich type natural language processing. Even though the morpheme component of the words pose the dominant vital part, The deep semantic of root word cannot not be predicted by that components. To come across these difficulties the lexical resource like WordNet is very useful. In this work the expected answer type can be exposed for the given question. But our assumption is that the previous or next phrase of the question term is the phrase where the question type is inhered. This assumption is precise for many other natural languages as for as the question statements are concerned. This work is to be extended for Question focus identification in future.

References

1. Anandan, P., Saravanan, K., Parthasarathi, R., Geetha, T.V.: Morphological Analyzer for Tamil. In: International Conference On Natural language processing (2002)
2. Lee, C., Wang, J.-H., Kim, H.-J., Jang, M.-G.: Extracting Template for Knowledge-based Question- Answering Using Conditional Random Fields. In: ACM SIGIR Workshop on Mathematical/Formal Methods in Information Retrieval MF/IR 2005 Salvador, Brazil, August 15-19 (2005)
3. Zhang, D., Lee, W.S.: Question Classification using Support Vector Machines. In: 26th annual international ACM SIGIR conference on Research and development in information retrieval, Toronto, Canada (2003)
4. Devi Poongulhali, P., Kavitha Noel, N., Preeda Lakshmi, R., Manavazhahan, A., Geetha, T.V.: Tamil WordNet 1st International Global Wordnet Conference, Jan. 21-25, 2002. CIIL, Mysore (2002)
5. Graesser, A.C., Person, N.K.: Question asking during tutoring. American Educational Research Journal 31, 104–137 (1994)
6. Lafferty, J., McCallum, A., Pereira, F.: Conditional random fields: Probabilistic models for segmenting and labeling sequence data. In: Proc. of the International Conference on Machine Learning (ICML) (2001)
7. Xin, L., Xuan-Jing, H., Li-de, W.: Question Classification by Ensemble Learning. IJCSNS International Journal of Computer Science and Network Security 6(3) (2006)
8. Pinto, D., Branstein, M., Coleman, R., King, M., Li, W., Wei, X., Croft, W.B.: QuASM: A System for Question Answering Using Semi-Structured Data. In: Proceedings of the JCDL 2002 Joint Conference on Digital Libraries (2002)
9. Rabiner, L.R.: A tutorial on hidden Markov models and selected applications in speech recognition. In: Proceedings of the IEEE. IEEE, Los Alamitos (1989); IEEE Log Number 8825949
10. Krishnan, V., Das, S., Chakrabarti, S.: Enhanced Answer Type Inference from Questions using Sequential Models. In: Proceedings of the Conference on Human Language Technology and Empirical Methods in Natural Language Processing, Vancouver, British Columbia, Canada, October 6-8,2005, pp. 315–322 (2005)
11. Li, W.: Question Classification Using Language Modeling, `citeseer.ist.psu.edu/576076.html`
12. Li Dan Roth, X.: Learning Question Classifiers International Conference on Computational Linguistics (COLING 2002), Taipei, Taiwan, 24 August (2002)

Analogical Translation of Medical Words in Different Languages

Philippe Langlais[1], François Yvon[2], and Pierre Zweigenbaum[2]

[1] Université de Montréal, Dept I.R.O., Québec, H3C 3J7 Canada
[2] CNRS, LIMSI, Orsay, F-91403 France
`felipe@iro.umontreal.ca, yvon@limsi.fr, pz@limsi.fr`

Abstract. Term translation has become a recurring need in many domains. This creates an interest for robust methods which can translate words in various languages. We propose a novel, analogy-based method to generate word translations. It relies on a partial bilingual lexicon and solves bilingual analogical equations to create candidate translations. We evaluate our approach on medical terms. To study the robustness of the method, we evaluate it on a series of datasets taken from different language groups and using different scripts. We investigate to which extend the approach can cope directly with multiword terms, and study its dependency to the size of the training set.

1 Introduction

New words are coined all the time, especially in technical domains. Among others, medicine is well-known for its propension to create new words to describe new diseases (*cardiomyopathy perivesiculitis*), interventions (*cystectomy*), microorganisms (*autoantibodies*), substances (*thiogalactosides*), etc. Many of these are named with complex words, built from existing morphemes: neoclassical compounds are probably the most characteristic type, but other word formation devices are also productive, *e.g.*, words derived from person names (*Wolffian*). The previous sentences list examples in English, but the same observation applies to a number of other languages [1,2], seemingly with a great degree of parallelism. For instance, one finds in Swedish: *tiogalaktosider* (*thiogalactosides*); Finnish: *kystektomia* (*cholecystectomy*); Russian: *аутоантитела* (*autoantibodies*); French: *périvésiculite* (*perivesiculitis*).

The question we address in this paper is then: are medical word formation devices parallel enough in different languages for it to be possible to guess the translation of a new word? For instance, given knowledge of a number of medical words in a source language L_S and their translations in a target language L_T, can one *generate* the translation w_T in L_T of an unseen word w_S in L_S?

This problem has been addressed by Schulz and colleagues [3], who wrote rules to *generate* words in Spanish from Portuguese medical words. Claveau [4] went further by using machine learning techniques to learn transducers from examples to generate French words from English medical words (and the reverse). These methods can be called "generative" as they build new target words from

A. Ranta, B. Nordström (Eds.): GoTAL 2008, LNAI 5221, pp. 284–295, 2008.
© Springer-Verlag Berlin Heidelberg 2008

previously unseen source words. They can rely on human expertise [3] or on machine learning methods [4].

Quite different, non-generative methods can also be used to *identify* word translations in parallel corpora [5] if such corpora can be found which contain the desired source words (and their translations). These word-alignment methods take advantage of the prior existence of translations, but are intrinsically limited by the availability of parallel corpora. They can be called "identification-based" methods, as they must be provided with data which contain the solutions to the problem (the target translations). Comparable corpora can also be used when parallel corpora are scarce (*e.g.*, [6]), but they make the task of translation identification more difficult and error-prone.

Both kinds of methods can be helped if a morphological analyzer of the source and/or target languages is available [7,8]: in that case, complex source words can be decomposed and the generation or identification of target translations is reduced to that of correspondences between component morphemes. However, it requires a substantial human investment to obtain a precise morphological analysis of derived and compound words and to specify the mapping between component morphemes in source and target languages (even though it may be partially helped by machine learning methods, *e.g.*, [9]).

The present work explores the use of a different generative method: analogical learning [10,11,12]. As the above-mentioned methods of this type [4] it is trained on an initial bilingual lexicon and relies on the formal similarity of medical words in some languages to propose new translations; in contrast to external methods, it can generate translations for unseen words. In this paper, we examine how this kind of method performs on medical words. We evaluate it on a series of datasets and compare it to an identification-based, non-generative method based on edit-distance.

This paper is organized as follows. We first present the datasets used for testing the method. We introduce the principles of analogical learning on which our system relies. We describe a series of evaluations which test different features of the datasets. We discuss their respective results, which show that the method performs as well on the different language and script pairs, in different translation directions, on both uni- and multi-terms, but depends to some extent on the size of the training set.

2   Datasets

We ran our experiments with several goals in mind. First, we wanted to check whether analogical learning is better suited for specific language pairs. Second, we were interested in observing whether it is more suited to translate into a morphologic rich language (such as Finnish) or the other way round. Third, we wanted to appreciate whether analogical learning is equally efficient when translating multiterms (terms with several words) as when translating uniterms. Last, we also wanted to gauge how important the quantity of training material is to the overall approach.

The UMLS Metathesaurus [13] is a large repository of medical terminologies, with over 1.5 million distinct concepts and over 5 million distinct terms in 17 languages (version 2008AA, March 2008).[1] A given concept may be labelled with terms from different languages. It is therefore a very interesting resource to extract bilingual medical lexicons. A difficulty however is that terms which label the same concept in different languages are not always linguistically translations of each other: they may correspond to different ways of referring to the same entity. For instance, UMLS concept C0027051 is labelled with *Myocardial infarction, Heart attack, Infarto miocardico, Infarto del Miocardio, Ataque al corazon,* among a total of 105 distinct strings; each term is tagged with its language, but there is no systematic tagging of which term is a translation of which other term. Therefore, we designed a series of filters to extract sets of bilingual term pairs from the UMLS Metathesaurus. Depending on the source terminologies, datasets of different sizes could be obtained.

Small size datasets: MeSH thesaurus. The Medical Subject Headings (MeSH) is the thesaurus used by the US National Library of Medicine to index the biomedical scientific literature in the MEDLINE database.[2] Its preferred terms are called "Main Headings" (synonym terms are called "Entry Terms"). We collected pairs of source and target Main Headings (TTY[3] = 'MH') with the same MeSH identifiers (SDUI). We did not collect pairs of entry terms because we do not know how to pair actual translations among the possibly numerous entry terms of a given main heading.

Russian MeSH is normally written in Cyrillic, but some terms are simply English terms written in uppercase Latin script (e.g., ACHROMOBACTER for English Achromobacter). We filtered out these terms (1,366), retaining only Cyrillic Russian MeSH terms (23,394).

Medium size datasets: MedDRA thesaurus. The Medical Drug Regulatory Activities thesaurus (MedDRA) is intended to describe adverse effects of drugs and other related terms. It contains different term types: high-level group terms (TTY = 'HG', 332 terms in English or Spanish), hierarchical terms (TTY = 'HT', 1682 terms) and lower-level terms (TTY = 'LT', 56580 terms). MedDRA also has preferred terms (TTY = 'PT', 17867 terms). We collected pairs of source and target terms of the same types (TTY = 'MH') with the same MedDRA identifiers (SDUI).

Large size dataset: SNOMED CT nomenclature
The Systematic Nomenclature of Medicine (SNOMED CT) has a large coverage of signs and symptoms, but also of anatomy, diseases and other medical concepts.

---

[1] The UMLS can be obtained at no cost from the National Library of Medicine at `http://www.nlm.nih.gov/research/umls/`

[2] The MeSH thesaurus and its translations are included in the UMLS Metathesaurus. Independently from the UMLS, the MeSH can also be browsed online at `http://www.nlm.nih.gov/mesh/MBrowser.html`. The French-English bilingual version can be seen at `http://ist.inserm.fr/basismesh/mesh.html` or at `http://www.chu-rouen.fr/ssf/arborescences.html`

[3] In the UMLS Metathesaurus tables, the TTY field codes the type of the term, with values depending on the source terminology.

SNOMED CT has full-form descriptor terms (TTY = 'FN', 311,313 terms in English / 310,311 in Spanish), preferred terms (TTY = 'PT', 311,313 / 310,311), synonymous terms (TTY = 'SY', 141,474 / 102,929). As in MeSH, we required that only preferred terms should appear in term pairs.

Data preparation. In each source, each word was lowercased, and pairs of identical words were discarded. Table 1 shows the number of terms for each source (column 2, *All terms*). We also prepared for each source its subset consisting of uniterms (terms composed of exactly one word, i.e., with no space) made only of alphabetic characters and possibly dashes, containing at least one lowercase character (column 3 of Table 1). It can be seen that MedDRA and SNOMED have a very small proportion of uniterms.

Table 1. Data sources: bilingual term lists. EN = English, FI = Finnish, FR = French, RU = Russian, SP = Spanish, SW = Swedish.

Dataset	All terms	Uniterms
mesh-SW-EN	19090	5928
mesh-FR-EN	19230	5091
mesh-SP-EN	21021	6240
mesh-FI-EN	21787	7013
mesh-RU-EN	23394	7842
meddra-SP-EN	67523	3598
snomedct-SP-EN	284255	10921

3   Analogical Learning

An *analogical proportion* is a relation between four items $[x : y = z : t]$ where x is to y what z is to t in a sense to be specified (see Lepage [10] or Stroppa and Yvon [11] for more detail). Here, formal relations between strings of characters are considered, *e.g.*, $[aortotomy : aortitis = spondylotomy : spondylitis]$. An *analogical equation* is an analogical proportion where an item is unknown, *e.g.*, $[x : y = z :?]$. Stroppa and Yvon [11] propose a method to solve analogical equations, *i.e.*, to generate the missing fourth item. Complex objects may also be considered in an analogical proportion, *e.g.*, pairs of words of the form (*source, target*) where *target* is the translation of *source* (these are entries in an existing bilingual lexicon). Given such an object with a missing part (*e.g.*, missing *target*), *analogical inference* can predict it by solving analogical equations. It proceeds in three steps:

(i) collecting triplets of word pairs whose first elements define with *source* an analogy;

(ii) solving the analogical equations between the corresponding second elements;

(iii) selecting the best candidate among these solutions.

Let us illustrate this with the word pair (*spondylitis, ?*) where we want to find as second term the French translation of *spondylitis*. The following analogical proportions are identified in (i): that written above, [*adenomalacia : adenitis = spondylomalacia : spondylitis*], [*arthropathy : arthritis = spondylopathy : spondylitis*], etc., where (*adenomalacia, adénomalacie*), (*adenitis, adénite*), (*spondylomalacia, spondylomalacie*), etc., are in our bilingual lexicon, but not (*spondylitis, ?*). Analogical equations such as [*adénomalacie : adénite = spondylomalacie : ?*] are thereby formed and solved in (ii), producing solutions among which *spondylite* (the correct translation). The same solution may be generated through multiple equations, therefore the frequency of each solution can be used to rank the solutions generated in (iii).

The main difficulties in this method stem from the very large number of analogical proportions that must be considered in (i) (it is cubic in the number of input objects), and have been addressed by sampling and by using suitable data structures.

4   Experiments

4.1   Experimental Setup

For each experimental condition, we computed the following measures [14]:

Coverage: The proportion of input words for which the system can generate translations. If N_t words receive translations among N, coverage is defined as $\frac{N_t}{N}$.

Precision: Among the N_t words for which the system proposes an answer, precision is the proportion of those for which a correct translation is output. The system proposes a ranked list of translations for each input word. Depending on the number of output translations k that one is willing to examine, a correct translation will be output for N_k input words. Precision at rank k is thus defined as $P_k = \frac{N_k}{N_t}$.

Recall: Is the proportion of the N input words for which a correct translation is output. Recall at rank k is defined as $R_k = \frac{N_k}{N}$.

Edit-distance [15] computes a distance between two words based on their common and distinct characters. Since in our setting, source and target words are often formally similar, given a list of potential target words, a candidate translation of an input word is the target word which is closest to it in terms of edit-distance. An ideal situation for this method is one where all correct translations are included in the list of potential target words. We built such a list by using the target part of each of our input bilingual lexicons, an extremely favorable situation for this method.

To study the applicability of the method to any medical term, not only those made of a single word (uniterms), we tested the methods both using the whole bilingual term lists and using their subsets consisting of only uniterms.

4.2   Results

The algorithm was applied to translate the different test sets, each consisting of a random 10% split of the prepared source bilingual term lists searching analogies (step i) in the SEARCH set, solving the resulting analogical equations (step ii) then ranking solutions according to frequency (step iii).

Analogy. Table 2 shows the coverage, precision and recall obtained on all types of terms from each language to English, then the same data for some of the reverse language pairs. P_1 and R_1 stand for precision and recall at rank 1, *i.e.*, when looking at the top candidate translation proposed by the algorithm. P_{25} and R_{25} refer to precision and recall at rank 25: this provides an idea of whether using a classifier to rerank candidate translations could find the correct translation among the top ones proposed by the present simple frequency ordering. Similar data is also displayed for uniterms only in Table 3.

Table 2. Generating translations through analogy for all types of terms. Coverage, precision and recall are shown as percentages. Correct is the percentage of terms that receive a reference translation by analogy. Because of the huge sizes of the full MedDRA and SNOMED terminologies, tests were only performed on a subset of the test material. However 90% of the whole terminologies were used to build analogies.

Dataset	Test	Coverage	Correct	P_1	R_1	P_{25}	R_{25}
All types of terms, Language X to English.							
mesh-FI-EN	2178	44.3	32.5	38.3	17.0	63.7	28.2
mesh-FR-EN	1923	38.2	29.5	45.5	17.4	69.3	26.5
mesh-RU-EN	2340	40.0	30.8	49.2	19.7	69.2	27.6
mesh-SP-EN	2102	43.3	35.1	50.5	21.9	73.1	31.6
mesh-SW-EN	1907	44.2	33.6	44.6	19.7	68.2	30.2
meddra-SP-EN	1589	73.4	62.9	19.0	13.9	53.4	39.2
snomedct-SP-EN	2000	60.1	49.0	35.0	21.1	62.9	37.8
All types of terms, English to Language X							
mesh-FI-EN	2178	46.5	31.7	34.0	15.8	54.7	25.4
mesh-FR-EN	1923	42.6	27.9	34.1	14.5	56.7	24.1
mesh-RU-EN	2340	46.7	33.4	36.8	17.2	60.7	28.3
mesh-SP-EN	2102	48.1	40.9	19.6	64.2	30.9	36.3
mesh-SW-EN	1909	43.8	31.9	38.0	16.7	64.2	28.1
meddra-SP-EN	1644	79.7	60.3	20.1	16.0	46.0	36.7
snomedct-SP-EN	1806	68.5	48.8	20.3	13.9	45.6	31.3

Edit-distance. Table 4 provides similar information collected with the edit-distance method. To complement the investigation of edit-distance, we observed that uniterms and their translations in close languages (such as French and English or Spanish and English) are very similar (less than 3 edit-operations on average). Differences can be substantial for more distant language pairs (such as Finnish and Swedish into/from English). Of course, for languages that do not share the same alphabet, terms differ drastically, which plugs edit-distance based

Table 3. Generating translations through analogy for uniterms

Dataset	Test	Coverage	Correct	P_1	R_1	P_{25}	R_{25}
Uniterms, Language X to English							
mesh-FI-EN	701	44.2	30.4	49.0	21.7	65.5	29.0
mesh-FR-EN	509	34.4	23.0	46.3	15.9	63.4	21.8
mesh-RU-EN	784	48.6	32.1	38.1	18.5	61.7	30.0
mesh-SP-EN	624	46.0	29.8	42.5	19.6	60.6	27.9
mesh-SW-EN	592	41.0	29.1	46.1	18.9	64.2	26.4
meddra-SP-EN	361	50.8	41.7	48.5	24.6	77.3	39.3
snomedct-SP-EN	1094	57.8	34.6	34.6	20.0	54.8	31.7
Uniterms, Language English to X.							
mesh-FI-EN	701	42.8	29.7	44.3	19.0	63.7	27.2
mesh-FR-EN	509	39.1	25.1	46.2	18.1	61.3	24.0
mesh-RU-EN	784	47.1	33.0	44.4	20.9	67.2	31.6
mesh-SP-EN	624	39.7	28.0	44.0	17.5	66.1	26.3
mesh-SW-EN	592	40.9	28.4	45.0	18.4	64.5	26.4
meddra-SP-EN	359	56.3	45.7	33.2	18.7	63.4	35.7
snomed-SP-EN	1094	56.6	34.2	33.1	18.7	55.6	31.5

approaches. In some exceptional instances though, the correct match may happen to be found; for instance, the unique case in mesh-RU-EN uniterms where edit-distance provides the correct translation is инъ-янъ (*yin-yang*), where инъ-янъ is the only Russian term in the MeSH thesaurus made of two sequences of three letters separated by a hyphen.

Multi-terms and their translations are much less correlated in terms of edit-distance. We computed that an average of 8 to 12 edit-operations distinguish multi-terms from their translations in the different language pairs that share the same alphabet. The SNOMED and MedDRA tasks (all terms) involve a more important deviation of the source terms and their translations. Therefore, we can expect edit-distance variants to perform very badly on these tasks. Besides,

Table 4. Identifying translations through edit-distance for the Language X to English translation direction. As edit distance always proposes candidate translations, its coverage is always 100% and $P = R$, so we simplify the table accordingly and only show values for precision at ranks 1 and 25.

Test	P_1	P_{25}	P_1	P_{25}
	all terms		uniterms	
mesh-SW-EN	33.8	37.8	70.0	74.8
mesh-FR-EN	71.8	77.1	84.6	89.6
mesh-SP-EN	81.5	89.1	85.8	89.7
mesh-FI-EN	33.6	38.0	71.2	76.8
mesh-RU-EN	1.0	1.1	0.1	0.8
snomedct-SP-EN	4.1	5.3	83.8	91.4
meddra-SP-EN	4.4	4.4	75.2	82.6

as underlined earlier, the proportion of (easier-to-handle) uniterms in these two large terminologies is much lower.

5 Discussion

Examples of successful analogies are shown in Table 5. Example 1 (fr-en) shows how a translation where a word ending is involved (*-ie* / *-ia*) leverages an example with a prefix switch (*exo-* ↦ *ecto-*), itself licensed by another word pair (*exosquelette* ↦ *ectosquelette*). This translation is indeed easy to find by edit-distance. The rest of those listed in Table 5 could not be found by edit-distance in our experiments. Example 2 (fi-en) pairs two formally unrelated words, *syöpägeenit* and *oncogenes*. Example 3 (fi-en) shows how an analogy on Finnish uniterms is parallelled by an analogy on English multiterms. In example 4 (fi-en), English terms involve commas and different word orders in analogy terms: *legislation, drug vs drug industry*. Example 5 (fi-en) has a hyphen and different word orders in Finnish and English. This example contains a digit, as does a rough 7% of the test terms in our dataset. Note that we do not treat digits in any specific way. Example 6 (fi-en) illustrates that different analogies can support the same translation.

Influence of parameters. The results do not evidence a strong influence of the language pair on analogical translation, whereas edit-distance is hindered by different scripts (Cyrillic) and (to a lesser extent) by more distant languages (Swedish, Finnish). This can be explained by several factors. A first factor is linked with the analogy method, which does not rely on a comparison of the source and target terms. A second factor may come from the chosen domain, medicine, where a part of the vocabulary is built in a more or less systematic way. A third factor may come from the fact that most of the terms in our international terminologies are translations of an initial version, generally in English.

Table 5. Example analogies supporting correct translations

	source/target	triplets for analogical equations
1	exocardie	<ectosquelette;ectocardie;exosquelette>
	exocardia	<ectoskeleton;ectocardia;exoskeleton>
2	syöpägeenit	<kasviproteiinit;syöpägeeniproteiinit;kasvit>
	oncogenes	<plant proteins;plants;oncogene proteins>
3	otsaontelo	<poskiontelotulehdus;poskiontelo;otsaontelotulehdus>
	frontal sinus	<maxillary sinusitis;frontal sinusitis;maxillary sinus>
4	elintarviketeollisuus	<lääkelainsäädäntö;elintarvikelainsäädäntö;lääketeollisuus>
	food industry	<legislation, drug;drug industry;legislation, food>
5	epha5-reseptori	<akvaporiini 1;akvaporiini 5;epha1-reseptori>
	receptor, epha5	<aquaporin 1;receptor, epha1;aquaporin 5>
6	epha5-reseptori	<alfa6beeta1-integriini;alfa5beeta1-integriini;epha6-reseptori>
	receptor, epha5	<integrin alpha6beta1;receptor, epha6;integrin alpha5beta1>

The translation direction has an impact on precision for some of the language pairs. For MeSH (all terms), precision is better when translating into English than the reverse. For MeSH uniterms, this is much less sensible. Globally though, analogy does not seem to be too much disturbed by translating into a rich morphological language.

Overall, analogical learning does equally well on uni- and multi-terms. This was expected since the method does not rely on the notion of word. For MeSH, between 23% (uniterms, French to English) to 40% (all terms, English to Spanish) of the test terms could be translated correctly by analogy. Many terms could not be translated because of a failure to identify analogies in the input space (step i).

For the MedDRA dataset, which is almost three times larger than the MeSH dataset, analogical learning could translate 63% of the Spanish to English *all terms* test set. Note however, that the precision is much smaller in that case. This is because many analogies are being identified during step (i), which in turn introduces many solutions. This clearly shows the need for a better filtering strategy (step iii) than the simple frequency-based ranking we considered in this study.

It is interesting to note, that for the SNOMED dataset, which is roughly four times larger than MedDRA, we witness a decrease of the number of correctly translated terms. If corpus size matters to a certain degree, what seems more important is the diversity of the phenomenon present in the search material.

Comparison with edit-distance. An interesting observation can be made when contrasting edit-distance and analogy variants. For uni-terms, edit-distance seems to be more appropriate when the languages share the same alphabet; it is the reverse for multi-terms. Translating multi-terms by analogy can lead to drastic improvements in precision and recall, as can be observed for the SNOMED and MEDDRA experiments, where edit-distance culminates at a recall of around 5% while analogy records a precision of 74% and a recall of 40% for the SNOMED dataset (rank = 25) and a precision of 55% and a recall of 31% for MedDRA (rank = 25). This clearly illustrates that analogy captures linguistic information that helps in translating multi-terms. The fact that it does not outperform edit-distance on single-terms (when using a single alphabet) is likely due to the nature of medical terms which share the same latin or greek roots, which facilitates the task of edit-distance-like approaches. Note however that edit-distance has access to the solution when translating, while analogy does not. Note also that for languages with different scripts (RU/EN), edit-distance simply fails to translate most of the terms. A transliteration step could alleviate this issue, but this would require specific resources for each language and script.

We investigated more closely whether the terms translated had a special configuration regarding edit-distance. We found out that the average edit-distance between terms and their reference translation is larger for the terms that we could not translate. The difference however, is not spectacular: in the order of one point for uniterms, and two points for multi-terms. This means that analogical learning is not especially biased toward translating "easy" terms.

Table 6. Average number of analogies found in the input space *nbi*, average number of target equations solved *nbe*, and average number of productive equations *nbp*, *i.e.*, equations with at least one solution. These figures are computed on the only words that received a translation by analogy for the X to English translation direction (similar figures are observed for the reverse direction).

	all terms			uniterms		
	nbi	*nbe*	*nbp*	*nbi*	*nbe*	*nbp*
mesh-FI-EN	55.5	28.3	25.4	7.8	6.3	5.2
mesh-FR-EN	63.2	26.2	23.7	6.4	5.8	4.9
mesh-RU-EN	43.4	28.6	25.4	30.3	8.1	6.8
mesh-RU-EN	37.5	29.9	26.3	30.3	8.1	6.8
mesh-SP-EN	30.2	27.4	25.3	15.8	6.7	5.5
mesh-SW-EN	60.3	18.8	16.5	17.8	7.5	5.9

Table 6 helps to appreciate the number of analogies identified in the input space, as well as the number of productive equations[4] formed in the output space. We call *productive* an equation which generates at least one solution. We observe that more analogies are identified while translating multi-terms. This might simply be due to the larger training datasets considered in this case. Another explanation could be that multi-terms exhibit strong construction patterns, as for instance in the case of *nervsystemets sjukdomar* in Swedish (*nervous system diseases*) that could be translated thanks to many analogies of the form:

[*hypotalamustumörer:nervsystemets tumörer =*
hypotalamussjukdomar:nervous system diseases]
⇒ [*hypothalamic neoplasms:hypothalamic diseases = nervous system neoplasms:?*].

[*ileumtumörer:nervsystemets tumörer = ileumsjukdomar:nervsystemets sjukdomar*]
⇒ [*ileal neoplasms:ileal diseases = nervous system neoplasms:?*]

We also observe that most of the equations formed in the output space produce at least one solution, which indicates that the inductive bias of analogical learning (an input formal analogy corresponds to an output one) seems to be adequate.

Compared to analogy, edit-distance had an easier task since all target words are included in the search list. Had we not added the list of target words, edit-distance would have had a much lower potential recall. A more realistic test would consist in using for a candidate list a large corpus or word list such as can be found on the Web.

Synthesis and related work. A precise comparison with Claveau and Zweigenbaum [4] is difficult since their TEST set was quite different from ours as it contained pairs of identical words. Their best attainable precision was 75% when

---

[4] We only count the output equations that are being solved. In practice, many equations produced can be ruled out without solving them, thanks to properties on formal analogies.

test words were randomly selected as in the present work, but included 10–12% of identical words. They do not report the corresponding recall.

The analogical method can generate translations for unseen words. The resolution of an analogical equation combines the known words in the equation to create a new, hypothetical word which solves it. Identifying and solving a large number of such analogical equations builds cumulative support for the most promising hypotheses. The frequency ordering used in this paper is a crude method for selecting the best translation; the use of a suitable classifier can boost selection (current experiments obtain a reduction of candidates by 90% with little or no loss in recall).

Another way to improve the analogical method would be to provide it knowledge on morphemes or "subwords," as prepared, *e.g.*, in [7]. This could be used to enforce morphemic boundaries when generating analogical equation solutions and therefore reduce the number of generated forms, or to perform a posteriori filtering of candidate translations in step (iii).

6   Conclusion

We introduced an analogy-based method to generate word translations and tested it to evaluate its potential on medical words. Its precision can be quite good once a stronger selection component is integrated in its last step (current upper bound at 81%, MeSH, sp-en). Its recall is lower, with an upper bound at 55% (MedDRA, sp-en) in the current experiments. It can be increased by a combination with complementary, existing methods based on attested words, such as edit-distance with a large word list. It has the distinctive feature of being able to generate translations for unseen words.

We checked that the analogy method is robust on a series of language pairs, including distant languages (Finnish) and different scripts (Cyrillic). We also verified that it can tackle the direct translation of multiword terms without having to first segment them into words.

Acknowledgments

We thank the anonymous reviewers of this paper for their helpful comments. This work has been partially founded by the Natural Sciences and Engineering Research Council of Canada.

References

1. Iacobini, C.: Composizione con elementi neoclassici. In: Grossmann, M., Rainer, F. (eds.) La formazione delle parole in italiano, Niemeyer, Tübingen, pp. 69–95 (2004)
2. Namer, F., Baud, R.: Predicting lexical relations between biomedical terms: towards a multilingual morphosemantics-based system. In: Stud Health Technol Inform., vol. 116, pp. 793–798. IOS Press, Amsterdam (2005)

3. Schulz, S., Markó, K., Sbrissia, E., Nohama, P., Hahn, U.: Cognate mapping - a heuristic strategy for the semi-supervised acquisition of a Spanish lexicon from a Portuguese seed lexicon. In: Proc 20th International Conference on Computational Linguistics (COLING 2004), Genève, Suisse, pp. 813–819 (2004)
4. Claveau, V., Zweigenbaum, P.: Translating biomedical terms by inferring transducers. In: Miksch, S., Hunter, J., Keravnou, E.T. (eds.) AIME 2005. LNCS (LNAI), vol. 3581, pp. 236–240. Springer, Heidelberg (2005)
5. Deléger, L., Merkel, M., Zweigenbaum, P.: Using word alignment to extend multilingual medical terminologies. In: Zweigenbaum, P., Schulz, S., Ruch, P. (eds.) Proc LREC Workshop Acquiring and representing multilingual, specialized lexicons: the case of biomedicine, Genoa, Italy,ELDA, pp. 9–14 (2006)
6. Fung, P., Yee, L.Y.: An IR approach for translating new words from non-parallel, comparable texts. In: Proceedings of the 36th ACL, Montréal, August 1998, pp. 414–420 (1998)
7. Hahn, U., Honeck, M., Piotrowski, M., Schulz, S.: Subword segmentation: Leveling out morphological variations for medical document retrieval. J. Am. Med. Inform. Assoc. 8, 229–233 (2001)
8. Namer, F., Zweigenbaum, P.: Acquiring meaning for French medical terminology: contribution of morphosemantics. In: Fieschi, M., Coiera, E., Li, Y.C.J. (eds.) Proc 10th World Congress on Medical Informatics. Studies in Health Technology and Informatics, vol. 107, pp. 535–539. IOS Press, Amsterdam (2004)
9. Creutz, M., Lagus, K.: Morfessor in the morpho challenge. In: Proceedings of the PASCAL Challenge Workshop on Unsupervised segmentation of words into morphemes, Venice, Italy (2006)
10. Lepage, Y.: Solving analogies on words: an algorithm. In: COLING-ACL, Montréal, Canada, pp. 728–734 (1998)
11. Stroppa, N., Yvon, F.: An analogical learner for morphological analysis. In: 9th Conf. on Computational Natural Language Learning (CoNLL), Ann Arbor, MI, pp. 120–127 (2005)
12. Langlais, P., Patry, A.: Translating unknown words by analogical learning. In: Proc. Joint Conference on Empirical Methods in Natural Language Processing and Computational Natural Language Learning (EMNLP-CoNLL), Prague, Czech Republic, pp. 877–886
13. Lindberg, D.A.B., Humphreys, B.L., McCray, A.T.: The Unified Medical Language System. Methods Inf. Med. 32(2), 81–91 (1993)
14. Baeza-Yates, R., Ribeiro-Neto, B.: Modern Information Retrieval. Addison-Wesley, New York (1999)
15. Levenshtein, V.I.: Binary codes capable of correcting deletions, insertions, and reversals. In: Soviet Physics Doklady, pp. 707–710 (1966)

Improving Chinese Pronominal Anaphora Resolution by Extensive Feature Representation and Confidence Estimation

Tyne Liang and Dian-Song Wu

Department of Computer Science
National Chiao Tung University, Hsinchu, 30010, Taiwan (R.O.C.)
{tliang,gis92807}@cis.nctu.edu.tw

Abstract. Pronominal anaphora resolution denotes antecedent identification for anaphoric pronouns expressed in discourses. Effective resolution relies on the kinds of features to be concerned and how they are appropriately weighted at antecedent identification. In this paper, a rich feature set including the innovative discourse features are employed so as to resolve those commonly-used Chinese pronouns in modern Chinese written texts. Moreover, a maximum-entropy based model is presented to estimate the confidence for each antecedent candidate. Experimental results show that our method achieves 83.5% success rate which is better than those obtained by rule-based and SVM-based methods.

Keywords: pronominal anaphora resolution, maximum entropy model, Chinese, discourse.

1 Introduction

As Chinese becomes widely used in the world, the techniques to facilitate Chinese text understanding are demanded. Among various kinds of language processing techniques, few approaches have been presented to resolving commonly-displayed pronouns in Chinese written texts. The reasons are attributed to the difficulties in extracting useful explicit semantic or syntactic clues from contexts. For example, Chinese nouns rarely contain morphological clues to indicate their gender or plurality features.

Essentially pronominal anaphora resolution relies on the ways to check those constraints between pronouns and their antecedent candidates. Among various kinds of constraints discussed in recent literatures, lexical, grammatical, and positional features are commonly addressed in [6, 10, 15, 16]. On the contrary, it is not easy to acquire semantic features or syntactic features from contexts if effective parsing or named entity identification tools are not available [4, 16, 17].

On the other hand, the ways to weight extracted features have been approached by heuristic rules or machine learning models. In general, rule-based methods have problems of portability and scalability while learning-based methods require a large well-tagged training corpora for satisfactory performance [11, 12, 13]. Besides, learning approach like SVM-based classification manipulates candidates by labeling positive or negative classes rather than estimating the likelihood that a candidate becomes an antecedent.

A. Ranta, B. Nordström (Eds.): GoTAL 2008, LNAI 5221, pp. 296–302, 2008.

In this paper, an effective approach to Chinese pronoun resolution is presented. In addition to the features commonly used in previous approaches, two innovative features are introduced by considering Chinese discourse structures. One is feature of coherence relations which are helpful to guide pronominal anaphora resolution [8]. The other is the feature of forward-looking centers associated with discourse utterances [5, 14]. Such discourse features will be extracted by implementing the presented heuristic rules with the help of outer resources. Moreover, our antecedent identification is implemented by a maximum-entropy based model which is motivated to yield global optimization of feature weighting [1]. The experimental results show that our method yields 83.5% success rate on 651 anaphor-antecedent pairs, enhancing 8% and 3% success rates respectively while compared to the general rule-based method presented in [15] and a SVM-based method. Besides, the experimental results show that the impact of the innovative discourse features is positive in enhancing the presented pronoun resolution.

2   The Pronoun Resolution

The presented resolution is implemented in the training phase and the testing phase. The training phase is mainly to train the presented maximum-entropy confidence estimation on the selected feature set. The testing phase involves the tasks to process texts, extract informative features from both contexts and outer resources, and finally determine antecedents. Table 1 lists the target pronominal anaphors to be resolved in this paper. Unlike English pronouns, Chinese pronouns remain the same in expressing nominative and accusative cases.

Table 1. The target pronominal anaphors

	Singular	Plural	Possessive (Singular)	Possessive (Plural)
Male	他(he, him)	他們(they, them)	他的(his)	他們的(their, theirs)
Female	她(she, her)	她們(they, them)	她的(her, hers)	她們的(their, theirs)
Neutral	它(it)	它們(they, them)	它的(its)	它們的(their, theirs)

2.1   Text Processing

Text preprocessing involves sentence segmentation, Part-of-speech tagging, noun phrase chunking and grammatical tagging. The sentence segmentation and POS tagging are processed by CKIP Chinese word segmentation system[1]. Noun phrase chunking is implemented by our finite-state machine chunker. All noun phrases appearing in the two sentences ahead of a target pronoun will be treated as antecedent candidates. This is because 94% antecedents identified in our training corpus are in two sentences ahead of their corresponding anaphors.

Since the text processing is implemented without any help of a parser, so we simply treat all noun phrases appearing in front of a verb as subjects and agents and those succeeding a verb as objects and patients. Other grammatical tags like gender, and number features for each noun phrase are implemented with the following heuristic rules.

---

[1] CKIP Chinese word segmentation system is available at http://ckipsvr.iis.sinica.edu.tw/

(1) Number identification procedure:

Step 1: Define symbols as follows:

  NP= an given noun phrase;

  HNP= head noun of the noun phrase;

  Q= set of quantifiers;

  P= set of collective quantifiers like {群, 夥, 堆, 對, 批};

  R= set of plural words like {都, 全, 全部, 全體, 皆, 所有, 每個, 雙方, 多數, 一些, 某些, 若干, 幾個, 數個, 許多, 諸多};

Step 2: If NP satisfies any of the following conditions, then return singular.

  i. HNP is a person name;

  ii. NP contains a title;

  iii. NP ∈ {[這|那|該|某|一] +{Q-P}+noun};

Step 3: Else if NP satisfies any of the following conditions, then return plural.

  i. HNP is an organization name;

  ii. The last character of NP∈ {們, 倆};

  iii. NP contains plural number + Q;

  iv. NP follows r, where r∈ R;

 Step 4: For other cases, the number feature associated with the NP is marked unknown.

(2) Gender identification procedure:

Step 1: Check each NP whether it is an animate with the help of CKIP lexicon[2].

Step 2: If its semantic tag is not mankind, then return neutral;

Step 3: Else if NP satisfies any of the following conditions; then return male;

  i. NP= person name+先生;

  ii. the first character of NP is "男";

  iii. the last character of NP is "父";

  iv. NP+的+female_title word;

  v. NP +他;

Step 4: Else if NP satisfies any of the following conditions; then return female;

  i. NP= person name+女士;

  ii. the first character of NP is "女";

  iii. the last character of NP is "母";

  iv. NP+的+male_title word;

  v. NP +她;

  vi. first-name contains any female character;

Step 5: For other cases, the gender feature is marked unknown.

2.2 Extensive Feature Representation

In this paper, each antecedent candidate is represented with a rich set of extracted features. As listed in Table 2, the features can be grouped into six categories. Among them, lexical, positional, grammatical and heuristic features are employed in our resolution as well as most of previous resolutions. However, our approach acquires more semantic features instead of syntactic features like parsing results used in [4, 17].

---

[2] CKIP (Chinese Knowledge Information Processing Group) lexicon is available at
http://www.aclclp.org.tw/use_ckip_c.php

The extracted semantic features include the named entities identified by the named entity identifier presented in [7]. Moreover, two other semantic features are also included in our rich feature set while we considering Chinese discourse structures. One is coherence relation feature and the other is forward-looking center feature. As pointed in [8], the establishment of coherence relation guides pronominal anaphora resolution, and vice versa. In this paper, we assume that a coherence relation exists between an antecedent candidate and a pronoun if they are in the same discourse unit which may cross sentences. The discourse unit is identified by checking whether there are explicit discourse markers collocating in the discourse unit containing an antecedent candidate and a pronoun. The collocating markers are those words of the discourse lexicon database presented in [3]. For example, "一方面" ("on the one hand") and "另一方面" ("on the other hand") are collocating markers linking the coherence relations among a discourse unit.

As indicated [5, 14], a discourse utterance is associated with forward-looking or backward-looking centers. Backward-looking centers are often omitted or realized as pronouns while ranking of forward-looking centers corresponds to the likelihood that a center becomes the primary focus of subsequent discourses. Considering Chinese language is called a topic-prominence language, we hence extract forward-looking centers as one kind of discourse features by implementing the following simple center-identification rules.

Table 2. The feature set

Type	Feature	Description (C: antecendent candidate; P: pronoun)
Lexical	Same_Pro	C and P are the same pronoun
	Per_Pro	P is a personal pronoun
	Non_Emb	C is not an embedded NP
	Reflexive	P is a reflexive of C
Grammatical	Gender	C and P have gender agreement
	Number	C and P have number agreement
	Animate	C is a animate entity and P is a male or female pronoun
	Role	C is the agent of a verb
	Parallel	C and P are the same grammatical roles
Semantic	NE_Per	C is a person name and P is a male or female pronoun
	NE_Org	C is an organization name and P is a plural pronoun
Positional	Same_Clause	C and P are in the same clause
	Same_Sent	C and P are in the same sentence
	Same_Para	C and P are in the same paragraph
	Near_NP	C is the nearest NP to P
	Clause_Lead	C is the first NP in the clause
	Sent_Lead	C is the first NP in the sentence
Heuristic	Repeat	C repeats more than once in text
	Definite	C follows a determiner
Discourse	Coherence	C and P are in the same discourse unit
	Fwd_cent	C is the forward-looking center

1. The first noun phrase in a sentence is treated as topic by default.
2. For each pronoun, all the noun phrases appearing in the preceding clause are treated as forward-looking center candidates.
3. If one of the candidates is the identified topic, the topic becomes the forward looking center; otherwise, the candidates are selected to be the center by following the priority rule, that is, subject-labeled candidate is firstly selected; an object-labeled candidate is the second one; the other candidates are the last ones.

2.3 Antecedent Identification

With a rich set of extracted features, each antecedent candidate is estimated by our maximum entropy base model. The candidate is selected as antecedent if it has top confidence value as defined in Equation (1). In the experiments, we employed YASMET[3], a language toolkit implementing a smoothing maximum entropy based model with a Gaussian prior [9].

$$confidence = Pr(x = positive \mid c) = \frac{exp(\sum_i \lambda_i f_i(c, positive))}{Z(c)} \tag{1}$$

$$Z(c) = exp(\sum_i \lambda_i f_i(c, positive)) + exp(\sum_i \lambda_i f_i(c, negative))$$

where

x: $x \in$ {positive, negative} and x labels c as positive or negative
c: an antecedent candidate for its corresponding pronoun
λ_i: the weight for feature f_i

$$f_i(c,x) = \begin{cases} 1, \text{if}(c,x) \text{ satisfied feature constraints} \\ 0, \text{otherwise} \end{cases}$$

3   Comparative Results and Analysis

The presented resolution is trained by a training corpus which contains 157 news documents extracted from a balanced corpus ASBC[4]. Another different set of 150 news documents is used as testing data for performance comparison. The resolution is evaluated in terms of success rate (Equation (2)).

$$success\ rate = \frac{number\ of\ correctly\ resolved\ anaphor\ \text{-}\ antecedent\ pairs}{total\ number\ of\ anaphor\ \text{-}\ antecedent\ pairs} \tag{2}$$

The proposed resolution is verified and compared to rule-based and SVM-based approaches. The rule-based method is implemented in the way as presented in [15] in which only four features, namely, number, gender, grammatical, and position are

---

[3] YASMET is available at http://www-i6.informatik.rwth-aachen.de/Colleagues/och/
[4] Academia Sinica Balanced Corpus is available at http://www.sinica.edu.tw/SinicaCorpus/

extracted and weighted manually. On the other hand, the SVM-method is implemented by using the toolkit LIBSVM[5] with the presented 21 features. Table 3 shows that our method yields better success rate to the rule-based method by considering more features at antecedent identification. On the other hand, a SVM-based approach essentially ignores the remaining antecedent candidates whenever one candidate is tagged to be positive, hence less success rate is obtained by the SVM-based resolution while compared to the presented method.

The impact of features is verified by implementing leave-group-out evaluation. Table 4 shows that grammatical features as well as semantic features are the first two important features. It also shows that the innovative discourse features are useful to enhance the pronoun resolution though they improve success rate slightly. The reason is that few inter-sentential discourse units were identified by the discourse marker based matching method. Improvement of discourse identification is expected in the future work. Besides, examining the resolution errors, we found that most of errors are attributed to text processing and gender identification. It is observed that Chinese pronoun "他" (he) is often incorrectly used for a female entity in Chinese texts.

Table 3. Performance evaluation

Method	Success rate
Wang & Mei (2005)	75.7%
SVM-based classifier	80.6%
Our method	83.5%

Table 4. Performance of leave-group-out evaluation

Excluded feature group	Success rate
Lexical	76.6%
Grammatical	73.7%
Semantic	74.6%
Positional	77.5%
Heuristic	81.7%
Discourse	80.7%

4   Conclusions

This paper addressed the commonly-observed pronominal anaphora in Chinese texts. An effective resolution approach is presented by using extensive feature representation and confidence evaluation. To our best knowledge, the presented resolution is the first approach to employ discourse coherence and center features. With real experiments, the innovative features are proved to be useful in enhancing resolution performance. Meanwhile, the maximal entropy based confidence evaluation indeed yields better resolution performance than the SVM-based and rule-based approaches.

---

[5] LIBSVM is available at http://www.csie.ntu.edu.tw/~cjlin/

References

1. Berger, A.L., Piertra, S.A., Pietra, V.J.: A maximum entropy approach to natural language processing. Compuational Linguistics 22(1), 39–71 (1996)
2. Bergsma, S., Lin, D.: Bootstrapping Path-Based Pronoun Resolution. In: Proceedings of the 21st International Conference on Computational Linguistics and 44th Annual Meeting of the ACL, pp. 33–40 (2006)
3. Chen, Shou-Yi.: Corpus-based Coherence Relation Tagging in Chinese Discourses, Master Thesis, National Chiao Tung University, Taiwan (2006)
4. Converse, S.P.: Resolving Pronominal References in Chinese with the Hobbs Algorithm. In: Proceedings of the 4th SIGHAN Workshop on Chinese Language Processing, pp. 116–122 (2005)
5. Grosz, B.J., Joshi, A.K., Weinstein, S.: Centering: A Framework for Modeling the Local Coherence of Discourse. Computational Linguistics 21(2), 203–225 (1995)
6. Lappin, S., Leass, H.: An Algorithm for Pronominal Anaphora Resolution. Computational Linguistics 20(4), 535–561 (1994)
7. Liang, T., Yeh, C.H., Wu, D.S.: A Corpus-based Categorization for Chinese Proper Nouns. In: Proceedings of the National Computer Symposium, pp. 434–443 (2003)
8. Kehler, A.: Coherence, reference, and the theory of grammar. CSLI Publications, Stanford (2002)
9. McCallum, A.K.: MALLET: A Machine Learning for Language Toolkit (2002), http://www.cs.umass.edu/~mccallum/mallet
10. Mitkov, R.: Multilingual Anaphora Resolution. Machine Translation 14(3-4), 281–299 (1999)
11. Ng, V.: Machine learning for coreference resolution: From local classification to global ranking. In: Proceedings of the 43rd Annual Meeting of the Association for Computational Linguistics, pp. 157–164 (2005)
12. Ng, V., Cardie, C.: Improving machine learning approaches to coreference resolution. In: Proceedings of the 40th Annual Meeting of the Association for Computational Linguistics, pp. 104–111 (2002)
13. Strube, M., Muller, C.: A machine learning approach to pronoun resolution in spoken dialogue. In: Proceedings of the 41st Annual Meeting of the Association for Computational Linguistics, pp. 168–175 (2003)
14. Strube, M., Hahn, U.: Functional centering. In: Proceedings of the 34th annual meeting on Association for Computational Linguistics, pp. 270–277 (1996)
15. Wang, H.F., Mei, Z.: Robust Pronominal Resolution within Chinese Text. Journal of Software 16, 700–707 (2005)
16. Wang, N., Yuan, C.F., Wang, K.F., Li, W.J.: Anaphora Resolution in Chinese Financial News for Information Extraction. In: Proceedings of the 4th World Congress on Intelligent Control and Automation, pp. 2422–2426 (2002)
17. Yang, X.F., Su, J., Tan, C.L.: Kernel-Based Pronoun Resolution with Structured Syntactic Knowledge. In: Proceedings of the 21st International Conference on Computational Linguistics and 44th Annual Meeting of the ACL, pp. 41–48 (2006)

A Grammar Formalism for Specifying ISU-Based Dialogue Systems

Peter Ljunglöf and Staffan Larsson

Gothenburg University, Dept. of Linguistics,
Renströmsgatan 6, S-41255 Göteborg, Sweden
{peb,sl}@ling.gu.se

Abstract. We describe how to give a full specification of an ISU-based dialogue system as a grammar. For this we use Grammatical Framework (GF), which separates grammars into abstract and concrete syntax. All components necessary for a working GoDiS dialogue system are specified in the abstract syntax, while the linguistic details are defined in the concrete syntax. Since GF is a multilingual grammar formalism, it is straightforward to extend the dialogue system to several languages. Furthermore, the GF Resource Grammar Library can be used to write a single concrete instance covering 13 different languages.

1 Introduction

1.1 The Information-State Update Approach

The GoDiS dialogue manager [1] is based on formal semantic and pragmatic theories of dialogue, and provides general and fairly sophisticated accounts of several common dialogue phenomena such as interactive grounding, accommodation, multiple conversational threads, and mixed initiative. GoDiS is based on the Information State Update (ISU) approach to dialogue management [2]. The ISU approach, which has been developed over the last 10 years in several EU-funded projects, provides a generalization over previous theories of dialogue management and allows exploring a middle ground between sophisticated but brittle research systems, and robust but simplistic commercial systems. In the ISU approach, a dialogue manager is formalized as:

1. an information state (IS) type declaration, indicating which kinds of information the system needs to keep track of
2. a set of dialogue moves, i.e., abstract semantic representations of utterances
3. information state update rules, which:
   (a) update the IS based on observed dialogue moves
   (b) select moves to be performed by the system based on the current IS

The IS is a structured object which can contain e.g. sets, stacks, records, queues, etc. This allows efficient scripting of ISU system applications. In GoDiS, which is based on a theory of Issue-Based Dialogue Management (IBDM), a single

A. Ranta, B. Nordström (Eds.): GoTAL 2008, LNAI 5221, pp. 303–314, 2008.

script (called a *dialogue plan*) can be used flexibly by the dialogue manager to allow for a wide range of dialogues. While it would in principle be possible to implement many GoDiS dialogues using finite state automata, the processes of implementing, debugging and modifying these systems would be prohibitive.

The main benefit of the IBDM account as implemented in GoDiS is the combination of advanced dialogue management and rapid prototyping (quick implementation, debugging and modification) enabled by cleanly separating general dialogue solutions from application-specific domain knowledge.

1.2   Examples of Flexible Dialogue

Below are some examples of dialogues enabled by a single dialogue plan in the IBDM framework. The examples are taken from an implementation of a cellphone application. The dialogue plan, in this case the plan for changing a phone number in the phone book, specifies a default order of system actions to take:

1. ask for the name
2. ask for the type of number (home, cellphone, or work)
3. ask for the new number
4. change the phone book entry for the given name and type to the new number

Example 1. In the first example, after requesting the system to change a number, the user gives initiative to the system and just answers system questions:

> U: Change phone number.
> S: Okay, let's see. What name?
> U: Lisa
> S: Okay. Home number and work number are available. Which number do you want to change?
> U: Home number
> S: Okay. What is the new number?
> U: 11 12 13.
> S: Okay. I have now changed Lisa's home number to 11 12 13.

Example 2. Alternatively, the user can combine the request with answers to some as-yet-unasked questions. The default ordering of system actions in the dialogue plan can thus be overridden:

> U: I would like to change Lisa's number to 11 12 13.
> S: Okay, let's see. Home number and work number are available. Which number do you want to change?
> U: The home number please.
> S: Okay. I have now changed Lisa's home number to 11 12 13.

Example 3. It is also possible to just throw the system some information, and it will try to figure out which action the user wants the system to perform. If there is more than one candidate, the system will generate a clarification question. (Here we are also using a plan for making calls and a plan for searching for phone numbers):

U: Lisa's home number
S: Lisa's home number. I don't quite understand. Do you want to make a call, change a phone number or search for a phone number?
U: Change phone number
S: Okay. What is the new number?
U: 11 12 13.
S: Okay. I have now changed Lisa's home number to 11 12 13.

Example 4. If we provide the application with additional plans, e.g. for reading SMS messages, it is possible for the user to take new initiatives (ask questions or request actions) at any point in a dialogue. The system will enter into a sub-dialogue, and when the sub-dialogue is finished it will return to the previous dialogue topic. There is no intrinsic limit to the number of simultaneous conversational topics that the system can keep track of:

U: I would like to change Lisa's number to 11 12 13.
S: Okay, let's see. Home number and work number are available. Which number do you want to change?
U: Check my messages.
S: You have got this SMS: "Hi! I have a new home number, it is 11 12 13. Love, Lisa". Let's go back to changing an entry. Which phone number do you want to change?
U: The home number please.
S: Okay. I have now changed Lisa's home number to 11 12 13.

In addition to the above, general techniques for dealing with problems of perception, understanding and acceptance enable both user and system to provide feedback at any point in the dialogue. Such feedback can be either positive (signaling successful perception, understanding and acceptance) or negative (signaling problems).

We want to stress again that all the dialogues above use the same single dialogue plan. That is, the addition of that single plan to the application domain knowledge module enables many different dialogues.

1.3   Adding Natural Language to GoDiS

As previously mentioned, GoDiS enables rapid prototyping of systems with advanced dialogue behavior. However, the GoDiS dialogue manager only communicates with the outside world using semantic representations called *dialogue moves*. The designer of the dialogue system must implement a translation between natural language utterances and dialogue moves, be it through a simple lookup table, or an advanced feature-based grammar. If the system is speech-based, it also needs a statistical language model or a speech recognition grammar.

These components have to be maintained. If we add a new concept, e.g., a new dialogue plan, we have to add new grammar rules for handling the actions, questions, answers, etc., that are associated with the concept. Each entity in the database has to exist, both in the speech recognition component, in the grammar and in the dialogue system. If the dialogue system is multilingual, we have to ensure consistency for each language.

There have been attempts of solving parts of these consistency problems. The Regulus grammar compiler [3] or the Grammatical Framework [4] can automatically create speech recognition grammars from a higher-level grammar, thus ensuring consistency between speech recognition and parsing. Both these formalisms have been used for building grammars for GoDiS systems [5].

One problem is still not sufficiently addressed: consistency between the dialogue system and the grammar. The dialogue moves that the grammar outputs from parsing have to conform to the dialogue moves that the GoDiS system recognizes; and the other way around: The grammar has to be able to translate dialogue moves from GoDiS into natural language utterances.

What we want is a single formalism where we can specify the complete dialogue system. There have already been some attempts of this, but not for ISU-based dialogue systems. In [6] it is shown that a simple GF grammar can be converted into a VoiceXML dialogue system. However, their translation can currently only handle small domains, and the resulting system has very limited dialogue handling capabilities. In this paper we show how a GoDiS dialogue system can be specified as a GF grammar. All components necessary for a full-fledged ISU-based dialogue system are then automatically generated from the grammar.

1.4   Grammatical Framework

Grammatical Framework [4] is a grammar formalism based on type theory. The main feature is the separation of abstract and concrete syntax, which makes it very suitable for writing multilingual grammars. A rich module system also facilitates grammar writing as an engineering task, by reusing common grammars.

The main idea of GF is the separation of abstract and concrete syntax. The abstract part of a grammar defines a set of abstract syntactic structures, called abstract terms or trees; and the concrete part defines a relation between abstract structures and concrete structures. This separation of abstract and concrete syntax is crucial for the treatment of dialogue systems in this article.

The abstract theory of GF is a version of Martin-Löf's [7] dependent type theory. A grammar consists of declarations of categories and functions. Categories can depend on other categories – the following declarations state that Request and Utterance are categories that depend on a Domain:

> **cat** Domain
> **cat** Request(Domain)
> **cat** Utterance(Domain)

Functions are declared by giving argument and result types. Function declarations can also bind variables to be used in dependent types. Here we state that an Utterance can consist of a Request, provided that the share the same Domain:

> **fun** request : (d:Domain)→ Request(d)→ Utterance(d)

Concrete Syntax. GF has a *linearization* perspective to grammar writing, where the relation between abstract and concrete is viewed as a mapping from abstract to concrete structures, called linearization terms.

Linearizations are written as terms in a typed functional programming language, which is limited to ensure decidability in generation and in parsing. The language has records and inflection tables; and the basic types are strings and inflection parameters. There are also local definitions, lambda-abstractions and global macro definitions. The parameters are declared in the grammar; they can be hierarchical but not recursive, to ensure finiteness.

The following things are declared in the concrete syntax:

- The *inflection parameters* have to be declared. E.g., a verb phrase request in a simple variant of Swedish can be in imperative or infinitive:
  param VerbForm = Imperative | Infinitive
- Each category should have a matching *linearization type*. E.g., a Swedish verb phrase request depends on the VerbForm:
  lincat Request = VerbForm $\Rightarrow$ Str
  lincat Utterance = Str
- For each function in the abstract we define its *linearization function*. An utterance for our Swedish requests can either be a direct Imperative, or an indirect ("I would like to" followed by an Infinitive):
  lin request(req) =
      variants{req ! Imperative ; "jag vill" ++ req ! Infinitive ++ "tack"}
- A category can have an optional *default linearization*, which is used for unknown terms of that category:
  lindef Request =
      table{Imperative $\rightarrow$ "gör någonting" ; Infinitive $\rightarrow$ "göra någonting"}

With these example definitions, the possible linearizations of the incomplete term request(_) are "gör någonting" ("do something") and "jag vill göra någonting tack" ("I want to do something please").

Multilinguality and Resource Grammars. It is possible to define different concrete syntaxes for one particular abstract syntax. Multilingual grammars can be used as a model for interlingua translation, but also to simplify localization of language technology applications such as dialogue systems.

The abstract syntax of one grammar can be used as a concrete syntax of another grammar. This makes it possible to implement grammar resources to be used in several different application domains.

These points are currently exploited in the GF Resource Grammar Library [8], which is a multilingual GF grammar with a common abstract syntax for 13 languages, including Arabic, Finnish and Russian. The grammatical coverage is similar to the Core Language Engine [9]. The main purpose of the Grammar Library is as a resource for writing domain-specific grammars.

Note that for ease of presentation we do not make use of resource grammars in our running example. The interested reader is referred to [10], for a survey of the GF module system and resource grammars.

2   The GoDiS Dialogue Manager

In this section we give a short description of the building blocks of the GoDiS dialogue manager. The purpose of this description is to give details on how to specify a GoDiS system. We are not trying to explain the internals of the dialogue manager, which is described thoroughly in [1].

The GoDiS system communicates with the user via *dialogue moves*. There are three main dialogue moves – requesting actions, asking questions and giving answers. All three moves take one argument – the action, question or answer that the move is requesting, asking or giving.

Apart from the three main moves there are also different kinds of feedback moves – confirmations, failure reports and interactive communications management. We will not dwell into how these moves function, except for noting that they are important for the dialogue flexibility demonstrated in section 1.2.

The basic building blocks in GoDiS are individuals, sorts, one-place predicates and actions:

- The sorts are ordered in an hierarchy of sub- and supersorts. Each predicate has a domain which is a specific sort.
- Each individual e belongs to a specific sort s, written e : s.
- A predicate p (with domain s') can be applied to an individual e:s, where s is a subsort of s', to form a proposition p(e). A proposition can be used in an answer, answer(p(e)), or a y/n-question, ask(?p(e)).
- A collection of y/n-questions can be asked as an alternative question, ask({?p(e), ?p(f), ... }).
- A predicate p can be eta-expanded to a wh-question ?x.p(x). Wh-questions can be asked, ask(?x.p(x)).
- An action a can be requested, request(a). After the action has been performed it is confirmed, confirm(a), or a failure is reported, report(fail(a,...)).
- From an action a or a question q we can form the special propositions action(a) and issue(q).[1] These propositions are mainly used when asking the user what to do, or in feedback moves.

To specify a GoDiS dialogue system, we have to give the following information:

- The sortal hierarchy, i.e., the subsort relation.
- The individuals and the sorts they belong to.
- The predicates and their domains.
- The actions.
- The dialogue plans.

Apart from these things we have to have an interface for communicating with the device. The only thing we assume about this interface is that it can accept actions (using the dev_do plan construct) and queries (using dev_query).

---

[1] The propositions can be read approximately as "action a should be performed" and "question q should be resolved", respectively.

Dialogue Plans. Dialogue plans have already been touched upon in section 1.2. They convey what the system can do and/or give information about. A dialogue plan is a receipt for the system, so it knows how to answer a specific question, or how to perform a given action. The dialogue plans can roughly be divided into three different kinds – actions, issues and menus.

An *action plan* is when the user wants to perform an action, e.g., change the number of a contact in the phone book. Action plans are usually built in the same way. First the system asks some questions to get enough information, and then the action is performed. As an example, this is a more formal version of the plan in section 1.2:

> *changeNumber:* findout(?x.nameToChange(x))
> findout(?y.typeToChange(y))
> findout(?z.newNumber(z))
> dev_do(changeNumber)

After the plan has finished, GoDiS reports to the user about the success or failure of the action.

An *issue plan* is when the user has (explicitly or implicitly) asked a question, which the system should answer. Issue plans usually follow the same pattern as action plans, except that instead of telling the device to execute an action, it is given a query to solve. Here is the example plan for searching for phone numbers:

> *?x.searchForNumber(x):* findout(?y.nameToSearch(y))
> findout(?z.typeToSearch(z))
> dev_query(?x.searchForNumber(x))

The result of the query is an answer to the question, which GoDiS automatically reports to the user.

A special kind of action plan is the *menu*, where the user can select from any of a given number of sub-plans which the system then performs. Note that these sub-plans can be menus themselves, which gives a hierarchy of menus.

> *managePhonebook:* findout({ ?action(addContact)
> ?action(deleteContact)
> ?action(changeNumber)
> ?issue(?x.searchForNumber(x))
> ?issue(?y.searchForName(y)) })

3 Specifying a GoDiS System as GF Abstract Syntax

In this section we show how all necessary components of a GoDiS dialogue system can be specified in the abstract syntax of a GF grammar. All GoDiS components can be automatically extracted from the grammar.

3.1   Menus, Actions and Issues

In our GF grammar we define a category Menu, and three categories depending on Menu, reflecting the actions, issues and sub-menus in a plan.

```
cat Menu
cat Action(x)      [x : Menu]
cat Issue(x)       [x : Menu]
cat SubMenu(x,y)   [x,y : Menu]
```

Each action and issue in our dialogue specification belongs to a menu. Now, the first thing we have to do is to define the menus in our dialogue system:

```
fun mainMenu, makeCall, managePhonebook : Menu
```

An action plan is specified by giving a function with result category Action(m) where m : Menu. An example is the plan for changing the phone number:

```
fun changeNumber : nameToChange → typeToChange → newNumber →
                                        Action(managePhonebook)
```

An issue in GoDiS is a wh-question ?x.P(x). This is reflected in the GF grammar where all issues are functions with the result Issue(m). Here is the issue plan for searching for a contact's phone number:

```
fun searchForNumber : nameToSearch → typeToSearch →
                                number → Issue(managePhonebook)
```

Note that there is a crucial difference between the arguments. All arguments except the last one represent information which the system asks the user for. The last argument represents the final answer of the query.

Each menu in the specification corresponds to a menu plan in GoDiS. The elements of a menu are specified by the argument m to the dependent types Action(m) and Issue(m). E.g., the menu managePhonebook consists of five choices, of which changeNumber and searchForNumber are already specified above. With this solution we do not have to specify the menu plans directly, but they can be deduced automatically from the menu argument to each action and issue.

Finally, the mainMenu in our example asks whether we want to make a phone call, or manage the phone book. Both these alternatives are menus themselves. This is specified by creating instances of the SubMenu type:

```
fun makeCallSubMenu : SubMenu(mainMenu,makeCall)
fun managePhonebookSubMenu : SubMenu(mainMenu,managePhonebook)
```

3.2   The Dialogue System Ontology

Everything else in the GF grammar specifies the ontology of the dialogue system. From the grammar we can extract the sorts and the sortal hierarchy, the individuals and the sorts they belong to, and the predicates and their domains.

Sorts. In our simple example we want to have two GoDiS sorts, names and phone numbers. Names are defined as a simple database:

fun anna, bert, charles, diane : name

In our setting a phone number is simply a sequence of small numbers (i.e., numbers below 100):

fun single : smallNumber → number
fun cons : smallNumber → number → number
fun 0, 1, 2, ..., 99 : smallNumber

Each of the GF types is automatically translated to a GoDiS sort, and each instance becomes a GoDiS individual. The complex functions create non-atomic individuals, so these are the accepted numbers in our GoDiS application:

single(n) : number **if** n : smallNumber
cons(n,m) : number **if** n : smallNumber **and** m : number

Note that the sort smallNumber will be created, which we do not use at all in our application. But this is no problem since it doesn't interfere with the sorts we are using.

User Answers. Not all sorts are intended to be used in communication. E.g., we do not want the user to give answers of the form answer(smallNumber(...)), but only of the form answer(number(...)). Therefore the grammar writer has to specify which sorts can be uttered as answers, by supplying the category Answer:

fun answerName : name → Answer
fun answerNumber : number → Answer

With these two definitions, the user can give answers containing names and phone numbers, but not small numbers.

Coercions and Subsorts. Each type that occurs as an argument in an Action or an Issue reflects a system-initiated question. E.g., the action for calling a phone number is:

fun callNumber : numberToCall → Action(makeCall)

From this specification, numberToCall will be translated to a one-place predicate in GoDiS. But GoDiS also needs to know the domain of this predicate. This is specified by a *coercion* function in GF:

fun coerceNumber : number → numberToCall

A function is a coercion if it, *i*) takes exactly one argument, and *ii*) is the only function with the same result type. We do not translate coercions to instance rules as we did for the sort of numbers. Instead we state that number is a subsort of numberToCall, which in GoDiS term means that any answer of the form answer(number(...)) is a relevant answer to the question ?x.numberToCall(x).

4   User and System Utterances in the Concrete Grammar

In this section we exemplify how it is possible to specify concrete linearizations of the abstract syntax, so that the final system can convert utterances to and from dialogue moves.

4.1   Linearizations of Dialogue Moves

In a GF grammar, each abstract function has a corresponding concrete *linearization* with the same number of arguments. E.g., the callNumber action, and the sort number, can have the following linearizations:

> **lin** callNumber(x) = "call" ++ *variants*{x ; "a number"}
> **lin** single(x) = x
> **lin** cons(x,y) = x ++ y

Now, the result of parsing the sentence "call twelve nineteen sixty" will be the GF term:

> callNumber(cons(12,cons(19,single(60)))) : Action(makeCall)

There is an automatic translation from GF terms to GoDiS dialogue moves, and the final result in this case will be:

> request(callNumber), answer(numberToCall(cons(12,cons(19,single(60)))))

Note that there is one alternative linearization of callNumber where the argument is not used. This means that parsing of "call a number" will return callNumber(_X), which is a GF term with a metavariable _X. The translation to GoDiS dialogue moves yields:

> request(callNumber), answer(numberToCall(_X))

This is equivalent to request(callNumber), since the second dialogue move is uninformative and will be ignored.

The GF linearizations are also used by the system; e.g., when it wants to raise a question or give an answer. The dialogue moves generated by GoDiS will be translated to (one or more) GF terms, which in turn are linearized to utterances. So, when the system wants to ask the question ?action(callNumber), it linearizes the term askAction(callNumber(_X)) to the resulting utterance "Do you want to call a number?".

> **fun** askAction : (m:Menu) → Action(m) → DialogueMove
> **lin** askAction(_)(x) = "Do you want to" ++ x ++ "?"

4.2   System Wh-Questions

In the grammar, the GoDiS predicates are specified as GF categories, not grammar rules. This means that a wh-question such as ?x.numberToAdd(x) does not correspond to a GF term, but to the category numberToAdd instead. Fortunately,

GF has a mechanism for specifying how to linearize unknown terms of a given category. For each GF category corresponding to a predicate we define a *linearization default*:

lindef numberToCall = "Which number do you want to call?"
lindef numberToAdd = "Which number do you want to add?"

When the GF linearizer comes across an unknown term of the category C, it uses the linearization default for C. This means that we can translate the dialogue move ask(?x.numberToAdd(x)) to a GF metavariable of type numberToAdd. GF then linearizes the metavariable to the utterance "Which number do you want to add?".

4.3   Using the GF Resource Grammar

To get more grammatically correct utterances (e.g., for congruence or different word order) we make use of complex linearization types in the GF grammar. One way to do this is to specify all grammatical parameters for the target language ourselves.

Another solution is to use the GF Resource Grammar Library for implementing the concrete syntax. The resource library is a common API for 13 languages, implemented as a large GF grammar. It can be used for writing grammatically correct domain grammars without needing perfect knowledge of the target language. Instead of writing linearization terms in the right-hand sides, we give a syntax tree from the resource grammar. As an example, the action for calling by number can be written:

lin callNumber(x) = mkVP (call_Verb)
                        (*variants*{x ; mkNP (a_Det) (number_Noun)})

Here, mkVP and mkNP are operations defined in the resource library, and call_Verb, a_Det and number_Noun are defined in the lexicon.

Finally, recall that a single abstract GF grammar can map to several concrete syntaxes. This can be used for writing multilingual dialogue system grammars. In particular, the GF Resource Grammar Library can be used to write a single concrete instance covering 13 languages.

5   Discussion

We have described how to give a full specification of an ISU-based dialogue system, as a GF grammar. The abstract syntax specifies the dialogue manager, and the concrete syntax specifies a mapping between GoDiS dialogue moves and natural language utterances.

Related Work. Some earlier attempts have been done on specifying dialogue systems in a single formalism. Most similar to our solution is [6], from which this article has borrowed some ideas. The advantage of our approach is that by compiling to GoDiS we get all the nice dialogue handling capabilities as exemplified in section 1.2.

Another inspiration has been [5], where some parts of a GoDiS system can be specified as an OWL ontology. The difference here is that in our system *all* necessary parts of a GoDiS system are specified in the GF grammar.

Future Work. The implementation is still only a prototype, and we plan to implement a full-scale version in the near future. A real-sized proof-of-concept dialogue system will also be implemented.

Multimodal dialogue systems as described in [11] are not currently handled, but we plan to extend the formalism to handle multiple modalities as well.

The abstract syntax of a GF grammar can be implemented as an OWL ontology [5]. We plan to explore whether it is fruitful to specify at least parts of a dialogue system in OWL.

References

1. Larsson, S.: Issue-based Dialogue Management. PhD thesis, Department of Linguistics, Gothenburg University (2002)
2. Traum, D., Larsson, S.: The information state approach to dialogue management. In: Smith, K. (ed.) Current and New Directions in Discourse and Dialogue, pp. 325–353. Kluwer Academic Publishers, Dordrecht (2003)
3. Rayner, M., Hockey, B.A., Bouillon, P.: Putting Linguistics into Speech Recognition: The Regulus Grammar Compiler. CSLI Publications (2006)
4. Ranta, A.: Grammatical Framework, a type-theoretical grammar formalism. Journal of Functional Programming 14(2), 145–189 (2004)
5. Ljunglöf, P., Amores, G., Burden, H., Manchón, P., Pérez, G., Ranta, A.: Enhanced multimodal grammar library. Deliverable D1.5, TALK Project (August 2006)
6. Bringert, B.: Rapid development of dialogue systems by grammar compilation. In: Keizer, S., Bunt, H., Paek, T. (eds.) Proceedings of the 8th SIGdial Workshop on Discourse and Dialogue, Antwerp, Belgium (September 2007)
7. Martin-Löf, P.: Intuitionistic Type Theory. Bibliopolis, Napoli (1984)
8. Ranta, A., El-Dada, A., Khegai, J.: The GF Resource Grammar Library (2006), http://code.haskell.org/gf/doc/resource.pdf
9. Rayner, M., Carter, D., Bouillon, P., Digalakis, V., Wirén, M.: The Spoken Language Translator. Cambridge University Press, Cambridge (2000)
10. Ranta, A.: Modular grammar engineering in GF. Research on Language and Computation 5(2), 133–158 (2007)
11. Bringert, B., Cooper, R., Ljunglöf, P., Ranta, A.: Multimodal dialogue system grammars. In: DIALOR 2005, 9th Workshop on the Semantics and Pragmatics of Dialogue, Nancy, France (June 2005)

Word Sense Disambiguation of Farsi Homographs Using Thesaurus and Corpus

Raheleh Makki and Mohammad Mehdi Homayounpour

Laboratory for Intelligent Sound and Speech Processing, Department of Computer
Engineering and Information Technology, Amirkabir University of Technology, Tehran, Iran
makki@aut.ac.ir, homayoun@aut.ac.ir

Abstract. This paper describes disambiguation of Farsi homographs in unrestricted text using thesaurus and corpus. The proposed method is based on [1] with some differences. These differences consist of first using collocational information to avoid the collection of spurious contexts caused by polysemous words in thesaurus categories, and second contribution of all words in the test data context, even those not appeared in the collected contexts to the calculation of the conceptual classes' score. Using a Farsi corpus and a Farsi thesaurus, this method correctly disambiguated 91.46% of the instances of 15 Farsi homographs. This method was compared to three supervised corpus based methods including Naïve Bayes, Exemplar-based, and Decision List. Unlike supervised methods, this method needs no training data, and has a good performance on disambiguation of uncommon words. In addition, this method can be used for removing some kinds of morphological ambiguities.

Keywords: Word Sense Disambiguation, Thesaurus, Corpus, Farsi Language.

1 Introduction

In every language, there are words whose pronunciation cannot be determined without notification of their senses in the contexts they occurred. Theses words are called homographs. A text to speech system needs to disambiguate homographs. Respect to above definition, a homograph is a word associated with multiple senses. So, homograph disambiguation problem is a word sense disambiguation (WSD) problem.

Word Sense Disambiguation (WSD) is the problem of assigning the appropriate meaning (sense) to a given word in a text or discourse [2]. Resolving the ambiguity of words is a central problem for language understanding applications and their associated tasks including, for instance, machine translation, information retrieval and hypertext navigation, parsing, text to speech, spelling correction, reference resolution, automatic text summarization, etc [3].

WSD is one of the most important open problems in the Natural Language Processing (NLP) field. Despite the large number of WSD systems for other languages specially English, it is a fact that because of the lack of labeled corpora and knowledge sources, to date no large scale and highly accurate word sense disambiguation system has been built for Farsi language.

A. Ranta, B. Nordström (Eds.): GoTAL 2008, LNAI 5221, pp. 315–323, 2008.

With regard to the approaches or strategies employed, there are three ways to approach the problem of assigning the correct senses to ambiguous words in context:

- a knowledge-based approach, which uses an explicit lexicon (MRD: Machine Readable Dictionary and thesaurus) or ontology (e.g. WordNet),
- corpus-based disambiguation, where the relevant information about word senses is gathered from training on a large sense-tagged corpus,
- A hybrid approach combining aspects of both of the aforementioned methodologies [4].

The major difficulty of a corpus-based approach, however, remains the data acquisition bottleneck [5]. So, the use of knowledge sources, including information about word senses, besides a corpus is proposed.

This paper describes disambiguation of Farsi homographs in unrestricted text using thesaurus and corpus. The proposed method is based on [1], but we use collocational information to avoid the collection of spurious contexts caused by polysemous words in thesaurus categories. Moreover, all words in the context of test sample contribute to the calculation of the conceptual classes' scores.

This paper is organized as follows: Section 2 is devoted to explain the algorithm used in this paper. Section 3 introduces the thesaurus and corpus used in our experiments. Section 4 reports the results of the proposed method and compares them with the results of three supervised corpus based methods that are implemented and applied to the selected homographs. Finally, Section 6 concludes and analyzes obtained results.

2   The Proposed Method

The method used in this paper follows the steps of the algorithm described in [1], but modifies it in collection of contexts and calculating the scores of conceptual categories. The basic algorithm, presented in [1], is based on the observation that declares if there is a context discriminator for the conceptual categories, we can use it to disambiguate the word senses that are members of these categories. So, for word sense disambiguation, we should at first determine the conceptual categories that the ambiguous word is a member of them. Then we can build a context discriminator for these categories, and since each sense of the ambiguous word belongs to one of these categories, use the discriminator for predicting the correct sense [1].

To determine conceptual categories, we can use a thesaurus. A thesaurus is a knowledge source that puts words in conceptual categories in a way that words belonging to a category are synonyms. Therefore, this knowledge source is proper for recognition of conceptual categories related to an ambiguous word. Now that the categories are identified, we should construct a discriminator for them. The steps of this task are illustrated in [1] as follows.

1. Collect contexts representative of conceptual categories
2. Identify salient words in the collective context and weight them
3. Use the resulting weights to predict the appropriate sense of an ambiguous word in new context

We followed these steps here with a little change in each step.

2.1 Identification of Certain Collocations and Collection of Representative Contexts

The goal of this step is to collect a set of contexts representative of conceptual categories related to the senses of ambiguous word. To do this, we look for occurrences of each member of the category in a corpus, and where one is found, extract concordances of k surrounding words. It's illustrated in [1] that conceptual categories extracted from thesaurus may include polysemous words. It's obvious that all the occurrences of this word in the corpus do not mean the same, and the contexts related to other categories should not be extracted. We replace the polysemous word in the categories with some of its certain collocations that are cues for one sense and related category. This avoids the collection of irrelevant contexts.

For instance, the Farsi word "شیر", belonging to one of the conceptual classes of the homograph "ببر" (tiger, cut, take), is a polysemous word. The word "شیر" means lion, milk, and tap in different sentences. The first sense, lion, relates to one of the conceptual categories of the homograph "ببر" (tiger) and the two last senses are related to other categories. So, instead of extracting the context of each occurrence of the word "شیر" in the corpus, we extracted each occurrence of the collocations: " ببر و شیر" (tiger and lion), "ببر و جنگل" (tiger and jungle), and etc. In other words, we extracted the contexts including these collocations or co-occurrence of these words.

Whereas the homograph is a member of all of its conceptual categories, we also used some collocations of it in the categories, and gathered more relevant contexts. For instance, the homograph "شکر" has two senses equivalent to sugar and thankfulness. Therefore it belongs to two conceptual categories corresponding to these senses. We used collocation "خدا را شکر" (thanks God) in the category related to thankfulness sense, and "قند و شکر" (sugar cubes) in the other sense.

To identify these certain collocations which are representative for a particular sense, we can extract the most frequent co-occurring words with the polysemous word from the corpus and use the knowledge of an expert to select certain collocations and assign them to the correct conceptual category. We also can extract a number of polysemous word's samples and label them with correct sense manually, then extract the certain collocations from this tagged set. In this way, we need to ensure that a collocation is a good representative for a particular sense and related category (sense$_i$). So, we calculated the amount of the following relation and if it was lower than a threshold, we ignored it.

$$Score(collocation) = \frac{\Pr(collocation \mid sense_i)}{\Pr(collocation \mid \sum_{j \neq i} sense_j)} . \tag{1}$$

2.2 Weighting All the Words in Collected Contexts

In the basic algorithm, for each word (w) appeared in the collected contexts of a Roget's thesaurus category (TCat), the following probability is calculated. Then the words with higher probability are selected as the salient words for that category, and the logarithm of their probabilities is considered as their weights [1]. In this paper we used this probability and also its logarithm. The only difference consists of keeping and weighting not only the salient words, but also all the words appeared in the contexts.

$$\frac{\Pr(w \mid TCat)}{\Pr(w)} . \tag{2}$$

2.3   Calculation of the Scores of Categories and Assigning the Correct Sense

In the basic algorithm, when the ambiguous word appeared in a novel context, the method assigns a score to each of the conceptual categories. This score is calculated based on the relation 2 which adds the weight of each of the salient words of a category (TCat) appeared in the test context, to the score of that category.

$$Score(TCat) = \sum_{w \ in \ context} \log(\frac{\Pr(w \mid TCat) \times \Pr(TCat)}{\Pr(w)}) . \tag{3}$$

Finally the category with highest score is assigned to the ambiguous word as the correct sense. We used the same strategy in this paper. The only difference is that all the words in test context, even those not observed in the collected contexts of a category contribute to the score calculation of that category. It means in score calculation of a category, each word in the new context adds its related weight determined in the previous step to the score of that category. For the words in test context (w) not observed in the collected contexts of a category (TCat), we added the following probability to the score of that category.

$$\Pr(w \mid TCat) = \log(\frac{1}{N(TCat)}) . \tag{4}$$

N(TCat) indicates the frequency of category TCat in the corpus. In other words it indicates the number of collected contexts for this category. This probability has a reverse relation with the frequency of the category. It is reasonable, because for the uncommon conceptual categories which appear less in the corpus, some words have little chance to occur in the small number of collected contexts.

3   The Thesaurus and Corpus Used in This Paper

In this paper, we used a raw corpus collected and organized by the Research Center for Intelligent Signal Processing in Iran (RCISP). This is the most important comprehensive corpus for Farsi language, and contains about one hundred million words. The texts of this corpus are gathered from different sources like newspapers, magazines, journals, Internet, books, theatre plays, itineraries, diaries, calendars, and letters. This corpus includes various domains such as economy, export, culture, sciences, etc. This corpus does not include semantic tags and is a raw corpus for our problem (WSD). Ten millions words of this corpus include Part Of Speech (POS) Tags [6]. We selected a subset of this corpus containing about 8 million words for our experiments and labeled it manually with semantic tags.

The thesaurus utilized here is the first one for Farsi words and expressions. It is designed and structured exactly like Roget's thesaurus with the same number of classes, sections, and heads. It also contains an index equal to Roget's thesaurus [7], [8].

4   Experiments

The described method was applied to 15 Farsi homographs. Conceptual categories are extracted from the thesaurus for each homograph and then the corpus is used for collection of contexts. So, this method is a hybrid approach. Table 1 shows the

Table 1. Performance of the proposed method in % applied to 15 Farsi ambiguous words

Word	Sense	Freq	Precision	Recall	Total Accuracy	MFS	WS
تن	Ton	2892	83.94	96.71	85.51	66.50	20
	Body	1457	90.66	63.28			
شکر	Sugar	267	96.62	96.25	94.97	70.63	30
	Thankfulness	111	91.07	91.89			
سیر	Garlic	1184	94.99	94.42	92.33	72.64	34
	Journey	446	85.43	86.77			
اشکال	Figures	264	79.06	82.95	80.89	51.02	44
	Defect	275	82.82	78.91			
خرد	Wisdom	209	87.44	93.30	89.68	51.35	20
	Tiny	198	92.39	85.86			
حلال	Lawful	82	94.05	96.34	92.66	75.23	20
	Resolvent	27	88.00	81.48			
نفس	Breath	204	87.91	78.43	91.37	73.33	40
	Oneself	561	92.45	96.08			
اشراف	Dominance	51	83.05	96.08	88.78	52.34	22
	Knight, Gentleman	56	95.83	82.14			
قسم	Oath	71	89.04	91.55	89.31	54.61	20
	Sort	59	89.65	88.13			
مهر	Punch	238	83.55	81.09	83.97	46.83	6
	A Solar Month	406	85.31	88.67			
	Love	223	81.77	78.47			
محرم	A Lunar Month	233	97.49	100.00	97.29	90.66	20
	Intimate	24	100.00	75.00			
جو	Atmosphere	329	96.41	97.87	95.72	74.10	28
	Barley	115	93.64	89.56			
شرف	Honor	89	97.73	96.63	96.35	65.44	38
	Soon Expected	47	93.88	97.87			
کرم	Cream	16	93.75	93.75	94.32	52.27	26
	Chromium	11	100.00	100.00			
	Worm	46	95.55	93.48			
	Generosity	12	85.71	100.00			
	Cream Colored	3	100.00	66.66			
سرم	My Head	93	97.89	100.00	98.47	70.99	34
	Serum	38	100.00	94.74			
Avg.	--	304.03	91.38	89.24	91.44	64.53	26.8

performance of this method. The first two columns show the homograph and its senses. The frequency of each sense appearing in the corpus is reported in the third column.

Next three columns report the evaluation measures: precision, recall, and total accuracy [9]. The last two columns show the baseline and the best window size. The baseline is the lower bound on the performance of word sense disambiguation [10], and is the performance of always choosing the most frequent sense. By window size we mean the number of words around the ambiguous word which are considered as the context words of test sample. The last row shows the average of each column. The performance column shows that this method clearly outperforms the baseline method.

For comparison, we implemented three corpus based methods and applied them to the same homographs. There are two possible approaches to corpus based methods: supervised and unsupervised. Supervised approaches use annotated training. So, training and evaluating them presupposes the existence of sense-tagged corpora, but they generally outperform unsupervised methods. Supervised methods can be classified into probabilistic, exemplar–based, and rule-based approaches [4]. We implemented a method from each approach. Then, we chose Naïve Bayes (NB), K nearest Neighbor (KNN), and Decision List (DL).

Space does not permit description of the details of these methods. In KNN implementation, features contribute to the calculation of the similarity between two samples with different weights. Similarly in classifying a new test example, each example of the set of nearest neighbors votes for its class with a weight proportional to its closeness to the test example [3], [11]. The decision list is implemented based on [12]. We also applied the basic algorithm to the homographs. In this experiment, we considered 3000 salient words for each conceptual category.

Table 2. Performance of the basic algorithm and corpus based methods in %

Word	Proposed Method	Basic Algorithm	Naïve Bayes	Exemplar Based	Decision List	No. of Examples
تن	85.51	82.02	95.33	92.08	95.05	4349
شکر	94.97	93.12	94.88	91.46	94.12	378
سیر	92.33	91.35	95.55	88.63	92.10	1630
اشکال	80.89	77.55	80.92	81.44	83.36	539
خرد	89.68	85.99	85.59	82.83	86.03	407
حلال	92.66	87.15	91.42	89.89	89.79	109
نفس	91.37	85.49	90.35	90.74	91.40	765
اشراف	88.78	82.24	89	86.82	86.41	107
قسم	89.31	80.15	90.77	92.35	89.4	130
مهر	83.97	71.86	88.00	85.69	84.55	867
محرم	97.29	94.96	96.17	96.26	95.86	257
جو	95.72	85.81	95.63	90.11	93.06	444
شرف	96.35	89.05	98.33	98.33	99.65	136
کرم	94.32	87.50	79.66	79.48	86.12	88
سرم	98.47	96.18	97.06	89.85	96.19	131
Average	91.44	86.03	91.24	89.06	90.87	689.13

Table 2 shows the performance of the proposed method in comparison with the basic algorithm and three corpus based methods. The first two columns show the homograph and the proposed method's performance. The performance of the algorithm presented in [1] by Yarowsky is shown in the third column as basic algorithm. Columns 4 to 6 report the results of Naive Bayes, Exemplar-based, and the Rule-based methods in order, and the last column shows the number of examples existing in the corpus for each homograph. We used 10-fold cross validation for performance calculation of these methods. The last row shows the average of each column.

The basic algorithm searches the whole thesaurus for identification of the conceptual classes relevant to an ambiguous word, and it is stated that this might increase the performance of the algorithm notably. Here, we considered only those categories under which the polysemous word is listed. We also performed all the steps of the algorithm on the inflectional forms of the words, since there was no reliable stemmer available to the authors.

As the last row of table 2 shows, by considering certain collocations of the homograph and ambiguous words in the conceptual categories, and making all of the words in the test context contribute to the score calculation of categories, the performance increases by 5.41%.

We can also use this method for removing the morphological ambiguity. Each NLP system needs a morphology module. This module may encounter words whose morphological structure cannot be determined without notification of their senses. For example consider the word "سرم". As stated in table 1, this word has two senses. When the word has the first meaning (my head), its morphological structure should be "Noun /سر/ + possessive pronoun /م/", and when it has the second meaning (serum), the morphological structure should be just "Noun /سرم/". We used the proposed method for removing this kind of ambiguity. To extract the conceptual categories for the first meaning, we used the related categories of the word's lemma, /سر/.

Corpus-based methods choose the correct sense of the ambiguous word with the highest probability or similarity computed on the basis of the training data. So, their performance is very sensitive to the number of training examples. Training examples should be a good representative for all the ambiguous word's samples. Then, the training set should contain adequate number of samples from different texts and domains.

For instance, consider the ambiguous word "کرم" with five senses described in table 1. This word occurred 88 times in the corpus. It's obvious that this number of training examples can't be a good representative for five senses. The last sense, cream-colored appeared 3 times. Regarding to table 1, Naïve Bayes disambiguates this ambiguous word with the accuracy of 79.66%, while the accuracy of the proposed method is 94.32%. Table 3 shows the precision and recall of all the applied algorithms for every sense of this ambiguous word. As expected, corpus based methods can disambiguate none of the samples of the fifth sense correctly, while the precision and recall of the proposed method for this sense are 100% and 66.66%. It means this method disambiguates 2 of 3 samples correctly. So, the performance of the proposed method is not dependent on the number of training examples, and it can be appropriate for identifying word senses which occur rarely.

Table 3. Precision and recall of all the applied algorithms to the ambiguous word "کرم" with 5 different sense

Sense of word "کرم"	No. of Samples	Basic Algorithm	Proposed Method	NB	KNN	DL
Precision of Cream	16	75.00	93.75	60.00	77.78	66.67
Recall of Cream		93.75	93.75	37.50	43.75	66.67
Precision of Chromium	11	84.61	100.00	100.00	100.00	78.57
Recall of Chromium		100.00	100.00	90.91	36.36	100.00
Precision of Worm	46	97.37	95.55	75.44	68.18	97.67
Recall of Worm		80.43	93.48	93.48	97.83	91.30
Precision of Generosity	12	80.00	85.71	88.89	100.00	80.00
Recall of Generosity		100.00	100.00	66.67	75.00	100.00
Precision of Color	3	100.00	100.00	0.0	0.0	0.0
Recall of Color		66.66	66.66	0.0	0.0	0.0

The average number of senses for Farsi homographs is 2.18 which is lower in comparision with English. For example, in the WORDNET, the average number of senses per noun for the most frequent 121 nouns in English is 7.8 [13].

So, It seems that the above applied algorithms should have lower performance on disambiguation of English words. But, the average number of senses per word is not the only factor that affects the performance of word sense disambiguation algorithms in a given language. Comprehensiveness of corpus and the quality of knowledge sources like thesaurus also affect the performance of the algorithms. Therefore, regarding to table 2, it can be concluded that imperfectness of used corpus and thesaurus might be one of the reasons that the average performance of the basic algorithm on disambiguation of Farsi homographs is lower than the performance reported in [1] for English homographs.

5   Conclusion

A method was proposed for word sense disambiguation of Farsi homographs. This method needs no sense tagged data. Therefore, we do not have to label the training data manually which is very expensive and time consuming. Comparisons show that from the point of homograph word sense disambiguation performance, the proposed method is comparable to supervised corpus based methods. Considering the lack of tagged corpora and knowledge sources for Farsi language and the difficulty of preparing them, and also considering the good results obtained from the conducted experiments in this paper, the proposed method seems to be well applicable to Farsi word sense disambiguation.

Moreover, the results show the proposed modifications added to the basic algorithm presented in [1], improve the homograph disambiguation performance by 5.41%. In addition, the proposed method can be used for removing morphological ambiguity and for disambiguation of word senses which occur rarely.

Acknowledgments. Authors would like to thank Mr. Jamshid Fararooy for his kind cooperation in this research and providing us the access to his valuable Farsi thesaurus in a machine readable format.

References

1. Yarowsky, D.: Word-sense disambiguation using statistical models of Roget's categories trained on large corpora. In: 15th [sic] International Conference on Computational Linguistics (Coling), Nantes, pp. 454–460 (1992)
2. Ide, N., Veronis, J.: Introduction to the Special Issue on Word Sense Disambiguation: The State of the Art. Computational Linguistics 24(1), 1–40 (1998)
3. Escudero, G., Marquez, L., Rigau, G.: Naïve Bayes and Exemplar-Based Approaches to Word Sense Disambiguation Revisited. In: 14th European Conference on Artificial Intelligence, ECAI, Berlin, Germany (2000)
4. Gausted, T.: Linguistic Knowledge and Word Sense Disambiguation, PhD dissertation, Groningen University (2004)
5. Gale, B., Church, K., Yarowsky, D.: A method for disambiguating word senses in a corpus. Computers and the Humanities 26, 415–439 (1992)
6. Bijankhan, M.: Farsi text corpus, Research Center of Intelligent Signal Processing of Iran (RCISP), http://www.rcisp.com
7. Fararooy, J.: thesaurus and Electronic transfer of Persian language content. In: 2nd workshop on Persian language and computer, Tehran, Iran (2004)
8. Fararooy, J.: Thesaurus of Persian Words and Phrases (1999)
9. Manning, C.D., Raghavan, P., Schutze, H.: An Introduction to Information Retrieval. Cambridge University Press, Cambridge (2008)
10. Gale, B., Church, K., Yarowsky, D.: Estimating upper and lower bounds on the performance of word-sense disambiguation programs. In: 30th Annual Meeting of the Association for Computational Linguistics, Newark, pp. 249–256 (1992)
11. Ng, H.T.: Exemplar-Base Word Sense Disambiguation: Some Recent Improvements. In: 2nd Conference on Empirical Methods in Natural Language Processing, EMNLP 1997 (1997)
12. Yarowsky, D.: Decision lists for lexical ambiguity resolution: Application to accent restoration in Spanish and French. In: 32th Annual Meeting of the Association for Computational Linguistics, Las Cruces (1994)
13. Ng, H.T., Lee, H.B.: Integrating Multiple Knowledge Sources to Disambiguate Word Sense: An Exemplar-based Approach. In: 34th Annual Meeting of the Association for Computational Linguistics, pp. 40–47. N.J. Association for Computational Linguistics, Somerset (1996)

Local Rephrasing Suggestions
for Supporing the Work of Writers

Aurélien Max

LIMSI-CNRS and Université Paris-Sud 11
Orsay, France
aurelien.max@limsi.fr

Abstract. In this article, we present a framework for obtaining rephrasings for short text spans. Good candidates include paraphrases, but also more generally phrases that could help a writer revise a text with some shifts in meaning. The presented framework uses as its knowledge source bilingual aligned phrases learnt from parallel corpora. We present several models for selecting rephrasings, and we evaluate the selection power of candidate rephrasings on *grammaticality*, *meaning preservation* and *authoring value*. The approach is then discussed and future work is described.

1 Introduction

One of the most difficult tasks for a writer, apart from content selection and planning, is finding the appropriate words. Some paraphrases may appear more natural to a native speaker, integrate better within the stylistic context of a discourse, or use terminology that is more adapted to the intended readers of a document. On the other hand, different rephrasings can introduce shifts in meaning that better convey what the writer actually wants to express. Therefore, automatic rephrasing techniques as a whole can be useful for writers, but with some control over how much meaning can be altered.

Today's users of word processors, the most commonly used authoring tools, get suprisingly very little help as regards such a need. Thesauri, dictionaries of synonyms or inverted dictionaries can provide some help at the lexical level by suggesting related words, and it remains the responsibility of the author to accept or not the changes in meaning. Grammatical checkers bring some help in checking that a text remains grammatical after it has been altered, but for this type of use this is mainly restricted to ensuring that correct agreements are enforced.

There has been a recent interest in automatic paraphrasing approaches, which has been motivated mostly by the needs for identifying paraphrases in information extraction tasks and generating text in text-to-text generation applications such as multi-document summarization. Most of the proposed approaches rely on the use of comparable monolingual corpora or parallel monolingual corpora. While comparable monolingual corpora can be easily collected, identifying highly reusable paraphrasing patterns from them is an active research issue. Parallel

A. Ranta, B. Nordström (Eds.): GoTAL 2008, LNAI 5221, pp. 324–335, 2008.
© Springer-Verlag Berlin Heidelberg 2008

monolingual corpora can be used to extract more reliable alignments, but this type of resource is extremely scarce and therefore cannot lead to large quantities of useful paraphrasing data.

In a strict sense, paraphrasing poses the difficult issue of meaning equivalence. Whereas the acceptability of lexical paraphrasing has started to receive some attention [1,2], assessing the acceptability in terms of meaning change for sentential paraphrasing is still a real challenge. In fact, systems attempting sentential level paraphrasings such as [3] use application contexts that are so restrictive that the chances of meaning alteration are very low.

Although paraphrasing aids would be undoubtedly useful for writers, we argue that rephrasing aids can assist in more general authoring needs. The current approaches to Machine Translation, and statistical approaches in particular (SMT), pay very little attention to modeling transfer of meaning between source and target languages, but can nonetheless prove quite useful if used appropriately. In particular, such systems can provide ranked translation completions for translators who can accept or ignore them, as in the TransType system [4]. There is nonetheless a recent resurge of interest for modeling source context in Statistical Machine Translation (e.g. [5,6]).

In this paper, we present an approach inspired from [7,8] which produces ranked rephrasing candidates for short text spans. Our prototype system is more specifically intended for integration within word processors to assist writers who can evaluate in use the appropriateness of the rephrasing candidates, but could also be used for unsupervised rephrasing of text.[1] The system makes use of the wealth of correspondances that can be extracted from large bilingual parallel corpora used in SMT systems. As in [7], it uses a pivot translation into a foreign language to find rephrasings in the same language. We use a log-linear framework typical of phrase-based SMT systems to integrate various models for features that may be of interest to a human writer. The relative contribution of each model is not optimized using an automatic evaluation metrics such as BLEU for translation [9], but can be tuned dynamically by the writer.

In the following section, we describe our framework for generating rephrasings of phrases based on translation into a pivot language, and various models that can be integrated into it. In section 3, we describe evaluation settings and report on our results on a rephrasing task. We describe related work in section 4, and finally discuss our approach and future work in section 5.

2   Rephrasing Based on Pivot Translation

2.1   Framework

The phrase-based approach to Statistical Machine Translation [10] relies on automatic alignments between phrases of words in two languages. Those alignments

---

[1] We have not evaluated our approach for unsupervised rephrasing of text. We believe that this type of application would only be sensible after some spotting of specific text spans, such as text spans that are unnatural but still comprehensible by native speakers, has been performed.

map contiguous groups of surface forms of words which do not have to correspond to linguistically motivated units.[2] Translation is performed on a sentence basis: a heuristic search attempts to find segmentations of an input sentence into phrases and the mapping into a target sentence by substituting source phrases by their possible translations and possibly reordering them. Search is guided by an evaluation function that combines different models whose relative weights are optimized on automatic translation evaluation metrics such as BLEU [9] using corpora not seen during training.

At the heart of this approach is the translation table that associates input phrases to the set of their possible translations together with their conditional probabilities and other information. Many approaches to phrase extraction rely on word-based alignements as a first step. For example, Och and Ney [12] use $1 \rightarrow N$ word alignments in both directions between two languages, symmetrize those alignments, and incrementally grow phrasal alignments by adding source or target words to the alignments that are only word-alignable to a corresponding word of the aligned segment. After phrase extraction, conditional probabilities are estimated, for example using maximum likelihood estimation.

Such $N \rightarrow M$ alignments can capture lexical translations (e.g. *exigeons* $\rightarrow$ *ask for, call for, demand, expect, request*, etc.) and phrasal litteral or idiomatic translations (e.g. *un bon début* $\rightarrow$ *a good approach, a good first move, a good starting point, a positive initiative, an encouraging start, the right road*, etc.), but can also capture noise depending on the alignment heuristics used (e.g. *les états candidats (candidate countries)* $\rightarrow$ *Member States, the candidate countries were to, the accession countries have called for, candidate, the*, etc.) Because different target phrases associated with a given source phrase can either represent paraphrases in all or some contexts or phrases with different meanings, approaches for disambiguating phrases during translation using source context have been recently proposed [5,6]. Among the main limitations of this type of phrasal alignments are their inability to model non-consecutive words in source and target sentences and to generalize the contents of phrases.

Bannard and Callison Burch [7,8] have used phrasal translation probabilities between two languages to find phrasal paraphrases by using one of the two languages as pivot as illustrated in Figure 1. Search of a paraphrase p_2 for p_1 is defined by equation 1, where the conditional probability is calculated over all possible *pivot* phrases:

$$\hat{p}_2 = \arg\max_{p_2 \neq p_1} P(p_2|p_1) = \arg\max_{p_2 \neq p_1} \sum_{pivot} P(pivot|p_1)P(p_2|pivot) \qquad (1)$$

---

[2] While early experiments have shown decreased performance when phrases in both languages were restricted to syntactic chunks [10], more recent results show that syntactically-motivated alignments can improve translation performance (e.g. [11]).

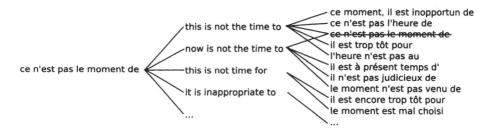

Fig. 1. Example of rephrasing for a French phrase using English as pivot

Callison-Burch [8] measured the importance of various factors impacting the quality of the paraphrases obtained.[3] Using manually built alignments yields a significant improvement in paraphrase quality, showing that if appropriate alignments are available the proposed approach can produce better paraphrases. Several languages can be used for finding pivot phrases, and using several simultaneously tend to improve alignment quality and therefore paraphrases themselves. Using a language model to find the paraphrase that maximizes its score in the original sentential context leads to improved fluency but to a decrease in meaning preservation. Lastly, restricting pivot phrases to those actually aligned in a test aligned bilingual corpus improves paraphrase quality, which illustrates the importance of disambiguating source phrases relatively to the pivot language.

In this work, we propose an integration of automatic rephrasing as an authoring aid. We use the log-linear framework traditionally used in SMT systems in order to integrate various models to score possible rephrasings. However, we do not use an automatic evaluation of rephrasing quality, as its definition depends heavily on the subjective appreciation of a writer, which implies that the weight of models cannot be optimized as done in SMT using metrics such as BLEU.[4] Equation 2 presents the formulation of the search for the rephrasing with the highest score, where M is the set of models used, h_m is the score of a model, λ_m is its weight and C represents sentential context.

$$\hat{p_2} = \arg\max_{p_2} \sum_{m=1}^{M} \lambda_m \log h_m(p_1, p_2, C) \qquad (2)$$

---

[3] In his experiments, Callison-Burch used 46 randomly chosen English phrases in multiword expressions present in WordNet (e.g. *at work*, *concentrate on*, *big business*), and 289 original sentences containing an occurrence of one of them and 1,366 unique sentences obtained through substitution. Evaluation was performed by two judges who had to assess the *adequacy* and *fluency* of paraphrases.

[4] As noted by Callison-Burch [8], there is currently no standard methodology for evaluating paraphrase quality directly, and task-based evaluation (e.g. for Machine Translation [8]) is often performed. Whereas working towards an automatic evaluation methodology of paraphrasing is a crucial research issue, it seems that applying such a methodology to rephrasing, which depends a lot on the intention of a writer, would be too limiting at this point.

2.2   Models for the Selection of Local Rephrasings

In this section, we describe the models that we have used for assessing several characteristics of automatic rephrasings. In contrast to most previous work we are aware of (e.g. [7,13,2]), we are not only interested in meaning preserving paraphrases, but more generally in rephrasings that may be of interest to a writer.

Model Based on Pivot Translation (Piv). We use the scoring of paraphrases by the pivot model proposed by Bannard and Callison-Burch [7], using a single language as pivot.[5]

$$Piv(p_1, p_2, C) = \sum_{pivot} P(pivot|p_1)P(p_2|pivot) \qquad (3)$$

Model Based on Language Fluency (Lm). We use a language model as a scoring function to measure the fluency of the substitution in context of the rephrased segment. As noted by Callison-Burch [8], modifying one part of a sentence might require other changes in the sentence for it to remain grammatical, but this is currently not taken into account by our proposed approach. Also, this type of model will tend to favor shorter phrases.

Model Based on Dependency Relationship Preservation (Dep). When substituting a part of a sentence with another phrase and if this substitution does not require other changes in the sentence, then the dependency relationships between words outside that phrase should be preserved. Moreover, dependency relationships crossing a phrase boundaries (i.e., whose governor was outside the phrase and dependant inside it, or the opposite) could still exist after such a substitution, possibly with a modified dependency target in the phrase. In figure 2, the original sentence has a SUJL relationship between *nous* and some target in the segment, and an OBJ relationship between some target in the segment and *voulons*. The same relationships are found when substituting *faire des efforts* with *consentir des efforts*. However, when substituting *faire des efforts* with *leurs efforts*, only the first relationship can be found. The ability to measuring this of course depends greatly on the capacity of the parser used to find dependency relationships, and on its robustness to agrammatical input.

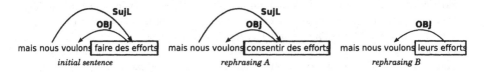

Fig. 2. Example of dependency relationships before and after phrase substitution

---

[5] Making use of context using the approach of [5] is part of our future work.

The score of our model is based on some proportion of the number of such dependencies found after substitution over the number of original dependencies:

$$Dep(p_1, p_2, C) = \frac{1 + |\mathcal{D}_1^{extra} \cap \mathcal{D}_2^{extra}| + |\mathcal{D}_1^{inter} \cap \mathcal{D}_2^{inter}|}{1 + |\mathcal{D}_1^{extra}| + |\mathcal{D}_1^{inter}|} \tag{4}$$

where $\mathcal{D}_1^{extra}$ and $\mathcal{D}_2^{extra}$ are the sets of dependency relationships of the form *(governor,relationship,dependant)* outside the rephrased segment, respectively before and after substitution, and $\mathcal{D}_1^{inter}$ and $\mathcal{D}_2^{inter}$ are respectively the sets of dependency relationships of the form *(target_outside_phrase,relationship)* crossing a rephrased segment boundary, respectively before and after substitution.

Model Based on Common Lemma (Lem). There will be cases when possible rephrasings will be very close to their original phrase. This model favors rephrasings that use different words, where words can be restricted to the lemmas of content words:

$$Lem(p_1, p_2, C) = \frac{1 + |\mathcal{L}_2| - |\mathcal{L}_1 \cap \mathcal{L}_2|}{1 + |\mathcal{L}_1 \cup \mathcal{L}_2|} \tag{5}$$

where $\mathcal{L}_1$ and $\mathcal{L}_2$ are the sets of full word lemmas respectively in $p1$ and in $p2$.

3   Experiments and Evaluation

We have used the recent version of the Europarl corpus [14] to derive phrasal alignments between French and English. From the 948,507 aligned sentences, some 42 million aligned phrase pairs of up to 7 tokens were obtained for French and English using Giza++ [15] and the **grow-diag-final-and** heuristics described in [10]. French was initially chosen as the source language as we had an easy access to native speakers for evaluation and access to a robust dependency parser, SYNTEX [16]. We used a 5-gram language model trained on the French part of the corpus using Kneser-Ney smoothing.

We have manually built a test corpus of 82 sentences from the Europarl corpus not used for extracting phrase alignments and learning the language model. A human judge was then asked to select one text span per sentence that would be a good candidate for rephrasing during text revision. Only phrases that belonged to the French-English translation table used were accepted (e.g. *dans de bonnes conditions, maintenir le contact, attendent avec impatience, la plus étroite, états candidats,* etc.) Because we did not have automatic evaluation metrics and in order to be able to reuse our evaluation corpus for further experiments involving different models without new human annotation, we have built a finite set of rephrasings for each *(sentence, segment to be rephrased)* pair. In order to limit the annotation work, we have kept at most the 20 first rephrasings obtained using the PIV model only (which introduces a bias in our experiments as not all possible rephrasings can be considered, but those are the best according to our baseline model). Two native speaker judges were then asked to evaluate each of the 1648 rephrased sentences on three characteristics related to their use in a revision task with a 5-level scale:

- **grammaticality/fluency:** is the rephrasing flawless French that can be used as is (5), does it contain various level of language flaws (4-2), or simply impossible to reuse (1).
- **meaning preservation:** does the rephrased sentence carry the same meaning as the original sentence (5), diverge to various levels in terms of information removed or added from the original sentence (4-2), or has a completely different meaning (1).
- **authoring value:** can the rephrasing be directly reused for revising a text (5), can the rephrasing be used with a minor change (4), does the rephrasing contain elements that could be used for a good rephrasing (3), does the rephrasing contains elements that could suggest a rephrasing (2), or is the rephrasing useless (1).

After the judges had completed manual annotation, smoothing of the scores was done by keeping mean scores for each sentence. We measured a value of 0.59 standard deviation for score absolute differences between judges for grammaticality, 0.7 for meaning preservation and 0.8 for authoring value. Those values suggest that judgments on grammaticality and meaning preservation can be done fairly objectively with reasonable inter-judge agreement, and that judging authoring value on the proposed scale was more difficult and more dependent on personal judgment.

Results of mean scores for the first rank solutions with various model combinations are reported in figure 3.[6] We used uniform model weights, but will discuss later how weights can be directly tuned by a user.

PIV alone has a relatively good performance in grammaticality, suggesting that alignments in both directions often associate phrases of syntactically comparable natures. Adding LM or DEP improve its performance, the first result being consistent with the findings of [8]. Whereas the combination PIV+LM performs better in grammaticality than PIV+DEP, it is interesting to note that DEP alone performs better than LM alone. Apart from showing the interest of DEP, this could mean that preferences by DEP and PIV are more similar than between LM and PIV. An explanation may lie in the fact that, by nature, language models favor texts that are locally more fluent (on a window of 5 words at most in the case of LM), but not necessarily texts that capture dependencies of longer range, which is precisely what accurate grammatical dependency relationships can capture. Combining with LEM, which was not expected to play a positive role for grammaticality, degrades grammaticality scores in all cases except when combining it with all other models. This model may select phrases which are not always correctly aligned or which would require changes in other parts of the sentence.

---

[6] Due to the limited search space, an exhaustive search can be performed which is therefore guaranteed to find the optimal solution according to a model combination.

	grammaticality	meaning	authoring value	mean
PIV (baseline)	4.46	4.18	3.62	4.09
LM	4.28	3.62	3.45	3.78
DEP	4.35	3.68	3.43	3.82
LEM	4.05	3.21	3.28	3.51
PIV+LM	**4.65**	4.06	3.82	4.18
PIV+DEP	4.58	**4.27**	3.66	4.17
PIV+LEM	4.37	4.00	3.76	4.05
LM+DEP	4.49	3.81	3.68	3.99
LM+LEM	4.28	3.59	3.56	3.81
PIV+LM+DEP	**4.65**	4.05	3.92	4.21
PIV+LM+LEM	4.61	4.02	3.97	4.20
PIV+DEP+LEM	4.57	4.17	**4.02**	**4.25**
LM+DEP+LEM	4.37	3.69	3.64	3.90
PIV+LM+DEP+LEM	**4.68**	4.09	**4.05**	**4.27**

Fig. 3. Mean results at first rank for various model combinations (uniform weighting)

PIV also has good performance alone regarding meaning preservation. In fact, only the combination PIV+DEP has a better performance, while DEP alone has a performance which is much worse than PIV. The nature of the corpus may explain in part a bias towards meaning preserving paraphrases with PIV alone: the parliamentary session transcripts of the Europarl corpus contain more paraphrases than polysemous phrases. Another explanation would be that phrases selected by our evaluator tended to have the same meaning as those with highest PIV scores. The complementary contribution of DEP may be explained by the fact that it selects rephrasings in which both dependencies outside the rephrased segment and dependencies connecting the segment with its context are preserved, and that this may correct cases where PIV would prefer some shifts in meaning. The degradation of performance observed when combining with LM is consistent with [8]. Finally, LEM can sometimes select good lexical synonyms, but segments containing several full words may more often correspond to different meanings. The following is an example for which annotators gave good grammaticality scores, but poor meaning preservation scores:

Original sentence: *ce n' est pas le moment de se montrer hésitant . (this is no time for the faint-hearted .[7])*

Rephrased sentence: *il est trop tôt pour se montrer hésitant . (it is too early to be hesitant .)*

Lastly, authoring value scores are lower, which can be explained by the fact that rephrasings with bad fluency and/or meaning preservation scores will be penalized here as well. The combination of all models yields the best result. PIV seems to have the most impact, but all other models also contribute, but possibly

---

[7] "Translation" from the Europarl corpus.

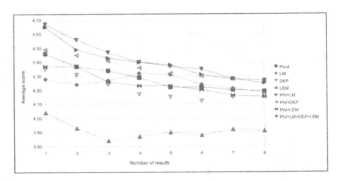

(a) Grammaticality mean scores

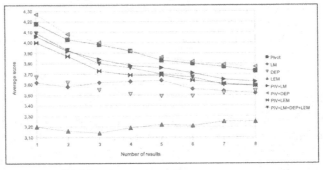

(b) Meaning preservation mean scores

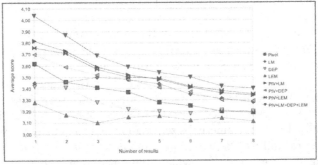

(c) Authoring value mean scores

Fig. 4. Mean scores depending on the number of results presented to the user

in different ways. This suggests that which model should be used (or its weight in our framework) could be chosen by a user. The following example illustrates a case where the rephrased sentence got an average meaning preservation score but a good authoring value score:[8]

---

[8] It is indeed the responsibility of an author to decide whether it is acceptable to rephrase *mesdames et messieurs* (*ladies and gentlemen*) with *mes chers collègues* (*my dear colleagues*).

Original sentence: *mesdames et messieurs* , *c' est maintenant l' heure de la pause et du dîner* (*ladies and gentlemen* , *we shall now stop for a break and something to eat*)

Rephrased sentence: *mes chers collègues* , *c' est maintenant l' heure de la pause et du dîner* (*my dear colleagues, . . .*)

Figure 4 shows mean results when presenting up to 8 rephrasings to a writer. It can be noted that model ranking for a given characteristics is almost constant.

4   Related Work

Monolingual comparable corpora have been used for automatic paraphrasing. For example, Barzilay and Lee [3] learned paraphrasing patterns as pairs of word lattices which are used to produce sentence level paraphrases. The corpus they used contained news agency articles on the same events, which allows precise sentence paraphrasing, but on a small sets of phenomena (and for a limited domain). Taking into account the fact that sentential paraphrasing is more likely to alter meaning, Quirk *et al.* [17] approached paraphrasing as monotonous decoding by a phrase-based SMT system. Their corpus consisted of monolingual sentences from a comparable corpus that were automatically aligned so as to allow aligned phrase extraction. Pang *et al.* [18] used parallel monolingual corpora built from news stories that had been independantly translated several times to learn lattices from a syntax-based alignment process. Lepage and Denoual [19] propose an approach in which initial paraphrases are found by translation equivalence in a bilingual corpus and new paraphrases are built by analogy.

Pivot translation as been proposed as an approach for paraphrasing phrases by Bannard and Callison-Burch [7], but to our knowledge no work has yet used bilingual corpora and Machine Translation for sentential paraphrasing, as this is too dependent on the overall quality of automatic translations. At the lexical level, Connor and Roth [2] used unsupervised learning to learn classifiers that indicate whether a word can be substituted for another word in a given context. Fujita [13] proposed a transfer-and-revision framework using linguistic knowledge for generating paraphrases in Japanese and a model for error detection.

5   Discussion and Future Work

In this article, we have presented a framework for obtaining rephrasings for short text spans. Good candidates include paraphrases, but also more generally phrases that could help a writer revise a text with some shifts in meaning. The presented framework uses as its knowledge source bilingual aligned phrases derived from parallel corpora. We have described several models for selecting rephrasings, and have shown in particular the value of models based on the preservation of dependency relationships.

There are several open issues to the presented work. First, there can be a strong bias introduced by the bilingual corpus used. Using Europarl with our pivot approach yields both generic and domain/genre-specific rephrasings, and it is important to be able to determine their appropriate context of use. It would also be interesting to investigate enriching this framework with phrases learnt from monolingual corpora from a given domain or genre, and to use features from the current text under revision. More generally, we would need to get some idea of the degree of possible reuse of a given rephrasing.

As shown by Callison-Burch [8], there is much to be gained by using better alignments. While it is unrealistic to rely on manually built aligned phrases given the broad definition of the notion of phrase, syntax-based alignments techniques (e.g. [11]) can provide more precise alignments that could in turn produce rephrasings that would be more grammatical and more useful to a writer. Information from the context of alignments could be used to learn classifiers to disambiguate the source phrase and get only pivot phrases that are compatible with the context of a given rephrasing, in similar ways as done for SMT [5,6].

Another issue concerns how text spans to be rephrased could be identified. In our experiments, we asked a writer acting as a revisor to manually select text spans. It appeared that, possibly due to lack of experience of our users with such an assistive technology, the choice of boundaries was not always optimal. In fact, enlarging the phrase spans by a few words on the left and/or on the right could sometimes yield much better candidates, which is partly due to the fact that context was not taken into account for selecting pivot phrases. We therefore intend to implement a search procedure that will attempt enlarging or shrinking segments up to a certain number of words and propose the new segment for consideration if it can yield a significantly better score. This also raises the issue of the automatic spotting of candidate text spans for revision, for example by using a language model to find very disfluent text spans.

In order to evaluate our framework in concrete use, we have started to develop an authoring prototype, which lets writers select text spans and obtain lists of possible rephrasings ordered by decreasing scores. Writers can directly tune the relative importance of the models used, so they can for example favor rephrasings that use different words and/or that are more or less fluent. Pivot phrases can be used for interactively disambiguating the original phrase and therefore restricting the set of possible rephrasings to those that are actually aligned to it. This feature might prove useful for writers writing in a second language and of course with sufficient knowledge of the pivot language.

References

1. McCarthy, D., Navigli, R.: SemEval-2007 Task 10: English Lexical Substitution Task. In: Proceedings of Semeval workshop at ACL, Prague, Czech Republic (2007)
2. Connor, M., Roth, D.: Context Sensitive Paraphrasing with a Single Unsupervised Classifier. In: Proceedings of ECML, Warsaw, Poland (2007)
3. Barzilay, R., Lee, L.: Learning to Paraphrase: an Unsupervised Approach Using Multiple-Sequence Alignment. In: Proceedings of NAACL/HLT, Edmonton, Canada (2003)

4. Foster, G., Langlais, P., Lapalme, G.: User-Friendly Text Prediction for Translators. In: Proceedings of EMNLP, Philadelphia, USA (2002)
5. Stroppa, N., van den Bosch, A., Way, A.: Exploiting Source Similarity for SMT using Context-Informed Features. In: Proceedings of TMI, Skovde, Sweden (2007)
6. Carpuat, M., Wul, D.: Context-Dependent Phrasal Translation Lexicons for Statistical Machine Translation. In: Proceedings of Machine Translation Summit XI, Copenhagen, Denmark (2007)
7. Bannard, C., Callison-Burch, C.: Paraphrasing with Bilingual Parallel Corpora. In: Proceedings of ACL, Ann Arbor, USA (2005)
8. Callison-Burch, C.: Paraphrasing and Translation. PhD thesis, University of Edinburgh (2007)
9. Papineni, K., Roukos, S., Ward, T., Zhu, W.J.: BLEU: a method for automatic evaluation of machine translation. In: Proceedings of ACL, Philadelphia, USA (2002)
10. Koehn, P., Och, F.J., Marcu, D.: Statistical Phrase-Based Translation. In: Proceedings of NAACL/HLT, Edmonton, Canada (2003)
11. Hearne, M., Ozdowska, S., Tinsley, J.: Comparing Constituency and Dependency Representations for SMT Phrase-Extraction. In: Proceedings of TALN, Avignon, France (2008)
12. Och, F.J., Ney, H.: The Alignment Template Approach to Statistical Machine Translation. Computational Linguistics 30(4) (2004)
13. Fujita, A.: Automatic Generation of Syntactically Well-formed and Semantically Appropriate Paraphrases. PhD thesis, Nara Institute of Science and Technology (2005)
14. Koehn, P.: Europarl: A Parallel Corpus for Statistical Machine Translation. In: Proceedings of MT Summit, Phuket, Thailand (2005)
15. Och, F.J., Ney, H.: A Systematic Comparison of Various Statistical Alignment Models. Computational Linguistics 29(1), 19–51 (2003)
16. Bourigault, D., Fabre, C., Frrot, C., Jacques, M.P., Ozdowska, S.: Syntex, analyseur syntaxique de corpus. In: Proceedings of TALN, Dourdan, France (2005)
17. Quirk, C., Brockett, C., Dolan, W.B.: Monolingual Machine Translation for Paraphrase Generation. In: Proceedings of EMNLP, Barcelona, Spain (2004)
18. Pang, B., Knight, K., Marcu, D.: Syntax-based Alignment of Multiple Translations: Extracting Paraphrases and Generating New Sentences. In: Proceedings of NAACL/HLT, Edmonton, Canada (2003)
19. Lepage, Y., Denoual, E.: Automatic generation of paraphrases to be used as translation references in objective evaluation measures of machine translation. In: Proceedings of International Workshop on Paraphrasing at IJCNLP, Jeju Island, Korea (2005)

Interactive Multilingual Web Applications with Grammatical Framework

Moisés Salvador Meza Moreno and Björn Bringert

Department of Computer Science and Engineering
Chalmers University of Technology and University of Gothenburg
meza@student.chalmers.se, bringert@chalmers.se

Abstract. We present an approach to multilingual web content based on multilingual grammars and syntax editing for a controlled language. Content can be edited in any supported language and it is automatically kept within a controlled language fragment. We have implemented a web-based syntax editor for Grammatical Framework (GF) grammars which allows both direct abstract syntax tree manipulation and text input in any of the languages supported by the grammar. With this syntax editor and the GF JavaScript API, GF grammars can be used to build multilingual web applications. As a demonstration, we have implemented an example application in which users can add, edit and review restaurants in English, Spanish and Swedish.

1 Introduction

Current multilingual web applications store a separate version of their content for each language. It is difficult to keep the information consistent and, in some cases, content available in one language is not provided in another. Adding a new language to the application requires translation of the available content from one of the existing languages to the new language.

We suggest a different approach to multilingual web applications, where the content is defined by a multilingual grammar and is created through syntax editing or parsing. Content created by a user who uses one language is automatically available in all the other languages supported by the grammar, and the content is consistent at all times. When the grammar is extended to cover a new language, all existing content is automatically available in that language.

To demonstrate this approach to multilinguality we implemented "The Restaurant Review Wiki", a web-based multilingual application in which users can add, edit and review restaurants in English, Spanish and Swedish. It uses GF grammars and the GF JavaScript API to provide multilinguality.

2 Grammatical Framework

Grammatical Framework (GF) [1] is a type-theoretical grammar formalism. GF grammars can describe both formal and natural languages and consist of an abstract syntax and at least one concrete syntax. The abstract syntax defines the

A. Ranta, B. Nordström (Eds.): GoTAL 2008, LNAI 5221, pp. 336–347, 2008.

scope of the grammar, i.e. all the expressions that can be built from it. The concrete syntax defines how the constructs in the abstract syntax are represented in a particular language. GF grammars can be multilingual, each language in the grammar having a separate concrete syntax. For any given grammar, GF provides parsing (going from a concrete to the abstract syntax) and linearization (going from the abstract to a concrete syntax). GF supports dependently typed and higher-order abstract syntax. These features are used, for example, to express conditions of semantic well-formedness. However, they are not used in this article since they are not supported in the implementations described.

GF includes a Resource Grammar Library [2] which defines the basic grammar of (currently) eleven languages. For each language, the Resource Grammar Library provides the complete morphology, a lexicon of approximately one hundred of the most important structural words, a test lexicon of approximately 300 content words, a list of irregular verbs and a substantial fragment of the syntax. The Resource Grammar Library has an API (Application Programming Interface) which allows the user to implement grammars for these languages easily. The API also provides tools to extend the resource grammars, for example, new words can be added to the lexicon. GF is freely available[1] and is distributed under the GNU General Public License (GPL).

2.1   An Example Grammar

To better explain GF grammars, consider a very small grammar that describes simple restaurant reviews. The abstract syntax defines what can be said in the grammar in terms of categories (**cat**) and functions (**fun**). In the example grammar, the abstract syntax (Figure 1) has four categories: Phrase (the start category), Item, Demonym and Quality. It also has some functions that construct terms in these categories. For example, the function *itemIs* takes an Item and a Quality as arguments and produces a Phrase, and an Item can be either *restaurant* or *food*. Examples of abstract terms produced by this abstract syntax are *itemIs* (*qualItem mexican food*) (*very good*) and *itemIs restaurant expensive*.

```
abstract Restaurant = {
    flags startcat = Phrase;
    cat Phrase; Item; Demonym; Quality;
    fun itemIs        : Item → Quality → Phrase;
        restaurant, food : Item;
        qualItem        : Demonym → Item → Item;
        italian, mexican : Demonym;
        very            : Quality → Quality;
        good, bad, cheap, expensive : Quality;
}
```

Fig. 1. Abstract syntax for the example grammar

---

[1] http://digitalgrammars.com/gf/

The concrete syntax specifies how the different abstract syntax terms are expressed in a particular language. There is a linearization type (**lincat**) for every category in the abstract syntax. The linearization type is the type of the concrete syntax terms produced for the abstract syntax terms in a category. Similarly, there is a linearization definition (**lin**) for every function in the abstract syntax. A linearization definition is a function from the linearizations of the arguments of an abstract syntax function to a concrete syntax term.

Figure 2 shows the English concrete syntax for the example grammar. The linearization type for all categories is $\{s : \mathsf{Str}\}$, that is, a record with a single field s of type Str (string). The linearization of the function *restaurant* is the concrete syntax term $\{s = \text{"restaurant"}\}$. The linearization of *itemIs* makes use of the linearizations of its argument terms of type Item and Quality. The linearization of the abstract syntax term *itemIs restaurant expensive* is the string "the restaurant is expensive".

> concrete RestaurantEng of Restaurant = {
>   **lincat** Phrase, Item, Demonym, Quality = $\{s : \mathsf{Str}\}$;
>   **lin** *itemIs i q* $= \{s = \text{"the"} + i.s + \text{"is"} + q.s\}$;
>   *restaurant* $= \{s = \text{"restaurant"}\}$;
>   *food* $= \{s = \text{"food"}\}$;
>   *qualItem d i* $= \{s = d.s + i.s\}$;
>   *italian* $= \{s = \text{"Italian"}\}$;
>   *mexican* $= \{s = \text{"Mexican"}\}$;
>   *very q* $= \{s = \text{"very"} + q.s\}$;
>   *good* $= \{s = \text{"good"}\}$;
>   *bad* $= \{s = \text{"bad"}\}$;
>   *cheap* $= \{s = \text{"cheap"}\}$;
>   *expensive* $= \{s = \text{"expensive"}\}$;
> }

Fig. 2. English concrete syntax for the example grammar

Figure 3 shows the Spanish concrete syntax for the example grammar. This concrete syntax is more complex because Spanish nouns have an inherent gender (masculine or feminine). Adjectives are inflected according to the gender of the noun they modify and the form of the definite article depends on the gender of the noun it modifies. Thus the category Item has a linearization type $\{s : \mathsf{Str}; g : \mathsf{Gender}\}$. In addition to the string field s, the record has a field g of type Gender, either Masc or Fem. The categories Demonym and Quality have a linearization type $\{s : \mathsf{Gender} \Rightarrow \mathsf{Str}\}$. The field s is here a function from Gender to Str. Some helper functions (**oper**) are also defined. For example, the function *adjective* takes a Str and returns a record of type $\{s : \mathsf{Gender} \Rightarrow \mathsf{Str}\}$. The abstract syntax term *itemIs (qualItem mexican food) (very good)* is linearized to "la comida mexicana es muy buena". If we replace the feminine noun *food* with the masculine noun *restaurant* the linearization changes to "el restaurante mexicano es muy bueno".

```
concrete RestaurantSpa of Restaurant = {
  lincat Phrase            = {s : Str};
         Item              = {s : Str; g : Gender};
         Demonym, Quality = {s : Gender ⇒ Str};
  lin itemIs i q  = {s = defArt ! i.g ++ i.s ++ "es" ++ q.s ! i.g};
      restaurant  = {s = "restaurante"; g = Masc};
      food        = {s = "comida"; g = Fem};
      qualItem d i = {s = i.s ++ d.s ! i.g; g = i.g};
      italian     = adjective "italiano";
      mexican     = adjective "mexicano";
      very qual   = {s = \\g ⇒ "muy" ++ qual.s ! g};
      good        = adjective "bueno";
      bad         = adjective "malo";
      cheap       = adjective "barato";
      expensive   = adjective "caro";
  param Gender = Masc | Fem;
  oper defArt : Gender ⇒ Str = table {Masc ⇒ "el"; Fem ⇒ "la" };
       adjective : Str → {s : Gender ⇒ Str} =
       . λx → {s = table {Masc ⇒ x; Fem ⇒ Predef.tk 1 x + "a" }};
}
```

Fig. 3. Spanish concrete syntax for the example grammar

To write the Spanish concrete syntax, the grammar writer had to take into account the morphological and syntactic features of the Spanish language. Even in this simple example, gender had to be considered; imagine a grammar in which number plus case is also involved, or polarity, or verb conjugation, or all of them at once. The larger the scope of the grammar, the harder it gets to properly handle the features of a language. That is why GF's Resource Grammar Library was implemented: to define the low-level morphological and syntactic rules of languages and allow grammar writers to focus on the domain-specific semantic and stylistic aspects. The idea is that if a grammar uses the Resource Grammar Library in a type correct way, it will produce grammatically correct output. The grammar writer still has to know the target language and the application domain in order to get the semantics and pragmatics right, since the grammar library only handles syntax and morphology. Figure 4 shows a Spanish concrete syntax for the example grammar which uses the Resource Grammar Library. The categories Phrase, Item, Demonym and Quality have the linearization types Phr (phrase), CN (common noun), A (one-place adjective) and AP (adjectival phrase), respectively. All linearizations use functions from the resource grammar, such as $mkN : Str → N$, $mkA : Str → A$ and $mkNP : Det → N → NP$.

3   Syntax Editing

A *syntax editor* (also known as *syntax-directed editor, language-based editor,* or *structure editor*) lets the user edit documents by manipulating their underlying

concrete RestaurantSpaRes of Restaurant = open SyntaxSpa, ParadigmsSpa in {
   lincat Phrase = Phr; Item = CN; Demonym = A; Quality = AP;
   lin *itemIs i q*   = *mkPhr (mkCl (mkNP defSgDet i) q)*;
     restaurant   = *mkCN (mkN* "restaurante");
     food   = *mkCN (mkN* "comida");
     qualItem d i = *mkCN d i*;
     italian   = *mkA* "italiano";
     mexican   = *mkA* "mexicano";
     very qual   = *mkAP very_AdA qual*;
     good   = *mkAP (mkA* "bueno");
     bad   = *mkAP (mkA* "malo");
     cheap   = *mkAP (mkA* "barato");
     expensive = *mkAP (mkA* "caro");
}

Fig. 4. Spanish concrete syntax using the resource grammar library

structure. Such editors can be constructed for any type of structured document, for example computer programs [3], or structured text documents [4].

In the context of GF, a syntax editor lets the user manipulate abstract syntax terms for a particular grammar, while displaying its linearization(s). Syntax editing with GF grammars is described in more detail by Khegai et al. [5]. To explain GF syntax editing we will make use of the grammar described in Section 2.1. There are two kinds of abstract syntax terms: complete terms, e.g. *itemIs restaurant good* and incomplete terms, e.g. *itemIs food* ?. A question mark in an incomplete term is a *metavariable*, i.e. a non-instantiated term. The metavariable in the incomplete term *itemIs food* ? is of type Quality. Syntax editing starts with a single metavariable and it is refined step-by-step until the desired complete term is constructed.

4 GF JavaScript Syntax Editor

This is a syntax editor written in JavaScript that can be used in any JavaScript enabled web browser. This allows the syntax editor to be embedded into web applications. It can also be used as a complete application by itself, for example, to explore, debug or test GF grammars interactively.

4.1 User Interface

The editor interface contains six panels (Figure 5):

Abstract syntax tree panel. Shows a tree representation of the abstract syntax term being edited. Selecting a node will highlight both the node in this panel and its corresponding linearization(s) in the linearization panel.

Linearization panel. Shows the linearizations of the current abstract syntax term in all the available concrete syntaxes. A string representation of the

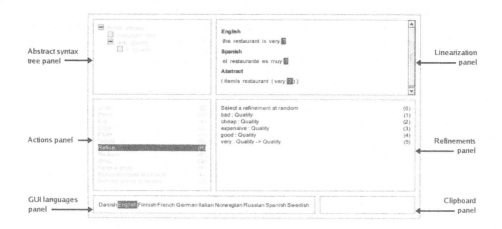

Fig. 5. GF JavaScript syntax editor

abstract syntax term is also shown. Clicking on a word in a linearization will select the corresponding node in the tree shown in the abstract syntax tree panel. Metavariables are linearized as question marks.

Actions panel. Used to show the actions available for the selected node (see Section 4.2). Actions not available for the selected node are grayed out.

Refinements panel. Used to show the available refinements or wrappers for the selected node whenever the "Refine" or "Wrap" action is selected.

GUI languages panel. Used to show and select the different languages available for the GUI (Graphical User Interface). Currently, three languages are supported: English, Spanish and Swedish. The goal is to support all the languages in GF's Resource Grammar Library. This interface localization is implemented using the approach described in Section 5.2.

Clipboard panel. Used to show the name and type of the term currently stored in the clipboard. The clipboard only holds one term at any given time.

4.2   Syntax Editing Actions

There are a number of actions that can be performed on abstract syntax terms. Some of the actions require no further explanation, among those we find: *Undo*, *Redo*, *Cut*, *Copy* and *Paste*. Some of the actions can be easily explained: *Delete* replaces an instantiated term with a metavariable, *Replace* is equivalent to *Delete* followed by *Refine*, except that it is treated as a single action in the edit history and *Refine the node at random* and *Refine the tree at random* respectively instantiate every metavariable in the subtree rooted at the selected node and the entire abstract syntax tree with type-correct objects selected at random. Finally, the following actions deserve a more in depth description:

Refine. Replaces a metavariable with a function of the appropriate type. The arguments of the function will all be metavariables. To refine a metavariable

of type Phrase (Figure 6(a)) we need to choose one function from those that
have the return type Phrase. Only the function *itemIs* : Item → Quality →
Phrase fits this requirement. This refinement will yield a term of the form
itemIs?? where the metavariables are of type Item and Quality (Figure 6(b)).

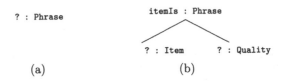

(a)   (b)

Fig. 6. Refining a metavariable of type Phrase

Wrap. Replaces an instantiated term of type T with a function which has at
least one argument of type T and a return type T. The original term is used
as the child corresponding to the first argument of type T; the remaining
children will be metavariables. In the example grammar, any term of type
Quality can be wrapped with the function *very* : Quality → Quality. Wrapping
the term *good* of type Quality, shown in Figure 7(a), with the function *very*
(Figure 7(b)) results in the term *very good* of type Quality (Figure 7(c)).
There is one exception: the top level node can be wrapped by any function
which has at least one argument of type T regardless of its return type.

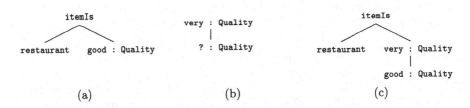

(a)   (b)   (c)

Fig. 7. Wrapping the abstract term *good*

Parse a string. Prompts the user for a string and tries to generate a type-
correct subtree by parsing it. On success, the node is instantiated with the
resulting subtree. GF grammars can be ambiguous, i.e. two abstract terms
can have the same linearization. When parsing an ambiguous string, GF
returns a list of abstract terms. In the syntax editor, the different trees
produced when parsing an ambiguous string are displayed in the refinements
panel so that the user can select one.

4.3   Implementation

We have implemented a GF JavaScript API that allows parsing, linearization,
type-annotation of meta-variables, and abstract syntax tree serialization and

deserialization to be done in JavaScript applications. This code is based on the existing GF JavaScript linearization implementation, which was originally used for output generation in GF-generated VoiceXML applications [6]. We have extended it with parsing functionality, by using the active MCFG parsing algorithm described by Burden and Ljunglöf [7].

The GF JavaScript API is now essentially an interpreter for PGF (Portable Grammar Format) [8]. PGF is a low-level format for type-theoretical grammars, and the main target of the GF grammar compiler. The GF grammar compiler has been extended to translate the PGF grammars it produces into a JavaScript representation, which is used by the GF JavaScript API. The JavaScript representation, which is isomorphic to the subset of PGF needed for type-checking, parsing and linearization, is used instead of the standard PGF form in order to avoid the extra computation needed to read PGF files directly in JavaScript.

On top of this API, the syntax editor implements the syntax editing actions, and facilities for supporting the editor user interface. One interesting addition is the support for associating parts of the linearization output with the abstract syntax sub-terms which generated them. Each node in the abstract syntax tree is given an identifier which encodes the path from the root of the tree to the given node. The linearization algorithm has been modified to tag each token that results from linearizing a node with that node's identifier. As a consequence, each token in the sequence of tokens produced by linearizing an abstract syntax tree will be tagged with the identifier of the node that produced it, and the identifiers of all its parent nodes. When the user selects a node in the tree, all tokens tagged with that node's identifier are highlighted. When a token is selected, the deepest node (i.e. longest identifier) which it is tagged with is highlighted.

5   Example Application: The Restaurant Review Wiki

The GF JavaScript API and the syntax editor described in Section 4 can be used together to build a multilingual web application. This section describes the Restaurant Review Wiki, a small demo application developed using these tools.

5.1   Description

The Restaurant Review Wiki is a restaurant database that allows users to add restaurants and reviews and view and edit the information in three languages (English, Swedish and Spanish). It is available online[2].

Users can add new restaurants and edit the information about existing restaurants. For each restaurant there is some basic information, such as address and cuisine, entered using standard HTML forms, and reviews which are created and edited by using the syntax editor as shown in Figure 8. The restaurant review grammar used in this application is an extended version of the grammar described in Section 2.1.

---
[2] http://csmisc14.cs.chalmers.se/~meza/restWiki/wiki.cgi/

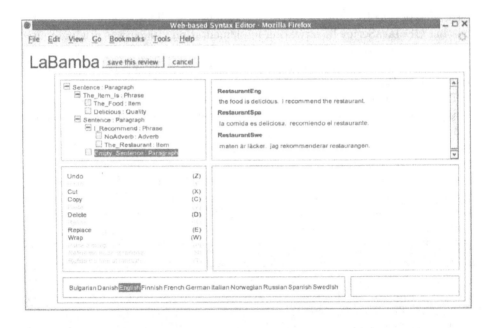

Fig. 8. Review editing page

When adding a new review, the abstract syntax term in the syntax editor is initially a single metavariable of type **Paragraph**. The user edits a review by stepwise refining the tree, by parsing a string or by some combination of these. For example, the user may parse a simple sentence such as "the food is delicious", and then use syntax editing commands to elaborate parts of it.

5.2 Implementation

Instead of storing the text in any language, the abstract syntax representation of the information is stored on the server and it is linearized by the client's browser upon request. The algorithms to linearize abstract syntax trees are efficient and with today's computing power the user should not be affected by delays caused by the linearization of the different multilingual elements of a page. Whenever a page is loaded, a linearizing function is called for every multilingual element in the page. This function takes the HTML element to linearize, a reference to the currently selected language and a grammar as arguments. It extracts the string representation of the abstract syntax term from the element, converts it into an abstract syntax tree, linearizes the tree using the concrete syntax for the currently selected language and stores the linearization in the element.

Two GF grammars are used by this application, one that describes the elements of web pages such as headers, field names, country names, cuisines, etc., and another that describes restaurant reviews.

5.3   Discussion

Advantages. Since the multilingual information is stored as its abstract syntax representation, all new content created by users is available for all languages immediately, and it is thereby consistent in all languages. In existing multilingual applications such as Wikipedia, multilingual content is created in parallel. This means that there is a different version of the information for each language and there is no guarantee that the information available for a particular language will be available in another nor that they will be consistent.

Having all the information in an abstract representation of a controlled language makes it possible to perform operations such as querying precisely and efficiently. For example, it should be easy to implement functionality that would let the user search for "cheap Thai restaurants close to the university".

Adding a language to the application means adding a concrete syntax for that language to the grammar. Once the concrete syntax is added, all existing information is automatically available in the new language. There is no need to translate the existing information by hand.

Disadvantages. The content that can be created using this approach is limited by the coverage of the grammar. This may be too restrictive and it may prevent users from effectively conveying their ideas through the content they create.

In this version of the application, new content is created by using the syntax editor, either by stepwise refining the abstract syntax tree or by parsing a string. The syntax editor has the advantage of generating content within the coverage of the grammar. The problem is that the editor is not very intuitive and it could be hard to use without training, a situation that could discourage potential users. Creating content by parsing is simple, but, if the user is not familiar with the grammar, producing valid content through parsing might be a difficult task unless the grammar has a very wide coverage.

Multilingual processing is done in the client rather than on the server. A JavaScript GF grammar may be larger than 1 MB, which could be a problem for devices with limited bandwidth or memory, such as PDAs or mobile phones. Also, devices with limited processing power may experience delays caused by the linearization of the multilingual elements in pages. Since the current version does linearization in the client even when viewing existing content, search engines may not be able to index the page using the linearized content.

If an abstract syntax used in an application is changed and the new version is not backwards compatible, it may no longer be possible to linearize the stored abstract syntax terms. If the coverage of the new grammar is a superlanguage of the old one, this problem can be solved by linearizing each stored term with the old grammar and parsing it with the new one.

Doing natural language processing client-side tends to stress the web browser implementations. The current state of web standards compatibility in browsers may lead to inconsistent behavior or performance in some web browsers.

6   Related Work

The Grammatical Framework (GF) provided, up until this point, two different syntax editors. The first provides the full functionality of GF but can only be used in machines that have the full GF system installed [1]. One use of this editor is as an integral component of the KeY formal program verification system [9]. The second, Gramlets [10], provides no parsing and no support for dependent types or higher-order functions but can be run on any machine that has a Java Virtual Machine (JVM) installed or in web browsers which have a JVM plug-in. Our syntax editor is more portable than the previous GF syntax editors, can be more easily integrated into web applications, and compared to Gramlets, it offers more functionality, most notably parsing. The syntax editor does not support the full GF language yet, as it only allows grammars which have no dependent types and no higher-order abstract syntax.

WYSIWYM [11] is a structure editor which displays natural language representations during editing. It now also has a JavaScript implementation[3]. Our editor is driven by a declarative specification of the language structure and generation rules. In WYSIWYM these components are built into the editor, which appears to make it more difficult to use the editor for new applications.

7   Future Work

Dependently Typed and Higher-order Abstract Syntax. For the syntax editor to support more advanced grammars, the GF JavaScript API should be extended to implement parsing, type-checking and linearization for grammars with dependently typed and higher-order abstract syntax.

Syntax Editor User Interface. New content is created using the syntax editor and, as mentioned before, this is too restrictive and could make users lose interest in the application. There is a need for a more intuitive interface which still guarantees that the content is within the domain of the grammar. One way to make the interface more easy to use is to add *completion*. The idea is to make the editor display a list of possible ways to complete the input that the user is typing, as is done in the GF-based WebALT exercise editor for multilingual mathematical exercises [12].

Server-side Processing. Instead of doing the multilingual processing in the client, it could be done on the server. This would be beneficial for devices with limited processing power, memory or bandwidth. Especially linearization of existing content should be off-loaded to the server, as this will also help search engines index the content.

8   Conclusions

We have implemented a syntax editor which provides the basic functionality of the Grammatical Framework (GF) in web browsers. It allows the user to stepwise

---

[3] http://www.itri.brighton.ac.uk/projects/WYSIWYM/javademo.html

create the abstract syntax trees described by a GF grammar through the use of special purpose editing actions, while showing linearizations of the trees in multiple languages. It can be used to test and debug GF grammars, or as a component in multilingual web-based applications.

To demonstrate how the syntax editor can be used to implement multilingual web applications, we also implemented "The Restaurant Review Wiki". It is a multilingual restaurant database in which users can add, edit and review restaurants in three different languages. The approach to multilinguality that we suggest makes all information available simultaneously and consistently for all the supported languages, and adding a new language is only a matter of adding a concrete syntax for that language to the application grammar. Additional work is required to make syntax editing more usable for untrained users, and to ensure that the technique works well in resource-constrained computing devices.

References

1. Ranta, A.: Grammatical Framework: A Type-Theoretical Grammar Formalism. Journal of Functional Programming 14(2), 145–189 (2004)
2. Ranta, A.: Grammars as software libraries. In: Bertot, Y., Huet, G., Lévy, J.J., Plotkin, G. (eds.) From semantics to computer science: essays in honor of Gilles Kahn. Cambridge University Press, Cambridge (2008)
3. Teitelbaum, T., Reps, T.: The Cornell program synthesizer: a syntax-directed programming environment. Commun. ACM 24(9), 563–573 (1981)
4. Furuta, R., Quint, V., Andre, J.: Interactively Editing Structured Documents. Electronic Publishing 1(1), 19–44 (1988)
5. Khegai, J., Nordström, B., Ranta, A.: Multilingual Syntax Editing in GF. In: Gelbukh, A. (ed.) CICLing 2003. LNCS, vol. 2588, pp. 199–204. Springer, Heidelberg (2003)
6. Bringert, B.: Rapid Development of Dialogue Systems by Grammar Compilation. In: Keizer, S., Bunt, H., Paek, T. (eds.) Proceedings of the 8th SIGdial Workshop on Discourse and Dialogue, Antwerp, Belgium, pp. 223–226 (2007)
7. Burden, H., Ljunglöf, P.: Parsing Linear Context-Free Rewriting Systems. In: Proceedings of the Ninth International Workshop on Parsing Technology, Vancouver, British Columbia, pp. 11–17. Association for Computational Linguistics (2005)
8. Angelov, K., Bringert, B., Ranta, A.: PGF: A Portable Run-Time Format for Type-Theoretical Grammars (manuscript, 2008),
   http://www.cs.chalmers.se/~bringert/publ/pgf/pgf.pdf
9. Beckert, B., Hähnle, R., Schmitt, P.H. (eds.): Verification of Object-Oriented Software. LNCS (LNAI), vol. 4334. Springer, Heidelberg (2007)
10. Johannisson, K., Khegai, J., Forsberg, M., Ranta, A.: From Grammars to Gramlets. In: The Joint Winter Meeting of Computing Science and Computer Engineering. Chalmers University of Technology (2003)
11. Power, R., Scott, D., Evans, R.: What You See Is What You Meant: direct knowledge editings with natural language feedback. In: 13th European Conference on Artificial Intelligence (ECAI 1998), pp. 677–681 (1998)
12. Cohen, A., Cuypers, H., Poels, K., Spanbroek, M., Verrijzer, R.: WExEd - WebALT Exercise Editor for Multilingual Mathematical Exercises. In: Seppälä, M., Xambo, S., Caprotti, O. (eds.) WebALT 2006, First WebALT Conference and Exhibition, Eindhoven, Netherlands, pp. 141–145 (January 2006)

Dependency Parsing by Transformation and Combination

Jens Nilsson[1] and Joakim Nivre[1,2]

[1] Växjö University, School of Mathematics and Systems Engineering, Sweden
[2] Uppsala University, Dept. of Linguistics and Philology, Sweden
jens.nilsson@vxu.se, joakim.nivre@vxu.se

Abstract. This study presents new language and treebank independent graph transformations that improve accuracy in data-driven dependency parsing. We show that individual generic graph transformations can increase accuracy across treebanks, but especially when they are combined using established parser combination techniques. The combination experiments also indicate that the presumed best way to combine parsers, using the highest scoring parsers, is not necessarily the best approach.

1 Introduction

Research in data-driven syntactic parsing in recent years has provided a wealth of knowledge. One conclusion of this research is that a well-chosen parsing representation is very important in order to achieve state-of-the-art accuracy. This observation holds for both constituency-based parsing and dependency-based parsing. Some examples with a constituency-based representation are Johnson [1] and Klein and Manning [2], where a graph transformation for instance can be deepening or flattening of phrases. For a dependency-based representation, both McDonald and Pereira [3] and Nilsson et al. [4] apply graph transformations in various ways, which concretely means moving dependency arcs in the training data or parser output. The graph transformations of all these studies are often fairly complex and usually tailored for a specific parsing algorithm, or motivated on linguistic grounds.

Another observation is that combining the output of various parsers is beneficial, and again this holds for both constituency-based parsing and dependency-based parsing. For instance, Henderson and Brill [5] report an improved accuracy when combining constituency-based trees of various parsers with a simple majority voting strategy, and Sagae and Lavie [6] also report increased accuracy for both constituency structure and dependency structure for the Penn Treebank.

The focus of this paper is on data-driven dependency parsing and the aim is to bring these two prominent techniques – graph transformations and parser combination – together. A set of new treebank independent graph transformations will be proposed here. In contrast to previously proposed graph transformations in dependency parsing, the transformations here are both simpler and more general, and neither linguistically motivated nor tailored for any specific parsing

A. Ranta, B. Nordström (Eds.): GoTAL 2008, LNAI 5221, pp. 348–359, 2008.

algorithm. In general, we will investigate the result when these generic transformations are applied one at a time for a dependency parser in order to find the transformations that are the most beneficial. We will also investigate whether the dependency trees of parsers based on different transformations can be combined to improve accuracy and how this can be done the most beneficially.

We begin with the necessary background in Sect. 2, followed by an introduction to the generic transformations in Sect. 3. Thereafter, in Sect. 4, parsing results for the general graph transformations for a wide range of languages are presented, both their performance individually and when they are combined using parsing combination techniques. We end with conclusions in Sect. 5.

2 Background

2.1 Transformations

As mentioned, choosing the right base representation is important for data-driven syntactic parsers. Graph transformations have been more prominent for constituency-based parsers, and the impact of individual graph transformations have been studied in detail by for instance Johnson [1] and Klein and Manning [2]. Another example is Bikel [7], who presents a detailed analysis of all graph transformations taking place in the Collins parser.

However, several studies have recently shown that accuracy can be improved for dependency-based parsers as well. The basic idea in dependency parsing is that the syntactic analysis establishes binary relations between the words of a sentence. This kind of analysis can be represented by a labeled directed graph, which is usually constrained to be a tree rooted at an artificial node prefixed to the sentence. A dependency tree is shown in Fig. 1, showing that the nodes (words) also are ordered by a linear precedence relation ($<$).

An arc $w_l \rightarrow w_j$ is projective iff, for every word w_j and arc $w_i \rightarrow w_k$ such that $i < j < k$ or $i > j > k$, there is a path from w_i to w_j ($w_i \rightarrow \ldots \rightarrow w_j$). A dependency tree is projective iff all its arcs are projective. Figure 1 is therefore non-projective, since the arc from *believe* to *What* violates the projectivity constraint.

Non-projectivity is an important phenomenon that many graph transformations in data-driven dependency parsing are designed to deal with. These graph transformations are motivated by constraints imposed by the parsing algorithm, that is, handling non-projectivity with projective parsing algorithms.[1] Hall and Novák [8], McDonald and Pereira [3] and Nilsson et al. [4] are some examples using projective parsing algorithms, where the two first studies present pure post-processing approaches. For instance, McDonald and Pereira use Eisner's second-order algorithm, which only derives projective trees. The post-processor

---

[1] Non-projective parsing algorithms are usually slower, and the amount of non-projectivity in existing treebanks is usually low enough to make projective parsing with pre-processing and post-processing a good choice in practice.

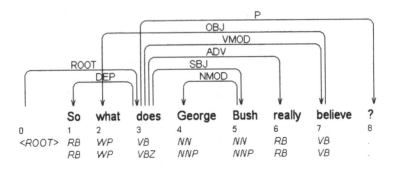

Fig. 1. Dependency tree derived from the Penn Treebank

then moves arcs in the tree to recover non-projectivity. This process iterates as long as the graph transformation increases the overall score of the tree and does not violate any tree constraint.

Nilsson et al. [4], on the other hand, apply a technique for recovering non-projectivity that complements post-processing with pre-processing. The transformation is known as pseudo-projective transformation, introduced by Nivre and Nilsson [9]. The preprocessor starts by identifying all non-projective arcs in the training data. These arcs are then lifted upward in the tree, one step at a time, until the entire dependency graph is projective. The lifting strategy is guaranteed to produce a projective dependency structure, which in practice seldom requires more than three lifts for a non-projective arc. The dependency labels of a lifted arc or surrounding arcs are augmented with additional information that partially encodes the original position the arc in the tree.

Pseudo-projectivity is one type of transformation that focuses on structures that are impossible for certain parsing algorithms to construct. However, the study of Nilsson et al. [4] also showed that transforming constructions that are difficult (although still possible) using a combination of pre-processing and post-processing can improve accuracy substantially as well. These transformations were targeting coordination and verb groups. For instance, they conclude that the annotation style applied by for instance Prague Dependency Treebank for coordination and verb groups can be more difficult to parse than a dependency structure inspired by Mel'čuk [10]. Even though their transformations improve accuracy, one drawback of their approach is that the transformations are not applicable to all dependency treebanks, but rather to treebanks annotating coordination and verb groups in a certain way.

Before presenting the generic transformations in Sect. 3, we will below discuss various combination approaches in dependency parsing.

2.2   Combining Dependency Parsers

There are a few papers describing strategies that combine the output of several dependency parsers into one single dependency graph. One example is Zeman and Žabokrtský [11], who present improved results in comparison to the best single parser for Czech. One observation is that their method can permit cycles in the combined dependency graph, unless explicitly forbidden.

The combination approach proposed by Sagae and Lavie [6] on the other hand avoids cycles implicitly, as it is based on the Chu-Liu-Edmonds algorithm for finding the maximum directed spanning tree given a dense weighted graph. The algorithm chooses, for each graph node, the incoming arc with highest weight. In case the resulting graph forms a tree, then it must be the maximum spanning tree. It must otherwise contain a cycle. The algorithm then contracts and replaces each cycle by one single node, and recalculates the weights of ingoing and outgoing arcs of the cycle. The algorithm recursively calls itself on the new graph, which is guaranteed to produce the same maximum spanning tree as in the original graph (Georgiadis [12]).

Chu-Liu-Edmonds algorithm have previously been used as a single dependency parser, where the weights are derived from a treebank directly (McDonald et al. [13]). For the combination approach, the weights are instead estimates based on the output of several dependency parsers, where the actual weighting strategy may differ. For instance, all arcs of all parsers can be given the same weight, or weighed in relation to each parser's overall accuracy.

Sagae and Lavie [6] also propose a weighting strategy where the weight of each arc depends on each parser's accuracy on the part-of-speech of the arc's dependent. Formally, given the output dependency graphs G_i ($1 \leq i \leq m$) of m different parsers for an input sentence x, a new graph is constructed containing all the dependency arcs proposed by some parser. Each arc a is weighted by a score $s(a)$ based on its popularity among the m parsers. The score $s(a) = \sum_{i=1}^{m} w_i^c a_i$, where w_i^c is the average labeled attachment score of parser i for the word class c of the dependent of a, and a_i is 1 if $a \in G_i$ and 0 otherwise.

This is the approach applied by Blended Malt (Hall et al. [14]), the top-scoring system of the CoNLL 2007 shared task [15]. It combines the output of a number of single parsers in this fashion. Three different parsing algorithms were applied in two directions, left-to-right and right-to-left, thus combining a total of six parsers. They report an improved accuracy (+1.4%) in comparison to their baseline (Single Malt), the best of the six single parsers.

3   The Generic Transformations

The generic transformations presented in this section – as well as the pseudo-projective transformations – are all instances of the same transformation methodology:

1. The graph transformation is applied to the training data.
2. A parser is trained on the transformed data.
3. New sentences are parsed.
4. The corresponding inverse transformation is applied to the output of the parser.

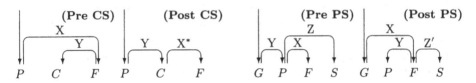

Fig. 2. CHILDSWAP and PARENTSWAP transformations

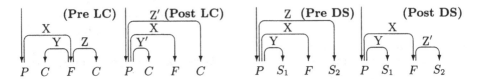

Fig. 3. LIFTCHILDREN and DESCENDSIBLINGS transformations

In contrast to the treebank dependent transformations in Nilsson et al. [4], the generic transformations are not constructed for a particular treebank annotation, but they are rather defined as general graph theoretic transformations. Four transformations and their corresponding inverse transformation are presented, which are denoted CHILDSWAP, PARENTSWAP, LIFTCHILDREN and DESCENDSIBLINGS. It is worth pointing out that this is just four types of transformations, where each transformation just as well could have been designed in a slightly different way. The exact behavior of a transformation is less important for the systematic parsing experiments in Sect. 4; the best transformations will nevertheless be found.

Each graph transformation starts in the same way by finding all tokens with a particular dependency type to its parent. The tokens are called the focus tokens (F). The transformation is then applied to the focus tokens in a bottom-up and left-to-right order.

3.1   ChildSwap

In the CHILDSWAP transformation, the general idea is to let the focus token and one of its left children exchange parents. In case the focus token has two or more left children, this transformation is defined to always take the leftmost child, whereas the transformation is not applicable when left children are missing. The transformation is illustrated in Fig. 2. F is the focus token, P its original parent and C its original leftmost child, where the picture **Pre CS** shows the situation before the swap and **Post CS** after.

Also, swapped focus tokens are given a new unique dependency label (X^*), which distinguishes them from unswapped focus tokens. This will facilitate the inverse transformation.

3.2   ParentSwap

The PARENTSWAP transformation is essentially the same type of transformation as CHILDSWAP, with the difference that the focus token and its parent exchange parents instead. That is, the new parent of P is its former grandparent (G), while F becomes the new parent of P. This is shown in **Pre PS** and **Post PS** in Fig. 2. A distinction between swapped and unswapped focus tokens is not really necessary here, since it is only tokens with the root as parent that lack a grandparent.

Whereas the transformation is relatively simple, the inverse transformation is more complicated as any child of the focus token in **Post PS** is the potential original parent. This is resolved by collecting a frequency list of all dependency labels of P (i.e. Y) in **Pre PS** during transformation. During the inverse transformation, the dependency type of the child with the highest frequency is then selected as the new parent of the focus token.

These pictures illustrate a potential problem with both swapping types, CHILDSWAP and PARENTSWAP. Depending on the linear order of the tokens involved in the swap, some arcs may introduce non-projectivity. In the situation in **Pre PS**, right siblings (S) of P entail non-projectivity, and these will thus be given F as its new parent. Hence, both swapping types are designed not to introduce additional non-projectivity.

3.3   LiftChildren

Figure 3 depicts the LIFTCHILDREN transformation. It simply lifts all children of the focus word upward one step, making them new siblings of the focus word. In order to facilitate the inverse transformation, the lifted tokens are distinguished from original siblings by augmenting their dependency types (Y' and Z').

3.4   DescendSiblings

The fourth and final transformation applied in this study is called DESCEND-SIBLINGS. If the arc of the focus token points to the left, its left siblings are turned into children of the focus token. Also, the corresponding right siblings of right pointing arcs are descended similarly during transformation. An example is shown in Fig. 3, where the arcs of S_2 are descended while the one for S_1 is left unchanged. Descended siblings are distinguished from original children by augmenting their dependency type (e.g. Z' for S_2). The inverse transformation is thus fairly simple.

4   Parsing Experiments

The generic transformations introduced in Sect. 3 will be empirically evaluated in this section. Their impact on the parsing result individually as well as when they are combined using the parsing approach by Sagae and Lavie [6] will be the focus of Exp I–III in Sect. 4.2 to Sect. 4.4.

4.1   Setup: Data and Parser

In the experiments, the ten treebanks of the CoNLL 2007 shared task [15] will be used (Arabic, Basque, Catalan, Chinese, Czech, English, Greek, Hungarian,

Table 1. Exp I, generic transformations, ** $= (p < 0.01)$ using McNemar's test compared to **Base**

	Ara	Bas	Cat	Chi	Cze	Eng	Gre	Hun	Ita	Tur
Base	73.7	74.0	87.3	83.5	75.6	86.3	73.2	77.5	82.5	78.9
Best	75.9**	-	87.0	83.6	76.1	86.3	73.9	77.4	82.5	78.8
Best Trans	CS	-	PS	DS	DS	CS	DS	CS	DS	CS
Label	Coord	-	SUBORD	DUMMY2	Pnom	VC	AuxP	LOCY	det	COORD.
Base + 9	75.0**	74.2	87.3	83.5	76.4**	86.3	74.5**	77.5	82.6	78.9
No inv. for Best	72.9	-	85.3	80.4	74.8	82.9	67.6	77.3	74.5	75.2

Italian and Turkish). The official training data sets for all treebanks has been divided into three parts. Data set T comprises 80% and is the ordinary training data in all experiments below. 10% is the development test set (D) used for parsers selection throughout Exp I–III. The remaining 10% (W) is reserved for estimating the arc weights of the parser combination. The weights are based on the labeled precision of the dependency types, which is a weighting strategy not applied by Sagae and Lavie [6].

All figures presented below are based on the official test data sets of the shared task with ~5000 tokens per language. The figures are the labeled attachment score (i.e. the percentage of tokens that are assigned both the correct head and the correct dependency label), where the ten parsed data sets for each parser have been concatenated into one file before evaluation.

We will use the open-source software MaltParser 1.0.4[2] for the experiments. The experiments have for simplicity used very similar settings to the Single Malt system in Hall et al. [14]. However, since a newer version of MaltParser is used, and since only 80% of the training data is used, the figures presented here will differ somewhat compared to theirs.

4.2   Exp I: Generic Transformations

We will in Exp I investigate how the accuracy is affected by the generic transformations and their corresponding inverse transformations. That is, can some of the transformations – despite their simplicity – increase accuracy (1) individually and (2) when the output of the individual parsers using one single transformation each are combined?

As mentioned, four transformations are implemented, all having focus tokens chosen according to its dependency label. Theoretically, the number of transformations for a treebank is four times the number of distinct dependency labels. We assume that the least frequent labels are more unlikely to have an impact (positive or negative) on accuracy, so we will throughout this paper only select transformations among the 16 most frequent labels for each treebank. Consequently, at most 65 ($4 \times 16 + 1$) parsers with one transformation each will be considered, including the parser without any generic transformations. Here in

---

[2] http://w3.msi.vxu.se/users/jha/maltparser/

Exp I, we will restrict the number of combined parsers to (1) the parser without any generic transformations, plus (2) the 9 parsers with transformations having the highest accuracy (on the data sets D).

Table 1 shows the evaluation of Exp I. The first row (**Base**) contains the figures without any generic transformations, which is our baseline. Row two (**Best**) presents the accuracies for the single best parsers. Selecting the best parser for the official test sets is *not* based on parsing the official test sets, but on both data sets D and W, i.e. the remaining 20% of the official training data not used for training. The two following rows show which transformation was applied for **Best**, and for which dependency label, where a dash means that no transformation outperformed the baseline on the development set $(D + W)$.

The impact of the transformations varies much between treebanks. For instance, Arabic has a statistically significant increased accuracy taking place for the label Coord (+2.2). This is an interesting observation, since this label is involved in coordination, which is one type of construction that the transformations in Nilsson et al. [4] target. The figures are not exactly comparable, as different training and testing sets have been used, but it is still worth noting that they reported an increased accuracy of (+2.1) for their coordination transformation on Arabic. As already mentioned, the difference is that the generic transformations presented here are not constructed for a specific type of annotation. Also Greek, with a similar annotation as Arabic, exhibits increased accuracy for some transformations involving coordination (e.g. Pred_Co for PARENTSWAP), but they are all slightly less prominent that the best Greek transformation.

For many other treebanks the baseline is at least as accurate as **Best** on the test set. Nevertheless, even though the increases for **Best** are not statistically significant for Czech (+0.5) and Greek (+0.7) (partly due the small test sets), the results indicate that these and other generic transformations can be beneficial.

The row (**Base+9**) aims to answer question (2) in the beginning of this section. It shows the accuracy when the baseline parser and the 9 best parsers with the highest accuracy (selected using the data sets D) for each treebank are combined. In comparison to **Base**, the accuracy increases for all languages. This again confirms previous studies, concluding that combining various parsers is beneficial, e.g. Sagae and Lavie [6] and Hall et al. [14], but it is for the first time shown that simple and generic transformations are beneficial while keeping all other settings unchanged. However, the situation is not as clear when determining its relationship to **Best**. Averaging over all languages, **Best** has marginally higher accuracy.

To summarize, treebank dependent and linguistically motivated transformations are not necessary in order to improve accuracy. Simple general transformations are often sufficient. Of course, the vast majority of these general transformations decrease accuracy. However, by applying them systematically like above, we are able to find the transformations that are beneficial. Finally, in comparison to the combination strategy in **Base+9**, simply selecting the single best parser is often at least as good.

Table 2. Exp II, no inverse transformation, where $^{**} = (p < 0.01)$ compared to **Base**

Base	Base+9	Base+9 - No Inv
79.2	79.6**	79.6**

4.3   Exp II: No Inverse Transformation

All generic transformations in Exp I combine pre-processing and post-processing according to the list in the beginning of Sect. 3. In this section, we will investigate the importance of the fourth step, the inverse transformation on the parser output. More precisely, how is accuracy affected when the output of the various parsers is not subjected to an inverse transformation?

The last row of table 1 (No inv. for **Best**) contains the accuracies of the single best parsers in column **Best** without performing the inverse transformation. These figures are consistently lower than **Best**, which clearly indicate the importance of the inverse transformation for the single parsers with transformations. When comparing these figures with **Base**, some noticeable observations can be seen, such as the substantial drops for Greek (-5.6) and Italian (-8.0). The inverse transformations are for these two and the other treebanks able to restore the accuracy, and for some treebanks even surpass **Base**.

When combining parsers without inverse transformations, one could expect the same behavior. However, this is actually not the case. Table 2 presents the accuracy for **Base** and **Base+9** for all ten treebanks, showing that **Base+9** outperforms **Base**. But the most interesting result is shown in the third column, **Base+9 - No Inv**. Here we have combined the baseline parser with the 9 highest scoring parsers (again selected using the data sets D) without performing inverse transformations. It is therefore plausible that the 9 selected parsers are not the same for these two combination strategies. **Base+9** has slightly higher accuracy but when rounded to one decimal, **Base+9 - No Inv** is comparable to **Base+9**.

The result can at a first glance seem somewhat surprising, but it can be explained by the adopted weighting strategy for the parser combination. The weights are estimated based on the precision of individual dependency labels. A transformation modifies the structure close to a certain dependency label. It is hence likely that the transformation yields a low weight to the dependency labels that often are involved in this transformation.

This, in turn, results in a low impact for these dependency labels during the parser combination. However, the remaining dependency structure is kept relatively intact, and is parsed differently compared to other parsers because of the transformation. This is beneficial irrespectively of whether an inverse transformation has been applied or not. In other words, the parser diversity is consequently a very important property, which Exp III below will investigate further.

4.4   Exp III: Selection Strategy

The results presented in Exp II indicate that the need of post-processing is important for the single parsers, while unnecessary when combining the parsers.

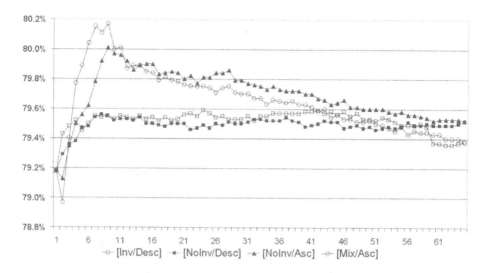

Fig. 4. Exp III, selection strategy, with the number of parsers at the x-axis

However, it is still unsatisfactory that **Best** and **Base+9** have virtually the same average accuracy in Exp I. In this final experiment, we will investigate whether the selection based on high accuracy, applied in Exp I, is the best strategy. In other words, can the moderate improvement in accuracy for **Base+9** in comparison **Best** (+0.4) be a result of suboptimal parser selection? Before we turn our attention to this issue, we will study whether ten is an optimal number of parsers to combine for **Base+9 - No Inv** and **Base+9**.

In Fig. 4, **Base+9** corresponds to the curve denoted [Inv/Desc], which means that the selection is based on the output for data set D with the inverse transformation, which is sorted in descending order, and where the parser combination uses the output with the inverse transformation. **Base+9 - No Inv** then corresponds to the curve [NoInv/Desc], meaning that the selection is based on the output for data set D without the inverse transformation, which are sorted in descending order, and where the parser combination uses the output without the inverse transformation.

Both these curves in Fig. 4 have very similar behavior, climbing in the beginning up to about 10 parsers. Thereafter, as more parsers with lower accuracies are added, no further real increase or decrease is recorded. So no more than 8–10 are in practice needed in order to reach the upper limit. The difference between the curves is negligible, which indicates that the additional complexity that the inverse transformations impose is not really worth the effort.

The diagram contains two more curves, and we will begin by looking at [NoInv/Asc]. Just as for [NoInv/Desc], the inverse transformations are not used at all, but the parsers are instead added in ascending order. That is, the baseline parser is first combined with the parser having the lowest accuracy without an inverse transformation, and then with the parser having the second lowest accuracy, and so on. This curve has a completely different appearance, as it has a much more clear peak at 9 parsers. More interestingly, the peak is located well above the two previous curves, despite (1) the unintuitive order in which new parsers are added, and (2) no inverse transformations. This result contrasts with the assumption that the best parsers should be combined first, in descending order.

The results so far should be enough to say that performing inverse transformations are in vain when combining parsers. However, the fourth and final curve [Mix/Asc] shows that this is a premature conclusion. The selection of parsers is here based on the parser outputs without inverse transformation sorted in ascending order, just like [NoInv/Asc]. The important difference is that it is not the parser outputs without the inverse transformation that are combined, but rather each parser's corresponding output with the inverse transformation. That is, [NoInv/Asc] and [Mix/Asc] selects the same parsers, but combines the parser outputs before and after the inverse transformation, respectively. This combination strategy outperforms the other three, having a peak at 9 parsers. Other logical combinations for parser selection exist (e.g. [Inv/Asc] and [Mix/Desc]), but none increases accuracy or our knowledge.

The main conclusion of Exp III is that we can in fact improve accuracy more by selecting the parsers in a way that seems unintuitive. Also, given an appropriate selection strategy, the inverse transformation is in fact beneficial.

The results can be compared to the best system of the CoNLL 2007 shared task, the Blend Malt (Hall et al. [14]), using 6 parsers (three parsing algorithms and two parsing directions), which reported an improved accuracy of +1.4 compared to their baseline, one single parser. The improvement for [Mix/Asc] compared to our baseline parser is +1.0 (from 79.2% to 80.2%), which is promising considering that no optimization of features and machine learning parameters has been performed for any parser besides our baseline parser. It is worth pointing out that our baseline has slightly lower accuracy compared to the single parser of Hall et al. [14], which partly is attributed to less training data (only 80%). Also, we conjecture that new generic transformations modifying the data even more than the ones proposed here will be even more beneficial.

5   Conclusion

We have shown that generic transformations not motivated linguistically and not tailored for a specific parsing algorithm can improve accuracy for several treebanks. We have presented four, and it is certainly possible to construct other types of generic transformations that also can improve accuracy.

The generic transformations were also combined using the approach presented by Sagae and Lavie [6], showing that they can be combined with an increased accuracy. We have also shown that the order in which various parsers are combined has a major influence. Our results indicate that the most apparent combination strategy – combining the parsers with the highest accuracy – is not the best way. Rather a more unintuitive strategy is better: use one well-performing parser as base, and then add the other parsers in ascending order, starting with the worst parser. This indicates that parser diversity is more important than high accuracy.

References

1. Johnson, M.: PCFG Models of Linguistic Tree Representations. Computational Linguistics 24, 613–632 (1998)
2. Klein, D., Manning, C.: Accurate unlexicalized parsing. In: Proceedings of ACL, pp. 423–430 (2003)
3. McDonald, R., Pereira, F.: Online Learning of Approximate Dependency Parsing Algorithms. In: Proceedings of EACL, pp. 81–88 (2006)
4. Nilsson, J., Nivre, J., Hall, J.: Generalizing Tree Transformations for Inductive Dependency Parsing. In: Proceedings of ACL, pp. 968–975 (2007)
5. Henderson, J., Brill, E.: Exploiting diversity in natural language processing: combining parsers. In: Proceedings of EMNLP, pp. 187–194 (1999)
6. Sagae, K., Lavie, A.: Parser Combination by Reparsing. In: Proceedings of HLT-NAACL, Companion Volume: Short Papers, pp. 129–132 (2006)
7. Bikel, D.: Intricacies of Collins' parsing model. Computational Linguistics 30, 479–511 (2004)
8. Hall, K., Novák, V.: Corrective modeling for non-projective dependency parsing. In: Proceedings of IWPT, pp. 42–52 (2005)
9. Nivre, J., Nilsson, J.: Pseudo-Projective Dependency Parsing. In: Proceedings of ACL, pp. 99–106 (2005)
10. Mel'čuk, I.: Dependency Syntax: Theory and Practice. State University of New York Press (1988)
11. Zeman, D., Žabokrtský, Z.: Improving Parsing Accuracy by Combining Diverse Dependency Parsers. In: Proceedings of IWPT-2005, pp. 171–178 (2005)
12. Georgiadis, L.: Arborescence optimization problems solvable by Edmonds' algorithm. Theoretical Computer Science 301, 427–437 (2003)
13. McDonald, R., Pereira, F., Ribarov, K., Hajič, J.: Non-projective dependency parsing using spanning tree algorithms. In: Proceedings of HLT/EMNLP, pp. 523–530 (2005)
14. Hall, J., Nilsson, J., Nivre, J., Eryigit, G., Megyesi, B., Nilsson, M., Saers, M.: Single Malt or Blended? A Study in Multilingual Parser Optimization. In: Proceedings of EMNLP-CoNLL, pp. 933–939 (2007)
15. Nivre, J., Hall, J., Kübler, S., McDonald, R., Nilsson, J., Riedel, S., Yuret, D.: The CoNLL 2007 Shared Task on Dependency Parsing. In: Proceedings of EMNLP-CoNLL, pp. 915–932 (2007)

Using Constraints over Finite Sets of Integers for Range Concatenation Grammar Parsing*

Yannick Parmentier[1] and Wolfgang Maier[2]

[1] CNRS-LORIA, BP 239, F-54506 Vandœuvre-Lès-Nancy Cedex, France
parmenti@loria.fr
[2] SFB 441 - Universität Tübingen, Nauklerstr. 35, D-72074 Tübingen, Germany
wo.maier@uni-tuebingen.de

Abstract. Range Concatenation Grammar (RCG) is a formalism with interesting formal properties (it has a polynomial parsing time while being more powerful than Linear Context-Free Rewriting Systems). In this context, we present a constraint-based extension of the state-of-the-art RCG parsing algorithm of [1], which has been used for the implementation of an open-source parsing architecture.

1 Introduction

Range Concatenation Grammar (RCG) [2] is a grammar formalism with attractive properties (*e.g.* closedness under complementation and intersection). Still, RCGs are computationally tractable: they can be parsed in polynomial time in the size of the input string and linear time in the size of the grammar [1]. Furthermore, as shown by [3], RCG can be used to encode different mildly context sensitive formalisms such as Multi-Component Tree Adjoining Grammar. RCG offers thus a uniform interface for comparing the properties of formalisms, and is a candidate pivot formalism for parser implementations.

In this context, we propose an extension of the state-of-the-art RCG parsing algorithm of [1] making use of constraint programming techniques. The extended algorithm has been implemented in an open-source parsing architecture for tree-based grammars [4]. Before presenting this extension, we first give a brief introduction to RCG.

An RCG is a set of clauses of the form : $A_0(x_{01}, \ldots, x_{0n_0}) \rightarrow \epsilon$ or $A_0(x_{01}, \ldots, x_{0n_0}) \rightarrow A_1(x_{11}, \ldots, x_{1n_1}) \ldots A_k(x_{k1}, \ldots, x_{kn_k})$ where x_{ij} is a concatenation of constants and/or variables and A_m is a predicate with arity n_m.[1]

As an illustration, consider the following RCG clauses:

$$(a) \quad A(X \ a \ Y \ Z) \rightarrow B(X,Y) \quad C(Z) \qquad (b) \quad B(\epsilon, \epsilon) \rightarrow \epsilon$$

(a) has a left predicate labeled A, whose arity is 1 and whose argument is made of the concatenation of the variable X, the constant a and the variables

---

* We are grateful to Laura Kallmeyer and three anonymous reviewers for useful comments on this work.
[1] For a formal definition of RCG, please refer to [2].

A. Ranta, B. Nordström (Eds.): GoTAL 2008, LNAI 5221, pp. 360–365, 2008.
© Springer-Verlag Berlin Heidelberg 2008

Y and Z. (b) is a clause whose left predicate is labeled B and whose arity is 2. Its two arguments are ϵ. (b)'s right member is empty (ϵ).

The idea underlying RCG is that the symbols (constants or variables) occurring in the argument of a clause are bound to ranges of the sentence by a substitution mechanism. Derivation in RCG corresponds to the *instantiation* of the clauses whose left predicate is distinguished (axiom of the RCG). In other terms, for each of the axiom clauses, we search for all the substitutions mapping symbols of the left predicate to ranges of the sentence. If such a substitution can be found (successful instantiation), then the left predicate of the clause is replaced by the right-hand side of the clause (the arguments of the right predicates are now bound to ranges). We then look for clauses whose left-predicate is one of these instantiated right predicates. These clauses are in turn instantiated. The derivation ends either when ϵ has been derived (success), or when no successful clause instantiation has been found (failure). In other terms, an input string w with $|w| = n$ belongs to $L(G)$ iff ϵ can be derived wrt w from $S(\langle 0, n \rangle)$.

To illustrate this, consider the RCG $G = \langle \{S, A\}, \{a, b\}, \{X, Y\}, S, P \rangle$ with:

$$P = \{ \ S(XY) \quad \rightarrow A(X, Y) \ , \ A(aX, aY) \rightarrow A(X, Y) \ ,$$
$$A(bX, bY) \rightarrow A(X, Y) \ , \ A(\epsilon, \epsilon) \quad \rightarrow \epsilon \qquad \}$$

which covers the copy language: $L(G) = \{ww \mid w \in \{a, b\}^*\}$. Considering the string $aabbaabb$, we have the following derivation (s refers to the substitution function):

Clauses	Instantiations
$S(XY) \quad \rightarrow A(X, Y)$	$s(X) = \langle 0, 4 \rangle \ (aabb) \ , \ s(Y) = \langle 4, 8 \rangle \ (aabb)$
$A(aX, aY) \rightarrow A(X, Y)$	$s(X) = \langle 1, 4 \rangle \ (abb) \quad , \ s(Y) = \langle 5, 8 \rangle \ (abb)$
$A(aX, aY) \rightarrow A(X, Y)$	$s(X) = \langle 2, 4 \rangle \ (bb) \quad , \ s(Y) = \langle 6, 8 \rangle \ (bb)$
$A(bX, bY) \rightarrow A(X, Y)$	$s(X) = \langle 3, 4 \rangle \ (b) \quad , \ s(Y) = \langle 7, 8 \rangle \ (b)$
$A(bX, bY) \rightarrow A(X, Y)$	$s(X) = \langle 4, 4 \rangle \ (\epsilon) \quad , \ s(Y) = \langle 8, 8 \rangle \ (\epsilon)$
$A(\epsilon, \epsilon) \quad \rightarrow \qquad \epsilon$	

2   Instantiating Predicates Using Constraints

The state-of-the-art RCG parsing algorithm our work is based on is a top-down parsing algorithm presented in [1]. The idea of this algorithm is to use the start predicate to trigger clause instantiations leading to the empty string. A complex step of this algorithm corresponds to the instantiation of a predicate. Indeed, when instantiating a predicate, we have to compute all possible substitutions between range variables and contiguous symbols of the input string.

To illustrate this, consider the predicate $A(XYZ)$ to be instantiated with respect to the input string $abcdef$. In this example, the number of possible instantiations is 28 (there are 3 contiguous range variables, that is to say 2 inner boundaries to be found, the first of these boundaries can occupy one of 7 positions: $\bullet abcdef$, $a \bullet bcdef$, etc., the second one has either to be equal or to follow –immediately or not– the first boundary, so the number of instantiations is $7 + 6 + 5 + 4 + 3 + 2 + 1 = 28$).

The complexity of the instantiation task depends on the size of the input string and the number of range variables to instantiate. More precisely [1] has shown that the maximum parse time complexity associated with a clause instantiation is $\mathcal{O}(n^d)$, where n is the length of the input string and d is the number of free boundaries (also called degree) in that clause: $d = max(k_i + v_i)$, k_i being the arity of clause i and v_i its number of range variables. In other terms, the parsing time complexity heavily depends on the instantiation time complexity (as shown in [1], the worst parsing time of a string of length n is $\mathcal{O}(|G|n^d)$).

In this context, we propose to encode predicate instantiation as a *Constraint Satisfaction Problem* (CSP). Note that [1] proposes to deal with the high time-complexity of clause instantiation by using some predefined specific predicates whose role is to decrease the number of free boundaries within ranges.[2]

In the above example, we had a unary predicate whose argument was made of 3 range variables XYZ. Another common form of argument is a mix of constants and range variables, such as in $aXYdZ$. In such a case, the constants can be seen as constraints (or *anchors*) on the values the free boundaries can be assigned. We will elaborate on this after a brief introduction to CSP.[3]

Constraint Satisfaction Problems. In the *constraint satisfaction* paradigm, a problem is described using a set of variables, each taking its value in a given domain. Constraints are then applied on the values these variables can take in order to narrow their respective domains. Finally, we search for one (or all) solution(s) to the problem, that is to say we search for some (or all) assignment(s) of values to variables respecting the constraints.

One particularly interesting sub-class of CSPs are those that can be stated in terms of constraints on variables ranging over finite sets of non-negative integers. For such CSPs, there exist several implementations offering a wide range of constraints (arithmetic, boolean and linear constraints), and efficient solvers. Examples of such implementations include the Oz/Mozart environment and the Gecode library.[4]

Instantiating predicates as a CSP. As mentioned above, an argument of a predicate to be instantiated contains range variables and/or constants, the latter acting like constraints on the boundaries between ranges.[5] To illustrate this, consider the instantiations of the predicate $A(aXYdZ)$ with respect to the input string $abcdef$. For this example, we only have 3 solutions, depending on where to put the boundary between ranges X and Y.

---

[2] The number of range boundaries could be reduced by binarizing the clauses mimicking CFG binarization. The benefit of this is unclear as it would increase the number of clauses to check for instantiation.

[3] For a detailed introduction to CSP, please refer to [5].

[4] See http://www.mozart-oz.org and http://www.gecode.org

[5] Note that (a) the RCGs we handle in our system are built automatically from lexicalized tree-based grammars, thus the arguments of a predicate often contain constants, nonetheless (b) the technique presented here does not depend on the presence of constants. These only reduce the search space of the CSP.

The idea underlying the interpretation of this instantiation task in terms of a CSP is to use the natural order of integers to represent the linear order imposed on ranges, and to define additional constraints reflecting the fact that constants (if any) are anchors for ranges of the input string. We do the following:

1. we define a model associating *boundary constants* with non-negative integers, and *boundary variables* with finite domains over non-negative integers,
2. we define constraints on these boundary variables,
3. we search for all assignments of values to these boundary variables.

Step 1. Let us define the input string w as follows: $w := b_0 s_1 b_1 s_2 \ldots b_{n-1} s_n b_n$ where s_i $(1 \leq i \leq n)$ is a constant symbol of the input string, and b_j $(0 \leq j \leq n)$ is a *boundary constant*. For convenience, we note $w[i] = s_i$. Every boundary constant is associated with an integer referring to its position in the string (boundary constants are ordered by the relation $(\leq, \mathbb{N})$). Thus $b_0 = 0$, $b_1 = 1$, *etc.*

In the same way, let us define an argument to instantiate *arg* as follows: $arg := B'_0 s'_1 B'_1 s'_2 \ldots B'_{m-1} s'_m B'_m$ where s'_i $(1 \leq i \leq m)$ is a symbol (range variable or constant), and B'_j $(0 \leq j \leq m)$ is a *boundary variable*. As before, we note $arg[i] = s'_i$. Furthermore, each boundary variable is associated with the finite domain $[0..n]$ (*i.e.* a boundary variable must match a boundary constant defined over the input string). Note that here we consider the case where all constants appearing in the input string and in the argument to instantiate occur only once (see *Nota bene* below).

Step 2. Once our model has been defined, we compute a constraint matrix M_C mapping boundary variables to boundary constants. Thus M_C is a $(m+1) \times (n+1)$ matrix where:

$$M_C[i,j] = \begin{cases} 1 & \text{if } arg[i] = w[j] \text{ or } arg[i-1] = w[j-1] \;\; (2 \leq i \leq m, 2 \leq j \leq n) \\ 1 & \text{if } (i,j) = (1,1) \hspace{4.5cm} (*) \\ 1 & \text{if } (i,j) = (m+1, n+1) \hspace{3.3cm} (*) \\ 0 & \text{otherwise} \end{cases}$$

The "1" in M_C represent boundary positions that are constrained by the input string. The lines marked (*) represent the fact the lower and upper bounds of the argument to instantiate must be respectively the lower and upper bounds of the input string. If we consider the previous example of the predicate $A(aXYdZ)$ to be instantiated with $abcdef$, we obtain the following constraint matrix:

$$M_C = \begin{array}{c|ccccccc} & b_0 & b_1 & b_2 & b_3 & b_4 & b_5 & b_6 \\ \hline B'_0 & 1 & 0 & 0 & 0 & 0 & 0 & 0 \\ B'_1 & 0 & 1 & 0 & 0 & 0 & 0 & 0 \\ B'_2 & 0 & 0 & 0 & 0 & 0 & 0 & 0 \\ B'_3 & 0 & 0 & 0 & 1 & 0 & 0 & 0 \\ B'_4 & 0 & 0 & 0 & 0 & 1 & 0 & 0 \\ B'_5 & 0 & 0 & 0 & 0 & 0 & 0 & 1 \end{array}$$

Step 3. We finally search for all assignments of values in $[0..n]$ to the boundary variables B'_j $(0 \leq j \leq m)$. In other terms, we search for all functions f such that:

$$f : \quad \mathbb{V} \quad \longrightarrow \quad [0..n]$$
$$B'j \; (0 \leq j \leq m) \longmapsto b_i \; (0 \leq i \leq n)$$

This search uses generic constraints reflecting the ordering of the boundary variables: $\forall (0 \leq i, j \leq m)$ $(i \leq j) \Rightarrow 0 \leq (f(B_i') \leq f(B_j')) \leq n$ and the specific constraints encoded in the matrix M_C:

$$\forall(1 \leq i \leq m+1, 1 \leq j \leq n+1) \quad (M_C[i,j] = 1) \Rightarrow (f(B_{i-1}') = b_{j-1})$$

In the latter formula, the indexes of the boundaries are shifted with respect to the matrix indexes (i, j) because M_C's rows and columns indexes start from 1 while the indexes of the boundaries start from 0. Considering our previous example, all B_i' are constrained by M_C, except B_2', which can take 3 values: 1 (b_1), 2 (b_2) or 3 (b_3), these are the 3 expected range boundaries.

Nota bene. Here, we gave a formal definition of the CSP-encoding. At first sight, the example we used looks trivial and one may wonder whether we really need all this formal tool, in other terms whether the complexity of instantiation has not been overestimated. To illustrate instantiation's complexity, one may think of arguments with duplicated constants, such as in the instantiation of $XaYaZ$ with $aaaad$. Which constant of the string refers to which constant of the argument to instantiate ? The approach presented here has to be generalized to deal with such cases. More precisely, we use a CSP to assign a constraining role to all potential anchors. For each of these assignments, we compute corresponding range instantiations using the CSP introduced above.

Finally, it is worth noticing that there doubtlessly exist several ways of instantiating RCG predicates (*e.g.* unification based solvers). The use of constraints over finite sets of integers offers a natural framework for handling ranges.

3   Conclusion and Future Work

In this paper, we paid a particular attention to the task of RCG predicate instantiation, on which the time complexity of RCG parsing heavily depends. We proposed to use techniques borrowed from the field of *constraint programming* to efficiently perform this task. The ideas presented here have led to the development of an open-source parsing architecture, which is currently used for designing a core Multi-Component Tree Adjoining Grammar for German [4].

In a near future, we would like to build a proof of correctness of the CSP-encoding and also to evaluate empirically the benefits of using CSP for predicate instantiation compared with existing approaches.

References

1. Boullier, P.: Range Concatenation Grammars. In: Proceedings of the Sixth International Workshop on Parsing Technologies (IWPT 2000), pp. 53–64 (2000)
2. Boullier, P.: Proposal for a Natural Language Processing Syntactic Backbone. INRIA report 3342 (1998)

3. Boullier, P.: On TAG and Multicomponent TAG Parsing. INRIA report 3668 (1999)
4. Kallmeyer, L., Lichte, T., Maier, W., Parmentier, Y., Dellert, J., Evang, K.: The Tübingen Linguistic Parsing Architecture (2008),
   http://sourcesup.cru.fr/tulipa
5. Schulte, C.: Programming Constraint Services. LNCS (LNAI), vol. 2302. Springer, Heidelberg (2002)

Analyzing Argumentative Structures in Procedural Texts

Lionel Fontan and Patrick Saint-Dizier

IRIT - CNRS,
118 route de Narbonne, 31062 Toulouse Cedex, France
stdizier@irit.fr

Abstract. In this short paper, we present the explicative structure as found in procedural texts. We focus in particular on arguments, and show how warnings, a type of arguments, can be extracted.

1 Introduction

Procedural texts consist of a sequence of instructions, designed with some accuracy in order to reach a goal (e.g. assemble a computer). Procedural texts may also include subgoals as well as lists of prerequisites, warnings, etc. Goals and subgoals are most of the time realized by means of titles and subtitles. The user must follow step by step the given instructions in order to reach the goal. Procedural texts are complex structures, they often exhibit a quite complex rational (the instructions) and 'irrational' structure which is mainly composed of advices, conditions, preferences, evaluations, user stimulations, etc. They form what is called the explanation structure, which motivates the goal-instructions structure. A number of these elements are forms of argumentation, they provide motivations and a strong and essential internal coherence to procedural texts.

In our perspective, procedural texts range from apparently simple cooking recipes to large maintenance manuals. They also include documents as diverse as medical notices, social behavior recommendations, directions for use, assembly notices, do-it-yourself notices, etc. The work we report here was carried out on a corpus in French. It is part of the TextCoop project, dealing with How-To question-answering.

We have already studied the instructional aspects of procedural texts and implemented a quite efficient prototype in the TextCoop project (Delpech et al. 2008). In this paper, after a short categorization of objects related to explanation found in a large corpus of procedural texts (about 8000 Web texts), we focus on the recognition of the argumentation structure. Argument recognition is a rather new research topic, and has many application, e.g. opinion analysis. Let us note some work in language processing concerning the recognition of arguments in the juridical domain.

2 Explanation Structure in Procedural Texts

First, in most types of texts, we do not find just sequences of simple instructions but much more complex compounds composed of clusters of instructions, that

A. Ranta, B. Nordström (Eds.): GoTAL 2008, LNAI 5221, pp. 366–370, 2008.

we call **instructional compounds**. These are organized around a few main instructions, to which a number of subordinate instructions, warnings, arguments, and explanations of various sorts may possibly be adjoined. All these elements are, in fact, essential in a compound for a good understanding of the procedure at stake. For example, explanations and arguments help the user understand why an instruction must be realized and what are the risks or the drawbacks if he does not do it properly. An example of an instructional compound is:

[*instructional compound* [*Goal* To clean leather armchairs,]
[*instruction* choose specialized products dedicated to furniture,
    [*advice* [*instruction* and prefer them colorless],
        [*arguments* they will play a protection role, add beauty, and repair some small damages.]]]]

Next, from our development corpus, we established a classification of the different forms explanations may take. Basically, the explanation structure is meant to help the user by making sure that he will effectively realize actions as they are specified, via e.g. advices and warnings. The main structures are facilitation and argumentation structures; they are either global (they are adjoined to goals, and have scope over the whole procedure) or local, included into instructional compounds, with a scope local to the instructional compound. These structures are summarized as follows:

- **facilitation structures**, which are rethorical in essence (Kosseim et al 2000) (Van der Linden 1993), correspond to *How to do X ?* questions, these include two subcategories:
  (1) user help, with: hints, evaluations and encouragements and
  (2) controls on instructions realization, with two cases: (2.1) controls on actions: guidance, focussing, expected result and elaboration and (2.2) controls on user interpretations: definitions, reformulations, illustrations and also elaborations.
- **argumentation structures**, corresponding to *why do X ?* questions. These have either:
  (1) a positive or neutral orientation with the author's involvement (promises) or not (advices and justifications) or
  (2) a negative orientation with the author involment (threats) or not (warnings).

In what follows, we will mainly concentrate on this second point, and in particular on warnings which are the most frequently encountered, besides advices (since there are rarely involvements from the author).

3 Identifying Arguments in Procedures

3.1 General Structure

Roughly, argumentation is a process that allows speakers to construct statements for or against another statement called the conclusion. These statements are called supports. the general form for arguments is : **Conclusion 'because' Support** (noted as C *because* S). Arguments may be more or less strong, they are in general associated with a certain weight. (Anscombre et al. 1981), (Moeschler 1985), (Amgoud et ali. 2001)

In the case of procedural texts, the representation is as follows. Let G be a goal which is realized via the sequence of instructions A_i, $i \in [1, n]$, whatever their exact temporal structure is. A subset of those instructions are interpreted as arguments where the conclusion is the instruction (A_j), associated with a support S_j that stresses the importance of A_j (*Carefully plug in your mothercard vertically, otherwise you will damage the connectors*). Their general form is: A_j *because* S_j (we use here the term 'because' which is more vague than the implication symbol used in formal argumentation, because natural language is not so radical). Supports S which are negatively oriented are warnings whereas those which are positively oriented are advices. Similarly to the principles of argument theory, but within the framework of action theory, if A_j is associated with a support of type warning S_j then if A_j is not realized correctly, the warning S_j is 'active' and attacks the goal G, i.e. it makes its realization more difficult if not impossible. Conversely, if S_j is an advice, it supports the goal G, making its full realization easier if A_j is executed.

As can be noted, our definition includes terms which are gradual: 'more difficult', 'easier', because in practice, failing to realize an instruction properly does not necessarily mean that the goal cannot be reached, but the user will just be less successful, for various reasons. In the natural language expressions of conclusions (the A_j) as well as of supports, there are many modals or classes of verbs (like risk verbs) that modulate the consequences on G, contrast:
use professional products to clean your leathers, they will give them a brighter aspect. with:
carefully plug in your mothercard vertically, otherwise you will most likely damage its connectors..
In the latter case, the goal 'mounting your own PC' is likely to fail, whereas in the former, the goal 'cleaning your leathers' will just be less successful.

3.2   Processing Arguments

From the above observations, we have defined a set of patterns that recognize instructions which are conclusions and their related supports. We defined those patterns from a development corpus of about 1700 texts of various domains (cooking, do it yourself, gardening, etc.). Let us focus here on warnings. The study is made on French, English glosses are given here for ease of reading. The recognition problem is twofold: identiying propositions as conclusions or supports by means of specific linguistic marks (sometimes we also found a few typographic marks), and then delimiting these elements. In general boundaries are either sentences or, by default, instructional compound boundaries. We have basically a unique structure composed of an 'avoid expression' combined with a proposition. The variations around the 'avoid expressions' capture the illocutionary force of the argument via several devices, here ordered by increasing force :

(1) 'prevention verbs like avoid' NP / to VP (*avoid hot water*)
(2) do not / never / ... VP(infinitive) ... (*never put this cloth in the sun*)
(3) it is essential, vital, ... to never VP(infinitive).

In cases where the conclusion is relatively weak in terms of consequences, it may not have any specific mark, its recognition is then based on the observation that it is the instruction that immediately precedes an already identified support.

Supports are propositions which are identified from various marks:

(1) via connectors such as: *sinon, car, sous peine de, au risque de* (otherwise, under the risk of), etc. or via verbs expressing consequence,
(2) via negative expressions of the form: *in order not to, in order to avoid, etc.*
(3) via specific verbs such as risk verbs introducing an event (*you risk to break*). In general the embedded verb has a negative polarity.
(4) via the presence of very negative nouns: *death, desease, etc.*

Some supports have a more neutral formulation: they may be a portion of a sentence where a conclusion has been identified. For example, a proposition in the future tense or conditional following a conclusion is identified as a support. However, as will be seen below, some supports may be empty, because they can easily be infered by the reader. In that case, the argument is said to be truncated.

Patterns are implemented in Perl and are included into the TextCoop software. We do not have space here to discuss about algorithms, but so far these are quite straightforward. From the above observations, with some generalizations and the construction of lexicons of marks, we have summarized the extraction process in only 8 patterns for supports and 3 patterns for conclusions. Arguments are tagged by XML tags. We carried out an indicative evaluation (e.g. to get improvement directions) on a corpus of 66 texts over various domains, containing 262 arguments. We get the following results:

conclusion reco	support reco	(3)	(4)
89%	86%	84%	81%

(3) conclusions well delimited (4) supports well delimited.

Besides identifying arguments (advices, warnings) in a text and other structure, a major application of this work is the acquisition of **domain know-how knowledge**, which is probably quite basic, but which could be subject to interesting generalizations. Obviously, to make this know-how operational, it is necessary to analyse it and transform it into a formal representation that supports inference.

3.3 Dealing with Empty Supports

Considering do-it-yourself and gardening texts, we noted that about 2/3 of the arguments are not supported. This very large number of unsupported arguments, in such typically procedural texts, can be explained by several factors: (1) procedural texts are more oriented towards action than control, (2) some supports, possibly complex, could in fact introduce doubts or confusions, (3) some explanations (supports) may be too complex to understand for a casual user, and (4) supports are sometimes sufficiently explicit in the conclusions (*do not scatter seeds by high winds ! = they won't go where you want them to go*).

Considering realized supports, we noted that they correspond to two main trends: (1) supports that express general requirements such as: efficiency of actions, security, ease of execution, adequate execution, speed, aesthetics, lower cost, etc. and (2) supports that cover more precise, domain dependent situations (*avoid pruning trees when temperature drops below zero*).

We have little room in this short paper to develop this section, but let us note here the directions we are investigating, which require different forms of inference. For empty supports corresponding to general requirements, we infer a generic support based on those requirements, e.g.: *mounting your computer: use a flat and clean surface.* induced support: 'for a better ease of execution'. From our observations (which need further confirmation and evaluation), generic supports are in general triggered by adjectives or by general purpose verbs used in the conclusion.

The second situation (empty support in a domain dependent situation) is more delicate and requires domain or lexical knowledge. We are investigating the use of principles of the Generative Lexicon (Pustejovsky 1991) for that purpose. Very briefly, *wind* has in its telic role several predicates like *push, take away, scatter, disperse, break, damage, ...* When applied e.g. to gardening, such as planting new flowers, since these are not so mobile when planted, a predicate like *break* or *damage* can be selected (selection principles in the Generative lexicon remain an open problem). Then from a statement such as: *avoid planting flowers by high winds* the support: *because wind will damage or break flowers* can be infered. This approach is quite complex but seems to be an interesting application to GL principles and data.

Acknowledgements. We thank the French ANR-RNTL research programme for supporting this project (TextCoop). We also thank very warmly Leila Amgoud for discussions around this project.

References

1. Amgoud, L., Parsons, S., Maudet, N.: Arguments, Dialogue, and Negotiation. In: 14th European Conference on Artificial Intelligence, Berlin (2001)
2. Anscombre, J.-Cl., Ducrot, O.: Interrogation et Argumentation. In: Langue francaise, L'interrogation, vol. 52, pp. 5–22 (1981)
3. Aouladomar, F., Saint-dizier, P.: Towards Answering Procedural Questions, Workshop KRAQ 2005, IJCAI 2005 Edinburgh (2005)
4. Delpech, E., Saint-Dizier, P.: Investigating the Structure of Procedural Texts for Answering How-to Questions, LREC 2008, Marrakech (2008)
5. Kosseim, L., Lapalme, G.: Choosing Rhetorical Structures to Plan Instructional Texts. Computational Intelligence. Blackwell, Boston (2000)
6. Moschler, J.: Argumentation et Conversation, Eléments pour une Analyse Pragmatique du Discours, Hatier - Crédif (1985)
7. Pustejovsky, J.: The Generative Lexicon. Computational Linguistics 17(4) (1991)
8. Vander Linden, K.: Speaking of Actions Choosing Rhetorical Status and Grammatical Form in Instructional Text Generation Thesis, University of Colorado (1993)

Natural Language Processing Across Time: An Empirical Investigation on Italian

Marco Pennacchiotti[1] and Fabio Massimo Zanzotto[2]

[1] Dept. of Computational Linguistics, Saarland University, Saarbrücken, Germany
pennacchiotti@coli.uni-sb.de
[2] DISP, Universitá di Roma Tor Vergata, Roma, Italy
zanzotto@info.uniroma2.it

Abstract. In this paper, we study how existing natural language processing tools for Italian perform on ancient texts. The first goal is to understand to what extent such tools can be used "as they are" for the automatic analysis of old literary works. Indeed, while NLP tools for Italian achieve today good performance, it is not clear if they could be successfully used for the humanities, to support the critical study of historical works. Our analysis will show how tools' performance systematically vary across different time periods, and within literary movements. As a second goal, we want to verify whether or not simple customization methods can improve the tools performance over the old works.

1 Introduction

Natural Language Processing (NLP) tools for morphological and syntactic analysis guarantee today high standards in terms of performance and robustness, so that they can be successfully used in a wide range of applications. Yet, despite the large availability of electronic editions of old literary works in the context of the TEI initiative [1], and despite the potential benefits, few attempts have been made so far to adapt NLP tools to the field of humanities (e.g. [2,3]), especially for Italian. For example, researchers in philology mostly use simple keyword search in context (KWIC) and dictionary query engines working on human annotated material, where the NLP contribution is minimal. The application of deeper automatic linguistic techniques would be valuable to build more sophisticated and useful tools for philological and literary studies.

A natural question is then why not much effort has been spent so far in adapting NLP tools to ancient texts. This cannot be only explained by the skepticism of researchers in the humanities over NLP applications in general. In our view, the core issue is that the humanistic and NLP research areas have different objectives. NLP research aims to build language models that cover the *most frequent* phenomena of *contemporary* natural languages. On the contrary, the goal of humanistic studies is to discover and analyse *odd* phenomena of *historical* natural languages. This makes difficult to adapt existing NLP models and tools on the humanities, discouraging any effort in that direction.

A. Ranta, B. Nordström (Eds.): GoTAL 2008, LNAI 5221, pp. 371–382, 2008.

Yet, a fruitful interaction between the two areas is possible. For example, researchers in the humanities could easily contribute in NLP whenever an odd phenomenon for an old grammar/lexicon is covered, by including its model in an existing NLP architecture. In turn, researchers in NLP could leverage these models, to customize the architecture to the particular language. In this framework, the first step to be done is to evaluate how far modern NLP machineries are from achieving good performance over ancient texts.

In this paper, we want to address the above issue, by studying the performance of basic NLP tools and resources (namely a standard dictionary, a morphological analyser and a part-of-speech tagger) over an historical language, and across different time periods and literary movements. Also, we want to verify whether or not simple customization techniques can help in achieving better performance over the ancient texts. We focus our attention on the Italian language, which for its lexical richness and its comparatively old story (the first forms of Italian date from the 10th century) represents an exemplar test set.

The paper is organised as follows. Section 2 describes work related to our investigation. In Section 3, we introduce the NLP resources we tested in our study, namely a syntactic parser and a dictionary of contemporary Italian. Section 4 describes the corpus of the ancient Italian texts we adopted as a test set. Section 5 reports and comments on the results of our experiments. Finally, in Section 6 we present possible future works to improve resource performance.

2   Related Work

Studies on the portability of NLP tools and resources to historical languages is still fairly limited. Rocio et al. [3] applied a standard grammar for contemporary Portuguese to automatically parse Medieval Portuguese, along with a specific lexical analyser to extend the coverage of the lexicon on ancient words. The good results demonstrated that partial parsing of ancient Portuguese texts is feasible by relying on tools for contemporary languages. Britto et al. [4] used a PoS-tagger similar to the Brill tagger [5], trained on a corpus of 130,000 manually annotated words, to annotate 25 of the 52 texts (2 million words) contained in Tycho Brahe corpus for Historical Portuguese. They obtained a precision of 95.45%, four points below standard performance on contemporary languages. More recently, Moon and Baldridge [2] proposed a semi-automatic approach to induce a PoS-tagger for Middle English from material taken from Present-Day English, lavereging bilingual boostrapping techniques [6], achieving an accuracy on the low 80ies. All these works seem to indicate that, in order to successfully use NLP tools on ancient texts, major adaptations on the lexicon and at other levels are needed. We are here interested to verify this hypothesis, in particular for a Romance language as Italian.

More widely, as regards electronic resources for historical texts, great efforts have been spent in recent years to create manually annotated corpora with lemma, morphological and part-of-speech information. Major examples are the Penn-Helsinki Parsed Corpus of Middle English [7] containing 1.5 million words in the period 1100-1500; the Corpus of Early Modern English [8] of 1.8 million words extracted from text of different type in the period 1500-1710; and the York-Toronto-Helsinki Parsed Corpus of Old English Prose [9], consisting of 1.5 million words. Resources also exists for other languages, such as Early New High German and Latin.

As for Italian, the *Opera del Vocabolario Italiano*[1] is manually building TLIO [10], a dictionary for ancient Italian, from the 9th to the 14th century, currently containing 18,000 entries, extracted from 1,960 literary works. The dictionary builds up on a corpus of around 3.5 million lemmatized and morphologically annotated tokens. The related query software *Gattoweb* is today one of the most used automatic tools for Italian philology, allowing to carry out keyword searches and KWIC over the corpus. Finally, the Corpus Taurinense [11] consists of 21 Italian texts from the 13th century (260,000 tokens), lemmatized, morphologically annotated and PoS-tagged in the EAGLES/ISLE format.

Unfortunately, so far there have been no significant researches explicitly dedicated to the development or customization of NLP tools for historical Italian, except some exploratory attempts using statistical methods reported in [12], where machine learning techniques have been used to semantically annotate the Italian novel *"Gli indifferenti"*. NLP tools for contemporary Italian, including the Chaos parser [13] adopted in our study, are instead of great interest for the Italian NLP community, as demonstrated by Evalita[2], an evaluation campaign of Italian NLP tools.

3   Contemporary Italian Dictionary and Parser for NLP

In this section we describe the two resources that are evaluated on the historical Italian texts. In Section 3.1 we shortly introduce the dictionary, while in Section 3.2 we describe Chaos, a syntactic parser for Italian.

3.1   Dictionary

The recognition of syntactic and morphological classes of words is one of the most important tasks in sentence interpretation. Even apparently monolithic syntactic parsers (e.g., [14,15]) perform part-of-speech tagging with specific models. For most part-of-speech taggers, one of the main problem is the treatment of unknown words. Morpho-syntactic lexicons are then one of the most important resources for the overall syntactic analysis. In romance languages morpho-syntactic lexicons are even more central. Unlike in English, in these languages each lemma may have a large number of forms. Simple stemming techniques cannot solve the problem, as forms of the same lemma can be very different. For example, the Italian form *"aiuterebbe"* (English: *"may help"*) and *"aiuta"* (*"helps"*) are two forms of the same lemma *"aiutare"* (*"to help"*).

---

[1] http://www.ovi.cnr.it/
[2] http://evalita.itc.it/

In our study we derive the dictionary from two morpho-syntactic lexicons included in the Chaos architecture: a manually-built generative morphology lexicon, and a corpus-induced lexicon.

Table 1. Italian morpho-syntatic lexicons

Generative morphology lexicon

		#
roots	nouns	10,658
	verbs	5,104
	adjectives	5,288
forms	nouns	16,567
	verbs	84,610
	adjectives	11,644

Corpus-induced lexicon

	#
forms	12,132

Generative morphology lexicon: This manually-built lexicon (see Table 1) includes ca. 22,000 lemmas: 10,658 nouns, 5,288 adjectives, 5,104 verbs, and other classes. Dictionary entries are organised as feature structures containing syntactic information and morphological information, specifying *gender*, *number*, *person*, *tense*, and *mood*. The generative lexicon produces 73,838 different forms, with an average ambiguity of 1.55. We included all the produced entries in our dictionary.

Corpus-induced lexicon: This lexicon has been built over a collection of articles of the Italian financial newspaper *Il Sole 24 Ore* and contains 12,132 words with an average ambiguity of 1.06. To find the interpretation of unknown words, we used a transformational part-of-speech tagger learner [5] producing 181 rules. Rules consist in a triggering condition and an emitted part-of-speech tag. For example, the rule *hassuf(ato)* → *VNP*, indicates that a word with the suffix *-ato* is likely to be a *VNP* – i.e. a verb in the past particle. Typical interpretations produced by this lexicon are impoverished compared to the generative morphology lexicon, as they include only the part-of-speech class information.

3.2   The Chaos Parser

Chaos [13] is a robust modular constituent-dependency parser for Italian, producing partial and possibly ambiguous syntactic analysis. In our study, we use the following module cascade: a *tokenizer*, matching words from character streams; a *yellow page look-up module* that matches named entities existing in catalogues; a *morphological analyser* that attaches (possibly ambiguous) syntactic categories and morphological interpretations to each word; a *named entity matcher* that recognizes complex named entities according to special purpose grammars; a rule-based *part-of-speech tagger*; a *PoS disambiguation module* that resolves potential conflicts among the results of the PoS tagger and the morphological analyser. Chaos also includes a *syntactic parser* based on modularisation and lexicalisation, whose study is not included in this paper.

We hereafter describe more in depth the morphological analyser M and the part-of-speech tagger POS, and their mutual interactions. Assume that $s = t_1 \ldots t_n$ is a tokenized sentence where t_i is a generic token. As a first step, Chaos activates the morphological analyser. The analyser is a function that works on tokens: given t, it produces the set of interpretations $M(t) = I$ that t has in the dictionary. These interpretations are considered unordered – i.e. the first interpretation is not necessarily the most plausible. Interpretations correspond to those described in the previous section. In a second step, the part-of-speech tagger is applied, by working on the whole sentence. Given a tokenized sentence $s = t_1 \ldots t_n$, it produces a sequence of PoS-tags $POS(s) = pos_1 \ldots pos_n$. At the end, for each token t_i there exists a unique interpretation pos_i. In a last step, the information from the PoS tagger and from the morphological analyser are harmonised. Given a token t_i in a sentence s, the preferred interpretation is the $l \in M(t_i)$ that is compliant with the PoS tag pos_i.

For example, consider the sentence *"the boat sinks"*. The morphological analyser produces the following interpretations for the token *sinks*: $M(sinks) = I_3 = \{[\text{lemma:sink,type:noun}], [\text{lemma:sink,type:verb}]\}$. The PoS tagger, after analysing the overall sentence, assigns the PoS-tag $pos_3 = Verb$ to the token t_3. In the last step, the interpretations in I_3 are reduced to those compliant with pos_3, i.e. $I_3' = \{[\text{lemma:sink,type:verb}]\}$. However, the PoS tagger is not a word sense disambiguator. Homograph forms with the same PoS (e.g., the noun *bank* as *institution* or *river bank*) are not disambiguated at this stage.

4   A Corpus of Historical Italian Texts

Our corpus of historical Italian texts is composed of 14 major Italian literary works, listed in Table 2.[3] We chose texts ranging across different time periods, literary movements, and genres, so that each of them could be somehow representative of a specific style. This allows to specifically evaluate the tools on movements, instead of generally on ancient Italian (though it must be clear that by studying a single piece it is possible to draw only indicative conclusions on a movement). The overall time range encompasses almost 700 year, starting with one of the first examples of written Italian (the *Rime* by the *Scuola Siciliana*), to a late work of the 19th century. It is here important to stress that by choosing such a different range of works, our goal is to give a very coarse-grained exploratory evaluation of the dictionary and the parser on different time periods, in order to investigate their applicability across time. However, we do not aim to draw final conclusions on the issue, which would require a much larger corpus of works. Also, we will not look in depth into philological explanations, as this should be left to an analysis requiring expertise in romance philology.

---

[3] All works are available in XML-TEI format at: *www.bibliotecaitaliana.it*

Table 2. Corpus of historical Italian texts adopted in the experiments

Author	Work	Year	Genre	Movement
Scuola Siciliana	Rime	1200	poetry	origins
Guido Cavalcanti	Rime	1275	poetry	Stilnovo
Giovanni Boccaccio	Decameron	1300	prose	
Dante Alighieri	Divina Commedia	1321	poetry	
Francesco Petrarca	Canzoniere	1348	poetry	
Lorenzo De'Medici	Canzoniere	1475	poetry	Renaissance
Ludovico Ariosto	Orlando Furioso	1532	poetry	Renaissance
Galileo Galilei	Dialogo sopra i due massimi sistemi	1632	prose	Baroque
G. Battista Basile	Le muse napolitane	1635	poetry	Baroque
Giuseppe Parini	Odi	1790	poetry	Illuminism
Vincenzo Monti	Poesie	1800	poetry	Neo-Classicism
Ugo Foscolo	Ultime lettere di Jacopo Ortis	1802	prose	Neo-Classicism
Vittorio Alfieri	Vita	1803	prose	Illuminism
Giovanni Verga	I Malavoglia	1881	prose	Verism

5   Resource Evaluation

In this section, we present an empirical evaluation of the dictionary and the parser on the corpus of ancient Italian works presented in Section 4.

5.1   Experimental Setup

We implement two different evaluation tasks: one to check the dictionary coverage; one to evaluate the Chaos morphological analyser and part-of-speech tagger accuracies. For the first evaluation task, we extract from the XML files all tokens – i.e. lists of characters separated by space and punctuation. From the collected tokens we derive a list of unique words (tokens without repetitions). Finally, for each word we check if there is an entry in the dictionary. We evaluate the dictionary coverage as the number of unique words in a literary work which have at least an entry in the dictionary.

For the second evaluation task we build a gold standard dataset over which to compute Chaos accuracies. The gold standard consists of a random sample of 42 sentences (3 for each work), manually annotated by two human experts. The annotators were asked to select for each word in the sentence, the correct morphological and part-of-speech classes. In case of ambiguity, the class that fits the contexts was chosen. We computed inter-annotator agreement over 3 sentences randomly extracted from the corpus, in order to assess the reliability of the gold standard. We obtained a Kappa value agreement of 0.87 for morphology and 0.63 for part-of-speech, corresponding respectively to *almost perfect* and *substantial agreement*. The accuracy of the tools has been computed as the percentage of correct predictions over the gold standard.

In both tasks we compare the performance of the tools on the ancient texts with the performance obtained on a contemporary Italian text, namely an

Table 3. Coverage of the modern dictionary; accuracy of the morphological analyser; and accuracy of PoS-tagger over different works

Author	# Words	Dict. coverage		morpho accuracy	PoS accuracy
Scuola Siciliana	8,751	2,387	27,3%	0.48	0.54
Guido Cavalcanti	1,978	941	47,6%	0.66	0.73
Giovanni Boccaccio	18,785	6,736	35,8%	0.74	0.90
Dante Alighieri	12,610	5,136	40,7%	0.72	0.75
Francesco Petrarca	6,946	3,094	44,5%	0.69	0.71
Lorenzo De'Medici	3,805	2,068	54,3%	0.83	0.81
Ludovico Ariosto	20,120	6,889	34,2%	0.62	0.68
Galileo Galilei	13,027	6,674	51,2%	0.77	0.77
G. Battista Basile	5,411	1,077	19,9%	0.52	0.56
Giuseppe Parini	4,030	2,250	55,8%	0.73	0.79
Vincenzo Monti	5,050	2,625	52,0%	0.74	0.84
Ugo Foscolo	8,567	4,610	53,8%	0.69	0.76
Vittorio Alfieri	13,277	6,627	49,9%	0.72	0.77
Giovanni Verga	8,250	4,019	48,7%	0.68	0.68
La Repubblica	*16.520*	*10.328*	*62.5%*	*0.91*	*0.97*

excerpt of the Italian newspaper *La Repubblica*. Such an evaluation will account for the portability of the tools – i.e. if there is a performance gap between historical and contemporary Italian.

5.2 Results

Results are reported in Table 3. Hereafter, we present both a *quantitative analysis* and a coarse-grained *qualitative study* of the results.

Quantitative Analysis. All ancient works show performance significantly lower than *La Repubblica*. Specifically, the average dictionary coverage on ancient works is 0.44, about 19% less than *La Repubblica*. The highest ancient work coverage is 0.56, still 7% less than the newspaper. Similar results are obtained for the Chaos' morphological analyser and PoS tagger, for which the average accuracies on ancient works are respectively 22% and 24% below *La Repubblica*.

The coverage of the dictionary is in general low. Regarding *La Repubblica*, this is due to the fact that the dictionary does not include proper nouns (which are clearly very common in newspapers) and modern foreign words (which are more and more present in contemporary Italian). Ancient texts present a much lower number of proper nouns, and no foreign words: in this case, the low performance are then completely due to the ancient lexicon.

The accuracy of the parser for *La Repubblica* is very high, somehow contrasting the above evidence on the dictionary. This indicates that the morphological analyser and the PoS-tagger successfully interact to find the correct analysis of words which are not present in the dictionary, by relying on the Pos-tagging rules encoded in the parser. For example the word *"logo"* is not present in the dictionary, but is still correctly recognized as a common noun by using contextual and morpho-derivational rules.

Parser accuracy over the ancient works is by contrast low, confirming the trend of the dictionary coverage. This suggests that PoS-tagging rules valid for contemporary Italian, cannot be straightforwardly applied to ancient texts. For example, given the fragment *"...d'amare domandassen pietanza"* (English: *"...would ask mercy for loving"*) (from *Rime della Scuola Siciliana*), the parser wrongly assigns the tag *common noun* to *"domandassen"*, because the word is not present in the dictionary, and then the parser backs-up to a PoS-tagging rule which states that a word following a transitive verb ("amare", *love*) must be a noun. Unfortunately, while this stands in general for contemporary Italian, it does not apply to many ancient examples.

Overall results support our initial claim that the dictionary and the Chaos parser for contemporary Italian are insufficient for the analysis of ancient texts, as there exists a significant gap in dictionary coverage between contemporary and ancient texts. PoS taggers cannot easily recover this gap. Default classification rules for unknown words learnt for contemporary Italian generally fail when used for historical Italian. We believe that this claim can be safely extended in general to all dictionaries and parsers for contemporary Italian. Indeed, our claim is in line with similar works for other historical languages. For example, Ricio et al. [3] show that the lexicons of Medieval and Contemporary Portuguese are substantially different, heavily impacting on parsing performance, despite the fact that the two grammars are quite similar. Also, Moon and Baldridge [2] prove that a straightforward application of parsers for contemporary English cannot be effective on Middle English, without applying strong adaptation strategies.

Diachronic/Synchronic Analysis. We were somehow surprised that there seem to be no correlation between genres and coverage, suggesting that poetry is not more complex than prose, at least from a lexicon perspective. Also, there is no correlation between performance and literary movements (one could expect that works of the same movement have stylistic similarities and by consequence similar performance).

Yet, as expected, there is a fairly high correlation between the age of the work and tools' performance: ancient works tend to have lower coverage than more recent ones. An exception to this trend is *Le Muse Napolitane*, which overall shows the lowest coverage, 19.9%. This is due to the fact that it is written in a dialect, whose lexicon contains many words which are not standard Italian.

The most ancient work is the *Rime* by the *Scuola Siciliana*, a collection of poetries of different Sicilian authors from the 13th century. The language of the Scuola is characterized by a richness in both quality and quantity. Indeed, these poets used to mix and assimilate different regional dialects, Latin, Langue d'Oc and Langue d'Oil. The result is a lexicon rich of different influences and forms, which is very distant from contemporary Italian. The performance of the tools are in facts very low: the dictionary covers only 27% of words, while the parser has accuracies close to 50%.

The following work, the *Rime* by *Guido Cavalcanti*, signals an important change in the Italian language, which in that time was evolving strongly towards the contemporary form. In the late 13th century the literary movement called *Dolce Stil Nuovo* put the basis for modern Italian, by importing substantial changes in the language phonology and morphology. This is why the performance of the tools on the Scuola Siciliana are so low if compared to all later works. For example, in the Scuola Siciliana we still find expressions derived from Latin such as *"flamma"*, *"plaser"* and *"dovero"'*, which in Cavalcanti are already changed in the contemporary Italian variants *"fiamma"*, *"piacere"*, and *"dovro"'*.

As for the 14th century, *Dante Aligheri*, *Francesco Petrarca* and *Giovanni Boccaccio* represent the final achievement of a strong and stable Italian linguistic system. The performance obtained by our tools are here difficult to explain with a coarse-grained analysis. Yet, what is interesting to notice is that the dictionary coverage is lower for Boccaccio, probably because of the extensive use of dialectal expressions to describe everyday life, that are today disused. The higher coverage on Petrarca can be justified by the fact that he tended to use a short and stable lexicon, without any concession to dialectal expressions and neologisms. This also explains why coverage on Dante is in between the other two authors. Dante, especially in the *Divina Commedia*, tended to introduce many neologisms, which today are in part lost and in part accepted.

The variable performance on the works from the Renaissance period (*Orlando Furioso* by *Ludovico Ariosto* and *Canzoniere* by *Lorenzo de'Medici*) reveal that there is no high consistency in the tools' performance among works of the same movement. Both the dictionary and the parser show much better results for the latter work than for the former. This supports the observation that it is not possible to draw conclusions on the applicability of tools for automatic analysis even on works of the same literary movement. A closer look at the two works reveals that the lexicons used by the two authors are very different. From the one side, the *Orlando Furioso* (edition 1532) was mainly written to address the taste of the overall Italian audience, and its vocabulary is then very tied to the Italian language of the 16th century, which was highly influenced by the old Latin and Greek languages. Indeed, the poem contains common content words such *"haver"* (contemporary Italian *"avere"*, English *"to have"*) and *"huom"* (contemporary Italian *"uomo"*, English *"man"*) which today are disused, and which are a direct derivation of Latin (respectively *"habeo"* and *"homo"*). On the contrary, the vocabulary used by *Lorenzo De'Medici* appears closer to contemporary Italian. A possible explanation is that one of the goal of *Lorenzo* was to disseminate the use of the "Fiorentino" dialect, which is the base of contemporary Italian, and that was in contrast with the tendency of that period.

A similar observation stands for the Baroque period, where we find two works (the *Dialogo* by *Galileo* and the *Muse* by *Giovan Battista Basile*) which highly differ from a lexical perspective. Indeed, the latter is a collection of dialectal poetries, which are distant from standard Italian. The former is a prose work whose main intent was to disseminate a scientific theory to the largest audience possible. It then sticks to the spoken language of the 17th century, that

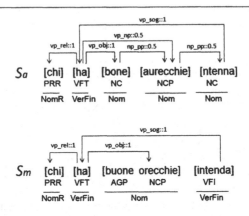

Fig. 1. Incorrect analysis of historical Italian (S_a) and correct analysis of contemporary Italian (S_m)

had consistently changed from the Italian of the 16th century, toward a form which is much more similar to contemporary Italian. This also explains why the performance over the *Dialogo* are much higher than over the *Orlando Furioso*.

More difficult is to follow the development of the Italian language in later periods, as different influences and movements start to merge together. A coherent analysis of the works from the Illuminism on (18th-19th century) would then require a deeper philological investigation, which is out of the scope of this work. We here only notice that in average the performance tend to increase with time, with the only exception of the latest work (*"I Malavoglia"*), whose performance are lower, due to the presence of many dialectal dialogs.

Reported results show that the accuracy of the tools is too low on historical Italian. This would strongly affect the overall syntactic analysis produced by the parser, because an incorrect PoS tagging has negative effects on the subsequent phase of the parsing process. For example, Fig. 1 reports the syntactic analysis for the ancient sentence S_a = *"chi ha bone auricchie 'ntenna"*, and the corresponding contemporary sentence S_m = *"chi ha buone orecchie intenda"* (English: *"if you have good ears try to listen"*). S_a and S_m have a similar grammatical structure. Yet, the fact that words are different leads to a completely different analysis. The analysis for sentence S_a is incorrect, while the analysis for S_m is *more* correct. The main problem in the analysis of S_a is the morpho-syntactic lexicon. Words such as *"bone"* (English: *"good"*), *"auricchie"* (English: *"ears"*), and *"ntenna"* (English: *"*try to listen"*) are not contained in the contemporary Italian lexicon. Two of them receive an incorrect part-of-speech tag: common noun (NC) instead of adjective (AGP) and common noun (NC) instead of verb (VFI). This is due to the fact that the PoS-tagger gives the noun tag (NC) as first hypothesis for unknown words. These type of errors completely mislead the syntactic analysis, as the figure shows.

6 Enhancing Resources for Ancient Italian

The previous section showed that the dictionary coverage and the accuracy of the morphological analyser and of the PoS-tagger are too low on historical Italian, thus strongly affecting the overall analysis produced by the parser. Hereafter, we propose some possible solutions to this problem, to improve the portability of the tools to historical Italian.

Manually build a lexicon for each period. This would be the most effective, but more costly solution, as the annotation should be carried out independently on every time period or literary movement having a definite lexicon. Previous similar experiences suggest that the effort is not feasible in a short time: for example, up to now and after more than 10 years of work, the TLIO dictionary contains lemmas only for the letters *A B C D E*, with a projected time to market of almost 50 years.

Leverage manually annotated corpora. A morpho-syntactically annotated corpus of historical Italian texts could be used to train reliable corpus-induced lexicons and PoS-taggers, as done in [4]. This solution is much more feasible than the previous one. Indeed, previous studies for contemporary and historical languages indicate that small sized corpora are sufficient to learn reliable NLP models. In this setting, active learning techniques could be highly valuable, as they allow to achieve a good compromise between accuracy and annotation effort.

Adapt existing models. A third viable solution consists in adapting current models for contemporary Italian, without going through a new learning phase and costly annotations. Rocio et al. [3] show for example that a simple **lexical analyzer** can turn a lexicon of contemporary Portuguese into a reliable lexicon for Medieval Portuguese, by using simple inflection rules. A similar approach could be used for historical Italian, lavereging adaptation rules for capturing morphological variations, such as : *-are* → *-ar*, to map *"amare"* and *"amar"*. Another adaptation strategy could rely on simple heuristic **string matching** functions. In facts, many contemporary words are small variations of ancient words – e.g. *"orecchio"* is adapted from *"auricchio"*. One of the best way of capturing these type of variations is using the Levensthein edit distance. We experimented such an approach on a dataset of 200 forms randomly extracted from the ancient Italian corpus (ca. 20 forms from each text). We obtained a coverage of 0.478 and an accuracy of 0.345.[4] Results indicate that string matching contributes to the task to some extent (it finds a good mapping for almost half ancient words), but at the cost of introducing potential noise (ancient words are often mapped to wrong entries in the dictionary).

As a future work, we will explore in particular the second and the third solutions. Also, we will measure the parser and dictionary performance over larger

---

[4] Given an ancient word w, we say that the Levensthein function *covers* the word if it finds the correct corresponding word(s) in the contemporary dictionary. Coverage is then defined as the percentage of ancient words which are covered, over the total number of words in the dataset. Accuracy is defined as the percentage of correct corresponding words over the dataset.

corpora, as the TLIO and the Corpus Taurinense, and investigate the performance of the whole parser chain, including a full syntactic analysis. Finally, we will activate collaborations with philologists, with the further goal of formalizng grammatical and lexical models for ancient Italian, and for studying a possible implementation of NLP-based tools for philological studies.

References

1. TEIconsortium: TEI P5: Guidelines for Electronic Text Encoding and Interchange. TEI Consortium (2005)
2. Moon, T., Baldridge, J.: Part-of-speech tagging for middle English through alignment and projection of parallel diachronic texts. In: Proceedings of the 2007 Joint-Conference on Empirical Methods in Natural Language Processing and ComputationalNatural Language Learning (EMNLP-CoNLL), pp. 390–399 (2007)
3. Rocio, V., Alves, M.A., Lopes, J.G.P., Xavier, M.F., Vicente, G.: Automated creation of a partially syntactially annotated corpus of medieval portuguese using contemporary portuguese resources. In: Proceedings of the ATALA workshop on Treebanks, Paris, France (1999)
4. Britto, H., Finger, M., Galves, C.: Computational and linguistic aspects of the construction of the Tycho Brahe Parsed Corpus of Historical Portuguese. Gunter Narr Verlag, Tubingen (2002)
5. Brill, E.: Transformation-based error-driven learning and natural language processing: A case study in part of speech tagging. Computational Linguistics 21(4) (1995)
6. Yarowsky, D., Ngai, G.: Inducing multilingual pos taggers and np bracketers via robust projection across aligned corpora. In: Proceedings of NAACL 2001: Second meeting of the North American Chapter of the Association for Computational Linguistics on Language technologies, Morristown, NJ, pp. 1–8 (2001)
7. Kroch, A., Taylor, A.: Penn-helsinki parsed corpus of middle english (2000)
8. Kroch, A., Santorini, B., Delfs, L.: Penn-helsinki parsed corpus of early modern english (2004)
9. Taylor, A., Warner, A., Pintzuk, S., Beths, F.: The york-toronto-helsinki parsed corpus of old english prose (2003)
10. Pollidori, V., Larson, P.: Il Tesoro della Lingua Italiana delle Origini(TLIO): il progetto lessicograco e i suoi risultati attuali. Franco Cesati Editore, Dordrecht, Germany (2005)
11. Barbera, Manuel Barbera, C.M., Marello, C.: Corpus Taurinense: italiano antico annotato in modo nuovo. Bulzoni Editore, Roma, Dordrecht, Germany (2003)
12. Basili, R., Di Stefano, A., Gigliucci, R., Moschitti, A., Pennacchiotti, M.: Automatic analysis and annotation of literary texts. In: Wokshop on Cultural Heritage, 9th AIIA Conference, Milan, Italy (2005)
13. Basili, R., Zanzotto, F.M.: Parsing engineering and empirical robustness. Natural Language Engineering 8/2-3 (2002)
14. Collins, M.: Head-driven statistical models for natural language parsing. Computational Linguistics 29(4) (December 2003)
15. Charniak, C.: A maximum-entropy-inspired parser. In: NAACL, Seattle, Washington (2000)

Statistical Surface Realisation of Portuguese Referring Expressions

Daniel Bastos Pereira and Ivandré Paraboni

Escola de Artes, Ciências e Humanidades – Universidade de São Paulo (EACH / USP)
Av.Arlindo Bettio, 1000 - 03828-000, São Paulo, Brazil
{daniel.bastos,ivandre}@usp.br

Abstract. Natural Language Generation systems usually require substantial knowledge about the structure of the target language in order to perform the final task in the generation process – the mapping from semantic representation to text known as surface realisation. Designing knowledge bases of this kind, typically represented as sets of grammar rules, may however become a costly, labour-intensive enterprise. In this work we take a statistical approach to surface realisation in which no linguistic knowledge is hard-coded, but rather trained automatically from large corpora. Results of a small experiment in the generation of referring expressions show significant levels of similarity between our (computer-generated) text and those produced by humans, besides the usual benefits commonly associated with statistical NLP such as low development costs, domain- and language-independency.

1 Introduction

Natural Language Generation (NLG) systems – which produce textual descriptions from usually non-linguistic input data - come to play when simple, 'canned' text is not sufficient, that is, when greater (i.e., closer to human performance) linguistic variation is required[1]. Designing a complete NLG system is a multidisciplinary, large-scale enterprise, often borrowing from fields such as Artificial Intelligence, Psycholinguistics and many others. In its simplest form, a typical NLG system can be viewed as a three-stage pipelined architecture as in Figure 1 adapted from [8]:

Starting from a high-level communicative goal of providing a textual description of a domain entity identified as 'john', the system builds up a plan to represent the input data. The plan is successively refined up to the point in which a mapping from semantic representation to text is drawn. This final conversion step, known as surface realisation, is the focus of the present work.

Surface realisation requires substantial knowledge about the structure of the target language, usually represented as a set of grammar rules or other linguistic constraints.

---

[1] For example, the STOP system [7] produces tailor-made smoking-cessation letters based on an input questionnaire filled out by the smoker, including her habits, concerns, previous attempts to quit, health problems etc.

A. Ranta, B. Nordström (Eds.): GoTAL 2008, LNAI 5221, pp. 383–392, 2008.

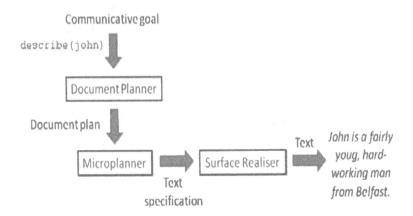

Fig. 1. The pipelined NLG architecture proposed in [8]

Designing a knowledge base of this kind may however be a costly, labour-intensive enterprise, which may be even harder for relatively (NLP-wise) resource-poor languages such as Brazilian Portuguese. Difficulties become even greater if we consider the case of multilingual applications, in which the resources for each of the languages involved would have to be built from scratch using expertise knowledge, and yet requiring periodical revisions as language use evolves.

As an alternative to this more traditional approach, we intend to develop a surface realisation component solely based on *n-gram* statistics, i.e., with no hard-coded linguistic knowledge. In doing so, we shall limit ourselves to the task of referring expressions surface realisation in the form of noun phrases (NPs.) Although it may look as if we were addressing a somewhat smaller or 'toy' problem if compared to e.g., the surface realisation of complete sentences in the form *subject-NP + verb + object-NP*, we will argue that this is not the case.

The remainder of this paper is structured as follows. Section 2 discusses the problem at hand, namely, the realisation of referring expressions as Portuguese text. Section 3 proposes a simple mapping from semantic properties to text units. Section 4 describes the statistical approach used in our work. Section 5 presents the results of a small evaluation experiment, and Section 6 summarizes our efforts so far.

2 Background

The generation of referring expressions is a critical subtasks in the NLG system, comprising content determination (choice between pronouns, definite descriptions etc, and in the latter the choice of semantic properties to be realised as text) and surface realisation proper. In this work we focus on the surface realisation of definite and indefinite descriptions, taking as input a semantic representation of the description to be generated, and producing output text in a target language.

As our input data, we use instances of descriptions taken from the TUNA corpus [4,9], a database of situations of reference collected primarily for the study of reference phenomena and referring expressions generation algorithms. Each of these situations consists of a target object (i.e., the intended referent), a number of distractors with their corresponding semantic properties (represented as attribute-value pairs), and a description of the target object. The descriptions were produced by 45 native or fluent speakers of English, participants of a controlled experiment with the sole purpose of identifying each intended referent[2].

We will initially focus on a small subset of TUNA descriptions originally distributed as training data for the GRE-2007 challenge[3], consisting of a collection of 239 descriptions in the Furniture domain[4]. The referents in this domain are pieces of furniture (sofas, desks etc.) of different sizes and colours, presented in a 3 x 5 grid so that their position within the grid was a likely referable attribute as well. The following Table 1 summarizes the existing attributes and their possible values.

Table 1. Attributes and their possible values in TUNA Furniture domain [9]

Attributes	Values
Type	chair, sofa, desk, fan
Colour	blue, red, green gray
Orientation	forward, backward, leftward, rightward
Size	small, large
x-dimension	1-5 (columns)
y-dimension	1-3 (rows)

TUNA descriptions are represented as uniquely identifying sets containing from 1 to 6 semantic properties (on average 3.03 properties per descriptions in our data set.) although most cases (95% in our data set) ranged from 2 to 4 properties. The following Table 2 shows the distribution of descriptions in the GRE-2007 training data according to the number of properties that they conveyed.

Table 2. Distribution of descriptions according to the number of properties in the Furniture domain

Properties	% of descriptions
1	3 %
2	21 %
3	48 %
4	26 %
5	1 %
6	1 %

Each individual property is an attribute-value pair as in <NAME="type" VALUE="chair">. The following is an example of one such description, which could be realised as "the large red chair, in the second column on the top".

---

[2] As opposed to, e.g., generating descriptions to achieve *intentional* goals [11].
[3] http://www.csd.abdn.ac.uk/research/evaluation/
[4] We are currently extending our work to cover instances of reference in the People domain (representing descriptions of photographs of people) also included in the TUNA corpus.

Example 1. Semantic representation of a description in TUNA [9]

```
<DESCRIPTION>
  <ATTRIBUTE ID="a295" NAME="size" VALUE="large" />
  <ATTRIBUTE ID="a296" NAME="colour" VALUE="red" />
  <ATTRIBUTE ID="a297" NAME="type" VALUE="chair" />
  <ATTRIBUTE ID="a299" NAME="y-dimension" VALUE="1" />
  <ATTRIBUTE ID="a301" NAME="x-dimension" VALUE="2" />
</DESCRIPTION>
```

Our goal is to produce a textual description (in Portuguese) from the above semantic representation that should ideally be as close as possible to human performance.
Additionally, we intend to do so without having to write – at least in this initial stage -
linguistically-motivated rules or natural language grammars.

Given that the attribute sets are the only portion of the TUNA corpus that is relevant to the present discussion (i.e., we disregard both target and distractors information entirely), one may ask why we use TUNA descriptions at all, as opposed to e.g.,
random sets of semantic properties. The reason is twofold: first, TUNA descriptions
are produced by humans, conveying valid combinations of properties that tend to co-
occur in real language use. Second, in a more recent version of the GRE challenge
data, descriptions are accompanied by the corresponding strings originally uttered (in
English) by the participants of each trial. In our view this data set may be useful for
evaluation purposes as we will discuss in Section 5.

3 Mapping Attribute-Value Pairs into Phrases

Our surface realisation approach requires evidence of the possible phrases that each
semantic property may relate to. For example, the property <NAME="size" VALUE=
"large"> may be realised as "big", "large" and so on, or, more dramatically, it may
for example change in gender and number in a Romance language. Since presently we
do not intend to write grammar rules, we are not interested in how this mapping is
actually done - this will be left to be decided by an underlying statistical language
model. Thus, our initial task is simply to compile a list of possible text realisations
represented as phrases for each semantic property in the corpus.

Two independent annotators started by producing individual lists of the most likely
phrases that could possibly be associated with every attribute–value pair in the corpus.
To prevent combinatory explosion (discussed in the next Section) we limited the word
choices when there was no structural difference among the alternatives. For example,
the property <NAME="orientation" VALUE="left"> would be mapped to both
"facing left" and "turned to the left", but it would be irrelevant for the present purposes to include an additional mapping to, say, "*orientated* to the left"[5].

Since at this initial stage we are only considering 1-to-n relations, the mapping annotation was straightforward. More complex (m-to-n) cases – those in which two or
more properties may combine to form a single text unit (e.g., the properties of being
human, young and male may be realised simply as "a young man" or even as "a boy")
- are rare in the Furniture domain and will be discussed elsewhere.

---

[5] The examples were kept in English for presentation purposes and do not correspond to literal
translations of the original Portuguese phrases that we have annotated.

Once the annotation task was accomplished, both lists were compared against each other and merged for completeness. The resulting list consisted of the set of 22 possible properties mapped into 41 phrases, including mainly prepositional (e.g., "facing backwards"), adjectival (e.g., "red") and noun phrases (e.g., "chair") with their possible gender and number variations. This data set - a valuable and potentially reusable output of this work in its own right - is the closest we intend to get to explicit knowledge representation at this stage.

The next step was to decide which and how phrases should be combined to form an output string. Since we do not intend to encode this kind of (linguistic) knowledge, we take an over-generation approach as follows. Given a non-linguistic input description represented as a list of semantic properties, we compute all possible (unordered) sets of phrases in which the description could be realised. For example, a description comprising two semantic properties <NAME="colour" VALUE="red"> and <NAME="type" VALUE="chair"> would be associated with two phrase sets: $s1=\{vermelho, cadeira\}$ and $s2=\{vermelha, cadeira\}$ to allow for the gender variation of the 'red' value in Portuguese. Next, we compute all possible permutations of each phrase set ($s1$ and $s2$ in the above example) that matched a pre-defined description template suitable to Portuguese phrase order[6], in the form

<determiner + type + colour + size + orientation + x-dimension + y-dimension>

once again with gender variation. Thus, the above semantic input would have the following four possible realisations, in which only (1) is well-formed.

Example 2. Possible surface realisations of <NAME="colour" VALUE="red"> <NAME="type" VALUE="chair"> as a Portuguese definite description.

1. *A cadeira vermelha.*
2. *A cadeira vermelho.*
3. *O cadeira vermelha.*
4. *O cadeira vermelho.*

It is important to notice that we use phrases – and not words - as our smallest text unit, and that even fairly long phrases such as "in the middle column" are to be treated as single units. In other words, given that our phrases are pieces of natural language provided directly by human annotators and that they should represent ideal word sequences, we do not consider permutations within phrases themselves. In fact, any attempt to do so would not only be unnecessary, but also prone to undesirable combinatory explosion.

The final step in our surface realisation process is to decide which of these (e.g., 1-4 above) alternatives is the most likely output string for the given set of properties. As we shall discuss, the selection procedure turns out to be trivially implemented with the aid of a statistical language model of Portuguese.

---

[6] Limiting the alternatives to those that match the template is only partially required in our approach, and indeed any robust language model should be able to find the most likely phrase ordering even without this simple heuristics, which is mainly intended to reduce the number of alternatives under consideration.

4 Statistical Surface Realisation

The simple idea that some word sequences are more *frequent* than others has lead to the concept of language modelling that is now widely used in NLP research, from parsing to Machine Translation (e.g., [1].) For example, we are more likely to read "he bough that book on Chemistry" than "that book on Chemistry he bought". Thus, a statistical language model (which in this example would be a model of the English language) can tell us that the first sentence is closer to well-formed English than the second, and that the second is still better than some random string, e.g., "bought on Chemistry that book he".

A statistical language model is a probability distribution $P(s)$ over a set of possible sentences s representing how often each individual sentence occurs in the modelled language. The most widely-used language models are those based on n-grams, in which the probability of a given word in a sentence is determined by the n-1 previous words. In a simplified form, we may compute probabilities based on a maximum likelihood (ML) estimate with some allowance for unseen instances. For example, in a trigram-based model, the maximum likelihood conditional probability PML of a word w_i given its two predecessors w_{i-2} and w_{i-1} in the text is defined as the counting (c) of occurrences of the trigram divided by the number of occurrences of its bigram constituent:

$$P_{ML} (w_i \mid w_{i-2}\ w_{i-1}) = \frac{c (w_{i-2}\ w_{i-1}\ w_i)}{c (w_{i-2}\ w_{i-1})}$$

This estimator is of course useless if a given instance has not been observed in the training data. In order to reserve some probability mass for unseen events (and also to improve the model accuracy), a wide variety of smoothing techniques have been proposed. Possibly the oldest of all, the Additive smoothing proposed by Lidstone in 1920 based on Laplace's Law [2] simply adds one unit to the observed counts, which effectively deals with the problem of data sparseness but generally presents a poor performance for allowing too much of the probability space to unseen events [6]. More effective estimators include the *Good-Turing* estimator (GT) [3], usually combining multiple-order models as the Jelinek-Mercer smoothing [5].

Probability values will be represented as the related measure of *cross-entropy*, which attempts to describe the *uncertainty* of the model (and hence lower cross-entropy values are better.) Cross-entropy values can be easily derived from probability estimates as follows. Given the probability $p(T)$ of a test set T containing w words, the cross-entropy $Hp(T)$ of a particular model on data T is

$$Hp (T) = (-1\ /\ w) * \log_2 p(T)$$

For a thorough review of statistical language models and smoothing techniques we report to [2]. Our own work is a straightforward application of these techniques. Given a set of all valid strings produced from a non-linguistic description as in Example 2 in the previous section, we simply evaluate each string against a statistical language model, selecting the most likely output string for the given input. For this purpose, we trained a simple bigram language model from the 40-million words in the NILC corpus [10] of Brazilian Portuguese using the tool described in [12]. Interestingly, although very representative of Brazilian Portuguese language use, the corpus mainly consists of newspaper articles whose descriptions are highly unlikely to resemble those rather schematic instances that we expect to produce from the TUNA data (e.g., "the green fan facing backwards" etc.).

5 Results and Evaluation

For each of the 319 instances of Portuguese descriptions in our data, we followed an over-generation strategy to produce the most likely surface realisations according to the NILC bigram language model described in the previous section. The resulting set of word strings comprises our *System* descriptions.

Evaluation proper was carried out by comparing each of the *System* descriptions to their human-produced counterparts, hereby called *Reference* descriptions. In order to build a *Reference* set, we take advantage of the training data made available with the REG-2008 Challenge, which include the actual English descriptions uttered by the participants in 319 TUNA trials. More specifically, two independent annotators manually produced a Portuguese translation of each of the 319 descriptions and, to facilitate agreement, the translations were also normalized, removing much of the noise that naturally occurs in raw data. This included a number of likely errors (e.g., "red chair in center *red*"), meta-attributes (e.g., "*first* picture on third row"), illegal attributes (e.g.., "the grey desk *with drawers*"), differences in specificity (e.g., "shown from the side" as a less specific alternative to both "facing left" and "facing right" values) and synonymy (e.g., "facing the viewer" as an alternative to "facing forward".) Moreover, given that definiteness cannot be worked out from the attribute set alone, all indefinite descriptions were changed to definite references.

Regarding the usefulness of this reference set, there are a number of due observations: firstly, given the differences between languages, our reference data set is not to be viewed as a resource for investigating language use as the original TUNA data set is intended to be, but rather as a standard of acceptable performance for a practical Portuguese NLG system. Moreover, since the translated descriptions were not produced in real situations of reference, we are aware that our results are not directly comparable to, e.g., the work carried out in the REG-2008 challenge in the evaluation of English descriptions, and that would remain the case even without normalization as we discuss later.

On the other hand, although the result of both translation and normalization tasks is a somewhat simplified set of Portuguese descriptions, this is not to say that these descriptions are tailored to match those that we intend to generate. In fact, one of the goals in the normalization task was to retain the most appropriate instances of reference, which included a large number of cases that we are not presently able to produce, e.g., those combining the *x-dimension* and *y-dimension* attributes in single references to corners, as in "in the upper right corner". We found that referring to a corner in these cases was far more appropriate - and indeed much more frequent in the data - than what our system will currently produce (e.g., "in the 5th column in the top row".)

Provided our *System*'s output and the *Reference* set, we followed the evaluation procedure applied in the more recent Referring Expressions Generation Challenge[7] (now called REG-2008) to compute Accuracy and String-edit distance scores for each *System-Reference* pair. Briefly, Accuracy is taken to be the proportion of generated string words that appeared in the *Reference* set, and String-edit distance is the traditional Levenshtein's metrics that takes into account the cost of insert, delete and substitute operations required to make the generated *System* string identical to the corresponding *Reference* (a zero distance value indicates a perfect match.) The results below were obtained using the *teval* tool provided by the REG-2008 team[8].

Table 4. Summary of the results of the evaluation experiment

Evaluation Criteria	All
Accuracy	0.24
String-edit distance	2.69

Overall, 103 instances (32.3%) of descriptions were incorrectly generated for lack of complete gender agreement caused by the fact that our simple bigram-based model cannot handle long-distance dependencies appropriately, as in "o sofá grande vermelha", in which the gender agreement between "sofá" and "vermelha" could not be established. Although we were presently unable to collect a sufficient large corpus of Brazilian Portuguese to improve these results, we believe that this could be easily fixed had we used a more expressive language model instead.

The above Accuracy scores are obviously low, but it should be pointed out that this measure, whilst useful in the context of a referring expressions generation competition, merely counts the number of system descriptions that match the reference set word by word. As for the String-edit distance, the present results seem reasonable given that our reference set contains descriptions of up to 12 words in length (5.62 on average.) More importantly, we found that these low scores were, to a great extent, due to a simple difference in word choice: for example, whenever the system chooses the word "line" but the reference set happens to use, e.g., "row", the simple String-edit measure – which does not account for synonymy – will penalize the system. In addition to that, it should be pointed out that this data set included 27 trials conveying illegal attributes or values represented in the corpus by the value 'others', which stands for any property expressed by the participant outside the scope of the experiment and which could not be expected to be realised by our system.

One striking difference between the system descriptions set and the reference set was the word order of (Brazilian) Portuguese adjectives. To our surprise, it is not clear in which order attributes such as *colour* and *size* should be realised in Brazilian Portuguese. For example, "a large red table" could be realised either as *type + colour + size* (e.g., "a mesa vermelha, grande") or as *type + size + colour* (e.g., "a mesa grande, vermelha".) As both alternatives seem equally acceptable, the choice may

---

[7] http://www.nltg.brighton.ac.uk/research/reg08
[8] At the time of writing we are carrying out a similar evaluation procedure using the REG-2008 *development* data set for the generation of definite descriptions in both Furniture and People domains, whose results will be discussed elsewhere.

depend on which property contrasts each of the distractors in the situation of reference. Whilst the present ambiguity probably reveals a weakness in our artificially-built reference set, it may also suggest that a much more sophisticated approach to Portuguese realisation is called-for, especially if compared to the generation of English descriptions, whose word order seems fairly standard. Further investigation on this issue is clearly required.

Finally, we would like to briefly return to the point made in Section 1 about the computational challenge of generating definite descriptions as opposed to whole sentences. We randomly selected a small subset of descriptions from the 2007 training data (22 instances, or about 10% of the total amount) and added a common subject and verb to each of them. Next, all possible permutations of each string were re-generated to produce whole sentences to be evaluated against the NILC bigram language model, the underlying assumption being that well-formed sentences following a *subject + verb + definite description* pattern as in "John bought a green table" should obtain the lowest cross-entropy values of all.

By manually examining the most likely output for each example, we found that in all (100%) cases the subject was followed by the verb (i.e., "John bought"), and that in only 5 cases (22.7%) the entire output string did not correspond to a well-formed sentence. Despite the small scale of this analysis, the results indeed suggest that, once a suitable sentence template has been somehow chosen, producing whole sentences may add little to the computational challenge of generating definite descriptions, and that a more expressive language model may enable the generation of unrestricted text in a similar fashion.

6 Final Remarks

In this paper we have described a simple application of statistical language models in the surface realisations of Portuguese referring expressions. Although at this stage we have arguably focused on the simplest cases (1-to-n mappings), results of a small evaluation experiment suggest that descriptions produced in this way are comparable to a human-produced reference set. Moreover, being a purely statistical approach, our work did not require the labour-intensive task of modelling grammar rules or linguistic knowledge of any kind, which may seem particularly attractive to NLP research in relatively resource-poor languages such as Brazilian Portuguese.

As future work we intend to expand our current approach to cover more complex cases of realisation, and possibly a more complex domain, ultimately leading to the design of a fully capable surface realisation component that could be embedded in a Portuguese Natural Language Generation system.

Acknowledgments

The authors acknowledge support from the University of São Paulo (USP "Ensinar com Pesquisa" programme), CNPq (grant nr. 484015/2007 9) and FAPESP (grant nr. 2006/03941-7.).

References

1. Brown, P.E., Pietra, S.A.D., Pietra, V.J.D., Mercer, R.L.: The Mathematics of Statistical Machine Translation: Parameter Estimation. Computational Linguistics 16(2), 79–85 (1993)
2. Chen, S.F., Goodman, J.: An empirical study of smoothing techniques for language modeling. Computer Speech and Language 13, 359–394 (1999)
3. Gale, W.A., Sampson, G.: Good-Turing frequency estimation without tears. Journal of Quantitative Linguistics 2, 217–237 (1995)
4. Gatt, A., van der Sluis, I., van Deemter, K.: Evaluating algorithms for the generation of referring expressions using a balanced corpus. In: Proceedings of the 11th European Workshop on Natural Language Generation, pp. 49–56 (2007)
5. Jelinek, F., Mercer, R.L.: Interpolated estimation of Markov source parameters from sparse data. In: Proc. of the Workshop Pattern Recognition in Practice, pp. 381–397. North-Holland, Amsterdam (1980)
6. Manning, C.D., Schütze, H.: Foundations of Statistical Natural Language Processing. MIT Press, Cambridge (2003)
7. Reiter, E., Robertson, R., Osman, L.M.: Lessons from a Failure: Generating Tailored Smoking Cessation Letters. Artificial Intelligence 144, 41–58 (2003)
8. Reiter, E., Dale, R.: Building natural language generation systems. Cambridge University Press, Cambridge (2000)
9. van Deemter, K., van der Sluis, I., Gatt, A.: Building a semantically transparent corpus for the generation of referring expressions. In: 4th International Conference on Natural Language Generation, INLG-2004 Special session on Data Sharing and Evaluation (2006)
10. Nunes, M.d.G.V., Vieira, F.M.C., Zavaglia, C., Sossolote, C.R.C., Hernandez, J.: A construção de um léxico para o português do Brasil: lições aprendidas e perspectivas. II Encontro para o processamento de português escrito e Falado. Curitiba, 61–70 (1996)
11. Jordan, P.W.: Can Nominal Expressions Achieve Multiple Goals?: An Empirical Study. ACL-2000, Hong Kong (2000)
12. Pereira, Bastos, D., Paraboni, I.: A Language Modelling Tool for Statistical NLP. In: 5th Workshop on Information and Human Language Technology (TIL-2007), Rio de Janeiro, 5-6 July, 2007, pp. 1679–1688 (2007)

Classification-Based Filtering of Semantic Relatedness in Hypernymy Extraction

Maciej Piasecki[1], Stanisław Szpakowicz[2,3], Michał Marcińczuk[1], and Bartosz Broda[1]

[1] Institute of Applied Informatics, Wrocław University of Technology, Poland
maciej.piasecki@pwr.wroc.pl
marcinczuk@gmail.com, bartosz.broda@pwr.wroc.pl
[2] School of Information Technology and Engineering, University of Ottawa
szpak@site.uottawa.ca
[3] Institute of Computer Science, Polish Academy of Sciences

Abstract. Manual construction of a wordnet can be facilitated by a system that suggests semantic relations acquired from corpora. Such systems tend to produce many wrong suggestions. We propose a method of filtering a raw list of noun pairs potentially linked by hypernymy, and test it on Polish. The method aims for good recall and sufficient precision. The classifiers work with complex features that give clues on the relation between the nouns. We apply a corpus-based measure of semantic relatedness enhanced with a Rank Weight Function. The evaluation is based on the data in Polish WordNet. The results compare favourably with similar methods applied to English, despite the small size of Polish WordNet.

Keywords: lexical-semantic relations, measures of semantic relatedness, wordnet construction, Polish WordNet, nouns, hypernymy extraction, supervised Machine Learning, classifiers, Rank Weight Function, filtering.

1 Introduction

Linguists who work on the manual construction of a wordnet or semantic lexicon would appreciate a tool that suggests, for a given word w, a set of words linked to w by lexical semantic relations. Among such relations, hypernymy is particularly important – it is, after all, the centrepiece of a wordnet hierarchy. Systems that make such suggestion seem to overwhelm linguists, though only few of the related words shown are of any interest. That is to say, it is not hard to extract many words that are somehow semantically related to w, but nuggets are rare in such plenitude. We seek a way of filtering raw suggestions that would strengthen the potentially most interesting elements.

Two main approaches to the automatic extraction of lexical semantic relations from corpora [1] are based on patterns and on clustering. For English, an almost fixed word-order language with limited inflection, manually constructed lexico-syntactic patterns were applied to the extraction of hypernymy; they gave good

A. Ranta, B. Nordström (Eds.): GoTAL 2008, LNAI 5221, pp. 393–404, 2008.

precision but low recall – see, for example, [2]. Mediocre recall can be an obstacle for linguists for whom the interesting cases are those of which they had not thought. The situation differs for an almost free word-order language with rich inflection, such as Polish. The preliminary experiments have shown that even achieving good precision in hypernymy extraction is a very demanding task for lexico-syntactic patterns. The patterns often extract indirect hypernyms.

Methods based on automatic learning of patterns from corpus, such as [1], can achieve much higher recall, with reasonable precision. The application of the patterns, however, is limited only to pairs of lexical units (LUs) that occur near each other in the same sentence in a specific lexico-syntactic structure. It is also still necessary to filter the final list, and additional knowledge is necessary to identify incorrect pairs.

Measures of Semantic Relatedness (MRSs) based on *distributional semantics* give high recall, theoretically limited only by the vocabulary of the corpus used. The main problem, however, is precision – or, to be exact, the lack of relation labels for identified pairs of semantically related LUs. On the list of LUs most related to a given unit one can find many semantic relations: synonymy and antonymy (with very similar distributional patterns), hypernymy, meronymy, metonymy, semantic linking by some situation type, and so on. For Polish, one can expect that, on average, in about 40% of cases the relation between nouns will be either close hypo/hypernymy or near-synonymy [3]. A linguist evaluated a sample of Polish adjectives and verbs [4]. Among 20 LUs deemed most similar to the given LU u – a majority of them in some wordnet relation to u – about a half were marked as very useful or useful. The other half were neutral or useless, and it is such suggestions that conceal the important results of applying an MSR.

Our main objective is to construct a function that gives the linguist a list of likely hypernyms of the given LU. We assume that the precision should be around 50% in order to make the user interested. MSRs achieved a good level of development for Polish – see the results in [5,4] – so we want to construct the function by filtering the result of an MSR for Polish nouns. A filter would remove from the lists all LUs except those considered close hyper/hyponyms of the given LU. We have set out to construct a classifier which assigns pairs of LU to two classes: *close hypernymy plus near-synonymy pairs* and *other*. A more fine-grained division into near-synonyms and close hypernyms seems to be extremely difficult on the basis of information extracted from corpora.

A supervised Machine Learning method of extracting hypernymy instances was proposed in [6,7]. Several modified versions of this method were analysed in [8]. A similar approach but using a different type of classifier was proposed in [9]. All these approaches, however, used lexico-syntactic relations directly as classifier attributes.

2   Classification Based on Condensed Information

In most methods of extracting hypernymy pairs, lexico-syntactic features are used directly to build a classifier. Typically, however, there may be tens of thousands of features that carry very sparse information. Moreover, in any such approach most of the information delivered to a classifier describes various aspects of semantic relatedness; only relatively few features express clues that may help identify particular types of semantic relation. Near-synonyms and close hyper/hyponyms of a LU u would be expected close to the top of the list of LUs most similar to u, generated by a good MSR.

Thus, we propose to extract hypernymy pairs in two phases:

1. extract the generic relation of semantic relatedness, modelled by some MSR,
2. identify hypernymy instances – pairs of LUs – on the basis of the results produced by the MSR.

The first phase uses all kinds of information that describes the semantics of LUs. The second phase concentrates on groups of semantically related LUs and applies specialised tests that distinguish specific lexical-semantic relations as subtypes of semantic relatedness.

An MSR of good accuracy can (by way of its high values) associate LUs that extremely rarely occur close by in the corpus at hand. Note that such occurrences are the precondition on any pattern-based method. MSRs condense information otherwise distributed among many lexico-syntactic patterns; in phase 2 we can concentrate on the most promising pairs.

The only assumption is the availability of a highly accurate MSR. Because we intended to experiment with Polish, we decided to use an MSR based on the *Rank Weight Function* applied to feature frequencies – henceforth MSR(RWF) – whose accuracy on Polish data surpasses various algorithms of MSRs generation [5,4]. Lacking a competent syntactic parser for Polish, we based MSR(RWF) on frequencies of lexico-morphosyntactic patterns implemented in a formal language of morphosyntactic Boolean constraints. Each type of constraint tests certain possible morphological and structural dependencies in the occurrence context, and is parameterised by a list of LUs. As an example, a constraint may test the presence of a *specific noun* (a constraint parameter) and a conjunction as parts of a coordinate noun phrase which includes the LU being described. A coincidence matrix $\mathbf{M}$ is created. Its rows correspond to nouns, columns to instances of constraint; cell $\mathbf{M}[\mathbf{n}, \mathbf{a}]$ stores the frequency of the occurrences of noun n, which meet the constraint instantiated by the LU a.

The constructed matrix of feature frequencies is filtered in order to eliminate features with high entropy and low information. Next, for each row vector a set of significant features is selected and transformed to rank value by RWF.

The second phase begins with the extraction, for the given LU u, of a set S of LUs most semantically related to u. Next, we need a classifier to select a subset of S that includes near-synonyms and close hypernyms of u.

3   Classifier Attributes

Instead of using frequencies of lexico-syntactic features collected from a corpus directly as attributes in learning the classifier, we wanted to identify a set of complex features that can give clues on the relation between two LUs. For a pair of LUs, the values of attributes are calculated prior to training or testing. This is done via co-occurrence matrices constructed on the basis of large corpora.

In search for attributes, we drew on information about the specificity of compared nouns, the extent to which they mutually share features, topic contexts in which they occur together and, last but not least, their semantic relatedness. We now present the complete list of attributes used; a and b are noun LUs.

1. *semantic relatedness* $MSR(a, b)$ – the value returned by an MSR,
2. *co-ordination* – the frequency of a's and b's co-occurrence in the same coordinate noun phrase,
3. *modification by genitive* – the frequency of a's modification by b in the genitive form,
4. *genitive modifier* – the frequency of b's modification by a in the genitive form,
5. *precision of adjectival features* – the precision of repeating b's adjectival features by the set of a's features (for the calculation method, see formula 1 below),
6. *recall of adjectival features* – the recall of repeating b's adjectival features by the set of a's features (for details, see formula 2),
7. *precision of modification by genitive* – the precision of repeating b's features, which express modification by a specific noun in genitive, by the similar features of a (the calculation method is similar to that in formula 1),
8. *recall of modification by genitive* – the recall of repeating b's features, which express modification by a specific noun in genitive, by the similar features of a ,
9. *global frequency* of a – the total frequency of a in the corpus,
10. *global frequency* of b – the total frequency of b in the corpus,
11. *number of significant adjectival features* of a – the number of adjectival features whose co-occurrence with a is statistically significant, e.g., according to the *t-score* measure,
12. *number of significant adjectival features* of b – the number of adjectival features whose co-occurrence with b is statistically significant,
13. *co-occurrence in text window* of a and b – the frequency of a and b co-occurring in the same text window, e.g., of the size ± 50 tokens,
14. *significance of co-occurrence in text window* of a and b – the statistical significance of a and b co-occurring in the same text window, e.g., on the basis of the *t-score* measure,
15. *adjectival specificity* of a – after [10], calculated here (see formula 3) as the average number of adjectival features for a single occurrence of a in the corpus,
16. *adjectival specificity* of b – calculated according to formula 3 ,
17. *adjectival specificity ratio* – the ratio of a's adjectival specificity to b's adjectival specificity.

In subsequent discussion, we use the term *relevant LUs* jointly for near-synonyms and close hyper/hyponyms that occur on the list of LUs most similar to the given LU a.

We pass to the classifier only those LUs whose value of semantic relatedness is higher in comparison to other pairs of LUs, but the exact value of MSR is still important. It is more likely that a relevant LU b will have a higher value of $MSR(a, b)$ – the attribute 1 – than non-relevant LUs.

The next group of attributes is meant to give the classifier information concerning directly the possible hypernymy and co-hyponymy relation between a and b. The co-ordination attribute (2) is based on a constraint that looks for syntactic co-ordination of a and b as constituents of the same composite noun phrase (NP). Only a limited set of conjunctions was manually selected: *ani* (*neither, nor*), *albo* (*or*), *czy* (*whether*), *i* (*and*), *lub* (*or*) and *oraz* (*and*). The value of (2) is the frequency with which the constraint is met for a and b co-occurring in the same sentence.[1] We also assumed that *co-ordination* is more frequent for potential co-hyponyms and hypernyms in some patterns.

A manual investigation of instance pairs of hypernyms in the IPI PAN Corpus of Polish [11] showed that, surprisingly, they often occur as the NP head and its noun modifier in the genitive case. Even more often there occurs meronymy expressed by the genitive modification. Thus, the classifier receives information on the frequency of this syntactic relation in both directions, when a is modified (3) and is the modifier (4). Both attributes are based on the same morphosyntactic constraint analysing the case of nouns and their positions; as no morphological agreement is required, the precision of the constraint is lower in relation to the constraints based on agreement.

The idea of the precision of repeating b's features by a's features, used in attributes: 5 and 7, is modelled after the MSR in [12]. We want to analyse the *additive precision* with which by using a's features we refer to ("retrieve") b's features. The precision is defined as follows:

$$P^{add}(a, b) = \frac{\sum_{i \in F(a) \cap F(b)} \mathbf{M}[a, i]}{\sum_{j \in F(a)} \mathbf{M}[a, j]} \tag{1}$$

where

- $F(x)$ is the set of features occurring frequently enough with x, according to a test of statistical significance, e.g., a *t-score* test, s
- $\mathbf{M}$ is a co-occurrence matrix that represents the given set of features; for attribute 5 the matrix of adjectives and adjectival participles $\mathbf{M}_{adj}$ is used, while for attribute 7 it is the matrix $\mathbf{M}_{Ng}$ of modification by nouns in the genitive case.

The additive recall of repeating b's features a's features, used in 6 and 8, is calculated similarly to P^{add} [12]:

$$R^{add}(a, b) = \frac{\sum_{i \in F(a) \cap F(b)} \mathbf{M}[b, i]}{\sum_{j \in F(b)} \mathbf{M}[b, j]}, \tag{2}$$

---

[1] The corpus is processed with the granularity of sentences – identified by a simple sentencer.

Additive precision and recall are calculated for each type of descriptive features separately, but the four attributes together are intended to show to what extent the description of a is included in the description of b. We assume that the possible descriptions of a hyponym are covered by the possible descriptions of its hypernym. Precision and recall allow us to test this dependency in both ways and measure its strength.

During the preliminary experiments, we noticed that nouns semantically related by situation type are difficult to distinguish from relevant nouns. In order to capture the difference, we added two attributes intended to signal a kind of topic similarity – the two nouns would be used in the description of the same topics. That is why the value of attribute 13 is the frequency of co-occurrence of a and b in a quite large context of ± 50. Moreover, there are no restrictions on these contexts. We want to record any co-occurrence. In attribute 14 this information is filtered and emphasised by the *t-score* test. However, we tested both versions as elements of a training/test vector.

With the next group of features we try to describe how specific both nouns are, and to get some information on the relation of hypernymy levels of a and b. First, the global frequency of a noun can say something about its generality – the attributes 9 and 10. Second, we also test the number of different significant adjectival features of both nouns – the attributes 11 and 12. Finally we apply to the description of both nouns a measure of adjectival specificity (15 and 16) following the proposal in [10] (a similar measure was proposed in [13]):

$$spec(a) = \frac{\sum_i \mathbf{M}_{adj}[a, i]}{globalTf(a)} \tag{3}$$

where $\mathbf{M}_{adj}$ is the matrix of co-occurrence with adjectives and adjectival participles, and $globalTf(a)$ is the total frequency of a in the corpus, that is to say, attribute 9

Some machine learning methods (C4.5, for example) would find it difficult to get the ratio of both specificity measures, so we explicitly added this ratio (17) to the attribute set.

4   Evaluation

The MSR for the experiments and the values of all attributes were generated from two corpora combined. One was the IPI PAN Corpus with about 254 million token. The other was a 116-million token *Korpus Rzeczypospolitej* (texts from a Polish daily) [14].

The MSR was the same as that proposed in [5], which uses a Rank Weight Function to transform frequencies into rank-based feature values. It was constructed on the basis of two types of lexico-morphosyntactic constraints:

- modification by *a specific adjective or adjectival participle*,
- co-ordination with a *a specific noun*.

All nouns, adjectives and adjectival participles from the combined corpora were used accordingly as the lexical elements of constraint instances. MSR(RWF) achieved the accuracy of almost 91% in WordNet-Based Synonymy Test working on the Polish WordNet (plWordNet) [3].

We used plWordNet as the main source of training/test examples. Following the general experimental paradigm of [6], we generated from plWordNet two sets of LU pairs: Known Hypernyms (KH) and Known Non-Hypernyms (NH). Our goal is to support linguists by presenting relevant pairs of LUs, so we were less strict than [6], and we included not only direct hypernyms in the set of Known Hypernyms. Two different divisions of the two groups, based on hypernymy path length, were used in the tests. Here are the data sets generated from plWordNet:

- **H** in results, the set of pairs: direct hypernym/hyponym, in all experiments included in KH – 2967 pairs in total,
- **P2**, pairs of LUs connected by a path of 2 hypernymy arcs included in KH – 2060 pairs,
- **P3**, pairs of LUs connected by a path of 3 or more hypernymy arcs, NH – 1176 pairs,
- **R** pairs of words randomly selected from plWordNet in such way that no direct hypernymy path connects them, NH – 55366 pairs.

After the first experiments, we noticed that the border space between typical elements of KH and NH is not populated well enough, especially considering its importance for Machine Learning. We manually annotated randomly selected pairs of LUs which occurred on the lists of the 20 LUs most similar to a given LU.

From this selection, 1159 pairs of words classified as non-relevant were collected into a set called **E**. In some experiments, we added **E** to NK, see below.

We experimented with two training sets combined from different data sets we have presented. Test sets were excluded randomly from training sets during ten-fold cross-validation. Training sets are named in Table 1 according to the following scheme: *KH, NH*. The first training set, named H+P2,P3+R includes only pairs extracted from plWordNet. It consists of 5027 KH pairs (H+P2) and 56531 NH pairs (P3+R) — 61558 pairs in total. Thus, in the case of this set, the test were done only on data already collected in plWordNet.

As plWordNet is rather small yet, the second training set was extended with the set **E** of manually classified pairs. We added only negative pairs, as we assumed that positive examples are well represented by pairs from plWordNet, while more difficult negative examples are hidden in the huge number of negative examples automatically extracted from plWordNet. The second training set consists of 5027 KH (H+P2) and 57690 NH (P3+R+E) — 62717 LU pairs in total.

In the experiments, we used Naïve Bayes and two types of decision trees, C4.5 and LMT. Naïve Bayes classifiers are probabilistic, C4.5 is in fact rule-based, and LMT combines rule-based structure of a decision tree with logistic regression in leaves. In order to facilitate a comparison of classifiers, we performed all experiments on the same training-test data set. Because we selected C4.5 as our primary classifier, and we generated examples from the same corpus, we did not introduce any data normalisation or discretisation. The range of data variety was also limited by the corpus used. The application of the same data to the training of a Naïve Bayes classifier resulted in a bias towards its more memory-based-like behaviour. According to the clear distinctions in the main group of the applied data sets, however, the achieved result was positive, see Table1.

All experiments were run in the Weka environment [15]. In each case, we applied tenfold cross-validation; the average results appear in Table1.

Because some classifiers, for example C4.5, are known to be sensitive to the biased proportion of training examples for different classes (here, only two), we also tested the application of random subsampling of the negative examples (NH) in the training data. The ratio KH:NH in the original sets is around 1:10. In some experiments the ratio was randomly reduced to 1:1 (the uniform distribution of probability was applied in drawing a new subset NH).

Table 1. Evaluation for both sets using tenfold cross-validation

	P	R	F_1	P	R	F_1
ratio		1:1			1:10	
Naïve Bayes						
H+P2,P3+R	89.80	47.10	61.79	46.30	45.80	46.05
H+P2,P3+R+E	84.70	59.10	69.62	34.60	53.50	42.02
C4.5						
H+P2,P3+R	82.10	77.50	79.73	66.90	43.10	52.43
H+P2,P3+R+E	81.70	78.40	80.02	60.70	39.90	48.15
LMT						
H+P2,P3+R	81.80	80.60	81.20	72.80	39.40	51.13
H+P2,P3+R+E	81.00	78.20	79.58	65.40	34.50	45.17

Precision and recall are calculated in Table 1 according to the description of examples extracted from plWordNet (H, P2, P3, R) or defined manually (E). The results achieved by both decision trees are very similar, and high according to all three measures. However, the inclusion of the set E decreases the result significantly in comparison to the high ratio $|R| : |E|$, that is to say, a small number of more difficult examples negatively influence the result. The R set includes more obvious and more closely semantically related pairs of LUs and is generated randomly from plWordNet, but E includes only tricky examples. That is why we ran additional tests on a separate set of LU pairs selected randomly from a set of lists of the 20 LUs most similar to the given LU generated by MSR(RWF). The set was annotated manually, and will be referred to as the *manual tesset* (M). The best classifiers according to Table 1 appeared to be biased towards positive decision, contrary to the classifiers trained on the 1:10 version of the learning data.

Below we present sample results of the classification selected from one of the folds of the tenfold cross-validation (classifier C4.5, ratio KH to NK 1:10, **E** included in NK).[2]

---

[2] Many words in these pairs are polysemous in both languages. The English translations "select" the intended meaning.

true positives: *akt* (*act*) – *ustawa* (*bill*), *bank* (*bank*) – *firma* (*firm*), *emocja* (*emotion*) – *smutek* (*sadness*), *intelekt* (*intellect*) – *przymiot* (*attribute*), *licencja* (*licence*) – *zezwolenie* (*permission*), *pragnienie* (*desire*) – *ochota* (*willingness*), *terytorium* (*territory*) – *kolonia* (*colony*), *warzywo* (*vegetable*) – *kartofel* (*potato*),

false positives: *celnik* (*customs officer*) – *policja* (*police*), *czynsz* (*rent*) – *oprocentowanie* (*interest*), *dochód* (*income*) – *dotacja* (*donation*), *nonszalancja* (*nonchalance*) – *rozrzutność* (*profligacy*), *odpad* (*waste*) – *produkt* (*product*), *problem* (*problem*) – *rodzina* (*family*), *temat* (*topic*) – *dostarczyciel* (*provider*), *zachwyt* (*admiration*) – *zdumienie* (*astonishment*),

true negatives: *człowieczeństwo* (*humanity*) – *prorok* (*prophet*), *licencja* (*licence*) – *zarządzenie* (*regulation*), *opis* (*description*) – *hipoteza* (*hypothesis*), *ślub* (*wedding*) – *kochanek* (*lover*), *tempo* (*speed*) – *sport* (*sport*), *trybunał* (*tribune*) – *sejm* (*diet (parliament)*),

false negatives: *linia* (*line*) – *ogonek* (*queue*), *konstrukcja* (*construction*) – *twierdza* (*fortress*), *nieprzychylność* (*unfriendly attitude*) – *emocja* (*emotion*), *podpora* (*support*) – *kula* (*sphere*), *zakochanie* (*infatuation*) – *emocja* (*emotion*).

We prepared the M set in order to go outside plWordNet with the tests and to look into the work of the classifiers from the point of view of their potential application in linguistic practice. As we wrote earlier, the set M was selected randomly from pairs of LUs with the highest value of semantic relatedness according to MSR(RWF). M consists of 2300 LU pairs with 1984 negative and 316 positive examples.

The C4.5 classifier trained on the sets KH=H+P2 and NH=P3+R+E with the ratio 1:10 achieved a 21.69% precision, a 50.32% recall and a 30.31% F-score. The percentage of false positives is still significantly below the level of 50%, which is a ratio that seems to be acceptable for a tool supporting linguists. The number of LU pairs presented to a linguists decreased drastically in comparison to MSR(RWF) alone, from 2300 to 733 – 31.87% of the initial list.

The results achieved on M for all classifiers were much poorer than the results on sets selected from plWordNet. We tried SVM as well, hoping for its usually good performance on numerical features without discretisation, but we have not achieved any valuable result.

Below we present examples of classifier decisions (classifier C4.5, ratio KH to NK 1:10, **E** included in NK).

true positives: *akredytacja* (*accreditation*) – *zezwolenie* (*permission*), *anegdota* (*anecdote*) – *opowieść* (*tale*), *dwója* (*bad (lowest) mark*) – *dwójka* (*dyad, pair*), *forteca* (*fortress*) – *budowla* (*edifice*), *forteca* (*fortress*) – *zamek* (*castle*), *incydent* (*incident*) – *zajście* (*incident*), *instrument* (*instrument*) – *przyrząd* (*example*), *owca* (*sheep*) – *jagnię* (*lamb*),

false positives: *abonent* (*subscriber*) – *odbiornik* (*receiver*), *cmentarz* (*cemetary*) – *zakwaterowanie* (*quarters*), *chwilka* (*fleeting moment*) – *berbeć* (*toddler*), *gniew* (*anger*) – *strach* (*fear*), *jesion* (*ash tree*) – *konar* (*bough*), *owoc* *(fruit) – grzyb (mushroom), palec (finger, digit) – nos (nose), paliwo (fuel) – odpad (waste),*

true negatives: *aktyw (activists) – przychód (income), kompletność (completeness) – zgodność (consistence, concordance), oś (axle) – kierunek (direction), otyłość (obesity) – nowotwór (cancer), ożywienie (animation) – postęp (progress),*

false negatives: *agenda (agenda) – przedstawicielstwo ((diplomatic) agency), alergia (allergy) – patologia (pathology), ankieta (survey) – badanie (investigation), komisariat (police station) – urząd (office), lądowanie (loading) – manewr (maneuver).*

A manual inspection of false positives in the results of classifier on the M set shows that many of them are co-hyponyms. They can be treated as positive answer from a linguists's point of view, but we tried to train the classifier not to select co-hyponyms as relevant pairs.

5 Conclusions and Further Research

The results achieved on the data extracted from plWordNet are very promising, especially when we compare them to the results of similar experiments in [6], where the highest value of F-score was 0.348. A direct comparison, however, is not possible, because we used examples of KH and NH generated directly from plWordNet, not from sentences in the corpora. Randomly generated pairs can include a larger percentage of obvious cases. On the other hand, plWordNet is much smaller than the Princeton WordNet [16] applied in [6], so a percentage of NH pairs are in fact relevant pairs not yet added to plWordNet. That produces substantial noise during training. The results achieved on the manually annotated set M and manually inspected show that the performance of the classifiers on 'real' data is lower. They have problems with distinguishing pairs of co-hyponyms from relevant pairs, produce higher percentage of errors for less obvious cases. Still, if we consider a task of delivering valuable suggestions to the linguists, we have achieved an enormous improvement in comparison with the lists of k most semantically related LUs. That is to say, a majority of the list elements are eliminated, but the error of elimination is small.

Because of the small size of plWordNet, it will be a laborious process to prepare a more difficult training set. In the case of each LU pair we can suspect that it is not yet described in plWordNet – building the set means extending the wordnet. Nonetheless, we plan to do it and to apply a bootstrapping approach in improving the classifier and extending the wordnet. We plan to derive several disjoint training sets – hyper/hyponyms at different distances, close and remote co-hyponyms, meronyms and so on – in order to construct decision classes with the increased precision. We want also to investigate ways of normalising and discretising attributes. Finally, our lack of success with SVM suggests search for additional attributes that could better discriminate among various types of lexical relations.

In contrast with [6], who use directly lexico-syntactic features, we propose a two-step approach. It is intrinsically based on MSR, on whose quality it depends to some extent. On the other hand, a good MSR can introduce a general description of relations among LUs and deliver knowledge derived from a very large number of contexts, not only direct LU co-occurrences. The complex attributes designed for the classifiers are a form of pre-processing. They express condensed information that facilitates the classifiers' decision processes. In order to compare our approach and that of [6], it would be necessary to re-implement the former with the same corpus and wordnet. The results achieved on the manual test set M shows that the present set of attributes does not give enough evidence for distinguishing near-synonyms and close hypernyms from co-hyponyms. More research is necessary on other possible sources of knowledge.

Acknowledgement. Work financed by the Polish Ministry of Education and Science, project No. 3 T11C 018 29.

References

1. Pantel, P., Pennacchiotti, M.: Espresso: Leveraging Generic Patterns for Automatically Harvesting Semantic Relations. In: [19], pp. 113–120
2. Hearst, M.A.: Automated Discovery of WordNet Relations. In: Fellbaum, C. (ed.) WordNet – An Electronic Lexical Database. MIT Press, Cambridge (1998)
3. Derwojedowa, M., Piasecki, M., Szpakowicz, S., Zawisławska, M., Broda, B.: Words, Concepts and Relations in the Construction of Polish WordNet. In: Tanács, A., Csendes, D., Vincze, V., Fellbaum, C., Vossen, P. (eds.) Proc. Global Word-Net Conference, Seged, Hungary, January 22-25 2008, pp. 162–177. University of Szeged (2008)
4. Broda, B., Derwojedowa, M., Piasecki, M., Szpakowicz, S.: Corpus-based Semantic Relatedness for the Construction of Polish WordNet. In: Proc. 6th Language Resources and Evaluation Conference (LREC 2008) (to appear,2008)
5. Piasecki, M., Szpakowicz, S., Broda, B.: Extended Similarity Test for the Evaluation of Semantic Similarity Functions. In: Vetulani, Z. (ed.) Proc. 3rd Language and Technology Conference, Poznań, Poland, Pozna, October 5-7, 2007, pp. 104–108. Wydawnictwo Poznańskie Sp. z o.o. (2007)
6. Snow, R., Jurafsky, D., Ng, A.Y.: Learning syntactic patterns for automatic hypernym discovery. In: Saul, L.K., Weiss, Y., Bottou, L. (eds.) Advances in Neural Information Processing Systems 17, Cambridge, MA, pp. 1297–1304. MIT Press, Cambridge (2005)
7. Snow, R., Jurafsky, D., Ng, A.Y.: Semantic taxonomy induction from heterogenous evidence. In: [19]
8. Kennedy, A.: Analysis and Construction of Noun Hypernym Hierarchies to Enhance Roget's Thesaurus. Master's thesis, School of Information Technology and Engineering, University of Ottawa (2006)
9. Zhang, M., Zhang, J., Su, J.: Exploring syntactic features for relation extraction using a convolution tree kernel. In: Proc. Human Language Technology Conference of the NAACL, Main Conference, ACL, pp. 288–295 (2006)
10. Caraballo, S., Charniak, E.: Determining the specificity of nouns from text. In: Proc. Joint SIGDAT conference on empirical methods in natural language processing (EMNLP) and very large corpora (VLC), pp. 63–70 (1999)

11. Przepiórkowski, A.: The IPI PAN Corpus: Preliminary version. Institute of Computer Science PAS (2004)
12. Weeds, J., Weir, D.: Co-occurrence retrieval: A flexible framework for lexical distributional similarity. Computational Linguistics 31(4), 439–475 (2005)
13. Ryu, P.M., Choi, K.S.: Taxonomy learning using term specificity and similarity. In: Proc. 2nd Workshop on Ontology Learning and Population ACL, Sydney, pp. 41–48 (2006)
14. Weiss, D.: Korpus Rzeczpospolitej. Corpus of text from the online edtion of Rzeczypospolita (2008), http://www.cs.put.poznan.pl/dweiss/rzeczpospolita
15. Weka: Weka 3: Data Mining Software in Java (2008), http://www.cs.waikato.ac.nz/ml/weka/.
16. Fellbaum, C. (ed.): WordNet – An Electronic Lexical Database. MIT Press, Cambridge (1998)
17. Agirre, E., Edmonds, P. (eds.): Word Sense Disambiguation: Algorithms and Applications. Springer, Heidelberg (2006)
18. Sojka, P., Kopeček, I., Pala, K. (eds.): Proc. Text, Speech and Dialog 2006 Conference. LNCS (LNAI). Springer, Heidelberg (2006)
19. ACL 2006, ed.: Proc. 21st International Conference on Computational Linguistics and 44th Annual Meeting of the Association for Computational Linguistics, The Association for Computer Linguistics (2006)

Similarity of Names Across Scripts: Edit Distance Using Learned Costs of N-Grams

Bruno Pouliquen

European Commission - Joint Research Centre
Via Enrico Fermi, 2749
21027 Ispra (VA), Italy
Bruno.Pouliquen@jrc.it

Abstract. Any cross-language processing application has to first tackle the problem of transliteration when facing a language using another script. The first solution consists of using existing transliteration tools, but these tools are not usually suitable for all purposes. For some specific script pairs they do not even exist. Our aim is to discriminate transliterations across different scripts in a unified way using a learning method that builds a transliteration model out of a set of transliterated proper names. We compare two strings using an algorithm that builds a Levenshtein edit distance using n-grams costs. The evaluations carried out show that our similarity measure is accurate.

Keywords. Transliteration, string similarity.

1 Introduction

String comparison is a known research area and has several applications: searching by similar string (allowing the words of the query to be slightly different from the one in the returned document), merging of database records, cognate identification and alignment (in the context of parallel or comparable corpora).

Our aim is to learn a discriminative transliteration model requiring no knowledge of the target language. In our project NewsExplorer [16], we identify an average of 450 new person names per day in different languages (including currently Russian, Bulgarian and Arabic). Evaluation has shown that about 11% of these (50 out of 450) are variants of names already stored in the database. In our setting, we thus need to decide for each of the new names, whether it is a variant of a known name (even when written in different scripts). Our approach is thus discriminative. We are not currently aiming at *guessing* the transliteration of a name (generative approach). In our work, we focus on the Levenshtein edit distance, and more precisely on a *cost-based* edit distance where the difference between two letters is not binary but depends on the *distance* between these two letters. This distance is the result of a statistical learning method.

In the course of years, we have compiled a list of person names across languages and scripts. We now make use of this list (compiled semi-automatically and constantly updated) to build a training set of name variants for a pre-selected language

A. Ranta, B. Nordström (Eds.): GoTAL 2008, LNAI 5221, pp. 405–416, 2008.

pair (example: Greek-English). Person names across scripts have the particularity to be transliterated and not translated (with some exceptions)[1]. Therefore they offer a good training set which we can use to learn transliteration models.

2 Related Work

Our work is situated between two disciplines: string similarity and transliteration.

A lot of work has been done on string matching (see [8], [5], [6], [2], [14], [17]). We will not focus on these techniques as our main goal here is to concentrate on similarity *across* scripts. We decided to use the most common measure: the Levenshtein edit distance. Other similarity measures include: Jaro [22], q-grams [20], longest common substrings (as used in [15]) and others. However, each of these metrics would require additional work to make them work on cross-script string comparison. We currently keep this for future work. Brill and Moore [4] have already worked on a very similar problem when building string-to-string edits (learned from examples) to improve a noisy channel spelling correction.

Transliteration is also a research area which has recently been focused on. Various work has been carried out on the transliteration of proper names: Knight & Grael [10] use phonetic information for Japanese to English transliterations, while AbdulJaleel & Larkey [1] make use of n-grams for transliteration from Arabic to English. Sherif & Kondrak [18] use a transducer on learned substring transliterations. While some applications focus on one specific language pair (using often phonetic dictionaries to get the right transliteration), in our context we want to match transliterations using only direct orthographical mapping and no phonetic representation. One reason for this is that we would have to build a string-to-phoneme mapping tool for several languages. The second reason is that phonetics are highly dependent on the origin of a name. The third reason is that it is usually not so accurate. Other work, like that of [12] and [3], trains the model on examples; they applied it to English-Chinese and Japanese Katakana-English, respectively, and achieved good results. However, they use a romanisation tool before comparing with English strings, which makes their approach difficult to generalise.

Most of the above-mentioned papers (except [3]) use the generative approach: creating the most probable transliteration for a name (i.e. what is the transliteration of "Εντίθ"?). We have chosen the discriminative approach: compute the similarity between two strings (i.e. is "Εντίθ" a transliteration of "Edith"?). In our approach, if a letter is similar to two different letters in the target script, we do not have to make a decision as we just want to look if one of the target letters is a part of the compared string.

Concerning string similarity and transliterations, we must mention the following papers: Freeman et al. [7] present the use of Editex [23], a variant of edit distance using groups of similar letters (character equivalence classes) and applied it to transliteration similarity from English to Arabic. The Arabic string is first romanised and the result is compared to English names using Editex. They use handwritten rules to normalise the English and Arabic names. One special case (the English 'ch') generates two different transliterations. This work is a nice attempt to overcome the *same-script*

---

[1] Entities others than person names are likely to be partially or entirely translated. i.e. *University of Oxford* is translated into Russian as Оксфордский университет /Oxfordski university/, and into Greek as Πανεπιστήμιο της Οξφόρδης /Panepistemio tis Oksfordis/.

limit of usual string metrics, but character groups of letters are not a real answer, as we have to pre-process both strings and even produce different paths.

In previous work (see [19]), we used a set of edit distances on different representations of the two names in order to automatically merge name variants as part of the NewsExplorer process. The names can be compared across scripts using a set of simple hand-written rules.

The main limit when comparing two strings in different scripts is specifically the letter-to-letter comparison. One alternative is to use phonemes and compare the two phonetic representations, as mentioned above. This solution is not applicable in our case (the name *Arthur Japin* has different phonetic representations when pronounced according to English, French, or Dutch pronunciation rules).

Another alternative consists of using trigrams or bigrams for transliterating and to compute character equivalence classes using n-grams instead of letters.

Klementiev et al. [9] use characters and bigrams as a feature representation for strings and learn correspondences between them in an active-unsupervised learning model to get new transliterations out of a comparable corpus of news. Li et al. [13] did similar work (applied to Chinese to English transliteration). They try to learn n-gram alignment probabilities out of a set of training pairs. Their n-gram transliteration pairs are learned by an Expectation Maximisation algorithm. They then use a Joint-Source Channel model to compare two strings, which outperforms the Noisy Channel Model.

Brill et al. [3] use trainable edit distance (as defined in [4]) to align Katakana and English term pairs. They first align Romanised Katakana strings with English strings using the standard edit distance. Then they learn common string-to-string probabilities in order to compute similarities between two transliterations. This work is very similar to ours, but they require a romanisation of the original Katakana pair, whereas we aim at being able to handle any script without relying on any transliteration tool.

3 The Name Transliteration Data

As part of the NewsExplorer system (see http://press.jrc.it/NewsExplorer, [16]), each day 450 new person names are recognised and inserted into the knowledge base. A name variant matching algorithm computes a distance between two names (even when they are not written in the same script) and out of the 450 new names recognised every day we automatically recognise about 50 names as being a variant of an existing person. The database contains now about 650,000 names. Some of these are available in different scripts: Arabic, Russian, etc. Some other name variants have been automatically gathered from the online encyclopaedia Wikipedia (for a complete description of the process see [19]).

Our material for training transliteration is taken from variants of person names collected out of NewsExplorer. Various transliterations are available: from non-Latin scripts (Russian, Arabic, Greek, Hebrew etc.) to Latin (English, French, German, Slavic languages, etc.). This data contains several variants of transliterations and not only one single standard form (both casual and regular transliterations, see [11]). While [21] identifies 32 variants for Libyan leader *Muammar Gaddafi*, NewsExplorer contains about 100 variants.[2]

---

[2] See http://press.jrc.it/NewsExplorer/entities/en/262.html

In comparison with other sources like Wikipedia, we can be sure that our material contains only person names that are most likely real transliterations and do not contain translations (see footnote 1).

Out of this database, we export a list of variants of the same person in two given languages. We can launch experiments for various language pairs such as English, French, Slovene, etc. to Russian, Arabic, Greek, Hindi, Japanese, etc.

NewsExplorer is compiling information in currently 19 languages including Russian and Bulgarian. The Cyrillic versions of person names are likely to have been collected by NewsExplorer, while other scripts like Japanese are usually from a Wikipedia page. This is the reason why in our experiments we focus on Latin-Cyrillic language pairs. As most readers are probably more familiar with Greek letters, we will present examples of transliterations in that language.

Our training set is a collection of transliterated names. It is important to notice that this set is 'noisy' in the sense that we may have examples that are not exact transliterations (like Μουαμάρ αλ Καντάφι /muamar al kadafi/ with *Muammar Abu Minyar al-Gaddafi*). The training set contains only full names of persons (i.e. both first and family name).

4 Method

Our aim is to compare names across scripts relying exclusively on the n-gram correspondence automatically learned out of a set of existing transliterated names. As the training set may contain non-exact transliterations, we decided to use the following algorithm:

(a) bootstrapping: initialise the similarity measure (see section 4.1)
(b) Select example pairs that are very similar (see section 4.2)
(c) Learn new n-grams out of these pairs (see section 4.3)
(d) Compute a new similarity measure (see section 4.4)
(e) Until convergence, go back to point (a) (see section 4.5)

	É	d	d	i	t
E	**0.5**	1.5	2.5	3.5	4.5
d	1.5	**0.5**	**1.5**	2.5	3.5
i	2.5	1.5	1.5	**1.5**	2.5
t	3.5	2.5	2.5	2.5	**1.5**
h	4	3	3	4	**2**

Using costs:
É→E =>0.5 -→h =>0.5 d→- =>0.5
C→C=>0
C→L=>1 when C≠L
Outputs the following alignment:

É	d	d	i	t	-
E	d	-	i	t	h

Fig 1. Cost-based edit distance

4.1 Cost-Based Edit Distance (Bootstrapping)

The core of our tool relies on the basic Levenshtein edit distance. To be exact, it is an adaptation of Editex [23], which makes use of a cost calculation. The dynamic programming approach computes the edit distance filling an array for each letter-alignment. Each cell of the array contains the minimum score of the three upper-left adjacent cells (we add to the score the cost of omission, insertion or replacement).

The basic edit distance algorithm can be written as follows:

```
dist(0,0)=0;
foreach i (0..length(s)) {
  foreach j (0..length(t)) {
    dist(i,j)=min(
          dist(i-1,j) + cost(s(i), '-'),     // insertion
          dist(i, j-1) + cost('-', t(j)),    // omission
          dist(i-1,j-1) + cost(s(i) ,s(j))   // replace
      );
  }
}
```

Where *cost(a,b)* returns a distance between the two characters (the value usually lies between 0 and 1). If character a or b is empty ('−'), then it represents the cost of omission or insertion of the other character. When computing the matrix, we can also build the path that best aligns the two strings (see example in Fig. 1).

4.2 First Alignment of Characters

We want to select translation pairs that are very similar. For each pair, we try to align the strings at character level. When nothing allows us to compare two strings (they are usually not in the same alphabet) we launch a shallow 1-1 character alignment. In order to reduce noise, we only make use of the strings that have the same length and where the first space is at the same position, such as the first alignment example in Fig. 2.

It should be highlighted that this first initialisation process works for language pairs which are likely to align one letter to another one (English-Russian, Arabic-English, Russian-Greek, etc.), but it is unlikely to work in other cases (Japanese Katakana to English for example). An alternative consists of bootstrapping the alignment with a matrix valorising empty alignments for vowels (some preliminary results indicate that the learning succeeds; see one example in Fig. 4).

Once all pairs have been aligned, we can compute the probability of alignment of each character pair. Each character pair probability is converted to a distance between 0 and 1. A character pair gets a distance of 0 if they always appear at the same position and a distance closer to one when they are rarely aligned. This distance matrix is then exported in order to be used in the next step.

This first shallow alignment produces a first distance matrix that we will now use in our edit distance for all our examples. For each translation pair, we compute the edit distance, converted into a similarity score (dividing the distance by the length of the longest string). If the similarity is not high enough (using an adequate threshold: by default 0.9) we skip this pair. Otherwise our edit distance algorithm outputs the path that minimises the distance. This path is a set of aligned characters. Non-corresponding characters are aligned with nothing ('−'). See Fig. 2 for some examples of alignments.

We sum all aligned character pairs and compute the distance between two characters as being the log of its frequency divided by the log of the maximum frequency found. This new distance matrix contains implicitly the cost of omission of characters. Once we have computed this first distance matrix, we can re-run the process.

4.3 Significant N-Gram Calculation

Most pairs of foreign scripts do not have a one-to-one transliteration (in Greek the 'θ' character corresponds to 'th' in Latin languages. Inversely, the Latin 'd' is often written in Greek using two letters: 'ντ'). We build a tool to try to 'guess' common 1-2 or 2-1 correspondences out of the path computed when using the 'cost' edit distance resulting of the previous process.

When focusing on empty alignments, the algorithm tries to compute its probability to be the result of a correspondence between a bigram and the previous letter or the following letter. If one of the bigrams appears often in the corpus, we replace it and re-run the process on the result. If computed bigrams do not have high probability to appear, we keep this empty alignment (some letters, like the letter 'ъ' in Russian are often not transliterated, so the alignment ъ→ – is correct).

To illustrate the process: having the four alignments listed in Fig. 2 with an edit distance containing substitution/omission costs of single characters, the algorithm tries to build all possible bigrams where an empty alignment was found (here: ί→ie, Ντ→D, το→o, θ→th, Λο→L, ού→u, θ→th, ε→he, γκ→g). In these examples the best candidate is 'θ→th' as it appears twice. We then replace the most common bigram and run the program on the result. Not only bigrams can be computed, but also more complex transliterations (like Τζ /tj/ → G learned out of alignments with *George*).

Σ	τ	α	ύ	ρ	ο	ς		Δ	ή	μ	α	ς
S	t	a	v	r	o	s		D	i	m	a	s

Ε	λ	ί	–		Ν	τ	ο	τ	έ
E	l	i	e		D	–	o	t	é

Λ	ο	ύ	θ	–	ε	ρ		Κ	ι	ν	γ	κ
L	–	u	t	h	e	r		K	i	n	g	–

Ά	ν	ν	α		Σ	μ	ι	θ	–
A	n	n	a		S	m	i	t	h

Fig 2. Examples of alignments on 4 translation pairs

We rerun the n-gram learning phase. Further recursive loops are likely to compute further n-grams. For example, when learning examples of Russian-German transliterations, after a few steps the algorithm 'learns' that the Russian letter 'ч' is likely to be aligned with the German 4-gram 'tsch' (as the Russian example in Fig. 4).

To avoid over-learning, we set a default threshold of 3 for the length difference between two n-grams, which allows the alignments 1-0,1-1,2-1,2-2,3-1,3-2,3-3,4-1,4-2,…, 5-2, etc.

4.4 Edit Distance Algorithm Using N-Gram Costs

A basic cost-edit distance when aligning *Εντιθ* with *Edith* based on the correspondences [E→E, ν→d, τ→–, ί→I, θ→t, –→h] will compute a distance of 2 between the two strings. The new algorithm compares potentially all the upper-left cells. The comparisons are not limited to characters, but to n-grams (like the one described in [4]). Now the use of n-grams allows us to improve the similarity as shown in Fig. 3. The new algorithm can be written as follows:

```
dist(0,0)=0;
foreach i (0..length(s)) {
   foreach j (0..length(t)) {
      min=MAXNUMBER;
      foreach a (alignments(s(i),t(j))) {
         cost=dist(i - a.i, j - a.j)
               + cost(substring(s, i - a.i, i),
                      substring(t, j - a.j, j));
         if (cost < min) {min=cost};
      }
      dist(i,j)=min;
   }
}
```

Performance: This new way to compute edit distance has a higher complexity. In theory, edit distance has a complexity of $O(n\ m)$. In practice, if we count the number of comparisons, the complexity is $O(3\ n\ m)$. Our new distance has a theoretical complexity of $O(n^2\ m^2)$. In practice, all alignments do not have to be tested for each cell. The simple improvement consists of computing all alignments of n-grams ending with the two characters of the current cell and try comparisons only with these alignments. The function $alignment(s_i,t_j)$ in the previous algorithm returns all possible n-gram alignments ending with the two letters s_i and t_j. The complexity is now $O(n\ m\ a)$ with a being the average number of possible alignments for the current cell In our experiments with English to Russian, $a=3.35$. When adding name parts in the training (see section 5), $a=4.14$.

	E	v	τ	í	θ
E	**0**	0.95	1.91	2.90	3.90
d	0.97	1	**0.30**	1.29	2.29
i	1.94	1.97	1.27	**0.30**	1.30
t	2.91	2.94	1.97	1.27	1.39
h	3.83	3.85	2.81	2.19	**0.40**

Using the following costs:
th→θ=>0.1, d→vτ=>0.3
Outputs the following alignment:

E	d	i	th
E	vτ	í	θ

Fig 3. N-gram based edit distance and alignment

4.5 Iteration of the Process

Once we have learned new n-gram costs, we compute again the new distance matrix. All the training transliterations are again compared with the same technique. It must be noted that few more examples can have a similarity higher than the threshold and that the alignments can be different than during the previous step.

After a few iterations the system does not learn new n-grams. The model becomes stable (in our Russian to English experiments the system stopped after 5 iterations).

5 Improvements

We made the choice to train our model on full names (containing both first and last names). This choice is questionable as most of other transliteration systems work on name parts only. The main advantage is that the method will still work for languages that do not use space (Chinese, Thai, etc.). Moreover it allows the system to learn some typical additional spacing in names. For example, the common prefix 'al-' (with different versions 'Al ', 'al ', 'El' etc.) in Latin versions of Arabic names is written without space in Arabic (i.e. the third example in Fig. 4). Other languages (like Farsi) may have variants with or without space or hyphens (for example: *Abdelaziz, Abdel-Aziz, Abdel Aziz* refer to the same first name).

When computing the distance between two n-grams, we face a basic problem: given the frequency of the alignment in our training corpus, what will be the distance? The basic idea is just to compute the ratio of this alignment given all other alignments for the same n-gram. Another parameter is the frequency of each n-gram. However, our goal is here to minimise the distance between two transliterations. If we keep the basic ratio, two known transliterations cannot have a distance of 0 because each source n-gram has very often several other possible transliterations. We decided to apply a weighting algorithm that artificially assigns a distance of 0 for the most common transliteration.

As observed by [18], the performance of a transliteration model can only improve when we add full name parts in the model (i.e. adding known transliterations of full words instead of relying only on the substrings or character correspondence). Our model is based on n-grams so we can directly add name part correspondences in the matrix. Without taking any external source, this can be done using our training set by looking at recurrent word alignments. We decided to automatically add first names (i.e. Дэвид→David) and also common last names (i.e. Смит→Smith). As for the learning of n-grams we first check that the two names are close enough to avoid adding some noise. Adding new n-grams leads to more computations when calculating the edit distance, so we also discard the name alignments that have an edit distance of 0 as this new n-gram-pair is identical to its corresponding sub-alignments. The unexpected result is that these new n-gram-pairs can also be recognised in the middle of a name, like in 'Дэвидсон ↔ Davidson' where the n-gram pair Дэвид→David brings better results than the combinations of Д→D, э→a, в→v, и→i, д→d). As shown in next section adding name parts does improve the performances.

6 Evaluation

We want to evaluate a similarity measure, not a transliteration method, so our evaluation will focus on comparing a set of source names (not part of the training set) to a set of target names. We suppose that the size of the target set is big enough to contain possible other similar names. We then evaluate if the top-scoring similar name (and having a similarity higher than a threshold) is really the expected transliteration.

Our training set is an export of the NewsExplorer data. We took all variants of person names in the Latin alphabet and build all alignments with all variants of the same person in the Cyrillic alphabet. This training set contains currently 33224 alignments out of 2374 different person names (These names are persons mentioned in the news over the past 3 years. Names are from various origins: European, Russian, East-European, Arabic, African. The transliteration alignment set is the result of a Cartesian product of all different variants of the same person).

To simplify the evaluation, we had to set a threshold to decide if a name is a transliteration of another. Using our trained similarity measure we computed the similarity between all transliteration pairs (from the same training set) and look for a minimum similarity that was able to recognise 95% of transliterations. The result is a threshold of 0.8.

We compiled four different test sets. The idea is to mix different sets: some contain Russian names in their Latin script, others Western European names in their Cyrillic script. Cross-matching sets allows to look for names that are supposed to be there or to look for names which are not supposed to be there.

[NewNames]: A list of 855 Russian-English transliteration pairs that where found in NewsExplorer later than the training of the Russian-English model. This list was manually validated to avoid wrong transliterations. It contains 515 unique Russian names and 774 unique English names. This test set is quite representative for our NewsExplorer-specific task (we want our model to be able to work equally in the future) as these names appeared in the news after the training.

[Lenta1k]: A list of 1299 transliterations that we compiled out of the Lenta newspaper articles (in news from 2006, validated manually). We excluded from this list several transliteration pairs that were already part of the training set. These transliterations contain usually non-Russian names.

[NExp3K]: A list of 3037 transliteration pairs taken from NewsExplorer data.

[Leaders] A list of Latin-script person names belonging to a government of any country of the world, compiled out of the "world leaders" page of the CIA Fact Book. This test set contains 5126 names and we decided to concentrate on 2 sub-tests: [leaders-fsoviet] and [leaders-4]. The first one contains 150 leaders of some of the former Soviet Bloc countries: Byelorussia, Bulgaria, Ukraine, Georgia and Russia. The second contains the first four persons of each country (as they appear in the document). In total, there are 772 names.

Our evaluation concentrates on trying to match one name against a list of other names. If there is a match which is more than the threshold (0.8), we decide that the two names are identical (transliterations of each other). An expert validated the automatic judgement and we summarise the results using standard precision/recall/F-measure in Table 1.

Table 1. Evaluation results

Source	Target	Matrix	Algorithm	Precision	Recall	F-Measure
NewNames	NewNames	ru-Lat	Basic	1	0.75	0.86
NewNames	NewNames	ru-Lat	n-gram	0.99	0.92	0.95
NewNames	NewNames	ru-Lat	n-gram+name parts	0.99	1	0.99
NExp3k	Lenta1k	ru-Lat	n-gram+name parts	0.74	0.91	0.82
Lenta1k	Lenta1k	Lat-ru	n-gram+name parts	1	0.98	0.99
leaders4	NExp3k	Lat-ru	n-gram+name parts	0.93	0.89	0.91
Leaders-fsoviet	NExp3k	Lat-ru	n-gram+name parts	0.8	0.98	0.88

The first line is a baseline result to evaluate the improvement due to our n-gram based edit distance compared with an edit distance based on a one-to-one character transliteration (We romanise Russian names using a standard conversion[3]). With the

---

[3] United Nations-recommended romanisation systems for Russian geographical names, available at http://www.eki.ee/wgrs/rom1_ru.pdf, (last visited 13/06/2008), with only two changes (Ë→E and Щ→Sh instead of the less common Ë→Ye and Щ→Shch).

basic algorithm the precision is actually very high but the recall very low, while our n-gram edit distance improves a lot the recall, adding a single error: Питер Брук aligned equally with *Peter Brock* (wrong) and *Peter Brook* (correct). Adding the name parts (see Section 5) outperforms previous algorithms. We kept this settings for all other evaluations.

Apart from the baseline, the recall is good except when we try to look up transliterations of international 'leaders'. The reason is that the CIA Fact Book writes full names (including middle names), while in NewsExplorer they have mainly usual names (CIA Fact Book contains *Muammar Abu Minyar al-Qadhafi* while NExp3K contains Муаммар аль-Каддафи /muammar al kaddafi/). The distance is then too high and makes the overall recall lower.

The precision is also good, except when we look up NewsExplorer names in the Lenta set. The reason is that our distance does not give any weight for last and first names and the distance between *Александр Стин* /aleksandr stin/ and *Alexander Vik* is quite small, mainly because they share the first name. The precision is not really high when matching former-soviet country leaders against NewsExplorer. Some of the Belarusian leaders have names which are similar to Russian names (examples: Belarusian Minister of Trade *Aleksandr Ivankov* and Russian painter *Aleksandr Ivanov*; Belarusian Minister of Statistics *Vladimir Zinovskiy* and Russian politician *Vladimir Zhirinovsky*). We can notice that precision is almost perfect when matching transliterations from the same set. This is expected. However, it also means that no other name comes as more similar than its own transliteration.

Another interesting mismatch is when the writing is quite different to the pronunciation. For example, the Korean name *Roh Moo-hyun* has a pronunciation closer to /no mu hjʌn/ and is transliterated in Russian as Но Му Хён (respecting the original pronunciation).

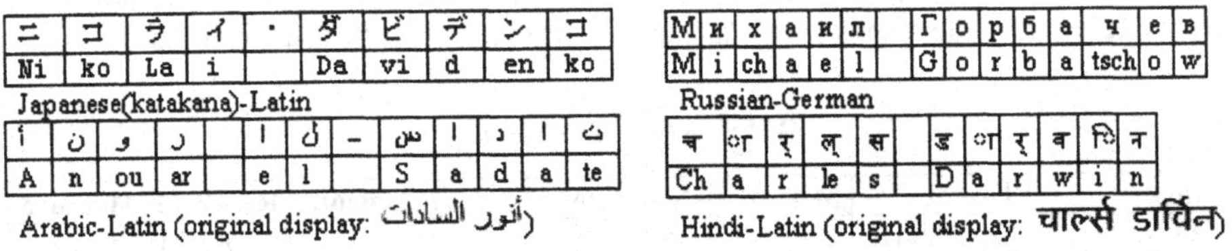

Fig 4. Examples of alignments using different trained transliteration models

7   Conclusion and Future Work

We have shown that our approach is able to learn transliteration models automatically relying exclusively on examples. The evaluation shows that our method outperforms standard edit distance. The result of such process can then compute similarities between names with quite high accuracy. However there are several improvements we will try to address in the future:

The way we learn n-grams is rather simple (we try to replace 0-1 alignments with 2-1). Other techniques have to be explored in order to guess further n-gram alignments (2-2 should be implemented). The current method is extremely fast to learn from examples. We could think of using this dynamic learning for some specific applications (i.e. learn the transliteration rules for German places in Russian). We have not tried the method on the Chinese script, which is an interesting challenge. It would also be interesting to compare our learning method with the one done by Brill & Moore [4] on the same test set.

Further techniques can improve the string similarity. For example, our evaluation suggests that we should give more weight to family names than to given names, and even less weight to middle names.

Our algorithm currently keeps the cases as we observed that the first letter of a name can be transliterated differently when it is placed at the beginning of a name or in the middle, as it has been highlighted for Arabic in [1]. Further experiments have to be launched to verify if ignoring the case improves the performance. Another option consists of adding the information whether the letter is at the beginning, in the middle or at the end of a name, like [4] who condition the probability on the position.

This work produced a promising tool that we can use for various applications like cognate identification, transliteration discovery (over the web or comparable corpora), or produce automatically transliterations, using different training corpora (which could produce different results if we trained transliteration to English, French, Italian or German). An interesting area of research is to learn on Latin script variants. This could help us to recognise declensions of names (*Toniego Blaira* referring to *Tony Blair* in Polish), or common variations of names (i.e. *François Chérèque* becoming *Francois Chereque* in English). Comparisons should then be done on a test set similar to the one in [15].

Acknowledgments. I am grateful to my colleague Ralf Steinberger without whom such a project would never happen, especially for the useful and original ideas he always has. Special thanks go to my colleague Jenya Belyaeva who helped with various evaluations. I am grateful to our colleagues from the Web Technology team for providing me with the precious multilingual news data, especially our team leader Erik van der Goot.

References

1. AbdulJaleel, N., Larkey, L.S.: Statistical transliteration for English-Arabic cross language information retrieval. In: CIKM, pp. 139–146 (2003)
2. Bilenko, M., Mooney, R., Cohen, W., Ravikumar, P., Fienberg, S.: Adaptive Name Matching in Information Integration, Intelligent Systems. IEEE, Los Alamitos (2003)
3. Brill, E., Kacmarcik, G., Brockett, C.: Automatically Harvesting Katakana-English Term Pairs from Search Engine Query Logs. In: Proceedings of the Sixth Natural Language Processing Pacific Rim Symposium, pp. 393–399 (2001)
4. Brill, E., Moore, R.C.: An improved Error Model for Noisy Channel Spelling Correction. In: Proceedings of the ACL 2000, pp. 286–293 (2000)
5. Christen, P.: A Comparison of Personal Name Matching: Techniques and Practical Issues, Technical Report TR-CS-06-02, Joint Computer Science Technical Report Series, Department of Computer Science (2006)

6. Cohen, W., Ravikumar, P., Fienberg, S.: A comparison of string distance metrics for name-matching tasks. In: IJCAI-2003 Workshop on Information Integration on the Web, Acapulco, Mexico, pp. 73–78 (2003)

7. Freeman, A.T., Condon, S.L., Ackerman, C.M.: Cross linguistic name matching in English and Arabic: alone to many mapping extension of the Levenshtein edit distance algorithm. In: HLT-NAACL 2006 (2006)

8. Hall, P.A.V., Dowling, G.R.: Approximate string matching. ACM Computing Surveys 12(4), 381–402 (1980)

9. Klementiev, A., Roth, D.: Named Entity Transliteration and Discovery in Multilingual Corpora. In: Learning Machine Translation (2006)

10. Knight, K., Graehl, J.: Machine transliteration. Computational Linguistics 24(4), 599–612 (1998)

11. Kuo, J.-S., Li, H., Yang, Y.-K.: Learning Transliteration Lexicons from the Web. In: Proceedings of 44th ACL, pp. 1129–1136 (2006)

12. Lee, C.-J., Chang, J.S., Jang, J.S.R.: Extraction of Transliteration Pairs from Parallel Corpora Using a Statistical Transliteration Model. Information Sciences (2006)

13. Li, H., Zhang, M., Su, J.: A joint source-channel model for machine transliteration. In: 42nd ACL, pp. 159–166 (2004)

14. Lindén, K.: Multilingual Modeling of Cross-Lingual Spelling Variants spelling variants. Information Retrieval 9(3), 295–310 (2006)

15. Piskorski, J., Wieloch, K., Pikula, M., Sydow, M.: Toward Person Name Matching for Inflective Languages (Forthcoming, 2008)

16. Pouliquen, B., Steinberger, R., Ignat, C., Käsper, E., Temnikova, I.: Multilingual and cross-lingual news topic tracking. In: CoLing 2004, Geneva, Switzerland, vol. II, pp. 959–965 (2004)

17. Ristad, E.S., Yianilos, P.N.: Learning string-edit distance. In: IEEE Transactions or Pattern Analysis and Machine Intelligence (1998)

18. Sherif, T., Kondrak, G.: Substring-Based Transliteration. In: 45th Annual Meeting of the Association for Computational Linguistics (ACL 2007), Prague, Czech Republic, pp. 944–951 (2007)

19. Steinberger, R., Pouliquen, B.: Cross-lingual Named Entity Recognition. In: Sekine&, S., Ranchhod, E. (eds.) Journal Linguisticae Investigationes, vol. 30(1), pp. 135–162 (2006) (Special Issue on Named Entity Recognition and Categorisation)

20. Ukkonen, E.: Approximate string-matching with q-grams and maximal matches. Theoretical computer science 92(1), 191–211 (1992)

21. Whitaker, B.: Arabic words and the Roman alphabet (last visit 18/03/2008) (2005), http://www.al-bab.com/arab/language/roman1.htm

22. Winkler, W.E.: The state of record linkage and current research problems, Technical report, Statistical Research Division, U.S. Bureau of the Census, Washington, DC (1999)

23. Zobel, J., Dart, P.W.: Partitioning Number Sequences into Optimal Subsequences. Jour. of Research and Practice in Information Technology 32(2), 121–129 (2000)

Turkish Language Resources: Morphological Parser, Morphological Disambiguator and Web Corpus

Haşim Sak[1], Tunga Güngör[1], and Murat Saraçlar[2]

[1] Boğaziçi University, Computer Engineering Department, Bebek,
34342 İstanbul, Turkey
hasim.sak@boun.edu.tr, gungort@boun.edu.tr
[2] Boğaziçi University, Electrical and Electronic Engineering Department, Bebek,
34342 İstanbul, Turkey
murat.saraclar@boun.edu.tr

Abstract. In this paper, we propose a set of language resources for building Turkish language processing applications. Specifically, we present a finite-state implementation of a morphological parser, an averaged perceptron-based morphological disambiguator, and compilation of a web corpus. Turkish is an agglutinative language with a highly productive inflectional and derivational morphology. We present an implementation of a morphological parser based on two-level morphology. This parser is one of the most complete parsers for Turkish and it runs independent of any other external system such as PC-KIMMO in contrast to existing parsers. Due to complex phonology and morphology of Turkish, parsing introduces some ambiguous parses. We developed a morphological disambiguator with accuracy of about 98% using averaged perceptron algorithm. We also present our efforts to build a Turkish web corpus of about 423 million words.

Keywords: Morphological parsing, Morphological disambiguation, Turkish, Web corpus.

1 Finite-State Morphological Parser

Morphological parsing is the problem of breaking a word such as *çocuklar* (children) into the constituent morphemes, *çocuk* (child) and *-lar* (plural suffix). To build a morphological parser, we need three components: a lexicon listing the stem words annotated with some information such as part-of-speech of the words to determine which morphological rules apply to them, a morphotactics component (morphosyntax) that describes the word formation by specifying the ordering of morphemes, and a morphophonemics component that describes the phonological alternations occurring in the morphemes during word formation. In finite-state morphology, all these components can be implemented using finite-state transducers.

To implement phonological rules, we used the two-level morphology formalism of Koskenniemi [5]. Two-level morphology is a formalism for describing morphological alternations. In this formalism, the phonological rules denote regular relations that can

A. Ranta, B. Nordström (Eds.): GoTAL 2008, LNAI 5221, pp. 417–427, 2008.

be represented by finite-state transducers. Two-level rules are applied in parallel or when implemented as finite-state transducers they can be intersected to a single morphophonemics transducer.

To show how two-level phonology is used to model phonological phenomena, we give an example for vowel harmony in Turkish [6]. In Turkish, the /a/ vowel in suffixes is realized as /a/ or /e/ in surface form depending on the word they are attached to. According to vowel harmony, the /a/ vowel changes its form to agree in backness with the preceding stem vowel. A two-level rule that describes this phenomena in the case of front vowels is given below.

A:e ⇒ @:FV [@:CONS | @:ε]* _

In this rule, "A" symbol is used for lexical representation of /a/ vowel in suffixes. "FV" symbol represents the front vowels /e/, /i/, /ö/, and /ü/. "CONS" symbol represents the set of consonants. "@" symbol means any symbol in the alphabet. This rule states that /a/ vowel (/A/ in lexical form) may be converted to /e/ vowel only if it is preceded with a surface front vowel followed possibly by a number of symbols having consonants and epsilon realizations in the surface form. The finite-state transducer realization for this rule is shown in Figure 1.

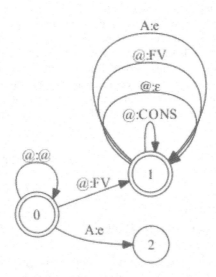

Fig. 1. Transducer for Turkish vowel harmony: "@:@" symbol represents any feasible lexical/surface pair absent in the transducer. "@" symbol represents any other symbol that is not used on any arc.

The lexicon and morphotactics can also be encoded into a single finite-state transducer as shown in Figure 2. This FST implements a simple nominal inflection for Turkish. The input side of this transducer encodes the morphological features to be returned as the morphological parse of the words. The output side is meant to be input to the phonological rules transducer, therefore it needs to be expanded to letter sequences. As you can see the output morphemes are marked with special symbols to encode phonological alternations in the rules transducer.

Fig. 2. A transducer for a simple Turkish nominal inflection

Given the morphophonemics and lexicon/morphotactics transducers, it is quite easy to build a transducer that implements a morphological parser. Simply, we compose the lexicon/morphotactics transducer with the morphophonemics transducer, then invert the resulting transducer to do morphological analysis rather than generation.

In this implementation, we aimed to build a morphological parser that is not dependent on any external system for running. We wanted to construct a finite-state transducer that implements a Turkish morphological parser and that can be embedded in other NLP applications. Therefore in this implementation, we did not use external systems such as PC-KIMMO and Xerox finite-state tools. For finite-state operations we used AT&T FSM tools [8], but these tools are not required for the parser to run.

We compiled a new lexicon of 54,267 root words. To compile this lexicon and to ensure the correct spelling of the words we used the Turkish Language Institution (TDK) dictionary.

An example output from the morphological parser for the word *alın* is given below:

alın[Noun]+[A3sg]+[Pnon]+[Nom]
al[Noun]+[A3sg]+Hn[P2sg]+[Nom]
al[Adj]-[Noun]+[A3sg]+Hn[P2sg]+[Nom]
al[Noun]+[A3sg]+[Pnon]+NHn[Gen]
al[Adj]-[Noun]+[A3sg]+[Pnon]+NHn[Gen]
alın[Verb]+[Pos]+[Imp]+[A2sg]
al[Verb]+[Pos]+[Imp]+YHn[A2pl]
al[Verb]-Hn[Verb+Pass]+[Pos]+[Imp]+[A2sg]

In the morphological parse output the first part is always the root word. Then the part-of-speech tag for the stem is given in brackets. These are followed by a set of lexical morphemes with the associated morphological features. The inflectional morphemes start with a + sign, and the derivational morphemes start with a - sign. The morphological features are given in brackets. If the morpheme is a derivational one, then the morphological features for that morpheme start with the part-of-speech of the derived word form. It is also possible that morphological features can be assigned in the absence of morphemes.

2 Morphological Disambiguation

A morphological parser for a language with complex morphology may return more than one possible analysis of a word. The ambiguous parses of an example word *alın* were shown in the previous section. As can be seen in that example, some of the parses have different root words and have unrelated morphological features due to the productive morphology of Turkish. This morphological ambiguity needs to be resolved for further language processing. Several approaches have been proposed for morphosyntactic tagging in inflective and agglutinative languages, e.g. [2,3,4,7,9,10,13].

An application of the averaged perceptron algorithm to the morphological disambiguation of Turkish text is described in [10]. In that study, a baseline trigram-based model of [2] is used to enumerate n-best candidates of alternative morphological parses of a sentence. Then the averaged perceptron algorithm is applied to re-rank the n-best candidate list using a set of features. In this study, we do not use a baseline model to generate n-best candidates. Instead, we do a Viterbi decoding of the best path in the network of ambiguous morphological parses of the words in a sentence using the averaged perceptron algorithm to train model parameters as explained in the next section.

The set of features that we included in the model are the same as in [10]. This feature set takes into account the current morphosyntactic tag (parse) and the history of the previous two tags. Therefore, we can do a left to right Viterbi decoding for the best morphological parse sequence for a sentence.

2.1 Perceptron Algorithm

A variant of the perceptron algorithm that can be applied to problems such as tagging and parsing is given in Figure 3. The algorithm estimates a parameter vector $\bar{\alpha}$ that can be used for mapping from inputs $x \in X$ to outputs $y \in Y$ using a set of training examples (x_i, y_i). In our setting, X is a set of sentences and Y is a set of possible morphological parse sequences. The algorithm makes multiple passes (denoted by T) over the training examples. For each example, it finds the highest scoring candidate among all candidates using the current parameter values. If the highest scoring candidate is not the correct one, it updates the parameter vector $\bar{\alpha}$ by the difference of the feature vector representation of the correct candidate and the highest scoring candidate. This way of parameter update increases the parameter values for features in the correct candidate and decreases parameter values for features in the competitor.

This algorithm can be set up for the morphological disambiguation problem as follows:

- The training examples are the sentence $x_i = w^i_{[1:n_i]}$ and the morphological parse sequence $y_i = t^i_{[1:n_i]}$ pairs for $i = 1,..,n$, where n is the number of training sentences and n_i is the length of the i'th sentence.

Inputs: Training examples (x_i, y_i)
Initialization: Set $\bar{\alpha} = 0$
Algorithm:
  For $t = 1,..,T$, $i = 1,..,n$
    Calculate $z_i = \arg\max_{z \in GEN(x_i)} \Phi(x_i, z) \cdot \bar{\alpha}$
    If $(z_i \neq y_i)$ then $\bar{\alpha} = \bar{\alpha} + \Phi(x_i, y_i) - \Phi(x_i, z_i)$
Output: Parameters $\bar{\alpha}$

Fig. 3. A variant of the perceptron algorithm

- The function $GEN(x_i)$ maps the input sentence to the candidate parse sequences.
- The representation $\Phi(x, y) \in \Re^d$ is a feature vector, the components of which are defined as $\Phi_s\left(w_{[1:n]}, t_{[1:n]}\right) = \sum_{i=1}^{n} \phi_s(t_{i-2}, t_{i-1}, t_i)$, where $\phi_s(t_{i-2}, t_{i-1}, t_i)$ is an indicator function for a feature that depends on the current morphosyntactic tag (morphological parse) and the history of the previous two tags. Then the feature vector components $\Phi_s\left(w_{[1:n_i]}, t_{[1:n_i]}\right)$ are just the counts of the local features $\phi_s(t_{i-2}, t_{i-1}, t_i)$. For example one feature might be:

$$\phi_{100}(t_{i-2}, t_{i-1}, t_i) = \begin{cases} 1 \text{ if current parse } t_i \text{ is al} + \text{Verb} + \text{Pos} + \text{Imp} + \text{A2pl} \\ \quad \text{and previous parse } t_{i-1} \text{ is a pronoun} \\ 0 \text{ otherwise} \end{cases}$$

- The expression $\Phi(x, y) \cdot \overline{\alpha}$ is the inner product $\sum_s \alpha_s \Phi_s(x, y)$.
- The function $\arg\max_{z \in GEN(x_i)} \Phi(x_i, z) \cdot \overline{\alpha}$ can be efficiently calculated using dynamic programming since the features that we use depend on only the current tag and the previous two tags.

For the application of the model to the test examples, we use the "averaged parameters" since they are more robust to noisy or unseparable data [1]. The averaged parameters γ are calculated by summing the parameter values for each feature after each training example and dividing this sum by the total number of examples used to update the parameters. With this setting, the perceptron algorithm learns an averaged parameter vector γ that can be used to choose the most likely morphological parse sequence of a test sentence x using the following function:

$$F(x) = \arg\max_{y \in GEN(x)} \Phi(x, y) \cdot \gamma$$
$$= \arg\max_{y \in GEN(x)} \sum_{s=1}^{d} \Phi_s(x, y) \cdot \gamma_s$$

2.2 Experiments

We used a morphologically disambiguated Turkish corpus of about 950,000 tokens (including markers such as begin and end of sentence markers). Alternative ambiguous parses of the words are also available in the corpus as output from a morphological analyzer. This data set was divided into a training, development, and test set. The training set size is about 750,000 tokens or 45,000 sentences. The development set size is about 40,000 tokens or 2,500 sentences. The test set size is also about 40,000 tokens or 2,500 sentences. The training set is used for parameter estimation and the development set is used to tune some of the parameters in the perceptron algorithm. The final tests were done on the test set.

The accuracy of the perceptron algorithm on the test set is 97.81%. For a comparison of accuracy of the Viterbi decoding with averaged perceptron with the trigrambased model of [2] and trigram-based model plus perceptron re-ranking as described in [10], see Table 1.

Table 1. Comparative Results on Test Set (40K tokens)

Method	Accuracy (%)
Trigram-based model [2]	93.61
Trigram-based + Perceptron [10]	96.76
Perceptron (this study)	97.81

3 Web Corpus

In the domain of language processing, we need large corpora for the application and evaluation of statistical methods. Such corpora are also important for empirical methods that the linguists and lexicographers use to infer information about language. There have been very few efforts to build a Turkish text corpus [11,12] and they were quite limited in terms of size and coverage to be successfully used in statistical natural language applications.

In this research, a large corpus for Turkish was built and cleaned using some heuristics and the morphological parser. The corpus is composed of four sub corpora. Three of these corpora (referred as *NewsCor*) are from three major newspapers in Turkish. The other corpus (referred as *GenCor*) is a general sampling of Turkish web pages. The combined corpus of these two corpora will be referred as *BOUN Corpus*.

For data collection from the web, we implemented a web crawler - an automated script to browse the web as used by the search engines. Since the collected data from the web is very noisy, we employed some automatic normalization and filtering methods to clean the corpus. We followed a multi step process to clean the corpus as described below:

1. Decode HTML entities
2. Trim white spaces at the start and end of the lines
3. Estimate letter sequence counts from a Turkish text and use these counts to filter documents
4. Remove duplicate lines to get rid of repetitions in web pages, such as text in navigation menus
5. Remove documents with less than 1,000 characters
6. Parse the documents using the morphological parser and remove those for which more than 25% of the words cannot be parsed

The normalization and filtering step removes about 60% of the text collected for *NewsCor* and 90% of the text collected for *GenCor*. This difference is expected since the web corpus data is very noisy when compared to the newspaper data.

The tokenization and segmentation of the corpus is often needed in language applications. Since the corpus is very large for manual operation, we employed automatic methods to tokenize and segment the corpus to sentences. The morphological parser that we have developed was very useful in this process. We used the parser as a computational lexicon to look for the words in the corpus.

For the encoding of the web corpus, we used the XML Corpus Encoding Standard, XCES (see http://xces.org) as used in [12]. We encode the corpus in paragraph and sentence level. We also plan to annotate the corpus linguistically in morphosyntactic level.

3.1 Contents of the Corpus

As stated before, Turkish web corpus is formed of four sub corpora. Three of these are from three major newspapers in Turkish and the other one is a general sampling of Turkish web pages. The statistics about the number of words (all words in the corpus), number of tokens (words and lexical units such as punctuation marks), and types (distinct tokens) are shown in Table 2. The percentages of tokens and types that can be successfully parsed by the morphological parser are also indicated. We can interpret the figures on the table from different points of view.

First, we observe that, due to the agglutinative nature of the language, the number of types is quite large. Turkish dictionaries on general domain have a typical size of 50,000-100,000 words. The number of types in the corpus being about 50-60 times larger than the typical number of (mostly) stems indicates that derived words are used commonly in written language.

Table 2. Web Corpus Size

Corpus	Words	Tokens	Types	Tokens parsed (%)	Types parsed (%)
Milliyet	59M	68M	1.1M	96.7	63.5
Ntvmsbnc	75M	86M	1.2M	96.4	55.8
Radikal	50M	58M	1.0M	97.0	65.7
NewsCor	184M	212M	2.2M	96.7	52.2
GenCor	239M	279M	3.0M	94.6	39.5
BOUN Corpus	423M	491M	4.1M	95.5	38.4

Second, a significant difference exists between the percentages of tokens and types successfully parsed. This is an expected result, since most of the tokens in the corpus are grammatical words and there is a relatively small amount of other kinds of tokens (punctuation symbols, proper nouns, etc.) that cannot be parsed. On the other hand, each distinct token is treated equally in the last column of the table, without taking frequencies into consideration. We see that the parser can return an analysis only for 38.4% of the types; the rest cannot be parsed. However, this percentage of types in fact constitutes 95.5% of the corpus. The main reasons for the unparsed types are the proper nouns that do not exist in the lexicon and the spelling errors in the corpus.

Another observation is about the cleanness of the corpus. When we compare *GenCor* with *NewsCor*, we notice a decrease in the number of words that can be parsed. The difference is about 2% in the case of tokens while it is much higher (12.7%) in the case of types. These figures indicate that *NewsCor* is much cleaner than *GenCor*, as might be expected. Also the analysis of the number of words, tokens, and types in the two subcorpora shows that *GenCor* includes more types that are not actually words and there are also some unparsed tokens with high frequencies on this subcorpus. These observations signal that the words used by general web users are more diverse than those used in news portals and some of these words seem to be accepted (due to their high frequencies) by the web community.

Finally, the performance ratios for the morphological parser are quite satisfactory. The success is 96.7% on *NewsCor* and it is slightly lower for *GenCor* due to special characteristics of the written text on the web.

3.2 Corpus Statistics

In this section, we will present statistical results about the corpus in order to get an idea about the coverage of a corpus of this size for an agglutinative language and also to observe the morphological characteristics of Turkish language. Figure 4 shows statistics about the types relative to the corpus size (number of tokens). As can be seen, the number of types is increasing continuously for both corpora and for the combined corpus. It seems that if corpus size is increased beyond the current size of 491M tokens, new types will still continue to emerge. This is supported by the evidence that when the corpus size was increased from 490M to 491M, 5,539 new types (of which 1,009 can be parsed successfully) have been added to the corpus. This is partly due to the productive morphological structure of Turkish and partly to the rich web environment. These facts indicate that the size of the current corpus does not cover all language usage. It should be extended until at least the number of types that can be parsed becomes stable, corresponding to the situation that nearly all possible derived forms are represented in the corpus. Adding more data beyond this limit will just cause an increase in the number of special tokens (e.g. proper nouns) and misspelled words.

Figure 5 shows coverage statistics with respect to the vocabulary size (number of types). The figure was obtained by first sorting the types in decreasing order of frequencies and then summing up the frequencies beginning from the topmost entry for the indicated vocabulary sizes. 50% of the corpus is formed of only about 1,000 distinct words. We observe that about 300K types are necessary in order to attain an acceptable coverage ratio (97-98%). The agglutinative nature of the language and the diversity of the web contents are the basic reasons of this result. The analysis of a similar statistic for the percentages of infrequent types shows that almost half of the types (about 2.0M) occur only once in the corpus. The number of types occurring less than 10 times is 3.4M and they represent 7.5M tokens in the corpus. Thus, the majority of types in the corpus are very infrequent and 98.4% of the corpus is formed of only 15.9% of the types.

To understand the source of the large number of types in the corpus, we give statistics for the stems and lexical endings (tokens stripped of their stems in lexical form such as +lAr+Hn) of the tokens that can be parsed in Figure 6. As the number of tokens considered reaches to the size of the corpus, the number of unique stems approaches to the size of our lexicon (54,267 root words). However, as can be expected, all the words in the lexicon do not appear in the corpus and even a corpus of this size does not contain any occurrence of 5,630 words. On the other hand, the number of unique endings increases steadily as new data are added. Note that the figure considers only the tokens that can be successfully parsed. Hence, this increase means that people freely derive new word forms by making use of suffix combinations not used before. This is an interesting result. Although we know that theoretically there is no limit on the number of derivations in Turkish, we might expect that in practice a (large) subset of all possible derived forms will cover the daily use of the language.

However, this expectation does not hold even for a set of nearly 500M tokens and about 9,000 new words, 40 stems, and 60 lexical endings emerge per 10M tokens at this size. When the whole corpus is considered, about 30 different words can be obtained from a single root form, which is an indication of the productive morphological structure of the language.

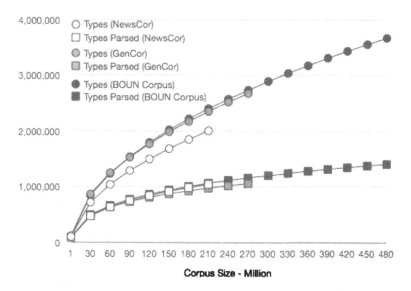

Fig. 4. Type statistics for subcorpora and combined corpus

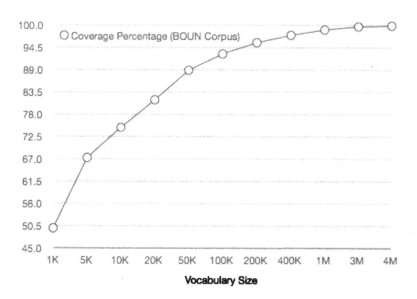

Fig. 5. Coverage statistics for subcorpora and combined corpus

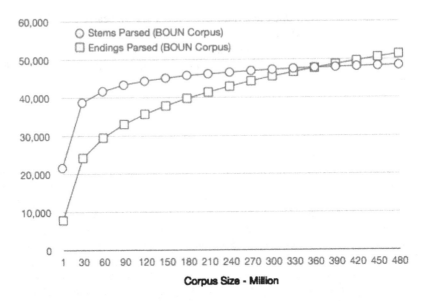

Fig. 6. Stem and ending statistics for subcorpora and combined corpus

4 Conclusions

In this paper, we presented some language resources and tools for Turkish that can be used to build Turkish NLP applications. We already used the morphological parser as a computational lexicon to implement a spell checker for Mac OS X. Our primary motivation in compiling these resources is to develop a large vocabulary speech recognition system for Turkish.

The language resources obtained as output of this research are: (i) A highly efficient finite-state morphological parser that does not depend on any other environment to run. It is one of the most complete parsers in terms of lexicon coverage, morphotactics, and morphophonemics; (ii) An efficient averaged perceptron-based morphological disambiguator that uses Viterbi decoding. The disambiguation accuracy of 97.81% is the highest accuracy reported so far for Turkish; (iii) A web corpus containing about 500 million tokens. The corpus has been cleaned using some heuristics and the morphological parser developed in this work and then converted to XCES XML format.

We believe that the methodologies described here for Turkish can be applied to other languages with complex morphology to build high-quality language resources. The resources obtained have the potential of being used as building blocks in large-scale language applications. As a future work, we plan to use the morphological parser and the disambiguator for linguistic annotation of the web corpus.

Acknowledgements

This work was supported by Boğaziçi University Research Fund under the grant numbers 06A102 and 08M103, and by TÜBİTAK under the grant number 107E261.

References

1. Collins, M.: Discriminative Training Methods for Hidden Markov Models: Theory and Experiments with Perceptron Algorithms. In: EMNLP (2002)
2. Dilek, Z.H.T., Oflazer, K., Tür, G.: Statistical Morphological Disambiguation for Agglutinative Languages. Computers and the Humanities 36(4) (2002)
3. Ezeiza, N., Alegria, I., Arriola, J.M., Urizar, R., Aduriz, I.: Combining Stochastic and Rule-based Methods for Disambiguation in Agglutinative Languages. In: COLING-ACL (1998)
4. Hajic, J., Hladka, B.: Tagging Inflective Languages: Prediction of Morphological Categories for a Rich, Structured Tagset. In: COLING-ACL, pp. 483–490 (1998)
5. Koskenniemi, K.: A General Computational Model for Word-form Recognition and Production. In: 22nd Annual Meeting on Association for Computational Linguistics, pp. 178–181 (1984)
6. Lewis, G.: Turkish Grammar. Oxford University Press, Oxford (2001)
7. Megyesi, B.: Improving Brill's PoS Tagger for an Agglutinative Language. In: Joint Sigdat Conference on Empirical Methods in Natural Language Processing and Very Large Corpora (1999)
8. Mohri, M.: Finite-state Transducers in Language and Speech Processing. Computational Linguistics 23(2), 269–311 (1997)
9. Oflazer, K., Tür, G.: Morphological Disambiguation by Voting Constraints. In: ACL, pp. 222–229 (1997)
10. Sak, H., Güngör, T., Saraçlar, M.: Morphological Disambiguation of Turkish Text with Perceptron Algorithm. In: Gelbukh, A. (ed.) CICLing 2007. LNCS, vol. 4394, pp. 107–118. Springer, Heidelberg (2007)
11. Salor, Ö., Pellom, B.L., Çiloğlu, T., Hacıoğlu, K., Demirekler, M.: On Developing New Text and Audio Corpora and Speech Recognition Tools for the Turkish Language. In: ICSLP (2002)
12. Say, B., Zeyrek, D., Oflazer, K., Özge, U.: Development of a Corpus and a Treebank for Present-day Written Turkish. In: 11th International Conference of Turkish Linguistics (2002)
13. Yüret, D., Türe, F.: Learning Morphological Disambiguation Rules for Turkish. In: HLT-NAACL (2006)

A Graph Partitioning Approach to Entity Disambiguation Using Uncertain Information

Emili Sapena, Lluís Padró, and Jordi Turmo

TALP Research Center
Universitat Politecnica de Catalunya
Barcelona, Spain
{esapena,padro,turmo}@lsi.upc.edu

Abstract. This paper presents a method for Entity Disambiguation in Information Extraction from different sources in the web. Once entities and relations between them are extracted, it is needed to determine which ones are referring to the same real-world entity. We model the problem as a graph partitioning problem in order to combine the available information more accurately than a pairwise classifier. Moreover, our method handle uncertain information which turns out to be quite helpful. Two algorithms are trained and compared, one probabilistic and the other deterministic. Both are tuned using genetic algorithms to find the best weights for the set of constraints. Experiments show that graph-based modeling yields better results using uncertain information.

1 Introduction and Motivation

Entity disambiguation resolves the many-to-many correspondence between mentions of entities in natural language and real-world entities. A real-world entity can be expressed using different aliases due to multiple reasons: use of abbreviations, different naming conventions (e.g. "Name Surname" and "Surname, N."), misspellings or naming variations over time (e.g. "Leningrad" and "Saint Petersburg"). Furthermore, some different real-world entities may have the same name or share some aliases. For instance, two citations of "J. Smith" in different documents may refer to different authors. In order to keep coherence in data extracted from text for further analysis, information integration is mandatory. This means, to determine when different mentions refer to the same real entity and when same mentions refer to different ones.

This problem arises in many applications that integrate data from multiple sources. Concretely, many tasks related to natural language processing have been involved in the problem, such as question answering, summarization, information extraction, among others. The entity disambiguation problem is also known as identity uncertainty, record linkage, deduplication, mention matching and many others.

Many techniques have been explored the Entity Disambiguation problem. Some of them use rules [1] while some others use string similarity functions [2,3]. In most works, the knowledge is manually defined, such as rules or weights [1,2], and only some works rely on the use of machine learning approaches [3,4]. Some techniques take advantage of an ontology structure, like clustering template elements [5], or exploiting relations [6,7].

A. Ranta, B. Nordström (Eds.): GoTAL 2008, LNAI 5221, pp. 428–439, 2008.

id	Name or alias	Relations with clubs
A	Tomasz Waldoch	Schalke (2001 - 2002)
B	Tomasz Waldoch	Bochum (1993 - 1999) Schalke 04 (1999 - 2006)
C	Waldoch	Bochum (1996 - 1998)

For example, we have three football players candidates to be the same real person with their relations with clubs in the table. A and B have exactly the same name but they are extracted from different sources so we are not sure if they are the same person. C is an alias of them, extracted from another document. A pairwise classifier would easily determine that A and B are the same person and also B and C, because they have played in the same clubs at the same time. However, determining if A and C are the same real entity may fail because a lack of information between them. If it happens, there will be a contradiction at the end of the process.

We also have that the element A has a relation with the club "Schalke" (element X) while element B has a relation with "Schalke 04" (element Y). These two clubs are also entities to disambiguate. We call this **uncertain information** because we can not ensure that they play in the same club, neither the opposite. If the classifier tries to determine if X and Y are the same club, it would need to know if A and B are the same person. However, if it tries first to disambiguate A and B it would need to know if X and Y are the same club. An iterative process seems to be more appropriate for this kind of information.

Fig. 1. Examples of pairwise classifier lacks

More recent works take advantage of some domain knowledge at the semantic level to improve the results. For example, [8] shows how semantic rules, either automatically learned or specified by a domain expert, can improve the results. [9] use probabilistic domain constraints in a more general model using a relaxation labeling algorithm to perform matching.

Most of these works face the problem as a pairwise binary classifier, where a pair of mentions of entities are classified as referring to the same entity or not. However, this point of view does not always take advantage of all the available information mainly due to two reasons:

– A classifier by pairs uses attributes of both elements, their relations and the constraints applied to them. This situation can cause misclassifying of some pairs of elements simply because of a lack of information. Consequently, this may lead the process to finish with contradictions in the results.
– In a binary classifier, it is not possible to use uncertain relations during the disambiguation process because the order of the pairs to classify may change the final result. Also, that uncertainty might make the process fail.

There is an example in figure 1. We call *uncertain information* or *uncertain relations* to the relations referring to an alias. In a data set where different entity types are related and each type has uncertainty (possible duplicates), we have to deal with uncertain relations.

As far as we know, three approaches in the state of the art deal with these problems. The first one consists in an iterative execution of the classification process like in the work of [6]. The second approach [10] defines the task with Markov logic networks and solve it doing logic inference with a MaxSAT solver. Third approach represents the problem as a graph for a subsequent partitioning [11,12]. We centered our work in the graph-based approach.

In this paper we propose a graph representation of the Entity Disambiguation problem taking advantage of already extracted uncertain information. We also propose the use of two iterative algorithms for resolution. On one hand, this point of view can overcome the difficulties of the pairwise classifiers because results do not fall in contradictions at the end of the process. On the other hand, using algorithms that work iteratively solving graph partitioning, one may use the information of uncertain relations in a more natural way.

The rest of the document is structured as follows. Section 2 presents an overview of related work. Section 3 formally defines the problem. The methodology employed is explained in section 4, and the algorithms are detailed in section 5. The last sections describes our experiments, results and conclusions.

2   Related Work

To the best of our knowledge, there are few works approaching multi-type entity disambiguation as a graph using uncertain information.

[11] defines a conditional model to disambiguate different entity types using, among others, the information offered by their relations. In this way, they propose a relational graph partitioning algorithm that ensures consistency in the decisions taken and also take advantage of uncertain relations. There is no previous purge in the data in order to reduce the execution costs. Other recent works [13,14] are based on the same idea.

[15] system and learning process is adaptive to any dataset. They deal with uncertain information using a structural connection strength measure, separately of feature functions. It can not have semantic constraints over relations such as time, kind of relation, and so on.

The algorithms used in these works are based in a greedy decision where, as in any greedy algorithm, wrong decisions at the beginning may unleash a bad performance. In our work we use two different algorithms that work iteratively and only take definitive decisions at the end of the execution. Other improvements presented here are a candidate selection system in order to reduce the execution costs and an homogeneous way to use attributes and relations between elements in any feature function.

3   Problem Definition and Representation

Entity Disambiguation problem consists of a set of references to entities (elements) that have to be mapped to the minimal collection of individual entities. Representing the problem in a graph we are reducing Entity Disambiguation to a graph partitioning problem given a set of constraints. At the end of the process, every partition will be a group of elements representing a real entity.

Let $G = G(V, E)$ be an undirected graph where V is a set of vertices and E a set of edges. Each element in our data is represented as a vertex $v \in V$ in the graph and an edge $e \in E$ is added to the graph for every pair of vertices representing elements which can potentially be the same entity.

The set of constraints between two elements is used to compute a variable weight value in each edge, which indicates how sure we are that the elements represented by the two adjacent vertices may be the same real entity. There are two kinds of constraints:

- **Fixed constraints.** Constraints that depend on static data. These constraints are comparisons about template elements attributes, relations, and other semantic rules. For example, two organizations having the same year of foundation or two people related with the same organization.
- **Variable constraints.** Constraints obtained from uncertain relations. These constraints may change their influence during the disambiguation process depending on the current state of the elements involved in the uncertain relation. For example, two people may be the same real person when the organizations related to them may be the same organization. If, during the disambiguation process, both organizations in the example tend to be the same real entity, both people will tend also to be the same person, and the other way round. *Variable constraints* are evaluated at each iteration during the disambiguation process and their weights are obtained depending on the involved elements state.

Finally, the edge weight used by the algorithms is the sum of the weight produced by the *fixed constraints* and the weight obtained evaluating the *variable constraints*. Negative weights indicates that the involved elements should not be in the same partition.

Let $\mathbf{x} = (x_1, ...x_n)$ be the set of elements to disambiguate. For each x_i, a vertex v_i is added to the graph. The elements may have some attributes and we write them as $\mathbf{x}_i = (x_i.a_1, x_i.a_2, x_i.a_3, ...)$ where, for instance, when x_i is an element of the type *organization*, $x_i.a_1$ is the attribute *foundation year*. The set of relations between two elements (x_i and x_j), even direct or indirect, are represented as $\mathbf{r}_{ij}$. Additionally, we have a vector $\mathbf{s}(t) = (s_1, ...s_n)$ containing the state of each vertex at iteration t. The state of a vertex v_i is s_i, a value indicating the partition where it is assigned.

Generally, edges weight for the graph partitioning is obtained before resolution like follows:

$$e_{ij}.weight = \sum_k \lambda_k f_k(\mathbf{x}_i, \mathbf{x}_j, \mathbf{r}_{ij}) \qquad (1)$$

where $f_k(\cdot)$ is a feature function that evaluates constraint k. It may use the information of the elements x_i and x_j, some of their attributes and their relations. And λ_k is the weight applied to the feature function. However, in our proposal we also utilize *variable constraints* that need to know the state of other vertices to be evaluated. Consequently, we call *fixed weight* to the weight contribution obtained in equation 1:

$$e_{ij}.wfix = \sum_k \lambda_k f_k(\mathbf{x}_i, \mathbf{x}_j, \mathbf{r}_{ij}) \qquad (2)$$

and we define the *variable weight* as:

$$e_{ij}.wvar(t) = \sum_k \lambda_k f_k(\mathbf{x}_i, \mathbf{x}_j, \mathbf{r}_{ij}, \mathbf{s}(t)) \qquad (3)$$

where t is the iteration number when the process is running. Adding $\mathbf{s}(t)$, we are providing new information to the feature function which is used to evaluate *variable constraints*. Finally, in each iteration, definitive weight is obtained as follows:

$$e_{ij}.weight(t) = e_{ij}.wfix + e_{ij}.wvar(t) \qquad (4)$$

This implies that algorithms used to resolve graph partitioning need to deal with dynamic weight values.

4 Methodology

The methodology used in our work for the Entity Disambiguation problem consists of four steps. First, to select the candidates. Second, to find the constraints between them to generate the graph. Once we have the problem represented in a graph, third step is to find the optimal weight combination for the feature functions that evaluate constraints. Finally, the graph partitioning problem is solved. The input of the process is a set of elements extracted from different sources that might be duplicated and the output is this set of elements grouped by the real entities they refer. Following subsections describe each one of these steps.

4.1 Candidate Selection

In order to avoid a graph where each vertex is adjacent to all the others, we generate a graph selecting elements candidates to be the same real entity. We select as candidates pairs of elements where one is an alias of the other. To do that we use the method of Alias Assignment developed by [16]. The method consists in training a Support Vector Machines pairwise classifier where each pair of elements is represented as a vector of features. These features are obtained using similarity functions such as string matching, edit distance and acronyms similarity. Also world-knowledge is used like city names in different languages for organizations or tipical nicknames for people. Depending on the kind of elements and their domain such as organization or people, we use different features.

Not all of the candidates have an edge between them because not all of them share an alias. For example, we have three elements of people named a) "Jason", b) "Jason Smith" and c) "Smith". Elements a and b will be adjacent vertices in the graph because "Jason" is an alias of "Jason Smith". The same happens with elements b and c. The vertices representing a and c won't be connected by any edge, however, they will be in the same subgraph so they may be, at the end, the same entity.

Then, we also link candidates that we are pretty sure that they are not the same entity, given that they already are in the same subgraph. These edges will have a negative weight which may help the algorithm. Following the same example, if "Jason" and "Smith" have different birth dates, they are also linked.

In this way, the whole problem representation as a graph consists of a set of subgraphs each of which is an entity disambiguation subproblem. Candidate selection is not a strictly necessary stage but helps reducing computational costs.

4.2 Constraints Evaluation

In the second step we generate the constraints applicable to the pairs of candidates. Using the ontology and the knowledge of the domain, an expert manually writes a set of rules that, when applied to a pair of elements, help to know whether they are the same entity or not. These constraints can be seen as soft rules and their influence or weight will be determined with Genetic Algorithms using training data in the next step. Constraints can be of any order, that is, any number of elements or pairs of elements may be involved in a constraint. Table 1 shows some examples of constraints.

Table 1. Example of constraints

Constraint	Kind of entity affected	Description	Kind of constraint
c1	Organization	Org_i and Org_j are likely to match if foundation dates are equal	Fixed
c2	Organization	Org_i and Org_j are likely to match if Per_l and Per_k are also likely to match and Per_l *belongsTo* Org_i and Per_k *belongsTo* Org_j	Variable
c3	Person	Per_i and Per_j are likely to match if they are related to the same organization	Fixed
c4	Person	Per_i and Per_j are unlikely to match if they are doing different events at the same time	Fixed

4.3 Finding Optimal Weights

The performance of the algorithms depend on the edge weights which, at the same time, depend on the constraint weights. In order to achieve good performance, it is mandatory to find a good constraint weight combination. Searching the space of constraint weight combinations is intractable here by an exhaustive search. Therefore, we use Genetic Algorithms for this task [17]. Other works have also used evolutionary algorithms to train similar processes successfully [18]. This step is only done for training, and it needs an annotated dataset. The graph is solved using different weight combinations and an evolutionary process is done evaluating each time the graph partitioning results. Once training is done, constraint weights are saved for further executions.

4.4 Solving Graph Partitioning Problem

Graph partitioning task determines the best partition assignment for the vertices, given a set of conditions. In this case, the conditions are the edge weights, which represent how strong are the involved constraints. Positive weights indicate that both adjacent vertices should be in the same partition, while negative weights indicate the opposite. The higher the weight, the harder the condition. The algorithms used (detailed in Section 5) iteratively look for combinations of partitions according to indications of edge weights.

5   Algorithms

We propose the use of two algorithms to entity disambiguation. The reason to compare a deterministic algorithm (Relax) with a probabilistic one (Ant) is the scalability. While a deterministic algorithm can ensure that the result is the best possible, for larger datasets it needs more resources and might be intractable. On the contrary, a probabilistic algorithm like Ants can achieve good performance (not the optimal) besides computational cost issues.

5.1   Relaxation Labeling Algorithm

Relaxation is a generic name for a family of iterative algorithms which perform function optimization, based on local information. They are closely related to neural nets and gradient step.

The algorithm has been widely used to solve AI problems [19] and also NLP problems such as from PoS-tagging [20], chunking, knowledge integration, and Semantic Parsing [21].

Relaxation labeling (Relax) solves our weighted constraint satisfaction problem dealing with variable *compatibility coefficients*. Each vertex is assigned to a partition satisfying as many constraints as possible.

5.2   Ants Algorithm

The ants algorithm is a multiagent system based on the idea of parallel search. A generic version of the algorithm was proposed in [22]. The algorithm faces the problem as a graph coloring problem, optimizing a global fitness function. In theoretical computer science, *"graph coloring"* usually refers to a very specific constraint satisfaction problem: assigning colors to vertices such that no two adjacent vertices have the same color. However, this algorithm is more general and optimizes a global fitness function using colors as a vertex state, and using local fitness function to decide the color of each vertex. Playing with local and global fitness functions one can adapt the algorithm to solve almost any problem of constraint satisfaction.

The algorithm works as follows. Initially, all vertices are randomly colored and a given number of agents (ants) is placed on the vertices, also at random. Then the ants move around the graph and change the coloring according to a local optimization criterion. The local and global fitness functions depend on the problem to solve and are the only part that normally needs adaption.

Each movement or decision taken by an ant has a probability of error, which prevents the algorithm falling in local minima.

The adaption of the algorithm to our entity disambiguation task is done by finding correct global and local fitness functions. Local *fitness* function is defined as:

$$Fit(v) = \frac{\sum_{i=0}^{m-1} e_i.weight - \sum_{j=m}^{l-1} e_j.weight}{\sum_{i=0}^{l-1} |e_i.weight|} \tag{5}$$

where vertex v has l adjacent vertices and $e.weight$ are the values of edge weights. From 0 to $m - 1$ are the edge weights corresponding to the adjacent vertices with the same color and from m to $l - 1$ are the ones corresponding to adjacent vertices with different color. Note that the values of the edge weights can be negative and their value is obtained as explained in section 3. If the obtained value is negative, $Fit(v)$ returns zero.

The global fitness function is then the sum of all the vertices fitness:

$$GlobalFitness = \frac{\sum_{i=0}^{n-1} Fit(v_i)}{n} \qquad (6)$$

where n is the total number of vertices. At the end of execution, vertices sharing a color are elements that refer to the same entity.

6   Evaluation Framework

We evaluated our approach to entity disambiguation using two datasets `Football` and `Cora`.

6.1   Football Dataset

We use data automatically extracted from different websites about football[1] (soccer). The entities to disambiguate are people (players, coaches, referees and presidents), organizations (clubs and federations) and teams. There are also other entities extracted like competitions, awards and matches that does not need disambiguation. Also relations (some of them, temporal relations) and events have been extracted from these websites (for example, players *belong to* clubs, teams *play* matches). Many players, clubs and teams have similar or identical names. In this situation, and when the information is extracted from different sources, one can not integrate the information only using similarities or name comparisons.

The whole data extracted consists of a high number of elements and relations as is summarized in Table 2. A representative part of the data has been manually labeled (last two columns in Table 2). We generated about 750.000 fixed constraints and 25.000 variable constraints of 33 different types (some examples in table 1). Each algorithm is trained and tested doing a five-fold cross-validation over the manually labeled data.

The reason to evaluate the system with this dataset is the existence of uncertain relations. During the information extraction process, some relations point to an alias that, at that moment, it is not possible to know which real entity is referring to (for exemple, "Robert" belongsTo "Manchester"). One does not know which Robert neither which Manchester). We save this relation as uncertain to use it in the subsequent disambiguation process. We have extracted different kinds of entities with relations between them what let us a good scenario to test our proposal.

6.2   Cora

In order to evaluate our methodology and algorithms in a dataset widely used, we choose Cora[2]. It contains about 1800 citations, with 600 different papers. We

---

[1] http://www.lsi.upc.edu/~esapena/data/footballdb.tar.gz
[2] http://www.cs.umass.edu/~mccallum/data/cora-refs.tar.gz

Table 2. Data used in the experiments

Kind of entity	# extracted elements	# Ambiguous elements	# Candidate pairs	# Elements labeled	# Real entities labeled
Person	22,828	17,721	207,275	888	326
Club	1,929	811	1,334	54	18
Team	1,830	682	1,049	53	21

disambiguate papers, authors and venues, but only papers are used for training and test because only papers are labeled. It is splitted in three non-overlapped parts (`fahl`, `kibl` and `utgo`) that we use for cross-validation.

7 Experiments

Three experiments have been done to evaluate our methodology and the algorithms proposed:

- **Comparing pair classification with graph partitioning.** The goal is to prove that the graph point of view and the use of uncertain relations achieve better results than pair classification. We train Support Vector Machines (SVM) to disambiguate entities as a binary classifier. Each pair of candidate elements is evaluated using the information of fixed constraints. We compare the results of SVM with the results obtained with Relax and Ants.
- **Comparing algorithms with and without using uncertain relations.** In this second experiment, the goal is to know how helpful is the use of uncertain information when disambiguating. We compare both algorithms Relax and Ants with and without using variable constraints.
- **Comparing Relax and Ants algorithms with Greedy Agglomerative Clustering.** The goal of this third experiment is to compare iterative algorithms with greedy and also corroborate that our proposed algorithms achieve state-of-the-art performance using a widely used corpus.

To evaluate the results we choose Purity and Inverse Purity measures and their harmonic mean F_1. In the Entity Disambiguation problem, the input is a set of elements and we are expecting a concrete association of them in the output. That is, we have to evaluate how correct are the groups of elements obtained. Purity (Pur) and Inverse Purity (IPur) are standard clustering measures that helps us to evaluate this kind of results. The precision of a cluster $P \in \mathbb{P}$ for a given category $L \in \mathbb{L}$ is given by $Prec(P, L) := \frac{|P \cap L|}{|P|}$. The overall value for purity is computed by taking the weighted average of maximal precision values:

$$Pur(\mathbb{P}, \mathbb{L}) = \sum_{P \in \mathbb{P}} \frac{|P|}{|D|} max_{L \in \mathbb{L}} Prec(P, L) \qquad (7)$$

$$IPur(\mathbb{P}, \mathbb{L}) = \sum_{L \in \mathbb{L}} \frac{|L|}{|D|} max_{P \in \mathbb{P}} Prec(L, P) \tag{8}$$

$$F_1 = \frac{2 * Pur(\mathbb{P}, \mathbb{L}) * IPur(\mathbb{P}, \mathbb{L})}{Pur(\mathbb{P}, \mathbb{L}) + IPur(\mathbb{P}, \mathbb{L})} \tag{9}$$

Pairwise precision and recall measures are not fully adequate for a partitioning problem. A good explanation of why Purity and Inverse Purity is more appropriate for this kind of evaluation can be found in [15]. In the results we only show the final F_1.

We use two baselines to compare the algorithms. Baseline *Join* groups all the elements of each subgraph. That is, all directly or indirectly connected candidates are considered to be the same real entity. It produces an Inverse Purity of almost 100%, depending on the goodness of the candidate selection process. Baseline *Disjoin* does the opposite, it separates all the elements as if each one was a different real entity. It obtains 100% Purity.

Also a Greedy Agglomerative Clustering (GAC) algorithm has been implemented in order to compare it with the performance of our proposed algorithms using the same information.

8 Results

The results obtained in the first experiment are shown in Table 3. As expected, if we evaluate the accuracy achieved by SVM, we obtain a performance that seems quite good: 85.8%. However, once pairs are classified, the final result has to determine which elements refer to the same real entity. We join all the pairs of elements classified as positive to obtain a set of groups (single-link). This last step generates large groups of elements because any missclassification causes merging of two groups. A few of these missclassifications cause this bad performance. Consequently, final results of SVM tend to be similar to the baseline *Join*. Both algorithms based in graphs outperform SVM thanks to the graph-based approach.

Table 3. Results of the first and second experiments in Football dataset. +*UR* means: using Uncertain Relations.

Algorithm	Join	Disjoin	SVM	Ants	Ants + UR	Relax	Relax + UR
F_1	8.2	12.3	53.6	75.6	79.2	81.5	83.7

The results obtained in the second experiment (Table 3) show that in both algorithms, Relax and Ants, the performance is better when uncertain information is used. Note that variable constraints represent only a 3% of the constraints in the Football dataset but they help the algorithms contributing with more information.

The third experiment (Table 4) shows how iterative algorithm Ants performs slightly better than Greedy Agglomerative Clustering (GAC) using the same information in Cora dataset. However, Relax does not achieve GAC performance and all three results are in an interval about 1.3%, which is not significant. A possible reason is because in Cora the most informative constraints are strings comparisions.

Table 4. Results of the third experiment in `Cora` dataset

Cora	GAC	Ants	Relax
fahl	86.6	**88.7**	88.0
kibl	96.8	**97.0**	95.7
utgo	**94.7**	94.2	92.4
Average	92.7	**93.3**	92.0

9   Conclusions

We have proposed two algorithms to the Entity Disambiguation problem and a graph-based modeling using uncertain information. Our hypothesis is that graph-based point of view can solve some of the troubles of pairwise classifiers. Experiments show that our modeling yields better results since combines more accurately the available information. Also, it is able to use uncertain information which turns out to be quite helpful.

Finally, we have seen that the proposed iterative algorithms achieve performance comparable to the state-of-the-art ones in a widely used corpus when no useful uncertain information is available.

References

1. Hernandez, M.A., Stolfo, S.J.: The merge/purge problem for large databases. In: SIGMOD 1995: Proceedings of the 1995 ACM SIGMOD international conference on Management of data, pp. 127–138. ACM Press, New York (1995)
2. Cohen, W., Ravikumar, P., Fienberg, S.: A comparison of string distance metrics for name-matching tasks. In: Proceedings of the IJCAI (2003)
3. Bilenko, M., Mooney, R.J.: Adaptive duplicate detection using learnable string similarity measures. In: KDD 2003: Proceedings of the ninth ACM SIGKDD international conference on Knowledge discovery and data mining, pp. 39–48. ACM Press, New York (2003)
4. Han, H., Giles, L., Li, H.Z.C., Tsioutsiouliklis, K.: Two supervised learning approaches for name disambiguation in author citations. In: Proceedings of the 2004 Joint ACM/IEEE Conference on Digital Libraries, 2004, pp. 296–305 (2004)
5. McCallum, A., Nigam, K., Ungar, L.H.: Efficient clustering of high-dimensional data sets with application to reference matching. In: KDD 2000: Proceedings of the sixth ACM SIGKDD international conference on Knowledge discovery and data mining, pp. 169–178. ACM Press, New York (2000)
6. Bhattacharya, I., Getoor, L.: Iterative record linkage for cleaning and integration. In: DMKD 2004: Proceedings of the 9th ACM SIGMOD workshop on Research issues in data mining and knowledge discovery, Paris, France, pp. 11–18. ACM Press, New York (2004)
7. Pasula, H., Marthi, B., Milch, B., Russell, S., Shpitser, I.: Identity uncertainty and citation matching. In: Processing (NIPS) (2002)
8. Doan, A., Lu, Y., Lee, Y., Han, J.: Profile-based object matching for information integration. IEEE Intelligent Systems 18(5), 54–59 (2003)
9. Shen, W., Li, X., Doan, A.: Constraint-based entity matching. In: Proceedings of AAAI (2005)
10. Singla, P., Domingos, P.: Entity resolution with markov logic. In: ICDM 2006, pp. 572–582. IEEE Computer Society, Washington (2006)

11. Culotta, A., McCallum, A.: Joint deduplication of multiple record types in relational data. In: CIKM 2005: Proceedings of the 14th ACM international conference on Information and knowledge management, pp. 257–258. ACM, New York (2005)
12. Han, H., Zha, H., Giles, C.L.: Name disambiguation in author citations using a k-way spectral clustering method. In: JCDL 2005: Proceedings of the 5th ACM/IEEE-CS joint conference on Digital libraries, pp. 334–343. ACM, New York (2005)
13. Bhattacharya, I., Getoor, L.: Collective entity resolution in relational data. ACM Trans. Knowl. Discov. Data 1(1), 5 (2007)
14. Wang, C., Lu, J., Zhang, G.: A constrained clustering approach to duplicate detection among relational data. In: Advances in Knowledge Discovery and Data Mining, pp. 308–319 (2007)
15. Chen, Z., Kalashnikov, D.V., Mehrotra, S.: Adaptive graphical approach to entity resolution. In: JCDL 2007: Proceedings of the 7th ACM/IEEE joint conference on Digital libraries, pp. 204–213. ACM, New York (2007)
16. Sapena, E., Padró, L., Turmo, J.: Alias assigment in information extraction. In: Proceedings of SEPLN-2007, Sevilla, Spain (2007)
17. Goldberg, D.E.: Genetic Algorithms in Search, Optimization and Machine Learning. Addison-Wesley Longman Publishing Co., Inc., Boston (1989)
18. Pelillo, M., Abbattista, F., Maffione, A.: An evolutionary approach to training relaxation labeling processes. Pattern Recogn. Lett. 16(10), 1069–1078 (1995)
19. Rosenfeld, R., Hummel, R.A., Zucker, S.W.: Scene labelling by relaxation operations. IEEE Transactions on Systems, Man and Cybernetics 6(6), 420–433 (1976)
20. Màrquez, L., Padró, L., Rodríguez, H.: A machine learning approach for pos tagging. Machine Learning Journal 39(1), 59–91 (2000)
21. Atserias, J.: Towards Robustness in Natural Language Understanding. Ph.D. Thesis, Dept. Lenguajes y Sistemas Informáticos. Euskal Herriko Unibertsitatea. Donosti. Spain (2006)
22. Comellas, F., Ozon, J.: An ant algorithm for the graph colouring problem. In: ANTS 1998 - From Ant Colonies to Artificial Ants: First international workshop on ant colony optimization, Brussels (1998)

Arabic Named Entity Recognition from Diverse Text Types

Khaled Shaalan and Hafsa Raza

Faculty of Informatics, The British University in Dubai, P.O Box 502216, Dubai, UAE
Khaled.shaalan@buid.ac.ae, hafsa.raza@gmail.com

Abstract. Name identification has been worked on quite intensively for the past few years, and has been incorporated into several products. Many researchers have attacked this problem in a variety of languages but only a few limited researches have focused on Named Entity Recognition (NER) for Arabic text due to the lack of resources for Arabic named entities and the limited amount of progress made in Arabic natural language processing in general. In this paper, we present the results of our attempt at the recognition and extraction of 10 most important named entities in Arabic script; the person name, location, company, date, time, price, measurement, phone number, ISBN and file name. We developed the system, Name Entity Recognition for Arabic (NERA), using a rule-based approach. The system consists of a whitelist representing a dictionary of names, and a grammar, in the form of regular expressions, which are responsible for recognizing the named entities. NERA is evaluated using our own corpora that are tagged in a semi-automated way, and the performance results achieved were satisfactory in terms of precision, recall, and f-measure.

Keywords: Information extraction; Named entity recognition; Arabic natural language processing.

1 Introduction

NER system is a significant tool in NLP research since it allows identification of proper nouns in open-domain texts. Larkey have conducted a study that showed the importance of the proper names component in language tasks involving searching, tracking, retrieving, or extracting information [9]. Another study by Crestan & de Loupy showed that named entity extraction helps users to browse large document collections more quickly and efficiently [2]. This seems plausible as, according to Gey 30% of the content-bearing words in news are proper names [5]. Abuleil [12] and Chinchor [11] stated that the valuable information in text is usually located around proper names, to collect this information it should be found first.

We have adopted the rule-based approach using linguistic grammar-based techniques to develop NERA. The approach is motivated by the characteristics and peculiarities of Arabic language. The recognition process takes two cycles, using the whitelist component and then applying the grammar rules. This open architecture approach provides flexibility and adaptability features in our system and it can be

A. Ranta, B. Nordström (Eds.): GoTAL 2008, LNAI 5221, pp. 440–451, 2008.

easily configured to work with different languages, NLP applications, and domains. We present the results of our attempt at the recognition and extraction of 10 most important named entities in Arabic script that is, the person name, location, company, date, time, price, measurement, phone number, ISBN and file name. The NERA system is evaluated using a reference corpus that is tagged with names in a semi-automated way. The achieved system performance results were satisfactory when evaluated against the standard measures; precision, recall, and f-measure.

The rest of this paper is structured as follows. Section 2 presents previous related work in Arabic NER. Section 3 describes the data collection methods used. Section 4 explains in detail our approach to NER in terms of system architecture. Section 5 is dedicated to show the reference corpora we built to carry out our experimental work. In Section 6 we present the results of our experiments, whereas in the Section 7 we highlight how our system NERA, provides solutions to challenges posed by Arabic language. Finally, in Section 8, we draw some conclusions and discuss future works.

2 Related Work

Name identification has been worked on quite intensively for the past few years, and has been incorporated into several products. Many researchers have attacked this problem in a variety of languages but only a few limited researches have focused on NER for Arabic text. This is due to the lack of resources for Arabic NE and the limited amount of progress made in Arabic NLP in general.

Maloney and Niv developed TAGARAB an Arabic name recognizer that uses a pattern-recognition engine integrated with morphological analysis. The role of the morphological analyzer is to decide where a name ends and the non-name context begins. The decision depends on the part-of-speech of the Arabic word and/or its inflections. The performance achieved for the Person NE recognition was 86.2%, 76.2% and 80.9% whereas for the Location NE it was 94.5%, 85.3% and 89.7% for precision, recall and f-measure respectively [7].

Abuleil presented a technique to extract proper names from text to build a database of names along with their classification that can be used in question-answering systems. This work was done in three main stages: 1) marking the phrases that might include names, 2) building up graphs to represent the words in these phrases and the relationships between them, and 3) applying rules to generate the names, classify each of them, and saves them in a database. The NE recognition accuracy was estimated in terms of precision by the author; People (90%), Location (93%) and Organization (92%) [12].

Samy has used parallel corpora in Spanish, and Arabic and an NE tagger in Spanish to tag the names in the Arabic corpus. For each sentence pair aligned together, they use a simple mapping scheme to transliterate all the words in the Arabic sentence and return those matching with NEs in the Spanish sentence as the NEs in Arabic. While they report high precision (84%) and recall (97.5%), it should be noted that their approach is applicable only when a parallel corpus is available [3].

Zitouni has adopted a statistical approach for the entity detection and recognition (EDR). In this work, a mention can be either named (e.g. John Mayor), nominal (the president) or pronominal (she, it). All are referring to one conceptual entity. The performance of this mention detection system is given by the author in terms of precision (64.4%), recall (55.7%) and f-measure (59.7%) [6].

3 Data Collection

For training and testing purposes, we have compiled corpora containing texts which are diverse in terms of domain, format, style and genre. This aims to ensure that the system can cope adequately with any kind of text, and that its future use is not limited to any particular text type. Techniques used for acquiring such data include:

- **Automatic collection of named entities instances and indicators from annotated corpora:** The Automatic Content Extraction (ACE[1]) and Arabic Treebank (ATB[2]) are some great resources that facilitate corpus based studies of many interesting linguistic phenomena in Modern Standard Arabic (MSA). These corpora were exploited for the data collection task. These corpora, which are tagged with great linguistic details, were first analyzed and the commonly occurring patterns were studied. These identified patterns were then used to extract useful data.
- **Name Database provided by government organization:** The person and company name dictionaries were also build from names collected from some organizations including Immigration Departments, Educational bodies, and Brokerage companies.
- **Internet Resources[3]:** Names were retrieved further from various websites[4] containing lists of Arabic names, company names and locations. Some of these names are Romanized (written using the Latin alphabet) and had to be transliterated from English to Arabic.

The NEs compiled by processing corpora, internet resources and various organizations, had to be further processed to ensure that the compiled data is clean. The raw data received had to be further processed to make it suitable for incorporation into the system.

4 The Architecture for NERA System

The NERA system was implemented through incorporation into the FAST ESP framework, [5]. Figure 1 shows the abstract architecture of the NERA system. The system requires two main processing resources: a *whitelist* (gazetteer) and a finite state transduction *grammar*. A *filtration mechanism* is also employed that enables revision capabilities in the system.

---

[1] ACE reference: http://projects.ldc.upenn.edu/ace/
[2] Treebank Corpus reference: http://www.ircs.upenn.edu/arabic/
[3] Web sites include: http://en.wikipedia.org/wiki/List_of_Arabic_names,
    http://www.islam4you.info/contents/names/fa.php, and
    http://www.mybabynamessite.com/list.php?letter=a
[4] Web sites include: http://en.wikipedia.org/wiki/List_of_Arabic_names,
    http://www.islam4you.info/contents/names/fa.php, and
    http://www.mybabynamessite.com/list.php?letter=a

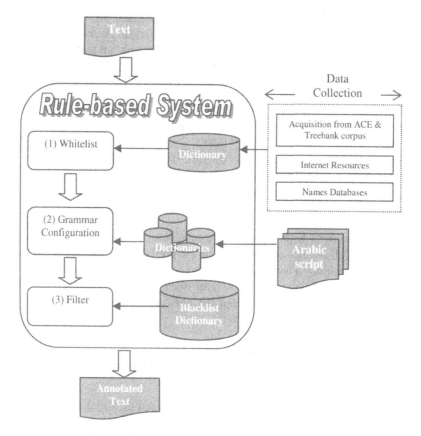

Fig. 1. Architecture of the System

4.1 Whitelist

The whitelist plays the role of fixed static dictionaries of various named entities. It is a mechanism that accepts matches which are reported as a result of an intersection between the dictionary and the input text. A Whitelist is a list of strings that must be recognized independent of the rules. It contains entries in the format:

عبدالرحمن قاسم الشيراوى|Abdulrahman Qasim Mohammed Alshirawi

The English transliterations of the Arabic names are included in the dictionary as meta-data in order to allow for incorporation with various applications.

4.2 Grammar

The grammar performs recognition and extraction of Arabic named entities from the input text based on derived rules. It describes patterns to match NEs, thereby annotations being created as a result. Due to the peculiarities and complexities in the Arabic language, grammar rules are a vital processing resource for the recognition system. For instance the lack of capitalization for proper nouns can be very well compensated by using NE indicators to formulate recognition rules. These NE indicators were obtained as a result of the deep contextual analysis of various Arabic scripts that were performed during the data collection phase. The indicators are referred to as trigger words within our system, forming a window around a named entity, which helps in identifying a NE within text but does not get recognized itself.

- Person Title: السيدة (Mrs.), السيد (Mrs.)
- Job title: الدكتورة (the doctor), أستاذ العلوم (the sciences professor)
- Company indicator: ذات مسئولية محدودة (LLC)
- Country Post-indicators: الاتحادية (the federal), الديمقراطية (the democracy)
- City Post-indicators: عاصمة المالية (the finance capital)
- Measurement: مللیجرامات (miligrams), كيلو مترات (kilometers)
- Price: جنيه مصري (Egyptian Pound), درهم إماراتي (dirham Emirati)

Moreover inflections within Arabic language can be well dealt with using handcrafted rules, which enables stripping off of the prefixes and suffixes from the stem word, prior recognition. Thus ensuring the recognition of the actual NE instance alone. For each type of named entity several rules were built and each one was applied in a particular order to ensure that the most comprehensive recognition result was achieved.

Example rule for *Person name* recognition

```
((honorfic+ws(location(ية|ي)+ws)?)+firsts_v
(ws+lasts_v)?ws+(number)?)
```

The above rule recognizes a person name composed of a first name followed by optional last name based on a preceding person indicator pattern, or the trigger words. The following name would be recognized by this rule:

الملك عبد الله	[The king Abdullah]
الملك الأردني عبد الله	[The Jordanian king Abdullah]
الملك الأردني عبد الله الثاني	[The Jordanian king Abdullah II]
الملكة الأردنية رانيا	[The Jordanian queen Rania]

Apart from contextual cues, the typical Arabic naming elements were used to formulate rules such as nasab, kunya, etc. Thereby the rules resulted in a good control over critical instances by recognizing complex entities.

Example rule for *Location* recognition

```
((مدينة | Administrative division) + ws)? + city name
+ws + direction
```

The rule above recognizes a city name (existing in the dictionary of city names). The following name would be recognized by this rule:

مدينة اغادير جنوب ... [Agadir City south of ...]

4.3 Filter

A *filtration* mechanism is used in the form of a *Blacklist* (rejecter) within the grammar configuration to filter matches, returned by rules, which appear after named entity indicators but are invalid entities. Consider the following example:

'وزير الخارجية العراقي الامين العام' [The Iraqi Foreign Minister the Secretary-General]

In this example, the words following the person indicator ('وزير الخارجية العراقي') [The Iraqi Foreign Minister]) that is, 'الامين العام' (the Secretary-General) is not a valid person name. The role of the blacklist, another set of rules, is rejecting such incorrect matches.

Apart from the *Blacklist* component certain heuristic *Filter rules* are used for postprocessing the system's extraction results in order to disambiguate extracted named entities. When applying a set of single-slot extraction rules to the input text i.e. sets of rules which extract particular types of named entity one after the other, one cannot exclude the possibility of identical or overlapping textual matches within the document, among different rules for different named entities. For instance, different sets of rules for extracting instances of both the named entities *person* and *location names* may overlap or exactly match in certain text fragments, resulting in ambiguous named entities. Among these named entities, the correct choice must be made. The *filter rule* is an intelligent way of specifying how to get the correct choice, with respect to the context in which the ambiguous situation may arise.

The following example illustrates an ambiguous situation in Arabic script:

احمد اباد لديه اهتمام بالغ بالفلسفة
(**Ahmed Abad** has a keen interest in philosophy)

In this example the bold text fragment represents both a person name and a location. Hence when NERA is applied here, both the Person and Location Extractors will return matches as 'احمد اباد' (Ahmed Abad). The developer can tune the system to resolve some kinds of ambiguous situations by the virtue of filter rules. One solution to disambiguate this situation is to use the following filter rule:

```
If a possible match M1 for a location entity intersects
with a match M2 that was previously reported by the
person extractor, then the match as a location name
will be discarded.
```

Thus in case of an intersection, the match for person names is preferred over location names. The filter rules defined within the system play a significant role to handle such situations and resolve ambiguity. However, it should be built upon careful analysis of the ambiguous situations in order to get accurate results.

5 Resources Build for Arabic NER within NERA

To develop the Arabic NER, we had to build our own corpora due to the unavailability of free Arabic corpora for research purposes. Moreover, the commercially available Arabic corpora are oriented towards newswire which we found lacks the coverage of the 10 named entities involved in our research. Further, we have also built the whitelist (gazetteer) component, which is a vital processing resource for many NLP tasks. Following, we present the main characteristics of the developed resources for Arabic.

5.1 Corpora for Person, Location, Date, Time, Price and Measurement NE

ACE (Automatic Content extraction, version 5.3.3 2005.05.31) and ATB (Arabic Treebank, version 2.0, LDC catalog number LDC2003T06) corpora by LDC are some great Arabic NLP resources. These corpora contain text taken from newswire documents and broadcast news which was used to create the entity tagged reference corpora for evaluating Person, Location, Date, Time, Price, and Measurement extractors within NERA.

For efficiency purpose the reference corpus build was divided into sets of test corpora, each being approximately 100KB in size. The total number of test sets for these named entities is 34, with 24 created from ACE corpus and 10 created from ATB corpus. The total size of the reference corpus is around 4MB composed of 300000 words. The size and content of the corpus is such that it contains a representative amount of occurrences of the following NE: Person name includes 500+ entities, location includes 500+ entities, date includes 394 entities, time includes 110 entities, price includes 400 entities, and measurement includes 386 entities.

5.2 Corpus for Company Named Entity

The ACE and ATB corpora do not include representative number of entities for company names. We sought another corpus, that is, Corpus of Contemporary Arabic (CCA[5]) [8]. We used CCA to create of the reference corpus for evaluating the *company extractor*. For building up the company test corpus we created two reference corpus set (each 100 KB in size) from randomly selected text from the CCA corpus. Both the two sets were hand tagged to mark company names within it. A total of *226 company name* instances have been hand tagged.

5.3 Corpus for Phone Number, ISBN and File Name Named Entities

Arabic available corpus resources are quite limited and restrained to coverage of the most important NEs such as person, location etc. Hence various Arabic websites (e.g. Real Estate, Newspaper etc) were analyzed to collect *Phone number, ISBN* and *file name* entities. The corpus build was hand tagged with 191 Phone number entities, 100 entities for ISBN, and 139 entities for File name.

5.4 Whitelists

NERA gathers three different manually built gazetteers or whitelist:
1. *Person Whitelist*: This contains a list of 263,598 complete names of people collected from DNRD (Dubai Naturalization & Residency Department), Brokerage companies, and existing Arabic corpora and internet resources. Further the names were split into dictionaries of first names with 175,502 names and last names with 33,517 names;
2. *Location Whitelist*: This consists of 4,900 names of continents, countries, cities, states, political regions, towns and villages found in the Arabic version of Wikipedia and other websites;

---

[5] CCA is freely downloaded online http://www.comp.leeds.ac.uk/eric/latifa/research.htm

3. *Organizations Whitelist*: This consists of a list of 273,491 names of companies including areas such as media and newspaper, construction, banks & insurance, airlines, telecommunications and many more.

6 Experiment

The evaluation of the NERA extractors was performed using our own reference corpora which highlight the Arabic resources built during this project work. Since the corpora were tagged in a semi-automated way, certain named entities were left untagged. In the recognition results these NEs were recognized correctly by the system, but since they were not tagged in the test corpora the evaluation tool marked these as false positives when in reality they were true positives. To overcome this issue, the entities marked as false positives by evaluation tool were extracted and re-tagged in the reference corpora. This iterative tagging of the corpus ensured quality. Moreover this tool can perform evaluation on a corpus with size limited to 100 KB. Hence the 5MB of evaluation corpora composed of 397,069 words was divided into 46 sets of corpus files.

6.1 Evaluation Method

We have adopted the standard evaluation measures in the IE community [1] (i.e. precision, recall and F-measures), to evaluate and compare the results. It was introduced to provide a single figure to compare different systems' performances.

6.2 Results

Table 1 summarizes the accumulative recognition accuracy, in terms of precision & recall, achieved by all the 10 extractors within NERA, against the reference corpora.

With respect to the extractors' person, location and company some of the entries within the whitelist component built were extracted from the same corpus used also for creating the reference corpora for evaluation. However, the evaluation results achieved are accurate since they indicated recognition of named entities not included in the *whitelist* but being recognized by the grammar rules within the pattern matching component.

Table 1. Accumulated accuracy of the 10 named entities

No	NE	Precision	Recall	f-measure
1	Person	86.3%	89.2%	87.7%
2	Location	77.4%	96.8%	85.9%
3	Company	81.45%	84.95%	83.15%
4	Date	91.2%	92.3%	91.6%
5	Time	97.25%	94.5%	95.4%
6	Price	100%	99.45%	98.6%
7	Measurement	97.8%	97.3%	97.2%
8	Phone Number	94.9%	87.9%	91.3%
9	ISBN	94.8%	95.8%	95.3%
10	File name	95.7%	97.1%	96.4%

One important factor that has greatly influenced the above achieved results is the non-standardization of written Arabic text. Majority of them are unstructured loaded with inconsistencies due to the lack of control over written forms of Arabic script. Standard practices in publishing written Arabic resources can help achieve far better accuracy results

7   Solutions to Challenges in NERA

7.1   Inflections

Arabic is a highly inflected language. So, within the handcrafted rules, we added the possibilities of breaking down the inflected form into a stem (or numeric figure) and affixes in order to recognize the stem as a name entity. Table 2 shows some inflected named entity examples which have been dealt with in the grammar file for the respective entity type.

7.2   Non-casing Language

Due to the lack of capital letters in Arabic script, we used keywords or indicator words to guide us to the place where one could find them in the text. The method adopted is to derive a set of heuristic rules that parse the phrases to extract the name entities. Some examples of keywords used for identifying the names are:

- o   Personal names (title): **Mr.** John Adams → السّيّد جون آدامز
- o   Personal names (job title): **President** John Adams → الرئيس جون آدامز

Table 2. Examples of inflections in Arabic text

Arabic Ex.	English Trans.	Entity Type	Affix (clitics)
بـ ٢٠,٢٦٦ دولارا	For $20,266	Price	'بـ' (baa)
الـ ٢٩٢٥ متر	The 2925 meter	Measurement	'الـ'(al)
بالولايات المتحدة	For the United States	Location	'بال' (baa, alif, laam)
ومصر	And Egypt	Location	'و' (Waw)
لهيئة الاذاعة البريطانية "بي بي سي"	for the British Broadcasting Corporation "BBC"	Company	'ل' (laam)

7.3   Spelling Variants

Spelling of translated and transliterated proper names in general tends to be inconsistent in Arabic text. Table 3 shows some examples of the inconsistency, although some can be considered as typos.

The extractor can handle, to some extent the above mentioned spelling variants. Such issues were dealt with within the context sensitive rules and dictionary build within the NERA system.

Table 3. Examples of variations in Arabic text

Arabic Ex.	English Trans.	Entity Type
أندونيسية / أندونيسيا	Indonesia	Location
جلدر / جيلد /غلدر /غيلدر	Guilder	Price (currency)
لوس انجيليس /لوس انجيلس/لوس انجلوس/لوس انجليس	Los Angeles	Location
رقم الموبيل: ٥٧٥٦٤٥٣ / الجوال: ٥٧٥٦٤٥٣	Mobile no: 3546575	Phone number
جوهانسورغ /جوهانسوبورغ/جوهانسبرغ/ جوهانسبورغ	Johannesburg	Location

7.4 Typographic Variants

The extractor is capable of recognizing variations in written Arabic text for the various named entities being recognized. Table 4 contains some example NE indicating typographic variations.

7.5 Ambiguity

This commonly found problem in Arabic script is encountered within NERA when ambiguous matches are returned by different extractors. Table 5 shows some of the ambiguous situations that the system can handle. These situations can be handled by specifying a filter rule that gives preference on one extractor over the other.

Table 4. Examples of typographic variations in Arabic text

Arabic Ex.	English Trans.	Entity Type	Typographic variation
أستراليا/استراليا	Australia	Location	drop hamza (initially, medially, or finally)
السعوديه/السعودية	Saudi Arabia	Location	two dots removed from taa marbouta
ليرة/ليره	Lira	Price	Two dots inserted on final haa
آسيا/اسيا	Asia	Location	Drop of the madda from aleph
إلاربع/الأربع	4th	Date (day)	Hamza (below or above aleph)

Table 5. Ambiguous examples

Ambiguous Ex.	English Trans.	Incorrect	Correct
فرنك سويسري 1.6985	1.6985 Swiss Franc	Person	Price
١٥ رمضان الكريم ٢٠٠٥	15th of Ramadan Al karim 2005	Person	Date
جاسم المتحدة للعقارات والصيانة العامه	Jussim united for real estate and general maintenance	Person	Company
١,٥ بليون دولار سنغافورة	1.5 billion Singapore dollar	Location	Price
شركة أرامكو السعودية	Saudi Aramco	Location	Company
في المساء اليزابيث الثانية	In the evening Elizabeth II	Time	Person
نقطة تحول في سبتمبر سنة ... ١٩٥٤... قدم مارتن	...a turning point in September 1954 Martin presented...	Measurement	Date

8 Conclusion

The work done in this project is an attempt to broaden the coverage for entity extraction by incorporating the Arabic language, thereby paving the path towards enabling search solutions to the Arabian market. Various data collection techniques were used for acquiring dictionary name lists. The rule-based approach employed with great linguistic expertise provided a successful implementation of the NERA system by accomplishing challenges posed by Arabic language. Rules are capable of recognizing inflected forms by breaking them down into stems and affixes. A filtration mechanism is employed in the form of a rejecter within the grammar configuration that helps in deciding where a name ends and the non-name context begins. Further the intelligent use of filter rules helps in dealing with ambiguity between named entities. We have evaluated our system performance using a reference corpus that is tagged in a semi-automated way. The average Precision and Recall achieved by NERA extractors for each named entity type, against the reference corpora were satisfactory.

Acknowledgement

This work is funded by the "Named Entity Recognition for Arabic" joint project between The British Univ. in Duabi, Dubai, UAE and FAST search & Transfer Inc., Oslo, Norway. We thank the FAST team. In particular, we would like to thank Dr. Petra Maier and Dr. Jürgen Oesterle for their technical support. Any opinions, findings and conclusions or recommendations expressed in this material are the authors, and do not necessarily reflect those of the sponsor.

References

1. Sitter, A.D., Calders, T., Daelemans, W.: A Formal Framework for Evaluation of Information Extraction, University of Antwerp, Dept. of Mathematics and Computer Science, Technical Report, TR 2004-0. (2004),
   http://www.cnts.ua.ac.be/Publications/2004/DCD04
2. Eric, C., de Loupy, C.: Browsing Help for a Faster Retrieval. In: Coling2004 proceedings, Geneva, August 2004, pp. 576–582 (2004)
3. Samy, D., Moreno, A., Guirao, J.M.: A Proposal for an Arabic Named Entity Tagger Leveraging a Parallel Corpus. In: International Conference RANLP, Borovets, Bulgaria, pp. 459–465.
4. FAST ESP, http://www.fastsearch.com/thesolution.aspx?m=376
5. Frederic, G.: Research to Improve Cross-Language Retrieval – Position Paper for CLE. In: Peters, C. (ed.) CLEF 2000. LNCS, vol. 2069, pp. 83–88. Springer, Heidelberg (2001)
6. Zitouni, I., Sorensen, J., Luo, X., Florian, R.: The Impact of Morphological Stemming on Arabic Mention Detection and Coreference Resolution. In: Proceedings of the ACL workshop on Computational Approaches to Semitic Languages, 43rd Annual Meeting of the Association of Computational Linguistics (ACL2005), Ann Arbor, Michigan, USA, pp. 63–70 (2005)

7. Maloney, J., Niv, M.: TAGARAB: A Fast, Accurate Arabic Name Recogniser Using High Precision Morphological Analysis. In: Proceedings of the Workshop on Computational Approaches to Semitic Languages, Montreal, Canada, August, pp. 8–15 (1998)

8. Al-Sulaiti, L., Atwell, E.: Extending the Corpus of Contemporary Arabic. In: Proceedings of Corpus Linguistics conference 2005. University of Birmingham, UK (2005)

9. Larkey, L.S., Jaleel, N.A., Connell, M.: What's in a Name?: Proper Names in Arabic Cross Language Information Retrieval CIIR Technical Report IR-278 (2003)

10. Maamouri, M.: Language education and human development: Arabic diglossia and its impact on the quality of education in the Arab region. In: The Mediterranean Development Forum. The World Bank, Washington (1998)

11. Chinchor, N.: Overview of MUC-7. In: Proceedings of the Seventh Message Understanding Conference (MUC-7) (1998)

12. Abuleil, S.: Extracting Names from Arabic Text for Question-Answering Systems. In: Proceedings of Coupling approaches, coupling media and coupling languages for information retrieval (RIAO 2004), Avignon, France, pp. 638–647 (2004)

A Noun-Predicate Bigram-Based Similarity Measure for Lexical Relations

Hyopil Shin and Insik Cho

Computational Linguistics Lab., Dept. of Linguistics, Seoul National University
Sillim-dong, Gwanak-gu, Seoul, Korea
hpshin@snu.ac.kr, iaminsik@gmail.com

Abstract. The method outlined in this paper demonstrates that the information-theoretic similarity measure and noun-predicate bigrams are effective methods for creating lists of semantically-related words for lexical database work. Our experiments revealed that instead of serious syntactic analysis, bigrams and morpho-syntactic information sufficed for the feature-based similarity measure. We contend that our method would be even more appreciated if it applied to a raw newswire corpus in which unlisted words in existing dictionaries, such as recently-created words, proper nouns, and syllabic abbreviations, are prevailing.

Keywords: Semantically-related words, similarity measure, lexical relations, noun-predicate bigrams.

1 Introduction

In large scale lexical database work like WordNet, building word relations such as synonymy, hypernymy, and antonymy lies in the core part of the work. Most work usually takes advantage of existing resources such as lexicons, and thesauri, or starts from scratch, which inevitably demands a lot of human effort and time to develop. Manually compiled lexicons or thesauri include very infrequent usages in a particular corpus[1], and are prone to be dependent on theoretical considerations and human judgment.

There has been much research on the automatic clustering of related words for lexical database and thesaurus constructions. Especially, many approaches to automatic detection of similar words have been widely pursued. One of the similarity measures is based on the distributional hypothesis or the distributional pattern of words, in which words that occur in the same contexts tend to have similar meanings. This approach links the semantics of words with their syntactical behaviors. Similar to [2], [1] adopted a syntactic parser and extracted dependency triples from the text corpus. The dependency triples extracted from a corpus can be features of the heads and modifiers in the triples. Then the similarity between two words was calculated with the information-theoretic similarity measure [1] suggested. This similarity measure can be used in a number of different domains, but requires a large-scale parsed corpus and dependency triples as features.

A. Ranta, B. Nordström (Eds.): GoTAL 2008, LNAI 5221, pp. 452–463, 2008.

On the basis of the similarity measure, we designed a new method of retrieving lists of semantically-related words. Even though the similarity measure was originally intended for similar words, due to the consideration of syntactical structures as features, the measure also comes up with lists of various lexical relations including synonyms, antonyms, hypernyms and hyponyms. The similarity measure we developed, takes into account distributions of words with features from grammatical relations, thus syntactic commonality between two words are likely to affect various lexical relations.

Unlike [1] and [3], we did not take advantage of a parsed corpus for feature extraction. We only considered noun-predicate bigrams with simple morphological features. This is because in our Korean data, only a small syntactically annotated corpus was available and no reliable syntactic parsers were available at the moment. Instead of using a parsed corpus, we focused only on morphologically tagged corpus in which morphological features and language-specific features were annotated. In an agglutinative language or a morphologically rich language like Korean, morphemes carry various grammatical relations such as subject, object, and oblique arguments as well as basic morphological information. We assumed that in SOV languages, window of a predicate and its single left element would suffice for a similarity measurement. Unlike English in SVO pattern, -1 window word of a predicate can vary from a subject of an intransitive verb, an object of a transitive verb to other oblique arguments such as a postpositional phrase, *John-eykey* (*to John* as in English counterpart). Predicate modifiers like adverbials and even connective verbs for compound verbs can occur at the -1 position. We took into account only nouns with or without case markers at the position as features and incorporated them into the similarity measure.

In this paper, we compare the syntactic contexts-based similarity and the simple bigram-based approach. We, then, demonstrate that the latter takes advantage of small numbers of features coming from a simple morphological analysis and produces significant lists of semantically-related words in the case of Korean. We also contend that the method, suggested here can deal with newly created words and special forms of words such as syllabic abbreviations that largely occur in newspaper articles and are hardly captured by manual work. Thus this approach can be used for domain-specific vocabulary or ontology constructions as well as general lexicon work such as automatic thesaurus and WorldNet constructions.

2   Related Work

Similarity is widely used in natural language processing. Many similarity measures have been proposed, such as the dice coefficient [4], the cosine coefficient [4], the distance-based measurements [5], the feature contrast model [6] , and the information-theoretic measurement[1] and [3] [1]. We only investigate two syntactic contexts approaches based on feature calculations.

---

[1] [7] discussed two kinds of similarity, relational similarity and attributional similarity. We only focus on word similarity. Other similarity measures have also been widely pursed.

2.1 The Information-Theoretic Measurement

[1] reviewed various kinds of similarity measures and suggested the information-theoretic measures, which made use of a parser to extract dependency triples from the text corpus and regarded the dependency triples as features of the heads and modifiers in the triples. For example, (*avert* obj *duty*) is a dependency triple which means that *duty* is an object of *avert*. Table 1 shows a subset of the features of *duty* and *sanction*. An 'x' in the *duty* or *sanction* column means that the word possesses that feature [1].

Table 1. Features of *duty* and *sanction* from [1]

Feature	duty	sanction	$I(f_i)$
f_1: subj-of(include)	x	x	3.15
f_2: obj-of(assume)	x		5.43
f_3: obj-of(avert)	x	x	5.88
f_4: obj-of(ease)		x	4.99
f_5: obj-of(impose)	x	x	4.97
f_6: adj-mod(fiduciary)	x		7.76
f_7: adj-mod(punitive)	x	x	7.10
f_8: adj-mod(economic)		x	3.70

Here $F(w)$ is the set of features possessed by w, and the commonalities between two words w_1, w_2 is $F(w_1) \cap F(w_2)$. And the similarity between two words is calculated as follows:

$$\text{sim}(w_1, w_2) = \frac{2 \times I(F(w_1) \cap (F(w_2))}{I(F(w_1)) + I(F(w_2))} \quad (1)$$

$I(F)$ is the amount of information contained in a set of features F. Assuming that features are independent of one another, $I(F) = -\sum_{f \in F} \log P(f)$, where $P(f)$ is the probability of features. When two words have identical sets of features, the similarity reaches the maximum value of 1, and when two words do not have any common feature, the minimum similarity 0 is reached.

According to the result from the work, [1] argued that the output showed good performance and revealed quite reasonable pairs of respective nearest neighbors. For example, the pair *captive* and *westerner* was very useful since it was very unlikely that any manually created thesaurus would list them as near-synonyms.

Despite the result, the syntactic dependency-based method has drawbacks. First, it is not easy to get reliable dependency triple sets from a large corpus. As a corpus gets larger, a lot of computing time and resources are required for feature extractions. Next, it is not certain what kind of syntactic information will function as discriminators to detect distributional similarities. In this approach, grammatical information such as subject, object, adjective modifiers were used to measure distribution-based similarity. Also the probability estimators for features have two problems. First English NPs that are syntactic subjects are much more likely to be pronouns, while NPs that are syntactic objects are much more likely to be non-pronominal. According to [8] based on the Switchboard corpus, 91% of English subjects are pronouns and 9% are non-pronouns. Likewise 34% of objects are pronouns, and 66% of objects, non-pronouns. Thus 'subj-of', and 'obj-of' may not be good candidates for features since pronouns at the positions are likely to diminish distinctive functions of the features.

2.2 Syntactic Contexts with the Weighted Jaccard Measurement

[9] suggested the notion of syntactic context and presented how syntactic information could be used to extract semantic regularities of word sequences. Following [10] 'attributes' which are the syntactic contexts of a word, they extracted syntactic information and made syntactic context more elaborate than [1] and [3]. They applied various semantic extraction techniques to the Brazilian Portuguese corpus from NILC (Inter-institutional Center of Computational Linguistics-USP/Sao Carlos/Brazil). Similarity was computed by measuring the syntactic information shared by 12,359 different nouns on the basis of 32,293 different attributes.

One of the most salient attributes in [9] experiments must be the specific prepositions to measure word similarity. In a Portuguese example *autorização à empresa* (*permission to the company*), *empresa* (*company*) was extracted as the attribute of *autorização* (*permission*). Information about prepositions was taken into account since they convey important syntactic and semantic information. This observation is a language-specific condition in syntactic contexts, which was not taken into account in [1]'s approach. Along the same line, we incorporate postpositional structures (prepositional phrases in English counterparts) into our experiments.

Even though [9] and [1] are common in the syntactic-based approach, they used different similarity measures. Unlike [1], [9] introduced the weighted Jaccard measure. The measure considers a global and a local weight for each attribute. The global weight considers how many different words are associated with a given attribute, and the local weight is based on the frequency of the attribute with a given word. The whole weight is the multiplication of both weights. The following is the weighted Jaccard measure between two words m and n.

$$WJ(w_m, w_n) = \frac{\sum_j \min(W(w_m \cdot att_j), W(w_n \cdot att_j))}{\sum_j \max(W(w_m \cdot att_j), W(w_n \cdot att_j))} \qquad (2)$$

The similarity, based on the weighted Jaccard measure of two words in Korean, *haksaying* (*student*) and *emeni* (*mother*) is calculated as follows.

$$WJ(w_m, w_n) = \frac{0 + 0.30099}{0.30094 + 0.47707} \approx 0.3868 \qquad (3)$$

[9] insisted that a syntactic-based approach opened up a much wider range of more precise contexts than does a simple windows strategy. Nonetheless, we should point out that to get very elaborate syntactic contexts, we also need much more specific and complicated linguistic information. The syntactic-based strategy requires a part-of-speech tagger for morpho-syntactic categories and a parser for basic phrasal groups or chunks. Like [1], this approach requires very reliable syntactic analysis, which seems not to be available in some languages.

Table 2. The weighted Jaacard between two Korean words *student* and *mother*

word	*student* (w_m), total attributes 100			
	Verb(reln):*f*	freq	*gw(f)*	$W(w_m, f)$
set of features	find-of(sub)	2	0.99970	0.30094
	comeout(mod)	2	0.99989	0.30099
word	*mother* (w_n), total attributes 113			
	Verb(reln):*f*	freq	*gw(f)*	$W(w_n, f)$
set of features	find-of(sub)	1	0.99970	0
	comeout(mod)	3	0.99989	0.47707

3 Word Similarity between Syntactic Contexts and Noun-Predicate Bigrams

As pointed out in the previous section, there have been many approaches to automatic discoveries of word senses. Following the distributional hypothesis that words that occur in the same contexts tend to be similar, syntactic contexts for feature vectors combine with similarity measures. [1], [3] and [9] showed various syntactic contexts and elaborate feature sets from the context. Our approach, however, makes use of simple noun-predicate bigram contexts and small numbers of feature sets originating from morphological analysis.

To validate our method, we compared the two approaches in Korean. We set up two contexts for our experiments. In the first context, following [1], [3], and [9], we considered syntactic contexts for feature extractions in Korean texts. We adopted the Sejong Korean corpus, which was an output of the national corpus project initiated by the Korean government for 10 years. The second context made use of only morphological information, and the experiment did not take advantage of syntactic analysis at all. Only predicates and -1 window words as arguments were considered. We describe two experiments in the following sections.

3.1 Syntactic Contexts-Based Experiment in Korean

We took the parsed Sejong Korean corpus for syntactic context experiment, which consists of 150,000 words. We converted the parsed trees into dependency structures, then we extracted grammatical relation sets from nouns and their dependent structures. We considered nouns occurring more than 10 times and we got only 6,686 nouns. Among the grammatical relation sets, we considered only subject, object, and modifiers as features following [1] and [3]. We excluded some predicates such as *ha-* (*do*), *toy-* (*become*), *iss-* (*be*), *eps-* (*be not*), *kath-* (*be like*), etc. from feature sets, because the predicates can combine with many kinds of nouns, thus diminish similarity values. Table 3 shows the similarity values of *ekkay* (*shoulder*) and respective nearest neighbors on the basis of [1]'s information-theoretic similarity measure described in (1).

Although this example shows some related words like *leg*, *head*, *neck* with lower probabilities, the general output turned out to be poor. According to our manual evaluation, most words produced lists of words in which relations are hard to find.

Table 3. Similarity value of *ekkay* (*shoulder*) based on the information-theroretic similarity

Word	Similarity value	Respective nearest neighbors	Features
shoulder	0.179791	Leg	mod-of (father), obj-of (expose)
	0.139527	Head	obj-of (shake)
	0.110426	Neck	obj-of (expose)
	0.102633	New	obj-of (take)
	0.102408	Friend	obj-of (take)

Table 4. Similarity value of *ekkay* (*shoulder*) based on the weighted Jaccard measure

Word	Similarity value	Retrieved word	Features
shoulder	0.14478	Neck	obj-of (expose)
	0.136577	Head	obj-of (shake)

We also checked the syntactic context approach with another similarity measure, the weighted Jaccard similarity measure by [9]. The following table shows the similarity values from the measure.

The result from the weighted Jaccard measure produced only two related words. With this result, we cannot judge which similarity measure is better. The average number of predicate types of nouns is only 7.97, which is too small to have distinctive features. With the corpus of 150,000 words, we could not make sure that the syntactic context-based approach could really contribute to word similarity in the case of Korean. A larger parsed corpus or more reliable parsers are not currently available.

Also we should point out that some grammatical features such as oblique phrases or postpositional phrases which are usually realized as prepositional phrases in English should be considered in Korean. The oblique phrases, however, were unlikely to be included in dependent structures because many of them are not arguments, but adjuncts, and the adjunct phrases are likely to be ignored in the dependency triples. This weakens the syntactic contexts-based approach in Korean.

3.2 Noun-Predicate Bigram-Based Experiment in Korean

Instead of the parsed corpus, we used the morphologically tagged Sejong corpus which consists of about 8,800,000 running words. First we searched words with V and E tags for predicates and inflectional endings respectively. Following [11] for the validity of web counts for a range of predicate-argument bigrams and [12] for the asymmetry between a verb and its object for collocations, we investigated noun-predicate bigrams in Korean. We chose one previous word of the predicate (-1 window word) and the -1 window word varies from noun phrases with or without case markers to verbs with compounding endings. Table 5 shows categories of -1 window words and their frequencies.

Table 5. -1 window categories and their frequencies

-1 word category with markers	frequency
nouns with obj-marker	294,864
nouns with oblique-marker	192,441
Adverbials	161,134
nouns with subj-marker	125,556
verbs with adnominal inflection	96,932
bound nouns[2] without markers	68,349
nouns with non-grammatical markers	59,139
nouns without markers	52,727
adjectives with adnominal inflection	31,766
nouns with subj-complement marker	20,036

The most frequent element occurring right before a predicate is a noun with the object marker *ul/lul*, which shows an example of transitive verbs. The oblique elements occupy the second highest frequencies, but were totally ignored in the syntactic context approaches.

Considering the frequencies above, features were extracted from noun phrases with/without grammatical case makers for the experiment. Other noun phrases with non-grammatical markers were excluded, because those noun phrases can combine with almost all the predicates. Noun phrases without case markers are ambiguous in that they can be realized as various grammatical relations. We specified the phrases as NullRelations. A total of 80 features were set up for our experiment. Table 6 shows some of the features with frequencies.

Table 6. Features for the morphology-based experiment and frequencies

Features	Freq
JKS: subj-of (predicate)	3,245
JKO: obj-of (predicate)	4,746
JKB-kathi: prepositional phrase 'like-' in English	248
JKB-eykey: prepositional phrase 'to-' in English	45
JKB-wa: prepositional phrase 'with-' in English	2,338
JKB-ulose: prepositional phrase 'as-' in English	20
NullRelation: no case markers	5.653

Following [1]'s similarity measure, a total of 6,600 noun-predicate bigrams were calculated. The result showed much more coherent word lists than those from syntactic contexts in the table 3. For example, the top 10 related words with respect to *ekkay* (*shoulder*) are listed in (4) in English counterparts.

---

[2] Bound nouns, also called dependent nouns, cannot stand alone. They always form a noun phrase with a preceding modifying element such as a pronominal modifier.

(4)

```
back (0.2077), waist (0.1650), neck (0.1620), head
(0.156232), leg (0.146328), chest (0.144231), forehead
(0.143842), body (0.137493), knee (0.129336), arms
(0.125568)
```

The notable thing from this experiment is that the bigram approach produced various lexical relations or respective nearest neighbors according to [1]'s terminology. Also sister words which can be hyponyms of certain word were widely detected. In the above example (4), all the words except *body* have sister relations in terms of *shoulder* and the words can be hyponyms of the hypernym, *body-part*.

4 Evaluation

4.1 Evaluation for Recall

To evaluate the bigram context method, similar work using the same corpus is necessary. Unfortunately there has been no such kind work in Korean as of yet. Instead we compared our word lists with synonym or near-synonym lists from a Korean dictionary and English-Korean dictionaries such as 'Yonsei Korean dictionary, Gumseong English-Korean dictionary, and Minjung English-Korean dictionary'. 4,877 entries from three dictionaries were chosen and the total number of synonym lists of the entries was about 4,000,000 with the average 8.14 synonyms per word. Out of 4 million related words, 40% of words matched with our lists. Since our lists contain not only synonyms but also antonyms, sister words, and hypernyms, 40% recall for synonyms is promising. The following table shows recalls according to the frequencies of synonyms from the three dictionaries.

Words occurring over 80 times showed more than 90% recall. This suggests that higher frequency words would have more types of predicates, thus features from predicates would also be increased.

Table 7. Recalls related to the frequencies in synonyms from three dictionaries

freq	Word pairs in 3 dictionaries	extracted pairs	recall
20	13,629	10,607	0.778267
40	7,551	6.365	0.842935
60	5,192	4,575	0.881163
80	3,820	3,441	0.900785
100	2,993	2,738	0.914801
120	2,211	2,066	0.934419
140	1,828	1,723	0.94256
160	1,539	1,450	0.94217
180	1,249	1,190	0.952762
200	1,083	1,030	0.951062

4.2 Manual Evaluation

We also manually evaluated about 22% random samples (1,488 words) from the test data consisting of 6,686 words. We chose the top-15 pairs of each word and manually checked lexical relations. Table 8 is an example of *cilpyeng* (*disease*) with top-15 retrieved words and similarity values.

Table 8. The top-15 words pairs of *disease*

word	Retrieved words with English translations	Sim. value	Manual checking
cilpyeong (disease)	cilhwan (disease)	0.38	Syn
	wuycangpyeng (gastroenterological ailment)	0.29	Hypo
	pokthong (stomachache)	0.27	Hypo
	hwuyucung (sequela)	0.25	Hypo
	cungsey (symptom)	0.24	Rel
	am (cancer)	0.22	Hypo
	paykhyelpyeng (leukemia)	0.21	Hypo
	allergy	0.21	Hypo
	pwucakyong (side effect)	0.21	Rel
	chensik (asthma)	0.20	Hypo
	ceonyembyeng (epidemic)	0.20	Hypo
	tangnyopyeng (diabetes)	0.20	Hypo
	pwunyel (cleavage)	0.18	Not
	noilosey (neurosis)	0.19	Hypo
	pyenhyek (revolution)	0.19	Not

Among manually checked relations, 'rel' means another kind of relation other than 7 word relations adopted here. 'Not' specifies unrelated words. Even though manual evaluation is a notorious task due to discrepancies among human annotators, the example above reveals that retrieved words from the similarity measure are quite reasonable. Only two words have nothing to do with *disease* and many of them belong to the category of 'hyponymy'.

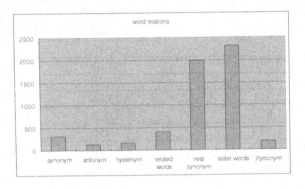

Fig. 1. Distributions of 7 relations

In our manual evaluation, 290 lexical items out of 1,488 do not have any lexical relations; all marked as 'not'. And the average number of relations per word is 3.70766 (24,7177%) in top-15 candidates. We set up 7 word relations including synonyms, antonyms, hypernyms, related words, near synonyms, sister words, and hyponyms. The distribution of the relation from manual checking is in Figure 1. Here, sister words are tentative candidates for hyponyms of a certain word. For example, the word *white* retrieves some color-based words like *green*, *red*, and *black*. Those words can be hyponyms of *color*. The sister words occupy the majority of lexical relations followed by near synonyms. This implies that our method can benefit hierarchical lexical work by linking sister words to the hypernym.

5 Discussion

Our experiment was based on the balanced corpus, called the Sejong Korean corpus. To validate our method and to check whether or not the method is corpus-sensitive, we conducted an experiment on the raw Korean newswire corpus, 'Hankyelye'. The corpus consists of newspaper articles over three years from 2001 to 2003. As a testbed we select some portions of the corpus, so 47,084,285 words and 4,316,876 bigrams were extracted, which was almost 6 times bigger than the Sejong corpus in size (8,800,000 words) and about 4.5 times bigger in the numbers of bigrams. The total number of extracted features is 43,313, which is about 1/100 size of the whole words. Since it is a raw corpus, we performed morphological analysis and repeated the same procedure for the experiment.

The result seemed to retrieve even more interesting lists of words than using the Sejong corpus. Instead of specifying detailed evaluations, we point out some notable facts from the experiment. Due to the properties of the newswire, retrieved lists of words contain lots of recently-created words, compound nouns, proper nouns, organizations, and syllabic abbreviations, which are unlikely to be listed in the existing lexicon. For example, *sonposa* is a syllabic abbreviation of **sonhaypohemsa** (*property insurance company*). This word widely appears in newspaper articles, but not in the dictionaries. Our method retrieved the following lists of words with similarity values.

```
(5) sonposa: sayngposa (0.14, life insurance company),
sicwungunhayng (0.10,general bank), pohemsa (0.10,
insurance company), yenlyengday (0.09, age)
```

Here *sayngposa* is also a syllabic abbreviation of **sayngmyengpohemsa**(*life insurance company*). This method enables us to reinforce many unlisted words and their relations in lexicon work. Also the wide coverage of lexicon can contribute to advanced NLP systems such as word sense disambiguation, information retrieval or search systems using lexical relations.

The final thing we need to mention is the size of the corpus and the numbers of features for this method. The features in this approach are extracted from a predicate and its noun arguments. We generally expect that the bigger corpus would have more predicates and arguments, thus more distinctive features would appear. Although our experiments with 8,800,000 and 47,084,285 words turned out to be a good size, the lower bound of the size for quality considerations should be carefully investigated.

The table 7 in 4.1 shows proportional frequencies to recalls. According to the table, words occurring over 80 times show more than 90% recalls. This implies that infrequent words are less likely to be captured as lexical relations. We should think about the threshold of the corpus size and frequencies of words.

6 Future Work and Conclusions

The method outlined in this paper demonstrates that the information-theoretic similarity measure and noun-predicate bigrams are effective methods for creating lists of semantically-related words for lexical database work. Our experiments revealed that instead of serious syntactic analysis, bigrams and morpho-syntactic information sufficed for the feature-based similarity measure. We contend that our method would be even more appreciated if it applied to a raw and a large-scale corpus such as newswire data. As seen in previous sections, various relations of unlisted lexical items were well captured.

The lists of semantically-related words, however, do not identify the relation of the included items. The lists still contain uncommon words as well as related words. At present, we manually validate retrieved words, thus automatic word clustering is required. There have been many approaches to word clustering, but most of them benefit from existing resources such as Roget's thesaurus, and WordNet[13], which hampers further research when the resources are not available. We are developing ways to significantly improve automatic word clustering within the semantically-related lists without largely resorting to the resources.

References

1. Lin, D.: An Information-Theoretic Definition of Similarity. In: Proceedings of ICML-1998. Madison, Wisconsin (1998a)
2. Alshawi, H., Carter, D.: Training and Scaling Preference Functions for Disambiguation. Computational Linguistics 20(4), 635–648 (1994)
3. Lin, D.: Automatic Retrieval and Clustering of Similar Words. In: Proceedings of COLINGACL 1998, pp. 768–774 (1998b)
4. Frakes, W.B., Baeza-Yates, R. (eds.): Information Retrieval, Data Structure and Algorithms. Prentice-Hall, Englewood Cliffs (1992)
5. Rada, R., Mili, H., Bicknell, E., Blettner, M.: Development and Application of a Metric on Semantic Nets. IEEE Transaction on Systems, Man, and Cybernetics 19(1), 17–30 (1989)
6. Tversky, A.: Features of similarity. Psychological Review 84, 327–352 (1977)
7. Turney, P.D.: Similarity of Semantic Relations. Computational Linguistics 32(3), 379–416 (2006)
8. Francis, H.S., Gregory, M.L., Michaelis, L.A.: Are Lexical Subjects Deviant? CLS-1999. University of Chicago (1999)
9. Gasperin, C., Gamallo, P., Agustini, A., Lopes, G., de Lima, V.: Using Syntactic Contexts for Measuring Word Similarity. In: Workshop on Knowledge Acquisition and Categorization, ESSLLI 2001 (2001)

10. Grefenstette, G.: Explorations in Automatic Thesaurus Discovery. Kluwer Academic Publishers, USA (1994)
11. Lapata, M., Keller, F.: Web-based Models for Natural Language Processing. ACM Transactions on Speech and Language Processing 2(1), 1–30 (2005)
12. Tapanainen, P., Piitulainen, J., Jarvinen, T.: Idiomatic Object Usage and Support Verbs. In: COLINGACL 1998 (1998)
13. Ide, N.: Making Senses: Bootstrapping Sense-tagged Lists of Semantically-Related Words. In: Gelbukh, A. (ed.) CICLing 2006. LNCS, vol. 3878. Springer, Heidelberg (2006)

German Compounds in Factored Statistical Machine Translation

Sara Stymne

Department of Computer and Information Science
Linköping University
Sweden
sarst@ida.liu.se

Abstract. An empirical method for splitting German compounds is explored by varying it in a number of ways to investigate the consequences for factored statistical machine translation between English and German in both directions. Compound splitting is incorporated into translation in a preprocessing step, performed on training data and on German translation input. For translation into German, compounds are merged based on part-of-speech in a postprocessing step. Compound parts are marked, to separate them from ordinary words. Translation quality is improved in both translation directions and the number of untranslated words in the English output is reduced. Different versions of the splitting algorithm performs best in the two different translation directions.

1 Introduction

Compounding in German is productive and very common. Compounds are written without spaces or word boundaries. In statistical machine translation compounds lead to sparse data problems, increasing the number of unseen words. For translation into German it is a problem since several English words can be translated as distinct words rather than as a compound. To deal with these issues, compounds can be split into their component parts prior to training and translation, and for translation into German merged back together.

This study investigates how different compound splitting strategies influence factored phrase-based statistical machine translation (PBSMT). Translation between German and English is explored in both directions. An empirical method for compound splitting is used, which only requires a mono-lingual corpus and a part-of-speech (POS) tagger. Compound splitting and merging are performed as pre and postprocessing steps of the factored PBSMT system. Contrary to previous studies, parts of the split compounds are marked as such, to distinguish them from other words, since the semantics of compounds are not always compositional. Compounds are merged using a novel strategy based on part-of-speech.

Compound splitting is evaluated both on one-to-one correspondence with English and on translation quality. The main aims are to explore marked compound splitting and to find out which versions of an empirical compound splitting method give best results for translation of sentences in both directions between English and German in a factored PBSMT system.

A. Ranta, B. Nordström (Eds.): GoTAL 2008, LNAI 5221, pp. 464–475, 2008.

2   Compounding

German compounds are formed by joining words without spaces or word boundaries. In addition, so called filler letters can occur between words, letters can be removed at the end of all but the last part of a compound, *umlaut* can be used, and there might be combinations of these. The term compound suffixes (*Kompositionssuffixen*) is used to describe these changes in [1], that also gives an overview of compound forms that occur in German noun compounds, based on a corpus study, summarized in Table 1.

Table 1. Compound suffixes in German

Type	Suffixes	Example
None		Risikokapital (Risiko + Kapital) *risk capital*
Additions	*-s -n -en -nen* *-e -es -er -ien*	Arbeitsplatz (Arbeit + Platz) *Place of employment*
Truncations	*-e -en -n*	Südwesten (Süden + Westen) *south-west*
Combinations	*-us/-en -um/-en -um/-a* *-a/-en -on/-en -on/-a* *-e/-i*	Museenverwaltung (Museum + Verwaltung) *Museum management*
Umlaut	*umlaut + -er*	Völkermord (Volk + Mord) *genocide*

3   Related Work

German compounds in SMT have been addressed in a number of papers, (see e.g. [2,3,4]).

Translation into English is explored in [2], that use an empirical method where words are split in all possible parts, and for each part a check is performed against a monolingual corpus if it exists as an individual word. Additions of *-s* and *-es* are allowed to occur at all split points. A number of versions of the algorithm are tested in order to choose the correct splitting options, based on word frequencies, POS or bilingual alignment information. They find that an eager splitting method, choosing the splitting option with the highest number of splits, gives best translation results for PBSMT, despite having low precision and recall on one-to-one correspondence. A frequency-based ranking method based on the geometric mean of word frequencies gives similar results for PBSMT. Compound splitting also improves the translation quality of a word-based SMT system. In this case using the geometric mean gives the best result, and the eager method gives worse result than no splitting at all. The systems are evaluated on NP/PPs, not on full sentences.

The same algorithm and in addition a rule-based method is used in [3]. In addition splitting is used only to improve word alignments. Both methods lead to improved translation quality. Both [2] and [3] integrate compound splitting by preprocessing training data and the text to be translated. No marking of compounds is used; the parts are treated as normal words.

In [3], compound splitting is also used for translation into German. They use the frequency-based version of the algorithm of [2] as in the other translation direction, and then merge compounds in a postprocessing step. The merging is based on two lists compiled from the German training corpus, a list of compounds and a list of compound components. If a word in the output is a compound component, they check if this word merged with the next is in the compound list, if it is, it is merged. A drawback of this method is that it only merges known compounds.

In addition [3] experiments with joining of English compounds based on POS or alignment data. All these methods lead to improved translation quality.

In [4], marking of split compounds is used in a factored PBSMT system with morphologically enriched POS-tags for German. A modified version of the splitting algorithm of [2] is used, which improved translation quality.

4   Processing of German Compound Words

German compounds are split in a preprocessing step and merged in a postprocessing step of translation.

4.1   Splitting Compounds

The splitting algorithm used in this study is the algorithm presented in [2], with a few modifications. Words are split in all possible places and a splitting option is chosen based on word frequencies from a monolingual corpus. The monolingual corpus is German Europarl text [5], with 1,467,291 sentences. It is POS-tagged and lemmatized using TreeTagger [6]. For the default algorithm the following changes from [2] have been made:

- The arithmetic mean of frequencies is used as default, rather than the geometric mean, in order to get more splits.
- Compound parts have to be of minimum three letters length.
- Words to be split are limited to content words: nouns, adjectives, adverbs and verbs. Proper names are, however, not split, since translating them in parts generally would give rise to errors.
- The last part of the compound must have the same POS as the full compound.
- The full list of compound suffixes in Table 1, except *umlaut*, is used
- In addition to surface form, lemmas are also used to calculate word frequencies. The reason for this is that compound parts often have the base form.
- Hyphenated words can only be split at hyphens.

The algorithm is varied by changing a number of parameters:

- The minimum length of words to be split and of compound parts is changed to 8 and 4 respectively.
- The scoring method is changed. In place of the arithmetic mean, the geometric mean of word frequencies is used or an eager method which choose the maximum number of parts. (These two methods are similar to the eager and frequency-based methods of [2])
- The number of parts per compound are restricted to maximum two and maximum two for all POS except nouns.
- All compound suffixes listed in Table 1, except *umlaut* are used, or only the 4 most common in the corpus study of [1], addition of *-s, -n, -en* or *-nen*.
- The restriction that the POS of the last part has to match the POS of the full compound is not used.

The splitting methods are summarized in Table 2. The methods differ in how many compounds they split, and in how many parts they split words, as is shown in Table 3, for the test text with a total of 55,580 words. The differences are large, with more than three times as many splits for the eager system as for the system with only common compound suffixes.

Table 2. Summary of the splitting options. The default method is shown with all settings, the other methods only show what differs from the default method.

Splitting	Word length	Part length	Scoring	No. of parts	Suffixes	POS match
default	6	3	arithm.	unlimited	all	yes
l8-s3	8					
l8-s4	8	4				
geom			geom.			
eager			eager			
nn2+				noun > 2		
max2				max 2		
common					common	
anypos						no

As pointed out in [2], parts of compounds do not always have the same meaning as when they stand alone. As an example they mention *Grundrechte* ('basic rights'), where the first part, *Grund*, usually translates as *foundation*, which is wrong in this compound.

To address this issue all compound parts but the last are marked with the symbol '#'. They are thus handled as separate words. Marking of parts also means that they can keep their compound form, since they are not treated as normal words. If marking were not used it would be desirable to remove or add compound suffixes, as is done to a certain extent in [7].

Parts of split words also receive a special POS-tag, based on the POS of the last word of the compound, and the last part receives the same POS as the full word. (1) shows an example of a split word.

Table 3. Number of compounds found in the test text for the different methods, showing both total, and number of parts per split compound

Method	Total	2	3	4	5+
default	4862	3642	971	211	38
l8-s3	4624	3404	971	211	38
l8-s4	2985	2674	294	17	–
geom	3689	3063	534	74	18
eager	7729	4539	2050	788	352
nn2+	4693	3776	709	171	37
max2	4383	4383	–	–	–
common	2542	2303	228	11	–
anypos	6739	4691	1606	356	86

(1)   Regierungskonferenz NN (*intergovernmental conference*) ⇒
Regierungs# NN-FL + Konferenz NN

4.2   Merging Compounds

For translation into German a postprocessing step is performed where compounds are merged. Since a factored translation system is used, merging can be based on POS. If a word has a compound-POS, and the following word has a matching POS, they are merged. If the next POS is a conjunction, a hyphen is added to the word, allowing for coordinated compounds as in (2). Else the compound markup is simply removed. The POS-based algorithm has the advantage that it can merge unseen compounds and handle coordinated compounds.

(2)   Wasser- und Bodenqualität
water and soil quality

4.3   Integration with Translation

The MT system used is a factored PBSMT system. In a factored system translation is not only based on surface form, but other features such as POS or lemma can be used in addition in different phases of translation (see [8]). The current system uses POS as an output factor, and two sequence models, a 5-gram language model and a 7-gram POS-model, see Fig. 1. The Moses toolkit [9] is used for decoding and training, SRILM [10] for sequence models and Giza++ [11] for creating word alignments. Minimum error rate training [12] is used for tuning of feature weights. In addition German contracted prepositions and determiners are split in a preprocessing step, and for translation into German merged in connection with true casing by running a second Moses instance.

All corpora are European Parliament texts [5]. The size of the corpora are 439,513 sentences for training, 600 sentences for tuning and 2000 sentences for testing[1].

---

[1] The test set is *test2007* from the ACL 2008 Workshop on Statistical Machine Translation, http://www.statmt.org/wmt08/shared-task.html

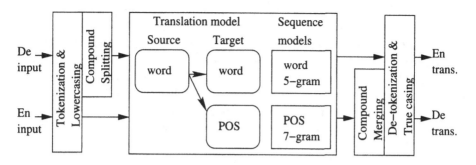

Fig. 1. Architecture of the factored system

Compound splitting is integrated in a preprocessing step for training and for translation from German. Compounds are split using the different versions of the splitting algorithm described in Sec. 4.1. For translation into German, compounds are merged in a postprocessing step.

5   Evaluation

The nine splitting methods described in Sec. 4.1 are compared to each other and to a baseline without splitting (*raw*) for one-to-one correspondence with English and for translation quality.

5.1   One-to-One Correspondence

To measure one-to-one correspondence I followed the evaluation method described in [2]. One-to-one correspondence occurs when the words in a German compound are translated as separate content words in English. In addition there

Table 4. One-to-one correspondence of split compounds compared to a manually annotated gold standard for the different splitting methods

Method	Correct		Wrong			Metrics		
	split	not	not	faulty	split	prec.	recall	acc.
raw	0	5000	174	0	0	–	0.0%	**96.6%**
default	99	4504	22	52	323	20.9%	57.2%	92.1%
l8-s3	99	4530	22	52	297	22.1%	57.2%	92.6%
l8-s4	120	4692	36	17	135	**44.1%**	69.3%	96.2%
geom	109	4614	33	31	213	30.9%	63.0%	94.5%
eager	43	4243	18	112	584	5.8%	24.9%	85.7%
nn2+	99	4521	24	50	306	21.8%	57.2%	92.4%
max2	133	4546	29	11	281	31.3%	**76.9%**	93.6%
common	99	4714	58	16	113	43.4%	57.2%	**96.3%**
anypos	99	4310	10	64	517	14.6%	57.2%	88.2%

can be inserted function words. As an example *Medienfreiheit* is in one-to-one correspondence with *freedom of the media*, since the two German parts *Medien* and *Freiheit* corresponds to two separate words, *media* and *freedom*. The lack of correspondence of the two function words, *of the*, is not considered.

A gold standard was created by manually annotating the first 5000 words of the test text for one-to-one correspondence with the English reference text. Out of the 5000 words, 174 were compounds in one-to-one correspondence with English.

The results of the one-to-one evaluation is shown in Table 4. The same categories and metrics as in [2] are used:

correct split: words that were correctly split
correct not: words that should not be split and were not
wrong not: words that should be split but were not
wrong faulty: words that were split but in an incorrect way
wrong split: words that should not be split but were
precision: (correct split) / (correct split + wrong faulty + wrong split)
recall: (correct split) / (correct split + wrong faulty + wrong not)
accuracy: (correct) / (correct + wrong)

The splitting options have their strengths on different metrics, with three different methods having the best results for the three metrics used.

Compared to the default method it can be seen that both imposing length restrictions and using the geometric mean increases the results on all three metrics. Limiting the number of parts makes a minor difference when nouns are excluded, but gives the highest recall when used for all POS. Using only common compound suffixes gives higher precision, whereas not using the POS restriction on the last word gives lower precision. No splitting actually gives the highest accuracy.

The largest error category is wrong splits. The splits in this category are reasonable, in the sense that all parts are meaningful German words, even if they are not in one-to-one correspondence with English. As an example, of the 323 wrong splits for the default system, 234 (72,5%) are reasonable. The erroneous splits often have parts that are common words such as *ich* ('I') and *ist* ('is').

Compared to [2], the two similar systems, eager and geom, have lower results on all metrics. This might in part be due to other changes made to the algorithm, such as allowing more compound suffixes, but can also be because these algorithms make more mistakes on full sentences than on NP/PPs.

5.2   Translation Quality

Translation quality is measured against one reference translation, using three metrics, BLEU [13], NIST [14] and METEOR [15].[2]

---

[2] The evaluation is case-sensitive. %BLEU and %METEOR notation is used. METEOR is used with the "exact" and "porter stem" modules, the WordNet-based modules for English are not used.

German ⇒ English

The results for translation from German into English can be seen in Table 5[3]. All systems with compound splitting get higher NIST and METEOR scores than the raw system, but only the geom system has a higher BLEU score than the raw system. The geom system, which is similar to the frequency-based system, that performed well in [2], has the highest score for all metrics. The eager system, however, performs poorly. This is probably because it makes more mistakes when used on full sentences than on only NP/PPs.

Table 5. Translation results for German ⇒ English

Method	BLEU	NIST	METEOR
raw	26.29	6.888	52.27
default	26.12	6.915	52.62
l8-s3	26.13	6.920	52.61
l8-s4	26.20	6.935	52.61
geom	**26.35**	**6.945**	**52.79**
eager	25.88	6.898	52.45
nn2+	26.10	6.923	52.61
max2	26.23	6.934	52.67
common	26.22	6.944	52.54
anypos	26.12	6.920	52.59

Two other systems that perform reasonably well are the systems with common compound suffixes and maximum 2 splits. Of these the common system has high precision and accuracy on the one-to-one evaluation and the max2 has high recall. Limiting the length of both words to be split and compound parts gives rise to small improvements in BLEU and NIST.

One improvement that can be seen in the systems with split compounds is that the number of untranslated words is reduced by more than half. The raw system has 733 untranslated words (1.25%), compared to 360 words (0.61%) in the geom system. Of the untranslated words in the geom system 45 (12.5%) are marked compound parts, which could possibly have been translated if marking were not used. Among the other untranslated words there are many proper names and unsplit compounds. The translation example in Table 6 shows an example of a sentence where the systems that split compounds, exemplified by geom, manages to translate a compound that is untranslated by the raw system.

English ⇒ German

The result for translation from German into English can be seen in Table 7. In this direction the systems with splitting had higher scores than the raw system

---

[3] As [3] note, only a small percentage of words are affected by compound splitting so significant changes in error measures can not be expected.

Table 6. Sample translation for German ⇒ English with and without compound splitting

Sentence type	Example
De original	... der Koordinierung der Außen- und **Sicherheitspolitiken**...
De preprocessed	... der koordinierung der außen- und **sicherheits# politiken**...
En with splitting	... the coordination of the foreign and **security policies**...
En without splitting	... the coordination of the foreign and **sicherheitspolitiken**...
En reference	... to coordinate the common foreign and **security policies**...

for all metrics and systems, except the eager system for BLEU. The eager system had the worst performance of the systems with splitting in this translation direction as well.

The best scoring systems in this direction are not the same as in the opposite direction. The default system and nn2+ had the highest scores. These systems have lower precision, just over 20%, on the one-to-one evaluation, than the systems that performed best in the opposite direction.

In this direction, imposing length limits on words to be split and compound parts led to worse translation results, as opposed to the other direction where it improved the results.

An example where the systems that split compounds handle compounds better can be seen in Table 8, exemplified by the default system. The default system manages to produce the desired compound, whereas the raw system produces two nouns instead.

Table 7. Translation results for English ⇒ German

Method	BLEU	NIST	METEOR
raw	19.31	5.727	26.53
default	**19.73**	**5.854**	27.05
l8-s3	19.63	5.833	27.02
l8-s4	19.56	5.821	26.96
geom	19.64	5.818	26.95
eager	19.16	5.788	26.75
nn2+	19.71	5.850	**27.07**
max2	19.66	5.837	26.98
common	19.67	5.824	27.03
anypos	19.62	5.853	27.01

Table 8. Sample translation for German ⇒ English with and without compound splitting

Sentence type	Example
En original	...of the **national states** than to represent genuine progress...
De with splitting	...der|art **national#|nn-fl staaten|nn** als|kokom echte|adja fortschritte|nn zu|ptkzu machen|vvfin...
De with splitting, postprocessed	...der **Nationalstaaten** als echte Fortschritte zu vertreten...
De without splitting	...von den **Nationalen Staaten** als echte Fortschritte zu machen...
De reference	...der Nationalstaaten zu bekräftigen, als dass sie einen wirklichen Fortschritt darstellt...

5.3 Discussion

The methods that improved translation quality most were different in the two translation directions. A method using the geometric mean of word frequencies performs best for translation into English, and limiting the number of splits to two and only using common compound suffixes also performs well. Methods using the arithmetic mean of word frequencies, and limiting the number of splits to two for all words but nouns worked best for translation into German. Limiting the number of compound suffixes gives good results in both directions.

Generally systems with more total splits perform better for translation into German, and systems with fewer splits perform better for translation into English.

One-to-one correspondence does not seem to be a good indicator for judging if a splitting method will improve PBSMT. In part this could be explained by the fact that the PBSMT system aligns word sequences, and thus can rejoin split words in the translation model. Another reason can be that a larger number of splits increases the chance of splitting unseen compounds into known parts at translation time.

Since compounds only make up a small proportion of all words the differences found between systems were small in many cases. Human analysis of translation output will be needed to shed further light on these small improvements. A small qualitative study of compound translation for a system using a similar splitting method indicates that translation of compounds is improved by splitting compounds [4].

6 Conclusion

A number of versions of an empirical compound splitting method have been explored for translation between German and English in both directions. Incorporating them into a factored translation system and marking compounds did give a small improvement of translation quality. Particularly the number of untranslated words are reduced by approximately half for translation into English. However, marking does lead to a small number of untranslated compound parts.

As in previous work, methods with high scores on metrics for one-to-one correspondence with English did not give the best translation results for German to English. This study shows that the same holds for translation in the opposite direction.

This study has also indicated that to achieve good translation results splitting should not necessarily be performed using the same method for translation in different directions.

Some of the methods that worked well have not yet been tried in combination, which would be interesting in future work. The methods can also be expected to work well for other compounding languages, such as Swedish or Italian.

References

1. Langer, S.: Zur Morphologie und Semantik von Nominalkomposita. In: Tagungsband der 4. Konferenz zur Verarbeitung natürlicher Sprache, pp. 83–97 (1998)
2. Koehn, P., Knight, K.: Empirical methods for compound splitting. In: Proceedings of the tenth conference of EACL, Budapest, Hungary, pp. 187–193 (2003)
3. Popović, M., Stein, D., Ney, H.: Statistical machine translation of German compound words. In: Proceedings of FinTAL - 5th International Conference on Natural Language Processing, Turku, Finland, pp. 616–624 (2006)
4. Stymne, S., Holmqvist, M., Ahrenberg, L.: Effects of morphological analysis in translation between German and English. In: Proceedings of the Third ACL Workshop on Statistical Machine Translation, Columbus, Ohio (2008)
5. Koehn, P.: Europarl: A parallel corpus for statistical machine translation. In: Proceedings of MT Summit X, Phuket, Thailand, pp. 79–86 (2005)
6. Schmid, H.: Probabilistic part-of-speech tagging using decision trees. In: Proceedings of the International Conference on New Methods in Language Processing, Manchester, UK, pp. 44–49 (1994)
7. Holmqvist, M., Stymne, S., Ahrenberg, L.: Getting to know Moses: Initial experiments on German-English factored translation. In: Proceedings of the Second Workshop on Statistical Machine Translation, Prague, Czech Republic, pp. 181–184 (2007)
8. Koehn, P., Hoang, H.: Factored translation models. In: Proceedings of the Joint Conference on Empirical Methods in Natural Language Processing and Computational Natural Language Learning, Prague, Czech Republic, pp. 868–876 (2007)
9. Koehn, P., Hoang, H., Birch, A., Callison-Burch, C., Federico, M., Bertoldi, N., Cowan, B., Shen, W., Moran, C., Zens, R., Dyer, C., Bojar, O., Constantin, A., Herbst, E.: Moses: Open source toolkit for statistical machine translation. In: Proceedings of the 45th Annual Meeting of the ACL, demonstration session, Prague, Czech Republic, pp. 177–180 (2007)
10. Stolcke, A.: SRILM - an extensible language modeling toolkit. In: Proceedings of the International Conference on Spoken Language Processing (ICSLP), Denver, Colorado, pp. 901–904 (2002)
11. Och, F.J., Ney, H.: A systematic comparison of various statistical alignment models. Computational Linguistics 29(1), 19–51 (2003)

12. Och, F.J.: Minimum error rate training in statistical machine translation. In: Proceedings of the 41st Annual Meeting of ACL, Sapporo, Japan, pp. 160–167 (2003)
13. Papineni, K., Roukos, S., Ward, T., Zhu, W.J.: BLEU: a method for automatic evaluation of machine translation. In: Proceedings of the 40th Annual Meeting of the ACL, Philadelphia, Pennsylvania, pp. 311–318 (2002)
14. Doddington, G.: Automatic evaluation of machine translation quality using n-gram co-occurrence statistics. In: Proceedings of the Second International Conference on Human Language Technology Research, San Diego, California, pp. 138–145 (2002)
15. Lavie, A., Agarwal, A.: METEOR: An automatic metric for MT evaluation with high levels of correlation with human judgments. In: Proceedings of the Second Workshop on Statistical Machine Translation, Prague, Czech Republic, pp. 228–231 (2007)

A Reordering Model for Phrase-Based Machine Translation

Vinh Van Nguyen, Thai Phuong Nguyen, Akira Shimazu, and Minh Le Nguyen

Japan Advanced Institute of Science and Technology
1-1, Asahidai, Nomi, Ishikawa, 923-1292, Japan
{vinhnv,thai,shimazu,nguyenml}@jaist.ac.jp

Abstract. This paper presents a new method for reordering in phrase based statistical machine translation (PBSMT). Our method is based on previous chunk-level reordering methods for PBSMT. Our method is a global reordering. First, we parse the source language sentence to a chunk tree, according to the method developed by [1]. Second, we apply a series of transformation rules, which are learnt automatically from the parallel corpus to the chunk tree over chunk level. Finally, we solve phenomena for the overlapping of phrases and chunks, and integrate a global reordering model directly in a decoder as a graph of phrases. The experimental results with English-Vietnamese and English-French pairs show that our method outperforms the baseline PBSMT in both accuracy and speed.

Keywords: Natural Language Processing, Machine Translation, Phrase-based Statistical Machine Translation.

1 Introduction

In machine translation, the reordering problem (global reordering) is one of the major problems, since different languages have different word order requirements. The statistical machine translation task can be viewed as consisting of two sub-tasks: predicting the collection of words in a translation, and deciding the order of the predicted words (reordering problem). Currently, phrase-based statistical machine translation [2,3] is the state-of-the-art of SMT, and uses widely distance-based reordering constraints such as IBM constraints [4], ITG constraints [5,4] and distortion limit [2]. With these models, PBSMT usually is powerful in word reordering within a short distance, however, long distance reordering is still problematic. A main criticism of PBSMT is that it does not make use of any linguistic information, while in linguistic theory, reorderings between linguistic phrases in different language pairs are well described.

In order to tackle the long distance reordering problem, in recent years, huge research efforts have been conducted using syntactic information. [6] shows significant improvement by keeping the strengths of phrases, while incorporating syntax into PBSMT. Some approaches have been applied at the word level [7]. They are particularly useful for language with rich morphology, for reducing data sparseness. Other kinds of syntax reordering methods require parsed trees,

A. Ranta, B. Nordström (Eds.): GoTAL 2008, LNAI 5221, pp. 476–487, 2008.

such as the work in [8,7,9]. The parsed tree is more powerful in capturing the sentence structure. However, it is expensive to create tree structure, and building a good quality parser is also a hard task. All the above approaches require much decoding time, which is expensive.

With PBSMT, the decoder takes much computation time because the reordering of phrases (many possible reorderings) is implemented in the decoding process. Therefore, the approach we are interested in here is to balance quality of translation and decoding time. Consequently, we use an intermediate syntax between POS tag and parse tree: *chunks* and *phrases*, as the basic units for reordering. An advantage of *chunks* is closer to *phrases* in PBSMT.

In this paper, we also focus on researching the ordering problem, and aim to improve both the quality of translation and computation time for decoding. Our method is a global reordering, and based on previous chunk-level reordering methods for PBSMT. First, we parse the source language sentence to a chunk tree. Second, we apply a series of transformation rules which are learnt automatically from the parallel corpus to the chunk tree over chunk level. Third, we solve phenomena for the overlapping phrases and chunks and integrate a global reordering model directly in the decoder, as a graph of phrases. Finally, we find the best translation sentence in this graph.

The rest of this paper is structured as follows. Section 2 reviews related works. Section 3 briefly introduces PBSMT. Section 4 introduces how to apply transformation rules to chunks, and how to deal with overlapping phrases and chunks. Section 5 briefly introduces the steps for generating a reordering graph of phrases. Section 6 describes and discusses the experimental results. Finally, conclusions are given in Section 7.

2   Related Work

To solve the reordering problem, [10] used a lexicalized reordering model as a feature in the log linear model of PBMT. However, their experiment showed that the lexicalized reordering model is not sufficient powerful to correctly guide long distance movements.

[7] presented a reordering model based on clause restructuring. They used this model in the preprocessing step of the PBSMT system. The weakness of this approach is that rewriting the input sentence, whether using syntactic rules or heuristics makes hard decisions that can not be undone by the decoder, because this model just applies to the preprocessing step. Hence, reordering is better handled during the search algorithm, and as part of the optimization function.

[11,12] applied Maximum Entropy (ME) model for phrase reordering. They used ME for estimating distortion probability. However, estimation is local, because the next phrase only depends on the current phrase. So, as a result, their systems are not robust to unseen phrases.

Several methods proposed use syntactic information to handle the reordering problem. Methods by [8,9], include tree-to-string translation rules extracted from parallel corpus with linguistic annotations. However, there are some problems with syntax-based models. The first one is the expense of computational time for decoding, because the source sentence or target sentence must be parsed to a tree. The second problem is that tree-to-string rules fail for non-syntactic phrase pairs (phrase pairs that are not subsumed by any syntax tree fragments (subtree)) because they require a syntax tree fragment over the phrase to be parsed. For example: a phrase pair for English - Japanese: "the teacher is" and "sensei wa" is a non-syntactic phrase pair, because "the teacher is" and "sensei wa" are not subsumed by syntax subtree.

Note that these models have radically different structures and parameterizations than phrase-based models for PBSMT.

[13] proposed a strategy to reorder a source sentence using rules based on syntactic chunks. This strategy demonstrated promising results when compared with the state of the art phrase-based system [2], in particular regarding computational time. Nguyen's strategy only reordered the phrases within each chunk of sentence, however. In other words, the chunks of a sentence were not reordered.

3   Brief Description of the Baseline Phrase-Based SMT

In this section, we will describe the phrase-based SMT system which was used for our experiments.

Phrase-based SMT, as described by [2], translates a source sentence into a target sentence by decomposing the source sentence into a sequence of source phrases, which can be any contiguous sequences of words (or tokens treated as words) in the source sentence. For each source phrase, a target phrase translation is selected, and the target phrases are arranged in some order to produce the target sentence. A set of possible translation candidates created in this way is scored according to a weighted linear combination of feature values, and the highest scoring translation candidate is selected as the translation of the source sentence. Symbolically,

$$\hat{t} = \arg\max_{t,a} \sum_{i=1}^{n} \lambda_i f_j(s, t, a) \tag{1}$$

where s is the input sentence, t is a possible output sentence, and a is a phrasal alignment that specifies how t is constructed from s, and $\hat{t}$ is the selected output sentence. The weights λ_i associated with each feature f_i are tuned to maximize the quality of the translation hypothesis selected by the decoding procedure that computes the argmax.

The log-linear model is a natural framework to integrate many features. The baseline system uses the following features:

- the probability of each source phrase in the hypothesis given the corresponding target phrase.
- the probability of each target phrase in the hypothesis given the corresponding source phrase.
- the lexical score for each target phrase given the corresponding source phrase.

- the lexical score for each source phrase given the corresponding target phrase.
- the target language model probability for the sequence of target phrase in the hypothesis.
- the word and phrase penalty score, which allow to ensure that the translation do not get too long or too short.
- the distortion model allows for reordering of the source sentence.

The probabilities of source phrase given target phrases, and target phrases given source phrases, are estimated from the bilingual corpus. [2] used the distortion model (reordering model), which simply penalizes non-monotonic phrase alignment based on the word distance of successively translated source phrases.

4 Reordering over Chunks

4.1 The Approach

We will extend the strategy of [13] to our new model. We will solve a reordering over chunks in PBSMT as a global reordering. First, we parse the source language sentence to a chunk tree. Second, we apply a series of transformation rules which were learnt automatically from the parallel corpus to the chunk tree over chunk level. Finally, we integrate a global reordering model directly in the decoder using a graph of phrases, and find the best translation sentence in this graph. When we integrate a global reordering model in the decoder to create a phrase graph, we must solve the overlapping phrase and chunk problem.

Our approach is similar to [14] except for the following important differences: first, we parse the source language sentence to a chunk tree, while they parse the source using chunking. Second, we use transformation rules with a hierarchial structure, so we will reorder over chunks more generally, while they use the rules without hierarchical structure. Finally, we solve phenomena for the overlapping phrases and chunks, while they do not mention this problem.

4.2 The Algorithm for Solving the Overlapping Phrases and Chunks

In this section, we will describe the heuristic algorithm for solving phenomena of overlapping phrases and chunks, generating a graph of phrases. With a given source sentence f, phrase p_{ij} of f from position i to position j and chunk c_{kl} of f from position k to position l, we state that phrase p_{ij} overlaps chunk c_{kl} if $(i \leq k$ and $l \neq j)$ or $(l \leq j$ and $k \neq i)$.

We conduct error analysis of the translation output of the "Over Chunks" system (the system which only implements reordering at chunk level) and observe that phrases which overlap chunks (those chunks are reordered) can be omitted in the decoding process. With the example in Section 4.2, the phrase "what characteristics does" can be omitted because this phrase overlaps two chunks: [what characteristics WHNP] and [does AUX] (an ordering of those chunks in a target sentence is [does AUX][what characteristics WHNP]). So, we need to find a solution to cover as many phrases as possible in the decoding process with reordering over chunk level. We use a simple idea: phrase is so close to chunk, we reorder approximately phrases based on chunks (a reordering of chunks is a reordering of phrases).

The algorithm to solve the phenomenon of overlapping phrases and chunks first implements reordering over all chunks, and then reorders k phrases separately based on reordering of chunks (the algorithm is described by $k = 2$ because the algorithm takes an expensive time with $k > 2$), and generates all possible paths in a graph of phrases. The efficiency of this algorithm is represented in Section 6.3. The algorithm is presented in Figure 1 as Algorithm 1.

Algorithm 1

Input: set of chunks ($\Delta = \{c_{kl}\}$)
         set of phrases ($\Gamma = \{p_{ij}\}$)

1: Reorder(Δ)
2: **for** ($i = 0 \rightarrow n - 1$)
3:   **for** ($p_{ij} \in \Gamma$)
4:     **for** ($c_{kl} \in p_{ij}$)
5:       **if** ($k' \notin [i, j]$ or $l' \notin [i, j]$) **then**
6:         $\Theta = \Theta \cup p_{ij}$
7: **for**($p_{xy} \in \Theta$)
8:   Reorder($p_{xy}, c_{kl} \notin p_{xy}$)
9: **for** ($p_{xy} \in \Theta$)
10:   **for** ($i = y + 1 \rightarrow n - 1$)
11:     **for** ($p_{ij} \in \Gamma$)
12:       **for** ($c_{kl} \in p_{ij}$)
13:         **if** ($k' \notin [i, j]$ or $l' \notin [i, j]$) **then**
14:           $\Omega = \Omega \cup p_{ij}$
15:   **if** ($p_{x_1 y_1} \in \Omega$) **then**
16:     Reorder($p_{xy}, p_{x_1 y_1}, c_{kl} \notin p_{xy}$ and $c_{kl} \notin p_{x_1 y_1}$)

Fig. 1. Algorithm for solving the overlapping chunks and phrases and generating a graph of phrases

Input: A set of chunks (Δ), and a set of phrases for an input sentence (Γ).

We assume that an input sentence is represented as $w_0 \ldots w_n$ where w_i is the i-th word in the input sentence. We denote p_{ij} to be phrase with a start position i and an end position j in an input sentence; c_{kl} be the chunk with a start position k and an end position l; $c'_{k'l'}$ be a reordered chunk of a chunk c_{kl} in a reordered sentence.

In line 1 in Algorithm 1, we implement a reordering over all chunks according to transformation rules to generate a possible reordered sentence. From line 2 to line 6, from left to right, we find all phrases p_{ij} ($0 \leq i < j \leq n$) in an input sentence which satisfy the conditions: at least a chunk c_{lk} which a chunk $c'_{l'k'}$ does not belong to $[l, k]$ in a reordered sentence. We consider a reordered position of c_{lk} as the reordered position of the phrase p_{ij} in a reordered sentence. We store those found phrases in a set Θ. In line 7 and line 8, we reorder each phrase p_{xy} of the set Θ and remaining chunks (the chunks which do not belong to p_{xy}) to generate a possible reordered sentence.

From line 9 to line 14 in Algorithm 1, with each phrase p_{xy} belonging to a set Θ, from left to right, we find all phrases p_{ij} ($y < i < j \leq n$ in an input sentence which satisfy the conditions: at least a chunk c_{lk} which a chunk $c'_{l'k'}$ does not belong to $[i, j]$ in a reordered sentence. We consider a reordered position of c_{lk} as the reordered position of the phrase p_{ij} in a reordered sentence. Line 15 and line 16, we reorder each phrase p_{xy} of a set Θ and each phrase $p_{x_1y_1}$ and remaining chunks (the chunks which do not belong to p_{xy}) to generate a possible reordered sentence.

For example

Input sentence: *what characteristics does the smart student have ?*
Chunks and tags: [what characteristics WHNP][does AUX][the smart student NP][have VP] [? .]
Positions of chunks: 0 1 2 3 4
Syntax tree: (SBARQ (WHNP (WP what NN characteristics)) (SQ (AUX does) (NP (DT the JJ smart NN student)) (VP (VB have))) (. ?))
(1) Position of the reordering over chunks: 23104 (using two transformation rules of English-Vietnamese: (SBARQ → WHNP SQ ?, 1 0 2) and (SQ → AUX NP VP, 1 2 0))

If we do not consider the phrases of an input sentence that overlap the chunks, we implement the reordering over chunks from an input sentence to a reordered sentence as in Figure 2a. So, two phrases can be omitted in the decoding process: "what characteristics does" and "does the".

[the smart student NP] [have VP] [does AUX][what characteristics WHNP] [? .] (according to (1))

Words and Phrases: "what", "characteristics", "does", "the", "smart", "student", "have", "?", "what characteristics does", "does the", "smart student", "student have".

Therefore, we need to solve the overlapping phrase and chunk problem. The algorithm for overlapping phrases and chunks is demonstrated in Figure 2. We use a black line to denote a chunk and a dotted black line to denote a phrase. We begin with the phrase "what characteristics does" because this phrase overlaps two chunks: [what characteristics WHNP][does AUX], where chunk [what characteristics WHNP] satisfies a reordered position do not belong to an interval $[0, 2]$ in the reordered sentence. Consequently, we consider the reordering of chunk [what characteristics WP] as the reordering of the phrase "what characteristics does". We implement similarly reordering of a phrase "does the" and "student have". We implement reorderings of the phrase "what characteristics does" and chunks [the smart student NP], [have VP], and [? .]. We have a possible reordered sentence shown in Figure 2b: *[the smart student] [have] "what characteristics does" [?]*.

The Figure 4 shows a part of the graph of phrases after reordering of the above example.

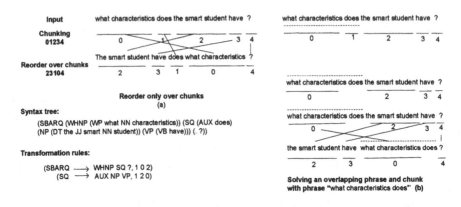

Fig. 2. Example for solving phenomena of overlapping Phrases and Chunks

5   Reordering Graph Generation

5.1   Parsing the Source Sentence

First, a POS tagger is usually used for chunk parsing. In our experiments, we used the tagger tool based on CRFs [15], then we used chunkparser-1.0 [1] to parse an English sentence to a tree. The main advantage of this method is not only fast computation time but also accuracy, which was about 85% with F1 score.

5.2   Transformation Rules

Suppose that T_s is a given lexicalized tree of the source language (whose nodes are augmented to include a word and a POS label). T_s contains n applications of lexicalized CFG rules $LHS_i \rightarrow RHS_i$ $(i \in \overline{1, n})$. We want to transform T_s into the target language word order by applying transformational rules to the CFG rules. A transformational rule is represented as $(LHS \rightarrow RHS, RS)$, which is a pair consisting of an unlexicalized CFG rule and a reordering sequence (RS). For example, the rule (NP → JJ NN, 1 0) implies that the CFG rule (NP→ JJ NN) in the source language can be transformed into the rule (NP→NN JJ) in the target language. Since the possible transformational rule for each CFG rule is not unique, there can be many transformed trees. The problem is how to choose the best one (we can see [16] for a description in more detail).

We use the method described in [16] to extract the transformation rules from the parallel corpus, and induce the best sequence of transformational rules for a source tree.

5.3   Applying Transformation Rules

First, we apply a series of transformation rules to the source tree for reordering over chunks. Next, we use the method described in Section 4.2 for solving phenomena of overlapping phrases and chunks. Finally, we generate a reordered graph of phrases, and find the best translation sentence in this graph.

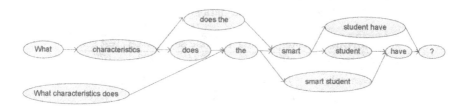

Fig. 3. A graph of phrases before reordering

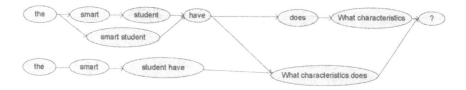

Fig. 4. A part of a graph of phrases after reordering

5.4   Graph Generation

For example, given a source sentence "what characteristics does the smart student have ?" in the above example in Section 4.2, we have a possible graph of phrases before reordering as shown in Fig 3.

After we apply a series of transformation rules (two rules: (SBARQ → WHNP SQ ?, 1 0 2); (SQ → AUX NP VP, 1 2 0)) and solve phenomena of overlapping phrases and chunks in the above example, we have a part of a possible phrase graph after reordering as shown in Figure 4.

All reorderings of an input sentence are encoded and stored in a graph of phrases. Each path is a possible reordering S', and given a reordering probability P. In this paper, the probability is computed using the transformation probability of the syntactic transformation model [16].

6   Experiment

6.1   Implementation

- We used chunkparser-1.0 [1] to parse a source sentence (English sentence) to a chunk tree.
- The rules are learnt from English-Vietnamese parallel corpus and Penntree Bank Corpus. We used the CFG transformation rules (chunk levels) for extraction from [16]'s method for reordering over chunks of an input sentence.
- Design of decoding is adapted from Moses [17]. In decoding, integration of an input sentence is handled as a graph of phrases.

Table 1. Corpora and data sets (sentences)

Corpus	Sentence pairs	Training set	Dev set	Test set
Conversation	16809	15734	403	672
General	55341	54642	200	499
Europarl	1288074	81920	480	1000

Table 2. Statistical information of reordering sentences in English sentences

Corpus	Sent	Sent with reordering
Conversation	672	215 (31.99%)
General	499	149 (29.86%)
Europarl	1000	244 (24.4%)

6.2 Data Sets

We conducted the experiments with English-Vietnamese pairs and English-French pairs. We used two English-Vietnamese corpora, one was collected from some grammar books (named "Conversation") and other one collected from daily newspapers (named "General"). These corpora, which include 16809 sentences and 55341 sentences for "Conversation" and "General", respectively, are split into training sets, development test sets, the test sets. For English-French pairs, we used a random part of the Europarl corpus [18] which is used in the WMT 07 shared task. This corpus contains over 1288074 sentences. The statistical information in detail about three corpora is shown in Table 1.

We tested 672 English sentences (test set of Conversation Corpus English-Vietnamese), 499 English sentences (test set of General Corpus English-Vietnamese), and 1000 English sentences (test set of Europerl corpus) for using CFG transformation rules (level over chunk). The statistics are shown in Table 2. The numbers of sentences which really were reordered over chunk level are 215 by 31.99 %, and 149 by 29.86 %, and 244 by 24.4 % "Conversation", "General", and "Europarl", respectively. Those results also showed that the problem of reordering over chunk levels is important with the language pairs for translation.

6.3 BLEU Score and Computational Time

We carried out the experiments on a PC with Pentium IV processor 2Gz, RAM memory 1GB. We ran GIZA++ [19] on the training corpus in both directions using its default setting, and applied the refinement rule "grow-diag-final" [2] to obtain a single many-to-many word alignment for each sentence pair. For learning language models, we used the SRILM toolkit [20]. For MT evaluation, we used the BLEU measure [21] calculated by the NIST script version 11b.

The translation results are presented in Table 3. The baseline system is a non-monotone translation system, in which the decoder does reordering on the target

Table 3. Translation performance for the English-Vietnamese and English-French tasks

Corpus	Method	BLEU score
Conversation	Baseline	35.66
	Over Chunks	36.12
	Over Chunks + Overlapping (OOC)	36.73
	Over Chunks + Overlapping + In Chunks	37.81
General	Baseline	34.07
	Over Chunks	34.69
	Over Chunks + Overlapping (OOC)	35.22
	Over Chunks + Overlapping + In Chunks	36.18
Europarl	Baseline	26.22
	Over Chunks	26.67
	Over Chunks + Overlapping (OOC)	27.16
	Over Chunks + Overlapping + In Chunks	28.01

language side (we adapted the beam search decoding algorithm [17]). The "Over Chunks" system is a translation system, which only implements reordering over chunk level. The "Over Chunks + Overlapping" system which combines reordering over chunk levels and solving the overlapping phenomena. The BLEU score of "Over Chunks" and "Over Chunks + Overlapping" systems are 36.12 and 36.73 absolute, which improved by 0.46 points and 1.07 points compared with the baseline of Conversation corpus. The BLEU scores of "Over Chunks" and "Over Chunks + Overlapping" systems are 34.69 and 35.22 absolute, which improved by 0.62 points and 1.15 points compared with the baseline of General corpus. The BLEU scores of "Over Chunks" and "Over Chunks + Overlapping" systems are 26.59 and 27.12 absolute, which improved by 0.45 points and 0.94 points compared with the baseline of Europarl corpus. Table 3 also shows the effect of a overlapping phrases and chunks. The "Over Chunks + Overlapping" systems improved by 0.61 points and 0.53 points and 0.49 points compared with "Over Chunks" systems of Conversation and General and Europarl, respectively. An improvement of "Overlapping" is well worthwhile. Those values showed that: (1) the improvement is higher with language pairs which are more different in word order; (2) PBSMT captures reordering quite well if there is a large amount of training.

After we implemented the reordering phrase over chunks, we used the method described in [13] to reorder in each chunk of our system, named "Over Chunks + Overlapping + In Chunks". The results are also shown in Table 3 which outperform that of OOC by 0.96 points and 1.08 points and 0.85 points absolute with "General" and "Conversation" and Europarl, respectively.

The computation time of OOC system is faster than that of baseline. We conducted the experiment with General and Europarl corpora. The results with

Table 4. Translation time for the English-Vietnamese "General" test set

Method	Computation time	Sec per sen
Baseline (decoding)	1489 sec	2.2 sec
OOC (pre-processing + decoding)	597 sec	0.88 sec

General corpus are shown in Table 4. The baseline system took 2.2 seconds per sentence and OOC system took 0.88 seconds per sentence. In short, the decoding time of our method is faster than that of baseline, by the approximate factor of 3 with the General corpus. With Europarl corpus, the baseline system took 4.91 seconds per sentence and the OOC system took 3.12 seconds per sentence.

7   Conclusion

In this paper, we have presented a new method for reordering in PBSMT. The experimental results with English-Vietnamese and English-French pairs show that our method outperforms the baseline PBSMT in both accuracy and speed. In future, we will solve the overlapping phrase and chunk problem generally, and more effectively.

Acknowledgments

We would like to thank to anonymous reviewers for helpful discussions and comments on the manuscript. The work on this paper was supported by the JAIST 21 century COE program "Verifiable and Evolvable e-Society".

References

1. Tsuruoka, Y., Tsujii, J.: Chunk parsing revisited. In: Proceedings of the 9th International Workshop on Parsing Technologies (IWPT 2005) (2005)
2. Koehn, P., Och, F.J., Marcu, D.: Statistical phrase-based translation. In: Proceedings of HLT-NAACL 2003, Edmonton, Canada, pp. 127–133 (2003)
3. Och, F.J., Ney, H.: The alignment template approach to statistical machine translation. Computational Linguistics 30(4), 417–449 (2004)
4. Zens, R., Ney, H., Watanabe, T., Sumita, E.: Reordering constraints for phrase-based statistical machine translation. In: Proceedings of the 20th International Conference on Computational Linguistics (CoLing), Geneva, Switzerland, pp. 205–211 (2004)
5. Wu, D.: A polynomial-time algorithm for statistical machine translation. In: Proceedings of ACL 1996, Santa, Cruz, CA, pp. 152–158 (1996)
6. Chiang, D.: A hierarchical phrase-based model for statistical machine translation. In: Proceedings of the 43rd Annual Meeting of the Association for Computational Linguistics (ACL 2005), Ann Arbor, Michigan, pp. 263–270. Association for Computational Linguistics (June 2005)

7. Collins, M., Koehn, P., Kucerová, I.: Clause restructuring for statistical machine translation. In: Proc. ACL 2005, Ann Arbor, USA, pp. 531–540 (2005)
8. Quirk, C., Menezes, A., Cherry, C.: Dependency treelet translation: Syntactically informed phrasal smt. In: Proceedings of ACL 2005, Ann Arbor, Michigan, USA, pp. 271–279 (2005)
9. Galley, M., Graehl, J., Knight, K., Marcu, D., DeNeefe, S., Wang, W., Thayer, I.: Scalable inference and training of context-rich syntactic translation models. In: Proceedings of COLING/ACL 2006, Sydney, Australia, pp. 961–968 (2006)
10. Koehn, P., Axelrod, A., Mayne, A.B., Callison-Burch, C., Osborne, M., Talbot, D., White, M.: Edinburgh system description for the 2005 nist mt evaluation. In: Proceedings of Machine Translation Evaluation Workshop 2005 (2005)
11. Xiong, D., Lui, Q., Lin, S.: Maximum entropy based phrase reordering model for statistical machine translation. In: Proceedings of ACL 2006, pp. 521–528 (2006)
12. Zen, R., Hey, H.: Discriminative reordering models for statistical machine translation. In: Proceeding of the Workshop on Statistical Machine Translation, pp. 55–63 (2006)
13. Nguyen, P.T., Shimazu, A., Nguyen, L.M., Nguyen, V.V.: A syntactic transformation model for statistical machine translation. International Journal of Computer Processing of Oriental Languages (IJCPOL) 20(2), 1–20 (2007)
14. Zhang, Y., Zens, R., Ney, H.: Chunk-level reordering of source language sentences with automatically learned rules for statistical machine translation. In: Proceedings of SSST, NAACL-HLT 2007 / AMTA Workshop on Syntax and Structure in Statistical Translation, pp. 1–8 (2007)
15. Lafferty, J., McCallum, A., Pereira, F.: Conditional random fields: Probabilistic models for segmenting and labeling sequence data. In: Proc. 18th International Conference on Machine Learning, pp. 282–289. Morgan Kaufmann, San Francisco (2001)
16. Nguyen, T.P., Shimazu, A.: Improving phrase-based smt with morpho-syntactic analysis and transformation. In: Proceedings AMTA 2006 (2006)
17. Koehn, P., Hoang, H., Birch, A., Callison-Burch, C., Federico, M., Bertoldi, N., Cowan, B., Shen, W., Moran, C., Zens, R., Dyer, C., Bojar, O., Constantin, A., Herbst, E.: Moses: Open source toolkit for statistical machine translation. In: Proceedings of ACL, Demonstration Session (2007)
18. Koehn, P.: Europarl: A parallel corpus for statistical machine translation. In: Proceedings of MT Summit 2005 (2005)
19. Och, F.J., Ney, H.: A systematic comparison of various statistical alignment models. Computational Linguistics 29(1), 19–51 (2003)
20. Stolcke, A.: Srilm - an extensible language modeling toolkit. In: Proceedings of International Conference on Spoken Language Processing, vol. 29, pp. 901–904 (2002)
21. Papineni, K., Roukos, S., Ward, T., W.J.Z.: Bleu: a method for automatic evaluation of machine translation. In: Proc. of the 40th Annual Meeting of the Association for Computational Linguistics (ACL), Philadelphia, PA, July,2002, pp. 311–318 (2002)

Interruption, Resumption
and Domain Switching in In-Vehicle Dialogue

Jessica Villing[1,*], Cecilia Holtelius[2], Staffan Larsson[1], Anders Lindström[3],
Alexander Seward[4], and Nina Åberg[5]

[1] Department of Linguistics, University of Gothenburg, Sweden
[2] Volvo Car Corporation, Sweden
[3] Mobility Services R&D, TeliaSonera, Sweden
[4] Veridict AB, Sweden
[5] Volvo Technology AB, Sweden
http://www.dicoproject.org

Abstract. The use of dialogue systems in vehicles raises the problem
of making sure that the dialogue does not distract the driver from the
primary task of driving. Earlier studies have indicated that humans are
very apt at adapting the dialogue to the traffic situation and the cognitive load of the driver. The goal of this paper is to investigate strategies for interrupting and resuming in, as well as changing topic domain
of, spoken human-human in-vehicle dialogue. The results show a large
variety of strategies being used, and indicate that the choice of resumption and domain-switching strategy depends partly on the topic domain
being resumed, and partly on the role of the speaker (driver or passenger). These results will be used as a basis for the development of
dialogue strategies for interruption, resumption and domain-switching
in the DICO in-vehicle dialogue system.

1 Introduction

The study reported on in this paper is part of the DICO project, the overall purpose of which is to demonstrate how state-of-the-art spoken language technology
can enable access to communication, entertainment and information services as
well as to environment control in vehicles[1]. The project group intends to demonstrate this primarily by means of working prototypes which promote safety in
driving while at the same time delivering ease-of-use in access to commercially
viable sets of on-line as well as in-vehicle services. To this end, the project has
developed a working prototype of a speech-based and multimodal dialogue system, which has previously been tested on real users both in simulator tests and
while driving in real traffic.

One specific question, which has arisen during these trials with the system
prototype, concerns how to deal with and even generate interruptions and topic

* The authors wish to thank Johan Jarlengrip, Volvo Technology AB.
[1] DICO is funded by Vinnova, project 2006-00844.

A. Ranta, B. Nordström (Eds.): GoTAL 2008, LNAI 5221, pp. 488–499, 2008.

shifts in the spoken dialogue between man and machine, e.g. in order to adapt to the current traffic situation in a timely fashion.

As can be expected, in human-human communication, this type of regulation is common and constitutes an integrated part of spoken communication. There are studies indicating that vehicle drivers are in fact very good at adapting their interaction to accommodate the cognitive demands of the combined tasks of driving and interacting through spoken language [1].

Researchers within the fields of vehicle safety and ergonomics have also proposed that in-vehicle spoken dialogue systems should adapt to the workload of the driver and suspend and resume dialogue accordingly [2] or even that the dialogue behaviour should be designed in such a way that a "neutral, small talk-like interaction results" [3].

The CHAT project [4] focused on robust, wide-coverage, and cognitive load-sensitive spoken dialogue interface, addressing issues related to dynamic and attention-demanding environments such as driving. Even if several of the dialogue and presentation strategies of CHAT are based on corpus data, it would not seem as if topic shifting, and strategies for suspending and resuming topic threads, has been studied in any detail. A limited set of implicit strategies for topic switching were investigated but not included in the final system. The CHAT system was not designed to monitor the driver's cognitive load; rather, general methods such as robust interpretation were designed to decrease cognitive load more generally.

It is the goal of this paper to investigate the strategies employed in human-human in-vehicle interaction for interrupting and resuming spoken dialogue, as well as strategies for changing the topic domain of the conversation. For this purpose, dialogues between driver and passenger in real traffic were recorded and videotaped under controlled conditions, where the driver's cognitive load was simultaneously measured by use of an indirect method.

We will first briefly describe the dialogue system which is begin further developed in the project, and describe some shortcomings which motivate the research presented here. We will then describe the experimental setup, as well as the transcription and annotation methods used. Finally, we will point to some future research directions motivated by our results.

2   The DICO Dialogue System

The dialogue manager in the DICO system is based on [5]. It enables flexible spoken human-machine dialogue by providing general solutions to several general dialogue management problems:

- Grounding: making sure that the system and the user are able to hear and understand each other
- Accommodation, enabling the user to
  - give information in any order
  - provide information without explicitly stating the task
  - clarify by responding to system clarification questions if there is some problem

- Mixed initiative: user can take initiative at any time
- Multitasking: switching between multiple simultaneous tasks
- Multimodality: Use speech and/or GUI or to interact

In addition, since DICO uses a domain independent dialogue manager, knowledge of dialogue is kept separate from domain-specific knowledge, which enables rapid prototyping of new applications.

The current version of the dialogue manager will prompt the user for answers to system questions until the user answers. This is clearly not a good strategy in the in-vehicle environment, since it risks increasing the cognitive load on the user by endlessly repeating e.g. a question when the driver is devoting her attention to the traffic:

USR> Call Lisa please
SYS> OK, Lisa. Do you want to use the home number of the mobile
phone number?
User enters roundabout and focuses all attention on the traffic
SYS> Do you want to use the home number or the mobile phone number?
SYS> Do you want to use the home number or the mobile phone number?
SYS> Do you want to use the home number or the mobile phone number?

...

One common way of dealing with this problem in in-vehicle speech systems is to repeat a message once, then wait for a fixed amount of time, and then give up. That this is not ideal either can be seen from the following (made-up) example:

USR> Call Lisa please
SYS> OK, Lisa. Do you want to use the home number or the mobile phone
number?
User enters roundabout and focuses all attention on the traffic
SYS> Do you want to use the home number of the mobile phone number?
Driver exits roundabout, and after a while the driver is ready to talk again
USR> Um, the mobile number please.
SYS> Sorry, I don't understand. What do you want to do?

In addition to lacking strategies for dealing with interruptions and resumptions, the dialogue manager offers rather restricted methods for switching between different topic domains. For example, to switch from the "telephone" application to the "audio system" application, the user has to provide explicit requests such as "go to the audio system". In cases where the system initiates a topic domain switch , this is also done in a rather stereotypical way ("returning to the telephone.").

It would clearly be useful to (1) add strategies for dialogue interruption and resumption, and (2) provide more convenient and natural means for switching between domains. In the context of the DICO project, the main point of smoothly managing dialogue interruptions, resumptions and domain switchings is to minimize the cognitive load of the driver.

3   Method

The goal of the test setup was to elicit driver–passenger dialogue which would feature a substantial and measurable number of instances of the different types of human speech-communicative strategies and linguistic devices known to be employed under cognitive load and other forms of driving-induced stress. One specific challenge was therefore how to make driver and passenger engage in natural dialogue and conversation of sufficient intensity that any additional distractions or increase in the cognitive load, due to driving or the surrounding traffic situation, would immediately compel the subjects to adapt their spoken language in ways which would be detectable from subsequent transcription of the conversation.

3.1   Subjects and Tasks

Eight subjects (two female and six male) between the ages of 25 and 36 were recruited internally with one of the partners, and were divided into driver-passenger pairs. The subjects had no previous experience from using speech technology or dialogue systems.

To meet the requirements mentioned above, the subjects were given two separate tasks, one navigation task and one memory task. In the navigation task the passenger simply had to instruct the driver on where to drive. The memory task was constructed so that the driver and passenger were to interview each other regarding personal background and interests during the drive, after which their individual ability to recall this information was scored using a fill-out form. Subjects were informed that their joint score would be the basis for a competition, to further encourage interaction, collaboration and thereby conversation. All tests were performed under real and challenging conditions, in relatively dense city traffic in central Gothenburg.

A previously unknown driving route was given to the passenger at the start, together with the interview sheet. The passenger was told only to give verbal driving instructions, spanning no more than one intersection ahead. Should the team lose track while navigating, they were instructed to find their way back to the pre-determined route and continue. The driver was told to focus on the main tasks and on driving for safety reasons, but was told also to perform the best he or she could in a so-called Tactile Detection Task (TDT), requiring the driver to press a button at irregular intervals. Each team was free to manage and solve the interview task in any way they saw fit. However, they were not allowed to take notes or use any other memory aids. Within the teams, each subject acted both driver and passenger, since the subjects were instructed to switch roles halfway into the test, which lasted for 60 minutes in total.

3.2   Test Environment and Data

The test car, a Volvo XC 90 (model year 2004), was equipped with a dual head-set microphone setup, enabling recording of driver and passenger on separate channels. Two digital video cameras were mounted inside the vehicle, one capturing a close-up of the driver's face, and the other capturing a wide-screen view of the road ahead. To measure driver workload, a system for performing a Tactile Detection Task was utilized in the test. The system consists of a buzzer attached to the driver's forearm and a response button attached to the index finger. At random intervals, the TDT issues a tactile stimulus to the driver and the driver is supposed to react as quickly as possible on each stimulus by pressing the response button. Driver distraction can then be measured dynamically in terms of user hit-rate and reaction latency, according to the method developed by e.g [6]. TDT furthermore enables capturing of driving-unrelated cognitive load, caused by other cognitive processes generated by the dialogue itself or by memory processing, even when car was not moving, e.g. at stoplights etc.

3.3   Transcription and Coding

For the transcriptions, the transcription tool ELAN[2] was used. ELAN is able to handle both audio- and video resources, and it allows annotation along multiple tiers (i.e. an utterance can be annotated with several independent annotation schema), both important features for this study. The annotation schema was designed to enable analysis of utterances related to interruption and resumption. The schema uses some notions from the MUMIN schema [7]. The notion of "utterance" we are using here is approximately "maximal syntactic phrase not interrupted by a long silence"; what counts as a "long silence" varies with context and has not been further operationalized.

The **domain-switch** tier is used for annotating utterances where the domain of the conversation changes. We distinguish three main domains of conversation in this task: navigation, traffic and interview. The following labels are used in the domain-switch tier:

– **navi:** A phrase which introduces or resumes talk about the navigation domain
– **traffic:** traffic (other than navigation)
– **interview:** interview
– **other**

Also, rather than marking whole segments with the domain tier, we only mark the first phrase in each domain segment.

The **sequencing** schema marks formal aspects of domain-switching utterances. The term "sequencing" refers to the mechanisms whereby a dialog is structured into sequences corresponding to different domains of conversation, and topics within these domains [7]. (Note that we do not currently annotate for topic switches within domains, as these are less well-defined than the domains.)

– **std-phrase** (sequencing function, standard phrase): A standardized, domain independent domain-switching phrase, e.g. "Let's see", "Where were we"

---

[2] http://www.lat-mpi.eu/tools/elan/

- **dom-spec** (sequencing function, domain-specific phrase): A domain-specific domain-switching utterance, e.g. "Turn right", "Wolfmother", "How was I supposed to drive, again?"
- **unsure** (sequencing function, phrase type not clear): A domain-switching phrase where it is unclear whether the phrase is a standard, domain independent phrase or a domain-specific phrase.

In addition to domain-switching and sequencing, utterances with feedback function were annotated with respect to form. Feedback utterances provide information regarding the perception, understanding and acceptance of an utterance. Three labels were used to distinguish forms of feedback utterances:

- **std-phrase** (feedback function, standard phrase): A standardized, domain independent phrase with feedback function, e.g. "Let's see", "mhm", "Okay", "Huh?", "What do you mean?", "Got it"
- **dom-spec** (feedback function, domain-specific phrase): A domain-specific utterance with feedback function, e.g. "To the left" (in response to "Turn to the left"). Typically contains a repetition or reformulation of the latest preceding utterance.
- **unsure** (feedback function, , phrase type not clear): A phrase with feedback function where it is unclear whether the phrase is a standard, domain independent phrase or a domain-specific phrase.

Note that "sequencing" and "feedback" are independent tiers; an utterance can thus be coded for both functions. For example, "Okay" can have both a feedback and a sequencing function.

The annotation schema has not been tested for inter-coder reliability, due to limited resources. Instead, annotators have discussed problematic examples and agreed on consensus decisions, sometimes altering the definitions in the annotation schema and altering previous annotations correspondingly. While full reliability testing would have further strengthened the results presented here, we believe that our results are still useful as a basis for future implementation and experimental work.

4 Results

As far as the authors are aware, this is the first investigation into the form of sequencing moves in in-vehicle dialogue. Although this was a fairly small-scale experiment, we believe that some tentative conclusions may be drawn from the transcribed data.

All in all 3590 driver utterances and 4382 passenger utterances were transcribed and coded. The drivers made 171 sequencing utterances, the passengers made 246.

Table 1 and 2 show the most common standard (i.e. domain-independent) phrases which were used utterance-initially when switching to a new domain. The data has been normalized for variations in pronunciation and in some cases

Table 1. Standard phrases for driver sequencing utterances

	Interview	Navigation	Traffic	Other
oops (*oj*)	0	1	8	3
alright[3] (*jaha*)	6	4	0	0
let's see (*ska vi se*)	2	5	0	0

Table 2. Standard phrases for passenger sequencing utterances

	Interview	Navigation	Traffic	Other
let's see (*ska vi se*)	7	9	0	0
alright (*jaha*)	6	1	0	2
okay	4	1	0	0

for variations in exact wording (the phrase "let's see"(Sw. "då ska vi se") has a number of variants, roughly paraphraseable as "now let's see", "let's see now" etc.). Table 1 shows that "oops"(Sw. "oj") is the most common sequencing phrase for the driver, and it is used as a single utterance to comment something in the traffic domain. It is however never used for switching to interview or navigation issues. "Let's see" is the most common phrase used by passengers. It is used for switching to the interview and navi domains (e.g. "Now let's see, sailing..."(Sw. "Nu ska vi se, segling...") or "Let's see here, keep right at the bridge"(Sw. "Ska vi se här, håll till höger vid bron")), but never for traffic or other domains.

Sequencing phrases that are domain specific, i.e. that can only be understood within a certain domain, are classified based on grammatical category according to the following schema[4]:

- DEC: declarative sentence
- INT: interrogative sentence
- IMP: imperative sentence
- ANS: "yes" or "no" answer
- NP: bare noun phrase
- ADVP: bare adverbial phrase
- INC: inomplete phrase

Figure 1 shows the frequencies of different kinds of domain-specific sequencing moves within the interview domain. Most common for both driver and passenger are declarative utterances, e.g. "Enemy of the enemy was the last I read" (re-raising earlier discussion about books). Second most common for drivers are incomplete phrases, e.g. "That was also favorite". For passengers noun phrases are second most common. For example, one passenger re-raises an earlier

---

[4] This schema was put together ad-hoc based on corpus observations and standard taxonomies of sentence types and grammatical categories.

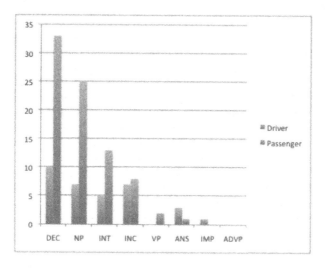

Fig. 1. Domain specific phrases for domain Interview

discussion about favorite music by simply saying "Wolfmother", which is the name of a previously discussed favorite band of the drivers'.

Figure 2 shows the kinds of domain specific phrases that are used within the navigation domain. Interrogative phrases are most common for drivers, e.g. "Should I go straight ahead here", while declarative phrases are most common for passengers, e.g. "Now you should turn left in the next crossing[5]".

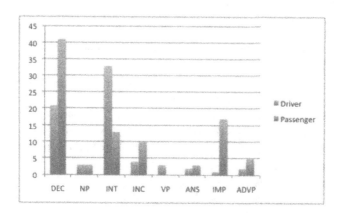

Fig. 2. Domain specific phrases for domain Navi

Figure 3 shows categories for domain specific phrases in the traffic domain. As can be seen the distribution is the same for both drivers and passengers. Declarative phrases are by far the most common, e.g. "And there you come and

---

[5] Note that this sentence has declarative form even though it is pragmatically a request.

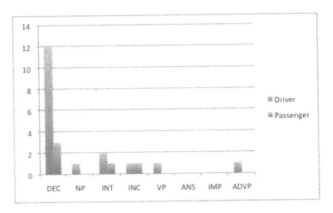

Fig. 3. Domain specific phrases for domain Traffic

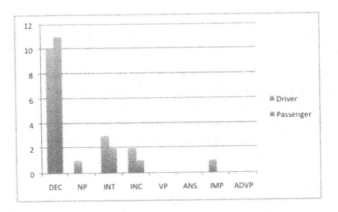

Fig. 4. Domain specific phrases for domain Other

I don't know who is driving"(Sw. "Och där kommer du och jag vet inte vem som kor") (driver talking to a fellow driver).

Figure 4 shows categories for all other domains. The distribution is similar to the traffic domain, and is also the same for both driver and passenger. Declarative phrases are most common here too, e.g. "It feels like I'm forgetting to press the button" (driver commenting the TDT button).

In addition to the phrases and words explicitly tagged as having a sequencing function, as shown above, it was also noted that in many cases, topic and domain shifts were also audibly distinguishable by virtue of prosodic cues and/or extra-linguistic sounds, such as lip smacks, inhalation noise etc. Two authentic examples from the corpus are shown below.

[INHALES] så nu är vi som tillbaks här igen
so now we are sort of back here again
[LIPSMACK] jaa det var fyra stycken där
yes you had four there

A search across all driver and passenger transcriptions for the extra-linguistic sound categories lip smack, breathing, sighing, coughing and throat clearing immediately preceded a domain shift was performed. Matches were found in 9% (10 instances out of a total of 166 domain shifts) of the driver transcriptions and 16% (18 instances out of a total of 244 domain shifts) of the passenger transcriptions. (It should perhaps be noted that sub-domain or topic shifts are not as yet explicitly coded, and consequently could not be included as contexts of the search.) Regardless of whether these sounds are produced at will or sub-consciously, a system which were able to detect them could use them as potential cues of an upcoming topic or domain shift.

5   Discussion

There some differences between the tables for driver and passenger standard phrases; for example, "oops"(Sw. "oj") is the most common standard phrase used for domain switching and dialogue resumption by the driver. It seems clear, since the phrase is mostly used when switching to the traffic domain, that this signal is motivated by real-time events in the environment, rather than planned ahead. We can perhaps make a conceptual distinction between "improvised" and "planned" sequencing moves. In addition, we can see that the improvised sequencing moves are motivated by the navigation task (since this is the domain that the dialogue switches to). "Let's see", on the other hand, is a good example of a "planned" sequencing move. It is frequently used by the passenger in both the interview- and the navi-domain, as well as the navi domain for the driver. This phrase seems to be used when the speaker a) believes that it is necessary to change domain (the driver do not know where to go or the passenger realizes that the driver has not got enough instructions) or b) believes that it is suitable to change domain (the driver knows where to go and the traffic situation is not too heavy, or the passenger believes that the driver should be capable of concentrating on something else but the driving task). "Alright"(Sw. "jaha") seems to have more of an eliciting function, declaring that the speaker is ready to change domain and encourages the hearer to make the first move.

As noted, passengers frequently used bare noun phrases when resuming a previous domain topic. Our hypothesis is that these NP re-raisings allude to a previously discussed topic, e.g. a question from the interviewers questionnaire which was interrupted by navigation- or traffic-domain dialogue. This is similar to the account of reduced "second-mention" forms for re-raising questions in dialogue put forward in [8]. Passengers usually use declarative phrases in all domains, which can be explained by the fact that it is the passenger who has access to information. In the interview and the navi domains the passenger have all the information about what questions to ask and which way to go. The driver also usually uses declarative phrases, in all domains but the navi domain where interrogative phrases are more common, since the driver frequently has to ask for information about where to go.

6 Future Work

We plan to add dialogue management strategies to the DICO dialogue manager to enable it to deal with phenomena like the ones described in this paper, and to evaluate the effect of these strategies on driver cognitive load in in-vehicle dialogue. The frequency lists are expected to be useful when deciding what to listen for from the user, how to react to sequencing signals from the user, and for generating natural-sounding sequencing moves from the system[6].

To fully adapt the dialogue to the driver's cognitive load, it would be very useful to get an estimate of this based on available information sources in the in-vehicle environment. We are working on using existing technologies for this, with the aim of connecting these technologies to the dialogue system and using it for optimizing system, behavior. A very interesting future research topic would be the detection of cognitive load from the speech signal, and for weighing together evidence from multiple sources. We envision the following kind of behavior:

USR> Call Lisa please
SYS> OK, Lisa. Do you want to use the home number of the mobile phone number?
User enters roundabout and focuses all attention on the traffic
USR> um... uh...
Driver exists roundabout, and after a while the cognitive load is sufficiently low to allow resuming the dialogue
SYS> Let's see. Lisa. Do you want to use the home number of the mobile phone number?

A relevant question in this context is whether user initiative should always override the system's estimation of the user's cognitive load. That is, if the speaker resumes the dialogue, should the system respond regardless of cognitive load? If so, how should it respond? Should it also take own initiatives or only do what's needed to complete the user's requests? These are questions which we hope to answer in future experiments.

References

1. Esbjörnsson, M., Juhlin, O., Weilenmann, A.: Drivers Using Mobile Phones in Traffic: An Ethnographic Study of Interactional Adaptation. International Journal of Human Computer Interaction, Special issue on: In-Use, In-Situ: Extending Field Research Methods (2007)
2. Nishimoto, T., Shioya, M., Takahashi, J., Daigo, H.: A study of dialogue management principles corresponding to the driver's workload. Biennial on Digital Signal Processing for In-Vehicle and Mobile Systems (2005)
3. Vollrath, M.: Speech and driving-solution or problem?. Intelligent Transport Systems, IET 1, 89–94 (2007)

---

[6] We are not claiming that system utterances should mimic human speakers in every way, only that knowledge of how humans express sequencing moves will be useful when designing the system output.

4. Weng, F., Varges, S., Raghunathan, B., Ratiu, F., Pon-Barry, H., Lathrop, B., Zhang, Q., Bratt, H., Scheideck, T., Xu, K.: et al.: CHAT: A Conversational Helper for Automotive Tasks.In: Ninth International Conference on Spoken Language Processing (2006)
5. Larsson, S.: Issue-based Dialogue Management. PhD thesis, Göteborg University (2002)
6. van Winsum, W., Martens, M., Herland, L.: The effect of speech versus tactile driver support messages on workload, driver behaviour and user acceptance. tno-report tm-99-c043. Technical report, Soesterberg, Netherlands (1999)
7. Allwood, J., Cerrato, L., Dybkjaer, L., Jokinen, K., Navarretta, C., Paggio, P.: The mumin multimodal coding scheme. Technical report, Center for Sprogteknologi, Copenhagen University (2004)
8. Cooper, R., Larsson, S.: Accommodation and reaccommodation in dialogue. In: Bäuerle, R., Reyle, U., Zimmermann, T.E. (eds.) Presuppositions and Discourse. Current Research in the Semantics/Pragmatics Interface. Elsevier, Amsterdam (2002)

Finite Matters

Verbal Features in Data-Driven Parsing of Swedish

Lilja Øvrelid

NLP-unit, Dept. of Swedish
University of Gothenburg

Abstract. This paper investigates the effect of a set of verbal features in data-driven dependency parsing of Swedish. Following an error analysis of a baseline parser, we show that the addition of information on verbal features such as tense and voice can give significant improvements over this baseline and, in particular, in the analysis of syntactic arguments. We furthermore show the importance of the binary property of finiteness for the parsing of Scandinavian and demonstrate that highly similar effects may be achieved with automatically acquired information.

1 Introduction

With the development of syntactic treebanks for a range of languages other than English, there is now considerable efforts in data-driven parsing and studies which highlight the effect of different linguistic properties of these languages are important for further improvements. In recent work on syntactic parsing of German, for instance, it has been debated whether certain structural properties of the language call for different parsing strategies or representational frameworks than the parsing of English (Dubey and Keller, 2003; Kübler et al., 2006). The Scandinavian languages share with German certain syntactic properties, such as a rigid verb placement in combination with word order variation, which make these languages interestingly different from English. In particular, the so-called V2-constraint requires that the finite verb be the second constituent of declarative main clauses and *finiteness* has been claimed to be a defining property of Scandinavian syntax in more theoretically oriented work (Holmberg and Platzack, 1995; Eide, 2008).

In strictly data-driven approaches to syntactic parsing, a grammar, whether handcrafted or induced, does not figure at all. The parser is trained on a treebank containing the correct analyses with respect to some representational framework, e.g, constituent analysis or dependency analysis and without a formal grammar to guide parsing, data-driven models typically condition on a rich linguistic context in the search for the most probable analysis.

In this paper we address the effect of a set of verbal features on the data-driven dependency parsing of Swedish, and in particular on the parsing of core grammatical functions such as subjects and objects. The parsing framework is deterministic classifier-based dependency parsing, more precisely the MaltParser system (Joakim Nivre and Nilsson, 2006), which achieved the highest parsing accuracy for Swedish in the CoNLL-X shared task on dependency parsing (Buchholz and Marsi, 2006).

A. Ranta, B. Nordström (Eds.): GoTAL 2008, LNAI 5221, pp. 500–509, 2008.

The paper is organized as follows. In section 2, we start out by briefly outlining some relevant syntactic properties of Scandinavian and we present the treebank and parser employed in section 3. Section 4 presents an in-depth error analysis of the results from a baseline parser, focusing on errors for syntactic dependents of verbs, like arguments and adverbials. The experiments presented in section 5 investigate the effect of additional information on the morphosyntactic properties of verbs, employing gold standard annotation. We evaluate the results both in terms of overall parse performance, as well as more detailed evaluation for individual dependency relations. We go on to assess the scalability of these results by employing automatically acquired verbal features. Finally, section 6 concludes and provides some suggestions for future research.

2 Scandinavian Morphosyntax

Before we turn to a description of the treebank and the parser used in the experiments, we want to point to a few grammatical properties of Swedish that will be important in the following. Like the majority of Germanic languages, but unlike English, the Scandinavian languages are *verb second (V2)*; the finite verb is the second constituent in declarative main clauses. Pretty much any constituent may occupy the sentence-initial position, as illustrated by (1)-(3).

(1) *Statsministern   håller ett tal   i   morgon*
     primeminister-DEF holds a   speech in tomorrow
     'The primeminister gives a speech tomorrow'
(2) *Ett tal   håller statsministern   i   morgon*
     a   speech holds primeminister-DEF in tomorrow
     'A speech, the primeminister gives tomorrow'
(3) *I   morgon   håller statsministern   ett tal*
     in tomorrow holds primeminister-DEF a   speech
     'Tomorrow, the primeminister gives a speech'

In (1) sentence-initial position is occupied by the subject, in (2) by the direct object, whereas we in (3) find an adverbial in sentence-initially. Word order in subordinate clauses, however, are not restricted by this constraint:

(4) *...eftersom statsministern nog   inte* **håller** *ett tal   i   morgon*
     since   primeminister enough not holds a   speech in tomorrow
     '...since the prime minister probably will not give a speech tomorrow'

Non-finite verbs follow the finite verb, but precede their complements and the presence of a non-finite verb introduces a greater rigidity in terms of interpretation of the clausal constituents.[1] With respect to core arguments, only subjects may intervene between a finite and non-finite verb, as in (6), and only objects may follow the non-finite verb, as in (5):

---

[1] In this respect Scandinavian differs from German, which positions non-finite verbs in clause final position.

(5) *Statsministern*   **ska hålla** *ett   tal*
    primeminister-DEF shall   hold   a   speech
    'The primeminister will give a speech'

(6) *Ett tal*   **ska** *statsministern* **hålla**
    a   speech   shall primeminister hold
    'A speech, the primeminister will give'

Main clauses consisting of a finite, transitive verb along with its arguments are thus structurally ambiguous, see (7), whereas the placement of a non-finite verb in the same clause clearly indicates syntactic functions, cf. (8) and (9):

(7) *Vem såg Ida?*
    who saw Ida
    'Who saw Ida / Who did Ida see?'

(8) *Vem   har sett Ida?*
    who   has seen Ida
    SUBJ   OBJ
    'Who has seen Ida?'

(9) *Vem   har Ida   sett?*
    who   has Ida   seen
    OBJ   SUBJ
    'Who has Ida seen?'

3   Data and Parser

Talbanken05 is a Swedish treebank in dependency format and contains both written and spoken language (Nivre et al., 2006a). The written sections of the treebank consist of professional prose and student essays and amount to 197,123 running tokens, spread over 11,431 sentences. Figure 1 illustrates the treebank annotation for the example sentence in 10.

(10) *Därefter betalar patienten   avgift med 10 kronor*
     thereafter pays   patient-DEF fee   with 10 krona-PL
     'Thereafter, the patient pays a fee of 10 kronas'

For each token, Talbanken05 contains information on word form, part of speech, head and dependency relation, as well as various morphosyntactic features. For verbs, the treebank distinguishes the categories of tense and voice, illustrated by the active, present tense verb *betalar* 'pays' in (10).

In the parse experiments, we employ the freely available MaltParser,[2] which is a language-independent system for data-driven dependency parsing. It is based on a deterministic parsing strategy, in combination with treebank-induced classifiers for predicting parse transitions (Nivre, 2006). The MaltParser system allows for explicit formulation of features employed during parsing by means of a feature model. As

---

[2] http://w3.msi.vxu.se/users/nivre/research/MaltParser.html

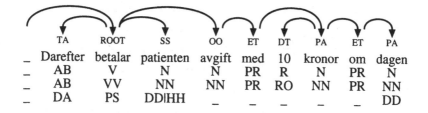

_	Darefter	betalar	patienten	avgift	med	10	kronor	om	dagen
_	AB	V	N	N	PR	R	N	PR	N
_	AB	VV	NN	NN	PR	RO	NN	PR	NN
_	DA	PS	DD|HH	_	_	_	_	_	DD

Fig. 1. Example (10) from Talbanken05 with dependency annotation

our baseline, we use the settings optimized for Swedish in the CoNLL-X shared task Nivre et al. (2006b) where the MaltParser system was the best performing parser for Swedish. The only parameter that will be varied in the later experiments is the information contained in the features used for the prediction of the next parsing action. The baseline parser employs information on part-of-speech, lexical form and previously assigned dependency relations.

4 Error Analysis of Baseline Parser

The written part of Talbanken05 was parsed employing the baseline parser described above, using 10-fold cross validation for training and testing. The overall result for unlabeled and labeled dependency accuracy is 89.87 and 84.92 respectively.[3]

Table 1. 10 most frequent error types in baseline experiment, where SS=subject, OO=object, AA=other adverbial, OA=object adverbial, ET=nominal post-modifier, RA=spatial adverbial, TA=time adverbial

Gold	System	Count
ET	OA	450
SS	**OO**	**446**
OA	ET	410
AA	RA	404
AA	OA	398
TA	AA	372
RA	AA	311
OO	**SS**	**309**
RA	OA	308
AA	TA	290

In an error analysis of the baseline parser we try to locate consistent patterns of errors. As Table 1 shows, the overall most frequent errors in terms of dependency relations involve either various adverbial relations or the core argument relations of subject

---

[3] Note that these results are slightly better than the official CoNLL-X shared task scores (89.50/84.58), which were obtained using a single training-test split, not cross-validation. Note also that, in both cases, the parser input contained gold standard part-of-speech tags.

Table 2. Position relative to verb for confused subjects and objects

Gold	Sys	before	after	Total
SS	OO	103 (23.1%)	343 (76.9%)	446 (100%)
OO	SS	103 (33.3%)	206 (66.7%)	309 (100%)

(SS) and direct object (OO). The errors in assignment of adverbial relations contain a fair number of PP-attachment errors (ET, OA). Furthermore, Talbanken05 makes numerous and fine-grained distinctions in adverbial functions (spatial, temporal, modal, comparative etc.), which clearly prove difficult for the parser to replicate.

The confusion of subjects and objects follows from lack of sufficient formal disambiguation, i.e., simple clues such as word order, part-of-speech and word form do not clearly indicate syntactic function. This is a direct consequence of the word order variation mentioned initially. As we saw in section 2, subjects and objects may both precede or follow their verbal head. These realizations are not, however, equally likely. Subjects, however, are more likely to occur preverbally (77%), whereas objects typically occupy a postverbal position (94%). Based on word order alone we would expect postverbal subjects and preverbal objects to be more dominant among the errors than in the treebank as a whole (23% and 6% respectively), since they display word order variants that depart from the canonical ordering of arguments. Table 2 shows a breakdown of the errors for confused subjects and objects and their position with respect to the verbal head. We find that postverbal subjects (after) are in clear majority among the subjects erroneously assigned the object relation. Due to the aforementioned V2 property of Swedish, the subject must reside in the position directly following the finite verb whenever another constituent occupies the preverbal position, as in examples (2)-(3) and the authentic error example in (10) above.

Following the error analysis, we may hypothesize that additional information regarding properties of the verb may contribute to the resolution of these types of ambiguities. As we saw in section 2, the V2-constraint is a categorical constraint in Swedish. The property of being data-driven entails that there is no grammar available for parsing where such a constraint may be stated explicitly. Rather, analyses produced by the parser are patterned on properties found in the treebank employed for training and these are the properties which we will be manipulating in the following experiments.

5   Experiments

Part-of-speech tag sets commonly make reference to the feature of tense, a category which is marked morphologically in Scandinavian, as in many other languages. In these experiments we will investigate the effect of verbal properties on the analysis of syntactic arguments, such as subjects and objects in a purely data-driven parser.

5.1   Experimental Methodology

All parsing experiments are performed using 10-fold cross-validation for training and testing on the entire written part of Talbanken05. Overall parsing accuracy will be reported using the standard metrics of *labeled attachment score* (LAS) and *unlabeled attachment score* (UAS), i.e., the percentage of tokens that are assigned the correct head *with* (labeled) or *without* (unlabeled) the correct dependency label, calculated using eval.pl with default settings.[4] Statistical significance is checked using Dan Bikel's randomized parsing evaluation comparator.[5]

We furthermore report accuracy for specific dependency relations, measured as a balanced F-score. In order to summarize improvement with respect to dependency relation assignment when comparing two parsers, we rank the relations by their frequency-weighted difference of F-scores.[6]

5.2   Gold Standard Features

The Talbanken05 treebank distinguishes the morphosyntactic properties of tense (present, past, imperative, subjunctive, infinitive and supine) and voice (active or passive) for all verbs. In order to investigate the influence of these various verbal features we performed a set of experiments testing the effect of this information. Three experiments were performed with different feature sets: only voice information (Voice), only tense information (Tense) and a final experiment where the categories in the tense feature were mapped to a binary distinction between finite and non-finite verb forms (Finite). The last experiment was performed in order to test explicitly for the effect of the finiteness of the verb.

Table 3. Overall results for experiments with gold standard verbal features, expressed as average unlabeled and labeled attachment scores

	Unlabeled	Labeled
NoFeats	89.87	84.92
Voice	89.81	84.97
Tense	90.15	85.27
Finite	90.24	85.33
Tense+Voice	90.15	85.28
Finite+Voice	90.24	85.38

Voice. A property of the verb which clearly influences the assignment of core argument functions is the *voice* of the verb, i.e., whether it is passive or active. As we see in Table 3, the addition of information on voice has little effect on the results and the overall difference from the baseline is not statistically significant. This is somewhat surprising as voice alternations have such confounding effects on the argument structure and argument realization of a verb. A closer look at the results, however, reveal that we do find an improved assignment for subjects and objects, as well as the passive agent relation following from the added information.

---

[4] http://nextens.uvt.nl/~conll/software.html

[5] http://www.cis.upenn.edu/~dbikel/software.html

[6] For each dependency relation, the difference in F-scores is weighted by its relative frequency, $\frac{Deprel}{\sum_i Deprel_i}$, in the treebank.

The improvement in analysis of the SS and OO relation is clearly linked to verbal argument structure; a passive transitive verb does not take an object whereas its active version does.

Tense. An experiment (Tense) was performed where we included information on verbal tense. The results in Table 3 show a significant improvement from the baseline ($p <$ .0001). The added information has a positive effect on the verbal dependency relations – ROOT, MS, VG, as well as an overall effect on the assignment of the SS and OO argument relations.

The most common error types indicate that the addition of information on tense improves on the confusion of the main argument types – SS, OO mentioned in the initial error analysis. We also find that head attachment of subjects in particular improves. The subject is always attached to the finite verb in the Talbanken05 analysis, so this is not surprising.

Finiteness. In order to ascertain the influence of finiteness, an additional experiment was performed where the various tense features were mapped to their corresponding class of 'finite' or 'non-finite'.[7] We see the results in Table 3 and find a significant improvement from the baseline ($p <$ .0001).

It is clear that the simple property of finiteness makes the relevant distinctions shown by the tense features. In fact, the mapping to a binary dimension of finiteness causes a further improvement ($p <$ .03) compared to the use of the total set of tense features. This supports the central role of finiteness in Scandinavian syntax, and V2-languages in general. As we recall, the finite verb provides a fixed position in the positioning and ordering of clausal elements. As Table 4 shows, the addition of finiteness information causes improved analysis for verbal relations, the core argument relations (SS, OO), as well as non-argument, adverbial relations (TA, AA, NA). These are all relations whose positioning is influenced by the finiteness of the verb.

Table 4. 10 most improved dependency relations with added information on finiteness, ranked by their weighted difference of balanced F-scores

Dependency relation		Freq	NoFeats	Finite
ROOT	root	.0649	86.71	88.03
SS	subject	.1105	90.25	90.91
VG	verb group	.0302	94.65	96.42
OO	direct object	.0632	84.53	85.31
+F	coordinated clause	.0099	52.07	55.45
MS	coordinated clause	.0096	63.35	66.63
TA	time adverbial	.0249	70.29	71.20
AA	other adverbial	.0537	68.70	69.04
++	conjunction	.0422	90.33	90.67
NA	negation adverbial	.0422	92.46	93.56

---

[7] Note that we are not equating tense and finiteness, since there are untensed forms which are still finite, e.g. the imperative (Holmberg and Platzack, 1995). Rather we map the present and past tenses, as well as the imperative to the class 'finite' and the rest to the 'non-finite' class.

In the initial error analysis we noted that errors which confused subjects for objects and vice versa were frequent and that these were typically caused by word order variation. We find that the addition of information on finiteness results in the correct assignment of 24.4% of the subjects which were initially confused for objects by the baseline parser. These are predominantly postverbal subjects (89.9%) which directly follow a finite verb. We furthermore find that 31.4% of the objects initially confused for subjects by the baseline parser and a fair number of these (45.3%) have a non-finite head verb.

Combined Features. The combination of the verbal features (Tense+Voice, Finite+Voice) causes a slight, but not significant improvement over the best of the individual features (Tense, Finite).

5.3   Automatic Features

In order to assess the scalability of the results detailed above, we performed an experiment where information on voice and finiteness was assigned automatically. For part-of-speech tagging, we employ the freely available MaltTagger – a HMM part-of-speech tagger for Swedish (Hall, 2003). The pretrained model for Swedish employs the SUC tagset (Gustafson-Capková and Hartmann, 2006). The SUC part-of-speech tag set distinguishes tense and voice for verbs.

The experiments with the gold standard verbal features described above clearly showed the benefit of mapping the tense values to a binary set of finiteness-features and this mapping was performed directly for the acquired features.[8] We find that the automatically assigned verbal features of finiteness and voice are very reliable, with accuracies of 97.6 and 96.9, respectively. However, the passive feature is infrequent and shows a quite low precision (74.0) due to syncretism in the *s*-suffix which is employed for both passives and deponent verbs. Deponent verbs are characterized by a passive *s*-suffix, but have an agentive semantics. Examples include *hoppas* 'hope', *trivas* 'enjoy'.

Table 5. Overall results for experiments with automatic features

	Gold standard		Automatic	
	Unlabeled	Labeled	Unlabeled	Labeled
NoFeats	89.87	84.92	89.87	84.92
Voice	89.81	84.97	89.83	85.00
Finite	90.24	85.33	90.15	85.23
Finite+Voice	90.24	85.38	90.12	85.26

It is interesting to note that the addition of the automatically acquired information on voice actually causes a small, but significant improvement in overall results (p<.03), in contrast to the gold standard experiment. Clearly, the overgeneration indicated by

---

[8] Present, past, imperative and subjunctive forms are mapped to the finite feature (FV), all other forms are mapped to the non-finite feature (ø).

the low precision actually captures generalizations which benefit the parse results. In parallel with the gold standard results, we find that the feature of finiteness causes a significant improvement in results (p<.0001). The results are somewhat lower, as is to be expected, but we find that it influences the analysis of the argument relations, as well as the verbal relations.

6 Conclusion

The above experiments have shown how properties of the verb are important in syntactic parsing of Swedish. An error analysis revealed consistent errors in the assignment of syntactic relations by the baseline parser. These errors were partly caused by structural properties of the language, and, in particular, word order variation.

The fact that the Scandinavian languages are V2-languages, which position the finite verb in second position, led us to design a set of experiments where we investigated the addition of information on the verbal properties of voice and tense. We found that the addition of tense, in particular, caused a significant improvement of overall results (p<.0001). In order to further test the extent to which tense may be reduced to finiteness, we performed an experiment where we mapped the tense features to features expressing the binary category of finiteness (finite/non-finite). We observed a further improvement of results (p<.03), supporting the central role of the property of finiteness in syntactic analysis of Scandinavian. We found an improved analysis for verbal dependency relations, as well as arguments and adverbials with verbal attachment. Corresponding experiments with automatically acquired features showed slightly lower, but similar effects, highlighting the scalability of the results.

It is clear that there are other linguistic properties which influence the assignment of syntactic relations in Swedish, such as the animacy and definiteness of arguments (Øvrelid and Nivre, 2007). The placement of adverbials are also characterized by variation in Scandinavian and in terms of future research, we would like to examine the analysis of adverbials and their interaction with verbal features as well as different features of syntactic arguments. Scalability continues to be a main concern and additions in terms of linguistic features should be acquired automatically instead of relying on gold standard annotation.

Bibliography

Buchholz, S., Marsi, E.: CoNLL-X shared task on multilingual dependency parsing. In: Proceedings of the Tenth Conference on Computational Natural Language Learning (CoNLL-X), pp. 149–164 (2006)

Dubey, A., Keller, F.: Probabilistic parsing for German using sister-head dependencies. In: Proceedings of the 41st Annual Meeting of the Association for Computational Linguistics (ACL), pp. 96–103 (2003)

Eide, K.M.: Finiteness and inflection: The syntax your morphology can afford on December 10, 2008 (2008), http://ling.auf.net/lingBuzz

Gustafson-Capková, S., Hartmann, B.: Manual of the Stockholm Umeå Corpus version 2.0. Dept. of Linguistics, Stockholm University (2006)

Hall, J.: A probabilistic part-of-speech tagger with suffix probabilities. Master's thesis. Växjö University, Sweden (2003)

Holmberg, A., Platzack, C.: The role of inflection in Scandinavian Syntax. Oxford University Press, New York/Oxford (1995)

Hall., J., Nivre., J., Nilsson, J.: Maltparser: A data-driven parser-generator for dependency parsing. In: Proceedings of the Fifth International Conference on Language Resources and Evaluation (LREC), pp. 2216–2219 (2006)

Kübler, S., Hinrichs, E., Maier, W.: Is it really that difficult to parse German? In: Proceedings of the 2006 Conference on Empirical Methods in Natural Language Processing (EMNLP) (2006)

Nivre, J.: Inductive Dependency Parsing. Springer, Dordrecht (2006)

Nivre, J., Nilsson, J., Hall, J.: Talbanken05: A Swedish treebank with phrase structure and dependency annotation. In: Proceedings of the fifth international conference on Language Resources and Evaluation (LREC 2006), Genoa, Italy, May 24-26 (2006a)

Nivre, J., Nilsson, J., Hall, J., Eryiğit, G., Marinov, S.: Labeled pseudo-projective dependency parsing with Support Vector Machines. In: Proceedings of the Conference on Computational Natural Language Learning (CoNLL) (2006b)

Øvrelid, L., Nivre, J.: When word order and part-of-speech tags are not enough – Swedish dependency parsing with rich linguistic features. In: Proceedings of the International Conference on Recent Advances in Natural Language Processing (RANLP), pp. 447–451 (2007)

Author Index

Lecture Notes in Artificial Intelligence (LNAI)

Vol. 4898: M. Kolp, B. Henderson-Sellers, H. Moura-tidis, A. Garcia, A.K. Ghose, P. Bresciani (Eds.), Agent-Oriented Information Systems IV. X, 292 pages. 2008.

Vol. 4897: M. Baldoni, T.C. Son, M.B. van Riemsdijk, M. Winikoff (Eds.), Declarative Agent Languages and Technologies V. X, 245 pages. 2008.

Vol. 4894: H. Blockeel, J. Ramon, J. Shavlik, P. Tadepalli (Eds.), Inductive Logic Programming. XI, 307 pages. 2008.

Vol. 4885: M. Chetouani, A. Hussain, B. Gas, M. Milgram, J.-L. Zarader (Eds.), Advances in Nonlinear Speech Processing. XI, 284 pages. 2007.

Vol. 4874: J. Neves, M.F. Santos, J.M. Machado (Eds.), Progress in Artificial Intelligence. XVIII, 704 pages. 2007.

Vol. 4870: J.S. Sichman, J. Padget, S. Ossowski, P. Noriega (Eds.), Coordination, Organizations, Institutions, and Norms in Agent Systems III. XII, 331 pages. 2008.

Vol. 4869: F. Botana, T. Recio (Eds.), Automated Deduction in Geometry. X, 213 pages. 2007.

Vol. 4865: K. Tuyls, A. Nowe, Z. Guessoum, D. Kudenko (Eds.), Adaptive Agents and Multi-Agent Systems III. VIII, 255 pages. 2008.

Vol. 4850: M. Lungarella, F. Iida, J.C. Bongard, R. Pfeifer (Eds.), 50 Years of Artificial Intelligence. X, 399 pages. 2007.

Vol. 4845: N. Zhong, J. Liu, Y. Yao, J. Wu, S. Lu, K. Li (Eds.), Web Intelligence Meets Brain Informatics. XI, 516 pages. 2007.

Vol. 4840: L. Paletta, E. Rome (Eds.), Attention in Cognitive Systems. XI, 497 pages. 2007.

Vol. 4830: M.A. Orgun, J. Thornton (Eds.), AI 2007: Advances in Artificial Intelligence. XIX, 841 pages. 2007.

Vol. 4828: M. Randall, H.A. Abbass, J. Wiles (Eds.), Progress in Artificial Life. XII, 402 pages. 2007.

Vol. 4827: A. Gelbukh, Á.F. Kuri Morales (Eds.), MICAI 2007: Advances in Artificial Intelligence. XXIV, 1234 pages. 2007.

Vol. 4826: P. Perner, O. Salvetti (Eds.), Advances in Mass Data Analysis of Signals and Images in Medicine, Biotechnology and Chemistry. X, 183 pages. 2007.

Vol. 4819: T. Washio, Z.-H. Zhou, J.Z. Huang, X. Hu, J. Li, C. Xie, J. He, D. Zou, K.-C. Li, M.M. Freire (Eds.), Emerging Technologies in Knowledge Discovery and Data Mining. XIV, 675 pages. 2007.

Vol. 4811: O. Nasraoui, M. Spiliopoulou, J. Srivastava, B. Mobasher, B. Masand (Eds.), Advances in Web Mining and Web Usage Analysis. XII, 247 pages. 2007.

Vol. 4798: Z. Zhang, J.H. Siekmann (Eds.), Knowledge Science, Engineering and Management. XVI, 669 pages. 2007.

Vol. 4795: F. Schilder, G. Katz, J. Pustejovsky (Eds.), Annotating, Extracting and Reasoning about Time and Events. VII, 141 pages. 2007.

Vol. 4790: N. Dershowitz, A. Voronkov (Eds.), Logic for Programming, Artificial Intelligence, and Reasoning. XIII, 562 pages. 2007.

Vol. 4788: D. Borrajo, L. Castillo, J.M. Corchado (Eds.), Current Topics in Artificial Intelligence. XI, 280 pages. 2007.

Vol. 4775: A. Esposito, M. Faundez-Zanuy, E. Keller, M. Marinaro (Eds.), Verbal and Nonverbal Communication Behaviours. XII, 325 pages. 2007.

Vol. 4772: H. Prade, V.S. Subrahmanian (Eds.), Scalable Uncertainty Management. X, 277 pages. 2007.

Vol. 4766: N. Maudet, S. Parsons, I. Rahwan (Eds.), Argumentation in Multi-Agent Systems. XII, 211 pages. 2007.

Vol. 4760: E. Rome, J. Hertzberg, G. Dorffner (Eds.), Towards Affordance-Based Robot Control. IX, 211 pages. 2008.

Vol. 4755: V. Corruble, M. Takeda, E. Suzuki (Eds.), Discovery Science. XI, 298 pages. 2007.

Vol. 4754: M. Hutter, R.A. Servedio, E. Takimoto (Eds.), Algorithmic Learning Theory. XI, 403 pages. 2007.

Vol. 4737: B. Berendt, A. Hotho, D. Mladenic, G. Semeraro (Eds.), From Web to Social Web: Discovering and Deploying User and Content Profiles. XI, 161 pages. 2007.

Vol. 4733: R. Basili, M.T. Pazienza (Eds.), AI*IA 2007: Artificial Intelligence and Human-Oriented Computing. XVII, 858 pages. 2007.

Vol. 4724: K. Mellouli (Ed.), Symbolic and Quantitative Approaches to Reasoning with Uncertainty. XV, 914 pages. 2007.

Vol. 4722: C. Pelachaud, J.-C. Martin, E. André, G. Chollet, K. Karpouzis, D. Pelé (Eds.), Intelligent Virtual Agents. XV, 425 pages. 2007.

Vol. 4720: B. Konev, F. Wolter (Eds.), Frontiers of Combining Systems. X, 283 pages. 2007.

Vol. 4702: J.N. Kok, J. Koronacki, R. Lopez de Mantaras, S. Matwin, D. Mladenič, A. Skowron (Eds.), Knowledge Discovery in Databases: PKDD 2007. XXIV, 640 pages. 2007.

Vol. 4701: J.N. Kok, J. Koronacki, R. Lopez de Mantaras, S. Matwin, D. Mladenič, A. Skowron (Eds.), Machine Learning: ECML 2007. XXII, 809 pages. 2007.

Vol. 4696: H.-D. Burkhard, G. Lindemann, R. Verbrugge, L.Z. Varga (Eds.), Multi-Agent Systems and Applications V. XIII, 350 pages. 2007.

Vol. 4694: B. Apolloni, R.J. Howlett, L. Jain (Eds.), Knowledge-Based Intelligent Information and Engineering Systems, Part III. XXIX, 1126 pages. 2007.

Vol. 4693: B. Apolloni, R.J. Howlett, L. Jain (Eds.), Knowledge-Based Intelligent Information and Engineering Systems, Part II. XXXII, 1380 pages. 2007.

Vol. 4692: B. Apolloni, R.J. Howlett, L. Jain (Eds.), Knowledge-Based Intelligent Information and Engineering Systems, Part I. LV, 882 pages. 2007.

Vol. 4687: P. Petta, J.P. Müller, M. Klusch, M. Georgeff (Eds.), Multiagent System Technologies. X, 207 pages. 2007.

Vol. 4682: D.-S. Huang, L. Heutte, M. Loog (Eds.), Advanced Intelligent Computing Theories and Applications. XXVII, 1373 pages. 2007.